F
7
.P99
1988

Puritans and Yankees

DATE DUE			

EARLY AMERICAN HISTORY

An eighteen volume series reproducing over three hundred of the most important articles on all aspects of the colonial experience

EDITED WITH INTRODUCTIONS BY
PETER CHARLES HOFFER
UNIVERSITY OF GEORGIA

A Garland Series

PURITANS AND YANKEES

Selected Articles
on New England Colonial
History 1974 to 1984

EDITED WITH AN INTRODUCTION BY
PETER CHARLES HOFFER

Garland Publishing, Inc.
New York & London
1988

Library of Congress Cataloging-in-Publication Data

Puritans and Yankees : selected articles on New England colonial history, 1974 to
1984 / edited with an introduction by Peter Charles Hoffer.
p. cm.—(Early American history)
ISBN 0-8240-6235-3 (alk. paper)
1. New England—History—Colonial period, ca. 1600–1775.   2. Puritans—New
England—History.   I. Hoffer, Peter C.   II. Series.
F7.P99   1988
974'.02—dc19   87-17215
                                                                                                    CIP

The volumes in this series are printed on
acid-free, 250-year-life paper.

Printed in the United States of America

CONTENTS

PREFACE

By maintaining that the continuity of the New England town was destroyed only late in the eighteenth century, the analytical school of New England history traced in the previous volume consciously put to one side two issues which would motivate the next wave of New England historians. The first of these issues was the growing sophistication, impersonality, and secularism of the formal structure of New England life in her courts, commercial institutions, and criminal laws. The second issue was the extent of conflict and the diversity of conflict within the towns. They simply were not all alike. In important books, David Grayson Allen, Stephen Innes, Gregory Nobles, and other younger scholars have probed the latter point,[1] while Bruce Mann, Hendrick Hartog, Douglas Jones, David Flaherty, and N.E.H. Hull have tested the former issue in books and articles.[2]

The articles in this volume do not repudiate the superb contributions of the articles in Volume Six, but instead add layers of complexity. The New England town's transition from agricultural village to market town, to mill town, or city, and perhaps back to marginal existence on the periphery of another, more successful town's outskirts, are now far better understood than they were even a decade ago. Within each of these towns were distinctions by age and class, distinctions in their turn affected by increasing commercialization. Historians have now made us aware that Connecticut towns are not the same as Massachusetts towns, that western Massachusetts towns are not the same as eastern Massachusetts towns, and even within the old settled belt of Bay Colony towns, individual communities might have had very different structure, development, and fate. In all, as one historian has written, the study of the towns is again "in disarray."[3]

Did the belief system of the New England community change as much as her demographic composition and her economic position? Here even the newest wave of scholarship fragments. Did a traditional "mentalité" preclude deep changes in affective behavior? Are intra-town lawsuits a measure of community unity? Does a decline in prosecution for sexual offenses mean a shift in communal mores, or a breakdown of local authority? Should conflict be viewed as the emergence of a new "affective individualism," or the end of Puritan hegemony? The success of the new scholarship in part lies in the range and fascination of the materials it has opened and the questions it has asked.

Recent scholarship has moved toward a middle ground in this controversy. Many of these small communities said yes to markets but no to the profit motive. Exchanges among farmers and markets in them were based upon need and use, rather than capital accumulation. There was plenty of buying and selling, but such transactions reflected traditional values rather than a proto-industrial ethos. Yet even these broad generalizations cannot be universally applied, for as Darrett Rutman has warned: "Bluntly put, the small places of early America ran the gamut from urbane metropolis to boondocks."[4]

Peter Charles Hoffer
University of Georgia

Notes

1. David Grayson Allen, *In English Ways* (Chapel Hill, 1981); Stephen Innes, *Labor in a New Land: Economy and Society in Seventeenth-Century Springfield* (Princeton, 1983); Gregory H. Nobles, *Divisions Throughout the Whole: Politics and Society in Hampshire County, Massachusetts, 1740–1774* (New York, 1983).

2. Bruce H. Mann, "Rationality, Legal Change, and Community in Connecticut, 1690-1760," *Law and Society Review* 14 (1980), 187–221; N.E.H. Hull, *Female Felons: Women and Serious Crime in Colonial Massachusetts* (Urbana, 1987). The other articles appear in this volume.

3. Gary Nash, "Social Development," in Jack P. Greene and J.R. Pole, eds., *Colonial British America* (Baltimore, 1984).

4. Darrett B. Rutman, "Assessing the Little Communities of Early America," *The William and Mary Quarterly*, 3d ser. 43 (1986), 178.

Community Custom and the Common Law: Social Change and the Development of Land Law in Seventeenth-Century Massachusetts

by DAVID THOMAS KONIG*

Whether or not historians of Puritanism still adhere to Perry Miller's view that an all-inclusive "orthodoxy" was imposed in Massachusetts in 1630, few would accuse the founders of that colony of failing to pay adequate attention to the most minute details of life in their holy experiment.[1] Because the Puritan commonwealth was a utopian experiment whose success or failure would demonstrate God's will to the world, every public activity was carefully conducted, scrutinized for its significance, and recorded for posterity. Their management of secular affairs—and in particular the land system—is, of course, assumed to have been part of this overriding scrupulosity.

But a close examination of the operation of that land "system" in one New England county (Essex, Massachusetts) reveals a far different picture. Contrary to the existing body of scholarship, order and regularity were not imposed on land arrangements until after 1660.[2] In reality, early land use was characterized by

*Assistant Professor of History, Washington University, St. Louis. The author is grateful for the support of part of this research by a grant from the Mark DeWolfe Howe Fund at Harvard University.

1. Miller's 2-volume work *The New England Mind* (Boston, 1935-53) stands as the classic statement of his position. For a brief assessment and criticism of Miller, see David D. Hall's "Introduction" to Miller's *Orthodoxy in Massachusetts* (rev. ed., New York, 1970).

2. One of the first discussions of these matters was Charles M. Andrews, *River Towns of Connecticut* (Baltimore, 1889). Although he included a map of lots in Wethersfield, he cautioned (p. 4) that in the center of town "allotments cannot in every case be absolutely ascertained, as the records are often vague and faulty." However, later historians were not as rigorous and ignored his warning. See, in this regard, A. C. Ford, *Colonial Precedents of Our National Land System as it Existed in 1800* (Madison, 1910), *passim*. Ford used Andrews' map—but not his text—to assert precedents from the seventeenth century for the Northwest Territory. Percy W. Bidwell and John I. Falconer, *History of Agriculture in the Northern United States* (Washington, D.C., 1925), p. 52, drew, in turn, on Ford's misinterpretation to maintain that early land

inexactness in distribution, inattention to recording, and neglect of the most basic statutory requirements of occupany and fencing. It was only in the last third of the seventeenth century that any stable or generally observed land system finally did emerge, and even then the process was a difficult one that revealed the inadequacy of both common law and English local custom in the New World.

The achievement of a stable land system in Essex County by the 1670's also casts doubt upon another received scholarly tradition—the tradition that Massachusetts was a jurisprudential wasteland before England imposed the common law upon it during the 1680's. Although the common law and English local custom did not play as large a role in pre-1680's Essex land dealings as we might have assumed, that county did not lack a body of law or "proper courts of law."[3] Both were well developed by the 1670's, and New Englanders raised loud and clear protests against their destruction by the Crown between 1684 and 1689. Their protests attest to the importance and competency of colonial law in Massachusetts; additionally, they point toward the need for an inquiry into the precise nature and role of the legal system in defense of which New Englanders were clamoring.

I. Confusion and Seeds of Dispute In The Early Years of Settlement

The land system first applied in Essex County was a hastily contrived one born of convenience and necessity. The super-abundance of land in the new world presented the first settlers with opportunities unimaginable in the England they had left. Arriving on a continent where much land was naturally clear or had been cleared by Indians, Englishmen rushed to apportion their new source of wealth. Prompt cultivation of the available land was necessary, of course, to avoid the "starving times" that had decimated earlier colonial settlements. As a result, scrupulous regard to detail was easily overlooked. Inexactness in allotment

---

arrangements possessed "remarkable regularity." For a more cautious opinion of this "system," see Herbert L. Osgood, *The American Colonies in the Seventeenth Century* (New York, 1904), I, 436.

3. The concept of a legal wasteland in colonial America before "reception" of the common law has been resurrected by Anton-Hermann Chroust, *The Rise of The Legal Profession in America* (Norman, Ok., 1965), I, 331. For a perceptive criticism of Chroust, as well as some suggestive thoughts on early American law, see Stanley N. Katz, "Looking Backward: The Early History of American Law," 33 *U. Chi. L. Rev.* 867-84 (1966).

and recording was tolerated, and little attention was given to the orderly plans which, it had been expected, were to be followed.

In this haste to divide and cultivate their land, the earliest farmers of Essex County naturally overlooked many realities. Although vast areas of land lay before them, not all of it was adequately fertile, and land which had been cleared by Indian burnings was of low productivity. In addition, not all land was suitable for the varied needs of a self-sufficient agriculture. Farmers needed more than just "land." They required well-drained land for plowing, as well as open grassy meadows to provide fodder for their livestock.[4]

The neglect of these necessities quickly became apparent. In Salem, for example, it was realized in 1637 that some men had been given "little or no marsh or medow ground." They had to be given land elsewhere, as did others who complained the following year. The extent of confusion in the earliest lotlaying was immense, for even those men who were official lotlayers were unfamiliar with the topography. Even the town surveyor of Salem and a neighbor were forced to request additional land as compensation in 1638 "in consideration that they had 50 Acres of rocks granted them formerly which are not of any use."[5]

With large amounts of land available, compensatory allotments were a common feature of the early Essex land system. Throughout the 1640's Salisbury took back land parcels in exchange for lots elsewhere within its limits, as in 1641 when it "ordered that Edward French should have 10 Acres on the east side of the Powow River in lieu of his 20 Acre lot granted upon the west side of the Powow River. . . ."[6]

This phenomenon was widespread in the county.[7] However, the process of land exchange was not as easy or conclusive as the first farmers seemed to assume. It was not always clear that

3

4. Bidwell and Falconer, *Agriculture,* pp. 7-8, 50-55.

5. "Salem Town Records," Essex Institute, *Historical Collections,* IX (1868), 45, 76, 78, 67 (Hereafter, "Salem Rec.," *EIHC*). For a similar complaint in Salisbury in 1639, see Salisbury Town Records, 1638-1902, p. 28. Typescript in the Essex Institute, Salem. (Hereafter, Salis. Rec.).

6. *Ibid.,* pp. 5-6, 68, 109.

7. Only Marblehead managed to escape such difficulties because in its first years it was almost exclusively a fishing community. As part of Salem in 1637 it was decided to grant only the standard small fisherman's plot to each resident there. No meadow or upland figured in its first distribution. Instead, allotments consisted of house and garden lots of two acres, with rights to common woods and pasturage for goats and cattle. Samuel Roads, Jr., *History and Traditions of Marblehead* (Boston, 1880), p. 12.

the original land grant was being relinquished. Frequently, town officials did not specify such an agreement, and the owners were glad to enjoy both the original and compensatory lots. In addition, selectmen optimistically assumed that the bustling development of their towns required highways and cartways across private property to reach outlying grants. Accordingly, they took land for such purposes and granted its owners other parcels. These highways were not always built immediately, and the reserved land was often reoccupied by the initial grantee or by a third party without challenge.[8]

In the earliest years of settlement, these Essex communities did not constitute a complete system, nor were they a finished society with long-established ways and orthodox modes of behavior. Patterns of permanent settlement were far from established, and entire settlements were abandoned in the 1620's as migrants cast about for satisfactory locations. Because the company's members were not committed to particular geographic locations, the Puritan leaders on both sides of the Atlantic tried to resettle the migrants elsewhere. Indeed, Cromwell's well-known suggestion that the colony move to the Caribbean was not considered fantastic.[9]

Many or the first generation, in fact, did not even contemplate permanent relocation, and regarded New England as only a temporary exile. Hugh Peter is probably the best known example of the many Essexmen who preferred to return to England during the Civil War. Although he preached at Salem from 1636 to 1641, Peter hurried off to his native country and quickly became a favorite of Cromwell. A Marblehead fisherman purchased Peter's 350-acre grant through his agent, while Peter's daughter in London believed the land to be hers.[10]

Such inattention to land matters was common because residential patterns were uncertain and frequently only temporary.

---

8. Edward Colcord of Hampton yielded land for a road in 1653, for instance, but the town did not lay out the path. In the meantime, another man occupied the land peacefully. *Colcord v. Drake* (1674), *Records and Files of the Quarterly Courts of Essex County, Massachusetts 1636-1683*, ed. George F. Dow (8 vol., Salem, 1911-21), V, 294 (Hereafter, *Essex Rec.*). See also *James v. Northy* (1672), *ibid.*, pp. 4-5; and *King v. Town of Lynn* (1673), *ibid.*, pp. 183-85.

9. Osgood, *Seventeenth Century*, III, 137-39.

10. Sidney Perley, *The History of Salem, Massachusetts* (Salem, 1926), II, 198. Similar confusion resulted from the activities of the fractious octogenarian minister Stephen Batchelor, who left behind his newly wed third wife as well as tracts of land in Lynn, Newbury, and Ipswich in order to return to England and marry yet a fourth time. Alonzo Lewis, *The History of Lynn* (Boston, 1829), pp. 54-56.

The occupancy of John Humphrey's enormous tract in Lynn, for instance, could be ignored when he abandoned it and returned to England because the town was severely depopulated in the 1640's. A large contingent had emigrated to Sandwich, Massachusetts, in 1637, and forty more families went to Long Island in 1640. When the end of the Great Migration halted the stream of repopulation, Lynn was dotted with abandoned tracts of land. So serious was the problem that in 1645 the town was unable to collect the colony rates it had been paying before, explaining that between two and three hundred acres of land were now "overrun with Sorrel."[11]

By the 1650's, officials of older towns like Salem and Lynn began to acknowledge that their land system was in a state of disarray and confusion. In 1650, for example, Salem tried to reserve its ungranted land in a certain area for use as commonage. The selectmen were unable to make a blanket reservation of the land, though, and revealed that much of what had been granted in the past was still unoccupied. In attempting to take possession of all land which "lyeth in comon," they had to make the provision that "such grants as have beene made before this order to perticular persons shall be made good unto them." A year and a half later the town allowed Jeffrey Massey additional acreage but was forced to caution him to "exceed not the quantitie nor take any *formerlie granted to other men*." Similarly, in 1653 land was granted subject to the provision that the man to whom it was formerly granted did not "quietlie possess and enjoy that 50 Acres laid out to him." Even when land was claimed much later by grantees, boundaries were laid out only reluctantly: Gervas Garford of Salem was given land in 1637, but he did not bound it for twenty years despite the colony's statutory requirement and the town's repeated prodding.[12]

A great deal of land was also abandoned in Salem by residents who did not leave the town. In 1644, one Guido Bayley was granted "so much of the swamp that lyes along by his lott over at Cape Annes Side as hee can ridde [drain] within three yeares next ensuing." Apparently the job was too large for him, because in 1653 he sold the land to Humphrey Woodbury. Bayley had abandoned the land, however, and he could not give a perfected deed to his grantee. Woodbury was not totally lax in certifying the claim, but all that he could do was enter a "caveat" with the county registry of deeds for a land transaction whose grantor held only dubious title.[13]

5

11. *Ibid.*, pp. 49, 52, 62, 72-78, 86-87.
12. Emphasis added. "Salem Rec.," *EIHC*, IX, 22, 164, 169, 173, 167, 204.
13. *Ibid.*, p. 129. Essex County Land Book (9 vols., handwritten copy

Imperfections of this sort existed—and were tolerated—because Essex was an unfinished society. It was not until 1686 that Salisbury, for instance, found it necessary to deal with "several obscurities for the securing of the justness" of claimants.[14] And there were obscurities in abundance all over the county. Not all of them waited until the 1680's for correction, but inexactness and incompetence were tolerated for what appears to be a surprisingly long time.

"Obscurities" occurred, in part, because of the lack of any uniform surveying system. There was no agreement, for example, as to whether straight lines or natural features should be used to separate land holdings. Zacheous Gould had assumed that his grant of three hundred acres in Reading was rectangular in shape, but to his dismay he later discovered that the lot of his neighbor in the next town had been laid out in a "circular form" whose arc subtracted from Gould's acreage.[15]

However, even an agreement to ignore natural features and employ straight boundaries might also leave questions unanswered. In Salem, for instance, some confusion existed as to whether a particular lot was rectangular or five-sided.[16] In Rumney Marsh (now the City of Chelsea, between Lynn and Boston) a problem unique to the new world arose: how to compensate for the variation of the meridian in North America. True north could be determined only by locating the magnetic north pole and applying a standardized figure to compensate for the difference between that reading and true (geographic) north. The variation used for readings in England could not be used in Massachusetts because of the different subtended angles formed by Boston and London between the two "north poles." Unfortunately, no agreement existed on how to compensate. Seventeenth-century surveyors appear to have used a variety of methods, some simply using the magnetic north alone, and others making their own allowance for the difference. Until John Winthrop IV produced a table of variations in 1763, the situation was prone to uncertainty and confusion.[17]

---

of the originals made in 1855 by the Essex County Commissioners. In the Registry of Deeds, Salem) I, 38.

14. Salis. Rec., p. 239.

15. *Gould v. Fuller* (1672), *Essex Rec.*, V, 84-85.

16. *Endecott v. Preston* (1690), Essex County Quarterly Courts, Records & Files, 1686-1692 (Manuscript vols. XLVI-LII, in the Essex County Court House, Salem. Hereafter, Essex Rec. MS.) LXIX, 3-21. See also *Lever v. Scales* (1682), *Essex Rec.*, VIII 267-70.

17. Mellen Chamberlain, *A Documentary History of Chelsea* (Boston, 1908), I, 269-70. Winthrop's table, covering the years 1673-1800 (because magnetic north changes yearly) can be found in the *Journals of*

It appears that exactness was not felt to be necessary in the actual surveying of the earliest grants. Thomas Fuller described the problems which beset him when he laid out a parcel of land in Rowley. Although he was trying to defend his accuracy when a dispute occurred many years later, his previous lack of scrupulous concern could not be concealed. Fuller related how

> my father did Charg us to bee suere that we make mesuere and an allowanc for the saigging of the lin and farder saith that I hard my father tendere andevere men to have the lin rune by Indifrant men and therewith to bee Conttent as they determined the case.

7

In the course of surveying, one of the measuring chains broke; it was not replaced and was used nonetheless. Significantly, the Andover men accepted Fuller's survey and did not insist on a subsequent measure by the proffered "Indifrant men."[18]

In Ipswich the laying-out of a lot to be used for the town's free school as revenue was done in an even more casual manner. The tract ran from one end of a creek over a swampy meadow. Assaying the task before them, the lotlayers were averse to slogging through the swamp, and they sent one man to do the unpleasant task of wading across to mark a tree on the other side. The mark was soon forgotten. No one knew where it was or seemed to care, for the work was never recorded. Looking back on their efforts many years later, one of the lotlayers confessed that there had been no general rule of surveying to follow at that time, and subsequently there was no way to clarify a situation which had existed unchallenged and unnoticed for decades.[19]

A significant feature of this early informality in land arrangements was the official inattention to statutory requirements as well as the disregard for any minimal regulation shown by private individuals. In 1634 the General Court had ordered that all land grants to freemen be recorded and a transcript be sent to it. Surveying was to be done in each town by a constable and four other freemen. The next year this requirement—indeed, it was a privilege, for it assured titles in writing—was extended to all grants made to those taking the oath of allegiance. What appears to be an orderly and regular system befitting the Puritan concern for orthodoxy in all aspects of life, however, was in practice rather less than that. By 1637 the widespread failure of local officials to follow the injunctions of 1634 and 1635 forced

---

the *House of Representatives of Massachusetts*, XL [1763-64] (Boston, 1970), 307.

18. *Selectmen of Andover v. Fuller* (1677), *Essex Rec.*, VI, 322-25.

19. *Epps v. Benet* (1678), *ibid.*, 404-10.

the General Court to act once more and demand "that some course bee taken to cause men to record their lands, or to fine them that neglect."[20]

Many towns responded nominally, at least—Salem threatened ten-shilling fines to all who failed to record their lots—but the widespread evasion continued. Many residents of Manchester did not bother recording their lots until 1689, for instance.[21] In Marblehead this laxity allowed great neglect and perhaps even fraud. Different people sold the same parcels of land, and others sometimes used the same share of commonage for many years with no problem. Yet remarkably, people in the first decades of Essex settlement made little or no effort to prevent this occurrence.[22] In Marblehead, for instance, Richard Norman bought a half share of commonage from Thomas Davis, while Richard Downing bought the exact same share from Henry Pease. In that same town, George Corwin was able to sell five shares of the town's cow common though he actually owned only three.[23] Salem at times was equally lax. A grant of land in 1654 was accompanied by the warning that the land was given "provided it was nott within any mans bounds before the said graunt"—the grantors, apparently, having no way of knowing whether it was.[24]

Neglect and evasion were possible in a society where such actions did not adversely affect the activities of others or the needs of society. If settlement could be encouraged by ignoring regulations, and if no one was harmed by the inexactness, few

20. *Records of the Governor and Company of the Massachusetts Bay in New England, 1628-1686*, ed. Nathaniel B. Shurtleff (5 vol., Boston, 1853-54), I, 116, 137, 201. (Hereafter, *Mass. Rec.*).

21. *Town Records of Manchester, From the Earliest Grants of Land, 1636 . . . until 1736* (Salem, 1889), p. 33.

22. In part, this situation may be attributable to the absence of any precedent in England, where no general deed registration system existed. However, even New Netherlands, which did have a precedent to draw upon, also did not act for many years and witnessed similar confusion. The office of surveyor-general was not created in other colonies until quite a while after initial settlement, too, although not as late as in Massachusetts, which waited until 1682. Richard B. Morris, *Studies in the History of American Law* (New York, 1930), pp. 69-71. Clarence W. Rife, "Land Tenure in New Netherlands," in *Essays in Colonial History Presented to Charles McLean Andrews* (New Haven, 1931), pp. 50-51. *The Colonial Laws of Massachusetts. Reprinted from the edition of 1672, with the Supplements through 1686*, ed. W. H. Whitmore (Boston, 1887), p. 296.

23. "Marblehead Town Records," Essex Institute, *Historical Collections*, LXIX (1933), 247-50. (Hereafter, "Marblehead Rec.," *EIHC*).

24. "Salem Rec.," *EIHC*, IX, 177.

people complained.[25] In this sense there was little "disorder" in early New England land patterns simply because divergence, variety, and neglect rarely brought people into sharp conflict or severely disrupted the orderly functioning of society. That did not mean, of course, that all land matters were carefully regulated, well-policed, and systematized into an orthodox conformity.

There was, then, great tolerance for violation of the law. Reserved town lands, for example, were commonly encroached on, and the towns' prerogative of making inviolate grants of land was frequently violated. In March 1636 Salem gave the following permission regarding a tract in Marblehead:

> John Peach ffisherman and Nicholas Mariott having fenced about five acres of ground on Marble Neck (*though contrarie to the order of the towne*) yet Its agreed that they may for the present improve the said place for building or planting, provided always that the propriety thereof be reserved for the right of the towne of Salem, to dispose of in processe of tyme to them or any other ffisher men, or others as shalbe thought most meet, yet soe as that they may have reasonable consideration for any chardge they shalbe at.

Despite the illegality of their action, Peach and Mariott had not been penalized, and they were promised compensation if the town ever took back the land.[26] A year later a similar case came to the attention of the town meeting, when it was pointed out that "John Pickering hath fensed in a portion of the Towns Land without Consent from the Towne." Seven men did protest and demand that he be fined twenty shillings. But they did not insist on his ouster, and even their limited demand for a fine failed at the town meeting.[27]

The unsanctioned appropriation of town land did not always go unpunished, but usually only small fines or rents were levied, such as the fee demanded of John Pickering. If permission were asked, moreover, even the fine might be omitted. When Humphrey Woodbury wanted some extra land near his own lot "as to mak him levell with other men" in 1637, the town of Salem agreed to his increasing his farm, "it being averred not to be prejudiciall unto any."[28]

Few encroachments were actually "prejudiciall." Often those that did cause problems were lots needed for public use, as in

---

25. A similar situation prevailed in New Netherlands. Many patroons were lax in requiring precision in the land dealings between their tenants. This inexactness, it seems, was thought to be a stimulus to rapid settlement. Rife, "New Netherlands," p. 62.

26. "Salem Rec.," *EIHC*, IX, 15 (emphasis added).

27. *Ibid.*, p. 46.   28. *Ibid.*, pp. 34-39.

1649 when a Salem man "enclosed a way for his use whereby divers men were forced to goe farr about to their lotts." Accordingly, it was "ordered that mr. Batter, mr. Gardiner, and Jeffrye Massy shall view and lay out the way."[29]

The important point is that much of what might have been disruptive in England—and which would become so decades later in Massachusetts—was, in those early years, still not "prejudiciall unto any." Most men in Massachusetts were content to "goe and live like lambs in a large place" without regulation. Frequently, encroachments on private land were easily solved by compensatory lots elsewhere. In 1657 Roger Hasscoll had a "difference" with William King and his neighbors over a highway through the former's property. Two appointed surveyors settled the matter by giving Hasscoll another parcel. King and his neighbors thus gained the access they needed to bring their grain to a mill, and Hasscoll did not suffer the loss of any land.[30]

Before the 1660's the problem of precise borders rarely led to serious confrontations requiring title trials. Instead, the occasional instances of land disputes were handled within the mechanism of town government. Eminent men were appointed and given "power to Issue" a resolution of the conflict. In the winter of 1656, to cite one example, Jeffrey Massey and Roger Conant were chosen for that purpose on two occasions in Salem.[31]

The 1650's began to witness some increasing concern for boundaries, but problems still could be settled by the arbitration of town leaders.[32] The only great concern in these early land arrangements, in fact, was the prevention of fraudulent land transfers; it was not the establishment and enforcement of precise boundaries.[33] Explicit assertion of borders was not felt to be necessary by many people in Essex. If someone needed wood, for instance, he might fell the required timber even if it was a "bound tree."[34]

The famous land recording act of 1640 reveals this preoccupation and the lack of concern for absolute boundary certitude.

29. *Ibid.*, pp. 105, 157-58.
30. John Cotton, *The Churches Resurrection, or the Opening of the Fift and Sixt Verses of the 20th Chapter of the Revelation* (London, 1642), pp. 25-26. "Salem Rec.," *EIHC*, IX, 205.
31. *Ibid.*, p. 189.
32. For examples of disputes solved in this manner, see *ibid.*, pp. 177, 205-06, 209.
33. For an example of an early grant in Salisbury showing the vagueness of boundaries, see Salis. Rec., p. 15. For a similar entry by the town of Salem, see "Salem Rec.," *EIHC*, IX, p. 14.
34. *Mansfield v. Newhall* (1682), *Essex Rec.*, VIII, 254.

According to its preamble, this law was "For avoyding all fraud-ulent conveyances, and that every man may know what estate or interest other men may have in any houses, lands, or other hereditaments they are to deale in." To assure its purpose, all land transactions were to be recorded; if not, they would be of no legal validity against anyone but the grantor. It is clear that this act was not intended to guarantee adequate surveying. In the first place, a clause restricted the recording as follows:

> And it is not intended that the whole bargaine, sale, etc., shalbe entered, but only the names of the grauntor and grauntee, the thing and the estate graunted, and the date; and all such entryes shalbee certified to the recorder at Boston within six months yearely.[35]

Secondly, at the revision of the law in 1648 and 1652 further limiting provisions were added. It was specified in 1648 that recording was necessary only "where the Graunter remains in possession." The reason for this qualification was that the convey-ance of title might not be apparent to the community if no physical transfer took place—especially if the land were not in use at all. The preamble to the 1652 statute sheds further light on this land system. Again, boundaries were not mentioned, and it was stated that more legislation was needed because "diverse within this jurisdiction are apt to rest upon a verball bargaine, or sale, for howses or lands of any valew." It was therefore necessary to prevent these "clandestine and uncertaine sales and titles."[36]

The function of the established system in the first three decades, therefore, was only to assure conveyances without specifying to what precise land the title pertained. It operated to guarantee payment to the grantor and protection to the grantee that the conveyance was not defective, and for this reason the registry of deeds sometimes recorded fishing contracts and other business dealings which had no relation to land.[37] Most transfers did record that a deed existed as part of a land transfer, but others did not indicate even that the grantee had obtained one.[38]

Indeed, it is likely that many grantors and grantees were not interested in exact limits and were using the registry only to certify land deals that were investments in future resale at

35. *Mass. Rec.*, I, 306-7. The best discussion of this act is Mark De-Wolfe Howe, "The Recording of Deeds in the Colony of Massachusetts Bay," 28 B.U.L. Rev. 1-6 (1948).

36. *Laws and Liberties of Massachusetts.* . . . ([1648] Cambridge, Mass., 1929), pp. 13-14. *Mass. Rec.*, IV, Part 1, p. 101.

37. Essex Land Book, I, 28.

38. *Ibid.*, p. 32.

a higher price. George Burrill bought six acres in Lynn from Josiah Stanborah and promptly sold it to Joseph Jenks for £17 in 1650. Burrill had not bothered to record his purchase from Stanborah, and Jenks did not record his purchase until 1654 when be mortgaged the six acres to John Gifford for £20. Gifford assigned his right to Edward Richards, who finally sold it to Henry Rhodes for £22. These last three transactions were recorded when they took place in 1654.[39]

Nevertheless, many men neglected to record even their titles and conveyances, and it became difficult to tell who owned neighboring property. A wooded plain in Salem was one such lot where people in the neighborhood believed different men to be its sole owner. There was no house erected on it, nor was it fenced. Daniel Southwick frequently cut wood there and called it "Davisons, or Captain Corwins plaine;" Corwin, for his part, regarded the land as common. Eleazer Taylor referred to it as "Barthollmews playne," while John Putman said that it was "reputed and comonly called Captain Trasks plain." However, at Trask's death the estate appraiser heard no mention that it had belonged to the deceased. No written proof existed to determine ownership, moreover.[40] It was with great accuracy, therefore—and no little understatement— that Thomas Hutchinson later wrote of his ancestors, "For the first twenty years, they used too little formality in their deeds and conveyances of the titles to land."[41]

II. *Pressures and Problems In the Restoration Era*

By the 1660's a convergence of historical factors caused the existing patterns of land management to change. The pressures of the colony's rapid growth and maturity, as well as events occurring in England, made it impossible to tolerate the informality and inattention to detail that had characterized the system. It became necessary, as a result, to bring uniformity and order to the divergent, conflicting practices in use. Decades of diversity, evasion, and development were finally followed by conformity, as New England society underwent changes that call into question the major assumptions of the "declension" model of Puritan historiography.[42] This change was not accomplished without difficulties,

---

39. *Ibid.*, pp. 53-57.

40. *Woolcott v. Trask* (1686), Essex Rec. MS, XLVI, 16-24.

41. Thomas Hutchinson, *The History of the Colony and Province of Massachusetts Bay*, ed. Lawrence Shaw Mayo (Cambridge, 1936), I, 383.

42. This model is set forth in Perry Miller's *The New England Mind: From Colony to Province* (Boston, 1953), especially Book I, "Declension."

though, and the system ultimately established was much different from what had been anticipated in 1630.

The confrontation of differing views and practices in a period of social change made Essex a highly litigious society, and its conflicts had to be resolved—and adjustments made—by legal action.[43] Land disputes alone made every meeting of the Essex courts a busy session: on the average, the courts handled twenty land title cases per year between 1672 and the removal of the charter in 1684,[44] as the county judiciary had developed an efficient and effective system for the preservation of social order amid change.

The stable patterns of provincial New England society slowly began to emerge when many of the conditions that had permitted the widespread neglect of precision in land arrangements were altered after 1660. One obvious factor was the diminishing supply of land. Naturally, land is not a limitless resource, and good land in particular soon became a scarce commodity in the older settlements of Essex County. At first, land hunger was rather easily satisfied, as the experience of Lynn illustrates. By 1638 that town had granted 8,680 acres to one hundred families. Although the total area of the town was twice that amount (18,000 acres), residents complained of a land shortage. It is safe to assume that the 8,680 acres were the total *useable* land within its borders, for much of Lynn was hilly and heavily wooded, and two large swampy marshes straddled the Saugus River in the center of town.[45] Settlement avoided these areas.

The General Court was able to satisfy the petitioning residents and granted them 6,400 acres next to the town, known as "Lynn End," which is now Lynnfield. Disposable undivided land was

13

43. The integral role of law and litigation in the process of social and political change after the medieval era has recently gained attention. For a perceptive discussion of this issue and the scholarship produced, see William J. Bouwsma, "Lawyers in Early Modern Culture," 78 *Amer. Hist. Rev.* 303-27 (1973).

44. This figure is a very conservative estimate. It includes only those whose goal was certification of title or boundary and not those seeking the recovery of damages. The number of cases in which title was the basis of the dispute was probably much higher for this reason. Also not included are debt cases involving rent: it is likely that many of the apparent "rent" cases arose from disputes about legitimate ownership. As a comparison on the use of the courts to decide title in another seventeenth-century colony, see Rife, "New Netherlands," pp. 60-62.

45. Lewis, *Lynn*, pp. 64-68. John Henry Sears, *The Physical Geography, Geology, Mineralogy, and Paleontology of Essex County, Massachusetts* (Salem, 1905), p. 21, Appendix A. The wooded areas of Lynn were kept as undivided common until 1708.

thus readily accessible in those early years, and the temporary lag in immigration during the 1640's halted population pressure for a time. By the 1660's, however, the pressure on land had resumed. Lynn no longer had an open frontier to its west, and all future land grants would have to be satisfied within its own limits. No more would it be able simply to expand "six miles into the countrey."[46]

As if these normal population pressures were not enough, matters were worsened by King Philip's War in 1675-76. In Salem alone twenty-three families were accepted as inhabitants after "being driven from there habetations by the Barbarios heathen" in 1675. Only one of these families was given free commonage and permission to stay indefinitely, and the rest were told that they could remain for only a year. Nonetheless, six of the latter group were still living in the town in 1683. Migration to the hinterland was temporarily halted by this struggle and the ensuing wars with France, and it did not resume its pre-war levels until the eighteenth century.[47]

Thus hard-pressed for land, Essex towns became more scrupulous toward their own permanent residents. The Salem town meeting began to show its concern for the dwindling supply of town land, and in 1673 it directed its selectmen "to take Care for the finding out and settling all such land as belongs to the towne In any part thereof. . . ." It now had become necessary to regulate and define arrangements which formerly had not required such attention. This practice soon became a routine one: in 1679 the town established a "Commitey to Search for Towne land within the bounds of Salem" and appointed subsequent ones in 1682, 1691, and 1693.[48]

Positive action accompanied these investigative efforts, as Salem officials became aware of the encroachments which had been made and tolerated for many decades. The surveying committee of

46. Commonwealth of Massachusetts, *Historical Data Relating to Counties, Cities and Towns in Massachusetts* (Boston, 1966), p. 41. For similar situations faced by Salem, Wenham, & Beverly, see *ibid.*, p. 58; and "Salem Rec.," *EIHC*, XLVIII, 348.

47. "Salem Rec.," *EIHC*, XLVIII, 20-21. Essex County Quarterly Courts, Records & Files, 1683-86 (3 boxes, in typescript at the Essex Institute, Salem. Hereafter, Essex Rec. TS), box 2, folder 11, leaves 69b-69mmm. On King Philip's War, see generally Douglas E. Leach, *Flintlock and Tomahawk, New England in King Philip's War* (New York, 1958), and Clifford K. Shipton, "The New England Frontier," 10 *New England Quarterly* 28 (1937).

48. "Salem Rec.," *EIHC*, XLII, 261; XLIII, 43; XLIX, 76; LXIV, 65; LXIX, 79; LXXXIII, 273, 275-76.

1673 found nine scattered lots belonging to the town. Among its other discoveries was a one hundred-acre tract "partly on Beverly bounds," of which eight "very good" acres had been cleared and planted with English grass. Moreover, the town officials reported:

> We found ther a bound tree newly Cut downe and hewed on the Sids. It was marked to deface the markes. We Conceave thear is Reason for the towne further to Enquire Concerning thatt matter. It is said to be the antient bounds between Edward Bishop and the towns Comon.[49]

The surveying discoveries of these later decades were not the only information of encroachments on town land known to the Salem officials, for they had tolerated other illegal actions for a long time. Only in 1658, though, did the town begin to reverse its earlier acquiescent policy, and on January 20 of that year it took the drastic step of tearing down all fences intruding on common land. Francis Skerry had been permitted to fence in "the potters lane" in exchange for a yearly rent of ten shillings, but in 1683 the town ended that agreement and commanded him to "leave it open for the townes use" once more. Many of the lots affected by this new type of action, moreover, were not just isolated planting or mowing lots. The importance of tearing down their fences and disseising their occupants was greater now because houselots, rather than planting or mowing lots, were affected: "Jonathan Southwicks fenc neare his house [was ordered] to be personally pulled down" by Salem officials in 1661. In a more serious case, Thomas Bell was ordered to tear down his house in 1683 because it was on town land, and if he refused the selectmen were authorized to sue him "for his Tres-passe and presumption." Suits such as these, with towns suing their own residents for encroachments on undivided land, appeared with increasing frequency in the decades after 1660.[50]

Essex towns were now taking a stronger stand in regard to land and were refusing to tolerate the easy informality of the earlier decades. For one thing, they finally began to pay closer attention to the recording of conveyances and to insist on the bounding of lots. Marblehead, for instance, had been independent since 1649, but it was not until 1669 that it ordered the recording of tenure by all persons holding land by grant from the time that the

---

49. Ibid., XLIII, 44-45; LXIV, 65; LXXXIII, 273, 277-79, 282.

50. Ibid., IX, 216; XL, 114; LXIV, 80, 207. On suits against residents, see, for example, Selectmen of Rowley v. Nelson (1672), Essex Rec., V, 86-87; Selectmen of Lynn v. Edmonds (1673), ibid., pp. 191-94; Sambourne [in behalf of the Town of Hampton] v. Tilton (1673) ibid., p. 237.

town had been part of Salem. If they failed to do so, they "shall afterward Claime no perticular Right to any Land otherwise then a Commoner." At the same time, significantly, the selectmen were directed to verify the exact boundaries of those lots. Salem had taken similar action in 1661, when it required all men with "former Graunts of land from the towne" to claim them from the selectmen. Failure would deprive them of any right to the land. Accordingly, Richard Hollingworth and John Tompkins requested their old and unoccupied grants finally to be laid out and recorded. Hollingworth's land had come to him from his father, while Tompkins had been granted his land sometime between 1637 and 1640, and he was now to lay it out "if he can tell wher to find it."[51]

More and more people were attempting to "tell wher to find" the land they had been granted by their town meetings or selectmen. The efforts of Andover in 1663 typified the problems involved. More explicitly than other towns, Andover confessed to its neglect of adequate procedure and recalled that

> the said inhabitants, att their first settling here, and since, hath not been soe carefull and exact, as they might and should have been, for the due and true recording of all such graunts, as have been made to particular persons, some being lost, some not entered, others imperfectly, which in time to come may prove troublesome and prejuditiall to the owners thereof. . . .

Andover was already beginning to experience problems of confusion and competition over land, and tried to control the situation by appointing seven towsmen to act

> whilst things are still fresh in memory, and all disputes and questions about the same may be prevented, and avoyded for time to come . . . [and] to view and examine all gifts and graunts made to particular persons, from the beginning of this plantation, until this present, with other claims by purchase or otherwise, and such as they find clear and certaine to allow and Confirme under their hands or the hands of some five of them, which being done, is to be recorded in the Towne book, and to be esteemed and accounted as valid and authentick, as if they had been entered and recorded at the time when they were graunted, though the day and year of such graunts be not mentioned nor remembered.

51. Salis. Rec., p. 189. "Marblehead Rec.," *EIHC*, LXIX, 252-53. "Salem Rec.," *EIHC*, XL, 109-10, 118; IX, 51, 65, 104. See also Haverhill's 1665 order to that effect: Essex Rec. TS, box 2, folder 10, leaves 61c-61h. Also, Topsfield's order in 1681: *Essex Rec.*, VIII, 319-23.

The town's statements reveal the problems confronting any effort to discover the real status of land claims after many decades of neglect. On the one hand the town noted that "things are still fresh in memory," but on the other hand that the time of "such graunts be not . . . remembered." In any disagreement or litigation where the date of earliest occupancy was crucial, a decision would be extremely difficult to make, and would pose unprecedented legal problems.[52]

The belated efforts of a town to create custom by declaring land tenures "as valid and authentick" as if legitimated by the passage of time were unavailing, however. Land was too scarce and valuable a commodity, and the dubious legality of such a declaration could not stand unchallenged. As a result, landholders and town officials turned to the county's legal system for guidance in correcting the disordered patterns of the previous decades. The intervention of the county court system was necessary because town powers of conflict resolution were inadequate to the task confronting them, and town meetings found that they were unable to employ the methods of the past. For example, compensatory lots could not be found in outlying areas of the town for men who had been mistakenly using common land as their own without any challenge. Similarly, if a farmer discovered that a lot he had been granted a quarter century earlier measured much less than what was specified, his town meeting could not simply let him take adjacent land when all surrounding acreage was being used by others. As new pressures and attitudes rendered town procedures useless, therefore, a new system had to be worked out in the courts.[53]

The conflict between town meetings and individuals over the diminishing supply of land was only a part of the struggle between proprietors and inhabitants which was to become so important at a later date. That issue, however, more properly belongs to the eighteenth century, when "the clear distinction was first made between the town and the proprietors and their respective functions were legally separated."[54] In the seventeenth century the county

17

---

52. *Poor v. Wright* (1681), *ibid.*, pp. 80-83. See also *Johnson v. Herriman* (1684), Essex Rec. TS, box 2, folder 10, leaves 61c-61h, for Haverhill.

53. In Newbury, *Gerrish v. Dummer* (1675), *Essex Rec.*, VI, 39-42, 64-66; *Dummer v. Jacquis* (1677), *ibid.*, VII, 318-22. In Wenham, *Poland v. Patch* (1679), *ibid.*, VII, 291-93. For further examples of how the county courts were replacing the town meeting as an instrument of conflict resolution, see David Konig, Social Conflict and Community Tensions in Essex County, Massachusetts, 1672-1692 (unpub. Ph.D. diss., Harvard University, 1973), pp. 109-229.

54. Roy H. Akagi, *The Town Proprietors of the New England Colonies.*

court disputes over undivided common land were generally not between proprietors and recently arrived squatters demanding their
share of new allotments. Rather, such conflicts involved men seeking to revive dormant rights, as in cases where land divisions had
been made to residents who had neither wanted nor bothered to
claim them.[55]

Just as town grants of commonage rights were being avidly revived, so too were claims to town land which had been granted to
stimulate the settlement of artisans who could perform essential
services for the town.[56] Perhaps the longest and most complicated legacy created by an abandoned enterprise was the famous
Saugus ironworks dispute. Given generous subsidies of land as well
as exemptions from taxes and militia duty for its employees, this
enterprise went bankrupt in 1652 after seven years of operation.
Its final contribution to the colony, wrote William Hubbard several
years later, was that "instead of drawing out bars of iron for the
country's use, there was hammered out nothing but contention and
lawsuits." Unable to obtain currency for its products, the ironworks
had sunk deep into debt, and creditors' actions dragged on for over
twenty years.[57]

Confusion and litigation over the defunct corporation's landholdings continued throughout the 1680's. Along with the disputes
at Swampscott over John Humphrey's farm, these efforts to straigh-
ten out the chaotic land situation left by John Becx and Company
dominated the affairs of Lynn in those years. The Essex magistrates
were confronted with a welter of conflicting claims that taxed their
ability to impose order over the confusion of forty years. Land sales
by contesting creditors had left duplicate grantees, and unoccupied
land had come under the control of squatters, too. The complexity

A Study of their Development, Organization, Activities, and Controversies, 1620-1770 (Gloucester, 1963), pp. 44-47. A Marblehead episode of
1674 appears to foreshadow the later social cleavage, but it is actually
the claim of men with legitimate but dormant rights to membership in
the commonage. James v. Bartlett (1674), Essex Rec., V, 278-83.

55. See, as an example, Fletcher v. Town of Salem (1673), Essex Rec.,
V, 173-74, in which a commonage share of 1649 was sued for in 1673.

56. For examples of millers, see Ely v. Grele (1685), Essex Rec. TS,
box 3, folder 12, leaves 9c-9h; and Osgood v. Challis (1679), Essex Rec.,
VII, 191. Land granted to sawyers caused the same problems. For a six-
year dispute in Haverhill over land "between the west bridge and a bridge
where a sawmill stood formerly," see Davis v. Swan (1679), ibid., VII,
191.

57. For a fuller description of the Saugus iron enterprise, see Bernard
Bailyn, The New England Merchants in the Seventeenth Century (Cam-
bridge, 1955), pp. 63-71. Hubbard's observation, from his General
History, is cited ibid., p. 69.

of the problem—legal and political, for some powerful men were involved—overwhelmed the abilities of the Lynn town meeting, and it was the county court which finally brought the issue to a close.[58]

These official or collective efforts to achieve order were paralleled by the efforts of neighbors—usually second generation New Englanders—to formalize their own land dealings and relationships with each other. For example, men began recording deeds in full at the county registry although not required to do so by law; the first such verbatim recording appeared in 1658.[59] In all types of private land matters, Essexmen were attempting to impose order where it never had existed.

A major reason for this new departure among individuals, as well as towns, was a subtle and distant one. With the ending of the Protectorate in England, a new meaning attached to the Puritan commonwealths in New England. The distressing religious developments of the Civil War years had gone far to disabuse American Puritans of their hopes that their own type of religious conformity could be established in England. Whether "old priests" or "new presbyters" ruled there after 1660, it could not be viewed as a place to return to. Less and less could England be considered "home" in quite the sense it had been in earlier times. New Englanders were no longer a small band of temporary exiles in a strange land awaiting their vindicated return to old Essex or old Suffolk. Instead, the concept of a "New England" as a permanent provincial society gradually began to emerge.[60]

While New Englanders now struggled to create a stable and permanent society in the New World, they discovered many problems left by the "counter-migrants" who had returned to England during the Puritan ascendancy there.[61] The land situation in the county had changed since those people had left, and the uncer-

19

---

58. One ironworks dispute which was relatively clear and touched on many other questions of land and society was *Newhall v. Appleton* (1684), Essex Rec. TS, box 2, folder 11, leaves 68a-68d. See also *Appleton v. Marshall* (1684), *ibid.*, folder 8, leaves 49u-49w. For another protracted ironworks dispute, see Joseph Armitage's series of suits against Thomas Savage in *Essex Rec.*, V, 89, 116, 194, 316.

59. Essex Land Book, I, 95-97.

60. For a perceptive description of this new state of mind, see Robert Middlekauff, *The Mathers. Three Generations of Puritan Intellectuals* (New York, 1971), chapter 6.

61. The "counter-migration" is described in William L. Sachse, "The Migration of New Englanders to England, 1640-1660," 53 *Amer.. Hist. Rev.* 251-78 (1948).

tain status of the land they had left behind now required more formal determination in the maturing society of the Restoration.[62]

The most involved land dispute which grew indirectly out of a counter-migrant's return to England was the disposition of John Humphrey's farm in Swampscott. This disagreement dragged on for many years and, in its origins, development, and conduct, reveals much about the formalization of land arrangements in the decades after the Restoration. In 1641, Humphrey sold most of his land to Lady Deborah Moody, but her occupation of it was brief, and she left it behind in a disarranged legal state when she migrated to Long Island. William Witter, meanwhile, had lived on the farm since 1630, and his neighbors the Ingalls family had been operating a tannery there since 1632; to their north, Edward Richards had settled on the farm in 1641.

Despite this unsettled state of title, no problems arose until 1675, when Ezekiel Needham purchased land from Richards and soon found that the town was claiming it for itself. Needham and Richards settled out of court,[63] but in 1680 William Witter's son Josiah sued Richards for trespass on "his inheritance left him by his father." A non-suit forced Witter to re-enter his action at a later session that year, but not before Richards got Thomas Marshall, an old resident of the town, to testify that the Witters never had bought the land. In the second entry of the case Witter claimed to have obtained the land by town grant in 1676 after the Needham-Richards case had revealed the uncertain status of titles in that area. Richards, on the defensive, denied the right of the town to grant that particular lot and attacked his neighbor's "Itching desire after it." Although Witter won his cause at the county court, he lost it on Richards' appeal to the Court of Assistants two years later.[64]

---

62. In 1642, for instance, John Bulfinch was granted land in Salem. He never fenced in his lot, and in 1658 he removed to "Chattam, County Kent, Old England." On his death over twenty years later, his daughter Katherine Bell of Charlestown claimed the land by suing John Batchelor for felling timber there. The defendant had purchased the parcel in 1674. Indeed, the lot had changed owners twice before. Despite her father's failure to fence, as well as his removal to England, Katherine put in a claim for the lot. *Bell v. Batchelor* (1681), *Essex Rec.*, VIII, 71-74.

63. *Needham v. Richards* (1675), *ibid.*, VI, 88. For a similar case in Hampton, see *Tilton v. Palmer* (1678), *ibid.*, pp. 427-28.

64. *Witter v. Richards* (1680), *ibid.*, VII, 315-16; VIII, 10. *Richards v. Witter* (1682), *Records of the Court of Assistants of Massachusetts, 1630-1692*, ed. John Noble and John F. Cronin (3 vols., Boston, 1901-28), I, 187.

Within four years the entire neighborhood was drawn into two major court cases concerning the area.[65]

Beyond the effort to bring order to the confusion left by the counter-migration, the turmoil at Humphrey's Farm reveals an important social development in Essex County: sons were refusing to acknowledge the casual and informal land arrangements of their fathers. As the acquiescent first generation of men like William Witter passed away, their landholdings were inherited by sons like Josiah who were eager to place relationships on a more formal basis—and perhaps increase their holdings in the process. Men of this sort could not be expected to rely on the tacit understandings which their fathers had held. Land was scarcer, and they did not share the assumptions about its utilization prevalent among the first generation. No longer was it absolutely necessary to put land promptly under cultivation to avoid starvation. No longer was it possible, they saw, to draw on large tracts of undivided land within town limits, or simply to expand further into the surrounding countryside.

21

At any rate, it might be said that the land usage sins of the fathers were being visited on the succeeding generation. Land might be used for decades by first-generation claimants, with any dispute being settled between the two parties without litigation. New pressures and resentments were emerging and their sons, by contrast, could not achieve such an agreement. Where earlier recipients had been content to leave such matters untouched, a subsequent—and less acquiescent—generation went to court.[66]

Old relationships were being formalized, whether by title trial or by the building of fences where none had existed before. Generally it was the appearance of new claimants—such as sons—that forced changes in the relationships. Land had been transferred frequently in the first years of settlement, but it was not until the Restoration that the new grantees began insisting on exactness and rejecting casual treatment of land tenure. In Salem, for instance,

---

65. *Farr v. Needham* (1684), Essex Rec. TS, box 2, folder 7, leaves 49e-49h. *Witter v. Farr* (1684), ibid., folder 8, leaves 60a-60g. For yet another dispute deriving from a Humphrey grant in Essex County, see *Edwards v. Maverick* (1681), *Essex Rec.*, VIII, 174-80, which concerned his daughter's claim to eight hundred acres in Marblehead.

66. One of Hugh Peter's lots in Salem offers an illustration of this process: *Norman v. Orne* (1685), Essex Rec. TS, box 3, folder 11, leaves 76e-76i. For another case, in which two brothers had made an exchange of land which was "only verball" and led to later dispute, see *Balch v. Price* (1680), *Essex Rec.*, VII, 388-91. On other litigious sons of acquiescent fathers, see *Bennett v. Pengry* (1674), ibid., V, 286; also, *Savage v. Hathorne* (1681), ibid., VIII, 195-203.

Francis Nurse bought a wooded area next to Zerobabel Endecott from James Allen and promptly challenged Endecott to prove that part of the adjacent area was not Nurse's, too.[67]

Another legal problem which confronted second and third generation Essexmen was that of buying or inheriting land of dubious title or uncertain seisin. The common law required a testator to be seised of land at his death. Similarly, a mere demandant was not entitled to sell his right of possession,

22

> lest pretended title be purchased up, and thereby lawsuits be promoted. For if a bare right of property or possession could be conveyed or transferred, men fond in speculating in lawsuits would no doubt buy them up for small sums and bring many vexatious actions; therefore, the law has wisely forbidden such conveyances.

However, the problem of effectual seisin beset a society whose land usage patterns were only finally beginning to stabilize. It was exceedingly difficult for grantors to be certain that they had not alienated (or been disseised of) land which they thought they were seised of and wished to sell. To settle matters such as these, open trials of title in the county courts became absolutely necessary. All interested parties were able to testify, and the court's decision stood as a relatively effective and public guarantee where none other existed.[68]

A land cause in 1682 revealed this process at work. In 1680 John Newhall and his nephew of the same name approached "ancient" William Edmonds, an original settler of the town of Lynn. They were very anxious to buy a certain lot from him, but Edmonds did not remember the status of the land very clearly. Nevertheless, he sold it to them on the condition that it was in fact still his own. Problems arose when Joseph Mansfield also laid claim to the land and sued the elder Newhall for trespass. As plaintiff, he maintained that Edmonds had sold the land over forty years earlier to "one Manton," from whom it eventually passed to the Mansfield family. Actual possession of the land was uncertain because it was located over two miles away from where Mansfield and Newhall lived, and

---

67. *Nurse v. Endecott* (1683), Essex Rec. TS, box 1, folder 1, leaf 2. For Haverhill, see *Davis v. Wells* (1679), *Essex Rec.*, VII, 190.

68. Nathan Dane, *A General Abridgement and Digest of American Law, with Occasional Notes and Comments* (Boston, 1824), IV, 8. In Essex practice, title was assured not only against the other party in the dispute, but—significantly—against everyone else, for successful litigants were almost never subsequently forced to defend their claims against other demandants.

across the broad Saugus River "neare to the fresh marsh" bordering Boston. Such were Edmonds' misgivings about the sale—especially after Mansfield refreshed his memory—that they had "broken his rest many nights," and he wrote to the Newhalls to drop the issue. "I have furder considered of it," he explained to them, "and matters brought to my minde about the Alienateing of it, and I would have you desist, and intreat you, not to make any trouble about it." His "Loveing Friends," however, pressed forward with their use of the land and successfully resisted Mansfield's suit. Edmonds, who as a first-generation New Englander was evidently dismayed by these actions of the younger Newhalls, rested his conscience by giving the purchase price to Mansfield.[69]

Landholders in Essex County generally also tried to assert effectual seisin of land by fencing what they believed to be their own. This was a recognized means of taking possession of land, because a fence (or a ditch serving as a fence) was evidence of possession adverse to another claimant's use of the land. Of course, the other claimant's "knowledge" of the fence would be hard to prove, but if the occupation was sustained without interruption for a long time while the claimant resided in the area, legal disseisin was achieved.[70]

Unbroken tenure was vital in such cases, but it often happened that old fences fell into disrepair and the land was occupied by another. Because conveyances were inoperative, if made while a grantor was out of possession, it was necessary to sue and prove that the fence was "sufficient." The sufficiency of fences was a difficult problem even where title was not at issue;[71] the problem was especially difficult when it was, and when the *continuous* fencing of up to thirty years had to be proved. An Ipswich case of 1678 is typical. William Fellowes had purchased a farm there in 1651 and erected a fence around it. Between then and 1678, the fence collapsed and the land was sold to Isaac Fellowes, who rented it to two tenants. Samuel Ayres, a neighbor, objected to their use of the land and fenced part of it as his own. The court upheld his claim that the land was his and that his fencing was sufficient to

23

---

69. *Mansfield v. Newhall* (two actions, 1682), *Essex Rec.*, VIII, 253-257.

70. Dane, *Abridgement*, IV, 25. See, for instance, *Appleton v. Rhodes* (1685), Essex Rec. TS, box 3, folder 13, leaves 85d-85e. *Assistants Records*, I, 276-77, 281.

71. The Salem town meeting was forced to order fallen fences repaired as early as 1637. "Salem Rec.," *EIHC*, IX, 40. Trespasses not testing title, as well as fencing requirements, are discussed more fully in Konig, Social Conflict, pp. 112-30.

disseise his neighbors, who had failed to maintain their fences for decades.[72]

The need to make conveyances operative, then, resulted in unavoidable title litigation. Essexmen were finding that effectual seisin required "notoriety," and that only the county courts could furnish it. Vacant or occasionally used lands—especially those in an outlying area of the town such as Edmonds' lot—were open prey to second- and third-generation residents who were more aggressive and less casual in their attitudes toward land. The large number of trespass cases which flooded the county courts of Essex attest to this fact. As Thomas Newhall noted of his opponent, Mansfield "knew full will his Case Could not be tryed but Title of land must come Inn." Samuel Weed of Salisbury wanted to settle the division of marshland with his neighbor, and he asked John Chase for assistance. According to Chase, Weed

> was at my house and desired me to joine with him to get a parsel of medo which Thomas Chefe [Chafee] hired of Mr. Roberd pike juner, which medo sammuell weed said mager pik claymed to be his but he had no rit to it and me would make him try his titel for it. he had cutt som of the gras on purpos to mak him try his titel.[73]

Although the procedure was not always an entirely friendly one, the use of amicable legal processes to try and assure title became common in the last decades of the seventeenth century. Two litigants, in fact, sent with their depositions a document in which they promised to try the title at court, and they added,

> we do covenant and promise that the case shall fairly goe on and procead, and that neither of us will in any way endeavor to hinder by nonsuit or other way the procedure of it.

Men might petition the court to appoint a committee to settle such a problem "that each man might know his own," but they usually went the full route of a court encounter, even when "it was all done in love."[74] If the action was not entirely collusive, sometimes it

---

72. *Ayres v. Pengilla* (1678), *Essex Rec.*, VII, 84-85. See also *Sanford v. Putnam* (1674), *ibid.*, 322-25.

73. *Appleton v. Newhall* (1684), Essex Rec. TS, box 2, folder 10, leaves 59b-59c. *Pike v. Weed* (1691), Essex Rec. MS, L, 46-49. See also *Johnson v. Herriman* (1684), Essex Rec. TS, box 2, folder 9, leaves 69c-69h, on a man's felling "timber for his own use on purpose to bring it to trial."

74. *O'Barrow v. Paule* (1691), Essex Rec. MS, XLIX, 87-93. *Petition of James Burnam* (1679), *Essex Rec.*, VII, 266. *Maverick v. Griggs* (1685), Essex Rec. TS, box 3, folder 13, leaf 86a.

resulted from a grantor's unwillingness to give a deed despite yield-
ing seisin of the land. Grantees were becoming highly conscious of
the need to certify their holdings and were ready to enter an action
to gain the documents they required—whether the original deed or
a recorded court decision.[75]

Dubious titles and occupancies were thus open prey all over
the county in the last decades of the seventeenth century. All the
cases so far discussed, however, were dwarfed in complexity and
acquisitive audacity by a series of lawsuits over land in Salem.
Lasting from 1674 to 1690, this dispute epitomizes the historical
trends of land usage throughout the period and the problems faced
by people in Essex County at the end of the seventeenth century.
The land in question was part of Governor John Endecott's farm
along the Crane River in Salem, where boundaries had not been set
out elaborately in the Governor's lifetime. Perhaps because of his
status, his neighbors acknowledged *his* interpretation of their borders, and no need was felt to formalize something which was already confirmed by the word of the eminent Endecott. Sometime
around 1660, for example, Richard Ingerson had rented a parcel of
land next to the governor's. One day, related Richard's son,

> the said Governor Endecott came to my father when we wear
> at plow and said to my father he had fenced in some of the
> said Governor Endecott's land. My father Replied then he
> would Remove his fence. Noe, said Governor Endecott, lett it
> stand and when you sett up a new fence we will settle in the
> bounds.

The governor had no fear that his understanding of the borders
would be challenged, for his neighbors were willing to abide by his
opinion.[76]

The governor's son and grandsons, however, were less able
to command this type of deference, and Nathaniel Putnam of
Salem found the uncertainty of boundaries to be an opportunity
for expansion and consolidation of his own holdings. Putnam's
"grand designe" to gain the land, as the Endecotts derisively
called it, hinged on the town book's ambiguous specification of the
border between Endecott's farm and Nurse's.[77] Putnam's claim,
of course, was vigorously challenged by the Endecotts. The gover-

25

---

75. *Bennett v. Pengry* (1674), Essex Rec., V, 286. *Holdred v. Scammon*
(1676), *ibid.*, VI, 140. *Newhall v. Knight* (1691), Essex Rec. MS, LI, 101.
76. *Endecott v. Preston* (1690), Essex Rec. MS, XLIX, 3-21.
77. The two main cases in this dispute, with the important depositions, are *Endecott v. Nurse* (1678), *Essex Rec.*, VII, 10-21 and *Endecott
v. Preston* (1690), Essex Rec. MS, LXIX, 3-21.

nor's widow Elizabeth testified that the Crane River (also referred to as a brook) was the northern bound of all the lots along its banks. Her family, she deposed at the first hint of dispute in 1674, had enjoyed their holdings

> without molestation or any disturbance or claime laid to it that I know of after which time [of the governor's removal to Boston] Nathaniel Putman or Putnam did fence in some small part of that ground which was on our side of the brooke and did fell trees on the same ground which was great offence to us. . . .

Putnam was equally prepared to present evidence of long usage. William Hathorne Sr. deposed that the brook was not the border of the two lots, which were actually bounded by "fouer straite lines, on fower poynts of the compass, and not as that brook runs."

The Endecotts replied that of the four landlords in the area, three agreed to the traditional interpretation of the brook as the boundary. Unlike Putnam, they

> ar Contented with what is honestly their owne, only Nathaniel Putnam who out of a Covetous humor not Caringe how he Ruienes other men thereby to inrich himselfe observinge some Improper and doubtful expressions in the Recording of Bishops farme and by his subtlety and Cunning Craft hath occasioned much trouble to the Courts and molestation of his neighbors.

Putnam, they concluded, had a

> grand designe, being to Catch what he can . . . [and] to devide or Cut in two that part of his [Endecott's] farme and to make it like unto a kites tayle the like president not being knowne in the Cuntry.[78]

Putnam's "grand designe" had capitalized on the indefinite boundary and title situation existing in the county. The older land system (if it can be called a "system") had proved inadequate before the many factors of change: population pressure on a limited amount of land, a new commitment to "New England" as a permanent society requiring established and stable ways, and the needs of a developing society to consolidate land for more efficient usage or to put it to different purposes.

Other men dealing in land in Salem were also coming to recognize that land arrangements were dangerously undefined and pre-

---

78. *Endecott v. Nurse, ibid.*

carious. Before buying land, they had to be sure that they would not lose their investment to a third party reviving a dormant claim or to a neighbor with land claims extending onto the newly bought land. Uncertainty of title reduced the value of any plot of land, however small; homeowners as well as prospective purchasers of land investments wanted perfect and unassailable title. Remarked Thomas Gardner about a house and land in Salem, he "would not give as much for the house as he would have done before the claim was made" to it by a third party.[79]

When Stephen Hasscoll contemplated buying the old Townsend Bishop farm, to cite another example, he went to Nathaniel Putnam and asked if he thought that it was safe to buy the land. Putnam was presently suing Robert Sanford over that site, and Hasscoll was negotiating with Sanford to buy it. Putnam's advice was cynical but sound. "You may let him [Sanford] have that land in Controversy," he answered, and suggested that Hasscoll could do better by suing the Endecott family over *their* uncertain tenures. "You may take twice as much from Mr Endecot," Putnam said, "and an acre of that land is worth two of the land" that Hasscoll was thinking of buying.[80]

Putnam's acquisitiveness was forcing all the men in that neighborhood to make their holdings certain. Not everyone was happy about this, of course. Putnam, for example, had told Sanford the same thing he had told Hasscoll: give up the suit to a dubious title and instead make a more certain case against Endecott. Answered Sanford, "I must not give away my land to him to take away another mans land. I did desire nothing but my owne."[81] Nevertheless, Sanford was constrained to enter a trespass action against Putnam at the county court in order to try the title of the lot in controversy as an attempt merely to gain secure title to his "owne" land.[82] Despite his aversion to the procedure, Sanford had been caught up in the necessary process of confirming land tenure by means of litigation.

The public acknowledgement and certification of title to land therefore became one of the Essex County court system's most important functions in the late seventeenth century. Only through the forum of the courts, by way of openly conducted litigation, could certainty of title be obtained and publicized. The statutory procedures to be followed in the occupation, usage, and conveyan-

---

79. *Price v. Williams* (1683), Essex Rec. TS, box 2, folder 6, leaf 33. See Also *Marshall v. Fellowes* (1684), *ibid.*, leaf 32.
80. *Nurse v. Endecott* (1683), ibid., box 1, folder 1, leaf 2.
81. *Endecott v. Preston*, n. 76 supra.
82. *Sanford v. Putnam* (1674), *Essex Rec.*, V, 322-25.

27

cing of land had become unenforceable. Even when followed, more-over, they proved to be inadequate at best and troublesome at worst. In the first place, full recording of the dimensions and limits of the land conveyed was not required, and would have been nearly impossible if it had been. Secondly, the system led to the very title disputes it was intended to prevent because it was easy to record the fraudulent sale of land. Apparently, no title search was demanded of grantor or grantee, and the recorder did not require absolute proof of title by the grantor. It was thus possible for a man with no legal title to a lot to sell it and have the transaction acknowledged by a magistrate and recorded by the county. Josiah Rootes (or Rhodes) did this in 1659 when he sold to Henry Kenny land that he knew belonged to his brother Thomas Rootes. Thomas had received the land by deed in 1655, but he had neither occupied the land nor recorded his receipt of the deed. It remained for him and Kenny to thrash out the problem before the courts in 1683.[83]

In large part the failure to record conveyances may be attributed to the fact that recording was required by law only "where the Graunter remains in possession." Given the casualness with which occupancy was treated in the early years, it is not difficult to see that misunderstanding could arise as to whether the grantee's entry and possession were actual and thus operative without recording. In Rowley this sort of problem occurred in 1672. Anthony Crosby had pledged an acre and a half to Richard Langhorne in 1661 as security for a debt. Crosby did not pay and thereby forfeited the land, but Langhorne never took possession. Crosby, as grantor, thus remained in possession of the land, and his conveyance to Langhorne was not operative because no recording was made of it. Crosby thereupon sold the land in 1665.[84]

III. Legal Divergence: The Failure of the Common Law as the Basis of Essex Land Jurisprudence

The land litigation in which the second generation of Essex settlers engaged spawned many novel and unanticipated legal problems for which the common law of England often provided inadequate answers. The common law of real property in England was a complicated body of rules containing many vestigial remains of medieval law. Called "an ungodly jumble" by Cromwell, the land law that was brought to Essex County in 1630 was heavily in-

---

83. *Rootes v. Kenny* (1683), Essex Rec. TS, box 1, folder 2, leaf 10. For a similar case involving another member of the Rootes family, see *Roades v. Appleton* (1685), *ibid.*, box 3, folder 12, leaf 75.

84. *Laws and Liberties*, pp. 13-14. *Langhorne v. Crosby* (1672), *Essex Rec.*, V, 80.

fluenced, of course, by local custom and included the varying practices of the many different manors from which the first planters
came.[85]

When this variety of English law was applied to the new
methods of land distribution and utilization in the new world,
though, its inadequacies quickly became apparent. Litigation was
necessary for the many individual disagreements for which no
general principles existed. The lack of principles resulted in decisions that were often contradictory, as technical questions of law
and procedure were largely ignored in the interests of fairness and
flexibility. As one historian has written of the Suffolk courts in this
period, "Decisions usually turned on issues of fact." Two centuries
ago Thomas Hutchinson had made the same observation of colonial
judges: "In civil actions," he wrote,

> equity, according to the circumstances of the case, seems to
> have been their rule of determining. Their judges had recourse
> to no other authorities, than the reason and understanding
> which God had given them.[86]

Part of the problem was that law brought to Essex from England sometimes provided no guidance at all in resolving the novel
legal issues that arose in the New World. One set of issues for which
English law gave no guidance arose out of the periodic division of
common lands in the various Massachusetts towns. It was not absolutely clear among Essex commoners if the purchaser of a lot originally laid out in a division of common lands also obtained the right
to the future allotments which an original grantee was assumed to
possess, or if the seller—because of his personal status as an original grantee—retained it. It was not clear, that is, whether rights to
allotments upon future divisions of common land could be held separate and apart from land obtained in earlier divisions.

Many people in the county were now eagerly seeking shares in
the commonage which their fathers had not cared about. Thomas
Elithorp of Rowley had bought one lot from a founder of the town,
but had sold it to Thomas Burckbee. The latter paid for it "partly
with a cow" before trying to back out of the deal. Actually, the land
and rights had little attraction for either of them: Elithorp later

---

85. As late as 1832 a British government commission observed "Each
manor had for itself a system of laws to be sought in oral tradition, or in
the court rolls or proceedings of the customary court, kept often by ignorant or negligent stewards." A. W. B. Simpson, *An Introduction to the
History of the Land Law* (London, 1961), pp. 217, 162.

86. Zechariah Chafee, Jr., "Colonial Courts and the Common Law,"
in *Essays in the History of Early American Law*, ed. David H. Flaherty
(Chapel Hill, 1969), p. 71. Hutchinson, *History*, I, 367.

renounced all right to land in Rowley, and Burckbee sold the lot to Joseph Jewett in 1654. In these last sales, Burckbee testified in 1672, he "never askt any deeds of it nor gave any when I sould it, nor troubled myself further about it." Elithorp's son John, though, renewed the family claim and successfully demanded that the town give him a full share in the next division of town lands.[87]

An even more complicated case arose when Anthony Carrell of Topsfield sued the purchaser of his commons share. Carrell had sold his share for thirty shillings to Thomas Baker, not expecting the town to make any further divisions. He did not leave the town, and continued to live on the houselot he had been granted. As a result, there was a question as to who deserved the new allotment— the original grantee still living on his old houselot, or the later purchaser of the commonage share. The problem was clarified only when local practices were explained to the court by another resident. He described that in the past, lot divisions "were denied to some who had not improved their lands at that time." Carrell fit the description of the customary practice, and the court rejected his suit.[88]

Where explicit proof of an original grant and subsequent conveyance of a right to a division of common land could be shown, the county courts generally decided in favor of the holder under the subsequent conveyance.[89] But in the many cases where no understanding at all, either written or implied, existed, the courts needed to formulate some rule of law to arbitrate the dispute between original and subsequent grantees of commons rights. In formulating a rule they could not turn to English precedent, since common lands in England, unlike those in Massachusetts, were rarely subjected to periodic divisions of new land among individual members of a corporation.[90] Instead, as in the Carrell dispute, the courts often

---

87. *Elithorp v. Pickard* (1672), *ibid.*, pp. 15-18. Attempts to revive claims might take many forms. For an example from Salisbury, see *Stevens v. Clement* (1692), Essex Rec. MS, LII, 47-54. Similar disputes arose concerning the early commonage grants made in Amesbury when part of Salisbury. *Weed v. Barnard* (1674), *Essex Rec.*, V, 296; *Fowler v. Weed* (1679), *ibid.*, VII, 274. On Rowley, see also *Longfellow v. Northend* (1679), *ibid.*, pp. 207-09; *Northend v. Longfellow* (1679), *ibid.*, pp. 209-16.

88. *Carrell v. Baker* (1673), *ibid.*, V, 133-35. For other cases of this sort in Rowley and Salem, see *Johnson v. Remington* (1674), *ibid.*, pp. 277-78; *Wicom v. Pickard* (1677), *ibid.*, VI, 364-66; *Howard v. Green* (1685), Essex Rec. TS, box 3, folder 13, leaves 84b-84f.

89. *Longfellow v. Pickard* (1678), *Essex Rec.*, VII, 122-23.

90. Collective purchase by commoners acting as a corporation was rare in English practice, and was confined to pasture land, which was then "stinted" or shared, of course, as common land among them. It was

turned to local town customs and transformed them into a new
body of law that would stabilize land dealings in Essex county.

Essex courts also found the common law to be of little help in
resolving disputes that arose when individuals who had been
granted land for a specific purpose, such as maintaining a mill,
continued to claim the land after they had ceased to fulfill the purpose. In 1637 John Goyt, for example, came to Cape Anne and
while there built a boat for John Humphrey. Goyt was not planning
to remain in the area, and when he told of his plans to leave for
"Mittapese," Humphrey and John Winthrop Jr. urged him to stay.
Goyt was a skilled laborer who could furnish the small shallops
necessary for communications and coastal fishing. To induce him
to stay they subsidized him with the grant of a cove at Marblehead
which served as an ideal business site for him and as a convenient
landing place for others to use. Goyt thus "satt downe at Marblehead" that year and began his work. Ten years later he sold the
cove by deed to one William Pitts, who sold it to Christopher Lattimore in 1659. Lattimore then sold it to Edward Holman, but the
latter upset things by fencing it in for his private use.

Holman was making a private claim to land which had been
attached to a public service no longer being rendered. He rested
his case on the validity of the deeds showing legal conveyance
from Goyt to Pitts to Lattimore to himself. Contrariwise, the town
of Marblehead brought two old residents to testify. These men,
Moses Maverick and John Peach Sr., had lived there since 1633.
Despite their insistence that the cove always had been considered
public property, Holman's enclosure was upheld.[91]

A seemingly contradictory result was reached in an analogous
case. In the 1640's Robert Clements of Haverhill had built a house
on a lot given him in return for grinding corn. On his deathbed he

31

---

not the practice of English landholders to act as a corporate body for
the acquisition of new land which then would be distributed as private
holdings in severalty. When new intakes were made from waste or de-
mesne (as in deparking), they were acquired by individuals acting as
individuals. It is important to emphasize the fundamental difference between English and early American agricultural conceptions here. In
Massachusetts, new divisions of town land were inseparably attached
to an individual's rights of commonage as well as to cutomary considerations. In England, on the other hand, all new intakes were regarded
as a "new thing" that could have no connection to past custom. While
legal distinctions between existing common and new intakes were basic
to English practice, it was the inviolate *connection* between the two that
characterized early American land arrangements. On the English background, see R. H. Tawney, *The Agrarian Problem in the Sixteenth Century* (New York, 1960 [1912]), pp. 95, 157-60, 245, 284-94.

91. *Hooper v. Holman* (1677), *Essex Rec.*, VI, 361-63.

acknowledged the town's ownership of the land. Nonetheless, his son sold the land to Daniel Ely. But another man—claiming the land by right of a subsequent town grant—had built a house there and refused all efforts to oust him. Fortunately, he located an old woman who could testify to Clements' deathbed cession. As an ancient settler of the town, her memory was accepted as proof of that particular town's traditional position; *viz.*, that "the land lying between the mill formerly called Mr. Clemansis mill and the street was Clemans no longer than he supplied the town by grinding."[92]

The inconsistency between the results of these two cases, together with the evidence of custom given in the latter, suggests that local town custom rather than a more widely applicable rule of common law was the basis for deciding them. Custom, in short, seems to have conferred title in Essex cases, even if custom was inconsistent with the rules of statute or of common law. One noteworthy example of this judicial disregard of statute and common law in a land cause was *West v. White,* in which the court rejected the suit of a man who had received possession of land by livery of seisin and had had his conveyance acknowledged and recorded by a magistrate pursuant to the recording act.[93]

A frequent situation in which Essex courts ignored common law rules arose when two individuals were in possession of the same land. It was very common for both the holder of title and the squatter to enjoy the use of the land at the same time. This simultaneous occupancy—which was a solecism at common law— was possible in an agrarian situation where grass was mowed only occasionally and only in certain spots of a large lot, or where cattle were pastured only occasionally. It was all the more usual in the early decades of settlement when owners of land in outlying areas of the town did not exclude others from using it while still nominally retaining the privilege of using it themselves.

The Essex County courts were frequently beset with such problems. Nathaniel Putnam's "grand designe" and the Nurse-Endecott dispute, for example, contained this feature. It was not unusual in these cases for both parties to bring men to court to attest to usage of the land many decades before, when they had been boys. When Sagamore Hill in Ipswich was contested in 1691, each side was able to obtain such witnesses. On one side, fifty-eight-year old Isaac Cummins told of learning forty years earlier that a house on the hill belonged to Daniel Hovey, the defendant in the action, and Thomas Metcalf testified that he had mowed the hill for the defendant "when I was a Lad and lived by Goodman

---

92. *Ely v. Grele* (1685), Essex Rec. TS, box 3, folder 12, leaves 9c-9h.
93. *West v. White* (1673), *Essex Rec.*, V, 174-75.

Hovey." On the other, Henry Bennett and Nathaniel Emerson told how Quartermaster Perkins and his son Abraham (the plaintiff) had enjoyed the land without challenge for over forty years.[94] Also in Ipswich, Thomas Boarman and Samuel Hunt had mowed the same lot for decades until Hunt finally said to the former, "Get you off my land, you Rogue." Hunt backed up his threat with a pitchfork, and Boarman judiciously decided on other ways of settling the matter. He replied, "you had better try the title to the Land another way" and then entered a court action against Hunt for mowing the land and "making void the title."[95]

Hunt, ironically, won the case at law, and his victory demonstrates a new world divergence from common law practice. The common law required that the person making the greatest use of the land be adjudged to have seisin thereof, provided his use had continued for the requisite statutory period. The rights of the second user, however, were also protected at common law, since he was accorded a right in the nature of a profit—a right, that is, to continue using the land as he had previously used it—provided he had used it for the statutory period. The Essex courts, however, sometimes rejected the common law rules (as they did for Hunt) and instead decided cases in a way that gave an unencumbered title to one of the competing users, even if he had not used the land for the full statutory period. Thus, when Edward Colcord of Hampton brought suit against Nathaniel Boulter and Francis Page, who had been cutting grass on his meadow "for twelve or fourteen years," in order to bar them from "endeavoring to alter the title," he found that their twelve year use was sufficient to give them title and for the court to reject his case.[96]

33

The policy of upholding titles unencumbered by rights in another emerged most clearly in a case that arose when the Manchester-Gloucester boundary was settled in 1672. Samuel Leach of Manchester then discovered that the land on which he had cut timber for many years actually lay in Gloucester. This tract had been granted to Gloucester's minister, the Reverend Richard Blindman,

94. *Perkins v. Hovey* (1691), Essex Rec. MS, LI, 36-39. Both sides claimed forty years because it was the period specified in the statute of limitations.

95. *Boarman v. Hunt* (1678), *ibid.*, VII, 85-87.

96. *Colcord v. Bouter* (1672), *ibid.*, V, 100. Other cases of this sort, granting title and barring further use of the land regardless of prior practice or arrangement, include the following: *Selectmen of Rowley v. Nelson* (1672), *ibid.*, pp. 86-87; *Ayres v. Pengilla* (1678), *ibid.*, VII, 84-85; *Neale v. Skerry* (1678), *ibid.*, pp. 107-08; *Fowler v. Nealand* (1681), *ibid.*, VIII, 151-52; *Savage v. Hauthorne* (1681), *ibid.*, pp. 195-203. *Marshall v. Fellowes* (1684), Essex Rec. TS, box 2, folder 6, leaf 32; *Orne v. Norman* (1684), *ibid.*, folder 10, leaves 68i-68m.

34

and it had passed to Richard Russell and then to Robert Knight. Leach and Knight were talking in 1678 when the former casually admitted that he had been chopping wood there for a long time and that he would continue to do so. The problem was a sticky one. Knight owned the land in question, "Kettle Cove," which in 1672 had been declared a part of Gloucester. Leach, although he acknowledged Knight's land rights in Gloucester, claimed to have enjoyed timber rights there by custom as a resident of Manchester. To settle the matter, Knight entered a trespass action against Leach in 1679. The court decided for the plaintiff, going against the defendant's insistence on the common law customary right in the nature of a profit. Leach was undaunted and soon filed for a review, "saying in a bragging way that he would keep the title of Kittle Cove in litigation for 20 or 40 years. . . ." The problem finally had to be settled at the Court of Assistants, where Knight won the appeal.[97]

The willingness of the courts to give title to an individual on the basis of an occupation of land for less than the common law statutory period emerged with comparable clarity in the litigation between Richard Dummer of Newbury and the town fathers. The litigation arose because Dummer claimed twenty acres more than he had fenced. Dummer tried and failed to get redress at a town meeting and in 1675 was impelled to "use some other meanes to recover my right, which is about twenty acres more than is fenced." He thereupon fenced the additional land and was sued by the town. Dummer was able to win his case and guarantee his legacy when he proved that his tenant had been using the land for eight years without a fence, and that there was "evidence of an old fence on the line by old posts and rails and many post holes."[98]

The new circumstances of life in Essex County thus had proved much of the common law inapplicable to land matters there. Land law was being modernized in England, but the common law forms of action were being designed for the problems of real property in England, and were ill-adapted for use in the new world.[99] Ejectment, which was becoming the most widely used form for trying title, was frequently inoperative in Essex despite its many resemblances to the form of title trial by trespass being used there. Ejectment was limited by certain provisions which severely restricted its application to the vexing land problems of Essex

97. *Knight v. Leach* (1679), *ibid.*, 198-201. *Knight v. Leach* (1680), *ibid.*, VII, 3-6. *Leach v. Knight* (1681), *ibid.*, VIII, 106-08. *Assistants Records*, I, 184, 194.

98. *Gerrish v. Dummer* (1675), *Essex Rec.*, VI, 64-66.

99. Samuel E. Thorne, "Tudor Social Transformation and Legal Change," 26 *N.Y.U. L. Rev.* 10-23 (1951).

County. Again, the reason was the abandonment or sporadic occupation of land for long periods of time. Ejectment was not available, for example, if the demandant's right of entry had been "tolled;" i.e., if a disseisor died while seised and his heir assumed possession of the land.[100]

When the common law was inapplicable, Essex courts often resorted to a quasi-equitable jurisdiction. The result was a sharp divergence of legal practices in Essex from the contemporary trends in English legal development. In seventeenth century England, the High Court of Chancery had become a leading target of legal reformers. Selden, for one, had commented that equity was determined by the length of the chancellor's foot, and English Puritans in general supported the efforts of Coke and the Parliamentarians to assert the supremacy of the common law over equity.[101]

American Puritans, on the other hand, found the equitable powers of the courts to be ideally suited to the conditions and needs of a new environment. The greatest reason for Puritan opposition to Chancery in England had been its employment to extend royal authority, rather than an ideological aversion to equity. American Puritans were perfectly willing to wield that type of power themselves. Indeed, Winthrop's famous defense of discretionary magistracy indicates a realization in Massachusetts that the law must be flexible and adaptable and not constrained by traditional limitations and customs deriving from a different situation.[102]

Other reasons also made equity more acceptable in Massachusetts than in England. The fundamental source of law and authority in Massachusetts was divine. Although the biblicism of early New England law has been over-emphasized, it is still valid to state that the legal system of the Bay Colony was based on God's authority— "an authority," wrote Woodruff, "in which the conscience of equity must have been supposed to inhere." Secondly, the powers of equity in Massachusetts were not wielded by a chancellor alone and did not derive from the opinion of a single man. When the Essex County courts made a decision based on equitable considerations rather than the common law, a jury was present and participating.[103]

---

100. Simpson, *Land Law*, p. 142. Another situation common in Essex and barring the use of ejectment was "deforcement." This affected squatter's land whose owner had never entered the land after gaining the right to it while the squatter was in possession. *Ibid.*

101. F. A. Inderwick, *The Interregnum, 1648-1660* (London, 1891), p. 223. John D. Eusden, *Puritans, Lawyers, and Politics* (New Haven, 1968), pp. 55, 163.

102. *Ibid.*, p. viii. John Winthrop, *History of New England*, ed. James Savage (Boston, 1853), I, 322.

103. Edwin H. Woodruff, "Chancery in Massachusetts," 5 *L. Q. Rev.*

The most important reason for the employment of legal powers formerly reserved to Chancery, though, was the demonstrated inapplicability of the common law to the varied and novel land problems in Massachusetts, and the ability of Essex Courts to use equity and custom to mold a new and more adaptable land law. This reliance on equity and community custom was a common sense response to the varying and unique needs of many different localities. Both in the situations they confronted and the equitable solutions they chose, the Essex County courts came to resemble English manorial courts very closely. Dealing with Essex freehold much in the manner copyhold had been treated, magistrates found manorial procedure —with its simplicity, its recording security, and its freedom from the technicalities of the common law—well suited to dealing with the bewildering novelties of their jurisdiction. The executive administration of the Essex courts was as "immense" as that of a court leet in England, and a description of English manorial courts can be applied to the quarterly sessions of Essex in their effort to impose order on the county's land arrangements:

> They employed various modes of action that we would not try to distinguish—rule making through by-laws, and ordinances, commands addressed to individuals and directing them to desist from conduct that was disapproved, or conviction for past misconduct with the penalty an amercement.

Like Essex courts, "these farmer courts could use 'equity' powers," and their juries, too, "acted in the confident belief that they had a general mandate to serve community interests in the ways that seemed best to them."[104] In Essex, where the insistence on strict legal forms and doctrines would have caused extensive hardship, the existence of a flexible legal system was essential. Allowing for individual consideration of each land disagreement on its own merits and according to local custom, it was a vital source of stability and order.

---

371 (1889). Thomas Lechford was appalled by the participation of a jury in the determination of equity matters. *Plain Dealing, or News from New England* [1642], ed. J. Hammond Trumbull (New York, 1970), p. 66.

104. John P. Dawson, *A History of Lay Judges* (Cambridge, 1960), pp. 231, 235, 244-45. Ironically, Coke had defended the right of a manorial lord to employ a type of equity in disputes among his copyholders: "he is not tied to the strict forme of the Common Law, for he is a Chancellor in his Court, and may redresse matters of Conscience upon Bill exhibited, where Common Law will afford no remedy. . . ." Sir Edward Coke, *The Compleat Copy-Holder, wherein is contained a Learned Discourse of the Antiquity and Nature of Mannors and Copy-holds* (London, 1650), p. 122.

36

IV. *The Legal Crisis of the Intercharter Period*

Despite the apparent chaos of incessant litigation, a system of order had emerged in Essex County. The loss of the colonial charter in 1684, however, overthrew that system and threatened to produce genuine disorder, for it was feared that the crown would demand enforcement of all the rigorous land requirements of the common law and thereby prevent landholders from obtaining certainty of tenure. To prevent this dangerous situation the General Court in 1685 suddenly passed an act officially confirming equity powers to all county courts, thereby permitting the continuation of equitable procedures. It explained that such an act was necessary because

> it is found by experience that in many cases and controversys betwixt partys, wherein there is matter of apparent equity, there hath been no way provided for releife against the rigour of the common law. . . .[105]

The General Court passed this law despite the revocation of the charter and the loss of legislative powers the previous year. As a result, the Dudley regime, established in 1686 passed its own judicature act for the Dominion. It, too, provided for equitable determinations, but the new court of chancery was a single high court for the entire colony and not a county equity court familiar with local custom and local realities. Instead of being made up of local magistrates with elected associates and a freely chosen jury, the new court was

> to be holden by the Governour or such person as he shall appoint to be Chancellor Assisted with 5 or more of the Councill who in this Court shall have the same power and Authority as masters of Chancery in England have or ought to have.

Moreover, appeals had to be sent out of the colony and directly to the King and Privy Council.[106]

The county courts were further undermined by the loss of their authority to decide any matter of title. This removal was a major alteration of traditional ways. No longer could titles be tried at a local

---

105. Massachusetts Archives, XL, 212-14 (Hereafter, Mass. Arch.). The preamble to the act noted that equity previously had been confined to the Assistants Court. This the legislature knew to be false, but it inserted it to counter English accusations that the colony had departed from its own codes, in which equity was reserved to the Assistants. After the Glorious Revolution, the county courts resumed these powers. *English v. Cromwell* (1690), Essex Rec. MS, XLIX, 69-78.

106. Mass. Arch., XL, 231-32. Viola F. Barnes incorrectly states that "the court of chancery established under the new system was a continuation of the one established in Massachusetts for the first time in 1685." *The Dominion of New England. A Study in British Colonial Policy* (New Haven, 1923), pp. 107-08.

court where one's elected justices sat in judgment. An itinerant
superior county court of common pleas was established in its place.
Although for Essex it held quarterly sessions at Salem and Ipswich,
it was distinctly different from the old charter's county courts.[107]
    First of all, this new court's lack of equity power made it im-
possible for Essex landholders to determine title in the way they had
come to expect. They resented the replacement of equitable determinations by the more rigorously technical common law and regarded it as "oppressive and injurous to the people." Title trials,
complained several former councillors after the revolution of 1689,

> must have had their Decision at the Ordinary Courts of com-
> mon law . . . whose matters of Equity and a Consideration
> transcending all Ordinary cases could not have a Proper Recog-
> nizance and due influence in the decision determination and
> judgment.

This change meant that title trials by collusive trespass actions
were no longer permitted. The Dominion jurists were well aware of
the local divergence from English ways, and they attempted—
with disturbing temporary success—to reverse that trend. John
Palmer, one of the judges of the Dominion's superior court system,
insisted on the application of common law forms to Essex land
causes and pointed out the legal absurdity of the old charter procedure. He wrote,

> 'Tis a Maxime, Volenti non fit injuria [Damage suffered by
> consent is no cause of action]; and when both Plaintiff and
> Defendant do, by a joynt consent, submit to the determination
> of the Court, or by their own negligence make default; Who
> hath the wrong? Where is the injury? This hath been a prac-
> tice so frequently used in your former Government (though
> under another name), that no body can be ignorant of it.[108]

In Connecticut, Gershom Bulkeley was more blunt when he criticized
his colony's pre-Dominion "abolition of the common and statute laws
of England, and so of all human laws except the forgeries of our own
popular and rustical shop and the dictates of personal discretion."[109]
    The success of the Dominion's effort to impose the common law
can be seen in the surviving records of the superior court of common

---

107. Mass. Arch., CXXVI, 250, 254, 257.
    108. Mass. Arch., XXXV, 155, 190. John Palmer, An Impartial Ac-
count of the State of New England (London, 1690), reprinted in The
Andros Tracts, ed. William H. Whitmore (Boston, 1868), I, 46.
    109. Gershom Bulkeley, Will and Doom, or the Miseries of Connecti-
cut by and under an Usurped and Arbitrary Power [1692], ed. Charles
J. Hoadly, Connecticut Historical Society, Collections, III (Hartford,
1895), 90.

pleas.[110] Common law forms are conspicuous by their presence. The fictitious litigants John Doe and Richard Roe made their first Essex appearances in an ejectment case of 1686, for example. Technical requirements of litigation were enforced, and court fees increased.[111] Popular distrust and resentment were obvious, as land litigation—so prevalent in court activity before 1684—was avoided and almost disappeared. Essexmen, it seems, were suppressing their conflicts out of fear that English practices would endanger their land arrangements.[112]

Their fears were well-founded, and were demonstrated by the retrial of the notorious "kites tayle" disagreement involving Nathaniel Putnam, Francis Nurse, and the Endecott family. The first two trials of title had been held under the old charter at the county courts; each time, Endecott's claim was upheld against Putnam's unconscionable —but legally sound—"grand designe." At the superior court session of September 1686, however, the action was tried again at Nurse's request. No equitable considerations were allowed, and Endecott lost his case at common law.[113]

Perhaps just as annoying to Essex landholders were the men constituting the superior court bench. Prior to the establishment of the Dominion legal system, the Essex county courts had a fairly stable bench. Since 1680, it was generally made up of Nathaniel Saltonstall of Haverhill, Daniel Denison of Ipswich, Robert Pike of Salisbury, Samuel Appleton of Lynn, and William Browne and Bartholomew Gedney of Salem. Gedney, Appleton, and Browne were carried over to assist at the superior court, and Daniel Epps of Ipswich and Richard Dummer of Newbury were added to it. Yet it was not these

39

<hr/>

110. These important records, which are nowhere cited in any monograph, guide, or bibliography of Massachusetts legal records, can be found included in the manuscript folios of the inferior court of common pleas at the Salem courthouse, Essex Rec. MS, XLV, 145 through XLVI, 136. They encompass two sessions of the superior court presided over by William Stoughton, John Usher, and Bartholomew Gedney at Ipswich, September 1686, and Salem, November 1686.

111. *Roe v. Doe "of the demise of Henry Rhodes"* (1686), *ibid.*, XLVI, 101-11. Court costs increased with the imposition of an additional one-shilling fee for "taxing cost" and greater insistence on the employment of writs and attachments, which also cost money. Recognizances, which had been required only in cases of appeal, were also sometimes required of plaintiffs in original actions. *Bowden v. Oak* (1688), *ibid.*, XLVII, 134-35. *Cross v. Manning* (1689), *ibid.*, XLVIII, 20-21.

112. In Salem a potential real property action was avoided when the parties settled the dispute amicably rather than submit to a common law title trial. *Shaw's Case* (1689), *ibid.*, pp. 28-29.

113. *Nurse v. Endecott*, n. 77 *supra*.

local men who caused problems, but rather the new presiding judges who made their own wills prevail over them.[114]

John Usher, Joseph Dudley, and William Stoughton were the councillors presiding at Salem and Ipswich, and their clerk was George Farwell. All of them were new to the county, and together they caused no little antagonism. One case from the Salem superior session of May 1686 was particularly outrageous. In January of that year Phillip Nelson served a writ of ejectment on John Pearson, Sr., to try the title to four and one-half acres of meadow and planting land and one-half share of a grist mill, all in Rowley. When the case came before the superior court in May, the jury decided in Pearson's favor. Dudley and Stoughton accepted the verdict, and clerk Farwell recorded it. However, Farwell was also Nelson's attorney, and when Pearson and his attorney Daniel Wicom left the courtroom Farwell removed the trial from the record and entered a new action. Dudley then sent the jury out again, and upon their special verdict he made a new decision in Nelson's favor. Wicom had no success at reversing this at the next superior session and had to appeal to the Governor and Council, the highest tribunal in the colony. Because clerk Farwell was not present when Wicom asked for the appeal, Wicom had to travel to Boston to enter it. There he paid the necessary fees to Dudley, who assured him that the appeal was duly entered. But "instead of hearing when our case should have a hearing," wrote Wicom after the uprising of 1689, "the next news came marshall [Jeremiah] Neale with an execution, which execution I understand was signed by Mr. Dudley."[115]

Incomplete as the Dominion records are for Essex County, they nonetheless reveal a genuine threat to the landholding and social system of the area which has not been recognized by historians. It is an historical commonplace that Andros challenged the validity of existing land claims in the colony, but the problem has been treated as between the Crown and individuals. Aside from making a belated effort to confirm their purchase of land from the Indians, though, Essex landowners did not bother to confirm their individual holdings with the Crown.[116]

114. *Essex Rec.*, VIII, 1, 24, 65, 150, 187, 241, 318, 394. Essex Rec. TS, box 1, folder 1, leaf 1; folder 2, leaf 1; folder 3, leaf 10; folder 4, leaf 18. *Ibid.*, box 2, folder 6, leaf 27; folder 7, leaf 48; folder 8, leaf 46.

115. Mass. Arch., XXXV, 137.

116. Only two men, Nelson of Rowley and John Small of Salem, requested title confirmation from the Dominion government for land within Essex County. Sidney Perley, *The Indian Land Titles to Essex County* (Salem, 1912), pp. 67-75, 77. Salem, Lynn, and Marblehead obtained Indian deeds for this purpose in 1684 and 1687. Confirmation of land claims with the Crown are discussed by Barnes, *Dominion of New Eng-*

Of even greater importance to landholders of Essex County, though, was the disruption of their accustomed system of determining title to land among individual, private citizens. By the 1680's colonial courts and jurisprudence had become essential to this aspect of their social organization, and the Dominion's disruptions were calamitous for the stability of their communities.

41

land, pp. 189-91. However, almost all of these were for grants in Maine, where title was more threatened by the claims of Mason to the area. Mass. Arch., CXXVI, 199; CXXVII, 236a, 239, 246, 254, 257, 258, 259, 278, 280; CXXVIII, 22a, 103, 109, 128, 137, 146, 174, 189, 200, 277, 296; CXXIX, 6, 66, 67, 69, 71, 98, 99, 111, 112.

DEATH AND THE PURITAN CHILD

DAVID E. STANNARD
American Studies Program
Yale University

FROM TIME TO TIME IN THE HISTORY OF MAN A NEW IDEA OR WAY OF LOOK-
ing at things bursts into view with such force that it virtually sets the terms
for all relevant subsequent discussion. The Copernican, Darwinian and
Freudian revolutions—perhaps, as Freud on occasion noted, the three most
destructive blows which human narcissism has had to endure—are among
the extreme examples of such intellectual explosions. Others have been of
considerably more limited influence: the concept of culture in anthropology
is one example, the frontier thesis as an explanatory device for American
history is another. At still another level is the seminal study of a particular
problem. An instance of this is the fact that throughout the past decade historians of family life have conducted their research in the shadow of Philippe Ariès' monumental study, *Centuries of Childhood,* a work that established much of the currently conventional wisdom on the subject of the
family in history.

One of Ariès' most original and influential findings was that childhood as
we know it today did not exist until the early modern period. "In medieval
society," he observed, ". . . as soon as the child could live without the
constant solicitude of his mother, his nanny or his cradle-rocker, he
belonged to adult society."[1] It was not until the 16th and 17th centuries, and
then only among the upper classes, that the modern idea of childhood as a
distinct phase of life began to emerge.

The picture Ariès sketched, drawing on such diverse sources as
portraiture, literature, games and dress, was predominantly one of French
culture and society; but it was clear that he felt his generalizations held true
for most of the Western world. Recent studies in colonial New England
have supported Ariès' assumption of the representativeness of his French

---

[1]Philippe Ariès, *Centuries of Childhood: A Social History of Family Life* (New York:
Random House, 1962), p. 128.

findings in extending his observations on medieval life to 17th and 18th
century Massachusetts; but the support for this contention is unsteady,
balanced as it is on much less substantive data than that on which Ariès' argument rests. The clothing of children as adults—only one strand of evidence in Ariès' historical tapestry—has been seized by some colonial historians and used as the principal basis for claiming that in 17th and 18th
century Massachusetts there was little or no distinction between children
and adults. "If clothes do not make the man," writes Michael Zuckerman,
"they do mark social differentiations"; and, adds John Demos, "the fact
that children were dressed like adults does seem to imply a whole attitude of
mind."[2] The phenomenon that both writers accurately describe, the similarity of dress for children and adults, may well suggest social differentiations and/or imply a whole attitude of mind—but not necessarily the one
claimed.

In the first place, to argue in isolation of other data that the *absence* of a
distinctive mode of dress for children is a mark of their being viewed as
miniature adults is historical presentism at its very best; one might argue
with equal force—in isolation of other facts—that the absence of beards on
men in a particular culture, or the presence of short hair as a fashion shared
by men and women, is a mark of that culture's failure to fully distinguish
between men and women. In all these cases there are alternative explanations, explanations that do not presuppose that special clothing for children,
or beards for men, or different hair lengths for adults of different sexes, are
universally natural and proper cultural traditions. As to the specific matter
of dress, children in New England were treated much the same as children
in England. Until age six or seven they generally wore long gowns that
opened down the front; after that, they were clothed in a manner similar to
that of their parents. Rather than this stage marking an abrupt transition
from infancy to adulthood, as Alan Macfarlane has pointed out it more
likely was merely a sign that children had then reached an age where sexual
differentiation was in order.[3]

Second, and most important, the supporting evidence that Ariès brings to
bear in making his case for the situation in medieval France generally does
not exist for colonial New England; when it does, it makes clear the fact
that there was no confusion or ambiguity in the mind of the adult Puritan as
to the differences between his children and himself. Puritan journals, autobiographies and histories are filled with specific references to the differences
between children and adults, a wealth of parental advice literature exists for

43

[2] Michael Zuckerman, *Peaceable Kingdoms: New England Towns in the Eighteenth Century*
(New York: Random House, 1970), p. 73; John Demos, *A Little Commonwealth: Family Life
in Plymouth Colony* (New York: Oxford Univ. Press, 1970), p. 139.
[3] Alan Macfarlane, *The Family Life of Ralph Josselin. A Seventeenth Century Clergyman*
(Cambridge: Cambridge Univ. Press, 1970), pp. 90–91.

the 17th century that gives evidence of clear distinctions between adults and children well into their teens, and a large body of law was in effect from the earliest years of settlement that made definitive discriminations between acceptable behavior and appropriate punishment for children, post-adolescent youths and adults.[4]

The matter of children's literature is one case in point. Ariès has argued, both in *Centuries of Childhood* and elsewhere, that in France "books addressed to and reserved for children" did not appear until "the end of the 17th century, at the same time as the awareness of childhood." Recently Marc Soriano has supported Ariès' contention by showing that prior to the stories of Perrault in the 1690s, French literature and folk tales were directed "almost entirely" at an adult audience, though of course children were exposed to them as well.[5] The situation was quite different in both old and New England in the 17th century, as William Sloane showed almost twenty years ago. Limiting himself to a definition of a child's book as "a book written *only* for children"—a limitation which excludes books which subsequently became children's fare and "works which are the tools of formal instruction"—Sloane compiled an annotated bibliography of 261 children's books published in England and America between 1557 and 1710.[6] It is true that most of the books listed would not meet Zuckerman's definition of a child's book as one which provides "a sequestered simplicity commensurate with a child's capacities," but that is not because children were viewed as synonymous with adults; rather, it is because 17th century New Englanders had a different view from that held by Zuckerman or other 20th century parents of the nature and capacities of children.[7]

The differentness of that view is crucial to this essay, and it will be developed at some length. But first it must be recognized that there were indeed children at home and in the streets of Puritan New England, and that this was a fact recognized—and never questioned—by their parents, ministers and other adults in the community. In many ways those children were seen and treated as different from children of today. In many ways they *were* different: to analyze, as this essay will, the Puritan child's actual and

[4]For a convenient collection of some of this material see Robert H. Bremner, ed., *Children and Youth in America* (Cambridge, Mass.: Harvard Univ. Press, 1970), 1:27–122.

[5]Philippe Ariès, "At the Point of Origin," in Peter Brooks, ed., *The Child's Part* (Boston: Beacon Press, 1972), p. 15; Marc Soriano, "From Tales of Warning to Formulettes: The Oral Tradition in French Children's Literature," ibid., pp. 24–25.

[6]William Sloane, *Children's Books in England & America in the Seventeenth Century* (New York: Columbia Univ. Press, 1955).

[7]Zuckerman, p. 77. It should be acknowledged that some of Ariès' contentions have been challenged within the French historical setting. On the matter of the presence or absence of an adolescent stage, for example, see the important essay by Natalie Z. Davis, "The Reasons of Misrule: Youth Groups and Charivaris in Sixteenth Century France," *Past and Present*, 50 (Feb. 1971); an extension of Davis' argument to 17th century London is Steven R. Smith, "The London Apprentice as Seventeenth-Century Adolescent," *Past and Present*, 61 (Nov. 1973).

anticipated confrontation with death is but one of many ways in which the extent of that difference can be seen. But it is too much of a leap, and there is no real evidence to support the contention that in 17th century New England, as in 15th and 16th century France, there was little or no distinction between children and adults.

Probably at no time in modern history have parents in the West agreed on the matter of the correct and proper approach to child-rearing. Certainly this is true of our own time, but it was equally so in the age of the Puritan.

"A child is a man in a small letter," wrote John Earle in 1628,   45

> yet the best copy of *Adam* before hee tasted of *Eve* or the Apple. . . . Hee is natures fresh picture newly drawne in Oyle, which time and much handling dimmes and defaces. His soule is yet a white paper unscribled with observations of the world, wherewith at length it becomes a blurr'd Notebooke. He is purely happy, because he knowes no evill, nor hath made meanes by sinne, to be acquainted with misery. . . . Nature and his Parents alike dandle him, and tice him on with a bait of Sugar, to a draught of Worme-wood. . . . His father hath writ him as his owne little story, wherein hee reads those dayes of his life that hee cannot remember; and sighes to see what innocence he ha's outliv'd.[8]

In view of this attitude among certain Englishmen of the 17th century—an attitude that, it appears, became prevalent in colonial Maryland and Virginia—it should come as no surprise to read in the report of a visiting Frenchman at the end of the century that "In England they show an extraordinary complacency toward young children, always flattering, always caressing, always applauding whatever they do. At least that is how it seems to us French, who correct our children as soon as they are capable of reason." This judgment was echoed a few years later by an Englishman reflecting on the customs of his people: "In the *Education* of *Children,*" wrote Guy Miege in 1707, "the indulgence of Mothers is excessive among the *English;* which proves often fatal to their children, and contributes much to the Corruption of the Age. If these be Heirs to great Honours and Estates, they swell with the Thoughts of it, and at last grow unmanageable." Had Miege been writing a bit later in the century he might have sought evidence for his assertion in the life of Charles James Fox who, at age five, had been accidentally deprived of the privilege of watching the blowing up of a garden wall; at his insistence his father had the wall rebuilt and blown up again so that the boy might witness it. On another occasion,

---

[8]*Micro-cosmographie or. A Piece of the World Discovered in Essays and Characters* (London, 1628), p. 5.

when the young Charles announced his intention of destroying a watch, his father's reply was: "Well, if you must, I suppose you must."[9]

But neither John Earle in 1628, nor Charles Fox in 1754 were Puritans; and neither Henri Misson in 1698, nor Guy Miege in 1707 were commenting on Puritan attitudes toward children. Had they been, their reports would have read very differently.

In 1628, the same year that John Earle was rhapsodizing on the innocence and purity of children, and on parental accommodation to them, Puritan John Robinson wrote:

> And surely there is in all children, though not alike, a stubbornness, and stoutness of mind arising from natural pride, which must, in the first place, be broken and beaten down. . . . This fruit of natural corruption and root of actual rebellion both against God and man must be destroyed, and no manner of way nourished, except we will plant a nursery of contempt of all good persons and things, and of obstinacy therein. . . . For the beating, and keeping down of this stubbornness parents must provide carefully for two things: first that children's wills and willfulness be restrained and repressed. . . . The second help is an inuring of them from the first, to such a meanness in all things, as may rather pluck them down, than lift them up.[10]

In place of Earle's child, seen as "yet the best copy of Adam before hee tasted of Eve or the Apple," the Puritan child was riddled with sin and corruption, a depraved being polluted with the stain of Adam's sin. If there was any chance of an individual child's salvation, it was not a very good chance—and in any case, the knowledge of who was to be chosen for salvation and who was not to be chosen was not a matter for earthly minds. "Because a small and contemptible number are hidden in a huge multitude," Calvin had written, "and a few grains of wheat are covered by a pile of chaff, we must leave to God alone the knowledge of his church, whose foundation is his secret election."[11] The quest for salvation was at the core of everything the devout Puritan thought and did; it was the primary source of the intense drive that carried him across thousands of miles of treacherous ocean in order to found a Holy Commonwealth in the midst of a

---

[9]Henri Misson, *Mémoires et Observations Faites par un Voyageur en Angleterre* (Paris, 1698), p. 128; Guy Miege, *The Present State of Great Britain* (London, 1707), p. 222; John Drinkwater, *Charles James Fox* (London: Ernest Benn, 1928), pp. 14–15. On the leniency of parental discipline in some families in the American colonial South see Edmund S. Morgan, *Virginians at Home* (Charlottesville: Univ. Press of Virginia, 1952), pp. 7–8, where an English traveler is quoted as saying of Maryland and Virginia: "The Youth of these more indulgent Settlements, partake pretty much of the *Petit Maitre* Kind, and are pamper'd much more in Softness and Ease than their Neighbors more Northward."

[10]*New Essays: Or, Observations Divine and Moral,* in Robert Ashton, ed., *The Works of John Robinson* (Boston: Doctrinal Tract and Book Soc., 1851), 1:246–48.

[11]John Calvin, *Institutes of the Christian Religion,* ed. John T. McNeill (Philadelphia: Westminster Press, 1960), 2:1013.

wilderness; it was his reason for being. And yet, despite his conviction of God's purposeful presence in everything he did or encountered, from Indian wars to ailing livestock, full confidence in his own or anyone else's salvation was rendered impossible by the inscrutability of his God. He was driven to strive for salvation at the same time that he was told his fate was both pre-determined and undetectable.

To be sure, Puritans believed there were signs or "marks," indications of God's will, that laymen and ministers alike could struggle to detect in their persons and in those of members of the congregation. But these signs were subject to interpretation and even feigning, and could never be regarded as more than *suggestions* of sainthood. Further, only very rarely was an apparent childhood conversion accepted as real by a congregation. Thus, Jonathan Edwards devoted a great deal of attention to youthful conversions during the stormy emotionalism of the Great Awakening, but only after first noting: "It has heretofore been looked on as a strange thing, when any have seemed to be savingly wrought upon, and remarkably changed in their childhood." And even James Janeway, whose *A Token For Children: Being an Exact Assessment of the Conversion, Holy and Exemplary Lives, and Joyful Deaths of Several Young Children*, was one of the best-read books of 17th and 18th century Puritans, admitted in a later edition that one of his examples of early spiritual development—that of a child who supposedly began showing signs of salvation between the ages of two and three—seemed to many "scarce credible, and they did fear [it] might somewhat prejudice the authority of the rest."[12]

But if conversion was unlikely at an early age, it was at least possible. Given the alternative, then, of apathetic acceptance of their children as depraved and damnable creatures, it is hardly surprising that Puritan parents urged on their offspring a religious precocity that some historians have interpreted as tantamount to premature adulthood. "You can't begin with them *Too soon*," Cotton Mather wrote in 1689,

> They are no sooner *wean'd* but they are to be *taught*. . . . Are they *Young?* Yet the *Devil* has been with them already. . . . They go astray as soon as they are born. They no sooner *step* than they *stray*, they no sooner *lisp* than they *ly*. Satan gets them to be proud, profane, reviling and revengeful, as *young* as they are. And I pray, why should you not be afore-hand with *him?*[13]

Puritan children, even "the very best" of whom had a "Corrupt Nature in them, and . . . an Evil Figment in their Heart," were thus driven at the

---

[12]Jonathan Edwards, *A Faithful Narrative of the Surprising Work of God*, in *The Works of Jonathan Edwards*, ed. C. C. Goen (New Haven: Yale Univ. Press, 1972), 4:158; James Janeway, *A Token for Children* [1679] (Boston: Caleb Bingham, 1802), p. 59.
[13]*Small Offers Towards the Service of the Tabernacle in this Wilderness* (Boston, 1689), p. 59.

earliest age possible both to recognize their depravity and to pray for their salvation. In the event that children proved intractable in this regard the first parental response was to be "what saies the Wise man, *A Rod for the fools back*"; but generally more effective—and more insidious—was the advice "to watch when some *Affliction* or some *Amazement* is come upon them: then God opens their ear to Discipline."[14] If Puritan parents carried out these designs with fervor it was of course out of love and concern for their children. But at least some of the motivation may well have had guilt at its source; as Mather and others were frequently careful to point out: "Your Children are Born Children of Wrath. Tis *through you,* that there is derived unto them the sin which Exposes them to infinite Wrath."[15]

48

We should not, however, pass too quickly over the matter of the Puritan parent's genuine love for his children. Even a casual reading of the most noted Puritan journals and autobiographies—those of Thomas Shepard, Samuel Sewall, Cotton Mather—reveals a deep-seated parental affection for children as the most common, normal and expected attitude. The relationship between parents and children was often compared with that between God and the Children of God. "That God is often angry with [his children]," Samuel Willard wrote in 1684, "afflicts them, and withdraws the light of his countenance from them, and puts them to grief, is not because he loves them not, but because it is that which their present condition requires; they are but Children, and childish, and foolish, and if they were not sometimes chastened, they would grow wanton, and careless of duty."[16] Indeed, in the same work in which Cotton Mather referred to children as "proud, profane, reviling and revengeful," he warned parents that "*They must give an account of the souls that belong unto their Families.* . . . Behold, thou hast *Lambs* in the *Fold.* Little ones in thy House; God will strain for it, —if wild beasts, and Lusts carry any of them away from the *Service* of God through any neglect of thine thou shalt smart for it in the fiery prison of God's terrible Indignation."[17]

Children, then, were on the one hand deeply loved, "Lambs in the Fold"; as Willard noted: "If others in a Family suffer want, and be pincht with difficulties, yet the Children shall certainly be taken care for, as long as there is anything to be had: they are hard times indeed when Children are denied that which is needful for them."[18] On the other hand they were depraved and polluted; as Benjamin Wadsworth wrote: "Their Hearts naturally, are a meer nest, root, fountain of Sin, and wickedness."[19] Even

[14]Cotton Mather, *The Young Mans Preservative* (Boston, 1701), p. 4; *Small Offers,* p. 62.
[15]*Cares About the Nurseries* (Boston, 1702), p. 32.
[16]*The Child's Portion* (Boston, 1684), p. 31.
[17]*Small Offers.* pp. 18–19.
[18]Willard, p. 16.
[19]"The Nature of Early Piety as it Respects God," in *A Course of Sermons on Early Piety* (Boston, 1721), p. 10.

most innocent infants, dying before they had barely a chance to breathe, could at best be expected to be given, in Michael Wigglesworth's phrase, "the easiest room in Hell."[20]

If the state of a child's spiritual health was an extremely worrisome and uncomfortable matter for the Puritan parent, the state of his physical health was not less so. In recent years historians of colonial New England have convincingly shown that the colonists of certain New England towns in the 17th and early 18th centuries lived longer and healthier lives than did many of their countrymen in England. This finding and the many others by these new demographic historians are important to our understanding of life in early New England; but in acknowledging the relative advantages of life in some New England communities compared with parts of England and Europe in the 17th century, we should be careful to avoid blinding ourselves to the fact that death was to the colonist, as it was to the Englishman and Frenchman, an ever-present menace—and a menace that struck with a particular vengeance at the children of the community.

Philip J. Greven's study of colonial Andover, Massachusetts is noteworthy for both the skill of the author's analysis and the stability and healthiness of the families whose lives he studied. As Greven explicitly points out, compared with Boston and other New England communities, Andover's mortality rate was exceptionally low, though it did climb steadily in the 18th century. It is worth dwelling briefly on the differences between Boston and Andover, because the power and sophistication of Greven's work can tend to suggest an implicit, and erroneous, picture of Andover as a representative New England town. It may or may not be representative of a certain type of Puritan community—a sufficient number of collateral studies have not yet been done to determine this—but demographically it was vastly different from Boston, the hub of the Holy Commonwealth. Mortality rates in Andover during the early 18th century, when those rates were on the increase, fluctuated within a normal annual range of about half those in Boston during the same period—somewhere between fifteen and twenty per thousand in Andover, somewhere between thirty-five and forty per thousand in Boston. Epidemic years are excluded from these calculations in both cases, but it should be noted that Andover's worst epidemic lifted the death rate to seventy-one per thousand, while Boston's worst epidemic during the same period pushed the death rate well over one hundred per thousand—or more than 10 per cent of the resident population.[21] In the 17th century, the smallpox epidemic of 1677–78, joined by the normal death

49

---

[20] *The Day of Doom* (London, 1687), stanza 181.

[21] Philip J. Greven Jr., *Four Generations: Population, Land, and Family in Colonial Andover, Massachusetts* (Ithaca: Cornell Univ. Press, 1970). For Greven's brief specific comparison of Andover and Boston, see pp. 196–97, note 14; detailed information on Boston can be found in

rate, probably killed off more than one-fifth of Boston's entire population. "Boston burying-places never filled so fast," wrote a young Cotton Mather:

> It is easy to tell the time when we did not use to have the bells tolling for burials on a Sabbath morning by sunrise; to have 7 buried on a Sabbath day night, after Meeting. To have coffins crossing each other as they have been carried in the street. . . . To attempt a Bill of Mortality, and number the very spires of grass in a Burying Place seem to have a parity of difficulty and in accomplishment.[22]

Indeed, if Andover fares well in comparison with mortality figures for English and European towns, Boston does not: it was not at all uncommon for the death rate in Boston to hover near or even exceed that for English towns like Clayworth that have been cited for their exceptionally high mortality rates.[23]

One of the problems with all these figures, however, is the almost inevitable underestimation of infant mortality; as Greven and other demographic analysts freely acknowledge, most infant deaths were unrecorded and their number can now only be guessed at. One such guess, a highly informed one, has been made by Kenneth A. Lockridge. In a study of Dedham, Massachusetts in the 17th and early 18th centuries, Lockridge found that an upward adjustment of 1/9 on the town's birth rate would most likely take account of unrecorded infant deaths.[24] If the same adjustment is made on the birth rate of colonial Andover a fairly accurate comparison of childhood birth and mortality rates can be made.

Although Greven traces a trend throughout the generations examined showing a steady drop in fertility and life expectancy rates as Andover became more urbanized, if we view the period as a whole the town remains a

John B. Blake, *Public Health in the Town of Boston, 1630–1822* (Cambridge, Mass.: Harvard Univ. Press, 1959), Appendix II; an excellent recent study is E. S. Dethlefsen, "Life and Death in Colonial New England," Diss. Harvard University 1972.

[22]Cotton Mather to John Cotton, Nov. 1678, in Massachusetts Historical Society *Collections*, series 4, 8 (1868), 383–84; contemporary estimates of the toll of the epidemic were made by John Foster and Increase Mather in Thomas Thatcher, *A Brief Rule to Guide the Common People* (Boston, 1678). See Blake, p. 20; for the population of Boston at the time and an estimate of the death toll of the disease, see Carl Bridenbaugh, *Cities in the Wilderness: Urban Life in America, 1625–1742* (New York: Capricorn Books, 1964 [orig. pub. 1936]), pp. 6,87.

[23]Peter Laslett, *The World We Have Lost: England Before the Industrial Age* (New York: Scribner's, 1965), pp. 146–47.

[24]"The Population of Dedham, Massachusetts, 1636–1736," *Economic History Review*, 19 (1966), 329. Cf. John Demos' estimate that in Plymouth Colony a 10 per cent infant mortality rate, though seemingly "surprisingly low," is a reasonable figure. Demos, pp. 131–32. Seventeenth century attitudes to early infant death are reflected in sources other than the formal records: on the first page of his *Journal* Thomas Shepard enumerated the birth dates, and in one case the death date, of his five sons—but Shepard had seven sons, the two not mentioned having died in infancy. See Michael McGiffert, ed., *God's Plot: The Autobiography and Journal of Thomas Shepard* (Amherst, Mass.: Univ. of Massachusetts Press, 1972), pp. 81, 33, 69.

good example of one of the healthier communities in New England. Using the Lockridge adjustment to include unrecorded infant deaths, the average number of children born per family in Andover throughout the century under discussion was 8.8. Of those, an average of 5.9 survived to adulthood. In other words, approximately three of the close to nine children born to the average family would die before reaching their twenty-first birthday. But, as Greven notes, the most vulnerable period in life was that "beyond infancy but prior to adolescence—the age group which appears to have been most susceptible, among other things, to the throat distemper prevalent in the mid-1730's." Again applying the infant mortality adjustment to Greven's figures, the rate of survival to age ten for all children born between 1640 and 1759 was approximately 74 per cent—with a generational high of 83 per cent and a low of 63 per cent, this latter figure of course indicating that at one point fewer than two out of three infants lived to see their tenth birthday. During the period as a whole, more than one child in four failed to survive the first decade of life in a community with an average birth rate per family of 8.8.[25]

Thus a young couple embarking on a marriage did so with the knowledge and expectation that in all probability *two or three* of the children they might have would die before the age of ten. In certain cases, of course, the number was more than two; Greven discusses instances when parents lost six of eleven children in rapid succession, including four in a single month, and four of eight children in less than a year—and this in a town remarkable for the relative health and longevity of its residents. In Boston the rate was much higher and even the most prominent and well cared for residents of that city were constantly reminded of the fragility of life in childhood. Thomas Shepard, for instance, had seven sons, three of whom died in infancy; the other four outlived their father, but he died at 43—having in that short time outlived two wives. As Joseph E. Illick has recently pointed out, Samuel Sewall and Cotton Mather each fathered fourteen children: "One of Sewall's was stillborn, several died as infants, several more as young adults. Seven Mather babies died shortly after delivery, one died at two years and six survived to adulthood, five of whom died in their twenties. Only two Sewall children outlived their father, while Samuel Mather was the only child to survive Cotton."[26]

It is important for us to recognize that conditions for living in colonial New England were sometimes superior to those in 17th century England and Europe. But it is equally important for us not to lose sight of the fact

---

[25]Greven, pp. 188–203.
[26]"Parent-Child Relations in Seventeenth-Century England and America," in Lloyd de Mause, ed., *The History of Childhood* (New York: Psychohistory Press, 1974). I am grateful to Professor Illick for allowing me to examine his manuscript prior to publication.

51

that the Puritan settlements were places where "winter was to be feared," as Kenneth Lockridge has written, where "harvests were a gamble that kept men's minds aware of Providence, plague arose and subsided out of all human control and infants died in numbers that would shock us today."[27]

It has often been noted by writers on the Puritan family that the prescribed and common personal relationship between parents and children was one of restraint and even aloofness, mixed with, as we have seen, an intense parental effort to impose discipline and encourage spiritual precocity. Parents were reminded to avoid becoming "too fond of your children and too familiar with them" and to be on their guard against "not keeping constantly your due distance."[28] Edmund S. Morgan has shown how this "due distance" worked in both directions, as when Benjamin Colman's daughter Jane wrote to her father requesting forgiveness for the "flow of affections" evident in some of her recent letters. Colman responded by urging her to be "careful against this Error, even when you say your Thoughts of Reverence and Esteem to your Father, or to a Spouse, if ever you should live to have one," and commended her for having "done well to correct yourself for some of your Excursions of this kind toward me."[29] Morgan has also seen the common practice of "putting children out," both to early apprenticeship and simply extended stays with other families, often against the child's will, as linked to the maintenance of the necessary distance between parent and child; "these economically unnecessary removals of children from home," he writes, probably resulted from the fact that "Puritan parents did not trust themselves with their own children, that they were afraid of spoiling them by too great affection."[30]

Morgan's suggested explanation for this practice seems logical and convincing, but there may have been an additional, deeper source for both this practice and the entire Puritan attitude toward severely restrained displays of fondness between parents and children. For children, despite the natural hold they had on their parents' affection, were a source of great emotional discomfort for them as well. In the first place, there was a very real possibility, if not a probability, that parental affection would be rewarded by the death of a child before it even reached puberty; the "due distance" kept by Puritan parents from their children might, at least in part, have been an instinctive response to this possibility, a means of insulating themselves to some extent against the shock that the death of a child might bring. This, of course, would be potentially true of any society with a relatively high rate of

[27] Lockridge, p. 343.
[28] Thomas Cobbett, *A Fruitfull and Usefull Discourse* . . . (London, 1656), p. 96.
[29] *The Puritan Family* (New York: Harper & Row, 1966), p. 107.
[30] Ibid., p. 77; cf. Demos, p. 74.

childhood mortality. But to the Puritan the child was more than a loved one extremely vulnerable to the ravages of the environment; he was also a loved one polluted with sin and natural depravity. In this, of course, he was no different from any other members of the family or community, including those Visible Saints viewed as the most likely candidates for salvation: Original Sin touched everyone, and all were considered polluted and not worthy of excessive affection. What is important here, however, is not that this dictum touched everyone, but that in the process it touched those most emotionally susceptible to its pernicious effects—the children of the zealous and devoted Puritan.

The Puritans of New England held as doctrine the belief that they were involved in a binding contract or "covenant" with God. This belief was complex and multifaceted, but one aspect of it viewed the entire community as having contracted a "social covenant" with God by which they promised strict obedience to his laws. Failure to obey on the part of any individual within the community could result in God's wrath being vented on the entire community. Thus, whenever signs of God's anger appeared, might they be comets or earthquakes or the deaths of eminent men, Puritans searched for the source of the divine displeasure and fearfully awaited future expressions of it. When the younger Thomas Shepard died in 1677, the Reverend Urian Oakes wrote in lamentation:

53

> What! must we with our God, and Glory part?
> Lord is thy Treaty with New England come
> Thus to an end? And is War in thy Heart?
> That this Ambassadour is called home.
> So Earthly Gods (Kings) when they War intend
> Call home their Ministers, and Treaties end.[31]

The depraved and ungodly child was, it is true, naturally repellent in his sinfulness; but more than that, the activity that might easily grow out of that sinfulness posed a very real danger to the well-being of the community. In response, understandably enough, the Puritan parent strove mightily to effect conversion or at the least to maintain a strict behavior code, but at the same time—when these effects were combined with the love he felt for his child, the tenuous hold the child had on life, the natural repulsiveness of sin—he may well have been driven to find ways of creating emotional distance between his offspring and himself.[32]

[31]*An Elegie Upon the Death of the Reverend Mr. Thomas Shepard* (Boston, 1677), p. 7; seeing portentous meaning in the deaths of eminent men was particularly common during the latter half of the 17th century as Puritans saw about them real and imagined signs of waning piety. For other examples see, for instance, James Fitch, *Peace the End of the Perfect and Upright* (Boston, 1673), p. 9; and Samuel Willard, *A Sermon Preached Upon Ezekiel* (Boston, 1679), p. 12.

[32]There is a large body of psychological and anthropological literature on related phenomena and it has been helpful in formulating some of the ideas in this section. On the effects of

But if separation was emotionally beneficial to the Puritan parent, it may have had precisely the opposite effect on the Puritan child. John Demos has recently speculated on the "profound loss" experienced by many Puritan children in the second and third years of life because of the fact that they were probably weaned at the start of the second year and very often witnessed the arrival of a younger brother or sister at the start of the third year.[33] This in itself, it might be argued, does not make Puritan children unique: the spacing of children at two-year intervals is common among many of the world's cultures, and weaning at twelve months is hardly an exceptional custom. But added to these practices was the conscious effort of Puritan parents to separate themselves from an excessively intimate relationship with their children. If this normal practice of separation was not enough, Cotton Mather was probably echoing a fairly common sentiment in viewing as "the sorest Punishment in the Family" the banishment of the child from the parents' presence.[34] Separation, however, can be both real and imagined, can be both present and anticipated. And, of course, the ultimate separation is death. This was a fact of which the Puritan parent was well aware and which the Puritan child, from the earliest age possible, was never allowed to forget.

May of 1678 was a month of great apprehension in Boston. The smallpox plague referred to earlier had entered the city some months before and had begun its relentless slaying of the population. By May hundreds had died and the governments of the colony and the town were hurriedly passing legislation aimed at holding down the spread of the deadly infection—people were directed not to hang out bedding or clothes in their yards or near roadways, and those who had been touched by the disease and survived were forbidden contact with others for specified periods of time.[35] The worst was yet to come: by the time it was over it was as though, proportionate to the population, an epidemic were to kill over a million and a half people in New York City during the next eighteen months. The city girded for it.

Only two years earlier New England had endured the devastation of King Philip's War, in which—not counting the enormous numbers of Indian

---

pollution fear see Mary Douglas, *Purity and Danger: An Analysis of Concepts of Pollution and Taboo* (London: Routledge & Kegan Paul, 1966); on the psychological problem of "approach-avoidance conflict," see, among many relevant monographs, W. N. Schoenfeld, "An Experimental Approach to Anxiety, Escape, and Avoidance Behavior," in P. H. Hoch and J. Zubin, eds., *Anxiety* (New York: Grune & Stratton, 1950), pp. 70–99; and Murray Sidman, "Avoidance Behavior," in W. K. Honig, ed., *Operant Behavior* (New York: Appleton-Century-Crofts, 1966), pp. 448–98.

[33]Demos, p. 136.

[34]"Diary," in Massachusetts Historical Society *Collections*, series 7, 7:535.

[35]Boston Record Commissioners, *Report*, VII, 119. Cited in Blake, p. 19; see also Bridenbaugh, p. 87.

dead—greater casualties were inflicted in proportion to the population than in any other war in subsequent American history.[36] Death was everywhere in 1678 when, on May 5, Increase Mather addressed his Boston congregation and prayed "for a Spirit of Converting Grace to be poured out upon the Children and *Rising Generation* in *New England*."[37] A decade later Increase's son Cotton would write, as I have noted earlier, that a particularly effective means of disciplining children was "to watch when some *Affliction* or *Amazement* is come upon them: then God opens their ear to Discipline." On May 5, 1678, the then teen-aged young man probably witnessed a particularly effective demonstration of this principle as it was directed toward an entire congregation.

Some years earlier—at first against Increase Mather's will, then later with his support—the churches of New England had succumbed to the need for what its detractors later called the "Half-Way Covenant," in which as yet unconverted adult children of church members were acknowledged as church members (with the right to have their own children baptized) but not as full communicants. Bound up with this change in the notion of Puritan exclusivity was the growing belief that, in his covenant with his holy children, God had promised to "be thy God, and the God of thy seed after thee."[38] In his sermon of May 1678, Mather alluded to this belief very early: "Now God hath seen good to cast the line of Election so, as that it doth (though not wholly, and only, yet) for the most part, run through the loins of godly Parents." It is well to remember here that before any comforts could be gained from this doctrine the Puritan parent had also to face the impossibility of ever being truly assured of his own election. But that is not the reason Mather cluttered his sentence with such awkward qualifications—"though not wholly, and only, yet ... for the most part." God remained inscrutable, and it was heresy to think otherwise; but also: "Men should not think with themselves (as some do) if their children do belong to God, then he will convert them, whether they pray for him or no, but should therefore be stirred up to the more fervency in cries to Heaven, for the blessing promised. *I* (saith the Lord) *will give a new heart to you, and to your Children,* yet you must pray for it."[39]

When he turned to address the youth of the congregation Mather mentioned explicitly the "affliction and amazement" that was at hand:

> Young men and young Women, O be in earnest for Converting Grace, before it be too late. It is high time for you to look about you, deceive not yourselves with false

55

---

[36] See Douglas Edward Leach, *Flintlock and Tomahawk: New England in King Philip's War* (New York: W. W. Norton, 1958), p. 243.

[37] *Pray for the Rising Generation* (Boston, 1678).

[38] John Cotton, *The Covenant of Gods Free Grace* (London, 1645), p. 19.

[39] Increase Mather, *Pray for the Rising Generation,* p. 12.

Conversions (as many young men do to their eternal ruine) or with gifts instead of Grace. . . . Death waits for you. There is now a Mortal and Contagious Disease in many Houses; the Sword of the Lord is drawn, and young men fall down apace slain under it; do you not see the Arrows of Death come flying over your heads? Why then, Awake, Awake, and turn to God in Jesus Christ whilst it is called today, and know for certain that if you dy in your sins, you will be the most miserable of any poor Creatures in the bottom of Hell.[40]

But Mather's most determined and terrifying words were reserved for the youngest and most vulnerable members of the congregation, those of less "discretion and understanding" than the other youths addressed. It was with them that the specter of parental and ministerial separation and betrayal was merged with the promise of death and damnation. "Beg as for your lives that the God of your Fathers would pour his Spirit upon you," he exhorted these littlest of children,

56

> Go into secret corners and plead it with God. . . . If you dy and be not first new Creatures, better you had never been born: you will be left without excuse before the Lord, terrible witnesses shall rise up against you at the last day. Your godly Parents will testifie against you before the Son of God at that day: And the Ministers of Christ will also be called in as witnesses against you for your condemnation, if you dy in your sins. As for many of you, I have treated with you privately and personally, I have told you, and I do tell you, and make solemn Protestation before the Lord, that if you dy in a Christless, graceless eatate, I will most certainly profess unto Jesus Christ at the day of Judgement, Lord, these are the Children, whom I spake often unto thy Name, publickly and privately, and I told them, that if they did not make themselves a new heart, and make sure of an interest in Christ, they should become damned creatures for evermore; and yet they would not repent and believe the Gospel.[41]

If there is one thing on which modern psychologists have agreed concerning the fear of death in young children it is that such fear is generally rooted in the anticipation of separation from their parents. Time and again experimental studies have shown that, as one writer puts it, "the most persistent of fears associated with death is that of separation—and the one which is most likely to be basic, independent of cultural, religious, or social background." "In children," this writer adds, "dread of separation seems to be basic."[42]

---

[40]Ibid., p. 22.

[41]Ibid.

[42]Marjorie Editha Mitchell, *The Child's Attitude To Death* (London: Barrie & Rockliff, 1966), p. 100; cf. Sylvia Anthony, *The Discovery of Death in Childhood and After* (London: Allen Lane, 1971), esp. chap. 8; Roslyn P. Ross, "Separation Fear and the Fear of Death in Children," Diss. New York University 1966; Eugenia H. Waechter, "Death Anxiety in Children With Fatal Illness," Diss. Stanford University 1968; and the now almost classic studies of J. Bowlby, esp. "Separation Anxiety," *International Journal of Psychoanalysis and*

There are, certainly, ways that children seem to have of defending against separation anxiety resulting from anticipation of death. One of these—one that has inspired poets down through the ages—is the expectation of reunion in death, a defense that makes separation a temporary matter.[43] But this was a defense denied the Puritan child. As if addressing this question directly, Increase Mather in 1711 remarked on

> What a dismal thing it will be when a Child shall see his Father at the right Hand of Christ in the day of Judgment, but himself at His left Hand: And when his Father shall joyn with Christ in passing a Sentence of Eternal Death upon him, saying, Amen O Lord, thou art Righteous in thus *Judging:* And when after the Judgment, children shall see their Father going with Christ to Heaven, but themselves going away into Everlasting Punishment![44]

As Edmund S. Morgan has pointed out, this verbal "picture of parent and child at the Day of Judgment . . . was a favorite with many Puritan ministers, for it made the utmost of filial affection."[45] It was probably not of much comfort to the Puritan child to hear that, if he was to be separated from his parents, he would at least still have the companionship of certain playmates—given the circumstances. For, as Jonathan Edwards put it in one of his sermons specifically addressed to young children: "How dreadful it will be to be all together in misery. Then you won't play together any more but will be damned together, will cry out with weeping and wailing and gnashing of teeth together."[46]

Another common defense against childhood fear of separation and death that is mentioned in the psychological literature is supplied by parental interjection that only old people die, not children.[47] Puritan children met precisely the opposite advice. The young "may bear and behave themselves as if imagining their hot blood, lusty bodies, activity, beauty, would last alwayes, and their youthful pleasures never be at an end," acknowledged Samuel Wakeman at a young man's funeral in 1673; "but," he warned, "*Childhood and Youth are vanity:* Death may not wait till they be gray-headed; or however, the earliest Morning hastens apace to Noon, and then to Night." From the moment they were old enough to pay attention children were repeatedly instructed regarding the precariousness of their

57

Psychiatry, Vols. 41 and 42 (1961), and "Childhood Mourning and Its Implications for Psychiatry," *American Journal of Psychiatry,* Vol. 118 (1961).

[43]Anthony (see note 42), p. 151.

[44]*An Earnest Exhortation to the Children of New England to Exalt the God of their Fathers* (Boston, 1711), p. 35.

[45]Morgan, pp. 178–79.

[46]Jonathan Edwards, unpublished sermon in Edwards' manuscripts in Yale University Library. Quoted in Sanford Fleming, *Children and Puritanism* (New Haven: Yale Univ. Press, 1933), p. 100.

[47]Anthony, p. 153.

existence. The sermons they listened to, the parents who corrected them, the teachers who instructed them, and eventually the books they read, all focused with a particular intensity on the possibility and even the likelihood of their imminent death. Further, those who died young, it was often noted, died suddenly—"Death is oftentimes as near the young man's back as it is to the old man's face," wrote Wakeman—and matter-of-fact repetitions of this ever-present threat joined with burning pictures of Judgment Day to hammer the theme home. "I know you will die in a little time," the esteemed Jonathan Edwards calmly told a group of children, "some sooner than others. 'Tis not likely you will all live to grow up."[48] The fact that Edwards was only speaking the very obvious truth did not help matters any.

Nor did the literalness with which Puritan children must have taken the descriptions of depravity, sin, imminent death, judgment and hell offer anything in the way of relief. At least since the early writings of Piaget psychologists have been familiar with the various stages of the child's sense of causal reality, one central and persistent component of which is termed "realism." Realism, as one writer puts it, "refers to the fact that initially all things are equally real and real in the same sense and on the same plane: pictures, words, people, things, energies, dreams, feelings—all are equally solid or insubstantial and all mingle in a common sphere of experience. . . . Realism does not imply fatalism or passive resignation, but simply a failure [on the part of the young child] to doubt the reality of whatever comes into awareness."[49] The children observed in the psychological experiments that gave rise to the identification of these stages of reality awareness were the children of 20th century parents, children living in, if not a secular universe, at least one in which a fundamentalist view of divine creation and judgment is largely absent. Puritan children, however, lived in a world in which their parents—indeed, the greatest scientific minds of the time: Bacon, Boyle, Newton—were certain of the reality of witches and subterranean demons. In 1674, surprised at Spinoza's skepticism regarding spiritual entities, a correspondent of the freethinking philosopher doubtless spoke for most men of his time, the famed "Age of Reason," when he replied: "No one of moderns denies specters."[50]

It has long been known that one component of death in the Middle Ages

---

[48]Samuel Wakeman, *A Young Man's Legacy* (Boston, 1673), pp. 6, 41; Edwards quoted in Fleming, p. 100.

[49]Joseph Church, *Language and the Discovery of Reality* (New York: Random House, 1961), pp. 15–16. For full discussion of this and other stages see Jean Piaget, *The Construction of Reality in the Child* (New York: Basic Books, 1954), and *The Child's Conception of Physical Causality* (Totawa, N.J.: Littlefield, Adams, 1966), esp. pp. 237–58.

[50]On the belief of 17th century scientists in the reality of the invisible world, see Lynn Thorndike, *A History of Magic and Experimental Science* (New York: Columbia Univ. Press, 1958), Vols. 7 and 8. The reference quoted is from 8:570.

was concern over the fate of the body of the deceased, and worry that a fully disintegrated corpse or one that had been destroyed in war might be unable to be present at the Judgment.[51] It is less well known, or less often acknowledged, that a similar literalism retained a hold on the Puritan mind into the 18th century. Thus in 1692 a highly respected New England minister could effectively deal with questions concerning the Last Judgment in the following manner:

> Where will there be room for such a Vast Multitude as Adam, with all his Children? The whole surface of the earth could not hold them all? Ridiculous exception! Allow that this World should Last no less than *Ten-Thousand* Years, which it *will not*; Allow that there are at once alive a *Thousand Millions* of men, which there *are not;* Allow all these to march off every *Fifty years*, with a New Generation rising up in their stead; and allow each of these Individuals a place *Five Foot* Square to stand upon. I think these are Fair Allowances. I would now pray the Objector, if he have any skill at *Arithmetick*, to Compute, Whether a Spot of Ground, much less than *England*, which contains perhaps about Thirty Millions of Acres, but about a *Thousandth Part* of the Terraqueous Glob, and about the *Three Hundred thirty third* part of the Habitable Earth, would not hold them all.[52]

In a world in which the presence of early death was everywhere, and in which the most sophisticated and well regarded adults expressed such a literal sense of spiritual reality, it is hardly surprising that children would respond with a deadly serious mien to reminders of "how filthy, guilty, odious, abominable they are both by nature and practice," to descriptions of parental desertion at the day of Judgment and subsequent condemnation to the terrors of hell where "the Worm dyeth not . . . [and] the Fire is not quenched," and to the exhortations of respected teachers to "Remember Death; think much of death; think how it will be on a death bed."[53] In such a world it is far from surprising that a girl of seven should react "with many tears"—and her father with tears of sympathy—to a reading of Isaiah 24, in which she would have encountered:

> Therefore hath the curse devoured the earth, and they that dwell therein are desolate: therefore the inhabitants of the earth are burned, and few men left. . . . Fear, and the pit, and the snare, are upon thee, O inhabitant of the earth. And it shall come to pass, that he who fleeth from the noise of the fear shall fall into the

59

[51]On this, with special reference to the catechistic treatment of such matters in the medieval text *La Lumiere as lais*, see C. V. Langlois, *La Vie en France au Moyen Age* (Paris: Librairie Hachette, 1928), 4:111–19.

[52]Samuel Lee, *The Great Day of Judgment* (Boston, 1692), pp. 19–20.

[53]Benjamin Wadsworth, "The Nature of Early Piety," p. 15; Solomon Stoddard, *The Efficacy of the Fear of Hell to Restrain Men From Sin* (Boston, 1713), p. 24; Joseph Green, *The Commonplace Book of Joseph Green* (1696), ed., Samuel Eliot Morison, Colonial Society of Massachusetts *Publications*, 34 (1943), 204.

pit; and he that cometh up out of the midst of the pit shall be taken in the snare: for the windows from on high are open, and the foundations of the earth do shake.

Nor, in such a world, should we consider it unusual that later in her youth this same girl would again and again "burst out into an amazing cry . . . [because] she was afraid she should goe to Hell," would "read out of Mr. Cotton Mather—why hath Satan filled thy heart, which increas'd her Fear," and would eventually be unable to read the Bible without weeping, fearing as she did "that she was a Reprobat, Loved not God's people as she should."[54]

The case of young Elizabeth Sewall is by no means unique. Puritan diaries and sermons are filled with references to similar childhood responses to the terrors of separation, mortality and damnation. As with so many other things Puritan, these fears seem to have reached a crescendo with the emotional outpourings of the Great Awakening in the 1740s.[55] But the fears were always present, following children into adulthood and combining there with the disquieting complexities of Puritan theology and Christian tradition to produce a culture permeated by fear and confusion in the face of death.

The Christian tradition that the Puritans had inherited counseled peace and comfort in one's dying hour. Elaborate procedures for coping with the fear of death had been devised throughout long centuries of experience. Extreme unction, the viaticum, indulgences, requiem masses, the prayers of family and friends—all these served the Catholic as a cushion against an excessively fearful reaction in the face of death. The relative optimism that grew out of this tradition was passed on, in different form, to much of Protestantism during the Renaissance and Reformation. Thus, Renaissance poetry on the theme of death, Edelgard Dubruck observes,

> . . . stressed immortality and the afterlife. The word "death" was often avoided and replaced by euphemisms . . . [and] depiction of the realistic aspects of death was carefully suppressed. . . . In the early sixteenth century, poets dwelt upon fame and immortality rather than death, and in the Reformation writings death had at least lost its sting, and both Lutherans and Calvinists insisted that death was at long last vanquished with the help of Christ.[56]

Although the Puritans inherited, and tried to live with, the *prescription* that a peaceful death was a good death, the deterministic pessimism of the faith was contradictory to Christian tradition and caused exceptional dis-

[54]Samuel Sewall, "Diary" in Massachusetts Historical Society *Collections*, series 5, V, 308, 419–20, 422–23, 437. See also the terrified reaction of Sewall's young son Sam to the death of a companion and his father's reminding him of the "need to prepare for Death," ibid., pp. 308–9.
[55]See the numerous references to violent childhood reactions to death in *The Christian History*, I and II (Boston, 1743–44); cited in Fleming.
[56]Edelgard Dubruck, *The Theme of Death in French Poetry of the Middle Ages and the Renaissance* (The Hague: Mouton, 1964), pp. 152, 154.

60

comfort as the devout Puritan awaited the end of his life.[57] To the adult Puritan the contemplation of death frequently "would make the flesh tremble."[58] To the Puritan child it could do no less.

Puritan New England, in this respect at least, seems a far cry from England in the same period, at least if Peter Laslett is correct when he writes that people there were "inured to bereavement and the shortness of life."[59] But in recognizing this, we should also be wary of finding in Puritan attitudes and behavior too much grist for our psychological mills. The fear of death, to many Freudians, is "closely interwoven with castration fear," a fear which "is so closely united with death fear that it has often been described as its origin." It is, writes psychoanalyst J. D. Howard, "purely . . . a secondary substitutive phenomenon of the castration fear which grew out of an inadequately resolved Oedipal conflict."[60] Turning to Freud himself, a more sophisticated interpreter with some knowledge of Puritanism might seize on the similarity between the Puritan requirement for uncertainty and his preoccupations with death, and Freud's treatment of uncertainty and obsessional neurosis.[61] But interpretations of this type are hopelessly bogged down by the arrogance and myopia of the historical present.[62]

61

The world of the Puritan—child and adult—was a rational world, in many ways, perhaps, more rational than our own. It is true that it was a world of witches and demons, and of a just and terrible God who made his presence known in the slightest act of nature. But this was the given reality about which most of the decisions and actions of the age, throughout the entire Western world, revolved. When the Puritan parent urged on his children what we would consider a painfully early awareness of sin and death, it was because the well-being of the child and the community *required* such an early recognition of these matters. It merits little to note that the

[57]For an extended treatment of this matter, see David E. Stannard, "Death and Dying in Puritan New England," *American Historical Review*, 78 (Dec. 1973), 1305-30.
[58]James Fitch, *Peace the End of the Perfect and Upright* (Boston, 1673), p. 6.
[59]Laslett, p. 96.
[60]J. D. Howard, "Fear of Death," *Journal of the Indiana State Medical Association* (1962), quoted in Hattie R. Rosenthal, "The Fear of Death as an Indispensable Factor in Psychotherapy," in Hendrik M. Ruitenbeek, ed., *Death: Interpretations* (New York: Delta Books, 1969), p. 171; the previous quotation is from Mary Chadwick, "Notes Upon the Fear of Death," in Ruitenbeek, p. 75.
[61]Sigmund Freud, "Notes Upon a Case of Obsessional Neurosis," Part II, *The Standard Edition of the Complete Psychological Works of Sigmund Freud*, James Strachey, ed. (London: Hogarth Press, 1957), 10:229-37.
[62]A particularly egregious example of this, with specific bearing on the subject at hand, is the apparent raison d'être of a new journal, *History of Childhood Quarterly*, as the interminable psychoanalytic explication of the theme that: "The history of childhood is a nightmare from which we have only recently begun to awaken." It is the insistent and quite serious claim of the founder and editor of this journal that prior to the 18th century there did not exist in Western history a single "good mother."

Puritans (and Bacon and Boyle and Newton) were mistaken in their beliefs
in hobgoblins; the fact is they were real to men of the 17th century, as real
as Ra and his heavenly vessels were to the ancient Egyptians, and at least as
real as the unconscious is to devout followers of Freud; and the responses to
that reality were as honest and as rational, in the context of the times, as are
the responses to reality of any parent today.

If children were frightened, even terrified, by the prospects of life and
death conjured up by their parents and ministers, that too was a natural and
rational response. As more than one Puritan writer suggested, to fail to be
frightened was a sure sign that one was either spiritually lost, or stupid, or
both.[63] Death brought with it, to all but a very few, the prospect of the most
hideous and excruciating fate imaginable. One necessary though by itself
insufficient sign of membership in that select company of saints was the
taking to heart of the warning to "beware of indulging yourselves in a stupid
secure frame."[64] Thus, wrote Samuel Willard with remarkably cool
detachment and insight,

> Here we see the reason why the People of God are so often doubtful, disquiet, dis-
> content, and afraid to dy (I put things together). The ground of all this is because
> they do not as yet see clearly what they shall be: It would be a matter of just
> wonderment to see the Children of God so easily and often shaken, so disturbed
> and perplexed in hours of Temptation, were it not from the consideration that at
> present they know so little of themselves or their happiness: Sometimes their son-
> ship itself doth not appear to them, but they are in the dark, at a loss about the
> evidencing of it to the satisfaction of their own minds, and from hence it is that
> many doubtings arise, and their souls are disquieted.[65]

Willard knew first hand of what he spoke. He was often the one chosen to
try to calm the fears of those who found the prospect of death too much to
bear; Judge Sewall in fact called him in to help with young Elizabeth's dis-
consolate weeping. It may be, despite their experience, that ministers and
parents like Willard were unaware of all the components that went into the
making of the Puritan child's fear of death. It was, as we have seen, a complex problem touching on a variety of matters which Puritan children and
adults alike had to face every day of their lives. But they did at least know
that when a young Betty or Sam Sewall broke down in tears over the prospects of death and damnation, the children—and they were children, not
miniature adults—were most often acting normally, out of their own
experience in the world, and in response to their parents' solemn, reasoned
warnings.

⁶³See, for example, Leonard Hoar, *The Sting of Death* (Boston, 1680), pp. 11–12.
⁶⁴Ibid.
⁶⁵Willard, *The Child's Portion*, p. 67.

THE STROLLING POOR: TRANSIENCY IN EIGHTEENTH-CENTURY MASSACHUSETTS

In 1790, William Bentley, the Salem diarist, observed two of the dominant changes occurring in Massachusetts society during the eighteenth century: the transiency of the poor and increased migration of economically diverse segments of the population:[1] Bentley noted that the Salem Selectmen debated "whether [or not] to warn Strangers out of Town in order to save the Town from the charges of the Poor. It is found in fact that the greater part of the whole property is in the hands of persons not Town born, and in the best streets even a majority of freeholders [are newcomers]."[2] To Bentley, migration had become a way of life in eighteenth-century Salem, and one result was a realignment of the rules for defining the social order. One could no longer expect that one's neighbors were, in Bentley's felicitous phrase, "Town born," and had grown to adulthood within the same town and presumably with the same set of values.

63

Bentley's observations of a changing social order were not simply the particularistic sentiments of a local diarist; they were the articulation of the passing of traditional Massachusetts society and the emergence of a more modern one.[3] This process of modernization in Massachusetts was by no means abrupt or dramatic. Indeed, it is more useful to view the middle and late decades of the eighteenth century as a period of transition. During this transitional stage, structural change, social values, and personal behavior fluctuated amidst the demands of passage from the more simple, face-to-face society of the seventeenth century. This essay seeks to examine three aspects of transiency migration during this transitional stage: the magnitude of transiency during the eighteenth century; the social and economic characteristics of transients; and the legal response to increasing numbers of transient poor persons.

During the eighteenth century, an increase in the number of transients in eastern and western Massachusetts coincided with the secular trend in westward migration and declining levels of residential continuity. This transition to increased mobility during the eighteenth century became even more firmly established during the nineteenth century. Mostly poor and of lower-class origins, eighteenth-century transients were found in both the congested eastern Massachusetts counties and the frontier. Moving very short distances from town to town and job to job, this class of transients confronted traditional communities with mounting problems of social welfare and control. The process of increased migration caused the towns to live in uneasy tension with a growing class of poor persons for several decades during the eighteenth century.

In response to this class of transients, new legal mechanisms were developed to limit their impact on the traditional towns. The towns relinquished some but not all of their customary responsibilities for the transient poor while society at large gradually assumed a greater proportion of the duties of care and control. These new legal mechanisms did not completely alter the care provided by families and towns, but they did make clear that Massachusetts society required more routinized means for sustaining social order than face-to-face, local society offered.[4] Thus the appearance of a visible class of transients and the rationalization of legal means of welfare and control during the eighteenth century represent aspects of the transition from traditional to modern American society.

64

I

In premodern Massachusetts, there was a remarkably wide divergence in the rates of population persistence, ranging from 50 to 83 percent (see Table 1).[5] This broad pattern of residential continuity was accounted for, however, by the first generation of settlers. Their rates of persistence (from available local studies) ranged from 52 to 83 percent. As time passed and the population expanded, the range of persistence in eighteenth-century Massachusetts narrowed to 50 to 69 percent. While the minimum rate of population continuity in premodern Massachusetts never fell below 50 percent, the maximum range varied quite dramatically over time. By the mid-eighteenth century, the overt residential stability found in some Massachusetts towns a century earlier had disappeared; taxpayers and their families began to move at a faster pace.

This mobility quickened even more during the early nineteenth century, as the secular patterns of persistence declined more sharply. From a longitudinal perspective, the decreased rates of the eighteenth century should be viewed as a transition to the more volatile rural and urban populations of nineteenth-century America.[6]

A useful index of eighteenth-century population redistribution through migration is the proportion of settlement dispersion occurring by geographic region. During the seventeenth century, almost all new settlements were formed in eastern Massachusetts. The western part of the colony remained relatively untouched except around Springfield and Northampton (see Table 2). By 1740, however, there was an absolute decline in settlement formation in the eastern counties as the white population began to shift to the west and the north. Almost 90 percent of the settlements founded between 1741 and 1780 were in the western counties.

Not all of the western settlements formed after 1741 were new; many were subdivisions which split off from older towns. While we normally think of the congested eastern towns as having to subdivide, the reverse was true

Table 1   Rates of Persistence in Selected Communities in Premodern
           New England*

Decade	Community**	Rate of Persistence	N	Range	Mean
				52-83%	67%
1643-1653	Rowley, Mass.	59%	(54)		
1648-1660	Dedham, Mass.	52%	(98)		
1660-1670	Dedham	78%	(91)		
	Hingham, Mass.	73%	(96)		
1676-1686	Windsor, Conn.	57%	(165)		
1680-1690	Dedham	73%	(113)		
1686-1696	Manchester, Mass.	61%	(34)		
1687-1695	Boston, Mass.	53%	(1224)		
1690-1700	Dedham	83%	(125)		
				50-69%	60%
1723-1733	Dedham	55%	(204)		
1731-1741	Wenham, Mass.	68%	(99)		
1741-1751	Beverly Mass.	50%	(302)		
	Wenham	58%	(113)		
1751-1761	Beverley	58%	(304)		
	Wenham	53%	(105)		
1754-1765	Hingham	69%	(331)		
1761-1771	Beverly	64%	(368)		
	Wenham	59%	(99)		
1780-1790	Boston	56%	(2225)		
1790-1800	Hingham	68%	(347)		

65

*   Computation of the persistence statistic displayed in this table was based on a
      determination of the number of persons listed in the first time period, and then a
      ratio of the persons who continued to the following time period was calculated.
      All persistence statistics in this table have been standardized to fit this method.

**   Sources, in order of listing, calculated by the author from *The Early Records of
      the town of Roxley, Massachusetts, 1639-1672* (Rowley, Mass., 1894), pp. v-x;
      Kenneth A. Lockridge, "The Population of Dedham, Massachusetts, 1636-1736,"
      Economic History Review XIX (1966): 322; Daniel Scott Smith, "Population,
      Family, and Society in Hingham, Massachusetts, 1635-1880," (Ph.D. diss., Univer-
      sity of California, Berkeley, 1973); Linda Auwers Bissell, "From One Generation to
      Another: Mobility in Seventeenth-Century Windsor, Connecticut," *William and
      Mary Quarterly* XXXI (1974): 79-110, Table VIII; calculated by the author from
      Manchester Town Records, 1636-1736 (Salem, 1889), pp. 30-31, 73; James A.
      Henretta, "Economic Development and Social Structure in Colonial Boston,"
      William and Mary Quarterly XXII (1965): 74-92; tax list and reconstitution data
      of Wenham, Massachusetts; tax list and reconstitution data of Beverly, Massachu-
      setts; Allan Kulikoff, "The Progress of Inequality in Revolutionary Boston,"
      William and Mary Quarterly XXVIII (1971): 402.

      All towns listed are located in Massachusetts unless otherwise noted.

Table 2   New and Subdivided Settlement Formation in Massachusetts, 1621-1860, by Geographic Region*

Region and type of settlement	1621-1660 Percent	N	1661-1700 Percent	N	1701-1740 Percent	N
East**						
New settlements	75	(36)	52	(14)	14	(8)
Subdivisions	19	(9)	22	(6)	48	(28)
East – Total	94	(45)	74	(20)	62	(36)
West†						
New settlements	6	(3)	19	(5)	20	(12)
Subdivisions		(0)	7	(2)	19	(11)
West – Total	6	(3)	26	(7)	39	(23)
Massachusetts, all						
New settlements	81	(39)	70	(19)	34	(20)
Subdivisions	19	(9)	30	(8)	66	(39)
Grand Total		(48)		(27)		(59)

	1741-1780 Percent	N	1781-1820 Percent	N	1821-1860 Percent	N
East						
New settlements		(0)		(0)		(0)
Subdivisions	10	(10)	42	(22)	68	(21)
East – Total	10	(10)	42	(22)	68	(21)
West						
New settlements	40	(38)	11	(6)	3	(1)
Subdivisions	50	(48)	47	(25)	29	(9)
West – Total	90	(86)	58	(31)	32	(10)
Massachusetts, all						
New settlements	40	(38)	11	(6)	3	(1)
Subdivisions	60	(58)	89	(47)	96	(30)
Grand Total		(96)		(53)		(31)

*   Compiled from Kevin H. White, *Historical Data Relating to Counties, Cities and Towns in Massachusetts* (The Commonwealth of Massachusetts, 1966). As used in this table, "date of settlement formation" is based on dates of founding of towns, districts, and plantations. In order to generate the most accurate time

Table 2   (cont.)

series of population dispersion using settlement formation as the index, I tried to use the earliest date of formation, particularly of districts and plantations. This definition of settlement formation — which focuses on the social organization of communities — offers the most useful way of portraying the dispersion of organized society by geographical area.

** Eastern Massachusetts includes all counties to the east of, but excluding, Worcester County: Barnstable, Bristol, Duke's, Essex, Middlesex, Nantucket, Norfolk, Plymouth, and Suffolk.

† Western Massachusetts includes all counties to the west of, and including, Worcester County: Berkshire, Franklin, Hampden, Hampshire, and Worcester. Several counties in Maine also received out-migrants, but they were omitted from this tabulation. Their inclusion would increase the proportion of new and subdivided settlements formed outside of eastern Massachusetts.

between 1741 and 1780: almost no towns subdivided in the east. Out-migration was the primary response to population growth in many eastern towns during the transitional period. (There were, however, rural-urban differences in the extent of out-migration in the east.) Ultimately, western migration declined after 1781 as economic adjustments were made and higher population densities accepted. But the transition to increased mobility had been made during the eighteenth century.

Migration increased during the eighteenth century as a natural but unwanted response to demographic pressures on available economic resources.[7] This change to greater geographic mobility was neither abrupt nor dramatic. It was a slow process intimately related to population growth and the need for land in traditional, agricultural society. Migration became a stopgap attempt to limit the population sizes of many Massachusetts towns, particularly the older farming towns in the eastern counties. Not until family limitation emerged during the nineteenth century as a more effective control on population size was geographic mobility loosened from its mechanistic relationship to population growth.

Precisely during the peak periods of eighteenth-century migration and settlement formation, the number of unwanted persons — transients — in two representative Massachusetts counties, Essex and Hampshire, increased dramatically (see Table 3). In Essex, located to the north of Boston along the coast and established during the seventeenth century, the rate of increase in the number of transient households doubled in each of the two decades following 1739-43 (from 56 percent in 1750-54 to 112 percent in 1760-64). Despite the higher absolute number of transients in Essex County, a rapid increase in the proportion of transients was common in Hampshire as well.

Located in western Massachusetts, Hampshire County underwent a substantial population growth during the eighteenth century. But during the

Table 3   Number of Transient Households Warned out of Essex and
           Hampshire Counties, 1739-1774, and the Rate of Increase or
           Decrease from the Previous Time Period

	Households warned and the rate of increase or decrease from previous time period				Average increase or decrease Percent
Dates	Essex County*		Hampshire County**		
	Percent	N	Percent	N	
1739-43	n.a.	(257)	n.a.	(50)	n.a.
1750-54	56	(400)	76	(88)	+ 58
1760-64	+ 116	(862)	+ 248	(306)	+ 139
1770-74	− 93	(58)	− 60	(122)	− 85

*   Taken from the Court of General Sessions of the Peace, 1726-96, Essex County,
       Massachusetts, Clerk of Courts Office, Salem, Massachusetts.
**   Taken from the Court of General Sessions of the Peace, 1735-81, Hampshire
       County, Massachusetts, Clerk of Courts Office, Northampton, Maasachusetts.
Note: The designation n.a. means that the proportional increase for the given time
       period was not available.

early 1760s, Hampshire witnessed a phenomenal increase in the proportion of
persons warned out as transients. The rate of increase was so much greater
than in any other time period in either Hampshire or Essex that it suggests
that the impact of a growing class of transients occurred later in the demographic history of this frontier county.[8] Once this time-lag is accounted for,
the ratio of transients in 1760-64 to the total population in 1765 in each
county was almost identical (.106 in Essex and .104 in Hampshire). By the
1760s social exclusion of the poor was as common on the frontier of Massachusetts society as in the older, more established, eastern counties.[9]
     The migration transition in eighteenth-century Massachusetts involved
both an increase in general population redistribution and a rise in transiency
mobility. The wandering poor person was not a completely new "type";
transients were found in smaller numbers in seventeenth-century towns. What
was new, however, was the existence of a class of the transient poor who
required economic assistance. This swelling population of dependent poor,
many of whom were single persons, confronted the traditional towns with
problems of poor relief. The visibility of eighteenth-century transients im-
plicitly challenged the traditionalism of the communal society; unemployment, single-person households, and residential mobility were not accepted
patterns of behavior.

During the eighteenth century, towns began to follow the practice of presenting the names and prior residential origins of transients to the courts of general sessions of the peace. Parents, their children, and servants (if any) were grouped together in the warnings which were prepared by local constables for the legal identification of all transients. Single persons were usually listed separately. The social unit warned out was the household, which consisted variously of a family, a single man or woman, or, more rarely, a family with a servant or slave.

The most distinctive feature of transient households in Essex and Hampshire Counties was the high proportion of single persons (see Table 4). The total proportions of single transients in Essex County ranged from 52 to 62 percent, while in Hampshire County there was a greater variation across time (from 26 to 54 percent). Although we do not know the ages of these single transients, their large proportion of the total suggests that many may have been young and unmarried — the most common characteristics of migrants.10 Yet we cannot rule out the possibility that some were older persons, such as widows, who were unemployable and migrating for better living conditions as dependent poor.

Transiency among single persons was not restricted by sex; almost equal proportions of men and women were warned in Essex while in Hampshire, again, there was more variation over time. These regional variations in the numbers of single men and women may be explained by the different demographic histories of the two counties. Essex, a demographically "older" county than Hampshire, had the most unbalanced sex ratio of all Massachusetts counties. In many Essex County towns, native sons migrated during the eighteenth century because of economic and population pressures. This outmigration reduced the supply of males and created a demographic imbalance. Hampshire, however, expanded after 1730, when the number of towns increased sixfold and the number of adult men and women was almost equal.11 Single transient women were perhaps more welcome in Hampshire because of the need for marriage mates in a developing area. In Essex, transient males were not the solution to a decline in available marriage mates because of their lower-class status. Caught between the pressures of increasing demands on economic resources and legal and moral strictures against the status of the single-person household, unmarried transients formed the major subclass of the dependent population.

The one-parent household was subject to very close scrutiny in eighteenth-century Massachusetts, particularly if headed by a woman. The overall proportion of one-parent families remained at a low level in both Essex and Hampshire, but the number of female-headed families almost tripled during the early 1760s. There may have been an incremental increase in widowhood following the French and Indian Wars which could account for this change.12

69

Table 4   Household Status of Transients in Essex and Hampshire Counties, Massachusetts, During the Eighteenth Century*

Household Status	1739-43		1750-54	
	Essex	Hampshire	Essex	Hampshire
Single persons				
Males	27%	28%	38%	33%
Females	27%	26%	30%	14%
Families**				
Two-parent	39%	38%	28%	42%
One-parent	7%	8%	4%	11%
Servants†	-		1%	-
Slaves	-		-	-
Total††	100%	100%	100%	100%
N	(257)	(50)	(400)	(88)

Household Status	1760-64		1770-74	
	Essex	Hampshire	Essex	Hampshire
Single persons				
Males	32%	30%	28%	11%
Females	31%	14%	24%	15%
Families				
Two-parent	29%	45%	40%	68%
One-parent	6%	10%	9%	6%
Servants	1%	-	-	1%
Slaves	1%	-	-	-
Total	100%	99%	101%	101%
N	(862)	(306)	(58)	(122)

*   Taken from the Court of General Sessions of the Peace, 1726-96, Essex County, Clerk of Courts Office, Salem, Massachusetts; Court of General Sessions of the Peace, 1735-81, Hampshire County, Clerk of Courts Office, Northampton, Massachusetts.

**   Almost all one-parent families were headed by females. In Essex County, 46 of 51 one-parent families in 1760-64 were headed by women. In Hampshire, 41 of the 52 one-parent families were headed by single mothers.

†   Since occupations were not included in the warning out, this is only a minimal estimate of the number of servants.

††   Percentages may not add to 100 percent due to rounding.

But mothers with illegitimate children also fell victim to banishment by communities attempting to avoid poor relief and enforce moral censure.[13] The late eighteenth century was a period of increased sexual activity, as the rise in premarital pregnancy rates in Massachusetts suggests. Prosecution for illegitimacy also reflected increased sexual activity as well as the moral authority of the towns and county courts.[14] It seems likely that transient single mothers fell within this category of socially excluded persons.

Not all transients were unmarried; families comprised the second largest category of unwanted persons. These transient families generally included only biologically related members: husbands, wives, and their children. Rarely were three-generational households, apprentices, servants, or slaves found among transient families.

Smaller than the average, premodern American family, transient families averaged just about four persons (see Table 5). Since family size is an indication of the relative age of the parents, it seems clear that married transients were as youthful on the frontier as in older, eastern Massachusetts. But there were demographic differences between transient families in each county. Proportionally more transient families lived in Hampshire than in Essex, and the average household size was larger in the west as well. These differences suggest that more families migrated to Hampshire County, presumably for better economic opportunities. Essex County, on the other hand, became more congested during the last half of the eighteenth century.[15] Part of this congestion may have resulted from transients who were trapped geographically and economically by old age, ill health, and poverty.

These distinctions showed also in the type of community more likely to take action against the transients. Since warnings out were related to a town's efforts to avoid the costs of poor relief, we would expect that in Essex County, where the economy was under stress, both the wealthy and poor towns would have warned out transients in equal proportions. The wealthy towns would be motivated by the desire to preserve their wealth and economic order; the less wealthy towns by the need to preserve what wealth was available. This, in fact, was the case in Essex County during the 1760s. There was almost no relationship between per capita warnings and per capita wealth. Transiency migration in Essex County was common to all towns, regardless of their wealth or population size.[16]

But in Hampshire County there was a stronger relationship between per capita warnings and per capita wealth. In part, this relationship reflects greater economic opportunities in Hampshire than in Essex. Transients clearly were attracted to Hampshire County, as its population growth and proliferation of new settlements suggest. Some communities were more attractive than others, but exactly which ones is not clear at this time. For example, the sick, the aged, and widows may have been drawn to those towns with well-developed charitable and institutional support. More generally, younger transients showed some sense of economic advantage in seeking places in

71

Table 5   Average Household and Family Size of Transients, 1760-64, and
            of Persons Listed in the Census of 1765, in Essex and Hampshire
            Counties, Massachusetts*

	Average household size	Average family size
Essex County		
1765 Census, whites only	5.34	n.a.
Transients, 1760-64	2.10	4.10
Hampshire County		
1765 Census, whites only	5.95	n.a.
Transients, 1760-64	2.65	4.03

*   Sources for transients, see Table 3. 1765 calculations are taken from data in
        Joseph B. Felt, "Statistics of the Population in Massachusetts," *Collections of the
        American Statistical Association* I, part II (Boston, 1845), pp. 149-51.

Note: Definitions of the relationships among family members are not available in the
        1765 Census. For this reason, I have adopted the term "household" to describe
        the average number of persons within each living unit. From the aggregated data
        available in the 1765 Census, "household" seems to be a more inclusive defini-
        tion than the term "family," which was used by the census takers. Within the
        census category of "family," servants, apprentices, possibly slaves, and three-
        generational families seem to have co-resided together. Also, the term "house-
        hold" permits us to categorize single individuals into separate households.

        The category of "average family size" omits single individuals and employs as the
        unit of analysis persons who were defined as biologically related members of the
        same family. While information of this type is not available from the census, it
        can be found in the warnings out. For a discussion of the definitions of family
        and household used here, see Peter Laslett, ed., *Household and Family in Past
        Time* (Cambridge, England, 1972), pp. 28-40.

Hampshire County, though they were often rebuffed.

Overriding these differences, however, was the fact that transients in both
counties came from the bottom of the social scale. Almost all of the Salem
transients listed in 1791 (mostly males) were working-class artisans and lower-
class mariners and laborers (see Table 6). Only a handful were in higher
occupational groups. Compared to the complete occupational structure of
Boston's males in 1790, the male transients from Salem were overwhelmingly
lower class. Yet an important variation occurs when we control for country
of origin. Nearly two-thirds of the foreign transients were mariners or fishermen while only about one-quarter of the domestic transients lived directly

Table 6 Occupational Status of Transients to Salem, Massachusetts, in 1791, by Residential Origins, Compared with the Occupational Structure of Boston, Massachusetts, 1790.

Occupational status	Residential origins of Salem transients, 1791* U.S.		Foreign		Total		Boston, 1790** all males	
	Percent	N	Percent	N	Percent	N	Percent	N
Government	-	(0)	-	(0)	-	(0)	3	(67)
Professional	-	(0)	1	(1)	1	(1)	9	(219)
Tradesmen	-	(0)	2	(2)	1	(2)	18	(474)
Clerical	-	(0)	1	(1)	1	(1)	3	(66)
Artisans	51	(59)	15	(12)	36	(71)	49	(1271)
Building crafts		(11)		(1)		(12)		(245)
Cloth trades		(17)		(2)		(19)		(289)
Food trades		(10)		(3)		(13)		(175)
Marine crafts		(6)		(4)		(10)		(219)
Metal crafts		(6)		(2)		(8)		(132)
Wood-workers		(3)		(0)		(3)		(106)
Miscellaneous		(6)		(0)		(6)		(205)
Service -		(0)		(0)		(0)	7	(183)
Mariners	24	(27)	61	(50)	39	(77)	5	(117)
Unskilled	25	(29)	20	(16)	23	(45)	7	(188)
Total		(115)		(82)		(197)		(2585)

73

* Calculated from "Salem Warnings, 1791," *Essex Institute Historical Collections* XLIII (1907): 345-52. Because of missing information as to occupations or residential origins, 26 males, 22 single women, and 14 widows were omitted.
** Calculated from Allan Kulikoff, "The Progress of Inequality in Revolutionary Boston," *William and Mary Quarterly* XXVIII (1971): 411-12, Appendix.

from the sea. Conversely, few foreign transients were artisans while a majority of domestic transients were dispersed among land- and sea-related crafts such as tailoring, ship's carpentry, and cabinet-making. Similar proportions of both domestic and foreign transients were unskilled workers.

Because Salem's foreign transients were primarily mariners, their transiency may have been a function of their occupations. On the other hand, the more balanced occupational profile of domestic transients suggests that they were attracted to Salem because of its diversified social structure. For example, the proportion of transient domestic artisans in Salem in 1791 was remarkably similar to the proportion of artisans in Boston. It is not surprising that skilled and semiskilled domestic artisans were drawn to a commercial town such as Salem; they sought economic opportunities where they were most available. More problematic was the future of unskilled laborers and husbandmen. These persons were least prepared to adjust to the economic life of a premodern, commercial town, and may have swelled the ranks of the transient poor.

Transient domestic artisans in Massachusetts should not be confused with English "tramping artisans" of the eighteenth and nineteenth centuries. Of course, their status as migrants was an important parallel, but English "tramping" was an organized form of unemployment relief and labor redistribution which operated with varying degrees of efficiency. In contrast, transiency in eighteenth-century Massachusetts was individualized and nonunionized. Some form of informal cooperation may have existed, particularly in the seaports of Salem and Boston, but nineteenth-century England had a more clearly defined subculture of migrant artisans.17

The low economic condition of Massachusetts transients raises the problem of whether they were capable of travelling long distances in search of employment or subsistence. An analysis of the residential origins of transients who entered three Massachusetts towns — Cambridge, Chelmsford and Salem — reveals two distinct types of migratory activity. First, foreign transients travelled long distances almost exclusively by water, immigrating from countries such as England or Ireland. Second, domestic transients relocated very short distances, usually not more than ten miles from the town of last residence. This pattern of the domestic transients was likely to have been a repeating one, so that some transients circulated from town to town.

Long-distance movement of transients from other countries depended on the geographic contiguity of the destination to the point of origin. Both Salem and Boston received distinct migratory streams of European transients during the late eighteenth century. Only a trickle of transients entered the seaport towns from outside Massachusetts (see Table 7).

The major stream of transients in seaport and inland towns was from within Massachusetts. Primary economic and population centers such as Salem and Boston received a majority of their transients from within Massachusetts. Smaller inland towns, removed from initial contact with foreign immigrants, also received almost all of their transients from within Massachusetts. The main exceptions were towns which dotted the borders, thus coming into contact with transients from neighboring states such as New Hampshire or Connecticut. Chelmsford, for example, a small, agricultural town located near New Hampshire, received nearly one-fifth of its transients from outside Massachusetts. Cambridge, however, recorded only a bare 2 percent of its transient population as coming directly from outside Massachusetts.

Thus the general pattern of transient migration in eighteenth-century Massachusetts was one of localized mobility, as transients moved from town

Table 7   Residential Origins of Transients in Three Massachusetts Towns
          During the Eighteenth Century

Residential origins	Cambridge* 1761-71	Chelmsford* 1761-71	Salem** 1791
Massachusetts	96%	82%	52%
Foreign	2%		36%
U.S., other	2%	18%	10%
Unknown	1%		2%
Total †	101%	100%	100%
Within ten miles	76%	64%	30%
Essex County	5%	6%	30%
Middlesex County	49%	72%	7%
Suffolk County	32%	4%	7%
N	(189)	(103)	(260)

75

*   Transients from Cambridge and Chelmsford represent male and female house-
     holds (single and married) who were warned by the Court of General Sessions of
     the Peace, 1761-71, Middlesex County, Clerk of Courts Office, Cambridge,
     Massachusetts.
**   Transients from Salem were warned by the local Selectmen. They represent male
     and female transients; marital status was not usually given. For sources, see Table
     6.
†   Percentages may not add up to 100 percent due to rounding.

to town within discrete local areas. The long migratory move — except for
foreign immigrants — was rare. More typically, transients circulated among
towns within a ten-mile radius. It is important to distinguish between localized mobility among rural and urban (or seaport) towns. Major population
sources such as Boston or Salem, with their large and diverse migratory
streams, drew transients from distances greater than ten miles. Of the transients entering Boston and Salem, however, about one-half were from within
ten miles.[19]
   In contrast to the urban areas, two rural Middlesex County towns, Cambridge and Chelmsford, received most of their transients from within ten
miles (see Table 7). With its close proximity to Boston, Cambridge was like a
way station for transients. Three-fourths of Cambridge's transients came from

40

within ten miles, and a third were from nearby Boston. Boston's transient migration stream seemed to feed directly into Cambridge, as a procession of migrants — many of foreign birth — paused briefly but moved on. Chelmsford, located outside of a large migration stream, experienced even fewer long-distance transients than Cambridge. Indeed, the county boundaries of Middlesex were as useful a guide to the extent of localized mobility into Chelmsford as the ten-mile radius (72 percent from within the County vs. 64 percent from within ten miles). Ultimately, the ten-mile radius provides the most useful measure of transiency migration. The nearer a town was to a major population stream, the more likely it was that the transient would cross a political boundary. Even during the transition from a traditional to a modern society, there was a pattern of rural to urban migration. Artisans, for example, were probably "pulled" across political boundaries to better opportunities; unskilled laborers may have been "pushed" from their jobs by poor working conditions or a declining economy.

Transiency thus reflected important but limited geographic mobility, which followed from frequently intense poverty and physical hardship. Constables and clerks conveyed a sense of poverty in some cases from which escape was almost impossible. William Pickett, for example, had been a prisoner in Canada during the French and Indian War. After suffering hardships of war and captivity, he returned to Springfield without even sufficient clothing. The London-born Pickett had been a servant before his capture during the war.[20]

Given the high proportions of single transients, it is plausible to suggest that many transients were ex-servants. Servitude of whites in Massachusetts usually was not permanent. At the end of their terms of service, men and women were often in their early twenties and ready to begin a new "stage" in their personal and economic growth. For example, over one-fifth of the privates from Essex County who served in the French and Indian War in 1758 were servants. For some, the experience of travelling to other parts of New England during military service may have opened up hitherto unknown opportunities for settlement. One such private, Daniel Buteman from Beverly, eventually appeared on the tax lists there, married a local woman and out-migrated.[21] The case of Buteman is but one example; the important point is that migration and military service were tied to improved economic opportunities for young ex-servants such as Buteman.

Others were less fortunate. Benjamin Baley, his wife, and their three children required poor relief from Topsfield in 1762. Baley bound himself to some Topsfield inhabitants who failed to fulfill their obligations, leaving him without a job, any form of income, and dependent upon the town.[22] Transients such as Baley, encumbered by economic responsibilities to the towns in which they settled, were taxed just as other inhabitants but lacked the ability to pay their shares. Appearance on an eighteenth-century tax list implied neither wealth nor residential stability. Peter Frost, for one, made an extreme choice when he was unable to solve his continuing problems of poverty and personal care. Frost, an Ipswich laborer, bound himself for life in 1700 to William Cogwell, Jr.[23]

Sickness plagued some transients. Reports of clerks commonly referred not only to their poverty but also ill health. The death of transients in unfamiliar towns was common; Samuel Graffam, for example, of Harpswell fell sick in Topsham and died there. In particular, young children were extremely vulnerable to the ardors of repeated migration. Jane Wing, a single mother, lost one of her three children in Bridgewater and the town reluctantly absorbed the cost of the burial.[24] The rigors of transiency — poverty, constant mobility, poor health, the inability to work, and few alternatives for improvement — confronted at least some of the transients of eighteenth-century Massachusetts with a circle of poverty which was difficult to break. Widows, the aged, children, and the mentally ill were most vulnerable to the conditions of transiency.

One ex-servant who fell into distress was Elizabeth Nicholson Stimson. Her history — brief as it is to us — reads like a microcosm of the transient's existence.[25] Elizabeth was born in Salem in 1775 but moved to Andover with her family in 1779. When she was fifteen or sixteen years old, Elizabeth left her family and worked as a "maid servant" for eight years, until 1798, primarily in Middleton but also in Reading. She lived on her wages, completed the term of service, and returned to Salem to live with her aunt. After a few months, she moved again, this time back to her father's home in Andover. There she lived until she married in 1799 at the age of twenty-four. With her husband, probably an itinerant mariner, she lived in Salem and bore three children until the entire family required poor relief in 1807. Elizabeth Stimson's mobility patterns seem typical of eighteenth-century Massachusetts: completely localized within a discrete geographical area. She married at an average age, but only after completing eight years as a servant. Precisely why she and her family required poor relief was not clear, but they, like hundreds of others, turned to the town for assistance in increasing numbers during the eighteenth century. Their ability to cope with poverty and illness depended in part on the institutional responses of the towns, the counties, and the General Court to the plight of the transients.

77

III

Both the rising numbers of transients and their economic dependency prompted institutions in eighteenth-century Massachusetts to develop new solutions to social welfare and control. During this transitional period, some continuity in traditional practices of welfare and control remained. But the thrust of the eighteenth-century response to the new class of transient poor was away from the seventeenth-century practices.

The seventeenth-century background of the institutional control of transients (as distinct from welfare) presents an incomplete record, but two themes emerge from the archives of the towns. First, the towns regulated very carefully the admission of new members. Viewed in this sense, close scrutiny of all types of migrants functioned to monitor the quality of potential townsmen and women in order to achieve a cohesive social order.[26] In addition to controlling the quality of new inhabitants, the regulation of transients was rooted in a suspicion of their possible criminal acts. Salem, for example, did not permit Indians in the town except during daylight hours, and constables were directed by the Selectmen to view as suspicious "night walkers" and others who were awake at unreasonable hours.[27] The most dangerous transients, often called vagabonds, required more specific public control. Persons who were unable to give "a good and satisfactory account of their wandering up and down" were included within this category.[28] They were subject to corporal punishment for their wanderings and returned to their legal residences. In this case, banishment was used because no police force existed which could maintain effective control over the more dangerous transients.

The second rationale for social control was economic; towns tried to minimize transiency in order to avoid responsibilities of poor relief. Theoretically, those persons most likely to require poor relief — foreign immigrants, ex-servants, the wandering poor, and the sick — could gain legal inhabitancy by residing for a specific length of time. Once a needy person was settled, his welfare was normally provided through families.[29] But the seventeenth-century towns took measures to prevent things from going this far. Ipswich, for example, regulated the flow of transients in a 1699 town law because such persons "may prove burdensome in several respects to the town." An earlier law in Wenham required a security bond from transients, while Salem sought to protect itself from economic burdens by permitting two joiners to enter the town in 1661 only because they had secure employment.[30] Employment defused the threat of poor relief, particularly if the transient was a servant and responsible to a master.

Local institutions monitored the activities of transients as well. Seventeenth-century churches and schools limited their participants to personally familiar inhabitants, as opposed to transients. In the 1640s, the elders of the church at Salem advised the newly formed Wenham Church to admit only those individuals "known [personally] to some of the congregation to be in Covenant elsewhere." In the small seventeenth-century communities, where relationships were conducted on a face-to-face basis, the distinction between personally familiar individuals and those without connections within the community was an important boundary between transients and residents. Ipswich went so far as to distinguish formally between the family and friends of town residents and unwelcome "strangers" who were outside of those networks. Even if transients lived side-by-side with local inhabitants, town institutions separated the transient. In Salem, transients could send their children to the local schoolmaster, but only at a fee of twice that of full inhabitants.[31]

While most of the evidence indicates that transients in seventeenth-century Massachusetts towns were treated with varying degrees of suspicion, it must be noted that the practice of geographic mobility was also an accepted one. Cambridge acknowledged the passage of travellers through that town by giving permission to Andrew Belcher in 1653 "to sell beer and bread for [the] entertainment of strangers and the good of the town." Such licensing was not uncommon. Similarly, the General Court recognized the status of the nonresident by creating special laws and courts to handle some of their financial and legal situations.[32] While geographic movement was a normal part of the life of some towns, particularly seaports such as Boston, transients held an ambiguous position — neither totally accepted nor completely rejected.

In most towns during the eighteenth century, resident dependents still received care in individual families. For dependents without families or close relatives, the usual practice was for Selectmen or overseers of the poor to pay residents for boarding disabled or indigent persons. Often dependents performed small household chores if physically able. Mary Cue, of Wenham, agreed "to keep" Aaron Jones for one year in 1745, a standard length of time for this contractual service. Her duties included providing Jones with food, "both in sickness and in health," as well as mending his clothes. For these services, the town paid her about four pounds and absorbed all medical expenses. By 1788 in Wenham, the care of local dependents remained with individual families but the town took steps to rationalize the economics of poor relief. Placement of dependents occurred through bidding, with the poor going to the family with the lowest bid. Wenham obtained care but at minimal public cost.[33]

Assistance of local dependents was an integral part of life in the Massachusetts towns, but these functions were performed with varying degrees of success and motives. On the one hand, care was extended to nonresidents such as widow Mercy Fiske, who entered Wenham without permission of the Selectmen in 1694. They nevertheless paid for a doctor and nurse to care for her.[34] Similarly, the smaller agricultural towns such as Manchester, Topsfield, and Wenham agreed to raise money to donate to the poor of Boston during the Revolution.[35]

On the other hand, disputes between towns and between individuals and towns over the responsibility for the care of the poor were common. The poor law of 1794 attempted to alleviate some of these questions of care by providing poor relief of up to three months for all persons. Indeed, one of the most striking features of the revised poor law was its meticulous provision for resolving disputes between towns. Usually the point of contention was the precise residential origin of the perons in need of care. Gloucester and Wenham, for example, disagreed over the legal residence of an "idiot boy" named Nathan Rolings, with Wenham claiming that he was brought into the town

79

44

illegally.[36] The plight of Rolings, who required some form of permanent care, suggests that social welfare by families in colonial Massachusetts also had its problematic side. One can easily imagine a boy like Rolings having been buffeted from town to town and family to family.

Even families did not always care for their own relatives who were in need. Wenham and Beverly had to negotiate a contract in order to force a non-resident son to care for his widowed mother. Also, the overseers of the poor of Marblehead petitioned the court of general sessions of the peace in 1752 to force the relatives of two "aged" women to care for them.[37] Avoidance of familial responsibility, while not the usual practice, clearly was a part of the colonial experience.

With overseers of the poor empowered to bind out transients as well as children, social welfare and social control converged. In both rural and urban towns, overseers bound children of the poor and idle into service. Boston's and Wenham's overseers turned naturally to the servant and apprenticeship system. Children as well as adult transients received food, shelter, clothing, perhaps some form of training, and varying degrees of emotional relationships.[38] What must be understood here, though, was the conjunction of family life and its values and the community's resolution of economic dependency through the labor system. Not only did overseers minimize their relief expenses; they maximized social order by dispersing potential transients into the community.

Another alternative — formal institutionalization — was not used extensively in Massachusetts until the early nineteenth century. But the practice of grouping dependents under the same roof existed throughout the eighteenth century. Early forms of institutionalization were found not only in large population centers such as Boston or Salem; small agricultural towns such as Manchester, Wenham, and Ipswich also experimented with group housing.[39] Known as a workhouse or poorhouse, the typical eighteenth-century institution frequently housed the local poor and transients together. Also, towns combined the use of houses for transients and the poor with family welfare. As early as 1719, Ipswich built a poorhouse but in 1734 recommended that the poor be placed in private homes and employed outside. The use of workhouses for both the housing and employment of "idle and indigent" persons became widespread enough in Massachusetts by 1750 to require the General Court to regulate their operations. This law permitted the housing of poor, vagrant, and idle persons because all were deemed socially harmful.[40]

Transients who did not work had long been a source of intense concern to the General Court. The Court labelled transient vagrants as disruptive persons, accusing them of luring children and servants away from their "callings and employments." As early as 1682, the Court singled out Boston as a haven for "idle persons in families as well as single persons."[41] Transient vagrants who required specific controls were not only perceived as bad in themselves but as menaces to others and to the social order. This control was not confined to the large eastern towns. The General Court passed a special act at the end of the eighteenth century for the removal of vagrants and "strolling poor people" from the District of Marshpee on Cape Cod. Marshpee, according to the Court, had become a place of shelter for the transient poor, and was populated primarily by Indians and blacks.[42] And generally the more traditional forms of social welfare and control which relied on personal familiarity and residential continuity provided a stark contrast to the needs of a growing class of transient poor during the eighteenth century. Despite the continuities of care on a local level, the more complex and routine legal mechanisms of the eighteenth century represented a shift from traditional approaches to welfare and control.

As the eighteenth century progressed, the control of transiency depended less on each town as a unique social entity and more on the legal administration of a routine system of welfare and control. The customary statutory settlement laws before 1739 permitted a legal settlement if an individual resided in a town for a specified number of months. After 1739, residency requirements stiffened Legal residency required the agreement of the town meeting or the Selectmen; even the payment of taxes did not create a de facto form of legal residence.[43] In practice, the control of the movement and settlement of eighteenth-century transients was an integral part of the social order. The granting of poor relief, the laws of settlement, and the practice of warning transients to leave town were interrelated aspects of the legal structure employed by towns in Massachusetts to preserve their social order.

Who held the responsibility for discovering the presence of transients and informing them that they had to leave a particular town? This important question of the legal responsibility for the detection of transients changed over the course of the eighteenth century. The purpose of the settlement and poor-relief laws — the social control of unwanted persons — remained substantially the same, but the methods for dealing with transients were transformed. While each town originally was accountable for discovery and notification, by the end of the eighteenth century the town no longer had the sole responsibility for transients in its midst. By focusing closely on the process of discovery and the burden of notification of the warnings-out system, we can ascertain the shifting legal relationships between the transients, the towns, and the county courts.

In 1692, the Province of Massachusetts enacted a settlement law which provided that persons not legally warned out of a town within three months became inhabitants, and entitled to poor relief.[44] This statute was a more formalized statement of seventeenth-century settlement laws passed by individual towns; however, it added several features to the legal process of the control of transiency and of poor relief. First, the burden of discovering the presence of transients was placed on the towns themselves. Eager to avoid poor relief, warnings were returned by towns to their county courts as proof that the town had warned out all transients. These procedures meant that the costs of the discovery of transients and the legal notification of their presence became functions of the town governments and secondarily of the county courts. In most towns, populations were small and transients easily identifiable. But in more populous towns, or those with a greater turnover of new persons such as Boston and Salem, identification of transients required more than the customary reliance on the face-to-face encounters of the agricultural villages. As early as 1670, the Salem Selectmen hired Thomas Oliver to go to each house once a month to inquire about the presence of "strangers."[45]

During the late 1720s and 1730s, the General Court altered the settlement and poor-relief laws by shifting the burden of discovery of the transients from the towns themselves to the local inhabitants who provided them with food and shelter.[46] Called "entertainment" laws, these statutes provided that transients could not remain in a particular town longer than twenty days without special permission from that town. Inhabitants who housed transients were required to give the town clerk a written description of the transient's personal characteristics or be subject to a forty-shilling fine for noncompliance. As a device for the control of transiency and reduction of poor relief, warnings out were used contemporaneously with the "entertainment" laws. The former prevented the transient from becoming a legal resident; the latter provided a source of indemnity against the poor relief of transients. This dual form of control regulated not only the transients but also cautioned local inhabitants before they rented rooms to transients.

The operation of this law was straightforward and local inhabitants seem to have cooperated. For example, in 1738, Richard Dodge, a lifelong resident of Wenham, notified the Selectmen that he had "taken in" Thomas Colwell, his wife, and their three children. The Colwell family migrated to Wenham from New Hampshire, were given a dwelling house by Dodge, and probably hired as servants. Because this family was employed, they were exempted from the twenty-day restriction. It was not unusual for Dodge to hire a servant family. Married in 1724, Dodge's wife Mary gave birth to seven children by 1738 — but only one was alive by the end of that year. Without maturing children in an agricultural economy, Richard Dodge was labor poor and in a position to need hired help for his farm.[47]

By 1767, the General Court removed the burden of discovery of transients from the towns and their inhabitants alike, placing it directly on the transients themselves. Instead of relying on local constables to warn transients through the county courts, the 1767 statute required all transients to inform the Selectment of their presence as they entered a town. Responsibility for being a transient came to rest with each migrant; status as a nonresident meant that persons were to submit themselves voluntarily to physical removal back to their towns of legal residence.[48]

Known transients were removed on authority of a warrant from a justice of the peace. Constables secured transients by warrants, and returned them from town to town until the transients reached their legal residences. If possible, the transient paid for the cost of this removal; otherwise, the town of legal residence bore the expense.49 The General Court absorbed the costs of persons to destinations outside of Massachusetts. One important exception to this law exempted apprentices and servants from removal if attached to a master or family; the labor system remained intact while physical removal controlled potentially harmful transients. An important implication of this statute was the decline of the system of warnings out processed through the county court. Legal notification that transients were nonresidents was no longer necessary under the 1767 law.

Not until the 1790s did the General Court fully rewrite the settlement and poor-relief laws in operation during the middle years of the eighteenth century. Indeed, it seems as though the Revolution and its aftermath temporarily interrupted — rather than caused — revision of the policies regulating transients. Drawing on the principles of the 1767 statute, the revision of 1794 provided for an even more routinized procedure for the removal of transients.50 The 1767 statute in effect had eliminated the warnings out as a device for controlling transiency, but some towns continued the practice both through the county court and local overseers of the poor. However, the 1794 statute specifically ended the warnings-out system, substituting a comprehensive procedure for the return of transients to their legal residences. With this added power of removal came expanded responsibilities; each town had to provide care and immediate relief for all persons regardless of resident status for a period of up to three months.

The shifting burdens of legal responsibility for the transients of eighteenth-century Massachusetts culminated in this statute of 1794. Poor transient persons became fully integrated into the legal structure but not the social order. Towns became legally responsible to the transients' need for care; yet these same towns also could employ removal procedures practiced earlier in the century. The difference was that the new procedures for removal provided the most efficient and least expensive method of removing transients and reducing the work of the county courts. Transients received some increased procedural rights, such as an appeal to the court for common pleas to contest removal, but the statute focused most extensively on the procedural aspects of removal, the control of dependent persons, and the arbitration of disputes among towns over questions of legal residences of transients. This revised law of 1794 clearly revealed continuities with past practices, but it also reflected divergences, particularly more precise, rational forms for the administration of poor relief. For while the 1794 poor law was a "legal institutionalization" of the transient poor, it also, paradoxically, maintained a resolution of dependency which relied heavily on the family.

By the end of the eighteenth century, local systems of welfare and control ultimately became integrated into the larger structure of Massachusetts society. The implications of this process of integration (by the General Court, the county courts, and the towns) suggest that the familiar communal assumptions of life in the premodern town experienced severe testing under the reality of increased transiency migration and economic stratification. Late eighteenth-century Massachusetts society was a dynamic one in transition; it was not a fixed, flat, "colonial" one. David Rothman, in his recent analysis of nineteenth-century penal and welfare practices uses a "noninstitutional" counterpoint based on a motionless view of colonial America as a contrast to the nineteenth-century society which "discovered" the asylum.[51] This leaves the impression that before 1800, social welfare was an unchanging, idyllic blend of assistance from one's family and neighbours. Rothman's point about the development of institutionalization during the nineteenth century is astute astute; the counterpoint, however, does not explain transitional change within the history of premodern systems of welfare and control. Rather than stressing a dichotomy between "colonial" and "Jacksonian" policies of social welfare and control, we must recognize a transitional period from the traditional forms to the more modern ones of the nineteenth century.

The eighteenth-century legal process of social control actively involved both the town and the county court. The role of the county court, however, did not supersede that of the town; the two interacted defensively in attempts to monitor transient migration, minimize poor relief, and preserve the social order. The decline in the use of warnings in 1767 and their disappearance from the revised poor law of 1794 as a technique of social and economic control represent part of the rationalization of the legal sanctions on transiency in Massachusetts. These more predictable, routine methods of limiting the economic and social impact of transients are characteristic of more modern societies.[52]

Social solidarity did not disappear as the towns shared their political authority with the county courts, but the boundaries of social interaction were redefined.[53] Localism, or the "Town born" in Bentley's words, was no longer a guarantee of homogeneity. The emerging social order in late eighteenth-century Massachusetts required support from general laws which defined transients as deviants from the cultural and economic norms of family life, residential stability, and secure employment. Banishment could no longer satisfy the needs of a transitional society. Increasing levels of transiency migration and reciprocal legal means of control indicate that premodern Massachusetts had passed from an explicitly communal society to a more complex, modern one. This transition was by no means complete by 1800. Yet the tensions of the structural change and legal adjustments pointed more in the direction of modern nineteenth-century America than toward communal continuity.

Douglas Lamar Jones
Brandeis University

IN SEARCH OF THE HISTORICAL CHILD: MINIATURE ADULTHOOD AND YOUTH IN COLONIAL NEW ENGLAND

ROSS W. BEALES, JR.
College of the Holy Cross

"I SHALL MISS THE LITTLE GROWN-UPS—WERE THERE NO CHILDREN IN those days?"[1] This question about an eighteenth-century portrait of four American children essentially states the widespread scholarly and anti-quarian view of children in colonial America. Not only is it assumed that co-lonial Americans treated their children differently than we do today, but it is also believed that they regarded their children as "miniature adults" and recognized no stage of development like twentieth-century adolescence. While this essay does not suggest that colonial Americans treated their children as we treat ours, it does conclude that notions of "miniature adulthood" and the absence of adolescence in colonial New England are, at best, exaggerations.

Much of the myth of miniature adulthood stems from the belief that children in colonial portraits appeared old and dressed like their parents. Until the Revolution, writes Alice Morse Earle, "as soon as a boy put on breeches he dressed precisely like his father—in miniature."[2] According to Arthur M. Schlesinger, "the older generation as late as Independence still displayed its basic assumption that children were miniature adults by con-tinuing to dress the young like little grownups. . . . The vital distinction be-tween youth and age as yet remained unrecognized."[3] Monica Kiefer finds that eighteenth-century children occupied "a submerged position in an adult

---

[1] Alice Morse Earle, *Child Life in Colonial Days* (New York: Macmillan, 1899), p. 50.
[2] Ibid., p. 62.
[3] Arthur M. Schlesinger, *The Birth of the Nation: A Portrait of the American People on the Eve of Independence* (New York: Knopf, 1968), p. 25.

setting"; only through the child's "gradual emergence" from that status would he come to occupy "a place of honor as a cherished social entity." Like other observers, she concludes that "as children of Colonial times were expected to behave like adults, they quite logically wore clothes appropriate for the role."[4] Michael Zuckerman also states that there was "no clear distinction between child and adult" in eighteenth-century Massachusetts. Children in Puritan portraits are "only scaled-down adults," who wear both wigs and the same clothes as their parents. "If clothes do not make the man," he asserts, "they do mark social differentiations; a distinctive mode of dress for children never developed before the Revolution." New Englanders did not believe that children had "distinctive needs and desires," and children were therefore given "no distinctive places or roles." Eighteenth-century Massachusetts children "did not live separated from the society in a protected preserve of carefree innocence; they were part of a single undifferentiated community."[5]

Accounts of childhood in early America are marked by condescension, sentimentality, and even blank incomprehension. In describing Cotton Mather's admonitions to his daughter, Earle confesses, "I hardly understand why Cotton Mather, who was really very gentle to his children, should have taken upon himself to trouble this tender little blossom with dread of his death." None of Earle's concern for Mather's "tender little blossom" appears in her discussion of Nathaniel Mather, whose diary contains the admission, "Of the manifold sins which then I was guilty of, none so sticks upon me as that, being very young, I was *whitling* on the Sabbath-day; and for fear of being seen I did it behind the *door*. A great *reproach* of God! a specimen of that *atheism* I brought into the world with me!" For Earle, "it is satisfactory to add that this young prig of a Mather died when nineteen years of age."[6]

Certain that modern parents know best how to rear children, authors like Earle believe that their knowledge is an appropriate standard by which to judge other cultures and eras. They insist that colonial child-rearing

[4]Monica Kiefer, *American Children Through Their Books, 1700–1835* (Philadelphia: Univ. of Pennsylvania Press, 1948), pp. 1, 94, 225.

[5]Michael Zuckerman, *Peaceable Kingdoms: New England Towns in the Eighteenth Century* (New York: Knopf, 1970), p. 73. None of these publications systematically examines either children's clothing or portraiture. One suspects that little precise information will be gleaned from such sources, for neither extant clothing nor portraits reveal everyday styles. Any extensive examination of portraits must take into account Philippe Ariès's finding with respect to French children: *"The first children's costume was the costume which everybody used to wear about a century before, and which henceforth they were the only ones to wear."* Ariès, *Centuries of Childhood: A Social History of Family Life,* trans. Robert Baldick (New York: Random House, 1962), p. 57.

[6]Alice Morse Earle, *Customs and Fashions in Old New England* (New York: Scribner's, 1896), pp. 13, 15.

practices were not only incorrect but also harmful. Arthur W. Calhoun thus emphasizes the ill effect of "precocity" on children. The seventeenth century was "an age of precocity," which was encouraged in America by Puritan theology and a scarcity of labor. Parents' "zeal for education," for example, "overstimulated and forced baby minds"; the churches encouraged "infantile conversion"; and, in economic life, children were overworked and exploited. In Calhoun's judgment, the Puritans failed "to make the child appear valuable or noteworthy to himself or others." Such a "curtailment of infancy" was both a "distortion" of and "a crime against childhood."[7]

Sandford Fleming argues that in Puritan society "children were regarded simply as miniature adults, and the same means and experiences were considered as suitable for them as for those older." This view of children resulted partly from the general attitudes of a society which lacked the benefits of modern psychology. Furthermore, Puritan theology "had banished the child, and classed everyone indiscriminately, infants and those of maturity, as sinners who were in urgent need of being saved from hell." The necessity of encouraging early conversions was particularly unfortunate in the century after the Great Awakening, when an "overdependence" on revival methods caused the "child mind" to develop "wrong" and "perverted" ideas of God. Indeed, the emotional excesses of revivalism "could hardly fail to do permanent physical, mental and spiritual injury to many of the children wrought upon."[8]

John Demos finds that childhood in Plymouth Colony lasted a short, but crucial, six to eight years. Although a child's first year was "relatively comfortable and tranquil," his second year was likely to be traumatic. Not only would he be weaned and later be confronted by the birth of a rival sibling, but his parents, heeding the repressive advice of minister John Robinson, would seek to crush his "assertive and aggressive drives." As Robinson warned, "surely there is in all children . . . a stubbornness, and stoutness of mind arising from natural pride, which must, in the first place, be broken and beaten down." Demos suggests that this early childhood experience, in which the desire for "autonomy" was beaten down, instilled a lasting sense of "shame and doubt" in the Puritan character. As a result, adult life in Plymouth Colony was characterized by numerous personal conflicts and court cases, especially incidents involving slander, defamation, and fear of public exposure.

[7]Arthur W. Calhoun, *A Social History of the American Family from Colonial Times to the Present* (Cleveland: Bobbs-Merrill, 1917), I, 105, 107, 108, 110, 111.
[8]Sandford Fleming, *Children and Puritanism: The Place of Children in the Life and Thought of the New England Churches, 1620-1847* (New Haven: Yale Univ. Press, 1933), pp. 16, 60, 66-67, 153, 188.

At about six to eight years of age, a child in Plymouth Colony became, in effect, a "miniature adult." Clothing symbolized this new status: previously dressed "in a kind of long robe which opened down the front," boys and girls now dressed very much like their parents. This implies "a whole attitude of mind," in which "there was no idea that each generation required separate spheres of work or recreation. Children learned the behavior appropriate to their sex and station by sharing in the activities of their parents." Six- or seven-year-olds began "technological" training, the boys perhaps working with their fathers at planting or fencemending, the girls helping their mothers with the cooking, spinning, or candlemaking. There may also have been some academic training, including more intensive religious instruction. The pattern of age at apprenticeship and service in other families also leads Demos to stress the years from six to eight, "the most common age for such arrangements."

Children's religious experiences also suggest miniature adulthood, for whole families attended the same church services, and "the young no less than the old were expected to digest the learned words that flowed from the pulpit." While nineteenth-century conversions typically occurred among young people in their teens, "no similar pattern" was found at Plymouth. In fact, many conversions apparently took place well before puberty. "Perhaps, indeed, a religious 'crisis' can more reasonably be connected with the whole matrix of changes customary for children at the age of about six to eight." Thus, with the evidence converging on this early age, it is likely that "the culture attached a very special importance to this particular time of life. Further 'proof' is lacking, but perhaps it was now that children began to assume the role of little adults."

After these crucial early years, the development of the child was relatively smooth. "The way to maturity appeared not as a cliff to be mounted in a series of sudden and precarious leaps, but as a gradual ascent the stages of which were quite literally embodied in the many siblings variously situated along the way." Adolescence was not the turning point that it is today, for "at Plymouth the 'teens' formed a period of relatively calm and steady progress toward full maturity." Courtships began during this stage of development, and following marriage, "the later years of life in Plymouth Colony brought, in most cases, no new departures of a major kind."[9]

*John Demos, *A Little Commonwealth: Family Life in Plymouth Colony* (New York: Oxford, 1970), pp. 69, 134–36, 138–40, 142, 146, 182. See also John Demos, "Developmental Perspectives on the History of Childhood," *Journal of Interdisciplinary History*, 2 (1971), 315–27, and Joseph E. Illick, "Child-Rearing in Seventeenth-Century England and America," in *The History of Childhood*, ed. Lloyd deMause (New York: Psychohistory Press, 1974), pp. 303–50. In his most recent discussion of the family, Demos emphatically states, "*Colonial society barely recognized childhood as we know and understand it today.*" "The American Family in Past Time," *American Scholar*, 43 (1974), 428.

Joseph F. Kett agrees with Demos's findings with respect to adolescence. "Verbal distinctions between childhood and youth" were "practically non-existent in the seventeenth century and still rare in the eighteenth." While there were numerous references to "youth" as early as the seventeenth century, the Puritans used "youth" as a noun rather than as a concept. Thus, their sermons commonly "mixed up children, youth, young people, and young men." Indeed, even if they experienced adolescence in a social sense, seventeenth-century "Puritans would have had difficulty coming to terms with it," for they viewed life as a highway rather than as a series of stages.[10]

Substantial agreement thus exists among authors who discuss attitudes toward children and adolescents in colonial New England. That New Englanders regarded and treated their children as miniature adults is, in C. John Sommerville's words, "one of the hoariest shibboleths."[11] Similarly widespread is the belief that there was no stage in human development comparable to today's adolescence.

Recently, however, David E. Stannard has suggested that "there is no real evidence to support the contention that in 17th century New England, as in 15th and 16th century France, there was little or no distinction between children and adults." He notes, for example, that Puritan journals, autobiographies, histories, and family manuals make "clear distinctions between adults and children well into their teens" and that the law definitely discriminated "between acceptable behavior and appropriate punishment for children, post-adolescent youths and adults."[12] Stannard's observations are confirmed by an examination of the language New Englanders used to describe the "ages of man," by legal distinctions among age groups, and particularly by religious thought and practice.

Colonial New Englanders included both children and youth in the "ages of man," with youth extending from the early teens well into the twenties. When Gilbert Tennent preached in Boston in 1741, he used four familiar chronological divisions in addressing his audience: "old" and "*aged Persons*"; "*middle-ag'd People*, of thirty Years old and upwards"; "*my younger Brethren*, of fourteen Years and upwards"; and "*little Children*, of six Years old and upwards."[13]

Tennent's age-groups approximated the concept of the "ages of man" held by New Englanders. These ages included old age, middle age, youth,

[10]"Adolescence and Youth in Nineteenth-Century America," *Journal of Interdisciplinary History*, 2 (1971), 285-86.

[11]"Bibliographic Note: Toward a History of Childhood and Youth," *Journal of Interdisciplinary History*, 3 (1972), 446, n. 25.

[12]"Death and the Puritan Child," *American Quarterly*, 26 (Dec. 1974), 457-59.

[13]Gilbert Tennent, *The Righteousness of the Scribes* ... (Boston: J. Draper for D. Henchman, 1741), p. 16.

childhood, and sometimes infancy. Anne Bradstreet, for example, wrote "Of the Four Ages of Man," while Ellis Gray spoke of the "Old, and the middle Aged, the Young and little Children." Samuel Moody included "infancy" when he warned that "Judgment shall be Universal with respect to Persons, *viz.* Youth as well as Children and Infants below them, and Middle, with Old Age above them...." Jonathan Edwards advised "every one that is yet out of Christ, and hanging over the Pit of Hell, whether they be old Men and Women, or middle Aged, or young People, or little Children, now [to] hearken to the loud Calls of God's Word and Providence." William Cooper also addressed "MANY of you *Children,* you *Young People,* you that are *middle aged,* and you that are *old....*"[14]

Edwards placed the upper limits of childhood at fourteen when he described the revival of 1735 at Northampton. It had been unusual for children to be converted, but now, he reported, "near thirty were to appearance so wrought upon between ten and fourteen years of age, and two between nine and ten, and one of about four years of age...." Thomas Shepard also saw the early teens as a dividing point. When his fourteen-year-old son was admitted to Harvard College in 1672, Shepard urged him to "Remember... that tho' you have spent your time in the vanity of Childhood; sports and mirth, little minding better things, yet that now, when come to this ripeness of Admission to the College, that now God and man expects you should putt away Childish things: now is the time come, wherein you are to be serious, and to learn sobriety, and wisdom in all your ways which concern God and man." While young Shepard ended his childhood at fourteen, Cotton Mather dared call himself a "youth" at thirty-one. "I am willing now," he told an audience of young people, "at an Age thus far Extending, to conclude my own *Youth,* with one Affectionate Endeavour more" to encourage youthful piety.[15]

The early teens were recognized as special years in other aspects of Puritan culture. The laws of Massachusetts, for example, established fourteen as the age of discretion in cases of slander. (Neighboring Plymouth Colony set the "age of descretion" at sixteen for slander and lying.) Fourteen was

[14]*The Works of Anne Bradstreet,* ed. Jeannine Hensley (Cambridge, Mass.: Harvard, 1967), pp. 51–64; Ellis Gray, *The Fidelity of Ministers* ... (Boston: G. Rogers for M. Dennis, 1742), p. 20; Samuel Moodey [sic], *The Vain Youth Summoned* ... (Boston: Timothy Green, 1707), p. 7; Jonathan Edwards, *Sinners in the Hands of an Angry God* ... (Boston: S. Kneeland and T. Green, 1741), p. 24; William Cooper, *One Shall Be Taken* ... (Boston: T. Fleet for D. Henchman, 1741), p. 21. See also George Whitefield, *The Lord Our Righteousness* ... (Boston: S. Kneeland and T. Green, 1742), pp. 26–28, and Perry Miller, "Jonathan Edwards' Sociology of the Great Awakening," *New England Quarterly,* 21 (1948), 62–66.

[15]Jonathan Edwards, *A Faithful Narrative of the Surprizing Work of God* ... (London: printed for John Oswald, 1737), in *The Great Awakening,* ed. C. C. Goen, *The Works of Jonathan Edwards,* 4 (New Haven: Yale Univ. Press, 1972), p. 158; Colonial Society of Massachusetts, *Publications,* 14 (1913), 193; Cotton Mather, *Early Religion* ... (Boston: B. H[arris] for Michael Perry, 1694), p. 2.

also the age for "chusing of Guardions." Sodomists were to be executed, but if one party was forced to commit sodomy or was under fourteen, he was only "seveerly punished."[16]

The "ages of man" and the different ages of legal responsibility might be dismissed, however, as mere conventions that had no real social meaning. Such an argument might be especially persuasive with respect to the law because of Puritan attempts to institute Mosaic law in New England. But another area of New England culture—religious thought and practice—provides abundant evidence to confirm the patterns of language and law described above.

Historians like Calhoun, Fleming, and Demos argue that Puritans treated the young and old equally and encouraged early conversion experiences. "The young no less than the old," writes Demos, "were expected to digest the learned words that flowed from the pulpit." John Cotton would have disagreed. "Bring them to Church," he urged, "and help them to remember something, and tell them the meaning of it, and take a little in good part, and encourage them, and that will make them delight in it." This suggests that because children's capacities were limited, loving parents should take care that children understood at least something. William Williams later warned that "because of the weakness of their Understandings, and narrowness of their Capacities, in their younger Years, Pains must be us'd to convey Truth in such a manner as they may be able to *conceive* of it, and not meerly learn Things by rote."[17]

Puritan descriptions of the age-groups from which God was most likely to call His elect show that infants and children were not miniature adults. God would not, of course, restrict His call to any one age-group. "Should God call onely children, middle aged men, or old men onely," explained Thomas Hooker, "then men would conceive that there were something in the persons that moved him to this, either the weakenesse of the child, or else the innocencie thereof did move God to shew mercy thereunto, or else that God did delight in the strength or in the gifts and parts of a young man, or if he should call men in their old age onely, then men might thinke that their experience and gravitie did move God to call them onely." God called "some in all ages and at all times, some young ones chosen, and some refused, some old men called, and others cast aside." The selection of some

91

[16] *The Laws and Liberties of Massachusetts Reprinted from the Copy of the 1648 Edition in the Henry E. Huntington Library*, intro. by Max Farrand (Cambridge, Mass.: Harvard, 1929), pp. 1, 5, 35; *Records of the Colony of New Plymouth in New England*, ed. Nathaniel B. Shurtleff and David Pulsifer (Boston: W. White, 1855–1861), XI, 63.

[17] John Cotton, *A Practical Commentary, or An Exposition with Observations, Reasons, and Uses upon the First Epistle Generall of John* (London: R. I. and E. C. for Thomas Parkhurst, 1656), p. 102; William Williams, *The Duty and Interest of a People . . .* (Boston: S. Kneeland and T. Green, 1736), pp. 63–64.

for salvation and others for damnation resulted not from particular men's natural qualities but "from the freenesse of Gods mercy."[18]

Despite its freeness, God's mercy was extended to some groups more often than to others. "Some are called in their youth, some in their middle age, some in their old age, some in their tender yeares, some in their riper age, some old, some young, but this is most true that those whom God doth call it is most commonly in their middle age before they come to their old age." According to Hooker, the middle age "hath better Materials . . . wherein, or whereupon the frame of Conversion may be erected, or imprinted by the stamp of the Spirit."[19]

92

The special fitness of middle age for conversion followed naturally from the attitude summarized by John Norton: "Though knowledg may be without grace, yet there can be no grace without knowledg." Infants were incapable of the knowledge that preceded grace. "In Infancy," explained Hooker, "a man lives little other than the life of a Plant, or Beast, feeding and sleeping, growing and encreasing; or else he takes up himself with delights of outward objects most agreeable to his Sences." This did not mean that God would not save infants, but rather that His manner of converting them was special. "Calling," said Norton, "is either extraordinary, as in Elect Infants, dying in their Infancy: or ordinary." Thus, in John Cotton's view, children were "capable of the habits and gifts of grace from their first Conception . . . , and the reason is, as soon as capable of sin, capable of grace." Hooker noted that there was "a number of children" whom it was God's purpose to save "according to election." They were to be saved, however, not because they were children but while they were children, for "all the men in the world are either vessels of mercy, or vessels of wrath, according to the good will of God." The operation of God's grace on infants was "extraordinary in mans account," but Hooker cautioned against curiosity, "for secret things belong to God," and man should be content to know "that some children are elected, and God will sanctifie them, and glorifie them; but the number, and manner, I leave that."[20]

A child who lived through infancy could exercise his understanding little more than an infant. In Hooker's opinion, a child of ten or twelve lived "the life of a beast," and it was "almost impossible" for him "to consider of the mysteries of life & salvation." In his "tender yeares" a man had "such a weake understanding" that he could "hold nothing." If a child was told of

[18]T[homas] H[ooker], *The Unbeleevers Preparing for Christ* (London: T. Cotes for A. Crooke, 1638), p. 195; Thomas Hooker, *Application* . . . (London: Peter Cole, 1656), p. 266.

[19]Hooker, *Unbeleevers*. p. 198; Hooker, *Application*. p. 268.

[20]John Norton, *The Orthodox Evangelist* . . . (London: John Macock for Henry Cripps and Lodowick Lloyd, 1654), "The Epistle Dedicatory," and p. 130; Hooker, *Application*. p. 268; John Cotton, *A Practical Commentary*. p. 100; Hooker, *The Covenant of Grace Opened* . . . (London: G. Dawson, 1649), pp. 24–25.

the wonders of salvation, it was "impossible unlesse God workes wonder-
fully that hee should receive them." However, when a man arrived at "the
ripenesse of his yeares, from 20. years untill he come to be 40. or
thereabouts," Hooker believed, "the Understanding begins to shew it self in
her operations: Invention is then most quick to apprehend, the Judgment to
discern, Memory to retain, and the Affections tenderest and nimblest to im-
brace any thing offered, and most pliable to be wrought upon." At this age
"a man is able to conceive and partake of the things of grace, and fadom
[sic] them, and the power of his understanding comes on whereby he is able
to embrace them." The middle years were therefore "the fittest time that
God should bestow his graces upon a man."[21]

Puritan ideas about the age-groups from which God called His elect were
borne out in practice. At Dorchester, Massachusetts, for example, in the
period 1640–1730, only thirty-four (8.9%) of the 382 new communicants
whose ages are known were under the age of twenty; only three, all girls,
were under seventeen (one each at age thirteen, fifteen, and sixteen). In the
same years, 202 (52.9%) of the new communicants were in their twenties,
and ninety-four (24.6%) were in their thirties.[22] At New Haven, in the years
1685–1739, only fifty-four (7.9%) of the 681 new communicants whose ages
are known were younger than twenty.[23] Data from eighteenth-century Andover and Norton, Massachusetts, and Norwich and Woodbury, Connecticut, reveal the same pattern.[24] One must conclude, therefore, that the
most famous conversion of the eighteenth century, that of four-year-old
Phebe Bartlet of Northampton, was a remarkable exception.[25]

Provisions for catechizing children in the churches at Dorchester and
Norwich also indicate that the Puritans treated children and youth
differently. At Dorchester in 1672, the minister compiled a list of "all
children & servants that weer under any famely government in order to ca-

93

---

[21]Hooker, *Unbeleevers*, pp. 199–200; Hooker, *Application*, p. 268.
[22]Based on data in the *Records of the First Church at Dorchester in New England, 1636–
1734*, ed. Charles Henry Pope (Boston: Geo. H. Ellis, 1891), and in genealogical materials cited
in Ross W. Beales, Jr., "Cares for the Rising Generation: Youth and Religion in Colonial New
England," Diss. Univ. of California, Davis, 1971, pp. 244–46.
[23]Based on data in the *Historical Catalogue of the Members of the First Church of Christ in
New Haven, Connecticut (Center Church), A.D. 1639–1914*, comp. Franklin Bowditch Dexter
(New Haven: The Church, 1914).
[24]Philip J. Greven, Jr., "Youth, Maturity, and Religious Conversion: A Note on the Ages of
Converts in Andover, Massachusetts, 1711–1749," *Essex Institute Historical Collections*, 108
(1972), 119–34; J. M. Bumsted, "Religion, Finance, and Democracy in Massachusetts: The
Town of Norton as a Case Study," *Journal of American History*, 57 (1971), 817–31; Gerald F.
Moran, "Conditions of Religious Conversion in the First Society of Norwich, Connecticut,
1718–1744," *Journal of Social History*, 5 (1972), 331–43; James Walsh, "The Great
Awakening in the First Congregational Church of Woodbury, Connecticut," *William and
Mary Quarterly*, 3d ser., 28 (1971), 543–62.
[25]On Bartlet, see Edwards, *Faithful Narrative*, in *The Great Awakening*, ed. Goen, pp. 199–
205.

techising or some other way of instruction." The names for 1672 did not survive, but the church records do contain a list of catechumens for 1676. Males aged thirteen to twenty-eight are separated from the younger males, designated "Children from 12 et infra" and as young as seven. The list of "young Maids," aged seven to thirty-one, is not so explicitly divided, although there are spaces between ages twelve and thirteen and between ages eight and nine. The church at Norwich decided that "all the Males who are eight or nine years of age, shall be presented before the Lord in his Congregation every Lords Day to be Cate[c]hised, until they be about thirteen years in age." At thirteen, the boys and girls attended "the Meeting appointed in private for their instruction," and they continued to meet as long as they lived "under Family Government of Parents or others" or until they became full communicants.[26]

Communion presupposed a degree of knowledge that children could not achieve. "Children are not capable sabjects [sic] of the Lords Supper," wrote John Cotton. "For receiving whereof, the Apostle requireth wee should examine and judge our selves." Among "men of years, the Spirit . . . worketh faith by the hearing of the Word, and by revealing and tendering Christ as the al-sufficient and onely way of life." Aware that individuals matured at different rates, Puritan thinkers did not set an arbitrary age when individuals might be said to arrive at the "years of understanding." As early as 1643, Richard Mather recognized the problem of "how long Children should be counted under age." He noted that the New England churches had no occasion to look into the question. "Onely this we thinke, that one certaine rule cannot be given for all, whereby to determine how long they are under age, but according as God gives experience and maturity of naturall understanding, and Spirituall; which he gives sooner to some then unto others." Mather was somewhat more specific a number of years later when he asked, "*Till what age shall they* [children] *enter into Covenant with their Parents, whether sixteen, twenty one, or sixty?*" He answered that "as long as in respect of age or capacity they cannot according to ordinary account, be supposed able to act in a matter of this nature for themselves, so long they shall enter in by means of their Parents covenant, because whilst they are children and in their minority, they are not otherwise capable of covenanting: When adult, they are to covenant in their own persons." Thirteen years of age was not too old for a child to be included in his parents' covenant, for Ishmael (Genesis 17:25) had been "admitted to the Seal by his Fathers covenant at thirteen years of age." Nevertheless, Mather cautioned, in "the bounding of adult and in-adult age, depending upon the

---

[26]*Records of the First Church at Dorchester*, ed. Pope, pp. 67, 183–85; James Fitch, *An Explanation of the Solemn Advice* . . . (Boston: S. Green for I. Usher, 1683), p. 69.

judgment of prudence, much is to be left unto the discretion of Officers and Churches in this case."[27]

Charles Chauncy agreed with Mather on this point. "It cannot be concluded," he wrote, "that all persons are to be looked upon as adult at the very same age, some persons coming to years of discretion before others; and some . . . having weaker parts and less means of instruction then others have, therefore we see not how there can be any *particular time* fixed when all *persons* shall be accounted adult, (or of age) to answer for themselves at this or that age, but a latitude must be allowed in this case."[28]

At Northampton, the congregation of Richard Mather's son, Eleazer, sought to "come to som[e] de[ter]mination respecting the continuing [or] expiring of the state of minority," but did not find it "limited in Scripture to any perticular yere or tyme." They therefore followed Richard Mather's advice and voted that "the fixing of Adult, and not Adult age bee left to the wisdome, discretion and judgment of the Elders of the Church from tyme to tyme, and as they upon tryall and Examination of the Ability and capacity of each person respectively shall determine them to bee in that state either of Adult or inadult, accordingly shall Such persons bee accounted and walked towards by this Church."[29]

Solomon Stoddard, Eleazer Mather's successor, departed significantly from the Mathers' point of view. Stoddard came to believe that the sacrament of the Lord's Supper was a "converting ordinance" that should not be restricted to God's visible saints; it should rather be offered to the regenerate and to the unregenerate alike with the expectation that it would help bring the latter to Christ. But Stoddard did not follow his doctrine to its logical conclusion, for it was said that he permitted only those who were "Civilized & Cathechised above 14 years old" to come to the Lord's Table.[30] He thus demanded good behavior, knowledge of doctrine, and a minimal age. In discarding an older conception about the purposes of the Lord's Supper, he also discarded a flexibility in assessing the age when individuals arrived at years of understanding. It was certainly easier to classify a person as "adult" or as "inadult" merely by his age than to examine the ability and capacity of each person under fourteen, but one wonders

[27] John Cotton, *The Grounds and Ends of Baptisme* . . . (London: R. C. for Andrew Crooke, 1647), pp. 16, 129; [Richard Mather], *Church-Government and Church-Covenant Discussed* . . . (London: R. O. and G. D. for Benjamin Allen, 1643), p. 22; [Richard Mather], *A Disputation Concerning Church-Members and Their Children* . . . (London: J. Hayes for Samuel Thomson, 1659), p. 13.

[28] Charles Chauncy, *Anti-Synodalia Scripta Americana* . . . (London, 1662), p. 23.

[29] Northampton Church Records, Feb. 2, 1668 (microfilm, Forbes Library, Northampton, Mass.).

[30] James P. Walsh, "Solomon Stoddard's Open Communion: A Reexamination," *New England Quarterly*, 43 (1970), 110, quoting Edward Taylor's MS Notebook (Massachusetts Historical Society).

whether this decision did not reflect a certain loss of spiritual energy, perhaps a waning of piety, that led to a less personal treatment of each soul. Put in slightly different terms, Stoddard's open communion and the arbitrary restriction of communion to persons over fourteen can be viewed as movement away from Puritanism's sect-like qualities toward an increasingly church-like form of religion.

Not all churches made such arbitrary distinctions among persons of different ages. At Barnstable, for example, the church baptized a sixteen-year-old boy "by vertue of his fathers Covenant bec[ause] upon examination, before the Elders & divers brethren of the Church thereto appointed, hee was Judged An Inadult person though 16 years old when his father Covenanted." Another case was that of Jane Bump, who, "being about fourteen or 15 years old, was examined, & being one of the family & looked upon in her minority, was Baptised." The minister declared seventeen-year-old John Howland "to be adult" and "that he could not baptize him on his mothers faith but finding In him Such pious dispositions declared that he Could baptize him on his own faith and Covenant." The members of the church agreed that John was "a Subject of baptism," but since "this was a new Case" and the members could not agree on the reasons why he should be baptized, they concluded that "this Instance [was] not to be made a precedant In time to Come." Jedidiah Lumburt's eighteen-year-old son was baptized at the West Parish of Barnstable "by vertue of his fath[er's] Covenant, for upon examination of him before the elders of the Church, he appeared not of maturity to act for himself," and "therefore he was Judged an In[adult?] & received baptism as one In minority."[31]

At Chelmsford, the church decided in 1657 that children might be baptized if they were under the age of fourteen or fifteen when their parents became communicants. Six years later, it was agreed that the minister and at least one other church member were to examine the knowledge and spiritual experience of children who had grown to years of discretion. As a result of this examination, some children were taken into communion, but others were found to have a better memory than a real understanding of doctrine. In this case, the age of discretion was probably regarded as sixteen years, for in 1666 the church agreed on a course of catechism for all persons under sixteen. Unmarried men over sixteen were given special treatment: they had the choice either of publicly demonstrating their knowledge of religion or of attending the catechism classes.[32]

[31] Barnstable, Mass., West Parish, Church Records, Jan. 18, 1683 (Massachusetts Historical Society); "Scituate and Barnstable Church Records," *New England Historical and Genealogical Register,* 10 (1856), 349.

[32] *The Notebook of the Reverend John Fiske, 1644-1675,* ed. Robert G. Pope, Publications of the Colonial Society of Massachusetts, 47 (Boston: The Colonial Society of Massachusetts, 1974), pp. 110, 186, 200.

These kinds of records confirm the practice of what men like Richard Mather and Charles Chauncy held in theory: that there was no set age at which a person might claim, merely by virtue of accumulated years, a new standing in the church. Recognition that an individual had arrived at years of understanding or at years of discretion depended on an examination of that understanding or discretion. Even Stoddard's church required an examination, for a person who sought communion had to be both fourteen and "Civilized & Cathechised." Persons under fourteen, regardless of their precocity, were automatically excluded from communion; persons over fourteen were only conditionally eligible for communion.

Language, law, and religious thought and practice thus suggest that New Englanders, far from regarding children as "miniature adults," recognized their immaturity. But what about individuals who were no longer children? Did "youth" in colonial New England in any sense resemble twentieth-century adolescence? "The adolescent as a distinct species," writes F. Musgrove, "is the creation of modern social attitudes and institutions. A creature neither child nor adult, he is a comparatively recent socio-psychological invention, scarcely two centuries old."[33] In contrast to this viewpoint, S. N. Eisenstadt observes that

97

> however great the differences among various societies, there is one focal point within the life span of an individual which in most known societies is to some extent emphasized: the period of youth, of transition from childhood to full adult status, or full membership in the society. In this period the individual is no longer a child (especially from the physical and sexual point of view) but is ready to undertake many attributes of an adult and to fulfill adult roles. But he is not yet fully acknowledged as an adult, a full member of the society. Rather, he is being "prepared," or is preparing himself for such adulthood.[34]

Eisenstadt's generalization is applicable to colonial New England, where the stage of development, commonly called "youth," resembled today's "adolescence."

In physiological terms, adolescence is the biological and sexual maturation of a child, extending from puberty to the achievement of full reproductive capacity. In a broader sense, adolescence includes both sexual maturation and the social and psychological development of the individual. Sociologically, adolescence has been described as "the transition period from dependent childhood to self-sufficient adulthood." It ends with the attainment of full adult status within the limits prescribed by one's culture, class, and sex. Adolescents and children are thus distinguished from adults

---

[33]F. Musgrove, *Youth and the Social Order* (Bloomington, Ind.: Indiana Univ. Press, 1965), p. 13. See also John Demos and Virginia Demos, "Adolescence in Historical Perspective," *Journal of Marriage and the Family*, 31 (1969), 632–38.

[34]S. N. Eisenstadt, "Archetypal Patterns of Youth," *Daedalus*, 91 (1962), 30.

by the adult activities from which they are excluded: for example, marriage and the rearing of families; economic self-sufficiency; participation in the political life of the community to the extent that their sex and station permit. Psychologically, adolescence "is a 'marginal situation' in which new adjustments have to be made, namely those that distinguish child behavior from adult behavior in a given society." Chronologically, adolescence continues "from approximately twelve or thirteen to the early twenties, with wide individual and cultural variations."[35]

98   The transition from the dependence of childhood to the self-sufficiency of adulthood was not made suddenly in early New England. This can be seen, for example, in the individual's gradual assumption of the legal rights and obligations of adulthood. Massachusetts children over sixteen, "and of sufficient understanding," were to be executed if they cursed or struck their parents. Likewise, "a stubborn or REBELLIOUS SON, of sufficient years & understanding (*viz*) sixteen years of age," risked capital punishment for incorrigible disobedience. Another law provided that "the minoritie of women in case of marriage shall be till sixteen years." Although Plymouth youths were eligible for militia service at sixteen, "noe single persons under twenty yeares of age either children or servants" could vote in "milletary concernments." In Massachusetts, twenty-one was the age both for "passing away of lands, or such kinde of hereditaments, or for giving of votes, verdicts or sentences in any civil courts or causes," and for making "Wills & Testaments & other lawfull Alienations of their lands and estates." A statute of limitations affecting inheritances in Plymouth Colony permitted minors to bring suit within five years of reaching twenty-one. Finally, in the town of Barnstable in Plymouth Colony, a person had to be either twenty-four years old or married in order to share in a division of the town lands.[36]

"Where land was abundant and labor at a premium," writes Bernard Bailyn, "it took little more to create a household than to maintain one. Material independence was sooner or later available to every energetic adult white male, and few failed to break away when they could." Oscar and Mary F. Handlin assert that "the passage of the child to adulthood ceased to be a gradual progression through well-defined stages and became a single great leap away from home."[37]

[34] Rolf E. Muuss, *Theories of Adolescence*, 2d ed. (New York: Random House, 1968), p. 4. See also David Matza, "Position and Behavior Patterns of Youth," in *Handbook of Modern Sociology*, ed. Robert E. L. Faris (Chicago: Rand McNally, 1964), p. 192.

[36] *The Laws and Liberties of Massachusetts*, pp. 1, 6, 12; *Records of the Colony of New Plymouth*, XI, 219, 225; George D. Langdon, Jr., "The Franchise and Political Democracy in Plymouth Colony," *William and Mary Quarterly*, 3d ser., 20 (1963), 519, citing Barnstable Town Records, I (Town Offices, Hyannis, Mass.).

[37] Bernard Bailyn, *Education in the Forming of American Society: Needs and Opportunities for Study* (Chapel Hill, N.C.: Univ. of North Carolina Press, 1960), p. 23; Oscar Handlin and

Recent studies show that Bailyn and the Handlins overestimate the ease with which the economic self-sufficiency of a separate household might be attained. "A man ready to marry," observes Kenneth A. Lockridge, "did not just go out and get a job; he prepared a farm of his own to support his family or else he made sure that he could expect to inherit the family home and acres."[38] The creation of a household, contrary to Bailyn's premise, often must have required considerable labor, parental assistance, and capital outlay. Land had to be acquired, cleared, and fenced; buildings, however rough in the first years, had to withstand New England winters; animals and tools, as well as household utensils and furnishings, were also needed.

Philip J. Greven, Jr.'s study of the first four generations in Andover, Massachusetts, documents the slowness with which sons achieved economic independence. The key to independence was land, and fathers often retained until death legal title to the lands on which their sons were settled. Those sons who purchased their shares of the paternal estate were more often than not "mature men rather than youths just out of adolescence or in their early twenties." Some sons, particularly in the third and fourth generations, did choose to leave Andover, and their fathers often helped them to achieve autonomy relatively early.[39]

Patterns of apprenticeship in New England also suggest that a "youth" of thirteen or fourteen would not assume autonomous economic status for several years. In the seventeenth century, according to Edmund S. Morgan, a boy typically chose his calling between the ages of ten and fourteen. Most apprenticeships required seven years of service to a master and lasted until the age of twenty-one.[40] Thus, while an individual made an early choice of his life-long occupation, his actual economic independence was delayed seven years while he learned the skills of his calling. And even if he were fully trained at the age of twenty-one, it is unlikely that a young man would have had the capital or connections necessary to establish his economic independence.

Political rights also came slowly. In Plymouth Colony, the revised laws of 1671 established twenty-one years as the earliest age at which a man might become a freeman. John Demos finds no "set age" at which men became

99

Mary F. Handlin, *Facing Life: Youth and the Family in American History* (Boston: Little, Brown, 1971), p. 17.

[38] Kenneth A. Lockridge, "The Population of Dedham, Massachusetts, 1636–1736," *Economic History Review*, 2d ser., 19 (1966), 343.

[39] Philip J. Greven, Jr., *Four Generations: Population, Land, and Family in Colonial Andover, Massachusetts* (Ithaca, N.Y.: Cornell Univ. Press, 1970), pp. 75, 126, 132, 135 (quotation), 222–23.

[40] Edmund S. Morgan, *The Puritan Family: Religion and Domestic Relations in Seventeenth-Century New England*, rev. ed. (New York: Harper, 1966), p. 68.

freemen, for his sample of sixty adult males achieved that status between twenty-five and forty. "This privilege and responsibility . . . was perhaps the last in the series of steps leading to full adult citizenship in the community." Delayed political adulthood followed naturally from the economic qualifications for freemanship and late economic adulthood.

Marriage was closely connected to economic independence, for marriage presupposed the ability to provide for a family. Parents played an important role in their child's choice of a spouse, for successful courtship, at least in the seventeenth century, depended on the parents' directing influence, goodwill, and skill in negotiating a marriage settlement. Like the ability to earn a living, marriage was often delayed until the middle twenties and later.[41]

"The most sensitive register of maturity," writes Greven, "is the age at marriage, since the responsibilities and duties involved in the establishment of a new family suggest the recognition that the married couple were ready to function as adults."[42] This insight is confirmed by other evidence. The provisions for catechizing at Norwich and Dorchester took special notice of unmarried non-communicants, who were apparently required to receive religious instruction either until they became communicants or until they married and set up independent households. The laws of Plymouth Colony also accorded special recognition to the married *vis-à-vis* the unmarried. A married man under the age of twenty could presumably vote in "milletary concernments," while his single counterpart could not. Finally, at Barnstable a single male had to wait until the age of twenty-four in order to share in a division of the town lands, while a married male under twenty-four was eligible for a share.

From these varied data emerge a picture of a prolonged "adolescence" or "youth" experienced by young people in colonial New England. Youth, in Benjamin Colman's words, was a "chusing time."

NOW O Young People is *your chusing time,* and commonly your *fixing time;* and as you fix it is like to last. Now you commonly chuse your *Trade;* betake your selves to your business for life, show what you incline to, and how you intend to be imploy'd all your days. Now you chuse your *Master* and your Education or Occupation. And now you dispose of your self in *Marriage* ordinarily, place your *Affections,* give away your hearts, look out for some *Companion* of life, whose to be as long as you live. And is this indeed the work of your Youth?[43]

[41] Demos, *Little Commonwealth.* p. 148, 152–57, 193; Lockridge, "Population of Dedham," p. 330; Greven, *Four Generations,* pp. 33, 35, 118, 120, 206, 208.
[42] Greven, *Four Generations,* pp. 31–32. See also S. N. Eisenstadt, *From Generation to Generation: Age Groups and Social Structure* (Glencoe, Ill.: Free Press, 1956), pp. 30–31, and Peter Laslett, *The World We Have Lost* (New York: Scribner's, 1965), p. 90.
[43] Benjamin Colman, *Early Piety Again Inculcated* ... (Boston: S. Kneeland for D. Henchman and J. Edwards, 1720), p. 33. See also William Cooper, *Serious Exhortations* ... (Boston: S. Kneeland and T. Green for J. Phillip and J. Edwards, 1732), p. 10.

For today's adolescent, at least in his idealized type, this "chusing time" presumably provides the opportunity to try out a number of life styles or roles, for the choices are abundant and the pressures for early decision are often not great. In this respect, adolescence has been called a "moratorium," during which the adolescent is dependent on parents and society, yet free from significant responsibilities. As a result, the adolescent in an age-stratified society is likely to be part of a peer-group based on age and having its own distinctive "culture."

In colonial New England, the range of choices open to youth was narrow, particularly outside Benjamin Colman's Boston, and decisions tended to be irrevocable: "as you fix it is like to last." As Demos points out, "the professional and 'artisan' classes were relatively small" in seventeenth-century Plymouth, "and the vast majority of the populace was engaged simply in farming. In the typical case, therefore, the choice of a calling was scarcely a choice at all; instead it was something assumed, something everywhere implicit in the child's surroundings and in the whole process of growth." Kenneth Lockridge suggests that "most men showed the typical peasant's satisfaction with the *status quo*. It worked for his father and for his father before him, why tinker with success? Why, especially when it could be dangerous?"[44] In addition to having limited choices, sons—to say nothing of daughters—were heavily dependent upon their parents both in timing and in making their choice of education or occupation, economic independence, and marriage. Under such circumstances, a son's bold assertion of independence from his parents or adoption of an alien life style was surely difficult if not unthinkable. Neither the desire nor the ability existed.

This is not to say, however, that elements of a distinctive youth "culture" did not exist in colonial New England. Ministers' descriptions of youthful behavior before and after the revivals of the eighteenth century reveal a deep strain of anxiety about the apparent collapse of family government and a rejoicing that the revival had prompted a measure of youthful self-control and reformation. Jonathan Edwards, for example, reported that there was "a time of extraordinary dullness in religion" just after the death of his grandfather, Solomon Stoddard. "Licentiousness for some years greatly prevailed among the youth of the town," many of whom were "very much addicted to night-walking, and frequenting the tavern, and lewd practices, wherein some, by their example exceedingly corrupted others." The youth "very frequently" gathered "in conventions of both sexes, for mirth and jollity, which they called frolics," and in which they often spent "the greater part of the night . . . without regard to any order in the families they belonged to: and indeed family government did too much fail in the town."

[101]

44 Demos, *Little Commonwealth*, p. 147; Lockridge, "Population of Dedham," p. 344.

The Northampton revival of late 1734 and 1735 radically changed the behavior of the town's young people. The conversion of a young woman, "one of the greatest company-keepers in the whole town," was "almost like a flash of lightning, upon the hearts of young people all over the town, and upon many others." As Edwards looked back on the revival, he expressed the hope that those young people who were "on other accounts most likely and considerable" had become "truly pious and leading persons in the ways of religion." Similarly "those that were formerly looser young persons are generally, to all appearance, become true lovers of God and Christ, and spiritual in their dispositions."[45]

102   This pattern of youthful reformation was repeated frequently during the Great Awakening. At Somers, Connecticut, "those *Youths* that delighted themselves in Frolicking and Mischief" were reported to "have wholly left it off" and reputedly found "more Pleasure and Satisfaction in serving GOD, than ever they did in the Ways of *Sin* and *Satan*." The young people of Halifax, Massachusetts, abandoned "all Frolicking and Carousing, and merry Meetings" and now "took more delight in going to a Meeting than ever they did to a Frolick." The minister of Wrentham rejoiced that the "*young People*" had "generally and voluntarily *done* with their *Frolicking and merry Meetings*" and bitterly lamented the time they had wasted in such pursuits. Even "some of the *late Ring-leaders* of their Merriment" shared these sentiments. The Awakening at Bridgewater convinced many of the young "of the Sin of spending away Days & Nights in Singing and Dancing, and other youthful Sins, which they were much addicted to before, and greatly delighted in." As a result they stopped "their youthful Practices, of Singing, Dancing, Company-keeping, which before they esteemed lawful Recreations, and took abundance of Pleasure in."[46]

These and other accounts of pre-revival patterns of youthful behavior—night-walking, frolicking, company-keeping, carousing, merry-meeting, dancing and singing—suggest that there were elements of a separate youth "culture" at least in eighteenth-century New England. If this culture was not so sharply separated from the adult world as today's adolescent "cultures," the explanation may be that Puritan youth did not live in as highly an age-stratified society as today's adolescents. This is probably the source of Arthur W. Calhoun's alarm at Puritan "precocity." Puritan hagiography includes accounts of children who learned their letters and catechism at remarkably early ages. Moreover, it was not unusual at Harvard and Yale

[45]Edwards, *Faithful Narrative,* in *The Great Awakening,* ed. Goen, pp. 146, 149, 158.
[46]*The Christian History, Containing Accounts of the Revival and Propagation of Religion in Great-Britain & America,* ed. Thomas Prince, Jr. (2 vols.; Boston, 1743–45), I, 241, 260–61, 398–99, 409.

for brothers of different ages to be in the same class, or for a class to contain members whose ages ranged from the early teens to the twenties.[47]

It thus appears that in colonial New England, childhood was not succeeded by "miniature adulthood" but by "youth," a lengthy transitional period preceding adult status. During this "chusing time," when the young were expected (in Thomas Shepard's words) to "putt away Childish things," the youth remained dependent on his elders for his education, for his choice of and training in a calling, and for the material means, usually land, which would support a family. While this dependence carried with it a measure of parental control, it also provided a moratorium, a freedom from adult responsibilities, during which the elements of a youthful "culture" might emerge.

What do these findings suggest about the history of family life in America? On the one hand, as Stannard argues, the Ariès paradigm of French parent-children relationships is not applicable to the American experience. In part, this may arise from America's relatively short history, and therefore the Ariès model can be tested only in the context of the longer Anglo-American experience. On the other hand, recent investigations suggest that the Ariès paradigm may not apply to England and may not even be wholly correct in terms of the French experience.[48] In any event, historians must re-examine parent-child and inter-generational relationships from the earliest American settlements through the nineteenth century. Recent studies offer some outlines of a new, possibly American paradigm. Greven's study of Andover shows that first-generation fathers exercised remarkably strong and enduring control over their sons' lives. If this relationship existed elsewhere, perhaps we can attribute it not only to an abundance of land but also to a high degree of religiosity among the first-generation settlers. The weakening of patriarchalism in successive generations would fit not only into the narrowing economic base of farming communities but also into the weakening or dilution of religious zeal, the "declension" which Perry Miller has so masterfully analyzed. The slackening of parental discipline, one symptom of the declension, gave the younger generation more latitude to

[47]The average age of entering students in the Yale College classes from 1702 to 1739 was 16.4 years. Six students were under the age of seventeen at graduation (the youngest being fifteen), while three were graduated at twenty-eight. Richard Warch, *School of the Prophets: Yale College, 1701–1740* (New Haven: Yale Univ. Press, 1973), p. 254. On the mixing of different ages in English and French schools, see Lawrence Stone, *The Crisis of the Aristocracy, 1558–1641* (Oxford: Clarendon, 1965), p. 681, and Ariès, *Centuries of Childhood,* p. 239.

[48]Natalie Zemon Davis, "The Reasons of Misrule: Youth Groups and Charivaris in Sixteenth-Century France," *Past and Present,* 50 (1971), 41–75; Steven R. Smith, "The London Apprentices as Seventeenth-Century Adolescents," ibid., 61 (1973), 149–61, and "Religion and the Conception of Youth in Seventeenth-Century England," *History of Childhood Quarterly,* 2 (1975), 493–516.

develop their own "culture," which at times might seem very much at odds
with parental authority. Both Marion L. Starkey and John Demos, for
example, identify a structural conflict between generations in Salem Village
in 1692.[49] Although their interpretations of the sources of this conflict are
markedly different, does not the conflict itself partly reflect the development of a youthful "culture" not subject to parental supervision and
control?

The most startling manifestation of weakened parental control can be
seen in the dramatically increasing rates of pre-marital pregnancies which
occurred from the late seventeenth to the mid-eighteenth century. Equally
dramatic, however, were the decreasing rates of pre-marital pregnancies
that took place a century later.[50] When the New Lights of the 1740's observed an apparent reformation of manners and morals among the youthful
converts of the Great Awakening, their rejoicing was perhaps premature,
for, at best, the reformation may have affected only the new converts. Nineteenth-century revivalists were more successful than their predecessors, for
early conversions were expected and widespread and may have contributed
to an alteration in pre-marital sexual behavior—at least among middle-
class Protestants. The submergence or temporary denial of adolescent
sexuality may have prepared the way for the "discovery" of adolescence in
the late nineteenth and early twentieth centuries, as well as the mistaken
belief that earlier generations treated their children as miniature adults. As
a result, the idea of "miniature adulthood" must be seen, not as a description of social reality, but as a minor chapter in the history of social thought.

[49] Marion L. Starkey, *The Devil in Massachusetts: A Modern Enquiry into the Salem Witch Trials* (New York: Knopf, 1949), and John Demos, "Underlying Themes in the Witchcraft of Seventeenth-Century New England," in *Colonial America: Essays in Politics and Social Development*, ed. Stanley N. Katz (Boston: Little, Brown, 1971), pp. 113–33.
[50] Daniel Scott Smith and Michael S. Hindus, "Premarital Pregnancy in America, 1640–1971: An Overview and Interpretation," *Journal of Interdisciplinary History*, 5 (1975), 537–70. See also James A. Henretta, *The Evolution of American Society, 1700–1815: An Interdisciplinary Analysis* (Lexington, Mass.: Heath, 1973), pp. 132–34.

The Public Law of a County Court; Judicial Government in Eighteenth Century Massachusetts.

by HENDRIK HARTOG*

INTRODUCTION

Throughout eighteenth century America counties were governed by courts held collectively by local justices of the peace. Formally described as courts of general (or quarter) sessions of the peace and popularly known as sessions courts, these courts were empowered "to hear and determine all matters relating to the conservation of the peace and punishment of offenders and whatsoever is cognizable by them by law."[1] To modern eyes their authority appears divided between a limited criminal jurisdiction over noncapital crimes and a more general obligation to act as regulatory agencies responsible for what Emory Washburn called the "prudential affairs" of county life.[2]

Historians have studied these courts from several vantage points. Often sessions courts have been seen as aspects of colonial court systems, standing with their civil law counterparts, the courts of common pleas, midway between the august superior courts of judicature and the lowly courts held by individual magistrates.[3] Some historians have emphasized their roles as enforcers of colonial criminal law;[4] others have looked to their significance as

---

* A. B. Carleton, J.D. New York University; graduate student in the history of American civilization at Brandeis University.

1. 1692-3 *Acts and Resolves of the Province of the Massachusetts Bay*, c. 33; 1699-1700 *Acts and Resolves*, c. 1.

2. Emory Washburn, *Sketches of the Judicial History of Massachusetts* (1840), p. 170; William E. Nelson, *The Americanization of the Common Law* (1975), pp. 13-16; L. Kinvin Wroth and Hiller B. Zobel, editors, *The Legal Papers of John Adams I* (1965), pp. xxviii-xliv.

3. *Op. cit. supra* note 2.

4. William E. Nelson, "Emerging Notions of Modern Criminal Law in the Revolutionary Era: An Historical Perspective," 42 *N. Y. U. L. Rev.*, 450 (1967); Julius Goebel, Jr. and T. Raymond Naughton, *Law Enforcement in Colonial New York* (1944).

judicial restraints on the exercise of governmental power.[5] To a growing number of social historians the administrative powers of the sessions courts provide one explanation for the emergence of the magistracy as a county elite.[6]

None of these treatments exhibit much concern for the integrity of an institution. Historians have written about sessions courts as aspects of larger structures or social networks. Yet what is most apparent from a passing understanding of eighteenth century legal thought is the degree to which local legal institutions were regarded as independent recipients of constitutional power and authority.[7] The terms of a modern positivist jurisprudence that considers law the command of a sovereign and unitary state have little relevance to a sessions court of the mid-eighteenth century. It was not as an aspect of a modern legal system—the public law analogue of a private law court of common pleas—that eighteenth century Americans viewed a sessions court. Nor did they see it as an administrative agency or as a court for the control of administrative action. The very notion of "Administration" as a specialized function of government would have had little meaning.

Colonial Americans thought of a sessions court as a court of government that "conserved the peace." A sessions court was an

5. Nelson, *op. cit. supra* note 4, at pp. 13-15; Michael Zuckerman, *Peaceable Kingdoms* (1970), at pp. 24-25 argues that county courts were an ineffective counterweight to the political authority of the towns; but see David G. Allen, "The Zuckerman Thesis and the Process of Legal Rationalization in Provincial Massachusetts," 29 *Wm. & Mary Quarterly* (3rd ser.) 443 (1972), and L. Kinvin Wroth, "Possible Kingdoms: The New England Town from the Perspective of Legal History," 15 *Am. Jour. Leg. Hist.* 318 (1971).

6. John M. Murrin, "Book Review," 9 *History and Theory* 226 (1972); Ronald K. Snell, "The County Magistracy in Eighteenth Century Massachusetts: 1692-1750," (unpublished doctoral dissertation, Princeton University, 1971); Charles S. Sydnor, *American Revolutionaries in the Making* (1952). For a later period see Robert M. Ireland, *The County Courts of Antebellum Kentucky* (1972); Tadahisa Kuroda, "The County Court System of Virginia from the Revolution to the Civil War," (unpublished doctoral dissertation, Columbia University, 1970); Charles S. Sydnor, *The Development of Southern Sectionalism 1819-1848* (1948).

7. John P. Reid, "In a Defensive Rage: The Uses of the Mob, the Justification in Law, and the Coming of the American Revolution," 49 *N. Y. U. L. Rev.* 1043, at pp. 1086-1091 (1974); Nelson, *op. cit. supra* note 4, at pp. 13-35. This eighteenth century perception is closely analogous to the insight of modern legal anthropology that all societies have a multiplicity of legal systems responsive to differing but overlapping publics. See Leo Pospisil, *The Anthropology of Law: A Comparative Theory* (1971), pp. 98-126, and Sally F. Moore, "Law and Social Change: the Semi-Autonomous Social Field as an Appropriate Subject of Study," 7 *Law & Society Rev.* 710 (1973).

institution of undifferentiated local governmental authority. In practice it made a single continuum of judicial action out of the disparate forms of criminal and administrative business that came before it, a continuum which made possible a judicial government of county life. The responsibilities of a sessions court were defined less by its formal legal jurisdiction than by the needs of governance. But it lacked executive powềr. As a court, it could only govern insofar as public business was brought before it. And so, it was dependent on its attractiveness as a place where county problems might be brought for resolution.

This article is based on the records of one such court, the Middlesex County (Massachusetts) Court of General Sessions of the Peace, over a 75-year period from 1728 to 1803.[8] An intensive study of these records reveals that during the second half of the eighteenth century the conception of undifferentiated judicial government that underwrote the power of a sessions court over county affairs gradually unravelled and was replaced by a modern conception of county government as an administrative agency. This transformation stands in seemingly direct opposition to the ideological and constitutional struggle of Revolutionary America to confirm the independent authority of local institutions against the will of the sovereign. Yet, this transformation was also the exact contemporary of that struggle.

In 1803 the Massachusetts legislature transferred the whole of what we would consider the legal jurisdiction of the various county sessions courts to the county courts of common pleas. The only responsibilities still held by the collective body of the justices of the peace were ones specifically related to county administration: maintaining jails and other county buildings, settling county accounts and raising taxes, granting licenses, and laying out, altering, and discontinuing highways.[9] The sessions courts had formally become administrative agencies, the direct precursors of the boards of County Commissioners who would later replace them.[10]

---

8. Out of the 75 years between 1728 and 1803, the whole record, plus all relevant file papers were read for 16 years spaced at five year intervals. Other parts of the record and file papers were read in a more cursory fashion. All records are located in the large vault of the Middlesex County Courthouse, East Cambridge, Massachusetts, under the supervision of the Clerk of the Superior Court, Mr. Paul Sostek.

9. 1803 *Acts and Resolves,* c. 154.

10. The original sessions courts were abolished in 1807. 1807 *Acts and Resolves* c. 11, as amended c. 57. For the next 20 years, the state experimented with a number of variants on the sessions court (see footnote 145, *infra*) until in 1828 the whole idea of a sessions court was replaced by an administrative agency: the County Commissioners. 1827 *Acts and Resolves* c. 77.

108

So ended the 110-year history of the Massachusetts courts of general sessions of the peace. Founded with the Second Charter in 1692, they had survived the Revolution without significant legislative amendment. In fact, almost their whole history was marked by a singular lack of legislative attention. Occasional acts were passed specifying the terms of a particular criminal offense cognizable by sessions courts, but until the late 1780's the General Court never tried to direct the activities of the courts. The General Court could indicate areas of province-wide concern through legislation which the courts were bound to enforce.[11] But, until well after the Revolution, neither the General Court nor the court system as a whole had direct control over the activities of county sessions courts.[12] The act which first established these courts, after declaring that they could hear any case relating to the conservation of the peace, made no attempt to define what that meant. The remainder of the act was limited to a schedule for the meetings of the various county courts and descriptions of how appeals might be carried to the Superior Court of Judicature, the process of jury selection, and the requisite format for appeals from the criminal judgments of individual magistrates.[13]

11. See, for example, rules forbidding the killing of game out of season: 1698-9 *Acts and Resolves*, c. 21; 1716-17 *Acts and Resolves*, c. 12; 1738-9 *Acts and Resolves*, c. 3.

12. One might argue that because the concept of a sessions court, like other local English legal institutions, was so well understood by English colonials there would have been little need for legislative interference. Goebel and Naughton in *Law Enforcement in Colonial New York*, for example, regard an American sessions court as little but a replication of its English namesake: the vehicle through which English justices became the "administrators of England" after the Glorious Revolution. Yet the origins of the Massachusetts sessions courts were mixed and we can trace significant aspects of the structure and practice of the courts back to the county courts of the Massachusetts Bay colony of the seventeenth century. Unlike their English courterparts, provincial sessions courts rarely had to compete with other local courts for control of a jurisdiction. See Sidney and Beatrice Webb, *The Parish and the County* (1963); William Holdsworth, *A History of English Law*, X (1938), pp. 126-339; Frederic W. Maitland, "The Shallows and Silences of Real Life," *Collected Papers*, I (H.A.L. Fisher, ed., 1911), p. 467. At the same time, the responsibilities of the Massachusetts courts were far less extensive and elaborate than those ascribed to their English counterparts. When a Massachusetts version of Burn's standard J. P. treatise was prepared in the early 1770's, the editor had to make radical excisions in the English text in order to make it acceptable for use in America. *An Abridgment of Burn's Justice of the Peace and Parish Officer* (J. Greenleaf, ed., 1773, Evans #12,702), introduction.

13. 1699-1700 *Acts and Resolves*, c. 1. Even those specifications in the act meant less than one might think. Consider the appellate process. In all

During the second half of the eighteenth century, the practice of the Middlesex Sessions ,Court changed dramatically. The continuum of judicial government was broken; the distinction between criminal prosecution and administrative regulation became increasingly rigid and specific. Local criminal practice was integrated into a state-wide system of criminal justice; county administration came to be seen as the dependent agent of the Commonwealth. Insofar as the court continued to administer county affairs, it became less and less of a legal institution. And, by the turn of the nineteenth century, the justices of the Middlesex Sessions Court were functioning almost exclusively as limited administrators of county affairs. A sense of general responsibility for county life had given way before a bureaucratic model of county administration.

109

Such a transformation may have important implications for the study of some of the loftiest themes of American legal and constitutional history: the centralization of legal authority, the dichotomous relationship of law and politics, the separation of powers. But it is a transformation that grew out of mundane legal business: out of fornication cases, road building and repair, poor relief, and a host of other petty crimes and public concerns. In order to understand how a court "conserved the peace" of a county and how that conception of county government slowly changed, we need to look to the business of such a court as a whole, to the interrelationships of the issues that came before it, and to the functional integration of its responses to those issues. We need, in effect, to think of a sessions court as a distinct institution located in a particular community. A sessions court, like any court, was an entity whose "central aspect" was ". . . organized activity, activity organized around the cleaning up of some job." To borrow the terms of Karl Llewelyn,

---

civil or criminal cases, "appeal" meant not a review at a higher level of the legal basis for a decision, but rather a new trial. Only in some regulatory cases would a decision of the sessions court be reviewed on *certiorari*, and even that was still a matter of some controversy when John Adams was practicing. *Legal Papers of John Adams*, I, pp. 301-304, 321-322. In England the principles of *certiorari* were settled earlier. Edith Henderson, *Foundations of English Administrative Law* (1963). But in mid-eighteenth century America appeal still had less to do with the functional integration of a legal system or the control of administrative discretion than with the ability of litigants to change the legal level of their dispute. As such it reflects the intensity of local control over local legal institutions.

Moreover, while appeals to the Middlesex Sessions Court from the decisions of justices of the peace were common, decisions of the sessions court itself were rarely appealed to the Superior Court of Judicature. Between 1692 and 1705, three cases were appealed. In the 16 years studied between 1728 and 1803, only 20 cases were appealed; in six of those 16 years there were no appeals taken at all.

we may think of institutions of "law-government" as those institutions which perform jobs necessary to the maintenance of group life and order.[14] And in order to understand the legal life of a sessions court of the eighteenth century we ought to specify the jobs that court performed and the techniques it used.[15]

The Middlesex County Court of General Sessions of the Peace met alternately throughout the year in three county seats: Charlestown, Cambridge, and Concord.[16] Most of the justices were laymen, which was typical of the benches of most county courts in colonial America.[17] Like the magistrates in other counties,[18] many of the Middlesex justices took their responsibilities to the sessions court seriously, attending regularly and continuously over long periods of time.[19] The purpose of this study is not to argue that this court was an archetypal sessions court. No doubt the putative typicality of the Middlesex court was compromised by the strong competitive authority of towns in Massachusetts.[20] At the same time, this article is based on the assumption that by trying to describe the work of this one court we can come to some understanding both of the strangeness of eighteenth century governmental practice and of the ways this legal institution began to change into something more familiar.

Part One

FOUR ASPECTS OF THE BUSINESS OF THE PEACE, 1728-1803

What was a court that conserved the peace? An initial answer might be that it was an informal, discretionary problem-solver—a

---

14. Karl N. Llewelyn, "Law and the Social Sciences — Especially Sociology," 62 *Harv. L. Rev.*, 1286, at p. 1289 (1949); for other statements of the law-jobs theory see William Twining, *Karl Llewelyn and the American Realist Movement* (1973), and Karl Llewelyn and Addison H. Hoebel, *The Cheyenne Way* (1941).

15. This is not to underemphasize the importance of a self-conscious legal tradition in the lives of colonists. Indeed, that tradition offers one explanation for the ability of the court to govern the county through the use of judicial forms and techniques. The value of the law-jobs approach, however, is that it directs us to the actual work of the institution instead of looking endlessly at its membership and structure.

16. During the Revolution and for a short time thereafter, the court met in Groton instead of Charlestown, where the courthouse had been burned by the British.

17. A number of attorneys, notably Edmund Trowbridge and Jonathan Sewall, were also Middlesex justices of the peace.

18. Snell, *op. cit. supra* note 6 (Suffolk and Hampshire Counties).

19. Several Middlesex justices — Thad Mason and Francis Foxcroft to name two — were in continuous and regular attendance for up to 40 years.

20. Zuckerman, *op. cit. supra* note 5; Murrin, *op. cit. supra* note 6.

gathering of local notables who settled county affairs under the guise of conducting a court. Yet, that is too cynical. The legal and regulatory practice of a sessions court was not a front. It was an essential aspect of county governance, a set of tools that in large part determined the work of the court. As those tools—those legal categories—changed, so too did the nature of county government change. But through the first half of the eighteenth century the varying, seemingly dichotomous categories of the practice of a sessions court were integrated into a unitary notion of government. In Part Two of this article we will consider more directly the notion of a judicial government of county life and the institutional context which for a time at least gave it legitimacy. But here in Part One let us look to the major categories of the business of the Middlesex Sessions Court: liquor licensing, poor relief (settlement law), fornication, and road building and repair. And let us consider how those categories were used by the court to effect its mandate to conserve the peace.

111

A. *Liquor Licensing.*

One of the seemingly routine tasks of the Middlesex Sessions Court was the distribution and regulation of licenses for the innkeepers and liquor retailers of the county.[21] Each spring the clerk of the court would send town selectmen a form with the names of all holders of licensed public houses in the town; the selectmen would be asked to return the form with the names of those persons approved for the following year written on the back. Based on these returns, the court would publish in late summer a list of all the licenses granted or renewed throughout the county for the next year. At other times during the year, persons might obtain a license by special permission of the court.[22] In all cases, licensees had to post bond and find sureties to ensure the good order of their houses.[23]

At least through the first half of the eighteenth century, this seemingly placid routine concealed a complex and continuing bat-

---

21. 1692-3 *Acts and Resolves*, c. 20.
22. See Petition of W. Willis, *MGS Record*, 9-28; usually such a petition was based on the prior special authorization of the General Court.
Throughout this article *MGS Record* refers to the extended record books kept by the clerks of the Middlesex sessions court and now housed in the large vault in the Middlesex County Courthouse in East Cambridge. *MGS File Papers* refers to the court papers kept in dated dockets — from 1737-8 to 1827—behind the glass cases along one wall of the same vault. File papers from before 1737 are kept in indexed manila envelopes. See note 128, *infra*.
23. In 1728 the required bond was 250 pounds plus two sureties at 25 pounds each.

tle between towns and the court which exercised a discretionary control over who would be licensed. The justices did not simply register the choices of the towns. They would vote on each name presented before the court. And town selections were frequently rejected.[24]

Not only were town choices often denied, but persons were regularly licensed who had not been approbated by a town and who in fact had been explicitly rejected by the selectmen. In August 1743, for example, the selectmen of Dracut were presented by the grand jury for insulting the dignity of the court. It seems that, out of a continuing sense of frustration, the selectmen had made the following licensing return to the court, to which the justices strongly objected:

> . . . These may certify that we the subscribers (are the Same that we was when the within named Robert was last licensed, and that he is the Same, and if you Honours are the Same, we expect the Same Fate: but) do except to [and] against the said Robert Hildreth as a person unfit for the Business and imployment of an Innholder by reason that he doth not keep good Rule [and] order in his House.[25]

Towns were not in control of the situation. Towns presumably had as great an interest as the court in the peace and order of tavern life. But the court would pay as much attention to petitions of private individuals or groups written either in opposition to particular town candidates or in support of persons passed over or rejected by town selectmen as they would pay to the expressed desires of towns.[26] Taverns were important centers of community life, and we might imagine that the court listened with particular care to petitions from isolated sections of a township. When the residents of a "remote" part of Hopkinton heard that the town selectmen had

---

24. Votes were tallied anonymously on the backs of town returns and petitions. It is impossible as a consequence to know whether justices aligned themselves geographically or by some other criterion on whether to grant or to withhold a license.

25. Presentment of the selectmen of Dracut, *MGS File Papers*, 8-43.

26. See for example, the petition of Francis Mooves, *MGS File Papers*, 1737-8 (no date), who "humbly shews that he has learnt the Art of Distilling Spiritts but can't Set up that Business Without Liberty from this Court to Sell the Same in Small Quantities. For there is no [one] that wants Twenty Gallons of such Liquors at Once and therefore I must Either Loose the Trade or the Benefit of Exercising it or must Sell without License and run the Risove [risk of?] of being Prosecuted, Neither of which you Pet. is willing to do . . ." The court accepted his petition, and he was licensed in July 1738.

refused to approbate their local innkeeper, a Mr. Qualls or Quarles, because he did not keep "Good Orders" on the Lords Day, they wrote to the court to defend his actions. They all lived "Remote from Meetting" with "nowhere to gow in the Intermishtion Season [winter] But to the Publick Hous. there being no other hous near but what are thronged with . . . relations." An open and nearby tavern was a necessity, particularly on Sundays, in a world of poor roads and hard winters. And the court felt free to renew the license of Mr. Quarles in spite of his apparent unGodly and unlawful conduct.[27]

To the Middlesex Sessions Court licensing was a matter of the highest importance. The license was a declaration of public trust and responsibility in a person—a declaration that a person could be relied on to keep the public order of the county. Those who sold liquor without a license flouted the authority of the court.[28] Those licensees who did not keep good order violated a public trust.[29] Both were dealt with severely. The court felt no obligation to renew the license of an innholder or retailer from year to year. The license was an "office"; it was not the property of the licensee. It was a delegated grant of authority to a specific person to keep a public house in a specified place for a designated period of time.

As much, the process of liquor licensing exemplifies the governmental authority of the sessions court. And so it remained in Middlesex County into the 1750's. But by the late 1760's the process had apparently changed. One cannot prove very much from an absence of information. But file papers conspicuously lack the sense of conflict and strife that earlier characterized licensing returns. Licensing had gradually become a routine process. Licensees were able to hold on to their licenses for longer periods of time, and we might suspect that they grew increasingly confident that their licenses would be renewed yearly. By 1768, a license could move with the holder to a new house[30] or be sold with an inn or store to a previously unlicensed person.[31] The license now belonged to the licensee.

With the end of the Revolution, licensing procedures of the Middlesex Sessions Court changed in more radical ways. The clerk no longer recorded the yearly list of licenses in the extended record of court business. Licenses were kept in a "minute" book with other matters of presumably "non-legal" interest. And in 1786 the Gen-

113

---

27. *MGS File Papers*, 7-38.
28. See Martha Bowen, fined, *MGS Record*, 8-33.
29. See Opening of a Tavern (Martha Bowen's house), *ibid.*, 7-33.
30. Petition of Edward Richards, *ibid.*, 3-68; Petition of Esther Rand, *ibid.*
31. Petition of Nathan Fuller, *ibid.;* Petition of Abijah Smith, *ibid.*

eral Court made the choices of town selectmen obligatory on the
justices of the sessions courts.[32] Decision-making power had been
shifted away from the members of the court.

By 1798 the court seemed reluctant to prosecute even those
presented for presuming to be a taverner without a license. Where
the court had once greeted such presentments with ten-pound
fines, the court now looked for excuses not to prosecute. Jonathan
Fay, the attorney for the Commonwealth, announced at the instiga-
tion of the court that he would only prosecute Samuel Tuttle insofar
as Tuttle had illegally sold one mug of liquor.[33] And in the case of
Jepthah Richardson, Fay would not prosecute at all.[34] Perhaps, as a
public institution, the Middlesex Sessions Court no longer wished to
stand in the way of a private individual's pursuit of his livelihood.

Such an extrapolation might bring us too close to an anarchic
capitalism presumably beyond the expectations of the men of the
sessions court. What had certainly happened, however, was that a
license had become private property. Previously, a public house
had been "public" in two senses: as a place open to the public and
as a public trust. But, by the 1780's and 1790's, the latter notion
had lost much of its force and the idea of a license came close to
implying a guarantee of a livelihood. In September 1783 the court
granted George Fretcham (or Feechum or Fecham), an innkeeper
imprisoned for debt, a writ of habeas corpus so that he "should be
present at the Court of General Sessions of the Peace . . . in order
to take out such a license to qualify him for an Innholder and also to
prevent others from taking license to his Great detriment [and] the
detriment of the public . . ."[35] The government of the county
could not "take" a license from a person.[36] The license was an individual's property, and it was not to be an instrument of public authority.

At one time the justices of the Middlesex Sessions Court had
used licensing to enforce a complex vision of the good moral order
of the county. But as license holders gradually gained property
rights in their licenses, the court lost its former discretionary
power. A "legalized" license could not be used to serve governmental ends.[37] And, in the years after the Revolution, the Middlesex
Sessions Court became, in fact, a routine registrar of licenses.

---

32. 1786 *Acts*, c.68.
33. *Commonwealth v. Samuel Tuttle*, *MGS Record*, 5-98.
34. *Commonwealth v. Jepthah Richardson*, *ibid.*, 11-98.
35. *MGS File Papers*, 9-83.
36. At least not without due compensation.
37. By the same token, an institution dedicated to those ends would not
be trusted with power in a society dedicated to the legalization of property
rights.

B. *Settlement and Poor Relief.*

In England the law of settlement was a central aspect of the jurisdiction of a sessions court.[38] Historians of provincial Massachusetts have usually looked to the town as the locus of poor relief (and its avoidance);[39] yet in Middlesex County, as in the rest of Massachusetts, the process of warning out a transient from a town was dependent on the statutory authority of the sessions court and the justices of the peace. If town selectmen, in their capacities as overseas of the poor, decided to warn out a transient, they began by writing out a warrant to the local constable ordering him to go search out the individual and "warn" the transient "to depart out of his or her House." Having done so, the constable would return the warrant to the selectmen with the following notation on the back: "I have warned the within named person . . . to depart out of this Town . . . according to warrant." The completed warrant was then sent to the sessions court with a petition that "this Caution may be Entred at this Court so that s[ai]d . . . [person] may never be any charge to the . . . town."[40] The court then entered the "caution" of the town into its record, specifying if possible the names of all children and dependents and the town from which the transient(s) came. Only a recorded caution gave a town the right to request a warrant from a magistrate that would order the direct physical removal of a transient.

Poor relief and settlement law were complementary aspects of a general process that defined and limited local responsibility for dependent individuals.[41] From the perspective of the town, the effectiveness of that process depended on the sessions court, on the power that the sessions court gave towns to control who would qualify to receive their relief. Eighteenth century society operated on a traditional principle that each community was responsible for its own poor.[42] But in a society of growing geographical mobility[43] it

115

---

38. See *Burrow's Settlement Cases: 1732-1776* (1777); Thomas Caldecott, *Report of Cases Relative to the Duty and Office of a Justice of the Peace, from Michaelmas Term 1776, inclusive to Trinity Term, 1785* (1786); citations in *Legal Papers of John Adams*, I, pp. 306-7.

39. See Zuckerman, *op. cit. supra* note 5, at p. 113; Josiah Benton, *Warning Out in New England* (1911).

40. *MGS File Papers*, 5-38.

41. Another aspect of poor relief was the requirement that towns support their aged, but only if no child or grandchild were found to do so; see Petition of Concord, *MGS Record*, 11-73.

42. See David Rothman, *The Discovery of the Asylum* (1971), pp. 3-56.

43. See Douglas L. Jones, "Geographical Mobility and Society in Eighteenth Century Essex County, Massachusetts," (unpublished doctoral dissertation, Brandeis University, 1975).

became increasingly important to distinguish those who were of the community from those who did not belong. And the towns relied on a statutory concept of "inhabitancy" as a way of determining eligibility. "Inhabitancy" meant more than legal residence; one was always an inhabitant of one's place of birth, at least until one gained an inhabitancy elsewhere; but to become an inhabitant of any other town became a more and more difficult process through the eighteenth century. For 30 years after 1739 an inhabitancy generally depended on the specific approval of the town meeting or the overseers of the poor.[44] But the law was murky, and towns appear to have been unsure whether the statutory definitions constituted an adequate limitation of their responsibilities.[45] Thus they relied on "warnings out", underwritten by the power of the sessions court to authorize removal, as the only effective means of controlling their liability.

There was also a different and more important sense in which the effectiveness of a settlement based system depended on the intervention of the court. Each town was inevitably and understandably parochial in its desire to limit the costs of its responsibility, and each community would try to push the care of more or less transient poor onto another community. The harshness of a warning out system was presumably mitigated by the fact that some town somewhere would have to take in and care for the transient poor; by definition everyone had an inhabitancy somewhere, no matter how many towns from which an individual had been warned out. The problem was that that inhabitancy might be virtually undiscoverable, particularly in a situation where there was no incentive for a town to volunteer itself as a poor person's home. And it was the responsibility of the court to find ways of allocating the costs of poor relief between towns by "discovering" where an inhabitancy lay.

In September 1758, for example, the Middlesex Sessions Court heard a petition from the selectmen of Concord that Elisabeth Parker, a poor woman with an infant child, had been transported to Concord from Groton. She was not, the selectmen declared, a proper resident of Concord, and they asked that Groton reimburse them for the costs of care and that Elisabeth Parker and her child be returned to Groton. In an attempt to resolve the dispute, the justices of the court asked themselves whether Elisabeth Parker

44. 1738-9 *Acts and Resolves*, c.9.

45. Retrospectively, the best evidence for their insecurity was the large numbers of towns in Middlesex County which continued to warn out newcomers even after the act of 1767 (c.17) had effectively made warnings out unnecessary since the burden of discovery had been placed on the transients themselves.

had lived in Concord long enough to subject Concord to liability for her support and that of her child. They decided that she had not, but they were equally unwilling to draw the apparent legal conclusion that Groton should therefore be made responsible for the past and future care of the mother and child. The court seemed to be saying that there was no resolution to the problem, and it "continued" its consideration of the case.

And in the records of the court for March 1759 we can read that because of the dilemma created by the court's earlier refusal to make an effective decision Elisabeth and her child had lived in the Concord House of Correction at the county's expense since the previous September. She remained unemployed, and all efforts to discover her "true" inhabitancy had failed. The court therefore decided that she should be discharged from confinement, and the town of Concord was ordered to take responsibility for her well being. It was, said the court,

117

> the incumbent Duty of the Selectmen or Overseers of the Poor of any Town in which an Indigent Person resides to afford to Such Person Such Relief as is necessary whether such person be an Inhabitant . . . or otherwise. And the town of Concord would be chargeable for whatever was not covered by her earnings until the Town to which she properly belong be ascertained.[46]

The court's ultimate decision to put the cost of supporting Elisabeth Parker and her child "temporarily" on the town of Concord may have been the consequence of considerable testimony that she had been an intermittant resident of Concord since 1740, although she had been properly warned out of both Concord and Groton. For our purposes, however, it is most important to note both that the court was the one institution mandated to deal with the kinds of inter-town conflict engendered by the warning out process and that the court constructed a solution which had less to do with abstract legal right than with the concrete political necessity of maintaining a system of poor relief.

At the same time, removal cases rarely came to trial in Middlesex County before the 1760's.[47] We might guess that persons were usually not removed from the towns they had been warned out of unless the justification for the removal was incontestable. But it is also likely that informal arrangements existed between the towns of the county, partially bypassing the court, that allocated respon-

---

46. *Concord v. Groton, MGS Record and File Papers,* 9-58 and 3-59.
47. Years in which the court decided removal cases included 1738(1), 1758(2), 1763(1), 1768(4), 1773(1).

sibility for transient poor. Indirect evidence for such a hypothesis can be drawn from a number of sources. One of the only pre-1758 removal cases to appear before the court was brought by the town of Reynham, which would not have been able to participate in any extra-judicial arrangements because of its distance from Middlesex County.[48] In the case of Elisabeth Parker, discussed above, Groton supported Elisabeth while Concord maintained the child after she had been removed with her infant to Concord. Only when that support was no longer forthcoming from Groton did Concord press suit.[49] And finally we should note a case in 1758 involving a petition by the town of Weston that a poor woman and child living in Waltham had been so badly neglected that the overseers of the poor of Weston had had to spend an "excessive" amount for their support. The fact that the town of Weston was supporting residents of Waltham was not in itself a cause for complaint.[50]

Within such an informal system, there would have been a place for the sessions court, if only as a final—though rarely used—decisionmaker, but its practical role was quite limited. The "cautions" listed by the court were not active instruments of the power and authority of the court. In contrast to the jealously guarded county prerogative of liquor licensing, "warnings out" remained a symbol of the discretionary authority of town selectmen. The purpose of a yearly licensing return was merely to advise the court of a town's wishes in a matter of common concern; the purpose of a petition that a town's "cautions" be entered into the court record, by contrast, was to control the size and constitution of the town's own corporate membership. And we may well imagine that the court would hesitate to set itself up as a regular arbiter of who was and who was not *of* a particular local community. It is evident that poor people were not the only ones warned out of towns. Until 1767 each town could develop its own criteria for who was to be warned out, and some towns warned out all newcomers, including men with slaves and large property holders. None of these cautions were ever rejected by the court; the court automatically entered a caution into its record.

A caution, moreover, did not mean that the person cautioned against was routinely forced to leave his or her home. Rather, the power the caution invested in the selectmen was probably perceived as a kind of reserve. A person once cautioned "may never be

---

48. *Reynham v. Hopkinton, MGS Record,* 3-38.
49. *Concord v. Groton, ibid.,* 9-58.
50. *Weston v. Waltham, ibid.,* 12-58; the file papers of this case suggest a rather horrible story of two transients being moved back and forth between two towns without clothing or even food; *MGS File Papers,* 12-58.

118

any charge" to the town from which he or she had been cautioned. But individuals were rarely forced to leave, except at the point when they actually became dependent and required the assistance of the community.[51]

Whatever the truth of this hypothesis of a partially informal system of poor relief and administration, it is clear that, during the 15 years immediately preceeding the Revolution, settlement cases did become an important and regular part of the business of the court. We might assume that growth in the quantitative level of transiency, a growth Douglas Jones ascribes to a gradual process of modernization, was at the root of the change.[52] Between 1728 and 1763, while the population of Middlesex County probably doubled, the number of cautions entered for a year grew from six individuals and three households in 1728 to 233 individuals and 118 households in 1763. And since a caution once entered was permanent in its potential implications, the latter figure surely underestimates the actual growth in the numbers of persons and families in the county "at risk" as a consequence of having been warned out of a town.

Perhaps the sheer numbers of persons labelled transients combined with the growing economic inequality of the society broke down the private and informal arrangements that might have previously existed between towns.[53] In any event, settlement cases assumed an increasingly legalistic tone. Costs of suit were high. The court made its decisions without a jury. And cases were resolved into a series of legal-factual queries which the justices posed themselves,[54] which in their increasing technicality and abstraction typify the growing rigor of settlement law. Where the questions asked in *Concord v. Groton* in 1758 were directly factual, in 1768 the court asked itself whether a warning directed against a whole family was adequate as to any single member of that family,[55] whether a warrent ordering removal of a transient could be issued by a justice who was a resident of the town requesting the warrant,[56] whether a boy gained an inhabitancy in a town in which he had been apprenticed (or did he retain the inhabitancy of his father

---

51. See *Woburn v. Lexington, MGS Record*, 3-68.

52. Jones, *op. cit. supra* note 43.

53. See James Henretta, "Economic Development and Social Structure in Colonial Boston," *Colonial America*, Stanley Katz, ed. (1971), 450.

54. See *Concord v. Groton, MGS Record*, 9-58.

55. *Woburn v. Lexington, MGS Record* and *File Papers*, 3-68.

56. *Natick v. Medway, ibid.*; see also the *Legal Papers of John Adams*, I, pp. 299-319.

throughout his apprenticeship),[57] and whether failure by a town to win a settlement suit against one town precluded it from suing another town.[58]

Consider the case of Mary Powers. In 1739, when she was either three or five years of age, she left Boston with her mother Anna to join John Macklewain, who may have been her father, in Lexington. They were immediately "warned out" and moved to Woburn where John married Anna and where they all lived for about seven years. In the fall of 1746 they moved back to Lexington, from which they were again warned out by the constable. Mary, however, remained in Lexington, and in 1766, nearly 20 years after she had last been "cautioned," the town selectmen applied for a warrant to remove Mary from Lexington. The warrant was granted, and Mary was taken to Woburn, whose selectmen petitioned the court that she be sent back to Lexington and that the town of Lexington reimburse Woburn for the costs of her care.

The only question the court raised was whether the caution entered in 1746 against "John Macklewain and his family" was sufficient as to Mary. And once that issue was resolved in Lexington's favor, Woburn had no other grounds to contest her removal. A warning once entered into the records of the court would retain its potency in spite of the permanency of the transient cautioned against. Mary had lived in Lexington continuously from 1746 until she was removed. She had spent the better part of her life in the town. But that fact was irrelevant to the legitimacy of her removal.[59]

To a degree settlement cases reflect the growing Anglicization of the legal practice of the province. Technical, legal cases of the sort described above had been typical of the business of English county courts for some time,[60] and perhaps the justices of Middlesex County were trying to model themselves on their English counterparts by taking a more direct interest in the poor relief of the county.[61] These cases also demonstrate something of the growing

---

57. *Stoneham v. Framingham, MGS Record,* 12-68; this case was complicated by the fact that James Holden's father was *non compos,* and his apprenticeship had been arranged and ordered by the selectmen of Stoneham.

58. *Natick v. Newton, ibid.,* 3-68.

59. *Woburn v. Lexington, ibid.,* 3-68.

60. See *Burrows Settlement Cases: 1732-1776* (1777).

61. As a young lawyer, John Adams made a rather careful study of English settlement law. And we can assume that he was not alone; settlement law was an important aspect of the training of any lawyer, and the justice of the peace manuals of Dalton and Nelson, and later Burns, that devoted many pages to problems of settlement and poor relief were among the first

control lawyers exercised over the legal system. Towns were inevitably represented by counsel during the 1760's and 1770's, often by ambitious and distinguished members of the Massachusetts bar.[62] And the technicality of these settlement cases may be one manifestation of the professionalization and growing technical competence of the lawyers of the province.[63]

Yet, in a society in which population and geographic mobility were increasing rapidly, such a legalistic approach to the allocation of poor relief would have only a limited future. A determination of proper inhabitancy by a sessions court could settle intertown disputes only so long as towns continued to exercise moral and legal authority over their inhabitants and so long as the governmental authority of a sessions court was unquestioned. But after the beginning of the Revolution, removal cases no longer appeared before the Middlesex sessions court. And with the Constitution of 1780 the locus of responsibility for public welfare slowly shifted to the Commonwealth. A 1788 act directed all disputes concerning the support of the poor to the courts of common pleas, where they rapidly became an ever more technical branch of town law. [64] A year later the legislature presented a definition of "settlement'" that clearly excluded sessions courts from any role in its application.[65] Most interestingly of all, in 1791 the legislature resolved that in future all corporations involved with the care of the poor in Massachusetts would have to contract directly with the state.[66] Towns retained a basic obligation to care for their poor and dependent, but it was increasingly an administrative responsibility based on the authority and the participation of the state.[67] The law of settlement and the

121

---

law books published in the colonies. In terms of the Middlesex court, however, the most important evidence for regarding the poor relief practice of the 1760's and 1770's as an aspect of what has been called the Anglicization of the Province is the existence of settlement cases. Presumptively some kind of procedure must have existed prior to the late 1750's to deal with intertown disputes over inhabitancy and dependency. But such a procedure, whatever it was, did not rely on the forms of English local government law. The cases heard by the court in the 1760's and 1770's did.

62. Jonathan Sewall and John Adams were frequently the contending counsel in settlement cases in Middlesex County. See *Woburn v. Lexington*, for example, *MGS Record*, 3-68.

63. John M. Murrin, "The Legal Transformation: the Bench and Bar of Eighteenth Century Massachusetts," *Colonial America*, Katz, editor, 415.

64. 1788 *Acts*, c.61; see for example *Town of Freeport v. Town of Edgecumbe*, 1 *Mass. Rep.* 458 (1805), and *Town of Topsham v. Town of Harpswell*, 1 *Mass. Rep.* 517 (1805).

65. 1789 *Acts*, c.14.

66. 1791 *Resolves* (May), c.92.

67. 1793 *Acts*, c.59.

administration of poor relief had become conceptually separate categories of governmental work. Poor relief was becoming rationalized into a larger administrative structure, and in that structure the sessions court had no place.

C. Fornication.

By every quantitative measure, fornication was the most important aspect of the criminal business of a sessions court throughout the history of provincial Massachusetts.[68] Over 40 percent of all prosecutions sampled for this study (including those that occurred in the 1780's and 1790's when fornication cases no longer appeared before sessions courts) were for fornication, and well over half of all the misdemeanants punished by the Middlesex court were fornicators. The crime was prosecuted almost three times more frequently than offenses against the Sabbath, which was the second most prosecuted category, and over six times as many persons were punished for fornication as were punished for violating a Sabbath rule. But even these measures underestimate the increasing relative significance of fornication in the Revolutionary period. While prosecutions for fornication remained roughly constant, prosecutions for other crimes dropped precipitously. In 1733 the court heard 67 criminal cases of which 26 were for fornication; in 1768 it heard 27 cases of which 20 were for fornication. And by 1783 the court prosecuted only three cases that were not for fornication. In a sense, fornication had become the only regular criminal business of the court.[69]

It is easy to appreciate the usefulness and significance of fornication prosecutions in a "puritanical" society. Sexual immorality challenged the moral order of community and family life. The existence of bastards and of children born within nine months of marriage[70] was a visible contradiction of the sacraments of marriage.[71] Moreover, a bastard born to a mother who could not support him or her would have to be supported by the town in which

68. 1692-3 *Acts and Resolves*, c.18; Nelson, *op. cit. supra* note 2, at p. 37.

69. Apparently, this relative growth in fornication prosecutions had already begun in the early eighteenth century; Snell, *op. cit. supra* note 6, at pp. 155-184.

70. As a general rule only fornicators who produced children were prosecuted, although the death of a child at birth would not free the parents from criminal responsibility.

71. Fornication was of course not the only area of court business that interacted with church affairs. To take only one example, the court oversaw towns in their obligation to maintain a minister. See Petition of Reverend Swift (Framingham refused to support him adequately), *MGS Record*, 5-38.

the child was born, whether or not the mother had a settlement in the town. Towns might be faced with growing costs that resulted from the immoral behavior of strangers. And fornication prosecutions were the only possible deterrent.

For most of the first half of the eighteenth century there is much evidence to indicate that fornication prosecutions were used to secure primarily religious and deterrent ends. During the 1720's and 1730's over 50 percent of all fornication prosecutions were against couples who had produced a child within nine months of their marriage. In 1728 seven-eighths of the fornication cases heard by the Middlesex court charged "fornication before marriage." All those who could be shown to have engaged in sexual immorality would be punished. Throughout this period it was conventional for the court to prosecute both husband and wife. At the same time, the court used its fines to distinguish between those who married and "saved the town" from any charge and those who did not. In spite of the fact that a fine would presumably be a greater burden on a young singlewoman than on a married couple, the fines for fornication before marriage would almost always be lower than those for fornication without marriage. In 1733, for example, fines for fornication before marriage averaged 17.5 shillings less than fines assigned to singlewomen.

Sometime during the 1740's, however, the nature of a fornication prosecution in Middlesex County began to change. Men were no longer prosecuted for the crime of fornication, although they were sued for bastardy. The number of women prosecuted for fornication before marriage declined similarly. From 1743 on, such prosecutions never constituted as much as ten percent of the fornication cases heard by the court in a year, and in most years the court heard no such cases at all.[72] In effect, only singlewomen with bastards were being prosecuted for fornication.

As the defendants in fornication cases became uniform, so did the fines charged the convicted. Where in 1733 fines had averaged over three pounds and had ranged as high as five pounds, by 1743 fines averaged only one pound and ranged from five shillings to two and one-half pounds. And in the years studied after 1743 the fines charged by the court continued to decline. In 1768 fines averaged a little more than five shillings and ranged only between one and ten shillings; and in 1773 the sessions court charged a uniform four-or five-shilling fine for the crime of fornication. In 1733 fornication had been punished with greater severity than obstruction of justice,

123

---

72. We might suspect that married women were prosecuted only when it was believed that their children were conceived with someone other than their husbands.

violations of the Sabbath, gaming, drunkenness, and assault; in 1738, attempted rape was treated as a less serious offense than fornication. By contrast, after 1768, fornication was always the least seriously punished of all the crimes sentenced by the Middlesex court.

We cannot know exactly why the structure of fornication prosecutions changed so dramatically. The changes were not the product of legislation. And while we know that between 1761 and 1800 an unprecedented 33.7 percent of all first births in families in a variety of Massachusetts communities occurred within nine months of marriage,[73] it is not at all obvious what consequences that fact would have on the criminal practice of the Middlesex sessions court.

Although we cannot be certain of the causes of change, we can know what the results of those changes were. Fornication prosecutions continued to serve the governmental aims of the court, but, during the second half of the eighteenth century, fornication prosecutions had only a residual moralistic purpose.[74] Fornication prosecutions were largely reconstructed as a form of public welfare law. They became 'a way of allocating the costs of illegitimacy. After 1758 towns had the right to bind out into servitude any woman with a bastard who refused "to reimburse or procure the reimbursement of charge or expense . . ." of raising her child.[75] Since the only way a woman could legally compel a man to support his bastard (in a suit for bastardy) was by first confessing to fornication, we can assume that there was a substantial inducement to confessions. And it is evident that the vast majority of all women accused of fornication

_124_

---

73. Daniel S. Smith and Michael S. Hindus, "Premarital Pregnancy in America, 1640-1966: An Overview and Interpretation," 5 *Jour. of Interdisciplinary Hist.* 537 (1975); Daniel S. Smith, "The Dating of the Sexual Revolution," *The American Family in Socio-Historical Perspective* Michael Gordon, ed. (1973), p. 323.

74. In his article, "Emerging Notions of Modern Criminal Law in the Revolutionary Era: An Historical Perspective," (pp. 453-4), William Nelson has argued that the prevalence of fornication prosecutions in preRevolutionary Middlesex County demonstrates a continuing moralistic — even Puritanical — impulse that stands in direct contrast with the economic concern with theft that dominated post-Revolutionary criminal justice. As we have seen, such a position can only be maintained in ignorance of the degree of change in the structure of fornication prosecutions between the early eighteenth century and the 1750's and 1760's. Most importantly, such an argument depends on an untenable comparison of pre- and post-Revolutionary criminal justice "systems". Until well after the Revolution, the misdemeanors heard by a sessions court were not part of a provincial or state-wide system, but aspects of local governance and order.

75. 1758-9 *Acts and Resolves*, c.17

confessed their guilt long before their children were due.[76] Fornication cases became a kind of registration procedure whose purposes
were only coincidentally related to the punitive assumptions of the
criminal law. A fornication case was less a criminal prosecution
than a part of an administrative process designed to redistribute the
costs of maintaining dependent bastards.

To understand how a fornication case was used to perform an
administrative task we should begin by identifying three competing
interests in such a case: the town, the mother, and the "putative"
father. The child had no direct interest in the case since someone,
whether town or family, would always be responsible for the costs
of his or her care. But each of the others had a distinct stake in the
resolution of the process. And it was the responsibility of the justices and juries of the court to underwrite a process that would
distribute the costs of maintaining bastards.

125

The overt motivation of the town was obvious: it was to avoid
having to support a child out of its public funds.[78] And, from a
certain perspective, it might be said that the whole process of a
fornication case was designed to insure the town against the cost of
raising the illegitimate children of resident women. Whether or not
the court "adjudged" any particular man to be the father of a child,
someone would have to put up a bond and find sureties "to save the
town harmless from any charge" for the cost of raising the bastard.
If no man were found or convicted, the father or brother of the
woman would post the recognizance.[79] If the woman were a "trans-

---

76. See the case of Esther Bemis in text above footnote 91, *infra*.

77. As such, the practice of the Middlesex court came to approximate
English models for the treatment of bastards. In Blackstone, although fornication was considered as part of a general category of crimes against God
and morality, the actual description of the offense was solely in governmental terms. Punishment was mandated for the woman, but only "if the
bastard becomes chargeable to the parish: for otherwise the very maintenance of the child is considered as a degree of punishment." William
Blackstone, *Commentaries*, IV (1767), p. 65.
The point is not that there was no element of retribution or religious belief
in fornication prosecutions of the second half of the eighteenth century, or
conversely that earlier cases may not also have served an administrative
purpose. Rather, it is that the common meaning of a fornication case in the
context of the larger practice of the court changed over time, and that the
process was changed in order to accomodate that new meaning.

78. The town may also have had a continuing concern for the threat to
peace and order represented by bastard children. But that concern, if felt,
was not expressed in the records and file papers.

79. See the Bonds of John Harrington and Eliakin Rice, *MGS Record*,
4-58, and the Bond of Anthony Jones, *MGS File Papers*, 11-68, who "has

ient" of whatever duration, she would be removed as soon as her pregnancy became obvious.[80]

The interests of the woman were also secured by the court process. A man convicted of bastardy under the relevant statute[81] had to pay half the costs of the mother's "lying-in", which included the costs of the birth and all expenses incurred by the mother during the first month of the baby's life, generally two shillings per week thereafter,[82] all costs incurred by the mother while prosecuting her claim against him,[83] a bond with sureties—usually of 50 or 100 pounds—to ensure performance of the court's order, and a similar bond to protect the town from cost. To all this the woman could lay claim by implicating a man in her confession. And fornication confessions were almost always the consequence of a voluntary examination before a single justice in which primary attention was paid to the identity of the father.[84] We might say that the fine ultimately paid by the mother to the sessions court was less a punishment than a fee paid to invoke the power of the county to secure the support of a putative father.[85]

126

---

given Security to the Selectmen of the Town of Hopkinton to their Satisfaction for all Charge that may Arise by a male child Born of his Daughter . . ."

80. Some of the settlement cases heard by the court dealt with women who were about to have babies at the time of their removal. In at least one case the dispute between towns was complicated by the fact that in the process of being removed from one town to a second town a woman gave birth to a child in a third town. *Reading v. Framingham, MGS Record,* 12-63. The woman in this case was married, but since her husband (James Holden) was destitute, the third town would have had to support her child as if the child had been born illegitimate.

Five years after *Reading v. Framingham* James Holden and his family were again removed from Framingham, this time to Stoneham. It appears from the file papers that the impetus for this second removal was the fact that Holden was being sued for bastardy in New Hampshire. Presumably if the woman in New Hampshire won her suit, the town of his inhabitancy would have had to maintain her child since James Holden was still destitute. *Stoneham v. Framingham, MGS Record* and *File Papers,* 12-68.

81. 1692-3 *Acts and Resolves,* c. 18, section 5.

82. Earlier in the century the charge might have been as high as five shillings per week. See *Gleason v. Rice, MGS Record,* 12-33.

83. Whether this included the actual fine she had to pay is unclear from the available file papers.

84. Any single woman might submit to voluntary examination but could not be compelled to testify before the child was born (presumably because the child might still be born legitimate). See *Burn's Justice of the Peace and Parish Officer,* p. 56.

85. Women paid fines even when children were born dead. One reason they did so was because payment of the fine entitled a woman to sue (for

Against the compelling interests of the town and the convicted fornicatress it would seem that an accused father—a man accused of bastardy—had very little chance. To be an "adjudged" father was to be placed at severe cost.[86] Moreover, the evidence needed to adjudge a man the father of an illegitimate child was far less than what we would today consider necessary for a paternity conviction. In general, only two kinds of evidence were needed: the accusation of the mother under oath and a deposition by a midwife or other woman present at the birth testifying to the fact that the mother had named the accused man while in the midst of labor.[87] In the case of *Cutler v. Hastings,* for example, Mary Cutler confessed to fornication and charged Sam Hastings with being the father of her child. At trial, upwards of a dozen depositions were filed by men who admitted to having had sexual intercourse with Mary or who had watched her have intercourse with others. "She was," said one deponent, "common to every one to Do what they pleased to her."

127

---

bastardy) to recover the costs incident to childbirth. See Millicent Russell, fined, *MGS Record,* 5-63.

86. A man's responsibility to pay half the costs of a lying-in would seem to offer the fornicatress an opportunity to enjoy a level of luxury that she could not otherwise have indulged herself. In August 1743 Mary Cheeney sent Richard King the following bill for her lying-in:

To Child Bed Linen	/10/
To Bringing the midwife and women	1/10/
To midwife fees	1/
To Lhouger [lager beer?]	2/
To biscake	1/
To entertaining the women	2/
To otemeal	/5/
To rice and chocolat	1/
To Rum and Spribes [spirits]	1/19/
To spices	/6/
To norsing	3/
To bording the nors	2/
To fire and candles	2/10/

All of which came to 28 pounds for which Richard King would have been charged fourteen pounds. The court in this case disallowed the lhouger, biscakes, the entertainment of women, the rice and chocolate, and the rum and spribes as excessive and awarded her ten pounds, five shillings, and six pence. *MGS File Papers,* 8-43.

87. The act creating the jurisdiction of the sessions courts over bastardy stated that a man would be adjudged the father when the mother continued "constant in such accusation being examined upon oath and put upon the discovery of the truth in the time of her travail . . ." 1692-3 *Acts and Resolves,* c. 18.

And another deposition asserted that at one time Mary had tried to induce an abortion. The only depositions which directly implicated Sam were filed by Mary's mother and sister. Even the midwife admitted that during labor (travail) Mary had only accused Sam after much prompting from her mother. Still, the court adjudged Sam Hastings to be the father of Mary Cutler's child and ordered him to pay one half the cost of her lying-in and two shillings per week thereafter and to post two bonds to secure his performance of.the court order and to protect the town.[88] It may be that the depositions introduced at Sam Hastings' trial constituted an obvious conspiracy to discredit Mary Cutler, or it may be that there was other evidence which is lost to us. We cannot judge the veracity of a 200-year-old deposition. For our purposes, though, the point is that Mary Cutler did not have to prove that Sam Hastings was the only man who could have been the father of her child. All she had to show was that she had had intercourse with him and that she believed him to be the father of her child. And the only substantive defense a man could raise against a bastardy accusation was that he had never had intercourse with his accuser.[89]

Presumably it was the "policy" of the court to identify putative fathers in order to force them to assume the costs of providing for their illegitimate children.[90] And we might assume that the means used for effecting that policy was the bastardy trial. Yet, throughout all of the 16 years of court business examined for this paper only 16 bastardy cases at all were heard by the sessions court; in only two years (1733 and 1768) were there as many as three such trials. Given the concerns of the court and the interests of the town and mother, one might well wonder why there were so few.
well wonder why there were so few.

The answer is that most men were willing to work out private arrangements with both town and mother in order to avoid the cost and public exposure of a trial. If a man came to a satisfactory agreement with both other parties, no trial would be held. The court was uninterested in the public declaration of guilt or innocence. Its concern was with the orderly perpetuation of a system for the support of bastards. And just as there were incentives for women to

128

88. *Cutler v. Hastings, MGS Record* and *File Papers*, 9-53.

89. In *Fisher v. Kneeland, ibid.*, 3-61, the court adjudged Kneeland guilty "nothing being offered appearing to the Court to induce them to think him innocent."

90. It is not at all clear that the magistrates even cared if the mothers of illegitimate children consciously looked to the wealth of their "suitors" in order to decide whom they would accuse. See depositions in *Boone v. Wheeler, ibid.*, 3-61 and *Gage v. Headly, ibid.*, 9-68, and *Legal Papers of John Adams*, I, pp. 325-329.

confess and to identify their lovers, so the court utilized a process which was designed to encourage men to arrive at a private understanding with the other parties to a fornication case. How it did so may be gathered from an examination of the chronology of an ordinary fornication case.

On September 20, 1782, Esther Bemis of Waltham went to the home of James Dix, J.P., in order to be voluntarily examined. She was pregnant, and her child was "likely to be born a Bastard and to be chargeable to the town of Waltham . . . and Ebenezer Swan jun. late of Cambridge . . . Blacksmith, now said to be Resident in Salem . . . is the father of said Child and [Esther] prays that he may be dealt with according to Law." Dix then made out a warrant to the sheriff, deputy sheriff, or constable of Cambridge ordering the apprehension of Swan so that he could be made to post bond for his appearance at the sessions court.

That same day the undersheriff reported that after "diligent"(?) search he had been unable to find Ebenezer Swan who had "escaped" to Essex County. Five days later, another justice of the peace, presumably from Essex County, wrote another warrant for the sheriffs of Essex County and the constable of Salem.

On September 29, Swan was "captured" and taken before John Pickering, J.P., in Salem, who ordered that Swan be conveyed to Middlesex County. But on September 28 (at least according to the file papers), Swan had already been taken before James Sullivan, a magistrate from Middlesex County, who had ordered him to put up bond of 200 pounds and to find sureties for a similar sum for his appearance before the Middlesex Sessions Court. This bond was renewed in December for his appearance at trial the following year.

Meanwhile, Esther Bemis had posted a ten-pound bond with an equal surety for her appearance at court. But on May 9, 1783 she sent the following receipt to the court:

> Received of Ebenezer Swan jun. the Sum of thirty pounds Lawful money, which is in full of all Demands I have upon him relating to a child I have charged him with being the Father of [and] I also discharge the said Ebenezer Swan jun. from all bonds, [and] all charges that may hereafter answer relating to said child . . .

And on June 3, 1783, Esther Bemis was fined six shillings and costs (which came to ten shillings and six pence) by the sessions court for fornication. No man was charged in the record of the court with being the father of her child.[91]

---

91. Esther Bemis, fined, *ibid.*, 6-83.

For Ebenezer Swan the rewards of coming to a private agreement with Esther Bemis were tangible.[92] He was free not just of the costs of prosecution but also of the recognizances and the continuing charges which a bastardy trial would have probably imposed. Moreover, he was never publicly charged; the fact that he had fathered a bastard could remain unacknowledged.[93]

There remained of course a number of bastardy cases, but these were less criminal prosecutions to establish the legal guilt of a man than attempts by accused men to prove their innocence of charges. In a sense they most resemble libel proceedings in which a man stood as a plaintiff hoping to prove that he had been wronged by the woman who had accused him. Because of the evidentiary burden a man had to overcome, these cases were often ones in which the man had direct evidence of his own innocence.[93a] And in every case his goal was to keep the woman from being allowed to take her oath and give evidence. In *Gage v. Headly,* John Adams, who acted as Josiah Headly's attorney, introduced evidence to prove that Lydia Gage was an unstable and unchaste woman, that she had accused several other men at the same time that she accused Headly and in fact could not make up her mind, that she accused Headly only because he had money, and that one of the other men she had previously charged might have blackmailed her. Against these claims, Lydia Gage's attorney introduced evidence that Headly had repeatedly tried to bribe her not to name him and that many townsmen of Lincoln had suspected that Gage and Headly were sleeping together. The court decided that Lydia should not be "admitted" to her oath, and Josiah was adjudged innocent of her accusation.[94]

---

92. We might assume that Swan had also reached an informal agreement with the town. In other cases file papers sometimes included either an oral (witnessed) or a written certification of satisfaction from the town.

93. There seems to have been a kind of progression of sanctions from unacknowledged agreement to bastardy trial. If, as in the case of Esther Bemis, the man made a settlement prior to trial he would not be named at all. If such an agreement were not complete at trial, the woman's charge would be recorded; however, even in most of the latter cases, no bastardy trial would ensue. Perhaps the public record of the charge acted as an incentive for the man to reach a settlement with town and mother in order to avoid further public exposure. Occasionally the court would order a man so charged to put up bond to protect the town from charge, even though there was no bastardy trial. We might guess that in that situation the man had reached an agreement with the woman without coming to a similar understanding with the town. See Mary Hayden, fined (bond of William Toy), *MGS Record,* 9-68.

93a. *Boone v. Wheeler, MGS Record* and *File Papers,* 3-61.

94. *Gage v. Headly, ibid.,* 9-68; *Legal Papers of John Adams,* I, pp. 325-329.

During the second half of the eighteenth century, the various aspects of the law of fornication were integrated by the Middlesex sessions court into an administrative process of increasing efficiency and rationality. The costs of prosecution, which had once depended on variables of time and distance, were gradually reduced. The punitive functions of a criminal law all but disappeared as fornication prosecutions became routinized and almost bureaucratic. In 1785 the General Court passed "An Act for the Punishment of Fornication, and for the Maintenance of Bastard Children," which, after restating the older punishments that the law of 1692 had mandated, announced that any woman guilty of fornication could choose to appear before a justice of the peace and pay him directly six shillings for a first offense or twelve shillings for any offense after the first. The justice would send a certificate which would be a "full bar" against any prosecution by the sessions court.[95] The registration procedure that the law of fornication had become was now formally decriminalized. Not a single woman was presented before the Middlesex Sessions Court for fornication after 1785. And within ten years women were able to institute paternity actions without even a prior confession before a justice.[96] Paternity suits—although still called bastardy cases—became essentially civil disputes handled in accordance with legalistic standards. From our perspective these changes constituted little more than a formalization of long-standing judicial practice and innovation. In Middlesex County, the largest part of the criminal business of the sessions court had long been effectively decriminalized.

D. Roads.

Central to any understanding of the Middlesex Sessions Court as a court of government is an appreciation of how it exercised its responsibilities over the roads and bridges of the county. In later years, county government would be seen as little else than a road-builder. And while this certainly would not be an accurate description of the preRevolutionary court, it is equally clear that throughout the eighteenth century road building and maintenance were important aspects of the work of the court.

The powers of a sessions court over roads and bridges seem to fall into three categories: the power to lay out county highways directly, a judicial capacity to prosecute towns and individuals criminally for harming or neglecting county bridges or highways,[97] and a general ability to decide any disputes that might arise be-

131

---

95. 1785 *Acts*, c. 66.
96. Nelson, *op. cit. supra* note 4, at p. 457.
97. County highways were roads that connected one town with another.

132

tween town and town, town and individual, or individual and individual over the construction and maintenance of county highways,
town roads or private ways. Yet such a tripartite division is deceptive. Prior to the 1790's the Middlesex court only infrequently exercised its power to lay out new highways. In many years it would
hear no more than one petition for a new highway or for an alteration in an old one. Its prosecutorial role against individuals was
equally limited. In both 1733 and 1738, in most ways peak years of
court activity, the court heard no presentments against any individual for encroaching on or harming a county highway or bridge.[98]
The court did prosecute towns with some frequency. In 1743, for
example, the sessions court heard six presentments against towns
of which five alleged failures in road or bridge maintenance.[99] But
prosecutions against towns were only formally criminal proceedings. Out of 29 presentments heard by the court in the years studied
between 1728 and 1803, towns were convicted and fined in only
three cases. The more usual procedure was for the court to order
continuances until the condition complained of was repaired.
Meanwhile the costs of prosecution would accumulate (which
would always be borne by the defendant town), so there was a
strong incentive for a town to obtain its discharge from the court as
quickly as possible.

We can best think of the whole of the court's road business in
the years prior to the Revolution as defined by its responsibilities as
a dispute settler and a regulator of the actions of others. Even when
the court laid out or altered a highway, the towns in which the way
was located were responsible for the actual construction work.
Towns, in fact, had a direct responsibility for the construction,
maintenance and repair of all public roads and bridges within the
county. And much of the court's work was directed to ensuring that
town selectmen fulfilled their obligations to town residents. Towns
had, for example, an obligation to lay out and open ways within the
town so that residents could get to public meeting from their
homes. A man or woman who felt that a town had unreasonably
refused to open a town way might petition the court for relief.[100] An
individual, moreover, could compel the financial support of a town
for his or her own private way, if it could be shown to be of common
"necessity and convenience." And conversely, a town could be held

<hr>

98. But see John Collidge, dismissed, *MGS Record*, 5-43.
99. See for example, Selectmen of Newton, presented, *MGS Record*, 3-43, 5-43, 12-43.
100. See Petition of Thomas Stone and others, *ibid.*, 4-38, 5-38, 7-38, 8-38; see also footnote 126, *infra*.

liable for damages sustained as a consequence of the construction of a town or county way.[101]

At the same time, the court also settled disputes that might arise between town and town or individual and individual. It would allocate the costs of maintenance between the various towns dependent on a bridge in the same way that it also decided how much two farmers should each contribute to the common upkeep of a private way they shared between them. Petitions and courterpetitions would be heard and no decision of the court would be so final that it could not be reopened by a new petition presenting new or restated information.[102] The gate Joseph Willson of Malden kept over the way leading to Wormwood Point, like many such encumbrances, was a continuing source of litigation between he and his neighbors. One year he would be permitted by the court to keep up the gate; the next year, responding to a different set of petitions, the court would refuse him authorization to do so.[103]

133

The activities of the sessions court were limited by the judicial nature of the institution. The court did not "act" so much as it ensured that the actions of others were both adequate and correct and that road business was conducted in an orderly manner. As such, the conduct of road business in Middlesex County typified a conception of a judicial government as one that is dependent on the actions of others.[104] The Middlesex sessions court built few roads prior to the Revolution. But it used its powers as a court to compel others to do what it felt had to be done. Dependent on petitions and cases, it could not plan or develop a policy. What it could do, however, was enforce a conception of order which included an obligation to maintain the roads of the county.

But by the 1790's this vision of stability and order had evidently disappeared. Massachusetts, like the rest of the new nation was already involved in the creation of a "transportation revolution,"[105] and Middlesex County had a central role—best exemplified by the Concord-Cambridge Highway and the Middlesex Canal—in that development. Road building quickly became far and away the most important substantive business of the sessions court. And the regulatory function of the court became secondary to its emerging direct responsibilities to the Commonwealth.

---

101. See Petition of Merriam Foskit, *ibid.*,5-28.
102. See text above footnotes 136 and 137, *infra.*
103. *MGS Record*, 3-37, 3-38, 5-38, 3-43.
104. Road and bridge building also exemplify the impossibility of distinguishing public from private responsibilities within a pre-modern theory of government.
105. See George Rogers Taylor, *The Transportation Revolution* (1951); Oscar and Mary F. Handlin, *Commonwealth*, (rev. ed., 1968).

134

In quantitative terms, the growth of the court's road building work in the 1790's was impressive. For the combined years of 1763, 1768, and 1773 the court had heard a total of ten petitions to build or alter highways; for the years 1793, 1798, and 1803 it heard a total of 82 such petitions. But we might argue that its self perception had already undergone a transformation in the years immediately preceeding the Revolution. It is of course risky to generalize from the limited business of the court in the Revolutionary era, but it does seem evident that the court entertained less business directed toward compelling or authorizing the actions of others in the 1760's and 1770's than it had in the 1730's and 1740's. Individuals no longer looked to the court for authority to act on their own; instead, both individuals and towns increasingly asked the court to assume direct responsibility for the creation of new roads. And when individuals petitioned the court for relief from governmental action, their petitions asked for money damages instead of direct relief from town or county action.[106] Road building was becoming an exclusive right of public government. Private individuals might receive compensation, but they could not determine the actions of town and county.[107]

Throughout most of the eighteenth century, the process of road building had been a relatively straightforward process.[108] A petition asking for a new road would be presented to the justices of the court, who would assign a committee of three justices from communities adjacent to the area for the requested road to make a report as to whether the proposed road was "necessary and convenient." If the committee reported in favor of the petition, a jury would be called to lay out the way. And the road would then be opened and declared a public highway.

With the growth of road building business at the end of the century, this process became vastly more complicated. The court had to choose between numbers of alternative and competing courses of action and between petitions and counterpetitions requesting damages for the consequences of the court's work. Not only were there more requests for roads, but the process of opening a road had become longer and more elaborate and costly.

---

106. See Petition of Josiah Richardson et al., *MGS Record*, 11-73.

107. In the nineteenth century most aspects of county road regulation were integrated into a private law of municipal liability and a law of takings. Towns would not be told what they had to do, but courts would hold them liable for their negligence. And similarly, eminent domain law made unnecessary prosecutions for encroachment and much of the rest of the regulatory practice of a sessions court.

108. Bridge building was a somewhat distinct process because of the continuing intercession of the legislature.

And in the course of these changes, the court grew specialized and the justices became increasingly skillful in the conduct of their work.[109] As other parts of the business of the sessions court disappeared or were legislated out of existence, the court came to exist only for the administration of the private affairs of the county and for road building. And one senses in the records of the court during these years a growing confidence in the capacities of the justices as road builders and planners.[110] During the 1790's, the Middlesex court received more petitions for alterations in town roads—16 in 1793 and 15 in 1798—than it received for new highways—12 and 11. Many of these petitions presumably arose from the need for more passable ways and from the unwillingness of towns to effect

135

---

109. Some parts of the process changed more slowly. Although diagrams and surveyors' records do begin to appear occasionaly in road building decisions, the basic manner of description and laying out had not changed. The committee appointed to lay out a road over Gravel Hill in Newton, *MGS Record*, 9-98, made its report as follows:

. . . Then we crossed over to the south side of the road to an oak tree which we marked and which is the easterly of a row of large trees and from this we drew a straight line to the most westerly tree but one in the row and from thence to an elm tree marked on the other side of a barn. By this line the whole row of trees is brought into the road, and it is of importance to the traveller both in summer and winter that they should be preserved. The north side of the road is a very steep bank formed by sinking the surface of the ground to make a road in the side of the hill. In the winter and spring those trees are found to be very serviceable in protecting the snow and in summer their shade is equally beneficial to shelter both men and cattle from the insufferable heat of such a situation. These trees form the northern border of a tract of land known in this neighborhood by the name of *Half-Moon*. Mr. Edward Jackson claims them as his property but nothing decisive on this subject being offered to us—the Committee have thought it best to leave the question of damages to be settled by the court when sufficient evidence of their being private property shall be obtained—but we are clearly of opinion that their utility to the road is of such magnitude that when the private shall be ascertained it would be more proper to pay for them than to suffer them to be removed.

110. The court became capable of minor innovation in its handling of road building business. When Daniel Whitney and others complained that a road laid out by the county in 1796 from Watertown to Menotomy was "erroneous and defective and peculiarly injurious to individuals" and petitioned that the defect could be cured by a small alteration in the road, the court traditionally would have appointed a committee to inquire into the necessity and convenience of the alteration as a prerequisite to any substantive action. Instead, in this and similar cases, the court went ahead and appointed a committee which would immediately lay out the altered road. *Ibid.*, 5-98.

improvements. But it is important to recognize that the effect of a court ordered alteration was that a town road became a county road. Once a town road had been altered by county order it became a responsibility of the county,[111] and we may assume that the purpose of many of these petitions was in fact to put roads under county control, given that many of the changes requested appear to have been petty and minor. As such, petitions for alterations would also be striking testimony to the replacement of the presentment and other "judicial" tools of the court by direct administrative action. Instead of using its power to prosecute and punish towns for not maintaining roads in good repair, the sessions court now acted as its own agency for action.

We might speculate that a most important contribution to the court's growing administrative ability was the replacement of "laying out" juries with committees of the court. Again, the roots of this change went back to the preRevolutionary period. In 1756, the General Court authorized sessions courts to replace road building juries with committees of five "disinterested" freeholders.[112] In itself this hardly deserves mention as a change in court procedures, the committee of five freeholders being merely a smaller jury. But, after the Revolution, the court began to draw these committees of freeholders entirely from the ranks of the magistracy itself. No longer was there any restraint by the community over the justices' control of the road building process. Usually the committee of three justices that had decided whether a way was "necessary and convenient" stayed on to become the nucleus of the committee of five justices assigned to lay out the road. And as the volume of cases grew towards the end of the century, such a delegation of responsibility meant of necessity that virtually every member of the county bench was regularly occupied as a member of road building committees. By 1803, the court still had a residual judicial function.[113] It still lacked some of the capacities of a modern administrative agency.[113a] But skills had been acquired, and the court had taken on much of the shape of the board of county commissioners that would later replace it.

136

---

111. 1786 *Acts*, c.67

112. 1756-7 *Acts and Resolves*, c.18.

113. As late as 1803 the court still heard a few presentments against towns for not maintaining highways and against individuals for encroaching on highways. *Commonwealth v. Eliakin Morrill, MGS Record*, 3-1803; *Commonwealth v. John Mann and David Bacon, ibid.*, 5-1803; *Commonwealth v. Chelmsford, ibid.*, 11-1803 (two presentments).

113a. The most important change still to come was the ability of the court to assume directly the costs of road construction. Until 1825 the court was still obliged to depend on towns to bear construction costs and damages for roads located within their borders. 1825 *Acts*, c.171.

Part Two

THE CHANGING NATURE OF JUDICIAL GOVERNMENT

In 1804, county courts of common pleas assumed the legal jurisdiction which had previously been exercised by sessions courts. All that remained of the sessions courts' previous responsibilities was a statutory set of administrative tasks. The Middlesex Sessions Court had become an essentially modern administrative agency. It stood as a realization of two of the central premises of modern governmental theory: the sovereignty of a centralized system of (state) authority in which counties and other units of local government are merely subordinate entities, and secondly, the need for a strict differentiation between judicial and administrative action.

One half century earlier, the Middlesex Sessions Court had been a very different institution. It could have conformed to no modern governmental model. It was neither a court enforcing and following legal norms and rules nor was it an administrator capable of taking initiative and formulating policy within strictly defined guidelines. It was, as we have said, a judicial government of county life. The categories of its practice that were studied in Part One were less aspects of a legal system than of particular county governmental responsibilities. And in this Part we will examine how the Middlesex sessions court interpreted those responsibilities; how it went about conserving the peace of the county; and how that conception of county government changed during the second half of the eighteenth century.

A. *The Use and Justification of an Undifferentiated Court of Government.*

Any analysis of a preRevolutionary sessions court has to begin with the fact that it was a local court run by local notables. Its mandate was to be a local problem solver. And while it would be bound to enforce relevant provincial legislation, such as penal laws and tax laws, the lack of integration between central and local levels of authority meant that sessions courts were often free to interpret that legislation to serve their own local government ends.

As our study of fornication cases demonstrated, the Middlesex Sessions Court perfectly exemplified this conception of a largely autonomous local institution. Criminal laws were transformed into a governmental practice through the exercise of the court's practically unrestrained discretion. Occassionally, the court would even move from discretionary reinterpretation to a limited, but explicit disavowal of the authority of the legislature over county affairs. In September 1768, for example, the owners of a milldam in Malden

137

petitioned the court to be relieved from their obligation to build a passageway ensuring the free passage of fish downstream. The owners of the dam recognized that there was a provincial statute which explicitly ordered them to maintain a right of way for fish, but they asked the court to excuse them both from compliance and from liability "because the Petit. do not think themselves obliged by Law to make such passage way . . . ," and they asked the court to appoint a committee of three disinterested persons to investigate the necessity of such a construction. The court agreed and appointed a committee which made the following report:

138

> that to open a passage way in the same Dam would be a much greater Damage to the Publick than the Fish that might [pass] through the Same Passage Way would be of Advantage, as it appears that there would be but few, if any.

This report was accepted by the whole court, and the prayer of the petition was granted.[114] The petitioners had asked the court to balance a clear legislative directive against the presumed benefits of not enforcing that statute. The petitioners had argued that statutory law, the law of the General Court, need not be the "law" of the Middlesex Sessions Court. And in this case the court evidently agreed. The responsibilities of a local court were distinct from those of central authority.

But the strongest evidence for a perception of local autonomy comes not from the cases of the Middlesex Sessions Court as such but from the extended records of those cases kept by the court. Until the late 1780's, when the clerk wrote a description of a criminal case into the record book he wrote in the margin the name of the person tried and the outcome—"Samuel Willis, fined," or Watertown, dismissed."[115]fi3 A case tried before the court would never be classiflied as "*D. Rex. v. —*" (or *Commonwealth v. —*") in the margin; nor was it so labelled in the body of the record.[116] The only time when the crown would appear in the formal record of a case would be if the defendant forfeited his or her bond (recognizance) and refused to appear for trial. Then the king's attorney would ask the court to issue a writ of *scire facias* ordering the forfeiture of the bond.[117] And the case would be described as a conflict between King and individual.

---

114. Petition of Huldah Paine et al, *MGS Record* and *File Papers*, 9-68.
115. *Ibid.*, 5-38.
116. File papers and presentments would occasionally carry a *D. Rex v.* ——heading or invoke the authority of the crown in the language of the indictment. See text above footnote 135, *infra.*
117. See *D. Rex v. Bigelo et al, MGS Record*, 5-38. In many cases the *scire facias* proceeding was probably a sham constructed because defen-

We might consider this practice as announcing that, if a defendant accepted the legitimacy of the county sessions court and abided by its rules, the crime of which the person stood accused would be viewed only from the context of the county and not as placing him or her in conflict with a larger society. More precisely perhaps, the practice reveals that the criminal jurisdiction of the court was perceived as being a primarily local criminal jurisdiction, as constituting a mandate to enforce the "peace" of the county. Such a criminal jurisdiction was only theoretically related to the enforcement of the King's law. So long as defendants accepted the authority of the court, their crimes remained local community responsibilities; only when that authority was denied would a defendant be placed in conflict with the crown and general public authority.[118]

The essence of local control of the court lay less in the court's independence from centralized authority, however, than in its dependence on the support of a local public. The Middlesex sessions court was a court of government; its responsibilities extended to all the public affairs of the county.[119] Like other forms of government in eighteenth century America, the court lacked executive power— the power to enforce its own directives. There were no police; con-

---

dant and complainant were settling their differences outside of court. Neither litigant wanted the case to come to trial so the defendant would not appear. The court would continue its consideration of the writ over several meetings until agreement had been reached by the parties. Then the complainant would refuse to prosecute his complaint, the defendant would pay the cost, and the King's Attorney would sign a *nolo prosequi*, and the writ would be quashed. See *ibid.*

118, We might speculate that refusing to place a defendant in direct conflict with the crown also reflected a continuing sense of a community of sinners. All men sinned, and the ordinary sorts of sins that were the particular concerns of a sessions court (drunkenness, fornication, assault, etc.) were hardly such as to justify separating a sinner from his or her community. The public shame of a trial before the local public would be punishment enough. What has been called the "battle model" of criminal procedure—in which defendant is pitted against the power of the state—was not essential to the conduct of a criminal trial in eighteenth century Middlesex County. See John Griffiths, "Ideology in Criminal Procedure, or a Third Model of the Criminal Process," 79 *Yale L. Jour.* 359 (1970). Trials were meant to reconstruct order and peace, not to destroy them. It is perhaps important to note that almost all criminal cases resulted in the imposition of fines. Out of the 411 criminal cases examined for this study as a result of which 311 persons were punished — two persons were ordered incarcerated and two persons were ordered whipped. In 12 other cases, whippings or servitudes of one form or another were imposed as alternatives to payment of fines.

119. See the listing made by Nelson, *op. cit. supra* note 2, at p.15.

stables were inefficient, often unwilling, and potentially subject to conflicting loyalties. "In the Anglo-American tradition of government . . . government did not have vast bureaucratic armies of officials to enforce its laws, but instead relied on its subjects to aid the few officials who did exist in their task of law enforcement."[120] Effective rule depended on the ability of the court to engage the community in its work.[121]

A court of government, a government by judicial forms, had to find ways of encouraging people to come into court. The sessions court could only govern if cases involving a wide range of issues were brought before it, whether by petition, presentment, or complaint. Its responsibilities lay in the maintenance of order, but that order did not presuppose harmony or "peace" at least as we would understand the term.[122] Instead, order depended on the court's capacity to control conflicts and keep them from becoming general and endemic. And order presumed the willingness of people to bring conflict into court.[123]

Were the residents of Middlesex County willing to bring their conflicts into court? At least through the first half of the eighteenth century, the answer is apparently yes. The range of cases heard by the sessions court was relatively extensive and wide. In 1728 the court heard and decided 30 criminal cases and 19 civil disputes involving nine different categories of criminal offense and 13 varieties of civil action or petition. In 1733 the court heard 67 criminal cases involving 18 defferent forms of offense. Throughout these years, membership on the bench of the court was very stable, and we might assume that the governmental authority of the court was rarely questioned. New Englanders, after all, were part of a broad

---

120. Nelson, *op. cit supra* note 2 at p.34.

121. This dependence on private action for the execution of governmental duties explains how county taxes could be so very low—often no more than 1/50th of the province tax—and usually between 300 and 500 pounds for the whole county. Zuckerman, *op. cit. supra* note 5, at pp.25-26, used this fact to argue for the insignificance of the county as a governmental unity. Yet the nature of county governmental action indicates that he probably drew an incorrect conclusion.

122. This conception of the "peace" is already evident in the earliest important treatise for justices of the peace, William Lambarde's *Eirenarchia*:

> For Justices of the Peace were not ordained . . . to the ende to reduce the people . . . to an universall unanimities (or agreement) of mindes . . . Neither is it any part of their office to forbid lawfull suites and controversies . . . But to suppresse iniuicus force and violence, movend against the person, his goods, or possessions. (1970(1581)), p.7.

123. We might therefore consider the conservation of the peace as a kind of transitory state between self-help and the abstract justice of modern law.

and self-conscious legal culture which would lend legitimacy to a government by case law.

Yet, however useful it may be to assume a self-conscious legal tradition, too much reliance on such a concept begs the important question of how the Middlesex Sessions Court conserved the peace, — how it governed. An institution that relies on a public to bring it the business on which its work depends will presumably create inducements and incentives for that business. And the criminal practice of the Middlesex court can be viewed as including a number of more or less explicit encouragements to criminal litigants and litigation. Assault cases were almost always treated as relatively minor crimes with fines as low as one or three shillings.[124] Complainants were never punished for prosecuting frivolous charges or even for using the court process as a form of harassment.[125] Perhaps, given the ultimate ineffectuality of public power — its inability to enforce obedience or prevent violence or even provide accurate information — the membership of the court preferred that persons who might use weapons to settle their grievances use the law as a kind of weapon. In that way a peace might be conserved.

There are a number of cases that might plausibly be seen as the products of what we might call instrumental accusations.[126] But the following case of "bad blood" offers a direct illustration of such a conception.

The Bloods were a family that lived on the fringes of civil society; they were commonly considered to be horsethieves, although

141

---

124. See Eph. Littlefield, fined, *MGS Record*, 9-38.

125. See Ebenezer Fletcher, Timothy Flether, Zechariah Fletcher, Thomas Wright, John Wright, Eph. Wright, Abiel Richards, and Ebenezer Patch, all fined, *ibid.*, 3-48 (after attacking the constable who had caught them killing game out of season, they proceeded to accuse the constable and his assistants of assault before a justice of the peace who had no way of knowing the circumstances. The J. P. ordered the constable and his assistants to post bond for their appearance before the sessions court on assault charges. At trial, the constabulary were dismissed from their bonds, but no mention was made of the circumstances of the accusation. See *MGS File Papers*, 3-48.).

126. In 1737 Thomas Stone and others petitioned the court to compel Framingham to pay the costs of constructing a road to their homes so that they could attend public worship. A committee of the court was appointed to report on the "necessity" of such a road, but, while the matter was under consideration, the grand jury presented Elizabeth, Thomas Stone's wife, for not attending public worship. The court ultimately accepted her excuse and dismissed her from the charge, but she was still obliged to pay the fees and costs of a trial. Elizabeth Stone, dismissed, *MGS Record*, 8-38; Petition of Thomas Stone et al, ibid., 4-38, 5-38, 7-38, 8-38.

they owned valuable property outside of Concord.[127] But what they seem to have spent much of their time doing was suing each other (as well as others) in court. They appear regularly in the pages of the sessions court. And between 1724 and 1734 Elizabeth and Robert Blood, brother and sister, sued one another for debt before the Middlesex inferior court of common pleas at least four times.[128]

In the course of one of those debt cases, Robert asked Samuel Blood, a cousin, to testify in his behalf against Elizabeth. Samuel refused, and several uncontradicted depositions by witnesses report that Robert then threatened to accuse Samuel and Elizabeth of lewd and wanton conduct and fornication. He seems to have carried out his threat, and Samuel countered by accusing Robert of defamation before Francis Fullam, a magistrate, who ruled that Robert was guilty and fined him ten shillings and ordered him to find sureties for his good behavior.

Robert appealed this decision to the sessions court, and in March 1733 the jury declared him not guilty. The justices evidently disagreed with the jury's verdict and declared that Robert would pay not just the fees and costs of trial (which as we shall see was normally expected of even a winning defendant), but also Samuel's court costs, all of whkch together totalled nearly 15 pounds.[129]

So perhaps the case should have ended, but nine months later, a presentment against Samuel and Elizabeth Blood for fornication came up for trial. There had evidently been neither pregnancy nor birth nor any other evidence of sexual intercourse, and both defendants were dismissed from the presentment and declared not guilty. But both were ordered to pay the fees and costs of their trial.[130]

The overt consequences of the case are lost to us. We do not know if Robert succeeded in injuring the reputations of Samuel and Elizabeth.[131] Nor can we tell if the conclusion of the second trial discredited Robert. To look only for the consequences of the case, however, is to lose sight of the latent instrumental function of this legal process. Robert used the law as an instrument of defamation. From his point of view the way to slander someone was through direct invocation of the criminal law. And for that purpose the justices and the grand jury of the Middlesex Sessions Court made their law available.

---

127. Mr. Robert Gross was kind enough to share this information with me in conversation.

128. See the file index in the Middlesex County Courthouse which was put together as a WPA project and completed through 1737.

129. *MGS Record* and *File Papers*, 3-33.

130. *Ibid.*, 9-33.

131. Whether or not Robert succeeded, five years later Elizabeth was successfully charged with fornication. *Ibid.*, 9-38.

We might even hypothesize that aspects of the legal practice of the Middlesex Sessions Court functioned to induce people to make instrumental accusations. Consider the way costs were assigned in criminal cases during the first half of the eighteenth century. As in the Blood case, defendants were automatically charged the costs of prosecution, whether or not they were convicted of the charges against them. These costs were hardly nominal, usually more than five times the amount of a fine that would result from conviction and frequently upwards of five pounds.

Such an approach to cost allocation is apparently contrary both to contemporary and modern conceptions of proper judicial process.[132] And we have no way of knowing why the Middlesex sessions court followed such a practice. We can, of course, always construct more or less plausible legal rationalizations for assigning costs automatically to the defendant. Its justification may have been found in a belief that even innocent defendants ought to pay for the privilege of being acquitted of a charge, or it may have resulted from a distrust of the trial as a test of truth, from a conviction that acquittal had less to do with guilt or innocence than with an ability to manipulate technical rules of evidence.

The court may also have had more practical reasons for charging defendants with the costs of their trials. The Court, we may presume, did not want to assume the costs of the trials. And charging those who had complained against acquitted defendants might discourage future complaints. Yet the practice went beyond not charging discredited complainants; to make a formal charge against a person was a way of ensuring that that person would be put to cost. Whether the complaint was true or false, the defendant would have to pay the costs of prosecution. And a defendant had no protection against a vindicative and unwarranted charge. Perjury was difficult to prove, since oathtaking was considered an almost conclusive presumption of truth.[133] And perjury was in any case not cognizable by the sessions court because it was a capital offense. As in the Blood case, the only legally sanctioned counterweight was a suit for criminal defamation held before a single magistrate, which would similarly impose all costs on the defendant in that case.

We cannot know why the practice existed. Still, such a practice would make particularly good sense in the context of a court concerned to govern by attracting disputes to it for resolution. Today we assume that in a court case litigants are primarily concerned to defend their rights, to achieve redress for wrongs done to them, and to assert their own interests against others. But was this the case in the Middlesex County of the first half of the eighteenth century? It

---

132. Goebel and Naughton, *op. cit. supra* note 4.
133. Nelson, *op. cit. supra* note 2, at pp. 25-26.

143

might well be that in a culture where rational self-interest was not an undisputed value, a court case was more directly justified as a way of hurting one's opponent. Perhaps one went to court not to resolve a dispute, not just to win it, but to beat someone else. And if that were the case a practice of forcing defendants to pay costs would be a powerful incentive to the use of the court.

During the first half of the eighteenth century "conservation of the peace" by the Middlesex Sessions Court had less to do with dispute settlement and the amicable resolution of conflict than with the maintenance of a county structure of authority.[134] The use of a system of criminal justice to serve private and extrajudicial ends was acceptable so long as that structure was not threatened. And indeed, the court's success as a court of government might by judged in part by its ability to make its process into a usable and acceptable substitute for private violence and self-help.

At the same time, violence itself did not constitute a particularly serious offense in the eyes of the justices and juries of Middlesex Court. As we have noted, assault cases were treated lightly, but, by contrast, cases of fraud and nonviolent economic crime were punished far more severely than their violent counterparts. The most severe fine meted out by the court in any case during the years studied for this paper was one in which the defendant was accused of "fraud and deceit" and of being a cheat. In December 1743 Phineas Blood (another Blood) was presented for

undirectly and fraudulently obtain[ing] a certain promissory note . . . whereby one Downing Chempney did promise to pay one Samuel Jones of Concord on his order the sum of five pound two shillings for Value received on demand and having so obtained the Same the Said Phineas . . . did fraudulently and deceitfully with an intent to deprive the said Samuel of his Right therein and to cheat and defraud him of the Value expressed in the said Note insert and interline the word Jun. therein and afterwards the s[ai]d Phineas . . . did deceitfully personate [and] assume to one Abraham Cutting to be the s[ai]d Samuel Jones Jun. and for the sum of forty shillings he then [and] there received of the s[ai]d Abraham Cutting for a Writing on the backside of the s[ai]d Note . . . all which Actings [and] Doings of the s[ai]d Phineas are a manifest Cheat [and] tend greatly to the Destruction of Trade [and] Commerce are in evil Example to others [and] contrary to law as also to the Peace Crown [and] Dignity of our Lord the King . . .

134. For the anthropological notion of "dispute settlement" see Laura Nader and D. Metzger, "To Make the Balance," *The Ethnography of Law* (Nader, editor, 1965).

Phineas Blood's appropriation of a five pound two shilling note and its sale for two pounds was treated as three separate offenses, and his punishments totalled as follows: fines of 55 pounds, or fifty pounds plus a whipping, treble damages of £22/7/9, and two recognizances for good behavior at 200 pounds plus equal sureties.[135] Secret and deceptive behavior was considered a greater threat to the order of the community than any act of violence. And the conservation of the peace was not therefore a responsibility that could be satisfied by the redirection and legalization of threatened violence.

An effective public law depended on the court's ability to attract business from all areas of county life. As a court of government, the Middlesex court evidently felt that it had to guarantee a hearing to anyone whose interests were affected by its decisions. There appears to have been no notion of *res judicata;* the court was willing to rehear cases long after all issues of substance ought to have been settled. The town of Billerica, Chelmsford, Groton, Dracut, and Westford wrangled for the better part of the century in court over their respective obligations for the upkeep on the Billerica Bridge.[136] And when Joseph Willson complained that he had not been fairly treated by the court because he had not been present when it ordered him to remove a gate from the highway running through his property — "had he been present at said Court he could have given such convincing Reasons of the necessity of upholding it, as would have induced the Court to continue it notwithstanding what was urged for its removal . . . — the court agreed to appoint a new committee to report on the particular circumstances Willson alleged, notwithstanding that he had been represented by legal counsel at the previous hearing.[137] A court of law would deny such a petition; a court of government could not afford to do so.

If the court tolerated the use of its machinery for purposes seemingly distant from the usual objectives of a legal institution, it did so because without that business it could not govern. Its authority depended on the willingness of its public to bring business, however motivated, before it. And the jurisdiction of the Middlesex Sessions Court was defined not by standards of justiciability, but by its responsibility for the "peace" of the county. In order to conserve that peace, the court's jurisdiction had to be wide and potentially

145

---

135. *MGS Record,* 12-43, 3-44.

136. See *MGS Record* and *File Papers* for 1731, 1738, 1761-63, 1771, and 1791; also 1699-1700 *Acts and Resolves,* c.25, and 1716-7 *Acts and Resolves,* c.5.

137. *MGS Record* and *File Papers,* 3-37 and 3-38; Willson was allowed to keep up the gate for one year, *ibid.,* 5-38.

unrestricted, insofar as the court dealt with matters of county concern. In effect, the criminal and administrative jurisdictions of the court constituted one continuous jurisdiction for the conservation of the peace of Middlesex County. Its criminal practice was less a part of a province-wide system of criminal justice than a repository of power for the use of a county government.[138] By the same token, much of its administrative practice was marked by a quasi-criminal manner of procedure.

Perhaps the best way of thinking about this integrated jurisdiction of the court is to imagine it as a kind of continuum. At one extreme stood such purely administrative business as petitions to build roads or the repair of county buildings; at the other extreme were particular cases of violent or economic crime. But in the middle lay the great majority of the business of the court; and in the middle categories like administrative or criminal were mixed and had only a technical meaning. Much of what we think of as the criminal practice of the court fell directly within this middle ground of moral and regulatory order. In all but three of the 16 years studied for this article moral and regulatory crime (which we may take as equivalent to Blackstone's categories of "Offenses against God and religion," and "Offenses against the public health and the public police.") constituted at least 70 percent of the criminal practice of the Middlesex Sessions Court; in every year studied between 1733 and 1783 those categories made up over 80 percent of the court's criminal trials. Yet even statistics of such magnitude do not reveal the full fusion of categories in ordinary practice. As we have noted, towns were frequently prosecuted for various derelictions in their public duties: for not having a schoolmaster or for not repairing bridges or roads or a pair of stocks. Yet these towns were rarely convicted. The only function of a trial was to coerce a town to repair the conditions complained of. How to describe such a process? Was it criminal or administrative?

In fact, this continuum of criminal and administrative action seems to lie at the heart of the justification of the court, for only through a fusion of procedures could it fulfill its mandate as a court of government. It was not a disguised administrative agency. It had no way of making policy, dependent as it was on single cases for its business.[139] At most, it acted as a regulator of the actions of others. The only way that the Middlesex Sessions Court could control the

---

138. We might then think of the traditional constitutional structure of the court in terms of a separation of powers model with power divided between the presentment power of the grand jury, the power of the justices to impose recognizance and costs, and the power of petit juries to order punishments.

139. Maitland, *op. cit. supra* note 12, at pp. 447-479.

affairs of the county, to maintain the peace as it were, was through its success in hearing a wide range of different issues. Cases had to come to it. And its success as a government depended on the willingness of its public to bring matters before it for determination.

B. *The Emergence of County Administration in Massachusetts.*

By the 1790's the Middlesex Court of General Sessions of the Peace was not a court of government. Dependent on the cases that came before it, the court had become a narrowly specialized administrative agency. The court heard relatively few cases dealing with the preservation of an orderly society; prosecutions for moral and regulatory crime had declined dramatically. While the population of Middlesex County more than doubled, cases of moral and regulatory crime declined from 59 in 1733 to only two in 1793.[140] The Middlesex Sessions Court no longer conserved the peace. The continuum of governmental business — from administrative action to criminal justice — that had furnished an earlier description of its practice had been broken. Only in road building did it exercise any of its former discretionary authority.

147

What had happened to cause such a change? Perhaps the most apparent causal agent in the transformation of the court was the new control exercised by the legislature over the affairs of the court. In the new world of post-Revolutionary America there was no place for a discretionary problem solver that was not tied to the sovereign people of the whole Commonwealth.[141] The "public" for the actions of the court had become, in effect, the General Court. And there is much evidence to suggest that the Massachusetts legislatures of the 1780's and 1790's felt a sense of discomfort with the very existence of an institution formally committed to an undifferentiated conservation of the peace. During these years sessions

---

140. An even more striking contrast emerges if we group all entries made by the clerk of the court into the extended record into three categories: county administration (including care of county buildings, taxes, and accounts allowed), road construction and alteration (*not* including criminal presentments for encroachment or neglect of roads and bridges), and all other business heard by the court (criminal prosecutions, dispute settlement, regulation). In 1733 those entires displayed the following pattern:

County administration	26
Road building	4
Other	132

In 1803, by contrast, the following pattern had emerged:

County administration	27
Road building	83
Other	27

141. See Gordon Wood, *The Creation of the American Republic* (1969).

courts were stripped of much of their previous authority. The General Court denied sessions courts any role in poor relief, declared that sessions courts were obliged to accept the licensing recommendations of town selectmen, and gave the accused fornicatress an attractive (even seductive) option to confession before such a court.[142] An undifferentiated and largely autonomous judicial government of county life had become an anachronism in the Commonwealth. And the Massachusetts legislature acted directly to diminish the significance of the anachronism.

148

The clash of old and new conceptions of county government occurred most dramatically in the act passed in 1804 which took away the legal powers of sessions courts. The very idea that criminal jurisdiction could be moved from one court to another would have outraged legislators of mid-eighteenth century America. It would have been seen as a usurpation of local liberties and a dangerous centralization of power. On the other hand, we can hypothesize that for legislators of the early nineteenth century, such a shift was little more than a rationalization of the legal system of the Commonwealth. A misdemeanor case would no longer be an instrument as well as an instance of local governmental authority; it was merely an aspect of a general, state-wide system of criminal justice — a lesser form of felony case perhaps. Legal powers belonged in one place; administrative powers in another. Sessions courts did not exist to conserve a locally defined peace; rather, they were to be the administrators of a limited number of centrally defined concerns.

Yet, even as we recognize the growing centralization of authority in post-Revolutionary America, it would be a mistake to rely entirely on the emergent role of the legislature as a complete explanation for the transformation of Middlesex county government. That transformation had been underway well before the beginning of the Revolution. Between 1728 and 1748, the court had prosecuted an average of 42 criminal cases per year; between 1753 and 1773 it heard an average of fewer than 25 such cases. And almost all of that decline was in categories of moral and regulatory crime which had earlier played such a formative role in the undifferentiated government of the court (See Table 3). Neither in 1763, 1768, nor in 1773 had the Middlesex Sessions Court heard any presentments against towns for road or bridge violations. Except in settlement-removal cases, which in quantitative terms were never a large part of the court's business, the court's work as a general

142. 1788 *Acts*, c. 61 (providing for the support of the poor); 1789 *Acts*, c. 14 (defining settlement); 1786 *Acts*, c. 68 (liquor licensing); 1785 *Acts*, c. 66 (punishment of fornication).

problem solver was very limited throughout this period. In the years before the Revolution the role of a discretionary problem solver had already narrowed considerably.

TABLE

The Declining Number of Trials for Violent, Economic, and Moral-Regulatory Crime

Mean number of criminal trials for the years:

	1728, 1733, 1738, 1743, 1748	1753, 1758, 1763, 1768, 1773	1788, 1793, 1798, 1803
Violent Crime	4.2	1.6	2.25
Economic Crime	1.8	1	2
Moral-regulatory Crime	36	22	5.75

One model of what had happened to the court might be drawn from the changes that occurred over our 75-year period in the allocation of costs in criminal trials. By the 1750's the practice of automatically demanding payment of costs from the defendant had changed to a system in which the loser, whether defendant or complainant, paid. A practice which we hypothesized had functioned to encourage the intrumental use of the court had been transformed into one by which the court was pictured as a neutral dispenser of abstract justice. The court's job was not to attract business; instead it was to wait for cases to come before it. The court was to be nothing but a "legal" decisionmaker — a determiner of right and wrong.

Forty years later cost allocation practices changed again. In the late 1790's the court began routinely assuming the costs of criminal trials on the petition of the losing defendant. And we might take this as a sign that the criminal law, at least as practiced by the Middlesex court was no longer an aspect of the conservation of the peace. It was neither an instrument of general government and public regulation, nor was it a way of controlling and managing the disputes of individuals, rather, criminal law had become a mobilization of the power of the Commonwealth, a direct and special invocation of governmental power and authority, for which government would take responsibility and pay the costs.

Together these two changes in the practice of cost allocation suggest a general periodization for the history of the Middlesex sessions court in the eighteenth century. A court of government became in the 1750's and 1760's a court of law which, after the Revolution, was transformed into a specialized governmental agency. Such a three-part characterization of the history of the court has much to recommend it, if only for its evocation of the changing significance of a court of public law. As a periodization, however, this abstraction is at least partially incorrect, for during the 1750's, 1760's, and 1770's, when we might presume than the court's role as a court of law was ascendant, significant parts of its business — notably liquor licensing and fornication prosecutions — were becoming increasingly routine and standardized.

There is in fact no precise line of development in the business of the court over the second half of the eighteenth century. During that period the court lost most of the business which had at one time formed its work. But the ways in which that business was lost were not uniform.

The Middlesex Sessions Court of the first half of the eighteenth century governed by manipulating an open-ended jurisdiction, one without sharp boundaries and one in which its responsibilities were defined inclusively. After the middle of the century, by contrast, the structure of sessions court work became increasingly concrete and specific. The formal statutory jurisdiction of the court had not changed; but the spheres of action considered to be the proper responsibility of the court narrowed and rigidified. Gradually, the categories of its former practice either became routinized or were legalized and integrated into doctrinal categories that were seen as being antithetical to a court for the conservation of the peace. The destruction of an inclusive and undifferentiated practice was fatal to the maintenance of an effective judicial government of county life. The court continued to respond to public problems — transiency and the prevalence of bastards in the 1760's and 1770's, inadequate road in the 1790's. But those were problems in which the specifically administrative skills of a sessions court had proved useful.

We might say therefore that the court was redefined not just by the intervention of central authority but also as a consequence of the changing needs of its local public. The society was more complex. No single institution could be responsive to all the varying demands and claims of a diverse population. And the desires of local communities may have been less for a general court of government than for specialized and increasingly efficient administrative agencies which could take initiative and serve county needs directly.

It may also be that the needs of the local public of the Middlesex Sessions Court had changed in a more radical way. During the first half of the eighteenth century, the court had conserved the peace in part by redirecting violence and conflict into institutionally acceptable forms. It did not seek an end to conflict, but it did presume to create a structure of authority which could encompass an open-ended variety of conflicts. Such an approach to the maintenance of order in the county was presumably justified by the implausibility of actually stopping conflict and imposing "peace". Disputes were as much the result of complex and unreachable psychological needs as they were the product of rational calculation and self-interest.[143] And the work of the court prior to 1750 might stand as a public manifestation of the private needs of its public.

But during the next half century we can hypothesize that the needs of the public of the Middlesex Sessions Court changed. The decline of the "Puritan" and the rise of the "Yankee" may have meant that new private outlets were now available to release energies and conflicts that had formerly focused on the court.[144] On the one hand, a general and open-ended public law could not effectively govern the the powers and actions of private individuals. On the other hand, the attitude to regulation and the conservation of the peace revealed in the court's work during the first half of the

151

---

143. A case which demonstrates both the pathological motivations of some complainants as well as standing as a kind of transition case toward a different conception of the role of the court is the case of *Fairbanks v. Fisk and Maxwell* in 1753. Fairbanks had gone before a J.P. to accuse Fisk and Fisk's laborer Maxwell of having pulled down a portion of Fairbanks' fence, of allowing Fisk's cattle to graze on Fairbanks' hay and English grass, and "that he the complaint is afraid both by nights and by day of having some private Injury done him [and] his Substance destroyed by the said Asa and Robert . . ." Fisk and Maxwell were each fined one pound and ordered to find sureties for their good behavior.

Fisk and Maxwell then appealed to the sessions court where a new trial was held. In the course of the trial several neighbors of the litigants testified that there had never been a fence where Fairbanks claimed that the two defendants had pulled one down. Only Fairbanks and his children testified in support of his accusation, and even Fairbanks' cousin, Job Fairbanks testified that the day after the two were supposed to have knocked down the fence he saw "there was but seven Lengths and there never was no more and that was all standing but one and it joyned not to any enclosure and there was nothing inclosed by said fence . . ." Fisk and Maxwell were judged not guilty and were dismissed without paying any fees or costs. Fairbanks' son was ordered to post bond for his appearance before the Superior Court of Judicature because he was "vehemently suspected" of being guilty of perjury. *MGS Record* and *File Papers*, 9-53.

The notion of litigation as a way of releasing private anxieties and tensions is developed in John Demos, *A Little Commonwealth* (1970).

144. Richard Bushman; *From Puritan to Yankee* (1967).

eighteenth century was no longer needed as a redirection of unre-
solvable conflict. The public of the court had changed and no longer
brought it the cases that once had sahped its governmental practice.

From this perspective, the practice of the Middlesex Sessions
Court at the turn of the nineteenth century symbolizes not just the
transformation but also the failure of a particular conception of
county government. A county court of government depended on the
allegiance of a local public. But by the late eighteenth century that
allegiance was not forthcoming. The wide ranging complaints, petitions, and presentments which had once created the governmental practice of the sessions court had disappeared. County government had become an institution of limited utility and value. The
essential notion that lay behind the conservation of the peace — the
notion of a responsibility for the general corporated affairs of a
county — had become alien and implausible. A local public had
grown unresponsive to the values represented by an undifferentiated judicial government. And so that older conception of a
judicial government of county life was replaced by a bureaucratic
model of county government, by a conception of an institution responsible only for specific categories of county action and administration.[145]

152

---

145. Judicial government presumably came to an end in 1804. But that
was not the end of the legislative restructuring of county government. In
1807 courts of general sessions were replaced by courts of sessions held by a
small number of specially appointed justices rather than all of the J.P.s in a
county. 1807 *Acts*, c.11, as amended c.57. In 1809 these courts of sessions
were themselves abolished and their remaining responsibilities added to
those of the courts of common pleas. 1809 *Acts*, c.18. In 1811 courts of
sessions were reinstated. 1811 *Acts*, c.81. In 1813 all of the courts of sessions except those in Suffolk, Nantucket, and Dukes Counties were
abolished again. 1813 *Acts*, c.197. And in 1818 they were re-reinstated.
1818 *Acts*, c.120. Commissioners of highways empowered to cause roads to
be built at county expense were created in 1825. 1825 *Acts*, c.171. And in
1828, the courts of sessions were abolished for the last time. County commissioners were created to assume the responsibilities of both courts of
sessions and highway commissioners. 1827 *Acts*, c.77.

Throughout this period of turbulent structural change the actual practice
of government in Middlesex County remained constant. Aside from a small
residual criminal practice, the institution of county government was already in 1803 almost identical with what it would become by 1828—or even
1838. The jobs of the sessions court at the end of the eighteenth century and
the beginning of the nineteenth century were the same jobs performed by
the later courts of sessions and by the county commissioners. All through the
first third of the nineteenth century the records of Middlesex County reveal
a rather dull and unchanging story of roads being built, jails and court
houses repaired and reconstructed, and taxes laid. The structure of authority may have changed; the business of county government had not.

Connecticut's Villages Become Mature Towns: The Complexity of Local Institutions, 1676 to 1776

Bruce C. Daniels

153

ACCORDING to the folk cultural view of American history, the town meeting was the only major governing body in the communities of colonial New England and was an eminently democratic institution. The men met, exchanged ideas, decided policy, and elected committees and officers. What could be more democratic? Professional historians, of course, have long pointed out the inadequacy of this view, specifically in its failure to deal with restrictions on voting, family dominance, the politics of deference, oligarchical officeholding, economic power, and other factors that influenced the meeting and its officers. While sophisticated in their perception of the complexity of the problem of town meeting democracy, however, these same historians are not as sophisticated about the character of town government.[1] The debate goes on at length about the nature of local power elites and social structures, but seldom are the institutions of local government described even briefly, let alone in their full complexity. Consequently, those who have not done research in local New England history have been entitled to assume that the town meeting was a simple governing body and the only significant one beneath the county level. Those working in the field know that local

Mr. Daniels is a member of the Department of History, University of Winnipeg. He is the author of *Connecticut's First Family: William Pitkin and His Connections* (1975), and holds a Canada Council Leave Fellowship for 1976-1977. He wishes to thank Christopher Collier for his help with this essay.

[1] An exception to this criticism must be made for Michael Zuckerman's excellent analysis of Massachusetts town meetings in *Peaceable Kingdoms: New England Towns in the Eighteenth Century* (New York, 1970), 154-186. Otherwise, analyses of local institutions in New England have not improved upon Edward Channing, *Town and County Government in the English Colonies of North America,* Johns Hopkins University Studies in Historical and Political Science, 2d Ser., X (Baltimore, 1884), 5-58; G. E. Howard, *An Introduction to the Local Constitutional History of the United States: Development of the Township, Hundred, and Shire* (New York, 1889); and Charles M. Andrews, *The River Towns of Connecticut: A Study of Wethersfield, Hartford, and Windsor,* Johns Hopkins University Studies in Historical and Political Science, 7th Ser., VII-IX (Baltimore, 1889). Such seminal studies as Charles S. Grant, *Democracy in the Connecticut Frontier Town of Kent* (New York,

institutions were complex and included other significant bodies besides the town meeting, but they have not communicated this knowledge in any comprehensive fashion, probably because they themselves are not fully aware of how the various local units meshed and worked together.[2] It is the intent of this article to correct that deficiency with regard to one colony, Connecticut, over the hundred-year span before the American Revolution.

Town government in Connecticut was simple at the inception of the colony but steadily grew in complexity through the colonial period. At first, the town meeting with its officers was the only local governing body. The proprietors, who were the owners of the common land, and the society, which was the governing body of the church parish, were not distinctly separated from the town meeting. Generally, all adult white men were

---

1961); Sumner Chilton Powell, *Puritan Village: The Formation of a New England Town* (Middletown, Conn., 1963); and Kenneth A. Lockridge, *A New England Town, The First Hundred Years: Dedham, Massachusetts, 1636-1736* (New York, 1970), while perceptive in their social, economic, and political analyses, do not attempt an institutional analysis. In *Democracy in Kent*, chaps. 8 and 9, Grant hints at the importance of the problem but does not develop this beyond passing references and skeletal outlines. Historians writing in the 19th century spent more time on descriptions of local government. See Frances Manwaring Caulkins, *History of Norwich, Connecticut* (Norwich, 1873), *passim*, and Elizabeth Hubbell Schenck, *The History of Fairfield*, 2 vols. (New York, 1889-1905), *passim*. The standard reference for town government, John Fairfield Sly, *Town Government in Massachusetts, 1620-1930* (Cambridge, Mass., 1930), is not as useful as Channing, Howard, and Andrews. The best recent analyses of New England's local institutions appear in three unpublished doctoral dissertations on colonial Connecticut, but they are based on only a small number of towns and are fragmentary. See Bruce C. Daniels, "Large Town Power Structures in Eighteenth-Century Connecticut" (Ph.D. diss., University of Connecticut, 1970); Bruce P. Stark, "Lebanon, Connecticut: A Study of Society and Politics in the Eighteenth-Century" (Ph.D. diss., University of Connecticut, 1970); and William F. Willingham, "Windham, Connecticut: Profile of a Revolutionary Community, 1755-1818" (Ph.D. diss., Northwestern University, 1972).

[2] Historians now recognize that it is incorrect to speak of *the* New England town; major differences existed among types of towns as well as among towns of different colonies. See Edward M. Cook, Jr., "Local Leadership and the Typology of New England Towns, 1700-1785," *Political Science Quarterly*, LXXXVI (1971), 586-608. The present article relies heavily on four of the older large towns—Farmington, Hartford, Middletown, and Norwich—as primary examples, and on the numerous secondary sources that study either a single town or one aspect of government in several towns. For broader statements that include most towns, my sources are the statutes of the General Assembly, which, of course, applied to all towns, and a sample of 30 towns whose records have been examined. These 30 composed 36% of the colony's 84 towns and included towns of every county, size, function, and age. I have not examined all their operations of government but have catalogued the towns' officers, noted the dates when those men were first elected, counted the number of town meetings and noted the subjects the meetings dealt with, and examined the records for information on town meeting election procedures.

proprietors, and each town was coterminous with a parish. Hence, the town meeting performed duties which would later be administered by two separately functioning bodies: the proprietors and the society. The freemen, voters in colony-level elections, who would eventually constitute a fourth local self-governing body, had a collective existence apart from the town meeting, but their membership was controlled entirely by the central government, and they were therefore more an extension of the colony government than a local institution. The original form of local government was thus simple, and it was unified in the town meeting.

Beginning as early as the last quarter of the seventeenth century, this unity was broken in the older towns as the other three corporate bodies—proprietors, freemen, and ecclesiastical society—emerged as separate governing units. The differentiation of institutions was not planned by either the central government or the towns; rather, it resulted haphazardly from the growth of population within each town and from the increase in the number of towns.

155

Nowhere was the unplanned character of institutional differentiation more apparent than in the roles the proprietors played in the towns which had been founded during the colony's first thirty-five years. Unlike the Massachusetts General Court, which organized and regulated town proprietors in the 1670s and 1680s, the General Court of Connecticut did not pass legislation dealing with the proprietors until 1723.[3] The proprietors' role in local government developed indigenously before that date. The proprietors began to separate from the town meetings because, as the towns grew in population, many inhabitants who were qualified to vote at a town meeting were not proprietors. The first recorded proprietors' meeting took place in Hartford in 1665.[4] There was, however, such confusion over who was and who was not a proprietor that the town finally declared that all inhabitants who paid town rates would be considered legal proprietors.[5] Hartford thus resolved its difficulty by making the membership of the town meeting identical with that of the proprietors.

The proprietors' evolution in Middletown was more typical of the older

[3] Roy Hidemichi Akagi, *The Town Proprietors of the New England Colonies: A Study of Their Development, Organization, Activities, and Controversies, 1620-1770* (Philadelphia, 1924), 55-59. The colony government was called the General Court until 1698, when it officially divided into two houses and was renamed the General Assembly. Hence I refer to the colony government as the General Court prior to 1698 and as the General Assembly thereafter.

[4] "Hartford Town Votes, 1635-1716," Connecticut Historical Society, *Collections*, VI (Hartford, 1897), 21, 32.

[5] Anthony N. B. Garvan, *Architecture and Town Planning in Colonial Connecticut* (New Haven, 1951), 68.

towns. The first mention of them as a separate group appears in 1686, about thirty-five years after the town was settled. At that time the town meeting substituted the phrase, "the proprietors grant," for the usual "the town grants" in a land distribution. In 1696 the qualifying phrase, "the town meeting also a meeting of the proprietors," shows that, although one meeting acted for both, a need was felt to legitimize its functions by giving it both titles. In 1715 a Middletown town meeting listed the names of 176 men who were proprietors, a number probably half of the total of the eligible town meeting voters. Two years later a town meeting divided the proprietors into four geographic groups and gave each some authority in settling land problems, although major questions regarding land divisions were to be decided by all four groups together.[6] Even though divided, the proprietors still did not meet separately from the town meeting; each fourth would be polled during a town meeting for a proprietary decision relating to its section. Between 1717 and 1733 the town members would shift hats and deal with proprietary matters at the same meeting, prefacing the action by "the proprietors vote" or "the town votes," according to the nature of the business. In 1733 the town meeting ceased to act on proprietors' business, and thereafter separate proprietors' meetings were held and separate records maintained. Middletown still had a sizable parcel of undivided land, and the new proprietors met frequently in the 1730s to dispose of it. In 1734, for example, they met six times, while the town meeting met only twice. They elected a three-man proprietors' committee and a clerk in 1733. The next year, they expanded the committee to five men and elected a moderator. By 1740 the proprietors had disposed of almost all of Middletown's undivided lands, and in the 1740s they held only five meetings, all of which were one-item meetings either to deal with a specific problem or to elect an officer to replace one who had died. After 1750 the proprietors' meeting ceased to be a force in Middletown, although it continued in legal existence until 1822, when it dissolved itself.[7]

Norwich's and Farmington's proprietors evolved into separate bodies later than Middletown's. In Norwich, although the town meeting performed proprietary functions, not until 1717 did it feel the need to legitimize them by using the phrase, "the proprietors and inhabitants." In 1718 Norwich, like Middletown, divided its proprietors into four groups: East Side, West Side, Crotch of River, and Southwest.[8] However, Norwich's town meetings contin-

[6] Middletown Town Meeting Records, City Hall, Middletown, Conn., Feb. 1680, Dec. 1715 and 1717.
[7] Middletown Proprietor Records, City Hall, Middletown, Conn., 1734, *passim*. There is no evidence to indicate how the proprietors' membership was established and how exclusive it was. William Rockwell was both proprietor and town clerk, but he signed his reports in the 1734 meetings records as "proprietors' clerk."
[8] Norwich Town Meeting Records, City Hall, Norwich, Conn., Dec. 1717, May 1718.

ued to perform proprietary functions until 1733, when the proprietors began to meet separately and to maintain their own records. Farmington started to separate its proprietors in 1727, when the town meeting appointed a committee to find out "who are ye proprietors of commons."[9] In 1733 this had apparently been ascertained, and the proprietors started meeting separately and keeping separate records. By 1736 the separate identities of the two groups were so clearly established that the town meeting records mention negotiations with the proprietors.[10] The Farmington proprietors, like those of Middletown, had a flurry of activity in the 1730s, meeting forty-two times from 1733 through 1739. By 1739 all but an inconsequential fraction of the lands had been distributed, and the proprietors did not meet again until 1746 and not thereafter until 1759. They dissolved themselves in 1786, when Bristol and Berlin were split off from Farmington.

The General Assembly gave little direction to the proprietors, though it was almost certainly responsible for the sudden and complete separation of town and proprietors everywhere in 1733. The assembly in 1723 had ordered the proprietors of each town to meet, but most towns ignored the order. In 1732 the assembly repeated this order and the towns, probably perceiving that the statute was meant to be enforced, all obeyed. The 1732 act also repeated and expanded a statute of 1727 that gave the proprietors the power to "make Rates to defray the necessary Charges" arising from their new responsibilities.[11] Most proprietors elected a clerk, a treasurer, a surveyor, and a proprietors' committee of three to seven members.[12] These elections, unlike those of the towns, were not annual; rather, the officers served either until they died or, though more rarely, until someone expressed dissatisfaction with their performance and asked for a new election.

A fundamental difference existed between the town proprietors of the seventeenth century and those of the eighteenth. In general, early seventeenth-century proprietors were residents who received their land free from the General Court, while those of the late seventeenth and early eighteenth centuries were speculators who bought the land from the assembly and frequently did not reside in the new towns.[13] The Narragansett War in 1675 divides the two periods. During the war a large tract of land east of the Connecticut River came into the possession of a small but influential number of speculators, who persuaded the assembly that the planting of towns would

157

[9] Farmington Proprietor Records, in Farmington Town Meeting Records, Town Hall, Farmington, Conn., I, Apr. 1727.
[10] Farmington Recs., Dec. 1736.
[11] J. Hammond Trumbull and Charles J. Hoadley, eds., *The Public Records of the Colony of Connecticut* (Hartford, 1850-1890), VII, 379, 137, hereafter cited as *Conn. Col. Recs.*
[12] Akagi, *Town Proprietors*, 63-66.
[13] *Ibid.*, 46.

furnish an investment opportunity for private citizens as well as income for
the colony.[14] In one example of proprietary speculation, 105,793 acres,
obtained from Massachusetts after a border dispute, were sold in 1716 at
auction by the assembly to William Pitkin, representing a group of in-
vestors.[15] These men surveyed the town site, built roads for it, and then
resold the land to settlers for a profit.[16] In 1737, however, the assembly
required every town proprietor to build a house on his land and fence at least
six acres within two years, and these stipulations usually prevented absentee
proprietors from owning land in a town after that period.[17]

158

There were two other major differences between the proprietors of early
seventeenth-century towns and those of towns founded after 1675. The later
communities differentiated town meetings and proprietary meetings from the
outset. In addition, beginning with Lebanon in the 1690s, the later towns
were settled in non-nucleated fashion, with most of the land parceled out
early.[18] Seventeenth-century proprietors had divided their lands more slowly;
some of them husbanded it over a one-hundred-year period. Among the
younger towns, however, Kent divided 32,000 of its 50,000 acres within the
first two years of its existence, and in Lebanon the proprietors distributed
virtually all of the land by 1730.[19] When they divided the land, they let their
powers go as well, so that in most of the eighteenth-century towns proprietors
were operationally defunct after twenty or thirty years, even though they
were still important in older towns like Farmington, Norwich, and Middletown in the 1730s when these towns were almost one hundred years old. But
even in the old towns most proprietors, carried along by the speculative
mania of the 1730s, gave away their powers through land divisions.

Because freemanship involved less complex duties and obligations, and

[14] Richard L. Bushman, *From Puritan to Yankee: Character and the Social Order in Connecticut, 1690-1765* (Cambridge, Mass., 1967), 83-85.
[15] Akagi, *Town Proprietors*, 181, 182.
[16] The standard authorities on New England and Connecticut proprietors believe that many Connecticut towns settled in the 18th century experienced contests between resident proprietors and absentee proprietors who still owned land within the town. See *ibid.*, 130-133, and Garvan, *Architecture and Town Planning*, 65-68. In the case of at least one Connecticut town, Kent, this struggle has been exaggerated. In Kent, although 25 to 41 men who bought proprietary shares never lived in the town, most of the absentee proprietors sold their shares quickly to residents. Thirty-two of Kent's first 40 settlers were proprietors, and even though many Kent settlers complained of being victimized by absentee proprietors, their real aim was to delay payments to the General Assembly or the original proprietors. Grant, *Democracy in Kent*, 15-20.
[17] Grant, *Democracy in Kent*, 21.
[18] Garvan, *Architecture and Town Planning*, 66.
[19] Grant, *Democracy in Kent*, 15; Stark, "Lebanon," 349.

required a less formal structure, than the proprietary, the development of the freemen as an organized body proceeded more uniformly. Connecticut, unlike Massachusetts, never required freemen to be church members but did require them to possess property of a certain value. The qualification was high at first—£30 in personal property—but was lowered to £10 estate in land in 1675.[20]

The early system, whereby prospective freemen had to travel to Hartford and be personally admitted by the General Court, was always burdensome for the individual seeking freemanship, and it became onerous for the court as the population of Connecticut grew. In 1678 the court met this problem by instructing the town selectmen to certify that each person applying to the court for freemanship met the property requirement and was of "honest, peaceable, and civil conversation."[21] Since the deputies would admit the applicant if they were satisfied with the selectmen's recommendation, control of the admission of freemen was thus shifted in practice to the town, although in theory it remained with the central government.[22] The laws regarding freemanship did not change until 1729, when the formal power of admission was transferred to the freemen of each town, owing to the administrative difficulty of central control.[23] In actuality, after this date the freemen usually delegated the admitting power to the selectmen, even though the selectmen were officers not of the freemen but of the town, which included the inhabitants as well. The selectmen met a few hours in advance of the freemen's meeting, examined oral applications for freemanship, and admitted those whom they found satisfactory. The assembly specified that the town clerk must record in writing the names of all new freemen.[24]

Until recently, historians commonly estimated that as few as 10 percent of the eligible adult white males were actually freemen.[25] It appears, however, that with the transfer of control over freemanship from the colony to

159

---

[20] David H. Fowler, "Connecticut's Freemen: The First Forty Years," *William and Mary Quarterly*, 3d Ser., XV (1958), 313-315.

[21] *Conn. Col. Recs.*, III, 24.

[22] Since it was not a requirement for a town selectman to be a freeman, a non-freeman selectman could theoretically recommend someone for freemanship. It is doubtful, however, that any selectman was ever not a freeman.

[23] *Conn. Col. Recs.*, VII, 250.

[24] The process is described in Grant, *Democracy in Kent*, 109.

[25] Many of the low estimates of freemanship stem from historians' acceptance of Ezra Stiles's remark that only one out of nine Connecticut men could vote. See Oscar Zeichner, *Connecticut's Years of Controversy* (Chapel Hill, N. C., 1949), 8, and George C. Groce, Jr., *William Samuel Johnson, Maker of the Constitution* (New York, 1937), 54. Lawrence Henry Gipson, *Jared Ingersoll: A Study of American Loyalism in Relation to British Colonial Government* (New Haven, Conn., 1920), 19, rejects Stiles's estimate and suggests that freemen may have numbered slightly higher than 25% of the adult white male population.

the locality the number of freemen increased. After 1729 in Farmington, Norwich, Lebanon, Kent, East Haddam, and East Guilford, 52, 47, 54, 51, 64, and 79 percent, respectively, of those eligible were admitted as freemen.[26] The cluster of the first four towns—differing in age, size, and location—at about 50 percent suggests that this was perhaps an average, even though East Haddam and East Guilford show that the percentage could go much higher. In all of these towns, however, at least 70 percent of the population could have qualified economically for freemanship, and admission after 1729 seemed almost effortless.[27] The actual figures were much lower undoubtedly because many men who lived a long distance from the meetinghouse did not normally attend meetings. The farther away a man lived, the less likely he was to be a freeman.[28] Connecticut towns were large geographically, and it was not unusual for an "outliving man" to have to walk ten or so miles over poor roads to attend a meeting—a formidable undertaking even in good weather.[29] Substantiating the thesis that many men did not think free-manship worth a tiring walk is the fact that admissions were always much higher in years of turmoil and controversy, when political interest might be aroused. From 1761 through 1765 Farmington admitted only twenty-six men, but forty in 1766, the year of the Stamp Act election. After declining to four in 1767 and seven in 1768, the number jumped to thirty-seven in 1770, the year of the next close colony-wide election.[30] Many of the qualified men who were not freemen were young men in their twenties who almost certainly would seek admission when political events touched them closely.

The freemen met twice a year—in the first week of April and of September. At each session they elected two deputies to the assembly. To

160

[26] Figures for Farmington are based on calculations made from the Freeman's List, Farmington Recs., 1730; for Norwich see Daniels, "Large Town Power Structures," 134; for Lebanon see Stark, "Lebanon," 208; for Kent see Grant, *Democracy in Kent*, iii; for East Haddam and East Guilford see Chilton Williamson, *American Suffrage from Property to Democracy, 1760-1860* (Princeton, N. J., 1960), 27.
[27] Grant, *Democracy in Kent*, iii; Stark, "Lebanon," 208, 209; Daniels, "Large Town Power Structures," Appendix I.
[28] Stark, "Lebanon," 217-219; Grant, *Democracy in Kent*, 113.
[29] All of Connecticut's early towns were larger than the 36-square-mile township which folk culture enshrines as the typical American town. Farmington, Norwich, Lebanon, and Kent were approximately 100, 96, 77, and 50 square miles, respectively, in 1776. Today eight whole towns and parts of three other towns have been carved from the original Farmington. East Haddam and East Guilford were former societies in other towns, and at 58 and 36 square miles, respectively, in 1776 were smaller than most Connecticut towns. This probably accounts for their higher percentage of freeman.
[30] In Farmington Recs. freemen are entered after the Dec. 1691 meeting. Stark, "Lebanon," 205, and Grant, *Democracy in Kent*, 113, also point this out.

emphasize that the freemen's meeting was legally distinct from the town meeting, the town meeting of Middletown addressed a petition to the Middletown freemen asking their deputies to act also as agents for the town. Similarly, Sharon's town meeting authorized the freemen's deputies to argue a case for Sharon at the next assembly.[31] In both instances, the deputies were not representatives of the town government specifically but of the freemen alone, and a special deputation of powers was required for them to act for the town.

At the September meeting each freeman could vote for up to twenty men as nominees collectively for governor, deputy governor, and assistants. The constable of each town tallied the votes and forwarded them to the colony secretary, who announced at the October session of the assembly the names of the top twenty vote-getters for the entire colony. At the April freemen's meeting each freeman could vote for one of these nominees as governor, one as deputy governor, and twelve as assistants. The results were announced at the May session of the assembly.[32] Many towns took advantage of the gathering of the freemen in April to hold a town meeting on "freemen's day," but to emphasize the separate character of the two meetings, the freemen's meeting was held in the morning and the town meeting in the afternoon.

Society government came into existence only when a town was divided into two or more parishes; in towns that had only one church the town meeting administered the parish. Societies increased markedly in the eighteenth century as parishes divided. In 1708, the year of the Saybrook Platform, there were forty-three parishes in thirty-three towns, but between 1708 and 1740, eighty-six new parishes were created while only thirty new towns were founded. Since the population of the colony increased 400 percent during that same period, the average number of inhabitants per parish rose from 380 to 760. By 1760, 187 parishes existed in seventy-one towns, and the population probably averaged 1,000 per parish. Only very small or very new towns had but one parish and therefore no society government, whereas large towns usually had five or six by the end of the colonial period.[33]

Until the 1720s societies were allowed to develop unstructured by central

[31] Middletown Recs., Mar. 1774; Sharon Town Meeting Records, Town Hall, Sharon, Conn., Oct. 1755.
[32] The whole process is described in *Conn. Col. Recs.*, IV, 11, 12.
[33] These numbers are based on Samuel H. Rankin, Jr., "Conservatism and the Problem of Change in the Congregational Churches of Connecticut, 1660-1760" (Ph.D. diss., Kent State University, 1971), 116, 117. Also see Bushman, *From Puritan to Yankee*, Appendix I. Hillel Schwartz, in "Admissions to Full Communion in the Congregational Churches of Connecticut" (typescript), Conn. Hist. Soc., Hartford, estimates that the average population of the societies in 1740 was approximately 850.

authority; thereafter, their functions were outlined by the assembly. Society voters had to be either freemen or full communicants of the church. A man might be a town voter but not a society voter. Societies were empowered by the assembly in 1728 to levy rates, choose officers, erect meetinghouses, hire ministers, and regulate society schools.[34] Law followed custom, for the societies were already performing all these functions. Beyond these broad delegations of powers there were no specific instructions. The assembly, for instance, did not stipulate what officers should be elected or what particular duties they should have. In practice most of the societies set up positions similar to some of those of the first towns. Once established, society government grew little, unlike the rapidly expanding government of the town meeting. Most societies elected a three-member governing board called the society committee, a clerk, a treasurer, two raters, and perhaps a three- or five-man school committee.[35] Although as early as the 1640s some town meetings chose a moderator, it was society government that regularized this practice.

Only the assembly could create a new society. It usually did so for one of two reasons. First, when one part of a town was geographically distant from the town center, and when that distant part acquired enough inhabitants to make a society viable, it might seek society status in order to bring neighborhood government and church services closer to home. Second, a society might become split in a dispute over doctrinal matters, the location of the meetinghouse, or the hiring of a new minister; if the split became irreconcilable, the minority might petition the assembly for separate society status.[36] Dissidents who sought a new society were usually opposed by the parent one, for old societies were reluctant to lose any sizable part of their tax base. In these cases the assembly would almost always appoint an ad hoc arbitration committee of three or four assistants and deputies. The location of a new meetinghouse was a common cause of dissension; even a distance of one or two miles could provoke bitter strife. Lebanon societies built eight meetinghouses in the eighteenth century; assembly arbitration was requested for six of them. Selecting a minister also caused frequent quarrels. Societies and candidates usually agreed that a majority vote for a new minister was not sufficient grounds for calling him to "settle amoung us." Unanimity was always striven for.[37]

[34] *Conn. Col. Recs.*, VII, 211. Most schools in towns with more than one parish were society schools, although in the larger towns the town meeting administered grammar schools.
[35] A good discussion of the structure of a society can be found in Stark, "Lebanon," 151.
[36] The best discussion of the controversies that created new societies is in Bushman, *From Puritan to Yankee*, 147-232. Also see Rankin, "Conservatism and the Problem of Change," *passim.*
[37] Stark, "Lebanon," 85, 88-92.

162

Religious and political questions were closely intertwined in the functions of a society, since the issues the society dealt with—building a meeting-house, hiring and paying a minister, running schools, and enforcing proper social conduct—while essentially political, were separated from religion only with difficulty. The distinction the colonists drew, however, was that the minister and church elders alone, as distinct from the society meeting, handled matters concerning doctrine, the covenant, and church membership and discipline. Ultimately, of course, the minister and elders could be replaced by action of a society meeting.[38]

Congregational localism assured the society a large measure of auton-omy, although it was always subject to interference from the town and the assembly.[39] When societies did ask for arbitration or had it forced upon them from above, they might reject the result and defy the assembly as the Amity Society of New Haven did when it rejected the assembly's choice of a site for a new meetinghouse on the grounds that the assembly was prejudiced. The efforts of the assembly were of limited value in solving local problems unless the society cooperated. Guilford did not ask for arbitration of a controversy concerning the selection of a minister, and when the assembly appointed a committee the society indignantly refused to acquiesce on the grounds that the assembly had no jurisdiction. The religious controversies of the 1740s not only shook the colony and splintered many societies but intensified societal autonomy. There is strong evidence, for instance, that the famous General Assembly law of 1742 that banned itinerant preachers was disobeyed in mass by the societies. The eighteenth-century movement in Connecticut toward a more pluralistic view of religion made central control of society affairs more difficult. One student of the subject believes that the victor in the religious disputes was "neither the New Lights nor the Old Lights but the local congregation, whose power was secured." Decisions from above were usually made only at the request of a society, and they were viewed "as merely advisory opinions" which could be accepted or rejected.[40]

163

The town meeting in the mature towns elected officers, appointed committees, and ratified decisions made by the town officers. Usually it was not an active part of the decision-making process, but in almost every town at some point in the eighteenth century a controversy propelled the town meeting into action as the forum not only for airing the controversy but also

[38] *Ibid.*, 28.
[39] Rankin, "Conservatism and the Problem of Change," 110, 111, shows that the churches managed to retain a great deal of individual autonomy even under the Saybrook Platform, which was designed to enforce uniformity, through county associations, upon an increasingly pluralistic religious structure.
[40] These details of the societies' independence are from Rankin, "Conservatism and the Problem of Change," 110, 111, 150-152, 246, 247, 316, 317.

for settling it. It was normal for a town to hold one, two, or three perfunctory meetings a year for a twenty-year period, then suddenly hold as many as eight significant meetings in a single year, and then return to its previous composure. Most new towns held frequent meetings, often as many as ten or twelve a year, but once the difficult task of setting up a town was accomplished, the meetings declined to three or fewer in normal years. Although the meeting usually chose not to involve itself in decision-making beyond electing officers, its frequent flurries of activity during controversies left no doubt where internal power ultimately lay.[41]

164

In most towns the only important meeting in a normal year was the one held in December to elect town officers. It often lasted two days and occasionally part of a third. If other meetings were held, they were often one-item meetings of short duration. Many towns held their second meeting on freemen's day in April to choose officers to replace any who had resigned, left town, or died. A third meeting was occasionally held, perhaps to appoint a special committee or to ratify some especially important decision by the selectmen. It was not rare for a town to hold only the December meeting; many towns went four or five consecutive years with only one meeting a year.

The temper of the town meeting depended on whether it was held under normal circumstances or had become politicized by local controversy. Under normal circumstances lack of attendance was often a problem. The Hartford annual meeting of 1769 adjourned for a week after merely selecting a moderator who then declared attendance too low to conduct any further elections. Waterbury, plagued by poor turnouts at town meetings during the 1740s and frequently forced to adjourn for that reason, tried to solve its problem by starting the meeting at 10 A.M. instead of 9 A.M. In Sharon, where inhabitants frequently refused to attend meetings on cold winter days, meetings were postponed "considering the extremity of the weather and the fewness of the people," and "on account of the great coldness of the season." When the Norwich meeting of August 1715 voted on a previously unannounced issue, twenty-five votes constituted a majority. The attendance must have been less than fifty in a town that had at least 2,500 inhabitants. In a petition to the next meeting thirty-two men complained that the calling for this vote was a "surprise" and stated that while they normally did not attend meetings, they would have done so had they known the vote was to be taken.[42]

[41] Connecticut's example of town meeting frequency suggests either that the pattern of the increased activity in two Massachusetts towns, described by Kenneth A. Lockridge and Alan Kreider, "The Evolution of Massachusetts Town Government, 1640 to 1740," *WMQ*, 3d Ser., XXIII (1966), 549-574, was unique to Massachusetts or that the two towns were atypical.

[42] Waterbury Town Meeting Records, City Hall, Waterbury, Conn., Dec. 1754; Sharon Recs., Dec. 1763, Jan. 1767, and Dec. 1776; Norwich Recs., Sept. 1716.

Meetings ranged from small quiet affairs with little debate to highly charged sessions almost impossible to control. In 1729, apparently in response to rowdy meetings, the assembly passed a law forbidding tumults and riotous behavior at them.[43] After one such meeting in Middletown the town voted that no one should "interrupt the meeting by disorderly speaking." In a 1709 election meeting in Farmington a committee was named to "keep the youth in order during the meeting." Most communities recorded votes with the succinct expression, "the town votes," but occasionally they would preface this with "after much deliberation" or "after great discourse," indicating a more than usually heated debate. Middletown recorded tallies "by unanimous vote" often for periods as long as ten years and then would distinguish a rare vote as "by majority vote." During the 1720s and 1750s Ridgefield usually recorded votes as unanimous—"yea universally" one clerk wrote—but during the 1730s and 1740s the town had a long series of votes which were "by major vote," indicating that town consensus, while desired, could break down for protracted periods. Voting on issues was frequently oral, but towns could go to great lengths to protect the anonymity of voters on sensitive questions. Norwich, in a secret ballot which was tailored so that even illiterates could vote, specified that marks on a ballot meant that a minister should be let go while a blank ballot meant that he should be kept.[44]

165

The election of town officers was the main business of the annual meeting after the founding years. Election procedures were never codified either by the General Assembly or by any town in its written records. From indirect and occasional evidence in the records we can surmise that procedures varied both from town to town and within towns. In 1712 Middletown proposed that the three selectmen be chosen "by nomination and then voting upon nomination." This was defeated, and instead the town voted by "papers." Five years later, Middletown chose officers by "nomination and by lifting the hand." The moderator instructed the meeting to "shout to nominate." Still a third method in Middletown was used for the election of selectmen in 1720. The voters queued up and each gave a name orally to the clerk, who declared a man elected when he had a majority of the meeting. Other towns employed this oral system, but if someone requested it the vote would be by "proxies" (written ballots). Although discussion of voting procedures was only occasionally recorded, and discussion of qualifications of candidates was never recorded, elections must have involved some debate.

[43] *Conn. Col. Recs.*, VII, 245.

[44] Middletown Recs., 1700-1720, esp. Dec. 1702; Farmington Recs., Dec. 1709; Ridgefield Town Meeting Records, Town Hall, Ridgefield, Conn., Dec. 1722, and 1720s-1750s, *passim;* Norwich Recs., Aug. 1715.

Election meetings lasted from nine or ten in the morning to four in the afternoon, and usually took at least two days.[45]

An election system known to have been utilized by several towns may have been widespread and could explain how the meeting handled the election of large numbers of officers. In 1765 the Farmington moderator told the selectmen "to bring in their nominations of town officers to the meeting *as usual.*" The selectmen must have prepared a slate of officers in advance. The meeting could add or subtract nominations, but the consistency of Farmington's officeholding patterns supports the view that a small group of men constantly controlled them. The Newtown meeting voted that the "selectmen shall nominate the selectmen" for the following year; Ridgefield "disapproved of the nominations published"; and Norwalk "brought in nominations"—all suggesting that a small group of men, usually the selectmen, nominated officeholders in advance. As further evidence supporting this hypothesis, elections were smooth and seldom contested after the fact. In five of seven towns examined—Fairfield, Hartford, Kent, Lebanon, and Middletown—there were no controverted elections during the eighteenth century; the other two towns in the sample, Farmington and Norwich, each had but one.[46]

In the founding years, when the town meeting was the sole local governing body, it elected at its annual meeting three or five selectmen who were the key executive officers, two constables who enforced the law, a clerk who kept the records, two ratemakers who assessed property for tax purposes, two surveyors of highways who maintained roads, two to four fenceviewers who inspected and maintained fences, and two or three packers and sealers who inspected local produce and certified its salable quality. These offices, though created by the General Assembly, were responses to practical local problems, and many towns elected an additional officer or two to answer other local needs.[47]

[45] Middletown Recs., Dec. 1712, 1717, and 1720; Ridgefield Recs., Dec. 1722, 1749, and 1751; Branford Town Meeting Records, Town Hall, Branford, Conn., Oct. 1781 and 1782; Norwich Recs., Feb. 1702.

[46] Farmington Recs., Dec. 1765 (italics mine); Newtown Town Meeting Records, Town Hall, Newtown, Conn., Dec. 1766; Ridgefield Recs., Dec. 1772; Norwalk Town Meeting Records, City Hall, Norwalk, Conn., Dec. 1748, 1752, and 1756; Farmington Recs., Dec. 1702; Norwich Recs., Dec. 1728, and adjourned meeting of Dec. 1728.

[47] Bruce C. Daniels, "Town Government in Connecticut, 1636-1675: The Founding of Institutions," *Connecticut Review* (1975), 39-40, points out that the colony government created most of the first town offices and was responsible for the similarity of all towns' institutions. However, Thomas W. Jodziewicz, "Dual Localism in Seventeenth-Century Connecticut: Relations between the General Court and the Towns, 1636-1691" (Ph.D. diss., College of William and Mary, 1974), shows that despite the colony government's formal control, local governments often resisted

The three major officers of the early towns were the selectmen, the constables, and the clerk. The selectmen had both judicial and executive functions; they served as judges in the lowest courts in the colony, with jurisdiction over petty criminal and civil cases, provided that neither the suit nor the fine exceeded forty shillings. In a Puritan colony, where men and women were concerned with their neighbors' morals, the selectmen, along with the constables, had the obligation of ensuring that each person's conduct conformed to social expectations. The constable supervised the "watch" and provided for the town's security, collected the colony tax, and arrested those who broke colony or town laws. The clerk, while not often involved in major decision-making, was of crucial importance; he was ordered by the assembly to "keep an entry of all grants, deeds of sale or mortgages of lands, and all marriages, births, deaths, and other writings brought to you and deliver copies when required." To the joy of historians, most clerks performed their duties well.[48]

As the towns grew in size and complexity, the kinds and numbers of officers needed to administer their affairs increased correspondingly. Much of the increase resulted from additions to the numbers of such officers as fenceviewers and surveyors of highways, required by expansion of settlement to the outer geographic limits of the towns. In addition, several new offices were created. Their functions were outlined by town practice and by the assembly.

The position of grandjuryman offers an interesting example of the evolution of a local office. In 1666 the General Court created four counties—Fairfield, Hartford, New Haven, and New London—each of which was a judicial unit presided over by a county court. In 1667 the General Court ordered each county court to appoint a "grand jury of twelve able men at least" from among the towns. These grandjurymen were to meet once a year with their county court and "make presentments of the breaches of any law."[49] They could also at any time make a presentment of a breach of law to a local justice of the peace, a magistrate appointed by the colony government. Most towns had at least one justice, who assumed the local judicial duties exercised earlier by the selectmen; large towns sometimes had two or more.

the direction of the central government, so that the two levels were "partners in localism." Zuckerman, *Peaceable Kingdoms*, argues that Massachusetts's central government closely controlled the towns until the loss of the original charter, whereas both Powell, *Puritan Village*, and Lockridge, *A New England Town*, present a model of greater town autonomy in Massachusetts. T. H. Breen, "Persistent Localism: English Social Change and the Shaping of New England Institutions," *WMQ*, 3d Ser., XXXII (1975), 3-28, notes that there was a tension between colony and local authorities. This probably was also true for Connecticut.
[48] Andrews, *River towns*, 110-112; *Conn. Col. Recs.*, II, 281, III, 53.
[49] *Ibid.*, II, 61.

Over the next forty-five years the General Court added to the grand-juryman's duties, making him a social constable in each town. Grandjurymen were required to assist the selectmen and constables in maintaining order and assuring high standards of moral conduct. At sessions between 1667 and 1712 the assembly frequently enjoined the selectmen, constables, and grand-jurymen to watch out for unacceptable social or moral behavior.[50] These injunctions were issued in Connecticut at the same time that Massachusetts took similar action. This is, of course, the period in which historians have seen the falling away of many people from strict Puritan codes of behavior. In 1679 Massachusetts created the local office of tithingman for each town to help combat this moral decay.[51] Grandjurymen were the Connecticut General Court's answer to the same problem. But unlike the Massachusetts tithingman, who was elected by the town meeting, the Connecticut grand-juryman was appointed by the county court. In 1712, however, the assembly ordered all towns to elect at least two grandjurymen a year, and at the December 1712 annual meetings all the towns complied. Grandjurymen were thus incorporated into the operating structure of every town.[52]

Similarly, the office of tithingman, borrowed from Massachusetts, was created by the General Assembly in 1721 to combat moral laxity. Hartford began electing tithingmen in that year, and many towns did the same in 1722 and 1723. From then on, the assembly always included tithingmen when it issued annual pronouncements about social control to town officers. It instructed the tithingmen to "carefully inspect the behavior of all persons on the Sabbath or Lord's Day" and to make "due presentment of any propha-nation." By 1732 all the towns were electing tithingmen, who assumed the same constabulary functions that grandjurymen had originally performed. Neither the tithingmen nor the grandjurymen were given additional duties (although the grandjurymen's duties at the county courts were elaborated) until 1761, when they were instructed by the assembly to meet with the constables once a year in June to discuss provisions for the effective enforce-ment of local morality.[53] This was a last and anachronistic institutional attempt to preserve the old moral facade of the Puritan village.

The town offices of lister and rater, although originally created by the assembly, developed their functions in response to local needs, and in a variety of ways. In the early seventeenth century the towns were ordered to elect ratemakers who assessed all townspeople's wealth for tax purposes. Originally, the selectmen, not the ratemakers, set the tax rates. Between 1675

168

[50] *Ibid.*, III-V, *passim.*
[51] Herbert B. Adams, *Saxon Tithing-men in America,* Johns Hopkins University Studies in Historical and Political Science, 1st Ser., IV (Baltimore, 1883), 8.
[52] *Conn. Col. Recs.*, V, 324.
[53] *Ibid.*, VI, 277, XI, 499.

and 1700, however, ratemakers took over that function in most towns. In some they kept the name of ratemakers, and in others they were newly designated as "listers and raters" or "list makers and rate makers." Between 1700 and 1720 some towns began to elect separate "listers" and "raters," while others still kept the functions combined. These changes took place without any interference by the General Assembly. Although the assembly did finally decree in 1724 that each town must elect between four and nine listers,[54] the towns still took eclectic approaches to the creation of financial officers. A few towns elected financial auditors such as the inspectors of Hartford and the auditors of Middletown, to whom the listers and raters were directed to report.[55]

169

The offices of moderator and treasurer were both shaped more by local needs than by enactments of the General Assembly. In the early years of the seventeenth century a selectman performed the functions of each position. Gradually, with no prodding by the legislature, the towns began to elect treasurers. Hartford chose its first treasurer in 1706, and by 1749, when Fairfield elected its first, the practice had become general. The moderator's office evolved similarly. In the founding years most towns did not designate a moderator, although Windsor did so as early as 1642. Instead, one of the selectmen usually presided over the meeting. Between 1680 and 1720, however, virtually every town began electing moderators, who might or might not be selectmen. Practice varied because the central government never prescribed rules concerning moderators. For instance, while in most towns the moderator was elected for a single meeting, Fairfield named its moderator to serve for a number of meetings in a year. Theoretically, the moderator was not presiding over two meetings but over two parts of an adjourned meeting. However, the two sessions were often months apart and may have considered totally different business. Middletown elected its first moderator in 1708, stopped electing the officer in 1712, and started again in 1720; Derby elected one man to serve continually as moderator during the town's pleasure.[56]

As grandjurymen, tithingmen, raters and listers, moderators, and treasurers were added to the roster of town officers, the number grew to sometimes staggering proportions, further increased by the addition of

---

[54] *Ibid.*, VI, 463, 464.

[55] See election meeting records in Hartford Town Meeting Records, City Hall, Hartford, Conn., 1721-1729, *passim*, and Middletown Recs., Dec. 1737.

[56] *Some Early Records and Documents of and Relating to the Town of Windsor, Connecticut, 1639-1703* (Hartford, 1930), Dec. 1642; Fairfield Town Meeting Records, Town Hall, Fairfield, Conn., 1734, 1756, *passim;* Middletown Recs., 1708, 1712-1719, 1720; Derby Town Meeting Records, City Hall, Derby, Conn., Dec. 1707.

branders, key keepers, rate collectors, and sealers. Not only were new officers added, but each multiple office had its numbers expanded. Towns averaged fifty to sixty officers in 1725, sixty to seventy in 1750, and seventy-five to ninety in 1776. Two separate phenomena were probably at work in this expansion: larger towns required larger administrations, and increased population produced more aspirants for office. Farmington, in what must have been an attempt to involve as many men as possible in town government, elected 206 in 1776. These included, in addition to the clerk and the treasurer, seven selectmen, twenty-two grandjurymen, twenty-two listers, ten constables, twenty-five tithingmen, fifty surveyors of highways, seven leather sealers, seven weight sealers, nine measure sealers, sixteen fenceviewers, eight key keepers, seven branders, nine collectors for rates, one packer, and four ratemakers.[57] It should be noted, however, that Farmington had the largest square mileage of any Connecticut town, and with 6,069 inhabitants it was the third most populous town in the 1774 census.

It was clearly growth that caused the proliferation of local deliberative bodies and their offices. The proprietors came into existence as a separate group as a town's population grew to include many nonproprietors. The societies were constituted because the growth of both population and divergent religious opinions created a need to divide parishes. The method of admitting new freemen was decentralized because the increase in size and number of towns precluded a central admission policy. It was necessary to have many town meeting officers—grandjurymen, tithingmen, listers, raters, moderators, and treasurers—because the growth in population and the diffusion from a nucleated center to outlying farmsteads made it impossible for the selectmen personally to perform all of these functions. Other town officers, such as surveyors of highways and fenceviewers, became much more numerous because expansion to the outer edges of the towns placed new demands upon the services which the towns provided.

As local government grew, the selectmen exercised increased authority. The assembly passed more and more general enabling acts delegating greater discretionary powers to the selectmen. As noted above, in 1690 the selectmen were given supervisory power over all other town officers and were told "to take cognizance of such as do neglect the duties of surveyor, hayward, fenceviewer," and so forth. In 1703 the assembly passed an act providing the selectmen with broad military power "to order what houses shall be fortified and what they do order shall be done forthwith." In 1708 they were delegated the extremely important power to levy a tax whenever the town's finances required it. An act of 1719 gave the selectmen virtually carte blanche

[57] Farmington Recs., Dec. 1776.

power over the administration of local welfare. An unusual grant of authority in 1715 permitted them to reduce or eliminate an individual's colony rate if, in their judgment, it constituted a hardship. Acts of the assembly passed in 1775 and 1776 enhanced the ability of the selectmen to deal with the problems of civil strife. They could issue warrants against suspected loyalists and confiscate the estate of anyone deemed a partisan of Britain. All persons who traveled between towns had to carry letters from their selectmen. Charles Grant's study of Kent led him to conclude that much of the local war effort in that town was directed by the selectmen.[58]

The authority of the selectmen was expanded not only by enabling acts from above but also by delegations from the town meeting. When Hartford elected new officers in 1706, the meeting directed them to report to the selectmen. In Farmington in 1708 the meeting gave the selectmen total control of town finances in a sweeping delegation of power and later empowered them to act as the town's agents in such external matters as relations with the assembly or with other towns. The Norwalk meeting in 1702 and again in 1704 put its weight behind the selectmen in all their decisions between meetings. As we have seen, in several towns, perhaps in most, the selectmen nominated all town officers, and in some they prepared an agenda for the town meeting. In Norwich, in the 1740s and 1750s, the many problems for which the town usually named ad hoc committees were turned over to the selectmen, and the number of such committees steadily declined.[59] Selectmen, although officers only of the town meeting, became involved in the affairs of the proprietors, the freemen, and the societies. They were the institutional factor that integrated all of the complex local structures and made them work. The assembly in 1713 gave the selectmen the right to judge land disputes; they had practical control over the admission of freemen; and they frequently stepped into society affairs when societies became embroiled in controversies.[60] Although the three other local deliberative bodies were clearly differentiated from the town meeting, the selectmen nevertheless exercised influence over them and kept them *a part of* town government, not *apart from* it.

171

[58] *Conn. Col. Recs.*, IV, 32, 455, V, 73, VI, 112, XII, 255, XV, 193-194; Charles J. Hoadly, ed., *The Public Records of the State of Connecticut*, I (Hartford, 1894), 228. Grant's study of Kent strongly supports the conclusions of this paragraph. The Revolutionary effort in Kent was mainly directed by the selectmen. Grant, *Democracy in Kent*, 134, 135. During the Revolutionary years the activities of the town meeting and of the selectmen greatly increased. The Revolution was obviously a "crisis" situation that politicized the town meeting.
[59] Hartford Recs., Dec. 1706; Farmington Recs., Dec. 1708; Norwalk Recs., Feb. 1702, Dec. 1709; Farmington Recs., Apr. 1710, Dec. 1736.
[60] *Conn. Col. Recs.*, V, 403; Rankin, "Conservatism and the Problem of Change," 169.

Other factors also served to integrate the elements of local government. Since the selectmen were the creatures of the town meeting and the meeting became a vital forum during controversies, it could also bind the structure together. Moreover, many persons were members of all four different organizations in a single town, and solutions to problems must often have been hammered out by the same men in four different forums. In most towns many large families were knit together in kinship networks that provided great cohesion. Nor should the widespread practice of multiple officeholding be overlooked. Frequently, a single individual held proprietary, society, and town offices simultaneously, and the freemen's deputies invariably held other local offices as well.[61] Leadership was indivisible, and leaders were expected to serve the public good in all the bodies of local government. All of these factors helped the selectmen to ensure that the meetings and offices that proliferated to meet the needs of rapidly growing towns did not result in fragmented local governments that might well have frustrated efforts to meet those needs.

The effects of the differentiation of local government on the townspeople and on town politics are not the concern of this inquiry. It may be, however, that institutional differentiation militated against other trends in the society of eighteenth-century Connecticut. From recent quantitative and demographic work on New England a picture is emerging of increasing social stratification, leading to the supposition that townspeople were becoming progressively alienated. Town populations grew; the gap between the wealthiest and poorest members of society increased; land became critically scarce; wealthy families grew in prestige and power, while younger sons of other families were forced to leave town to seek their future; and in the older large towns, major officeholding patterns became more oligarchical.[62] All of

[61] The importance of plural officeholding and of large family units is well known to historians. See Bruce C. Daniels, "Family Dynasties," *Connecticut's First Family: William Pitkin and His Connections*, Connecticut Bicentennial Series. XI (Chester, 1975), and "Democracy and Oligarchy in Connecticut Towns: General Assembly Officeholding, 1701-1790," *Social Science Quarterly*, LVI (1975), 460-475.

[62] For the growth of economic inequality see Bruce C. Daniels, "Long Range Trends of Wealth Distribution in Eighteenth-Century New England," *Explorations in Economic History*, XI (1973-1974), 123-135, and James A. Henretta, "Economic Development and Social Structure in Colonial Boston," *WMQ*, 3d Ser., XII (1965), 93-105. Alice Hanson Jones, "Wealth Estimates for the New England Colonies about 1770," *Journal of Economic History*, XXXII (1972), 98-127, and Jackson Turner Main, *The Social Structure of Revolutionary America* (Princeton, N. J., 1965), show the economic inequality in the Revolutionary era. For the decline of land availability and its effects see Philip J. Greven, Jr., *Four Generations: Population, Land and Family in Colonial Andover, Massachusetts* (Ithaca, N. Y., 1970); Kenneth A.

these factors are indicative of a stratifying society with declining opportunities for most people. The ideological and political trends of the eighteenth century, however, led men to have higher expectations of participation in public life.[63] While demographic factors weighed heavily against increased involvement in decision-making, institutional differentiation probably worked in the opposite direction. The expansion in the number of officers elected in each town, the growth of neighborhood government in the form of societies, and the increased openness of freemanship all meant more opportunities for involvement in public affairs. It is true that the transfer of powers over land from the town meeting to the proprietors resulted in a narrowing of the political arena, since the proprietors were a smaller, more select group. This, however, ceased to be a factor in all but the newest towns after the 1740s when the common lands were all divided. Hence, the only institutional factor contributing to the closing of the polity in the late colonial towns was the low level of activity of the town meeting and the corresponding enhancement of the functions and authority of the selectmen. Yet it should be remembered that despite the important increase in the selectmen's executive powers, the relationship between them and the town meeting was much the same as that between the seventeenth-century minister and congregation described by Samuel Stone: "a speaking *Aristocracy* in the face of a silent *Democracy*."[64] And, although content in normal times to allow the selectmen to be the speaking aristocracy, the "silent democracy" made its voice heard whenever an issue politicized it. When this potential involvement is added to the growth in local offices, neighborhood governments, and freemanship, one must conclude that the institutional arrangements of local government on the eve of the Revolution were more in agreement with the growth of participatory ideology than with the contrary demographic trends.

173

Lockridge, "Land, Population, and the Evolution of New England Society, 1630-1790; and an Afterthought," in Stanley Katz, ed., *Colonial America: Essays in Politics and Social Development* (Boston, 1971), 467-491; and Darrett Rutman, "People in Progress: The New Hampshire Towns of the Eighteenth-Century," *Journal of Urban History*, I (1975), 268-292. For the growth of family influence and oligarchical officeholding see Daniels, "Family Dynasties," "Large Town Office-holding in Eighteenth-Century Connecticut: The Growth of Oligarchy," *Journal of American Studies*, IX (1975), 1-12, and "Democracy and Oligarchy," *Soc. Sci. Qtly.*, LVI (1975), 460-475.

[63] See Bushman, *From Puritan to Yankee*, and Zeichner, *Connecticut's Years of Controversy*, for these ideological and political currents.

[64] Quoted in Perry Miller, *Orthodoxy in Massachusetts, 1630-1650* (Boston, 1933), 186.

Notes and Documents

Law Reform in England and New England, 1620 to 1660

G. B. Warden

I N the seventeenth century Sir Edward Coke and his disciples believed that the common law of England represented the "perfection of human reason"; as a result, there was no compelling need or justification for tampering with its intricacies. Lawyers participated extensively in the disputes over parliamentary and royal sovereignty but showed little enthusiasm for substantive changes in legal procedure. At times, leaders like Oliver Cromwell and Sir Matthew Hale suggested that law reform was a nice idea but not really practicable or desirable on a large scale. Historians of the law have tended to follow this lead in arguing that the Puritan Revolution had little influence on English law. Sir William Holdsworth's sixteen-volume history of English law devotes only a few pages to law reform during the period of the Civil Wars, the Commonwealth, and the Protectorate. Theodore F. T. Plucknett's survey disposes of the subject in a few sentences.[1] Traditional legal histories give the impression that law reform and revolution were not proper activities for the gentlemen of the bench and bar.

Other historians, however, have devoted more serious attention to the movement for law reform in seventeenth-century England. Several excellent monographs have illuminated the extraordinary variety of legal grievances in Stuart England and the even greater diversity of legal reforms proposed after 1640, affecting nearly every dispute at the time about politics, the constitution, society, economics, and religion. Such indispensable studies have pro-

Mr. Warden lives in Cambridge, Massachusetts.

[1] Matthew Hale, "Considerations Touching the Amendment or Alteration of Lawes," *Hargrave Law Tracts* (London, 1787), 249-289; William S. Holdsworth, *History of English Law*, VI (London, 1966 [orig. publ. 1903]), 142-163, 410-430; Theodore F. T. Plucknett, *A Concise History of the Common Law*, 5th ed. (Boston, 1956), 54. See also C. R. Niehaus, "The Issue of Law Reform in the Puritan Revolution" (Ph.D. diss., Harvard University, 1958); Goldwin Smith, "The Reform of the Laws of England, 1640-1660," *University of Toronto Quarterly*, X (1941), 469-481; Stuart E. Prall, *The Agitation for Law Reform during the Puritan Revolution, 1640-1660* (The Hague, 1966).

vided much of the information explored in this essay. But the general impression still remains that, despite innumerable grievances and suggested proposals, law reform in England had few substantial results until the nineteenth and twentieth centuries.[2]

This essay argues that the Puritan Revolution had a profound, immediate effect on English law, if the term "English law" includes the legal reforms proposed and actually adopted by the English people who emigrated to New England before 1660. Curiously, most histories of the seventeenth century rarely connect events in England and New England in any detailed, comparative fashion. Yet, studies of the causes of the Puritan Revolution in England and of the reasons for establishing communities in New England make clear that both movements arose from the same set of social, economic, religious, political, constitutional, and legal conditions prevalent in England between 1558 and 1640.[3] Like many recent social historians, analysts of law in early New England have occasionally traced legal patterns, practices, and precedents back to England. But interpretations emphasizing cultural continuity in the transplantation of English law do not completely explain why

175

[2] G. B. Nourse, "Law Reform under the Commonwealth and Protectorate," *Law Quarterly Review*, LXXV (1959), 512-529; Donald Veall, *The Popular Movement for Law Reform, 1640-1660* (Oxford, 1970); R. Robinson, "Anticipations under the Commonwealth of Changes in the Law," in *Select Essays in Anglo-American Legal History*, I (Boston, 1907), 467-491, hereafter cited as Robinson, "Anticipations under the Commonwealth"; F. A. Inderwick, *The Interregnum* (London, 1891), 153-248; Alan Harding, *A Social History of English Law* (London, 1966), 265-282; David Underdown, *Pride's Purge: Politics in the Puritan Revolution* (Oxford, 1971), 275-296; Blair Worden, *The Rump Parliament, 1648-1653* (Cambridge, 1974), 105-160; Mary Cotterell, "Interregnum Law Reform: The Hale Commission of 1652," *English Historical Review*, LXXXIII (1968), 689-704; Barbara Shapiro, "Law Reform in Seventeenth Century England," *American Journal of Legal History*, XIX (1975), 280-312.

[3] Standard English histories such as those of S. R. Gardiner, Godfrey Davies, G. M. Trevelyan, and Christopher Hill rarely mention New England except in relation to the development of the Navigation Acts and the peripheral influence of Roger Williams. But see Carl Bridenbaugh, *Vexed and Troubled Englishmen, 1590-1642* (New York, 1968), 434-473; Wallace Notestein, *The English People on the Eve of Colonization, 1603-1630* (New York, 1954); John Gorham Palfrey, *History of New England during the Stuart Dynasty* (Boston, 1858-1890), I-II; Alan Simpson, *Puritanism in Old and New England* (Chicago, 1955); N. C. P. Tyack, "Migration from East Anglia to New England before 1660" (Ph.D. diss., University of London, 1951); Arthur Percival Newton, *The Colonizing Activities of the English Puritans* (New Haven, Conn., 1914); Theodore K. Rabb, *Enterprise and Empire: Merchant and Gentry Investment in the Expansion of England, 1575-1630* (Cambridge, Mass., 1967); Robert Brenner, "The Civil War Politics of London's Merchant Community," *Past and Present*, No. 58 (Feb. 1973), 53-107; Sumner Chilton Powell, *Puritan Village: The Formation of a New England Town* (Middletown, Conn., 1963); and John W. Thornton, *The Historical Relation of New England to the English Commonwealth* (Boston, 1874).

New Englanders adopted many practices that had few or no precedents in English legal procedures. Conversely, interpretations explaining such deviations as rough-and-ready responses to wilderness conditions fail to account adequately for those legal patterns that were continued. Other explanations based on the influence of Puritan thinking or the social backgrounds of the settlers provide some clues to why the New Englanders adopted or adapted legal practices in highly selective fashion. But most studies fail to appreciate the full relation of legal developments in New England to the law reform movement in England during the same period.[4]

176

If revolutionary reforms in England and the early settlement of New England arose from similar conditions, then the results of those movements can be and need to be considered in a comparative perspective. Accordingly, this essay will explore simultaneous legal developments on both sides of the North Atlantic because they involved exactly the same set of substantive legal issues and fit together as parts of the same revolutionary impulses. Obviously, there were crucial differences of time, space, physical environment, and social conditions affecting the Anglo-American law reform movements. Rather than preventing comparison, however, those differences vividly illustrate the results of legal change in the two regions during the Puritan Revolution.

Law reform was not a sudden innovation of the Puritan Revolution; as long as a legal system had existed in England, there had been proposals to alter and improve it. Many important changes had already begun in Tudor legislation regarding religious establishments and control of the poor. But those changes only vaguely resembled "reforms" in the usual sense of the word. Tudor legislation mainly enhanced the power of the state, with few demonstrable benefits for most subjects of the realm. Similar laws relating to uses, wills, enrollments, prerogative courts, monopolies, and the consolidation of criminal statutes affected large numbers of people but mainly as objects of state control. Such regulations partially reflected a movement toward codification taking place in many European states at the time in response to the need for centralized authority and uniform expectations about state-applied sanctions.[5]

[4] See Roscoe Pound, *The Formative Era of American Law* (Boston, 1938), 6-7; George Lee Haskins, *Law and Authority in Early Massachusetts: A Study in Tradition and Design* (New York, 1960), 163-221; Joseph H. Smith, ed., *Colonial Justice in Western Massachusetts (1639-1702): The Pynchon Court Record* ... (Cambridge, Mass., 1961); and articles by Haskins, Zechariah Chafee, Richard B. Morris, and Julius Goebel, in David H. Flaherty, ed., *Essays in the History of Early American Law* (Chapel Hill, N.C., 1969).

[5] G. R. Elton, *Reform and Renewal: Thomas Cromwell and the Commonweal* (Cambridge, 1973), 129-157; Barbara Shapiro, "Codification of the Laws in Seventeenth-Century England," *Wisconsin Law Review*, No. 2 (1974), 428-465.

In England, as elsewhere, changes in the legal powers of the state involved constitutional and political contests between monarchs and magnates, with only occasional reference to those outside the traditional centers of coercive power. In constitutional legal theory, a primary goal of reformers in England and New England after 1620 was to eliminate Stuart pretensions to the divine right of kings. In England this impulse took the drastic form of executing Charles I and abolishing the monarchy. Yet the antagonism to unlimited executive authority quickly led to self-defeating contradictions. Charles was hardly cold in the grave before the crown was offered to Cromwell. He refused it, but, even so, within a few years a hereditary protectorate was established, differing little from the monarchy, which was itself restored in 1660.[6]

177

The failure to abolish monarchy and establish an acceptable legislative sovereignty in constitutional law occurred in part because of bitter factional disputes within Parliament. But the issue also involved fundamental antagonisms over covenanted popular authority. The notion of a primitive, mythical contract between rulers and subjects had appeared in writings of continental natural-rights theorists. Yet in 1642, when Henry Parker asserted that all temporal authority derived from God had been originally vested in the people, not in the monarch or the state, the idea encountered a storm of outrage and provoked a barrage of pamphlets with legalistic counter-arguments. The theory, necessity, and practical application of a popular contract reappeared with even greater force in the new model army's *Agreement of the People* after 1647. Moderate Presbyterians in Parliament agreed with Cromwell's followers in refusing to endorse the popular covenant as the source of sovereign constitutional authority and the basis for a national government. Even as late as 1689 the best legal scholars in the House of Lords could find no historic evidence of a compact between king and subjects that James II had allegedly violated; coronation oaths came close, but they did not amount to a mutually binding contract. In Locke's writings, of course, the idea of a primitive contract had a powerful political influence, but it still remained a metaphor derived from theory rather than from history.[7]

[6] J. W. Gough, *Fundamental Law in English Constitutional History* (Oxford, 1961 [reprint from 1955 corrected ed.]), 48-139; J. R. Tanner, *English Constitutional Conflicts of the Seventeenth Century, 1603-1689* (Cambridge, 1962), 51-200; Conrad Russell, *The Crisis of Parliaments, 1509-1660* (London, 1971), 285-397.

[7] J. W. Gough, *The Social Contract* (Oxford, 1936), 62-136; Henry Parker, *Observations upon some of his Majesties Late Answers and Expresses* . . . [London, 1642], 1-13; John Spelman, *A View of a Printed Book* . . . (Oxford, 1642), 5-6, 13; D. Digges, *An Answer To A Printed Book* . . . (Oxford, 1642), 1-3; Digges, *A Review of the Observations* . . . (Oxford, 1643), 3-4; [Thomas Morton], *Christus Dei, the Lords Annoynted. Or, A theologicall Discourse, wherein is proved, that the regall or monarchicall Power of our Soveraigne Lord King Charles is not humane, but of divine Right, and that God is the sole efficient Cause thereof and not the People* . . . (Oxford, 1643), 3, 8-9; *Animadversions upon those Notes which a late*

In New England the fact of emigration put the settlers beyond the reach of royal power and produced a practical nullification of royal prerogative in church and state as a central element of constitutional sovereignty. In ecclesiastical and civil matters, the motto "No bishop, no king" was a practical reality in New England. Most pronouncements from early New England about constitutional authority affirmed that temporal authority was derived from God, manifested in the people, and by them delegated to duly chosen representatives and magistrates. Outside of Rhode Island, Puritan writers in New England hastened to condemn leveling or a "mere" democracy, preferring instead a balanced, mixed government that combined elements of monarchy, aristocracy, and democracy. Although magistrates in New England, individually or collectively, could act as arbitrarily as the most autocratic Stuart, no writer ever dared to eliminate the popular element entirely from any acceptable constitutional formulation.[8]

The New Englanders not only accomplished the theoretical goal of the English Puritans' constitutionalism. They also applied it in over a dozen popular civil covenants, which survive from early New England communities. Almost all of the covenants were approved well before the *Agreement of the People* in England. Even more remarkable are the starkly different groups that adopted civil covenants as the basis for the social, political, and religious foundations of their communities—royalists in Maine, New Hampshire, and Rhode Island; moderates in Connecticut, Springfield, and Dedham; separatists in New Plymouth; antinomians in Portsmouth; strict scriptural adherents in New Haven and Guilford. (Even Samuel Gorton's frenetic followers in Warwick, Rhode Island, who denied the constitutional validity of civil covenants, agreed not to have an agreement.) All of these civil covenants preceded the communities' church covenants. Some appealed to divine authorization as sanction for the agreements, others paid lip service to royal authorization, and a few cited no other authorization than the will of the subscribers.[9] Although it is unclear how binding these covenants were upon

178

Observator published upon the seven Doctrines and Positions which the King by way of Recapitulation layes open so offensive (London, 1642), 5; Henry Parker, *Animadversions Animadverted* ... [London 1642], 6; William Ball, *A Caveat for Subjects moderating the Observator* ... (London, 1642), 2-3, 6-7; William Haller and Godfrey Davies, eds., *The Leveller Tracts, 1647-1653* (London, 1944); A. S. P. Woodhouse, *Puritanism and Liberty: Being the Army Debates (1647-9) from the Clarke Manuscripts* ... (London, 1951); Don M. Wolfe, *Leveller Manifestoes of the Puritan Revolution* (London, 1944).

[8] Edmund S. Morgan, ed., *Puritan Political Ideas, 1558-1794* (Indianapolis, 1965), 75-225.

[9] William Brigham, ed., *The Compact with the Charter and Laws of the Colony of New Plymouth* ... (Boston, 1836), 19-20; Henry M. Burt, ed., *The First Century of the History of Springfield: The Official Records from 1636 to 1736* ... , I (Springfield, Mass., 1898), 156-160; Don Gleason Hill, ed., *The Early Records of the*

the original subscribers and later settlers, it is important that such diverse groups felt they had to make such explicit written statements about the foundations of their civil polity, anticipating the most revolutionary demands of political reformers in England at the time. Though not entirely demo- cratic, the New Englanders' acknowledgment of the express consent of the governed contrasted sharply with the failure of similar appeals in England at the time.

Once in power, magistrates whose authority was derived from God and had been signified by the choice of voters often did not feel an obligation to comply with every popular demand. As in England, the political history of seventeenth-century New England included examples of legislative or execu- tive tyranny. Political disputes occurred because voters and their representa- tives kept harking back to the letter or spirit of the civil covenants when the magistrates transgressed them. Limited by such explicit covenants, the magis- trates frequently found themselves powerless to oppose popular sentiment. Indeed, unlike England, the New England colonies subjected the legislators and executives to annual elections. No New England governor could veto legislation or legislative adjournments. No executive had any independent power to appoint judges and other officials. All judges and executive officers were subject to impeachment.[10] By these fundamental mechanisms New Englanders could minimize most of the abuses of executive power at issue under the Stuarts and the Protectorate. Through the theory and practice of fundamental civil covenants, with explicit limitations on executive and legis- lative authority, the New Englanders went far beyond English reformers in achieving the most important constitutional goals of the Puritan Revolution.

179

Town of Dedham, Massachusetts, III (Dedham, 1892), 2-3; Nathaniel Bouton, ed., Provincial Papers: Documents and Records Relating to the Province of New- Hampshire . . . 1623-1686, I (Concord, 1867), 126, 131-134, 110; Charles Thornton Libby, ed., Province and Court Records of Maine (Portland, 1928), I, 5, 75, 133-134; Charles Edward Banks, History of York, Maine . . . , I (Boston, 1931), 82; John Russell Bartlett, ed., Records of the Colony of Rhode Island and Providence Plantations in New England, 1636-1663, I (Providence, 1856), 14, 52, 70, 89, 112, 156- 157; J. Hammond Trumbull, ed., The Public Records of the Colony of Connecticut, Prior to the Union with the New Haven Colony, May, 1665 . . . , I (Hartford, 1850), 20-21; Charles J. Hoadly, ed., Records of the Colony and Plantation of New Haven from 1638 to 1649, I (Hartford, Conn., 1857), 11-19; Bernard Christian Steiner, A History of the Plantation of Menunkatuck and the Original Town of Guilford, Connecticut (Baltimore, 1897), 24-25.

[10] For a sample of political disputes see Robert Emmet Wall, Jr., Massachusetts Bay: The Crucial Decade, 1640-1650 (New Haven, Conn., 1972). For limitations on executive powers see Brigham, ed., New Plymouth Laws, 36-38; Bouton, ed., Provincial Papers of New-Hampshire, I, 122-153; Trumbull, ed., Public Records of Connecticut, I, 21-26; Hoadly, ed., Records of New Haven, 20-62; and Bartlett, ed., Records of Rhode Island, I, 157-158, 191-195; contrast with Libby, ed., Maine Province and Court Records, I, 14-42.

Another grievance of Puritan reformers in England concerned voting qualifications and the proper units of legislative representation. Moderates in England were generally content with the forty-shilling freehold qualification for voting in certain elections. Levellers and other extreme reformers argued unsuccessfully for an even broader franchise. Others advocated secret balloting rather than voice votes. Some experiments were tried after 1649 to increase the size of Parliament and alter the bases of representation, but none had any lasting effect.[11]

In New England, alternatives to property qualifications were more varied and more successful in expanding the franchise. Church membership was required for voting in Massachusetts and New Haven; the Bay Colony later allowed a property qualification, the effect of which is still being debated. In Rhode Island, heads of families had the franchise. Connecticut and Plymouth had at first no specific requirement other than approval by town selectmen or taking an oath of allegiance. Such changes did not approach universal manhood suffrage, but recent studies estimate that at a minimum between a third and a half of the adult males could vote, perhaps double or triple the proportion in England at the time.[12]

All the New England colonies adopted the township as the basic unit of legislative representation. The towns also had delegated powers usually reserved to the legislative assembly or county governments in Virginia, Maryland, and England itself. Annual elections, local by-laws, rotation of officers, access to town meetings and town offices by nonfreemen—all reflected the degree to which New Englanders tried to give substance to their original civil covenants and to popular authority in the actual operation of the civil state.[13] Practice did not exactly reflect democratic theory, but in voting and representation the New Englanders went much farther than their English counterparts dared to go.

In arguments about constitutional law and adjudication during the Puritan Revolution the demand for codification recurs persistently. Moder-

180

[11] See Tanner, *English Constitutional Conflicts*, 176-189; C. B. Macpherson, *The Political Theory of Posesssive Individualism* (Oxford, 1962), 279-292; and Haller and Davies, eds., *Leveller Tracts*, 59-61, 78, 112, 151, 322-323.

[12] For a review of the dispute over voting in Massachusetts see B. Katherine Brown, "The Controversy over the Franchise in Puritan Massachusetts, 1954 to 1974," *William and Mary Quarterly*, 3d Ser., XXXIII (1976), 212-241; George D. Langdon, *Pilgrim Colony: A History of New Plymouth, 1620-1691* (New Haven, Conn., 1966), 81-90; Isabel MacBeath Calder, *The New Haven Colony* (New Haven, Conn., 1934), 106-129; Richard S. Dunn, *Puritans and Yankees: The Winthrop Dynasty of New England, 1630-1717* (Princeton, N.J., 1962), 105-106; and Charles M. Andrews, *The Colonial Period of American History* (New Haven, Conn., 1934-1938), II, 7, 11, 27, 104-107.

[13] Michael Zuckerman, *Peaceable Kingdoms: New England Towns in the Eighteenth Century* (New York, 1970), 10-45.

ate and extreme reformers agreed that English statutes and common-law decisions were obscure, prolix, and inconsistent. Reformers yearned for a succinct, clear statement of the law, despite objections from professional lawyers, and they pointed to the legal codes of Normandy, Paris, Geneva, and states in Germany and the Netherlands as examples. One reformer claimed that all of English law could be put into a pocket-sized book so that Everyman could plead his own case. The bar and bench remained cool toward such proposals, however, and the codification movement concentrated more on negative criticism of existing law than on detailed, comprehensive models. Although parliamentary law reform committees began at least to discuss the subject, wartime politics prevented any successful action.[14]

It is not entirely coincidental that the most detailed model of a code published in England during the Puritan Revolution came from New England. Although a biblical code proposed by John Cotton had been rejected by Massachusetts and New Haven, the English printing gave the misleading impression that it had been officially adopted. A second English edition in 1655 was published by William Aspinwall, an Antinomian from Massachusetts and Rhode Island who became a Fifth Monarchy Man in England.[15]

181

[14] Shapiro, "Codification," *Wis. Law Rev.*, No. 2 (1974), 448-456. The most extensive English attempt at a code appears as an appendix to [A. Booth], *Examen Legum Angliae: or, The laws of England examined by Scripture, antiquity, and reason* (London, 1656), but see also pp. 4, 38, 53, 84-85, 124, 150. One could, of course, consider the Book of Orders in the 1630s as a form of codification. See Thomas Garden Barnes, *Somerset, 1625-1640: A County's Government during the "Personal Rule"* (Cambridge, Mass., 1961), 172-202, as well as William Lambard, *Eirenarcha* . . . (London, 1602), and Michael Dalton, *Countrey Justice* . . . (London, 1618). For other comments on the subject see Francis Bacon, *The Elements of the Common Lawes of England* (London, 1639), ii-v; Charles George Cock, *English-Law . . . with an Essay of Christian Government* (London, 1651), v-vi, 4, 69-70, 78-84, 101-187; William Medley, *A Standard Set Up* . . . (London, 1657), 15; William Sheppard, *Englands Balme* (London, 1657), 4-6; Francis Whyte, *For the Sacred Law of the Land* (London, 1652), 30-31, 43-44; Robert Wiseman, *The Law of Laws: Or, The Excellency of the Civil Law* . . . (London, 1657), 2, 97-173; T. Faldo, *Reformation of proceedings at Law* . . . (London, 1649), 21; and Henry Robinson, *Certaine Proposals in Order to a New Modelling of the Lawes, and Law-Proceedings* . . . (London, 1653), 3-5. See also Veall, *Popular Movement*, 87, 93, and Robinson, "Anticipations under the Commonwealth," 481-482.

[15] For the text of the 1641 code and Aspinwall's 1655 preface see "An Abstract of the Laws of New-England, as they are now established," Massachusetts Historical Society, *Collections*, 1st Ser., V (1798), 173-191. In addition see Worthington C. Ford, "Cotton's 'Moses His Judicials'," *Mass. Hist. Soc., Proceedings*, 2d Ser., XVI (1903), 274-284; and J. F. Maclear, "New England and the Fifth Monarchy: The Quest for the Millennium in Early American Puritanism," *WMQ*, 3d Ser., XXXII (1975), 238-240. See also Hugh Peters, *Good Work for a Good Magistrate. Or A Short Cut to Great Quiet* (London, 1651), 32; J[ohn] Cooke, *The Vindication of the Professors and Profession of the Law* . . . (London, 1646), 18, 25; and Edward Rogers, *Some account of the life and opinions of a Fifth-Monarchy Man* (London, 1867), 96.

Endorsement of such a code by the extreme fringe of the reform movement perhaps explains in part why moderate Englishmen rejected biblical codification.

The failure of the codification movement in England stands in marked contrast to the orgy of code-making that took place in the New England colonies. Plymouth had a topical code in 1636. Massachusetts followed an alphabetical arrangement in 1641 and 1648. Even heretical Rhode Island adopted a code in 1647, based heavily on Michael Dalton's *Countrey Justice*. Connecticut in 1650, New Haven in 1655, and New Hampshire in 1679 adopted modified versions of the Massachusetts codes. The disorganized settlers in Maine did not enact a code, but by annexation in 1651 they became subject to that of Massachusetts. These codes provided models for similar enactments in New York, New Jersey, and Pennsylvania later in the century.[16] That such diverse jurisdictions in New England had both civil covenants and civil codes illustrates how successfully fundamental changes of the law reform movement bore fruit in New England while falling on barren ground in England. One may argue that these codes lacked the technical rigor of European civil codes, but they apparently served the major purpose for which they were intended. They outlined a coherent constitutional authority and structure in the civil state, were in plain writing for everyone to see and use, provided a guide for conducting political and judicial affairs, gave some protection to civil liberties, and allowed opportunities for amendment. In short, the New England codes represented a remarkable achievement of the Puritan Revolution.

Reforms of constitutional theory, limited executive authority, civil covenants, voting qualifications, legislative representation, and codification could,

[16] For the texts of the codes see Brigham, ed., *New Plymouth Laws*, 36-54; William H. Whitmore, comp., *The Colonial Laws of Massachusetts* ... (Boston, 1887), 33-61; Max Farrand, ed., *The Laws and Liberties of Massachusetts* ... (Cambridge, Mass., 1929); Trumbull, ed., *Public Records of Connecticut*, I, 509-563; Bartlett, ed., *Records of Rhode Island*, I, 147-208; Hoadly, ed., *Records of New Haven*, II, 561-616; and Bouton, ed., *Provincial Papers of New-Hampshire*, I, 382-413, 444-451. See also the articles by Wolford, Haskins, and Ewing, in Flaherty, ed., *Essays in the Hist. of Early Am. Law;* and Samuel Ward, *Jethro's Justice of Peace* (London, 1627), 71-72. See also Haskins, *Law and Authority in Early Mass.*, 113-140; George L. Haskins, "Codification of the Law in Colonial Massachusetts: A Study in Comparative Law," *Indiana Law Journal*, XXX (1954), 1-17; Stefan A. Riesenfeld, "Law-making and Legislative Precedent in American Legal History," *Minnesota Law Review*, XXXIII (Jan. 1949), 103-144; Isabel M. Calder, "John Cotton and the New Haven Colony," *New England Quarterly*, III (1930), 82-94; F. W. Grinnell, "Some Forgotten Massachusetts History about Codification and its Relation to Current Legislative and Judicial Problems," *Massachusetts Law Quarterly*, I (1916), 319-339; and Thornton, *Historical Relation*, 70.

of course, go only so far in changing the sources of law and the substantive grievances which law reformers wanted redressed. Equally important was the necessity of changing the structure, processes, and content of judicial administration. Law reform pamphlets called constantly for the decentralization of courts, away from Westminster and shire towns to every village. This was not only a secular technical reform but also a biblical imperative, for in Israel there had been judges at every city gate. The expense and delay of taking cases back and forth to Westminster, the low monetary limit for removing suits out of the county courts, the too frequent use of writs of error on trivial technicalities—all seemed to make the law more remote from the people. Ironically, one of Parliament's earliest reforms aggravated the problem; in abolishing prerogative courts like the Court of Requests and the councils of Wales and the Marches, Parliament had left many areas without a convenient forum for justice. Strict biblical reformers wished the population of the realm to be divided into multiples of ten, fifty, one hundred, and one thousand; each group would have a judge and would allow appeals to the judges of the larger groups, up to a "Sanhedrin" of seventy, who in biblical fashion would be lawgivers, judicially and legislatively. At the local level, reformers wanted weekly or monthly courts in every town and village.[17] None of these demands, however, took the form of concrete proposals, and none was implemented in England.

183

The reform of Chancery reflected the major anomalies of changing judicial administration in the realm. Some advocated its complete abolition. Others wished only to expedite its technical procedures. As a court without juries, Chancery was anathema to many reformers, although equity in its popular sense was devoutly desired. One alternative proposed that common law courts should also dispense equitable relief. Extremists wished to make law subordinate to equity throughout the realm, and biblical purists wanted to abolish juries as unscriptural. During the Protectorate, Chancery was put out of business temporarily, despite objections that the court's large backlog

[17] See, in general, Nourse, "Law Reform," Law Qtly. Rev., LXXV (1959), 512-514; Veall, Popular Movement, 35-43; Robinson, "Anticipations under the Commonwealth," 468-469, 473-476; and Shapiro, "Law Reform," Am. Jour. Legal Hist., XIX (1975), 284, 288, 290, 292, 294, 304. See also Booth, Examen Legum Angliae, 78, 89-91, 105-109, 110-111, 147-148; Cock, English-Law, 4, 29, 68, 86, 88, 125, 134-140, 160; Medley, A Standard Set Up, 15-18; Peters, Good Work, 24, 29, 38, 39, 41, 44-51; Henry Robinson, Certain Considerations in Order to a More Speedy, Cheap, and Equall Distribution of Justice throughout the Nation ... (London, 1651), ii, v, 3-11; Sheppard, Englands Balme, 20, 28, 36, 59, 63; Ward, Jethro's Justice, 56; Whyte, For the Sacred Law, 58ff; George H. Sabine, ed., The Works of Gerrard Winstanley ... (New York, 1965 [orig. publ. 1941]), 62-63; Robinson, Certaine Proposals (1653), 5, 8; Henry Parker, Jus Populi. ... (London, 1644), 44-46; and Haller and Davies, eds., Leveller Tracts, 43, 108, 122.

reflected the popularity and utility of equitable reliefs to large numbers of litigants.[18]

Among the defects of the common law courts, none seemed more obvious than their technicalities, delays, and expense. Despite ingenious objections from professional lawyers, reformers demanded and temporarily succeeded in making English rather than "law french" the official language of court records. Others cried in vain to prevent cases from being dismissed because of trivial errors in pleading. Codification was part of the impulse to simplify and clarify the law and its procedures. Extreme reformers attacked the whole legal profession as parasites, vipers, locusts, and creators of the law's inhumanity. Some advocated the abolition of legal fees or their strict regulation. A few wished the state to pay both lawyers and doctors. One proposal demanded that legal fees at Westminster be used to subsidize public education in every town.[19] No realistic changes in pleading and judicial administration occurred, however, until the 1830s and 1870s.

In New England, the same proposals did not have to overcome ancient institutions and vested professional interests. Codification in all the New England colonies helped make the law accessible and intelligible. The township as the basic unit of governance provided the most immediate forum

[18] See Veall, *Popular Movement*, 35, 87, 179, 181-185; Robinson, "Anticipations under the Commonwealth," 471-472; Stuart E. Prall, "Chancery Reform and the Puritan Revolution," *Am. Jour. Legal Hist.*, VI (1962), 28-44; Stanley N. Katz, "The Politics of Law in Colonial America," *Perspective in American History*, V (1971), 258-261; Shapiro, "Law Reform," *Am. Jour. Legal Hist.*, XIX (1975), 282-283, 293, 301-302; and Nourse, "Law Reform," *Law Qtly. Rev.*, LXXV (1959), 524-525. See also Booth, *Examen Legum Angliae*, 10; Cock, *English-Law*, 45-46, 68, 86, 88, 165; Robinson, *Certain Proposalls in Order to the Peoples Freedome and Accomodation* . . . (London, 1652), 1, 20; Sheppard, *Englands Balme*, 21, 65; Whyte, *For the Sacred Law*, 31-33; Cooke, *Vindication*, 26; and Robinson, *Certaine Proposals* (1653), 3, 23.

[19] See Nourse, "Law Reform," *Law Qtly. Rev.*, LXXV (1959), 516, 519-520; Veall, *Popular Movement*, 30-51, 190, 200-211; Robinson, "Anticipations under the Commonwealth," 477, 481; Theobald Matthew, "Law-French," *Law Qtly. Rev.*, LIV (1938), 358-369; Shapiro, "Law Reform," *Am. Jour. Legal Hist.*, XIX (1975), 283, 284-285, 288, 290, 292-293, 294, 299, 302, 305, 306; William Cole, *A Rod for Lawyers* . . . (London, 1659); [Benjamin Nicholson], *The Lawyers Bane; or, the Lawes Reformation, and New Modell* . . . (London, 1649); Booth, *Examen Legum Angliae*, vi, 14, 89, 100-101; Cock, *English-Law*, 25, 42-43, 47, 68-69, 76, 88, 90, 134, 146, 165; John Cook, *Unum Necessarium: or, The Poore mans Case* . . . (London, 1648), 65-66; Medley, *A Standard Set Up*, 18; Peters, *Good Work*, 33, 34, 42-43; Robinson, *Certaine Considerations*, i, 1, 10; Sheppard, *Englands Balme*, 18, 20, 22, 37, 54, 212; Whyte, *For the Sacred Law*, 38; Cooke, *Vindication*, i, 58; Robinson, *Certaine Proposals* (1653), 8, 17; Ball, *A Caveat*, 7; Haller and Davies, eds., *Leveller Tracts*, 82, 89, 121, 138, 144, 167; Christopher Hill and Edmund Dell, eds., *The Good Old Cause: The English Revolution of 1640-1660* (London, 1949), 50, 333, 389-393, 435-436; and Rogers, *Some Account*, 53, 87-95.

for justice, by resident commissioners for small causes in Massachusetts, town courts in Rhode Island, and local judicial circuits among the Connecticut River towns. Massachusetts created county courts with appeals to the Court of Assistants or General Court.[20] The available records show clearly that the local courts of New England handled a huge volume of civil cases, so that litigation with frequent appeals and reviews became the people's second favorite indoor sport.

The New England codes provided opportunities to deviate from strict technicalities in pleading, giving later commentators the erroneous impression that early court practices were too crude and primitive to be respectably legalistic. The codes declared English to be the only official language of the law. The codes and subsequent statutes allowed courts to dispense legal remedies and equitable relief without having to conduct separate trials. Rhode Island, Plymouth, and New Haven provided arbitration to settle disputes out of court. For ten years Massachusetts prevented anyone from accepting fees for legal advice; Thomas Lechford, the colony's only practicing lawyer, was disbarred for jury-tampering. Massachusetts later allowed legal fees, but it and other colonies limited them by statute. Massachusetts also barred lawyers from sitting as deputies in the General Court. Anti-lawyer sentiment extended to Rhode Island, where a grand jury cited Samuel Gorton for contempt of court after he dared to call a judge a "lawyer." Juries were allowed to give special verdicts, as well as the Scottish "not proven." The records suggest that juries and judges did not draw sharp distinctions between matters of law and fact. Judicial tenure subject to annual election or legislative appointment in effect meant "during good behavior."[21] All in all,

185

[20] Haskins, *Law and Authority in Early Mass.*, 212-213; Albert Mason, "A Short History of the Supreme Judicial Court of Massachusetts," *Mass. Law Qtly.*, II (1916), 82-100; Elwin L. Page, *Judicial Beginnings in New Hampshire, 1640-1700* (Concord, N.H., 1959), 44-64; Amasa M. Eaton, "The Development of the Judicial System in Rhode Island," *Yale Law Journal*, XIV (1905), 148-170; Donald Lines Jacobus, "Connecticut's Colonial Committee System," *Connecticut Bar Journal*, XI (1937), 359-365; Dean B. Lyman, "Notes on the New Haven Colonial Courts," *ibid.*, XX (1946), 178-189. See also Herta Prager and William W. Prince, "A Bibliography on the History of the Courts of the Thirteen Original States, Maine, Ohio and Vermont," *Am. Jour. Legal Hist.*, I (1957), 336-362.

[21] Edwin H. Woodruff, "Chancery in Massachusetts: The Colony, 1628-1691," *Law Qtly. Rev.*, V (1889), 370-386; Frederick G. Kempin, Jr., "Precedent and Stare Decisis: The Critical Years, 1800 to 1850," *Am. Jour. Legal Hist.*, III (1959), 28-54; William M. Maltbie, "Judicial Administration in Connecticut Colony before the Charter of 1662," *Conn. Bar Jour.*, XXIII (1949), 147-158, 228-247; Henry H. Townshend, "Judicial Administration in New Haven Colony before the Charter of 1662," *ibid.*, XXIV (1950), 210-234; James Bradley Thayer, "A Chapter of Legal History in Massachusetts," *Harvard Law Rev.*, IX (1895), 1-12; Erwin C. Surrency, "Report on Court Procedures in the Colonies, 1700," *Am. Jour. Legal Hist.*, IX (1965), 172-176; Nathan Matthews, "The Results of the Prejudice against Lawyers in

the changes in structure, process, and substance of judicial administration accomplished almost all the major goals vainly sought by law reformers in England at the time.

Criminal penalties were also objects of grievance in England. Moderate reformers bewailed the enormous number of capital offenses and the death penalty for one-shilling crimes. Biblical extremists wished to abolish benefit of clergy and introduce capital punishment for adultery, sodomy, and blasphemy. Torture, oaths ex officio, strict sequestration of juries, and prohibitions on counsel and witnesses all received their share of criticism.[22]

The New Englanders achieved more success in reforming criminal law than did their English cousins. While the number of capital offenses actually increased in England after the Puritan Revolution, New Englanders eliminated the death penalty for such minor offenses as poaching, fence-breaking, and thefts over one shilling in value. Massachusetts, at least, made banishment a capital punishment (as a symbolic "decapitation" from the body politic), thus mitigating the severity of the few remaining capital crimes. The New Englanders did extend capital punishment to such biblical crimes as adultery and imposed more severe sanctions on gambling, races, duels, bigamy, and other diversions, but though statutory criminal penalties may look like evidence of a severe moral autocracy, the records indicate that judges and juries rarely inflicted the stated penalty for major crimes.[23] Moreover, procedural reforms and easier access to civil litigation for settling disputes minimized the chances that normal social friction would end in violence and criminal activity. Amid new socioeconomic conditions, the results of criminal reform in New England met almost every need expressed in England during the Puritan Revolution.

Massachusetts in the Seventeenth Century," *Mass. Law Qtly.*, XIII (1928), 73-74; Theodore F. T. Plucknett, "Book Review," *NEQ*, III (1930), 159; Kenneth W. Porter, "Samuel Gorton: New England Firebrand," *ibid.*, VII (1934), 405-444; Thomas Lechford, *Plain Dealing: or, News from New-England...* (London, 1642), III (Mass. Hist. Soc., *Colls.*, 3d Ser., XXIII-XXIV [1833]), 84-85.

[22] Veall, *Popular Movement*, 2-10, 17-27, 138, 140, 160, 235, 237; Nourse, "Law Reform," *Law Qtly. Rev.*, LXXV (1959), 514, 517, 519-522; Booth, *Examen Legum Angliae*, 53, 75, 79, 91-92, 119-123, 125, 128-131; Cock, *English-Law*, 161-162, 169, 177-178, 187; Cook, *Unum Necessarium*, 43-44, 46, 53. Peters, *Good Work*, 52-53, 56, which includes the proposal that felons be put in galleys rather than in jails; Robinson, *Certain Proposalls* (1652), 25-26, proposes substituting a swimming test for benefit of clergy. Sheppard, *Englands Balme*, 59-63, 95-97; Whyte, *For the Sacred Law*, 7-8; Cooke, *Vindication*, 18; Haller and Davies, eds., *Leveller Tracts*, 152, 325.

[23] Edwin Powers, *Crime and Punishment in Early Massachusetts, 1620-1692: A Documentary History* (Boston, 1966); David H. Flaherty, "Law and the Enforcement of Morals in Early America," in Fleming and Bailyn, eds., *Law in American History*, 203-253; Francis Fane, *Reports on the Laws of Connecticut*, ed. Charles M. Andrews (Hartford, 1915), 44-45; Haskins, *Law and Authority in Early Mass.*, 174-177, 204-212.

. The most pervasive object of reformers arose out of problems of indebtedness and property. A few English pamphleteers called for changes to
protect creditors, but most legal and economic complaints sought greater
protection for the more numerous class of debtors. Far from favoring a
radical repudiation of debts, the reformers sought instead to provide easier
means by which debtors could satisfy their obligations without harsh penalties and frustrating technicalities. Most English writers condemned distraint of debtors' property other than for arrears in rent. Most condemned
imprisonment for debt if the debtor could plead without fraud that he had no
assets other than necessaries. Others protested against the technical restriction
that prevented specialty debts such as sealed contracts from being assignable
by or to a third party other than the crown. Some reformers wished to
establish firmly the "equity of redemption," allowing debtors extra time to
prevent foreclosure of mortgages.[24]

Legal reforms to minimize the possibility of getting into debt and to
facilitate getting out of it invariably involved the technicalities of property
laws. Leaseholders and copyholders complained against the economic burdens in wardship, waste, forfeits, escheats, and entry fines. Primogeniture
prevented large amounts of real property from being used to satisfy the debts
of a decedent's estate, frustrating legitimate creditors and placing in-
ordinately heavy burdens on personal property and younger children. Under
certain conditions, freeholds could not be used to relieve the indebtedness of
living persons. Entails had the same effect of encumbering a debtor's personal
property and thwarting creditors. Moreover, such technicalities protecting
real property stimulated landlords and lawyers to invent even more ingen-
iously fraudulent conveyances, uses, fictitious actions, and other devices
annoying to both debtors and creditors.[25]

187

[24] Richard Ford, "Imprisonment for Debt," *Michigan Law Review*, XXV
(1926), 24-49; A. W. B. Simpson, "The Penal Bond with Conditional Defeasance,"
Law Qtly. Rev., LXXXII (1966), 392-422; Shapiro, "Law Reform," *Am. Jour.
Legal Hist.*, XIX (1975), 285, 290, 296, 308; Robinson, "Anticipations under the
Commonwealth," 488; Veall, *Popular Movement*, 13, 63, 149-150; Nourse, "Law
Reform," *Law Qtly. Rev.*, LXXV (1959), 515, 519-520, 523; Booth, *Examen Legum
Angliae*, 41, 49, 74, 134; Cock, *English-Law*, 47, 68, 76, 162-166, 168; Cook, *Unum
Necessarium*, 47-48; Peters, *Good Work*, 23, 34, 39, 98; Robinson, *Certain Pro-
posalls* (1652), 10, 18-23; Sheppard, *Englands Balme*, 89-90, 144, 193, 212-213; Faldo,
Reformation, 4-13; John A. Robert, *The Younger Brother His Apologie* . . .
(Oxford, 1634), 4; Robinson, *Certaine Proposals* (1653), 5, 20-23; Haller and
Davies, eds., *Leveller Tracts*, 152, 324-325.

[25] Veall, *Popular Movement*, 2, 52-55, 58-64, 84, 213-218; Shapiro, "Law
Reform," *Am. Jour. Legal Hist.*, XIX (1975), 289, 307; Robinson, "Anticipations
under the Commonwealth," 474, 488-490; Booth, *Examen Legum Angliae*, 14, 29-
30, 41, 62-63, 87-88; Cock, *English-Law*, 47, 48, 68, 71, 90, 152-153, 170-171, 174;
Edward Coke, *The Compleate Copy-Holder* . . . (London, 1650); Medley, *A Stan-*

An initial step to end such abuses was a widespread proposal for open public registration of all lands, conveyances, wills, contracts, mortgages, debts, and the administration of decedents' estates. That proposal foundered in a sea of verbiage in the parliamentary law reform committee, although Parliament adopted ordinances that recognized equity of redemption and assignability of specialty debts. The Restoration settlement ending feudal incidents applied mainly to the king's major tenants without benefitting copyholders and tenants of other landlords. Most of the reforms in property law proposed during the Puritan Revolution did not achieve any substantive results in England until 1926.[26]

188   In New England, legal reforms concerning debt and property succeeded not only because of the settlers' zeal for reformation but also because of economic conditions based on an abundance rather than a scarcity of land. All the New England colonies except Rhode Island abolished primogeniture and provided equal distribution of both real and personal property to all children, male and female, except for the scriptural double portion for the eldest son. With variations from colony to colony over the years, both real and personal property were liable for satisfying debts. Massachusetts, Plymouth, and Connecticut provided for registration of deeds and conveyances. Probate administration was decentralized in the county courts or town courts in Rhode Island and New Haven. Entails were not officially abolished, but with abundant land they were usually unnecessary and could be easily barred. Equity of redemption and assignability of specialty debts were recognized. Massachusetts, Connecticut, and New Haven allowed the common law courts to "chancer" penal bonds, reducing severe penalties to more reasonable amounts. Such measures minimized the necessity of imprisonment for debt; in distraint, goods and lands could be transferred to the creditor at appraised value without recourse to public sale.[27]

dard Set Up, 20; (London, 1650); Parker, Of a Free Trade 7; Peters, Good Work, 31, 77; Robinson, Certain Considerations, 7; Robinson, Certain Proposalls . . . (London, 1950); (1652), 19, 21; Sheppard, Englands Balme, 89, 153, 193; Whyte, For the Sacred Law, 3; Sabine, ed., Works of Winstanley, 4-5, 13; Robert, Younger Brother, 2-38; John Spelman, Two Treatises . . . (London, 1663), 3, 5; Haller and Davies, eds., Leveller Tracts, 153, 279, 325; Hill and Dell, eds., Good Old Cause, 43-52, 65, 85-97, 401, 413-424, 435-436.
[26] Veall, Popular Movement, 220-221, 235; Robinson, "Anticipations under the Commonwealth," 486-487; Nourse, "Law Reform," Law Qtly. Rev., LXXV (1959), 519-520; Booth, Examen Legum Angliae, 113, 133; Cock, English-Law, 68, 156, 170-171; Peters, Good Work, 28; Robinson, Certain Considerations, v; Sheppard, Englands Balme, 141, 178; Henry Robinson, The Office of Addresses and Encounters . . . (London, 1650), 4-6; Robinson, Certaine Proposals (1653), 19, 21, 23. See also R. R. A. Walker, "The Genesis of Land Registration in England," Law Qtly. Rev., LV (1939), 547-551.
[27] See Richard B. Morris, Studies in the History of American Law (New York, 1930), 69-125; Stefan Riesenfeld, "The Enforcement of Money Judgments in Early

Even without banks, corporations, or a stable currency, New Englanders could still get into debt. Indeed, almost all their economic transactions had to be on credit, but the availability of land and other legal reforms produced a sweeping though subtle transformation of socioeconomic values, groups, and processes. Property was no longer a scarce preserve of the privileged few; it became a negotiable commodity accessible to almost everyone and profoundly altering the relations between the sexes and the generations. Debt was no longer a sudden catastrophe or permanent enslavement, but a necessary way of life. Society still had its haves and have-nots, but few economic or legal institutions existed to perpetuate warfare between them. Legal reforms smoothed the way for reconciling differences over property and debts, and decreased the chances that social disputes would generate individual or collective violence. New England still had its poverty, crime, and persecutions, but in a new environment and in contrast to the ultimately futile hopes of the Puritan Revolution in England, legal reforms in New England reduced the possibility that power—social, economic or political— could be permanently monopolized by a few or within a perpetually petrified institutional hierarchy.

189

Why did the law reform movements have such different results in England and New England between 1620 and 1660?

Emigration and environment alone do not completely account for the differences. The lack of established institutions in New England doubtless contributed to the success of the law reform movement there, but not as the sole or determining influence. After all, Englishmen in Virginia and the West Indies confronted wilderness conditions but in general managed to recreate legal systems and social institutions along traditional English lines.

Nor does there seem to be a sufficient qualitative difference in the reforming zeal and ability of the Puritan leaders of England and New England to explain why the reform movements had such different outcomes. English law reformers criticized the legal system with more sophistication and perseverance than the New Englanders did, but the New Englanders compensated by solving problems with varied, concrete experiments.

American History," *Michigan Law Rev.*, LXXI (1973), 691-738; George L. Haskins, "The Beginnings of the Recording System in Massachusetts," *Boston University Law Review*, XXI (1941), 281-304; Haskins, "The Beginnings of Partible Inheritance in the American Colonies," *Yale Law Jour.*, LI (1942), 1280-1315; S. Laurence Shaiman, "The History of Imprisonment for Debt and Insolvency Laws as They Evolved from the Common Law," *Am. Jour. Legal Hist.*, IV (1960), 208; David T. Konig, "Community Custom and the Common Law: Social Change and the Development of Land Law in Seventeenth-Century Massachusetts," *ibid.*, XVIII (1974), 137-177; and Warren F. Cressy, "Title of Record," *Conn. Bar Jour.*, 1 (1927), 37-40.

One crucial difference between the two law reform movements was related to a problem of information about the legal difficulties needing reformation. The explosive increase of pamphlet literature in England after 1640 gives the impression that those who wrote and read about legal reform shared a body of knowledge about the status of the common law and its intricacies. That impression may be very misleading. Studies of literacy among the English population indicate that a large majority of the people could neither read nor write.[28] If so, many Englishmen might not have been able to express their grievances about the law, and, in return, educated law reformers might not have been able to communicate to a wider audience exactly what changes were needed. Even the literate part of the population frequently complained about inaccessibility of the central court records and decisions; the decisions of the common law were written in a peculiar orthography, in a quasi-foreign language, and were not published for wide circulation. Though many Englishmen may have had a nodding acquaintance with legal doings in manorial courts or borough corporations, a working familiarity with complicated legal documents at a high level was probably beyond most people's capabilities. The English law reform movement, therefore, may have suffered from an insuperable handicap from the start. It would have been difficult to reform the law in general and the common law in particular if most of the people, including even their leaders, were basically ignorant of the law, its technical problems, and the wide range of possible solutions.

The rather select group who emigrated to New England probably enjoyed a higher degree of literacy, university education, and familiarity with practical legal procedures, problems, and solutions. Roger Williams had been a protégé of Sir Edward Coke. John Winthrop had been a manor lord and an attorney at the Court of Wards and Orphans; he had been interested in law reform since 1624. Thomas Dudley had been a court clerk at Westminster and, succeeded by his son-in-law Simon Bradstreet, steward to the earl of Lincoln. Nathaniel Ward, author of the Massachusetts code of 1641, had studied at the Inns of Court before entering the ministry; he had drafted a reformed legal code as early as 1618. Richard Bellingham had been recorder at Boston in Lincolnshire. Even two of early New England's famous outcasts—Thomas Morton and Thomas Lechford—played a part as trained lawyers in the informal legal education of the settlers. Though most New Englanders may have had little familiarity with the common law, their acquaintance with local manor courts and borough customs provided practical experience with community regulation and the settlement of disputes.

[28] See Shapiro, "Law Reform," *Am. Jour. Legal Hist.*, XIX (1975), 311, and Lawrence Stone, "Literacy and Education in England, 1640-1900," *Past and Present*, No. 42 (Feb. 1969), 99-102.

190

Realistic legal reforms could flourish in New England because the educated reformers could rely on the people's familiarity with the proposed reforms.[29]

In similar fashion, discussions of the reform of the English common law, both contemporary and subsequent, have conveyed the impression that a general, uniform body of immemorial custom, written or unwritten, prevailed throughout the realm. It may be better to recall that the common law was essentially the law as interpreted by the king's four central courts at Westminster and that many parts of the realm enjoyed exceptions or deviations from common law practices. Even Coke, the champion of the common law, recognized that fourteen other systems of law operated in England— admiralty, the law merchant, canon law, equity and manorial law, to name a few. In addition, it is debatable that seventeenth-century Yorkshiremen, Cornishmen, East Anglians, and Londoners enjoyed the same local customs or similar degree of allegiance to uniform national institutions, many of which were rather recent inventions of the Tudors.[30] The complicated diversity of local legal and socioeconomic practices at the time doubtless hindered the achievement of a lasting political consensus and uniformity of reform sentiment in the legal profession and among informed laymen.

Yet, the New Englanders who achieved practical legal reforms also had a wide variety of regional backgrounds and local experiences. At a later date New England may have achieved the appearance of a uniform, homogeneous society, but in the early years of settlement many New England communities had to cope with the problems of coordinating people who came from different localities and had varied experiences with local regulation. Even in religion disagreements flourished about many points of doctrine and church polity. Consequently, like environmental influences, the varying degrees of social, economic, and cultural diversity or homogeneity alone do not fully explain why legal reforms failed in England but succeeded in New England.[31]

191

[29] Samuel Eliot Morison, *The Founding of Harvard College* (Cambridge, Mass., 1935), 359-410; Julius Goebel, "King's Law and Local Custom," in Flaherty, ed., *Essays in the Hist. of Early Am. Law*, 88-89, 95-100; Kenneth A. Lockridge, *Literacy in Colonial New England: An Enquiry into the Social Context of Literacy in the Early Modern West* (New York, 1974).

[30] Harding, *A Social History of English Law*, 216-261; Joan Thirsk, ed., *The Agrarian History of England and Wales*, IV (Cambridge, 1967), 1-112, 161-199; Goebel, "King's Law," in Flaherty, ed., *Essays in the Hist. of Early Am. Law*, 84; Bridenbaugh, *Vexed and Troubled Englishmen*, 13-82, 202-208.

[31] The extant immigrant lists show a preponderance of East Anglians but are woefully incomplete. Some of the confusing problems of diversity and homogeneity appear in Darrett B. Rutman, *American Puritanism: Faith and Practice* (Philadelphia, 1970), 9; T. H. Breen and Stephen Foster, "Moving to the New World: The Character of Early Massachusetts Immigration," *WMQ*, 3d Ser., XXX (1973), 190-192, 220-222; T. H. Breen, "Persistent Localism: English Social Change and the

In the classic but debatable formula of Sir Henry Maine, legal change, or at least its coordination with social change, occurs through legal fictions, equity, and legislation.[32] Such a formula does not exactly fit the law reform movements during the Puritan Revolution. Legal fictions may have provided elements of change on a small scale, but a frequent complaint of the time was that the common law had too many fictitious elements already, and many reformers were not satisfied with small changes. Other reformers believed that equity in its popular rather than technical sense would provide a panacea for the law's deficiencies, but the lack of juries and the alleged arbitrariness of equity's technicalities in the Court of Chancery could not solve all the legal problems of the time. In England as in New England, legislation might have provided a major mechanism for substantial legal change, but Parliament's travails between 1641 and 1660 allowed little chance for the expression of legal grievances and the implementation of legal reforms. The Levellers, in particular, protested against the type of law and justice dispensed by the unreformed parliaments. If Cromwell and feuding sects had formed stronger political coalitions in Parliament, legislation might have produced legal reform, despite objections from the professional bar and suspicious laymen.

Another mechanism for legal reformation remained generally unacceptable to the English. Many of the proposals demanded in England and enacted in New England were adaptations from the Roman civil law—partible inheritance, codification, and land registration, for example. But importations of civil law aroused the xenophobia of many Englishmen, and notions of the "Norman yoke" even led extreme critics to condemn the common law itself as a foreign corruption of pure Anglo-Saxon legal institutions. Of course, to most Puritans civil law smacked too much of Romish influence.[33]

In New England, however, magistrates and clergy had fewer qualms about adopting elements of the civil law as practiced by proper Calvinists in Scotland and especially by Dutch reformers in the Netherlands. Codification and partible inheritance in the civil law were also acceptable because they or their close analogues could be based soundly in scripture as well. The experience of many Puritan clergymen as chaplains in Germany and the

---

Shaping of New England Institutions," *ibid.*, XXXII (1975), 19-20; Timothy H. Breen and Stephen Foster, "The Puritans' Greatest Achievement: A Study of Social Cohesion in Seventeenth-Century Massachusetts," *Journal of American History*, LX (1973), 5-22; Stephen Foster, *Their Solitary Way: The Puritan Social Ethic in the First Century of Settlement in New England* (New Haven, Conn., 1971), 29-40. See also n. 35 below.

[32] Henry Sumner Maine, *Ancient Law: Its Connection with the Early History of Society and Its Relation to Modern Ideas* (New York, 1972), 11.

[33] J. G. A. Pocock, *The Ancient Constitution and the Feudal Law: A Study of English Historical Thought in the Seventeenth Century* (London, 1957), 30-55, 88-181; Christopher Hill, *Puritanism and Revolution* (London, 1958), 58-125.

Netherlands before 1630 may explain in part why elements of civil law found their way into the New England codes and other legal reforms.[34]

In England, law reforms to some degree had to confront such impediments as other legal systems, political factionalism, popular suspicions, social hierarchies, and military upheavals. In chicken-and-egg fashion, law reform could not occur without a concomitant reformation of social institutions, economic conditions, and political processes. In the early 1640s few English reformers looked beyond the immediate needs of reforming religion and executive authority. Although grievances abounded about the nature of society, the economy, and political influence, explicit complaints and proposed reforms appeared only later, failed to attract more than fragmented factions, and could not harmonize beneficial changes over the wide range of divisive problems facing the realm.

In New England, however, it was far easier to experiment with reforms answering most of the social, religious, economic, political, and legal grievances that had provoked emigration in the first place. As contributing influences, the relatively empty landscape and absence of old social hierarchies allowed experimentation to begin on a large scale, though not without dissension, divisiveness, and early failures. In this context, the diversity of the emigrants' backgrounds, instead of being a crippling handicap, provided a wide array of alternatives to choose from. Distance and difficulties of travel prevented close supervision and interference from king, bishops, and unfriendly factions in England. The self-selection of the emigrants combined with their common allegiance to some type of reformed religion to make social, economic, political, religious, and legal reforms succeed in New England.

Many historians of New England may be surprised or disconcerted by this consideration of early legal reforms within a context of revolutionary change. Recent studies of the region's communities have tended to emphasize the degree to which the settlers peacefully "transplanted" patterns of traditional agrarian communal life to the New World, while older histories argued that the settlers invented new institutions as a response to the wilderness environment.[36] Naturally, the newcomers did not suffer from mass

[34] Douglas Campbell, *The Puritan in Holland, England, and America: An Introduction to American History*, II, 4th rev. ed. (New York, 1893), 377-391, 414-418, 437-443, 452-455.

[36] In general, the recent local studies that have emphasized the continuity of stable, communal traditionalism in New England have paid little attention to the change, turmoil, mobility, and dislocations now being revealed in studies of English communities in the Tudor-Stuart period. See John Demos, *A Little Commonwealth: Family Life in Plymouth Colony* (New York, 1970), 2-11; Kenneth A. Lockridge, *A New England Town, The First Hundred Years: Dedham, Massachusetts, 1636-1736* (New York, 1970), 1-22; John J. Waters, "Hingham, Massachusetts, 1631-1661: An East Anglian Oligarchy in the New World," *Journal of Social History*, I (1968), 351-

193

amnesia after leaving England; during the early years of settlement many elements of family values, community life, and agricultural economics reflected continuity with the settlers' experience in England. Although the physical environment facilitated experimentation, few today would argue that the wilderness was a sole, deterministic causal force. Whatever social continuities or environmental influences there may have been on a local level, at a higher level of public organization and public law it is patently difficult to dismiss as merely coincidental the close congruence of social, economic, political, and legal reforms advocated by revolutionary writers in England and actually adopted in New England.

194

Admittedly, the surviving documents and early chronicles of New England present an overwhelming impression of moderation, conservatism, and dread of revolutionary tendencies in the new settlements. There were, however, compelling reasons why Bradford, Winthrop, Hooker, Davenport, and other leaders tended to obscure the true nature of their experiments and give the impression that nothing very radical was going on. First, they dreaded interference from England—from the king and bishops in the 1630s, from hostile Presbyterians in the 1640s, and even from Cromwell's tolerant Independents in the 1650s. Although for a while in the early 1640s many New Englanders hoped their experiments would kindle a shining beacon for England to follow, it quickly became apparent that England's leaders and factions did not heed or appreciate the New England Way. Thus, the true character of New England's independence in church and state needed to be concealed by obfuscation and deceptively moderate pronouncements.[36] In enacting almost all of the major reforms proposed during the Puritan Revolution, what the New Englanders actually did differed sharply from what they said they were doing.

Second, New England's officials were keenly aware that the region's independence and deviations from English law, if overtly proclaimed in revolutionary terms, might only encourage local dissidents to fragment the experiment into chaos. In cautiously adopting most of the programs of the

370; Zuckerman, *Peaceable Kingdoms*, 3-7, and especially Rutman, *American Puritanism*, 53-88. Exceptions are Powell, *Puritan Village*, 1-116; and David Grayson Allan's *After English Ways* (forthcoming). For critiques of the frontier's influence on early law see Smith, ed., *Colonial Justice in Western Massachusetts*, 157-158; and Goebel, "Law Enforcement in Colonial New York," in Flaherty, ed., *Essays in the Hist. of Early Am. Law*, 369-374.

[36] The clearest statement of the early New Englanders' deceptively moderate rhetoric is Richard B. Morris, "Massachusetts and the Common Law: The Declaration of 1646," in Flaherty, ed., *Essays in the Hist. of Early Am. Law*, 135-146. See also James Savage, ed., *John Winthrop's History of New England, 1630-1649*, I (Boston, 1853), 57, 79, 100, 109, 135, 137, 146, 153, 154, 161, 166, 170, 175, 187; Perry Miller, *Errand into the Wilderness* (Cambridge, Mass., 1956), 1-15; and Andrews, *Colonial Period of American History*, I, 400-429, II, 155-156, 173-174.

Puritan Revolution, New England also had to face challenges from almost every conceivable part of the political and religious spectrum: atheistic fishermen, Anglican royalists, Presbyterians, Seekers, "Familists," Separatists, Quakers, Antinomians, Fifth Monarchy Men, parliamentary republicans, Indian tribes, and outspoken individualists like Thomas Morton, Christopher Gardiner, Anne Hutchinson, Samuel Gorton, Thomas Lechford, Robert Child, Roger Williams, William Coddington, and William Pynchon.[37] To prevent outside interference and to legitimize their authority in the eyes of a diverse population spreading over the land, New England's leaders had to hide the independent nature of their actions behind a facade of conformity and moderation.

Though the moderate tone of early New England writings might deceive contemporary critics (and historians) for a while, the region's independence, its revolutionary enactments, and its deviations from English law, custom, and practice remained subjects of judicial and administrative debate for the remainder of the colonial period. Over the years, as memories of the early reforms faded, it was inevitable that new challenges from English officials and the changing socioeconomic conditions of a maturing society would erode and moderate the earlier innovations. Royal approval of later laws, appeals to the Privy Council, piecemeal legislation modifying earlier codes, the development of a professional bar, the lack of local law reports, and other changes tended to make the early reforms less immediately familiar to the people, less acceptable to English authority, and less independent of English legal practices. Even on the eve of the American Revolution, however, judges and attorneys were still debating the degree to which local laws did or did not conform to English law.[38]

195

[37] Savage, ed., *Winthrop's History*, I, 53, 56-58, 61, 70, 72-74, 82-86, 107, 117, 122, 132, 139-141, 146, 150, 156-158, 160-162, 166, 170, 177-179, 181, 185, 192-193; Andrews, *Colonial Period*, I, 430-495, II, 1-17, 31-36, 92-99; Wall, *Massachusetts Bay;* Breen and Foster, "Puritans' Greatest Achievement," *JAH*, LX (1973), 5-22.

[38] Fane, *Reports of Laws of Conn.*, ed. Andrews, 3, 5, 43-54; Harold D. Hazeltine, "Appeals from Colonial Courts to the King in Council, with Especial Reference to Rhode Island," American Historical Association, *Annual Report for 1894* (Washington, D.C., 1895), 299-350; Frank Strong, "A Forgotten Danger to the New England Colonies," *ibid., 1898* (Washington, D.C., 1898), 79-94; Louise Phelps Kellogg, "The American Colonial Charter," *ibid., 1904* (Washington, D.C., 1904), 192-333; John M. Murrin, "The Legal Transformation: The Bench and Bar of Eighteenth-Century Massachusetts," in Stanley N. Katz, ed., *Colonial America: Essays in Politics and Social Development* (Boston, 1971), 415-449; Joseph H. Smith, *Appeals to the Privy Council from the American Plantations* (New York, 1950), 522-653; Samuel M. Quincy, ed., *Reports of Cases Argued and Adjudged in the Superior Court of Judicature of the Province of Massachusetts Bay, between 1761 and 1772* (Boston, 1865), 9, 12-25, 42-48, 57, 70-72, 81-83, 106, 111, 133, 140, 163, 225, 238, 259-260, 286-288, 297, 313, 361, 370-381.

Ironically, in the 1760s Thomas Hutchinson, New England's champion of English authority, began publishing his history of Massachusetts and the documents vividly illustrating the region's early independence from England in religion, politics, society, economics, and law. In a classic case of publishing and perishing, Hutchinson the historian provided critics with the historic evidence that ultimately ruined Hutchinson the governor. The imperial debate led the colonists to reexamine the origins of their experience and awakened memories of the seventeenth century's revolutionary tendencies, as expressed, for example, in John Adams's *Dissertation on the Canon and Feudal Law.*[39] If only for a while and if only in part, a second revolution was needed to revive the revolutionary reforms of the first settlers.

196

[39] Thomas Hutchinson, *History of the Colony and Province of Massachusetts-Bay*, ed. Lawrence Shaw Mayo (Cambridge, Mass., 1936), I, 408-458, III, 266-267; Thomas Hutchinson, *A Collection of Original Papers Relative to the History of the Colony of Massachusetts Bay* (Boston, 1769); *The Speeches of His Excellency Governor Hutchinson, to the General Assembly of the Massachusetts-Bay* (Boston, 1773); Charles Francis Adams, ed., *The Works of John Adams . . .* , III (Boston, 1856), 448-464.

Land Tenancy and Social Order in Springfield, Massachusetts, 1652 to 1702

Stephen Innes

H ISTORIANS have emphasized the prevalence of freehold land tenure in seventeenth-century New England. Their accounts draw sharp contrasts between conditions in England that made for widespread tenancy—limited landholding, primogeniture, and restricted opportunities for spatial mobility—and the New England system, in which each town distributed large amounts of land to its inhabitants and the rule of partible inheritance supplied a patrimony for even the youngest son. In New England, moreover, an abundance of unsettled but attractive land outside the boundaries of established towns enabled those in straitened circumstances to seek their fortune elsewhere. Accordingly, land tenancy was rare; New Englanders enjoyed a measure of economic and social independence unknown in the Old World.

The amplitude of land, we are told, minimized social inequality and muted social tensions. In Dedham, Massachusetts, for example, the "incomparable abundance of land" enabled sons to "expect a patrimony which would keep [them] from having to rent land or work for another man or beg in the streets."[1] In Andover, by 1662, land allotments provided the town's earliest settlers with "land on a scale impossible for most of them to have anticipated . . . in England."[2] A resident of such communities could expect to receive approximately 200 acres during his lifetime; according to the most recent study, "an estimate of 150 acres for the typical early inhabitant of an eastern Massachusetts town is a reasonable figure."[3] Consequently, in these

Mr. Innes is a member of the Department of History at the University of Virginia. He wishes to thank Professors T. H. Breen and Margot Stein and Miss Juliette Tomlinson for their helpful criticism. He also wishes to acknowledge the generous financial assistance of the Society of Colonial Wars in the state of Illinois. Earlier versions of this article were presented at a symposium at the Newberry Library in Chicago, December 11, 1975, and at the Workshop in Economic History at the University of Chicago, December 3, 1976.

[1] Kenneth A. Lockridge, *A New England Town, The First Hundred Years: Dedham, Massachusetts, 1636-1736* (New York, 1970), 70-71.
[2] Philip J. Greven, Jr., *Four Generations: Population, Land, and Family in Colonial Andover, Massachusetts* (Ithaca, N.Y., 1970), 59.
[3] Kenneth A. Lockridge, "Land, Population and the Evolution of New England

towns the "distribution of wealth [was] relatively even and the spectrum of social rank narrow"; they composed a society of "one class, one interest, one mind."[4] Estate inventories generally ranged between £200 and £400. The average farm in England, by contrast, contained approximately 40 to 45 acres, and estate inventories of typical farmers rarely exceeded £50, while the estates of the aristocracy were valued in the tens of thousands of pounds.[5] In England tenants were many; in New England, few—or so it is said.

Yet in seventeenth-century Springfield, Massachusetts, land tenancy played a prominent role in shaping the town's socioeconomic structure. During any one year between 1652 and 1702, over one-third of the town's adult males were renting some or all of their lands, housing, or livestock. And much as rural peasants in pre-revolutionary France leased their holdings from the village's seigneur, Springfield's tenants leased predominantly from the town's largest landowner, John Pynchon.[6] In 1685, for example, 49 out of a total of 120 male inhabitants rented land or housing from Pynchon.[7] Of that same 120, 113 (94.2 percent) rented from Pynchon at some point in their lives. Between 1652 and 1702, 142 renters paid Pynchon over £4,000 for 1,500 contract years.[8] His annual income from rent receipts during this time

198

Society, 1630-1790; and an Afterthought," in Stanley N. Katz, ed., *Colonial America: Essays in Politics and Social Development* (Boston, 1971), 469-471. See also Greven, *Four Generations,* 59, and Sumner Chilton Powell, *Puritan Village: The Formation of a New England Town* (Middleton, Conn., 1963), Appendices VI and VII.

[4] Lockridge, *New England Town,* 70, 73, 76.

[5] W. G. Hoskins, *Provincial England* (London, 1963), 151-160; Mildred Campbell, *The English Yeoman Under Elizabeth and the Early Stuarts* (New Haven, Conn., 1942), chaps. 3, 4; Lawrence Stone, *Family and Fortune* (Oxford, 1973), 288-291.

[6] For a description of landlord-tenant relations in pre-revolutionary rural France see Thomas F. Sheppard, *Lourmarin in the Eighteenth Century: A Study of a French Village* (Baltimore, 1971), chaps. 1, 6, and Laurence Wylie, *Chanzeaux: A Village in Anjou* (Cambridge, Mass., 1966). While it is uncertain if Pynchon was the only landlord in 17th-century Springfield, he was the only resident engaged in large-scale, systematic leasing.

[7] John Pynchon's Account Books, 1652-1702, 6 vols., Connecticut Valley Historical Museum, Springfield, Mass., hereafter cited as Account Books. Because of their wide range of subject matter and attention to detail, these account books constitute one of the most informative sources extant for 17th-century social and economic history. They are apparently the only account books for an inland New England town now available to scholars. They make it possible to reconstruct economic and social relationships in ways impossible with more traditional types of evidence.

[8] Account Books, I-VI; 1685 tax list, inscribed "Anno Dom. 1685. An Estimate of the Plantation, both of Mens' Houses and Lands, in Springfield," Tax Collector's Office, Springfield City Hall, Springfield, Mass., hereafter cited as 1685 Tax List. The number of contract years has been calculated by totaling each contract year paid for every rental, even if some were coterminous; that is, if a man rented a 30-acre lot

ranged from £100 to £150, in addition to value derived from tenants' improvement of his land. Men rented from Pynchon primarily because he owned a disproportionate share of the town's lands—particularly the most productive and accessible acreage. His holdings in Springfield approached 2,000 acres, while the average Springfield resident in the seventeenth century held less than 70, much of it infertile or remote. Surprisingly, the inhabitants of this frontier village experienced a land shortage.

Tenancy was both a consequence and a cause of economic inequality. Men rented because their own lands were inadequate or because they lacked sufficient capital to begin farming an independent freehold. But by renting they frequently consigned themselves to economic and social stasis or, worse, to downward mobility. Instead of raising their status, tenants usually enriched Pynchon. The result, revealed dramatically in tax lists, probate inventories, and land distribution patterns, was a progressive stratification of Springfield society. Rather than evolving toward the one-class or middle-class social structure that historians have found in other early New England towns, Springfield become economically and socially polarized. It became divided between rich and poor, creditors and debotors, landlords and tenants—and the principal creditor and landlord was John Pynchon.[9]

Pynchon achieved power through a combination of inherited privilege, fortuitous circumstances, and entrepreneurial skill. In 1652 a religious dispute with the authorities of Massachusetts Bay caused William Pynchon, Springfield's magistrate and founder, to return to England. Much of his economic and political power devolved upon his twenty-six-year-old son John, who assumed control of his father's approximately 300 acres and

for six years and a yoke of oxen for the same six years, his total contract years would be 12. It is probable that the rental periods were considerably longer than the statistics cited suggest, because only the years in which Pynchon actually entered the payment for the rent in his account books were used in the sample. Repeatedly, in the account books, a contract is signed for a lease of 5, 7, 11 years, etc., but no subsequent payments are recorded. Although Pynchon was, for the period, an assiduous bookkeeper, it is likely that many payments were not recorded—or were recorded in day books that have not survived. To ensure the integrity of the statistics in this analysis, all contracts without recorded payments have been ignored. In addition to the 142 Springfield tenants, 58 residents of other valley towns also rented from Pynchon. Usually they leased lands or housing within their own communities although some rented within Springfield itself. These non-Springfield tenants were important to Pynchon, both as sources of income and as potential sources of social influence. However, because the focus of this article is on Springfield, and not Pynchon himself, these renters are not included in this analysis.

[9] John J. Waters finds similar divisions in Barnstable ("The Traditional World of the New England Peasants: A View from Seventeenth-Century Barnstable," *New England Historical and Genealogical Register*, CXXIX [1976], 3-21).

lucrative fur-trading network. The General Court also appointed him to serve on a commission designed to carry out the magistrate's functions. This commission—which the Court typically appointed for frontier communities that lacked an elected magistrate—continued until 1665, presiding over all civil and criminal disputes, selecting juries, and administering oaths. John parlayed these powers and his father's bequest into economic and political dominance.

By 1665, John Pynchon had acquired a significant measure of control over Springfield's inhabitants. His positions of authority included those of magistrate, judge of the county court of Hampshire, major (and later lieutenant colonel) of the militia, and moderator of almost every town meeting from 1661 to 1694. In addition, he controlled Springfield's economy by his vast landholdings and by his ownership of the town's only general store and all of its corn mills and saw mills. His general store not only was Springfield's sole source of manufactured imported goods but functioned as a bank and as a clearinghouse for the distribution of goods and services.[10] In an agricultural society that relied heavily on cereal grains for food, Pynchon's monopoly of the corn mills was an especially significant source of power. Most important, through his shipping and trading enterprises Pynchon linked the town's domestic economy to the outside world. Indeed, wherever a Springfield resident went—to the town meeting, the county court, the magistrate's session, the trained band, the mills, or the general store—he found John Pynchon.

Various groups within the town were directly dependent on Pynchon for their livelihood. These groups included tenants, debtors, and wage laborers, all of whom relied to a large extent on satisfactory relations with Pynchon for economic survival. In the aggregate these dependents numbered well over two hundred men between 1652 and 1702, and usually included approximately one-half the adult male population at any one time. Of the seventy-two men on the 1665 List of Springfield Inhabitants, forty (56 percent) were economically dependent on Pynchon—as tenants, debtors, wage laborers, or some combination of the three. Of the seventy-six inhabitants entered on the 1672 List of Springfield Town Meeting Voters, thirty-two (42 percent) occupied one or more of these statuses; fifty-six (47 percent) of the 120 inhabitants listed as taxpayers in 1685 can be so classified.[11]

[10] The store served as a bank because Pynchon was the only Springfield resident with sufficient liquidity to offer credit to others. It functioned as a clearinghouse for the same reason: inhabitants paid each other for goods and services through credits at the general store. As these various functions suggest, historians have overlooked the importance of the general store as a village institution in colonial America.

[11] Stephen Innes, "A Patriarchal Society: Economic Dependency and Social Order in Springfield, Mass., 1636-1702" (Ph.D. diss., Northwestern University, 1977), dependency tables.

Anthropologists describe the socioeconomic relationship which Pynchon had with many of these dependent men as patron-client contracts, defined as "an informal contractual relationship between persons of unequal status and power, which imposes reciprocal obligations of a different kind on each of the parties."[12] As patron, Pynchon exchanged the fruits of his status and power for the loyalty of his clients. He rented them land, provided employment, and lent money. His clients, for their part, accordingly accepted certain restrictions on their behavior. Those tenants whose rent was in arrears, men chronically indebted to Pynchon, and wage laborers dependent on him for employment were not likely to oppose his wishes in the town meeting or elsewhere.

As a corporate entity, the town depended on patronage from Pynchon. When the town meeting was unable to secure sufficient funds to build a new mill, school, or house of correction, or when it wanted to construct a storage chamber over the meeting house or undertake sheep-raising or swine-raising projects, Pynchon stepped in and provided the requisite funds. In return, the town granted him extensive tracts of land, toll privileges at the proposed mill, and the labor of citizens.[13] The inhabitants also accorded Pynchon the deference befitting his station. They addressed him as the "Worshipful Major Pynchon" and granted him such privileges as exemption from labor on public works.

The linchpin of Pynchon's dominance was his commanding position as mediator between Springfield and the outside world.[14] As magistrate, he held

201

[12] Sydel F. Silverman, "Patronage and Community-Nation Relationships in Central Italy," *Ethnology*, IV (1965), 172-188. See also George M. Foster, "The Dyadic Contract: A Model for the Social Structure of a Mexican Village," *American Anthropologist*, N.S., LXIII (1961), 1173-1192, and "The Dyadic Contract in Tzintzuntzan, II: Patron-Client Relationships," *ibid.*, LXV (1963), 1280-1294; J. A. Pitt-Rivers, *The People of the Sierra* (Chicago, 1961), 154-155; Morton H. Fried, *Fabric of Chinese Society: A Study of the Social Life of a Chinese County Seat* (New York, 1953), 224, 227; and Michael Kenny, "Patterns of Patronage in Spain," *Anthropological Quarterly*, XXXIII (1960), 14-23. For an excellent discussion of the relationship of cliency to the formation of village factions see Edit Fel and Tamas Hofer, "Tanyaket-s, Patron-Client Relations, and Political Factions in Atany," *Am. Anthropologist*, N.S., LXXV (1973), 787-800.

[13] Henry M. Burt, *The First Century of the History of Springfield: The Official Records from 1636 to 1736* (Springfield, 1898-1899), I, 61, 72, 280, 303-304, 352-355, II, 221. These volumes include the Springfield Town Records from 1636 to 1736 and the source will be cited hereafter as *Springfield Town Recs.*

[14] The anthropological literature that deals with mediators is extensive. See Silverman, "Patronage and Community-Nation Relationships," *Ethnology*, IV (1965), 172-188; Eric R. Wolf, "Aspects of Group Relations in a Complex Society: Mexico," *Am. Anthropologist*, N.S., LVIII (1956), 1065-1078; Clifford Geertz, "The Javanese Kijaji: The Changing Role of a Cultural Broker," *Comparative Studies in Society and History*, II (1960), 228-249; T. H. Breen, "Persistent

the highest office in the community; he also sat on the Bay Colony's council in Boston, over 100 forested, mountainous miles away. His affluence gave him leisure, wherewithal, and special reason to play the roles of power that linked the locality to the province. If the General Court wanted new plantations established in the Connecticut Valley, negotiations conducted with the Mohawks or with Connecticut, or boundaries laid out, it invariably turned to Pynchon. He also served as Springfield's advocate at the Court when the town requested lower taxes or disputed with its neighbors over land. By informal communications with other leaders Pynchon kept himself and his village abreast of provincial and even international events. Springfield learned of wars with the Dutch or the machinations of politics in London from letters he received from Governor John Winthrop, Jr., of Connecticut and Captain Sylvester Salisbury, commander-in-chief at Fort Albany.[15]

202

Likewise, through his commercial enterprises Pynchon linked the local economy to the outside world. He accumulated and transshipped surplus wheat, cattle, and timber from his own farms and from farms of residents throughout the valley. His position was especially advantageous because foodstuffs and livestock constituted the principal form of payment both for goods purchased at his store and for rents on his land. In return, he imported ironwares and linens—commodities always in short supply in the colonies. Pynchon thus achieved command over both export and import operations in the upper Valley.

The town and provincial governments rewarded Pynchon's services with generous land grants. When Springfield allocated land to its inhabitants, Pynchon invariably received the lion's share. In the allotment of the "inner commons" in 1699, the town awarded him 133 rods of mile-long strips; the next largest recipient, Pynchon's nephew John Holyoke, was given only 26

Localism: English Social Change and the Shaping of New England Institutions," *William and Mary Quarterly*, 3d Ser., XXXII (1975), 9; and Peter Laslett, "The Gentry of Kent in 1640," *Cambridge Historical Journal*, IX (1947-1949), 148-164. For an analysis of the extraordinary power of a magistrate in early Massachusetts see John M. Murrin, "Anglicizing an American Colony: The Transformation of Provincial Massachusetts" (Ph.D. diss., Yale University, 1966), 155-156.

[15] John Winthrop, Jr., to John Pynchon, Nov. 9, 1674, *Winthrop Papers*, XVII (Massachusetts Historical Society, *Collections*, 4th Ser., XXXVI-XXXVII [Boston, 1863-1865]), 9; John Pynchon to Capt. Salisbury, July 20, 1678, in E. B. O'Callaghan and J. H. Brodhead, eds., *Documents Relating to the Colonial History of the State of New York*, XIII (Albany, 1881), 511. Men functioned as mediators in other New England towns as well. John Winthrop, Jr., played this role in Ipswich, Massachusetts, and Mystic and New Haven, Connecticut. See Richard S. Dunn, *Puritans and Yankees* (New York, 1971), 70, 74-79. John Otis III also apparently functioned as a mediator in Barnstable, Massachusetts. See John J. Waters, Jr., *The Otis Family in Provincial and Revolutionary Massachusetts* (Chapel Hill, N.C., 1968), 46.

rods.[16] The General Court was equally generous. During the period 1659-1685, Pynchon received from the Court over 8,170 acres (predominately located outside Springfield) for services performed by him or his father William.[17] In 1659, the Court granted Pynchon 1,000 acres, and seven years later "for severall services past" it awarded him an additional 500.[18] In 1681, "in consideration of his paines formerly in runing our patent line," the Court gave him an island in the Connecticut River below Enfield Falls.[19] The suspension of the first Massachusetts charter in 1684 did not curtail Pynchon's receipt of additional lands. On June 4, 1685, the Court granted Pynchon, William Avery, and Hezekiah Usher a total of 1,000 acres in the Connecticut Valley, and later that day, "in answer to his petition," it gave "the quantity of eight miles square [5,120 acres] to Major John Pynchon."[20] He eventually owned land in every Massachusetts town in the Valley, in addition to 2,288 acres at Groton, Connecticut, and part of the island of Antigua in the West Indies.[21] At his death in 1703, in a community where almost half of the estate inventories were valued under £100, the value of Pynchon's real estate holdings alone exceeded £8,000.[22]

Local and provincial power reinforced each other. Because both the local community and the provincial hierarchy saw Pynchon as an indispensable man, they rewarded him with land commensurate with his worth. This in turn increased his power, both in the community and beyond. The result was a spiral effect in which power brought land and land brought more power.

203

[16] "Coppy of Mens Lots in the 2d Division," Apr. 1699, Springfield Public Library.
[17] N. B. Shurtleff, ed., *Records of the Governor and Company of the Massachusetts Bay in New England* (Boston, 1853-1854), IV, Pt. 1, 402, Pt. 2, 306; *ibid.*, V, 482-486, hereafter cited as *Mass. Recs.*; Massachusetts Archives, XLV, 82, Archives Dept., State House, Boston. Pynchon also may have received an additional 1,000 acres from the Court after his extensive losses sustained during King Philip's War in 1676; see J. G. Holland, *History of Western Massachusetts* (Springfield, 1845), I, 309. Pynchon and two other men received a grant of 10 sq. miles in 1659 for what proved to be an abortive effort to establish a fur trading post 40 miles west of Springfield; see Arthur H. Buffington, "New England and the Western Fur Trade, 1629-1675," Colonial Society of Massachusetts, *Transactions*, XVIII (1917), 176-177. Theodore B. Lewis underestimates Pynchon's landholdings in "Land Speculation and the Dudley Council of 1686," *WMQ*, 3d Ser., XXXI (1974), 255-272.
[18] *Mass. Recs.*, IV, Pt. 1, 402, Pt. 2, 306.
[19] *Ibid.*, V, 329-330.
[20] *Ibid.*, 482; Mass. Archives, CXII, 414A.
[21] Account Books, II, 238-239; Samuel Willys to Connecticut General Court, Oct. 1687, "Private Controversies 1642-1716," MS, Ser. 1, III, doc. 258, Connecticut Archives, Connecticut State Library, Hartford, Conn.
[22] Hampshire County Probate Records, Box 119, No. 40, Hampton County Court, Springfield, Mass.

Pynchon used some of this land for speculative purposes; the rest he let out to tenants.

Land shortage, above all other causes, drove Springfield inhabitants to rent from John Pynchon. Unlike other New England towns whose commons were not exhausted until the mid-eighteenth century, Springfield experienced a shortage almost from the beginning.[23] By 1655, there were already so many landless men in Springfield that the community devised a separate system for taxing them.[24] Many towns consistently discouraged emigration from the town center, but Springfield passed legislation designed to facilitate this process and thereby lessen the demand for land.[25] As early as 1664, the town meeting unhappily concluded that "there are diverse Persons in this Town who have but little land."[26] Fathers complained they had insufficient land to provide an inheritance for their sons. Moreover, because of widespread dissatisfaction within Springfield over land distribution policies, the committees responsible for land grants were in continual disarray. During its first three decades the town continually vacillated over the question of which institution—the board of selectmen, a special ad hoc committee, or the entire town meeting—should have responsibility for allocating land.[27]

From 1636 to 1685 the mean acreage possessed by a head of a household in Springfield fluctuated between 45 and 70 acres, less than half the acreage of Dedham and Andover. In its simplest form, the reason why most men had so little land was that John Pynchon and his kinsmen had so much. The only alternative for men with insufficient lands was to rent or to leave, and although Springfield's first generation experienced an exceedingly high rate of physical mobility, by the 1660s most inhabitants chose to stay. Of the seventy-two men entered on the tax list of 1664, fifty-five (76 percent) would die in Springfield. In 1672, seventy-six male inhabitants lived in Springfield; sixty-one (80 percent) of them remained in the town for the duration of their lives. By 1685 the situation again changed as inhabitants began to leave Springfield in greater numbers. Of the 120 residents on the tax list of that year, only seventy-six (63 percent) remained permanently in the town. Pressures on Springfield's land supply, brought about by the maturation of the town's second generation, undoubtedly played a role in this increase.

---

[23] Lockridge, "Land, Population and the Evolution," in Katz, ed., *Colonial America*, 467-484; Charles S. Grant, *Democracy in the Connecticut Frontier Town of Kent* (New York, 1961), 97-103.

[24] *Springfield Town Recs.*, I, 245.

[25] *Ibid.*, 248-249. To encourage settlement of Woronoco, then under Springfield's control, the town rebated one-half the rates assessed there.

[26] *Ibid.*, 318.

[27] *Ibid.*, II, 81.

Fathers who were themselves tenants or debtors were not in a position to bequeath a sufficient patrimony to the next generation.[28]

Patterns of unequal land distribution appeared with the town's founding and intensified as the century progressed. The 1646 tax list reveals that three men dominated the town's landholdings: William Pynchon, the founder, and his sons-in-law, Henry Smith and Elizur Holyoke. These three held 510 acres, more than 25 percent of the lands granted. Of the forty-two land-owners, Pynchon, with 237 acres, had the largest holding. After Pynchon, Smith, and Holyoke, the next largest holding was the minister's 67 acres. The average acreage was 47.9.[29] Although Springfield's early land distribution patterns were not demonstrably more inequitable than those of other towns at a similar stage, the concentration of so much land in the hands of a single family was unusual; and it prefigured the future.

205

The 1685 tax list reflected the culmination of the tendencies evident in 1646. Of a total of approximately 9,000 acres held by 120 persons, John Pynchon owned over 1,800 (20 percent). The acreage of the next largest landowner, Japhet Chapin, was 365. Pynchon held more land than the collective acreage of the fifty-two smallest owners, or 43 percent of the total number of male freeholders. The bottom 10 percent possessed less than 1 percent; the bottom 20 percent, 4.2 percent; and the bottom 30 percent, 8.6 percent. With Pynchon's holdings subtracted from the whole, the average acreage was 66. Forty-nine men held estates smaller than 50 acres, and sixteen owned under 25 acres.[30]

The landholdings of many of Springfield's inhabitants, in addition to being small, were often infertile or remote. Although the town possessed some of the best land in the Connecticut Valley, this land was concentrated in small areas of approximately four square miles on the west side of the river, two square miles south of the town center, and something less than two

[28] *Ibid.*, II, 76-77, 115-116; 1685 Tax List.

[29] *Springfield Town Recs.*, I, 190-191.

[30] 1685 Tax List. Because the tax list is in a poor state of preservation, portions of it are difficult to decipher. Louis Seig estimates that Pynchon's landholdings were closer to 2,000 acres ("Concepts of Change and the Historical Method in Geography: The Case of Springfield, Massachusetts" [Ph.D. diss., University of Minnesota, 1968], 112-116). The problem of assessing landholdings is compounded by the town's practice of listing rented land among a man's holdings if the rental contract required him to pay taxes on it. Because it is not always possible to distinguish rented land from owned land on the tax list, in these calculations all lands under a man's name are assumed to be his own. As this was not always the case, the patterns of land distribution were more inequitable than these statistics suggest. Estimates of the number of acres necessary to provide adequately for a family of seven vary greatly, largely because the relevant evidence is fragmentary and often ambiguous. Speculations range from 28 to 100 acres, depending on such variables as soil fertility, agricultural techniques, access to markets, and dietary habits.

square miles north of the center. Much of the remainder was composed of woodlands, unimprovable pine barrens, marshes, and terrain so rugged as to be useless for farming. John Pynchon's holdings were concentrated in the best planting fields: the "Plaine" north of the center, the "third division," Chicopee Field, and the area southwest of the Agawam River. Men without allotments in these fields were consigned to outlying or unproductive lots.[31] Consequently, rather than work infertile lands or make the daily trek to distant fields, many turned to Pynchon to rent. In a 1676 petition to the General Court for relief from garrison duties, the town declared that "many are forced to hyre land here, there own being so remote."[32]

206 The unequal distribution of land is reflected in estate inventories. From 1650 to 1705, the town of Hampshire County probated the estates of seventy Springfield decedents.[33] The distribution of wealth in these inventories parallels the patterns found in the tax lists. With adjustments made for indebtedness, the total value of the probated estates was £22,843. Of this amount, Pynchon's estate totaled £8,446 (37 percent). The top 5 percent of the decedents controlled £11,721, or 51 percent of the inventoried wealth. The bottom 20 percent held estates valued at a total of £243 (1 percent), and the bottom 50 percent controlled £1,951 (8.5 percent). The bottom sixty-two men (89 percent of the decedents) held a total of £8,547 (37.4 percent). Pynchon thus controlled as much wealth as the bottom 89 percent of the group. Only three men other than Pynchon held estates valued in excess of £800. Ensign Benjamin Cooley died in 1684, with holdings of £1,241. Pynchon's brother-in-law, Elizur Holyoke, died eight years later, leaving an estate of £1,187. Quartermaster George Colton's estate was valued at £847. At the other extreme, thirty decedents, or 43 percent of the total, left estates of less than £100, fifteen of which were valued below £50. Six men died with assets valued under £25; four of these died as town charges. Only 24 percent of the decedents, seventeen men, left estates within the supposedly normative £200 to £400 range.[34]

For the purposes of this analysis, tenants are grouped according to the degree of their dependency on Pynchon for economic sufficiency. Because the

[31] 1685 Tax List.
[32] Springfield Petition to General Court, Aug. 30, 1676, Conn. Valley Hist. Mus.
[33] Hampshire Co. Probate Recs., I-IV. Many Springfield decedents never had their estates inventoried. However, if the conventional wisdom among quantitative historians is correct, those dying young or poor were the most likely to be excluded.
[34] Ibid. For an excellent comparative view of the social structure of another Connecticut Valley town see Linda A. Bissell, "From One Generation to Another: Mobility in Seventeenth-Century Windsor, Connecticut," WMQ, 3d Ser., XXXI (1974), 79-110.

forms of dependence were complex and variegated, it is not logical simply to categorize tenants according to the number of acres leased or the duration of the rental period.[35] A tenant is classed as dependent whenever some dimension of his rental—its size, scope, character, duration, costs, or obligations—indicates that he was unable or unwilling to subsist without the lease.

The forms of dependency varied greatly. Some tenants leased 80-acre farms, complete with housing, orchards, livestock, and tools, for twenty years or longer—often at a rent as high as £22 yearly. Others rented a single acre of meadow for one year at six shillings. Most leases fell between these extremes. A typical renter might hold 15 acres, some housing, and a yoke of oxen for between twelve and sixteen years. Most tenants possessed lands of their own as well; they leased to supplement, not supplant their holdings. In addition to oxen, tenants rented horses, bulls, cows, sheep, and pigs. Some leased corn or saw mills from Pynchon, at charges up to £18 a year. Artisans rented their tools from him; a blacksmith leased everything in his shop. To his more affluent tenants Pynchon rented fur-trading rights, warehouse space, and shares in oceangoing vessels.[36]

In addition to their rent, tenants assumed a variety of ancillary obligations. They were responsible for constructing and maintaining fences on the rented land, and frequently for the taxes as well. Moreover, Pynchon often required his tenants to clear and "bring to plowing" all or part of the leasehold. Some contracts also stipulated that the tenant would erect housing, barns or sheds. Finally, Pynchon received half and sometimes all of the offspring of the rented livestock.

Tenancy in seventeenth-century Springfield was often a swift route to economic hardship. In a frontier agricultural society the labor involved in clearing land, erecting fences, and nurturing livestock was a significant capital investment. Only by this investment could most men climb the economic ladder. But labor for someone else's benefit was counterproductive, for if, after clearing and plowing the land, constructing fences and sometimes buildings, raising stock and paying rent and taxes, a tenant surrendered his lease, all money and labor invested were lost.[37] Similarly, cows, horses, pigs, and sheep were valued as much for the offspring they produced as for their daily utility. Tenancy tended to impoverish those who were already economi-

[35] Pynchon's occasional failure to include the size of the lot rented in the contract further complicates any appraisal of average acreage patterns.

[36] Unless otherwise stated, all the following information on tenancy is drawn from John Pynchon's account books.

[37] Aubrey C. Land discusses similar problems experienced by tenants in the tidewater South during the 18th century in "Economic Base and Social Structure: The Northern Chesapeake in the Eighteenth Century," *Journal of Economic History.* XXV (1965), 639-654.

cally vulnerable. Many became chronic debtors, and a large number lost sizable amounts of land, housing, or livestock to Pynchon for their debts, thus further stratifying the society.

There was another side to tenancy. It enabled some individuals to raise their standard of living, even though at the price of increased dependence on Pynchon. Like tenants in eighteenth-century New York, men without sufficient capital to purchase the land, provisions, and equipment required to start their own freehold, saw tenancy as an attractive alternative to the life of a wage laborer. Indeed, some men may have come to Springfield specifically in order to rent from Pynchon. However, unlike tenants in New York, who apparently received equity for their improvements of the leasehold and thus were rewarded for their time and labor, Springfield's tenants built and cleared only for the landlord's ultimate benefit.[38] Tenancy in Springfield enabled some men to move up from laborer to husbandman, but the renter's long-term prospects were frequently circumscribed by an inability to gain enough wealth to become independent.

John Pynchon's account books make it possible to identify six classes of renters in Springfield: (1) fifteen tenant farmers (characterized by Pynchon as "My Farmers"); (2) fifty-two dependent renters; (3) thirty short-term dependent renters; (4) nine long-term independent renters; (5) thirty-one short-term independent renters; and (6) five who rented animals exclusively. Of these, the tenant farmers were the most dependent.

The tenant farmers leased self-contained, fully equipped farms for extended periods at high rents. Their only contribution to the arrangement was labor. Pynchon supplied the lands, housing, barns, draft and dairy animals, and tools. The cost was accordingly high: £18 yearly was the most common sum, an amount often equal to the value of half or more of the tenant's harvest. Pynchon's fifteen tenant farmers collectively paid for a total of 226 contract years, with total payments of £1,093. The average duration of their rental period was fifteen years.[39] Most began renting from Pynchon while in their late twenties or early thirties and continued in some kind of contractual relationship with him as long as they remained in Springfield.

Isaac Morgan's experience as a tenant farmer was typical. Morgan first rented land from Pynchon in March 1672, when he leased 3½ acres in the Chicopee section of the town.[40] After his marriage the next year, he sought additional lands and equipment. On December 25, 1673, he rented a 42-acre farm from Pynchon for a term of eleven years. Pynchon provided "sixty

[38] For considerations of New York tenancy see Sung Bok Kim, "A New Look at the Great Landlords of Eighteenth-Century New York," *WMQ*, 3d Ser., XXVII (1970), 581-614; Patricia U. Bonomi, *A Factious People: Politics and Society in Colonial New York* (New York, 1971), 179-228.

[39] Account Books, I-VI.

[40] *Ibid.*, V, 421.

loads of dung to mend the land" and agreed to "build a house for the said Isaac Morgan to dwell in to the End of the term." He also supplied "a Barne . . . Three cows, a yoak of oxen and a horse together with a Cart, and wheels, yoak and Plough and chaine and all irons for the teams . . . [and] 80 apple trees for the said Isaac's use."[41] Morgan, for his part, agreed to clear and plow all the upland as well as pay both the town rates on the livestock and rent graduated up to £22 yearly.[42]

In 1667 John Petty, another tenant farmer, leased Pynchon's 80-acre "Tenement Farme" complete with oxen, on the west side of the river. Petty held the farm for ten years, paying an annual rent graded from £8 to £16. At the expiration of his lease—and after an abortive attempt to buy a house, homelot, and 27 acres of upland from Pynchon—he paid £3 10s. yearly for the rest of his life for the use of the second leasehold.[43] Petty rented Pynchon's lands because his own were inadequate; his real estate at his death in 1680 was valued at only £46.[44] From 1667 to 1680 Petty paid Pynchon for a total of twenty-one contract years, with payments in excess of £160. In a society where estate inventories typically did not exceed £150 and the annual wage for a farm laborer was £8, £160 was an extraordinarily large sum to transfer to one man during a lifetime. It consigned Petty to permanent tenancy.[45]

Jonathan Ball's career as a tenant farmer paralleled Petty's in many ways. In 1677, at age thirty-two, he leased an 80-acre farm in joint tenancy with Samuel Taylor. They held the farm until 1684, paying an annual rent of £18. In 1684 Ball rented two acres of meadow at sixteen shillings, and in 1688 he leased 11 acres of Pynchon's most fertile land on the west bank of the river at £3 8s. yearly. Ball held this land until Pynchon's death, fifteen years later.[46] By that time he had paid for a total of twenty-five contract years, with cumulative payments in excess of £145. This period of extended tenancy is attributable, as with Petty, to insufficient lands. The 1685 tax list shows that Ball possessed only 29 acres, despite the fact that he was forty years old and had been married twelve years. Moreover, probably less than half of this land was actually under tillage: 16 of Ball's 29 acres were located in a virtually inaccessible section of Springfield known as the "Pickle."[47]

With annual rents as high as £22, Pynchon recognized the economic value

209

[41] *Ibid.*, 422-423.
[42] *Ibid.* King Philip's followers destroyed the farm when they attacked Springfield in 1676. Morgan continued to rent from Pynchon, however; during his 16-year rental career he leased additional plowland, meadow, and oxen.
[43] *Ibid.*, V, 424-425. Petty also rented land from the town. See *Springfield Town Recs.*, I, 415.
[44] Hampshire Co. Probate Recs., II, 16.
[45] Account Books, III, 154-155, V, 62-63, 424-425.
[46] *Ibid.*, V, 524-525, VI, 18-19.
[47] 1685 Tax List.

of his tenant farmers. In a letter to his son Joseph, describing the burning of much of Springfield by King Philip's Indians in 1675, he underscored his reliance on income derived from tenants and debtors.[48] After relating the town's and his own losses, he cited the destruction visited on his tenants, particularly the farmers: "Four of those houses and barns... which were burnt in this towne belongeth to me also. So God hath laid me low. My farmers are also undone, and many in this town that were in my debt utterly disabled, so that I am really reduced to great straits."[49] In a letter to the Reverend John Russell of Hadley, Pynchon lamented the burning of "houses and barns I had let out to tenants."[50]

The second class of tenants, the dependent renters, was the largest and most important category of renters in Springfield. The fifty-two men in this group paid for 894 contract years, with total payments of £2,133. Their rental careers lasted an average of seventeen years; their average lifetime payments exceeded £44, in addition to rates and labor.[51] Each dependent renter was in some vital way reliant on his lease for economic sustenance. The group included both selectmen and men drawn from the town's poorest families.

Edward Foster's experience as a dependent renter illustrates how some men used tenancy to make the transition from laborer to husbandman. Foster originally came to Springfied as an indentured servant and first rented land from Pynchon in 1668, but he remained a tenant almost continuously until 1702.[52] During this time he paid for thirty-six contract years, with total payments of £153. In the late 1660s and early 1670s Foster leased a 3½ acre-homelot and 10 acres of bottom land. His rent for these holdings was over £5 yearly—approximately half his former annual income as a laborer. In 1673 Foster signed a contract with Pynchon that significantly altered his tenancy status. Now, rather than a two- or three-year lease, Foster agreed to a ten-year rental period. If he had envisioned his earlier leases as temporary expedients until he secured sufficient land of his own, he evidently abandoned that hope in 1673. The new contract consolidated all of Foster's

---

[48] For an account of the Indian attack on Springfield and the resultant social dislocation see Mason A. Green, *Springfield, 1636-1886; history of town and city* ... (Springfield, Mass., 1888), 581-582. Pynchon's fleeting plans to quit the town because of the losses he sustained were greeted with alarm in Boston. Gov. John Leverett immediately dispatched a letter reminding the Springfield magistrate that the future of the town lay in his hands. Leverett to John Pynchon, Sept. 8, 1675, in "Letters of Gov. Leverett," *NEHGR*, XLVIII (1894), 319.
[49] John Pynchon to Joseph Pynchon, Oct. 20, 1675, Conn. Valley Hist. Mus.
[50] Mass. Archives, LXVII, 282.
[51] Account Books, I-VI.
[52] Joseph H. Smith, ed., *Colonial Justice in Western Massachusetts (1639-1702): The Pynchon Court Record* ... (Cambridge, Mass., 1961), 225, hereafter cited as *Pynchon Court Rec.*

existing leases, along with additional meadow land, and called for rents of £7 yearly. He held this lease for the next eighteen years, until 1690. He subsequently rented five more acres in the rich Cold Spring Bottom for thirty shillings annually, which he paid for the next seven years.[53] Foster, like the tenant farmers, was apparently driven to rent because his own holdings were insufficient. In 1685 he owned only 25 acres, six of which were located in a distant and barren section known as None Such.[54] Although the remainder of his lands included some of Springfield's most fertile acreage, Foster nonetheless felt compelled to rent.

Other dependent renters similarly demonstrated by the scope and duration of their leaseholds that they looked to Pynchon and not to the town meeting for the lands they required. In 1689 John Kilum signed an agreement with Pynchon that is almost indistinguishable from the type of contract held by the tenant farmers. Pynchon "Lett out to John Kilum for 15 years land over Agawam . . . 45 acres." The contract specified the Kilum would "cleare and improve at least 15 acre," build "a good timber house and silo," and plant an orchard. Pynchon agreed to provide boards for the floors and the exterior of the house. The contract also required Kilum to build and maintain fences and pay all rates up to ten shillings. After fulfilling these obligations and paying up to £5 in rent, Kilum was expected to "leave all Tennentable" at the expiration of the lease.[55]

Such leading figures as selectmen and deputies to the General Court were also numbered among the dependent renters. John Dumbleton, a selectman for sixteen terms and a militia officer, was one of Pynchon's most valued tenants.[56] During a rental career that lasted from 1652 to 1692 and included fifteen separate contracts, he paid for a total of sixty-six contract years, with payments of £117.[57] He leased at various times over 50 acres, as well as oxen, bulls, and horses.[58] Abel Wright, like Dumbleton, was firmly entrenched in the town's leadership. Selectman, militia lieutenant, and representative to the General Court, Wright clearly enjoyed the esteem of his fellow inhabitants.[59] He, too, rented from Pynchon. Between 1668 and 1695, he paid Pynchon for

[53] Account Books, III, 184-185, V, 58-59, 474-475, VI, 54-55.

[54] 1685 Tax List.

[55] Account Books, VI, 228-229. Kilum held this land for 9 years, during which time he and Pynchon renegotiated the rent from £5 to £7 10s. annually. Kilum subsequently leased a total of over 30 acres of plowing and meadow land, some at joint tenancy. In 1693 he leased 11 acres in joint tenancy with Thomas Jones for £3 8s. yearly. By the time of John Pynchon's death in 1703, Kilum had paid for 16 contract years with lifetime payments in excess of £66.

[56] *Pynchon Court Rec.*, 266.

[57] Account Books, I, 67-69, II, 164, III, 181, V, 50-51, 182-183, 540, VI, 196.

[58] *Ibid.*, III, 181. Dumbleton owned 50 acres of excellent land in 1685, but it was apparently inadequate to meet his needs.

[59] *Pynchon Court Rec.*, 313, 387.

211

thirty-one contract years, renting plowland, meadow, oxen, and bulls. His payments totaled £56, in addition to rates and labor. In 1668 Wright leased land which Pynchon two days earlier had taken for debts from Benjamin Dorchester. The contract provided that if, at the expiration of the term, Wright "can attain to buy the land he is to have it before another." Unfortunately for Wright, he was unable to buy the land at the specified time, and he continued to pay the thirty-eight shillings annual rent for the next eighteen years.[60]

Although the dependent renters included men drawn from both the town's leadership elite and the servant class, most tenants came from a large middle group, composed of men who were usually freemen but rarely civil leaders. The substance and diversity of their experiences are illustrated by the rental careers of several farmers, millers, and artisans: Lazarus Miller, Philip Mattone, John Barber, Increase Sikes, Henry Rogers, Anthony Dorchester, John Stewart, and James Mun. During his rental career, which was cut short by his death at age forty-two, Lazarus Miller rented over 77 acres of upland and meadow as well as housing, orchards, and oxen. Between 1680 and 1697, he engaged with Pynchon for twenty-two contract years.[61] He, too, rented because his own lands were inadequate. In 1685 he held 64 acres, all in the distant and infertile section known as Block Bridge. This land was valued at only two shillings, fivepence per acre in contrast to values of up to sixty shillings per acre in the planting fields immediately across the river. And, largely because he was compelled to rent, Miller forfeited any prospects for upward mobility. At his death his entire estate was valued at an unremark- able £34, only £11 of which was in real estate. His outstanding debts to Pynchon totaled £18.[62]

Philip Mattone rented eighteen cow commons and four sheep commons

---

[60] Account Books, III, 116-117, V, 102-103, VI, 174, VI, Index, 4. Pynchon rarely allowed land to stand unproductive long. On Feb. 20, 1667, he sold Frances Pepper "that alotment which I bought of William Brooke (a few days ago)." *Ibid.*, III, 138. In April 1667, when Pynchon took all of Samuel Marshfield's land and housing on the east side of the Connecticut River for debts, he immediately rented the land to Nathaniel Ely for £8 yearly. *Ibid.*, 108. Wright held 160 acres in 1685; it seems surprising, therefore, that he rented under conditions that suggest economic distress. However, an examination of the location and valuation of Wright's lands reveals that much of his acreage was either remote or unsuitable for cultivation. His 160 acres were valued at £49, an average of only 6s. per acre.

[61] Account Books, V, 490-491, VI, 190-191, VI, Index. In 1680 Miller rented a 10-12 acre lot, an orchard and a house in Chicopee Plain and held it for two years, paying £3 10s. rent. In 1684 he leased a 24 acre lot, also in Chicopee Field, at £1 10s. In 1694 he leased a 30 acre lot, 10 acres of which were already broken up. His rent was £1 15s. yearly as well as fences and rates. In addition, he was to clear the remaining land and build a shelter. His widow was unable to redeem his debts to Pynchon after his death in 1697.

[62] Hampshire Co. Probate Recs., III, 38.

which Pynchon owned in Deerfield. His obligations under his eleven-year lease were considerable. In addition to a rent graduated up to £4, he agreed to pay all rates, maintain the fences, and build "a good dwelling house strong substantial and well Built and completely furnished," with dimensions of 30-by-20-by-10-feet as well as a barn of at least 48-by-24-by-14-feet.[63] The contract stipulated that Mattone "compleate and furnish the same before the End of the term, then leave and deliver all up in good repair." He was thus required to make a significant capital investment with the prospect of abandoning it all to Pynchon—a particularly revealing example of how wealth was transferred to Pynchon by both rent and labor. Although Mattone moved to Deerfield, apparently because his 40 acres in Springfield were inadequate to his needs, he scarcely improved his prospects for upward mobility by his disadvantageous arrangement with Pynchon. At his death in 1696 his estate was valued at £87, only £23 of which were in lands.[64]

John Barber rented, at least in part, because in 1678 he had lost 12 acres of his best land to Pynchon for debts of £15. His rental career extended from 1671 to 1696, during which time he paid £88 for over 50 acres of Pynchon's rich bottom land on the west side of the river, land that consistently demanded the highest rental payments charged by Pynchon.[65] Increase Sikes, another dependent renter, leased land, oxen, and a saw mill during a rental career that lasted from 1669 to 1696 and cost him £86 for twenty-two contract years.[66] Henry Rogers, between 1674 and 1699, leased at various times over 30 acres of upland and meadow. He paid £53 for thirty-seven contract years.[67]

Millers and artisans often turned to Pynchon to supply their needs. Anthony Dorchester rented Pynchon's corn and saw mills for annual payments of £13 and £18 respectively.[68] John Stewart, the town blacksmith, leased all his tools and materials from "1 greate anvill" down to "a spring lock" and "21 pairs of horseshoes."[69] The dependent renters also included

---

[63] Account Books, V, 536-537. Pynchon agreed to supply two cows in addition to the land. As this passage reveals, the word "commons" clung to some lands formerly held in common even after they passed into private ownership.

[64] Hampshire Co. Probate Recs., III, 27.

[65] Account Books, V, 42-43, 292, VI, 222-223. Barber's rental career gained momentum with the passage of time. In the 1670s and 1680s he paid an average of £3 annually in rent; but in the 1690s this figure rose to £6, in addition to rates and labor.

[66] Ibid., III, 173, V, 417-419, 546-547, VI, 120-121.

[67] Ibid., V, 464-465, VI, 88.

[68] Ibid., I, 128-129, 296, II, 136-137, III, 105, 252, V, 132, 352-353, 528.

[69] Ibid., II, 282-283, III, 136-137, V, 90. Stewart never escaped chronic, debilitating indebtedness to Pynchon. In 1663, for a debt of £23 2s. 4d., Stewart mortgaged to Pynchon his house, orchard and all his lands for payment within two years. Pynchon foreclosed on Feb. 21, 1670, although he allowed Stewart "Liberty to Live in the house till mid-summer" (ibid., 282, III, 137).

men so clearly impoverished that they could afford to rent only small parcels of land. Characteristically, these men leased the same small lot for extended periods. James Mun rented a four-acre lot from 1688 to 1700, at an annual payment of between one and two pounds. In 1685 Mun owned only 19 acres, valued at £8 18s.[70]

The third class of tenants was the short-term dependent renters—men who relied on leases from Pynchon to help them through brief periods of economic dislocation. These thirty renters paid approximately £240 for 218 contract years. The average duration of their rental period was seven years; their average total payment was £8.[71] Their dependency on Pynchon is illustrated by the scope and substance of their contracts. Joseph Marks, although he paid for only seven contract years, rented a 20-acre lot in Chicopee Field (for £3 10s. yearly), a shed, a yoke of oxen, a mare, and a gun.[72] Miles Morgan's nine contract years included leases for a house, 25 acres, oxen, a bull, and a cow.[73] Ebenezer Graves rented a 21-acre lot in Chicopee in joint tenancy with his brother in 1689; and from 1691 to 1694 he paid Pynchon up to £7 yearly for the use of lands on the west side of the river.[74] Thomas Copley leased a saw mill and a corn mill between 1681 and 1685. The mills were held at halves: Copley tended and maintained the mill, while Pynchon helped defray maintenance costs. The two men divided the tolls equally at year's end.[75]

The short-term dependent renters included a high percentage of joint or multiple tenancies. Under these leases the tenants divided expenses, profits, and labor according to a prearranged formula. John Burt, Benjamin Knowlton, and Thomas Mirrick rented an 11-acre lot in the third division from 1689 to 1693 "at thirds."[76] Victory Sikes and John Warner leased meadow land over the Agawam River for £4 10s. yearly. Pynchon required that Sikes and Warner "cleare off all trees and brush from the mowing lands."[77] Because joint tenancies involved relatively small investments, they were commonly utilized by Springfield's more impoverished residents.[78]

---

[70] Ibid., VI, 86-87; 1685 Tax List.

[71] Account Books, I-VI.

[72] Ibid., VI, 130-131.

[73] Ibid., I, 77, 265, III, 142-144, 240, VI, 26. Morgan frequently worked as a teamster for Pynchon. See Henry Morris, "Miles Morgan," Connecticut Valley Historical Society, Papers and Proceedings, I (1876), 250-262.

[74] Account Books, VI, 156, 172.

[75] Ibid., V, 170-171, VI, 48.

[76] Ibid., VI, 178.

[77] Ibid., VI, 106.

[78] It is not possible, however, to equate joint tenancies with impoverishment. Ebenezer and Daniel Graves were clearly among Springfield's dispossessed. Both were landless on the 1685 tax list. Similarly Benjamin Knowlton who, married for 10

The fourth category of tenants, the long-term independent renters, included nine men who rented small plots of land for extended periods, usually twelve to fourteen years. Their annual rents, in addition to rates and labor, averaged between one and two pounds. As a group, they paid for 118 contract years, with average payments of £11. In contrast to the dependent renters, whose economic well-being was contingent in some fundamental way on leases from Pynchon, renting for this group was clearly a supplemental activity. They rented because it was convenient and profitable to do so. Their dependence on Pynchon, therefore, was less direct than that of any of the first three groups.

Henry Chapin, the son of Springfield's first deacon, was typical of these renters. In 1673 he leased Pynchon's wet meadow on Chicopee plain at twelve shillings annually. Although the contract specified a term of seven or eight years, he held this meadow for the next twenty-two years.[79] Chapin, who bought 200 acres from Pynchon in 1659 and was the third largest landholder on the 1685 tax list, obviously rented out of choice and not necessity.[80] So did Joseph Ashley, who rented three lots between 1678 and 1687, two of them for at least nine years each.[81] Ashley, like Chapin, rented only to supplement his own holdings. He owned 86 acres in the most highly assessed section of the town in 1685; at his death in 1711 his real estate was valued at £209.[82]

The fifth set of tenants, the one least dependent on Pynchon, was the short-term independent renters. These were individuals who, like the long-term independent renters, rented for reasons of convenience and not necessity, but for limited periods, usually three years or less. The thirty-one men in this group paid Pynchon for a total of eighty-five contract years.[83] These tenants were drawn from Springfield's more affluent families. Japhet Chapin, a brother of Henry Chapin, held 365 acres in 1685—second only to Pynchon in the size of his holdings. During an intermittent rental career that extended from 1665 to 1695, Chapin leased a 5½-acre lot, a 4-acre lot, meadow, and a bull.[84] George Colton, quartermaster in the militia, selectman, and represen-

215

---

years in 1685, owned only 16 acres. At his death in 1690, his land was valued at only £13. (Hampshire Co. Probate Recs., II, 61). John Burt and Thomas Mirrick, however, were manifestly not among Springfield's poor. Burt owned 72 acres of excellent land in 1685; Mirrick, 110 acres. 1685 Tax List.

[79] Account Books, III, 156, V, 22-23, 208, VI, 44.

[80] Deed, John Pynchon to Henry Chapin, Mar. 9, 1659-1660, Conn. Valley Hist. Mus.

[81] Account Books, V, 444-445, VI, 28-29.

[82] 1685 Tax List: Hampshire Co. Probate Recs., III, 243-244.

[83] Account Book, I-VI. There were, in addition to the 31 renters in this group resident in Springfield, approximately 20 short-term independent renters from other valley towns.

[84] Ibid., III, 57-58, V, 13, VI, 44.

tative to the General Court, died in 1690 leaving an estate valued at £847—the fourth largest of any Springfield decedent in the seventeenth century.[85] Colton rented "a little red stonehorse" in 1654 and meadow on Freshwater River between 1663 and 1667.[86]

The sixth and last group of renters, those who leased animals exclusively, was composed predominantly of non-Springfield residents. Of the twenty-six men in this category, only five lived in Pynchon's home town. The average duration of a lease was between three and four years; rents rarely exceeded £2 annually, in addition to all rates, charges, and labor.[87] Draft animals—oxen or stone-horses—were the most frequently rented livestock, though leases of dairy cattle, mares, swine, and sheep were not uncommon. Renters in this group were usually drawn from the poorer families. Judah Trumble, for example, was a subsistence farmer who tilled his small plot with a yoke of oxen which he leased from Pynchon for £2 annually for seven years.[88] As with all livestock leases, Trumble paid all the rates and charges on the oxen and was responsible for replacing them if they were injured or destroyed while in his service. Another renter, John Crowfoot, leased a young mare for three years in the 1680s. Pynchon required Crowfoot to give him all foals that reached two years of age.[89] In 1692 Pynchon "lett out a cow. . . to William Booth" for seven years at ten shillings annually.[90] Similarly, Symon Rumnell rented "a sanded sow" for three years "at halves," and Pynchon received one-half the increase. In 1692 Pynchon yielded to John Woodward's "entreaties" for a yoke of oxen.[91] Because animals were fundamental to the operation of any farm, these renters' dependence on Pynchon was correspondingly high.

The town and debt records of Springfield reveal widespread economic hardship within the community. In 1667 the town meeting appointed a committee to "consider of the necessitous Condition of some famelys in the Plantation," whom several inhabitants thought needed relief. In 1669 Springfield's minister, Pelatiah Glover, threatened to leave because, the selectmen observed, "he apprehends that Wee are not able comfortably to maynteyne him." In 1685 the town asked the General Court to "consider our poverty" in a petition for rate relief. In an effort to improve fiscal health by reducing expenditures, Springfield adopted austerity measures in 1686. For the "satisfaction and ease of the town respecting charges" the inhabitants

[85] Hampshire Co. Probate Recs., III, 68-70.
[86] Account Books, I, 140, II, 244-247, III, 60.
[87] Ibid., I-VI.
[88] Ibid., V, 342-343.
[89] Ibid., VI, 122.
[90] Ibid., 91.
[91] Ibid., 35.

216

enjoined the selectmen from contracting any bargain in excess of £20 without "first advising with and consulting the Town, and having their Approbation concerning the same."[92]

The most compelling evidence of hardship in seventeenth-century Springfield is the incidence of chronic indebtedness reflected in estate inventories and Pynchon's account books. Not all debt is detrimental, of course. In a barter economy, people became indebted to each other simply for the day-to-day exchange of goods and services, or for loans made for capital improvements. However, the distinction here is between this normal indebtedness and the kind of chronic, disabling indebtedness which is not redeemed through regular transactions. Chronic indebtedness was likely, ultimately, to cost an inhabitant his lands, home, or livestock. Many inhabitants died with debts equal to a third or more of their estates. For the poorest inhabitants this indebtedness was particularly devastating. The combined assets of the lowest 10 percent of the decedents, £55, were significantly lower than their combined debts of £200.[93] Jonathan Taylor, Sr., died in 1683 with an estate of £40, and £47 in debts, predominatly owed to Pynchon. Symon Sacket, landless when he died in 1659, left an estate valued at £35 with debts of £30—£24 of which was owed to Pynchon. Benoni Atchinson was also landless at his death in 1704. His estate was estimated at £11, his debts at £19. He ended his life as a town charge. Sam Thomas's estate, probated in 1703, was valued at £5. He was "much in debt"; his shirt and britches "had been lent to him by the town." One chronic debtor, James Osborne, who "prejudice[d] himself and his family by disadvantageous bargaynes." was enjoined by the town meeting from making any contract in excess of ten shillings without the approval of the selectmen.[94]

John Pynchon was the principal creditor of most of these men. The indebtedness entries in his account books lay bare the processes of wealth transfer in early Springfield. Because Pynchon's control of the town's economy was so extensive, Springfield residents found at least occasional indebtedness to him inescapable. Those who avoided becoming indebted as tenants often saw their economic fortunes imperiled through chronically unbalanced ledgers at the store. Many inhabitants were eventually able to redeem their debts through crop surpluses or labor; others, however, were not so fortunate. Frequently these men were compelled to repay their debts by transferring land to their creditor. As Pynchon enlarged his holdings at the expense of those who owned much less, the town became increasingly stratified.

Between 1655 and 1702, over forty of Springfield's inhabitants lost a total of approximately 1,000 acres, in addition to houses, mills, and livestock, for

[92] *Springfield Town Recs.*, I, 359, II, 101, 171.
[93] Hampshire Co. Probate Recs., I-IV.
[94] *Ibid.*, II, 39, III, 90, 116; *Pynchon Court Rec.*, 241-242. 263.

debts to Pynchon totaling £1,134.[95] Many who lost property in this way rented them back from Pynchon. Moreover, Pynchon's ledgers included a substantial number of men who never lost land to him but who were deeply indebted to him over extended periods and thus subject to his control.

Griffith Jones, the town tanner, was typical of those who lost large-scale capital goods to Pynchon for debts. Jones's indebtedness ultimately cost him the very means of his livelihood. In 1663, "for debts" of £3 57s. 1d., Pynchon took his house, homelot, orchard, tanhouse, tanning vats, 15 acres, and a yearling calf.[96] In 1666 Pynchon similarly took Hugh Dudley's "house and lot, 7 acres and ½ over the great River and so cleare my books."[97] Roland Thomas, in 1668, lost 50 acres in Chicopee for debts of £48.[98] John Stewart, the blacksmith, also lost his house, homelot and all his land in 1670 for debts of £25 1s.[99] In 1675, in "settling what he owes me," Pynchon took all of William Brooks's 153 acres in Springfield to offset debts of £60.[100] In 1685 Pynchon secured an execution on the estate of the recently deceased Timothy Cooper for a debt of £130.[101]

Land executions were not limited to Springfield's poorer residents. Elizur Holyoke, Pynchon's brother-in-law, town clerk, representative, selectman, and probably the second most powerful man in the town, lost his half-share in the corn mill and the adjacent land for a debt of £121 18s. 8d. in 1664.[102] Samuel Marshfield, Springfield's representative to the General Court for three terms and a selectman for sixteen years, twice lost large parcels of land to Pynchon for debts. In 1667 Pynchon took "his house and land, viz: all his housing and all his land on this side of the great River. . . to Cleare the debt of £53.14.06." Again, two decades later, Pynchon informed Marshfield that it was time to pay the "ancient debt for goods had of me when I went to England." The debt totaled over £150; to redeem it, Pynchon declared, "I accept as followeth: 15 acres of Land in the Meadow over Agawam River more or less, 12 acres in the Pike over the River, 10 acres of Meadow and 10 acres of upland at Nonesuch: 20 acres more or less at Enfield, 50 acres at the Falls joining to that of Wm. Brooks. His part of the Sawmill at Schnounga-nock. . . with the Saw wholy to be mine."[103] At his death six years later, Marshfield was landless; his estate was valued at only £66.[104] The economic demise of a man of Marshfield's stature throws into sharp relief the perils intrinsic to Springfield's economic structure.

[95] Account Books, I-VI.
[96] Ibid., II, 173.
[97] Ibid., III, 176.
[98] Ibid., 159.
[99] Ibid., II, 282, III, 137.
[100] Ibid., V, 27.
[101] "Records of Execution." Conn. Valley Hist. Mus.
[102] Springfield Town Recs., II, 22.
[103] Account Books, III, 111, VI, 188-189.
[104] Hampshire Co. Probate Recs., III, 2.

The consequences of indebtedness and land forfeiture for the lives of the debtors and their families were often calamitous, as the unhappy experiences of John Mathews, Jonathan Taylor, Nathaniel Ely, and Obadiah Miller show. By the mid-1660s Mathews, a cooper and dependent renter, owed Pynchon a current debt of £20 and "an old account in an old book, £20.17.10." The old account, Pynchon testily observed, "hath been due to me 4 or 5 years and I now bring to account." Pynchon had tried without success to collect the debt in livestock two years earlier. In 1665 he wrote, "I should have had the two Beasts long ago which are now 2 cows besides the increase of them." After finally taking the animals, Pynchon rented one of them back to Mathews for forty shillings yearly.[105] By 1667 Mathews's already tenuous economic condition had deteriorated still further, and he was compelled to mortgage his house and lands to Pynchon for payment of a debt of £45 within three years. Mathews subsequently was unable to redeem the debt, and the land was forfeit.[106] At his death in 1684 he left an estate of only £8, all in movable goods. The management of the deeply indebted estate was awarded to Pynchon.[107]

Jonathan Taylor's experience parallels Mathews's in many ways. By the 1660s he was in serious financial difficulty with Pynchon. In 1668 he rented a house and 7½ acres on the west side of the river, which Pynchon had taken for debts from Hugh Dudley. The agreement stipulated that Taylor would "repair the house by thatching it." Two days later Pynchon asked his tenant to pay some old debts. After Taylor's apparent declaration of inability to do so, Pynchon reiterated that "it had bin due a great while and now it was tyme to pay it." Taylor agreed that the debt was due but "propounded noe way of pay." When Pynchon proposed to "take your 4 acres of land which you offered me a while ago," Taylor replied that he "knew not how to part with it." Pynchon's entry in his account book continues: "Noe said I, are you not willing to pay the debt[?] He said he could not due it till next yeare: said I, I think it tyme you should pay it now, and though you have bin on my debt a long time yet, I will give you £12 for that land; he said he thought it was too little and would not let it go so, and said he could not tell how to pay me till next year."[108] When Taylor died in 1683, his estate was valued at £40, only £5 of which was in land. His unpaid debts amounted to £47.[109]

219

[105] Account Books, III, 86. During a rental career that extended from 1664 to 1679, Mathews paid for 35 contract years, with lifetime payments in excess of £71. He leased 7½ acres of meadow for 13 years, paying Pynchon "10 good tight barrels" for its use. He also rented plowland, a home lot, an orchard, and cows.

[106] John Mathews Deed to John Pynchon, Apr. 22, 1667, Hampshire County Deeds, 1638-1699, A, 72. Mathews may have sought solace in drink. On Jan. 22, 1661, he was fined 10s. for being "found drunken and bereaved of his understanding which appeared both in his speech and behavior" (Pynchon Court Rec., 249).

[107] Hampshire Co. Probate Recs., II, 30-31.

[108] Account Books, III, 174-175.

[109] Hampshire Co. Probate Recs., II, 39.

Nathaniel Ely rented his house and lands from Pynchon for £8 yearly.[110] By 1666 he was indebted to his landlord for more than £130, and it was agreed that Ely would pay £5 per £100 on the annual unpaid balance. Subsequently, either to supplement his income or because he despaired of farming, Ely turned his house into a tavern.

Obadiah Miller's economic difficulties were similar to those of Mathews, Taylor, and Ely. In 1666, while in his late thirties, Miller lost 6 acres to Pynchon for a debt of £4. Unable to subsist without the land, Miller then rented it back for twenty shillings annually, although Pynchon maintained that "it be worth much more." In March 1668, Miller lost 9 more acres for debts of £17. A month later, this process continued. Pynchon's account book relates a curious and somewhat pathetic scenario involving Miller and his wife Joanna: "Goodwife Miller came to me with her husband and said she was willing I should have the land. But she thought I gave too little, and in further discoursing and owning my debt to have been long due, she was willing to agree to the sale, if I allowed her 11s she owes for kersey, which I agreed to and so yield them to, and so both were willing and the price for the land is £18. 1s."[111] Fourteen years later, the Miller family lost an additional 80 acres and a yoke of oxen to Pynchon "for the debts [of] £54.0.0."[112]

The wider social and political ramifications of Pynchon's dominant position in Springfield remain conjectural pending further research. Critical questions include the nature of political authority, the degree of autonomy within the town meeting, the inhabitants' perception of Pynchon, and the effects of dependency on both social cohesion within the larger community and family interaction within the household. Fragmentary evidence (in the form of court records) does suggest that Springfield did not enjoy the strong communitarianism characteristic of Dedham and Andover: physical assault, family feuds, slander, drunkenness, witchcraft accusations, and fraud occurred with some regularity throughout the period. Whether these levels were abnormally high remains uncertain in the absence of a comparative framework. For the same reasons, we need more information relating to the incidence of economic dependency in other communities. Answers to these questions will illuminate the central problem of Springfield's typicality in relation to other seventeenth-century towns and thus broaden our understanding of the social variety of early New England.

[110] Account Books, III, 108, 109. Ely paid Pynchon £116 for 18 contract years; he held the house and lands from 1668 to 1685.
[111] Ibid., 179. Springfield Town Recs., II, 605-606.
[112] Account Books, V, 543.

The Worlds of Roger Williams

*by Sydney V. James**

*I desire not to sleep in security and dream of a
nest which no hand can reach, I cannot but
expect changes, and the change of the last enemy,
Death. Yet dare I not despise a liberty which the
Lord seemeth to offer to me, if for mine own and
others' peace.*[1]

It is time to recapture some appreciation of the
complexity of Roger Williams's existence. A
simple approach may serve to make a start — an
attempt to distinguish the worlds in which he
spent his days, to untwist the strands that made
up the rope of his life.

The effort is worthwhile because his career has
been simplified too much and has been treated
too freely to make it the vehicle for a message.
His thoughts have been analyzed as having a
changeless consistency. He has been honored as
the hero of a cause or quality that made him
stand alone against his contemporaries — as the
champion of soul liberty, the pioneer of separating state from church or church from state, as a
paragon of individualism, or a friend of Indians.
Sometimes his career has been narrated to bring
out only those episodes or opinions that yield
simple conclusions. Williams inevitably sounds
rather like a crank. He probably had a touch of
that quality, but he had no obsessive personality
or monomania, no compulsion to set himself
constantly against the rest of mankind.

The distorted portrayals cannot be completely
corrected. Only fantasy or clairvoyance can pre-
tend to conjure up the "real" Roger Williams.
With so many allusions to now lost documents,
the surviving evidence warns against offering

more than a rough sketch with many parts left
vague. For instance, Williams's political theories,
which — to judge from his actions — surely
developed during the decades of dealings with
authority, exist only in fragments or in remarks
tangential to other subjects. No more than a
handful of his business transactions can be discovered in the extant letters. And there are no
details — gamey or otherwise — of his sexual
behavior. Psychohistorians, perhaps fortunately,
face rough sledding.

Still, some qualities of Williams's life are fairly
clear in the surviving evidence. Read in a
straightforward fashion, his letters reveal a man
who lived simultaneously in worlds that often
remained distinct. Even his framework of thought
could change almost completely when he turned
from one subject to another, as from fortunes of
the Puritan movement as a whole to public affairs
of the town of Providence. His views kept developing in the light of experience, most obviously
perhaps with regard to Indians. He shifted easily
between mentalities appropriate to his main
occupations: small-scale trader, public leader, and
preacher. Those who describe him as a paragon
of intellectual consistency, a man driven as few
ever have been by the implications of his ideas,
must leave a great deal out of the reckoning.

Williams lived in at least six distinct, though
sometimes overlapping, worlds of public life.
These were the worlds of the higher ranks in
English society, the Puritan movement, the
English settlement of New England, the Narragansett Indians, the colony of Rhode Island, and
the town of Providence. During the seventeenth

*Professor of history at University of Iowa, Sydney
James is author of *Colonial Rhode Island* (1975).

century, each was a stage for exciting events. A man acting on all six necessarily pursued the scripts of so many different dramas.

Williams also had several kinds of private relationships to other people. These included his family ties, his network of friends, and his pastoral duties in a church during the short time he had one. Little can be said of these relationships. His two years as a pastor — as distinguished from a preacher, which he was much of his adult life — have produced only evidence about his disagreements with Massachusetts authorities. Devoted parishioners in Salem stood behind him for a while in his insistence on congregational autonomy, freedom from secular interference, and separation from the Church of England; several of them followed him to Providence. This information, however, is all that is known about his ministry and the internal character of the church under his care.

Disappearance of Williams's incoming letters has closed the door on examining most of his many friendships. Even his relations with the John Winthrops, senior and junior, are impossible to understand because only his letters to them remain. Williams's words to the elder Winthrop manifested either reciprocated personal regard or deference before high standing and power. Lacking any sample of the response, both possibilities remain open. Quite likely the younger Winthrop and his wife were intimate with Williams, but the intimacy had no basis of equality.

Within his own family, Williams probably was conventionally affectionate, responsible, and attentive, although he left very little evidence to lend substance to this impression. In a way now out of fashion, he expressed his fondness for his wife by writing a book telling her how to improve her spiritual life. He worried about the epilepsy of one of his sons. Information on these private relations, like Williams's financial affairs, exists in stray fragments that may only suggest accurate impressions.

For better or worse, the public stages, the larger realms in which Williams's career unfolded, must be explored without much knowledge of his private traits.

Our first glimpse into Williams's life reveals his place in English society and his ambitions. We see something surprisingly close to a social climber. His earliest surviving words are in letters written in 1629 to Lady Joan Barrington. In a web of kinship connecting the Puritan gentry and aristocracy, Lady Barrington was, among other things, Oliver Cromwell's aunt. Williams, by contrast, had been born into the lower or middling ranks of commercial London. Partly through the favor of Lord Edward Coke, he had obtained a university education and with it something close to the rank of gentleman. Williams had entered the ministry and later became family chaplain to one of Lady Barrington's relatives and neighbors. He mingled freely in the company of the upper class so long as he remembered that he was not truly a member and behaved in ways suitable to his calling.

As a result of this mingling, Williams developed an affection for Lady Barrington's niece, Jane Whalley, and asked the aunt to approve his courtship. In a very deferential letter, he delicately acknowledged "some indecorum for her [niece] to condescend to my low ebb." But he politely pointed out that Jane Whalley's meager financial prospects equalled his own and he emphasized his devotion to the ministry, a vocation that made the match barely thinkable.[2] The marriage would have moved him into the circles of the gentry, and Lady Barrington would have none of it. She even forbade him further admission to her house.

Williams responded with an abrupt shift away from conventional deference. He assumed the role of pastor with a vengeance. Where formerly he had compared Lady Barrington to the biblical Sarah and the stars in the sky, he suddenly accused her of worldliness and disdain for the pious, especially ministers. "Certainly, Madame," he wrote, "the Lord hath a quarrel against you." He called on her to repent and reform without delay. "Remember, I beseech you, your candle is twinkling and glass near run. The Lord only knows how few minutes are left behind."[3]

He recovered and contented himself with a suitable wife, a clergyman's daughter of respectable standing but no social eminence. The marriage brought some improvement in Williams's social position. He could enter upper class society but could not obtain membership.

This episode might be dismissed as a burst of youthful optimism touched off by romance, which met frustration. Yet in 1652 he tried again

222

223

Barrington Hall at Hatfield Broad Oak in Essex.

Barrington Hall, Essex, England.

to raise himself on the English social scale. The incident resembled the familiar story of the Englishman who went to the colonies to make his fortune and then returned home to claim high rank, except Williams had neither grown rich nor planned to stay in England. He had another frustrating exchange of letters with a high-ranking lady, this time Lord Coke's daughter, Anne Sadleir, by whom he wished to be regarded as a brother.

Williams's grounds are revealing. Her father, he claimed, had referred to him as a son. He also presented his piety and devotion to "the ministry of Christ and the soul freedom of the people." But he had stronger claims than these. He was a man of high responsibilities on an official mission from an American colony. He was a published author — he sent her a copy of his latest book. He was a hero of English colonial expansion. "It hath pleased the Most High," he wrote, "to carry me on eagles' wings through mighty labors, mighty sufferings, and to vouchsafe to use so base an instrument (as I humbly hope) to glorify

himself [in] many of my trials and sufferings, both amongst the English and barb[arians]." As a result of his endeavors in religion and government, he had the confidence of powerful men in England, including Sir Henry Vane and Oliver Cromwell himself.[4]

Williams had a strong case, but it failed to impress Mrs. Sadleir, who was a passionate royalist and militant devotee of the non-Puritan wing of the Church of England. An exchange of letters followed in which she tried politely at first to dismiss him, while privately saying he should hang at Tyburn.[5] Again assuming his pastoral voice Williams told her what to read so that she would adopt his religious opinions.[6] Finally she turned on him in an angry letter matching his erudition with her own, and the episode came to a close.[7] For some reason, she saved his letters and the drafts of her replies.

Williams had some consolation for Mrs. Sadleir's treatment. Sir Henry Vane and his lady invited him to their country seat in Lincolnshire for an extended visit. This visit was his last known venture into the English upper class. After his return to America in 1654, he held a high position for a few years, but then largely withdrew from official duties and became increasingly a local figure.

Throughout his life, he regarded himself as a partisan — even a leader — of the Puritan cause and watched its fortunes closely. This aspect of his life had two or three parts. The familiar one is his determination to purify Puritanism, a zeal that resulted in his banishment from Massachusetts and easy entry into radical religious circles and offices of the mighty in England during the Puritan Revolution and the Protectorate. Scholars have written at length about this aspect of Williams's life and it needs no further comment. Only one point requires emphasis: he saw his disagreements with Massachusetts authorities and others as strictly family quarrels. He even hoped for something of a reconciliation when he wrote a book against Quakerism and sought to follow the book's success in Massachusetts by publishing some sermons.[8]

The Puritan cause held Williams's loyalties and intellectual interest throughout his life. When the Long Parliament began its work in 1640, opening the door to success for reform, he — like John Winthrop and many others in America — eagerly grasped at every bit of news from the mother country. Williams interpreted the upheaval between 1640 and 1660 in light of traditional concepts of Christian history, making a few adjustments to emphasize the New England experiment's importance in showing the way and also to offer his brand of Puritanism as the ultimate goal. He expressed his point of view in this exclamation on the stabilization of Cromwell's regime in 1652:

Praised be the Lord, we are preserved, the nation is preserved. The Parliament sits. God's people are secure — too secure. A great opinion is that the kingdom of Christ is risen and (Revel. 11) the kingdoms of the earth are become the kingdoms of our Lord and of his Christ.

Cautiously, he added, "others have fear of the slaughter of the witnesses yet approaching."[9]

Back in Providence he received letters from his friends in England conveying news that he exchanged with John Winthrop, Jr. Williams had reports of the tottering of the Protectorate and the

impending slaughter of witnesses when the Restoration approached — a time, as he understood it, to fear for the whole Protestant cause. The Pope had brought peace among his nations, except Portugal, while the Protestant countries warred among themselves. "The common enemy, the Romish wolf," he wrote, "is very high in resolution and hope and advantage to make a prey on all, of all sorts, that desire to fear God." He concluded that God had passed "an irrevocable sentence of amputations and cauterizations upon the poor Protestant party."[10]

In his last surviving letter, written shortly after political turmoil touched off by the Popish Plot allegations, Williams was still trying to fit the pattern of events into a grand design. "We have tidings here," he wrote, "of Shaftesbury's and Howard's beheading; and contrarily, their release, London's manifestations of joy, and the king's calling a Parliament." The contradictions could not be resolved in Providence. He finally turned away, saying, "But all these are but sublunaries, temporaries, and trivials. Eternity, O eternity, is our business."[11]

Related to his lifelong commitment to the Puritan cause was Williams's dedication to the English colonization of America. Here again an element in his outlook seemed at odds with his well known zeal for creating a refuge for victims of religious persecution. Both sides of his thinking were real, however.

Diplomacy with Indians in southern New England became the most famous manifestation of his devotion to general English advancement. Although he included Providence and Rhode Island interests in these negotiations, from the start he sought advantage and safety for all English settlers. This sense of solidarity with the rest he explained in 1638. To John Winthrop he pleaded that God's "wisdom and pity be pleased to help you all, . . . to remember that we all are rejected of our native soil, and more to mind the many strong bonds with which we are all tied than any particular distaste each against other."[12] The unifying ingredient for Williams was the Puritan movement.

Several years later he carried this thought to astonishing lengths. As president of the colony he had helped to keep independent from Massachusetts, he professed to officials in Boston a desire

224

for a comprehensive government in New England. This goal had been latent, perhaps, in his collaboration with the Winthrops but it became overt in 1655: "I cordially profess it before the most high, that I believe, if . . . ourselves and all the whole country by joint consent were subject to your government," he wrote, "it might be a rich mercy."¹³ At other times, before and after this occasion, he explored the possibility of bringing John Winthrop, Jr. into power as governor over Rhode Island and some territorial combination.

Williams gave up such projects in the later 1650s after the orthodox Puritan colonies resumed religious persecution of Quakers and Baptists. Preserving an autonomous Rhode Island again claimed his constant devotion. Late in life he defended the heterodox colony as one where he could bear witness against the churches and ministries of the neighboring jurisdictions. These institutions, he said, were "but state policies and a mixture of golden images unto which" the magistrates, "were [their] . . . carnal sword so long, . . . would musically persuade or by fiery torments compel to bow down as many as that great type of inventors and persecutors Nebuchadnezzar did."¹⁴ Thus he resumed his earlier conception of his purpose to maintain a religious refuge in New England.

Similarly, Williams's attitudes toward his Indian neighbors fluctuated, probably as a result of his experiences, but in ways that were sometimes indirect. Very little information survives concerning his commercial dealings of long duration with the Wampanoags and the Narragansetts. Record of his diplomatic endeavors and his evaluations of the natives are complicated by his propensity to romanticize danger and squalor he encountered, his tendency to make contradictory comments, and probably his reluctance to express himself candidly on some points.

When he undertook diplomatic missions for the English colonists at large, he reported to John Winthrop or whoever was governor of Massachusetts. Mostly, his tone was matter-of-fact, his judgments cautious. Williams, at first, had no high opinion of the senior chief sachem of the Narragansetts, Canonicus, whom he described in English as "very sour" and in Latin as a fretful and rude old man.

He never wholly reversed this opinion. At least he enjoyed a better relationship with the old potentate's junior partner and nephew, Miantonomi.¹⁵ In spite of his opinion of Canonicus, Williams usually took the Narragansett side in controversies among the Indians of southern New England.¹⁶

He displayed a touch of credulity when he heard of a potential alliance between the Pequots and the Mohawks. Believing Mohawk meant "man-eaters in their language," he imagined a horrifying possibility. "I sadly fear," he wrote, that "if the Lord please to let loose these mad dogs, their practice will render the Pequots cannibals, too."¹⁷

Hoping to convert them to Christianity, perhaps Williams wanted to think the Indians were malleable in their ways. After less than a year of what he reported only as diplomatic missions among them, he wrote John Winthrop that he saw "many a poor Indian soul inquiring after God," announcing that "I have convinced hundreds at home and abroad that in point of religion they are all wandering."¹⁸

Winthrop accused him of taking the Narragansetts' side in all controversies and believing whatever they told him. Probably offended, Williams replied, "I am not yet turned Indian," and he began what later became a frequent practice of emphasizing natives' ways that he abhorred to offset what he said for them. He called them "proud and angry and covetous and filthy, hating and hateful," modifying the indictment by adding, "as we ourselves have been till kindness from heaven pitied us."¹⁹

Within a dozen years Williams reversed himself on the value of bringing Christianity to the Indians but not on their uglier traits. By 1649 he became convinced that the introduction of civilized ways would have to precede the Gospel and he declared that it would be unfit to regard any Indians as English subjects until they renounced barbarism for what he called civility.²⁰

He polarized these two conditions of humanity emphatically during the 1640s and 1650s. Conceding some important virtues to the Indians he knew — though none to their enemies — he made surprisingly sweeping statements, such as, "All Indians are extremely treacherous," and called the Mohegans "the dregs of mankind."

From a contemporary copy of Williams's letter listing his gifts to Miantonomi.

Another group he described as "barbarous scum and offscouring of mankind." He spotted particular evils and on occasion summed up the situation by saying, "Barbarians are barbarians."[21]

These comments probably voiced not only Williams's actual appraisal but also frustration in his efforts to negotiate harmony in southern New England. Narragansetts, Niantics, Mohegans, and the governments of Connecticut and Massachusetts, kept wrangling among themselves, occasionally with tragic results. Nothing could persuade Massachusetts that the Narragansetts were behaving honorably, nothing could restrain Ninigret of the Niantics from adventures that stirred up trouble in various directions. Probably, Williams felt used rather than useful.

A long statement he made in 1677 after the Narragansetts and their rival nations had been nearly destroyed in war suggests his frustrations. After all that had happened, Williams remembered himself neither as a wary diplomat serving English colonization, nor as a civilized man patronizing barbarians, but as a tool of Canonicus. In a striking passage, Williams wrote:

I gave him and his youngest brother's son, Miantonomi, gifts of two sorts: First, former presents from Plymouth and Salem [that is, before Williams's move to Providence]; Two, I was here their counselor and secretary in all their wars with the Pequots, Mohegans, Long Islanders, Wampanoags. They had my person, my shallop and pinnace, and hired servant, etc., at command on all occassions, transporting fifty at a time, and lodging fifty at a time at my house. I never denied them aught lawfully they desired of me. Canonicus laid me out ground for a trading house at Narragansett with his own hand, but he never traded with me, but had freely what he desired — goods, money — and so that 'tis simple to imagine that many hundreds [value in pounds sterling?] excused me to the last of that man's breath, whom, dying, sent for me and desired to be buried in my cloth of free gift. And so he was.[22]

These disclosures appear in a letter written long after the fact and for the purpose of asserting Williams's views on how he obtained land from the Narragansett sachems by gift rather than purchase. Still, the letter has the ring of truth — or perhaps, half-truth. Williams no longer felt constrained to depict himself as masterful in his dealings with the sachems and admitted how much he had to do for them. He failed to include in the reckoning a reasonable appraisal of what they had done for him by giving land and keeping the peace that allowed Rhode Island towns to grow in the shadow of more powerful neighbors. Presenting himself as put upon more than can be justified by the record, he may be excused in light of his advancing years, the frightful losses in King Philip's War, and his embittered controversy with William Harris.

The Roger Williams who was a leader in the colony of Rhode Island needs little explanation. Several of his achievements are well known, such as his procuring the first charter and helping to obtain its reconfirmation against a patent making William Coddington governor for life on Aquidneck. In these endeavors Williams acted as an emissary for the colony in London.

At home, Williams's principal role in the colony's public business was as president in the years following 1654. He became president at a trying time when the colony had just been mostly reunited.

Coddington's patent shattered Rhode Island leaving three different governments asserting authority, two on the island and one on the mainland. To complicate matters, a number of English and Indians between the centers of Providence and Warwick earlier had joined with Massachusetts. Putting the pieces back together again required the work of many hands and Williams did more than his share. Before he returned from England, he persuaded Sir Henry Vane to send an appeal for unity.[23] Unrecorded bargaining, deliberation, and soul-searching led to a restoration of a single government under the first charter. Williams took office as its president.

There remained hard feelings, particularly on Coddington's part. Just how these were placated was not recorded — no doubt on purpose. Williams probably used his talent as peacemaker and accomplished much to soothe antagonisms.

His public responsibilities included dealing with the Massachusetts adherents. The frustrating, often comic and ironic story has been already well told. Williams by dignified arguments did little or nothing to persuade the officials in Boston to abandon their citizens south of the border. Reasoning gave way to confusion when scuffling and shouting began over which colony was to capture, hold prisoner, and try a sometime Pawtuxet resident named Richard Chasmore, accused of various crimes. Providence men carried the day by rescuing Chasmore from Massachusetts officials who boldly passed through town. The miscreant was held for trial under Rhode Island jurisdiction. Williams probably suffered, and rightly so, as a consequence of his demands that his neighbors turn Chasmore over to the invading officers. He surely lost prestige by failing to impose his policy, formulated with hopes of a New England unification under the Massachusetts government.[24] After this fracas he left high office and went back to informal methods for encouraging cooperation for the public good, most often within his own town. That he had a genuine gift for appealing to people's consciences cannot be denied.

Roger Williams as leading citizen of Providence presents a distinctive cluster of traits, preoccupations, and ideas about his place in the world. In the early years he devoted much thought to the rudiments of life — where to build his house, whom to welcome as neighbors, how to make a living, how to organize the nascent community at Providence. It is impossible to follow his steps precisely. What he wrote to John Winthrop about the problems he perceived in government and the ways he thought of solving them commonly appeared — if in modified form — in the town records. It appears as though he exerted leadership successfully on many occasions. Perhaps his most important objective was the policy of giving uniform land rights to all admitted as settlers of the town. To preserve this policy he had to allow special advantages to the first twelve men who joined him, thus creating the situation that caused his most protracted quarrel.

His brief service as religious leader, unfortunately, is known imperfectly. He wrote nothing about it that survives. The evidence is indirect at best, hearsay at worst. After departing from his past to embrace adult baptism by dipping, he later believed that the ministerial office no longer had devine sanction. For years he groped spiritually for an understanding of what worship might be authorized by God. Eventually he decided that he might speak publicly as preacher, though not serve as pastor of a church.[25] Toward the end of his life he delivered sermons regularly to anyone who attended at Cocumscussoc.[26] Conceivably, he might have also preached in Providence, though there is no evidence to suggest that he did.

He never abandoned the sermonic tone to his neighbors. His first extant epistle advocated that townsfolk submit disputes within the community and within the colony to impartial arbitrators.[27] His most famous letter on civil authority was a secular homily. To explain why religion and conscience should not be touched by the civil government, he compared the situation to that of a ship, where the captain needed authority for the good of all only over the actions of the crew and passengers, not their beliefs.[28]

If Williams preached civic duty to his fellow citizens in Providence, he also expressed himself to them in four other modes — blunt, avuncular, kindly, and vituperative. Sometimes he addressed them in the simplest terms, as in these recommendations: "I pray the town to provide some easy way for the trying of small causes" and "that the fee appointed in this town to an attorney may be moderated."[29]

The avuncular manner is illustrated by some advice to William Field, who had been in controversy with an Indian over the price of some land rights. After persuading the Indian to settle for a small sum, Williams wrote to Field, "Methinks I see a finger of the Most High in this providence. Formerly he demanded above £25 as I remember, [now] will rest with 25s. The wheel may turn again, and if this providence be neglected, there may not peace be had for many pounds."[30]

His protective manner appeared frequently. On one occasion he asked the town meeting to exert a "fatherly care" over three women. The first, an adult, inclined toward matrimony with a young man of unsettled ways and cloudy background. Because both her father and mother had died, Williams wanted the town to assume the customary parental duty of inquiring into the

suitor's fitness and deciding whether to allow or forbid the marriage. The second was a widow with young children to raise, for whom the town should make sure that her husband's intentions for his family should be carried out. The third was a woman who had gone insane. Williams wrote to the town meeting: "My request is that you would be pleased to take what is left of hers into your own hands and appoint some to order it for her supply, and, if it may be, some public act of mercy to her necessities stand upon record amongst the merciful acts of a merciful town, that hath received many mercies from heaven and remembers that (we know not when) our wives may be widows and our children orphans, yea, and ourselves be deprived of all or most of our reason, before we go from hence, except mercy from the God of Mercies prevent it."[31]

The vituperative mode, along with some redeeming sides of Williams's character, came out in his long dispute with William Harris, a dispute that made Williams a leader of part of the town against the rest. The contest brought out Williams's ugliest sentiments — outrage at having his memory attacked and his importance denigrated, self-pity used for manipulative ends, and an intense hatred rendered more vivid by skill in using words. He probably twisted the truth to serve his passion, something he did on no other discernible occasion. Among the choice attacks on Harris, Williams wrote, "his tongue is as foul as his pen with constant and loathsome revilings of all that cross him," adding the snide assertion that since Harris had been disfranchised by the town of Providence, "he hath lived in the woods until the year 1656 or thereabouts and, as some of his friends have often said, like another Nebuchadnezzar, not fit for the society of men."[32] Perhaps the best was Williams's description in 1679: "That prodigy of pride and scorning, W. Harris, who being an impudent morris dancer in Kent, under the cloak of scurrilous jests against the bishop got into a flight to New England, and under a cloak of separation got in with myself, till his self ends and restless strife and at last his atheistical denying of heaven and hell made honest souls to fly from him."[33]

Paradoxically the long contest showed Williams at his best, as an unselfish champion of honesty in dealings with the Narragansetts, as a man

Nar: 22. 11. 50 (so calld)

Wellbeloved friends: Lo: respect to each of
you presented with heartie desires of yor
present & eternall grace. I am sorrie y^t
I am occasioned to trouble you in ye midst
of many y^o other Troubles: yet upon ye Experience of y^o wonted Lo: kindnes & Gentle-
nes toward All men & my selfe also. I
pray you heare me patiently // I had pur-
posed to have psonally attended this Court
& to have presented (my selfe) these few
Requests following, but being much Lamed
& broken with such Travells I am forced
to present you in writing these 5 Requests

The first 4 Concerne others, living & dead amongst vs
the 5th Concernes my Selfe. // First then I pray be
pleased to review ye Propositions betweene vs &
o^r dead freind John Smith, & since it hath pleased
ye God of all mercies to vouchsafe this Towne & other
such a mercie by his meanes: I beseech you studie
how to put an End to y^t Controversie depending
betweene him (as I may so speake) & his: &c I beseech you
have referd ye Busines to some of o^r Lo: Neighbours
amongst you: But since there are some Obstructions
I beseech you put forth yor wisdomes who know
more waies to ye Wood then One: Eas ye first &
appoint others or some other Course, y^t ye Dead
clamour not from his Grave agst vs, but y^t ye Country about vs may Say y^t Providence is not only
a wise but a gratefull prople to ye God of Mercies & all his Instrum^ts of mercy toward vs. //

First page of Williams's letter to the Providence town meeting asking it to meet its Christian duty in caring for three women residents.

ardent to provide a refuge for victims of religious persecution, and as a political preacher of self-restraint and contentment with sufficiency. It is hard to avoid drawing from this nasty wrangle a respect for the man's sense of civic responsibility and his willingness to get into a dirty fight instead of retreating into the purity of extremist principles that would have isolated him from his community.

What is the meaning of the diversity within Roger Williams's life? His many worlds illustrate the flimsiness of the common notion of an older, simpler America — a notion that casts a bland golden glow on the past. Surely there have been pockets of bucolic isolation in America, but Roger Williams did not live in one. It is hardly possible to imagine a life — especially the life of a man residing in a town of a few hundred souls — acted out on more diverse stages; where events of cosmic dimensions occupied his thoughts on one stage, only to be quickly supplanted on another by the smallest details of neighborliness. To make his life a logical consistency under these conditions was all but impossible.

Williams did not have an extraordinary variety of elements in his life. He probably did have a few more matters to keep track of than his neighbors, and he dramatized the elements of his life by moving physically from stage to stage more often than others did. In seventeenth-century America, most adults had a profusion of concerns, if only because of the need for many skills in a nearly self-sufficient mode of living and the challenge of creating communities rather than inheriting them. Most men had to think of English neighbors, Indians, governments, prices in distant markets, politics in England, and the possibility of war — all of which inescapably affected their lives, even if they had no special religious causes to complicate their thoughts. Williams was a seventeenth-century American on a grand scale, not an oddity.

To find such a figure in the little town of Providence might seem improbable on first reflection, only because such eminent persons are rare everywhere. A glance at some of Williams's neighbors reveals a surprising number similarly caught up in the turbulence of the times. Williams's brother Robert remains a shadowy man, yet surviving evidence about him hints

strongly at thoughts churned up by religious radicalism during the Puritan Revolution. And there was Gregory Dexter, the London printer who emigrated when Williams returned from his first mission to the imperial capital. Dexter had been in the midst of the spiritual ferment and probably cast his lot in Providence as a place of like-minded persons. Or consideration might be given to John Throckmorton who wandered in trade and religion; the minister Thomas James who stayed only briefly; the mysterious Edward Cope; or Richard Scott, who married a sister of Anne Hutchinson and became the town's first well-known Quaker. Nearly any individual in early Providence about whom information can be found lived a storm-tossed life on both sides of the Atlantic, often in two or more communities in the American colonies, and often in shifting relation to the flows and eddies of the Puritan movement.

Actually Roger Williams was like his neighbors in many ways, exemplifying their characteristics in a greater degree. He was more active than they in the religious developments of his day, more persistent and rigorous in pursuing ideas, more widely traveled, more honored or at least more observed in his community and colony, more burdened with public responsibilities, more attentive to the grand events in Europe, better able to gain influence in England, slower to reconcile himself to being an obscure American, and far more gifted at articulating his thoughts. He was not the serene gray giant that extends a granite benediction over Providence from Prospect Terrace, but an intense man, active on many stages during a long public life. He was sincere and even prophetic in the summer of 1636 when he wrote, "I desire not to sleep in security and dream of a nest which no hand can reach." For him, Providence was the point where six worlds met, much more a base for action than a refuge.

230

1 Roger Williams to John Winthrop, c. Aug. 1636, in John Russell Bartlett, ed., "Letters of Roger Williams, 1632-1682," *Publications of the Narragansett Club*, 6 v. (Providence, 1866-1874) 6: 6 (hereafter cited as NCP 6). Texts of this and the other letters quoted in this article have been modernized in spelling and punctuation, manuscript abbreviations have been expanded, and numerals have been spelled out where suitable. Citations are to published rather than manuscript texts.

The idea for this article came from reading the unpublished manuscript edition of Williams's letters edited by Bradford F. Swan, whose erudition I have used frequently. His labors were immensely valuable providing useful notes and convincing estimates of the dates of undated letters.

An earlier version of this article was presented as a lecture at the Rhode Island Historical Society on April 27, 1978.

2 RW to Lady Joan Barrington, c. Apr. 1629, *New-England Historical and Genealogical Register* 43 (July 1889): 316-318.

3 RW to Lady Barrington, 2 May 1629, *New-England Hist. and Gen. Reg.* 43: 318-320.

4 RW to Anne Sadleir, probably Apr. 1652, NCP 6: 237-240.

5 NCP 6: 253.

6 Sadleir to RW, n.d.; RW to Sadleir, probably summer 1652; Sadleir to RW, n.d.; RW to Sadleir, n.d., probably winter 1652/3; NCP 6: 240-249.

7 Sadleir to RW, n.d., NCP 6: 249-252.

8 RW to Winthrop, 24 Oct. 1636; RW to Thomas Hinckley, 4 July 1679; RW to Simon Bradstreet, 6 May 1682; NCP 6: 7-13, 396-398, 403-406.

9 RW to Gregory Dexter, 8 Sept. or 7 Oct. 1652, NCP 6: 236. Scriptural citation is to Rev. 11: 15. Note that the prophesying and the killing of the witnesses occurs before this verse in Rev. 11: 3-7.

10 RW to John Winthrop Jr., 6 Feb. 1659/60; RW to Winthrop Jr. 8 Sept. 1660; NCP 6: 307-308, 310-312.

11 RW to Bradstreet, 6 May 1682, NCP 6: 406.

12 RW to Winthrop, c. 14 June 1638, NCP 6: 105. Cf. RW to General Court of Massachusetts, n.d., probably Oct. 1651, NCP 6: 231.

13 RW to General Court of Massachusetts, 15 Nov. 1655, *Hutchinson Papers*, 2 v. (Boston, 1865), 1: 310.

14 RW to Hinckley, 4 July 1679, NCP 6: 396-397.

15 RW to Sir Henry Vane and Winthrop, c. 1 May 1637, NCP 6: 16-17.

16 E.g., RW to Winthrop, c. 9 Sept. 1637, NCP 6: 62-63.

17 RW to Winthrop, 3 July 1637, NCP 6: 14.

18 RW to Winthrop, 28 Feb. 1637/8, NCP 6: 88. Cf. RW to Winthrop, between July and Dec. 1632, NCP 6: 2.

19 RW to Winthrop, c. 14 June 1638, NCP 6: 101.

20 RW to Winthrop Jr., 25 Oct. 1649; RW to General Court of Massachusetts, 5 Oct. 1649; NCP 6: 186, 270-272, 275-276.

21 RW to General Court of Massachusetts, 5 Oct. 1654; RW to Winthrop Jr., 6 Feb. 1659/60; RW to Sir Robert Carr, 1 Mar. 1665/6; NCP 6: 276, 307, 321, 323.

22 RW to a Special Court of Commissioners, c. 17 Nov 1677, in Henry Martyn Dexter, ed., *Roger Williams's "Christenings make not Christians," 1645*, Rhode Island Historical Tracts, No. 14 (Providence, 1881), 57.

23 Vane to Inhabitants of the Colony of Rhode Island, 8 Feb. 1653/4, NCP 6: 257-258.

24 Bradford F. Swan, *The Case of Richard Chasmore alias Long Dick* (Providence, 1944).

25 Edmund S. Morgan, *Roger Williams, The Church and the State* (New York, 1967), 39-56.

26 RW to Bradstreet, 6 May 1682, NCP 6: 404.

27 RW to Town of Providence, 31 Aug. 1648, NCP 6: 149-151.

28 RW to Town of Providence, n.d., perhaps 1654, NCP 6: 278-279. Cf. RW to the Town of Providence, c. Aug. 1654; RW to Daniel Abbott, 15 Jan. 1681/2; NCP 6: 262-266, 401-403.

29 RW to Town of Providence, c. 1 Nov. 1655, *R.I.H.S. Publications*, N. S. (1900) 8: 161.

30 RW to William Field, 13 Sept. 1649, *R.I.H.S. Proceedings*, 1877-1878 (1878), 62-63.

31 RW to Town of Providence, 22 Jan. 1650/1, NCP 6: 207-209; Bradford F. Swan, "Roger Williams and The Insane," *Rhode Island History* 5 (July 1946) 65-67.

32 Remonstrance and petition of Town of Providence to Governor and Council of Rhode Island, 31 Aug. 1668, *Early Records of the Town of Providence*, 21 v. (Providence, 1892-1915) 15: 122. That this document was written by Williams is shown in *Early Records* 3: 129.

33 RW to Hinckley, 4 July 1679, NCP 6: 397-398.

The Historical Journal, 24, 2 (1981) pp. 339–360
Printed in Great Britain

CRIME AND SOCIAL CONTROL IN PROVINCIAL MASSACHUSETTS*

DAVID H. FLAHERTY

University of Western Ontario

232

The first object of this article is to present some findings from an analysis of criminal activity in an early modern society, as measured primarily through various records of the Massachusetts Superior Court of Judicature, Court of Assize, and General Jail Delivery (the Assizes) from its creation in 1692 to the eve of the American Revolution. Since the amount of serious criminal behaviour revealed by this evidence seems small, the article will then seek to identify the most important components of the system of social control over criminality evidently at work in provincial Massachusetts. These include a conscious effort to maintain a homogeneous population, a pattern of collective settlement in townships, an effective system of prosecuting serious breaches of the criminal law, the commitment of elite groups in town, church, county, and province to law and order, and the role of the family in teaching and assuring appropriate behaviour.

The topic of social control over serious crime is distinct from the general issue of the maintenance of social order in society at large. Thus a number of variables of importance to the latter do not receive extended discussion in these pages, which focus on the crucial variables that are the central subject matter of this essay. For example, a number of influences and institutions promoted a general sense of personal morality and inculcated moral standards that obviously helped to discourage criminal activity. Schooling, the Congregational churches, puritan ideology, the growth and spread of what Norbert Elias has called the civilizing process in the early modern world, the characteristics of shame and guilt cultures, concepts of deference and hierarchy[1] – all

* This is a revised version of a paper first delivered at the annual meeting of the Organization of American Historians, Boston, Massachusetts, 19 April 1975. The Canada Council and Charles Warren Center at Harvard University have supported this study financially. Special thanks are due to my colleagues in the United States history seminar at the university of Western Ontario, and especially Richard S. Alcorn, for their constructive criticisms. In 1978–9 I had the stimulating experience of presenting a version of this paper to audiences at the universities of Edinburgh, Sussex and Oxford.

[1] See, generally, Emil Oberholzer, Jr, *Delinquent saints. Disciplinary action in the early congregational churches of Massachusetts* (New York, 1956); David H. Flaherty, *Privacy in colonial New England* (Charlottesville, Va, 1972), pp. 9–18; Norbert Elias, *The civilizing process. The history of manners* (Oxford, 1978), esp. pp. 79, 82, 137, 186–90, 201; James Axtell, *The school upon a hill. Education and society in colonial New England* (New Haven, Conn., 1974).

of these promoted 'moral' and 'upright' behaviour without having as much direct relevance to the amount of serious crime as the system of law enforcement and the absence of economic incentives to theft.

Deviant behaviour in Massachusetts was measured through an examination of approximately 1,500 criminal cases brought before the Assizes from 1693 to 1769.[2] In addition this essay utilized other sources for the period from 1690 to 1760, including statutes, legislative records, lower court records, correspondence, diaries, and newspapers. Since the crimes prosecuted at the Assizes included such offences as murder, riot, burglary, counterfeiting, and theft, the argument advanced in this essay applies primarily to deviant behaviour which may be characterized as 'serious'.[3] For the three decades studied most intensively, a total of 493 prosecutions appeared in the records of the Assizes, including 369 (74·8 per cent) original cases and 124 appeals.[4] Persons were found guilty in 187 (50·7 per cent) of the original prosecutions, an average of 6·2 persons per year found guilty at the Assizes for the entire province. The Appendix tables accompanying this essay present comparable data for the entire period from 1693 to 1769.

The data on the number of specific cases before the Assizes over a period of more than seventy-five years suggest that the level of deviant behaviour in society remained low.[5] The assertion that it was unusual for a person to commit

233

[2] The various records of the Superior Court of Judicature and the accompanying file papers are located in the office of the Clerk of the Supreme Judicial Court, Suffolk County Court House, Boston, and are described in David H. Flaherty, 'A select guide to the manuscript court records of colonial New England', *American Journal of Legal History*, xi (1967), 108–10.

[3] On the basis of the enabling statute of 1699 the jurisdiction of the Superior Court of Judicature included 'all pleas of the crown and all matters relating to the conservation of the peace and punishment of offenders...and generally of all other matters, as fully and amply to all intents and purposes whatsoever as the courts of king's bench, pleas and exchequer within his majesty's kingdom of England have or ought to have' (*The acts and resolves, public and private, of the province of the Massachusetts Bay*, ed. A. C. Goodell [Boston, 1869–1922], I, 370–2), (hereafter cited as *Mass. Acts and Res.*). Thus any criminal matter could and did come before the Assizes, but in practice the court primarily dealt with major offences, including all felonies and capital crimes. The Assizes enjoyed concurrent jurisdiction with General Sessions of the Peace in theft cases and such matters as assault. A modest trend to make certain crimes capital minimally expanded the jurisdiction of the Assizes during the early eighteenth century. Most petty offences on the docket of the Assizes came on appeal from General Sessions. The latter rarely tried serious crimes of any sort.

[4] The following considerations prompted the selection of three particular decades (1700–9, 1720–9, 1740–9) for intensive study: the desire to compare complete decades required starting some time after the creation of the Superior Court of Judicature in 1692; the wish to focus on the less-studied first half of the eighteenth century suggested beginning in 1700; the bulk of the existing records, as well as ease of comparison, inspired the choice of alternate decades.

[5] The figures for original prosecutions during the 1720s yield the following crime rates for 1725, a year in which the total population of the province of Massachusetts Bay was approximately 100,000: 12·5 prosecutions per 100,000 in the population and 4·7 convictions. The comparable figures for 1745, when the total population was 168,829, are 9·2 prosecutions per 100,000 and 5·3 convictions. Only Suffolk county had a substantial increase in original prosecutions from the 1720s to the 1740s.

The evidence of a declining crime rate at the Assizes and General Sessions in the first half of the eighteenth century coincided with a rapid increase in the volume of civil litigation. David Grayson Allen pointed out that in the court of Common Pleas for Middlesex county 'between

a crime refers only to behaviour defined as serious in contemporary law. It excludes crimes like piracy and smuggling, which were not prosecuted in the common law courts, and a narrow range of minor offences tried by county courts of General Sessions of the Peace and individual justices of the peace. It is beyond dispute that the society faced insurmountable problems in trying to stamp out such minor offences as fornication.[6] The burden of office, ignorance, corruption, fear, friendship, and indifference were detrimental influences on law enforcement; the resistance of human beings to moral regimentation in particular hardly needs comment. But although this study has not attempted to quantify all of the cases at General Sessions for every county to develop a complete portrait of the total amount of crime before the courts, enough records of General Sessions have been examined to indicate that 'serious' crime is not in fact hidden away at the inferior court level.[7] Individual justices of the peace settled only the most trivial criminal complaints.

Despite inadequate comparative data, the conclusion that the rate of known serious crime was low is not unusual. This condition now seems typical of several rural societies in early modern times in western Europe and North America, including Scotland, Sweden and seventeenth-century England.[8] It seems likely that conditions in Massachusetts simply mirrored life in ordinary English counties, although it is clear from the New York crime rates that rurality itself does not guarantee low levels of deviance.[9] It is also apparent that the instrumentalities of social control were stronger and more successful

234

the first and fifth decades of the eighteenth century, the number of cases increases tenfold, from an average of seven to seventy-five per quarter session' ('The Zuckerman thesis and the process of legal rationalization in provincial Massachusetts', *William and Mary Quarterly*, 3rd ser. xxix [1972], 456). In this context the docket of the Superior Court of Judicature in Middlesex county for January 1742, was typical of the imbalance between civil and criminal litigation: there were eleven continued civil actions, 104 new civil cases, and three criminal prosecutions; none of the latter led to actual trials (Superior Court of Judicature, minute book 48).

[6] The argument concerning the limited capacity of colonial law enforcement with respect to minor criminal matters is developed in Flaherty, *Privacy in colonial New England*, pp. 189–218, and in Flaherty, 'Law and the enforcement of morals in early America', *Perspectives in American history*, ed. Donald Fleming and Bernard Bailyn, v (Cambridge, Mass., 1971), 201–53.

[7] The author has examined the records of every county court of General Sessions for this period. The dreary round of minor prosecutions for Sabbath-breaking, illegal sale of liquor, fornication, theft, assault, and other miscellaneous matters discourage serious study in their entirety. The records quantified to date are those for Suffolk county from 1726 to 1731 and from 1744 to 1753 and for Middlesex from 1720 to 1724 and from 1740 to 1744. The 206 offences for 1720–4 in Middlesex broke down as follows: assault, 5·3%; theft, 5·3%; fornication, 62·6%; public worship, 11·7%; and miscellaneous, 15·0%. For 1740–4 the comparative figures for 120 crimes were: assault, 3·3%; theft, 4·2%; fornication, 28·3%; public worship, 16·7%; miscellaneous or unknown, 21·7%; and killing wild deer, 25·8%.

[8] See, in general, Bruce Lenman and Geoffrey Parker, 'Crime and control in Scotland, 1500–1800', *History Today*, xxx (1980), 13–17; Jan Sundin, 'Education-control-composition-punishment. Function of Swedish parish administration before 1850' (unpublished manuscript, university of Umea, Sweden, 1979); James A. Sharpe, 'Crime in the county of Essex, 1620–1680' (D.Phil. thesis, Oxford, 1978); Pieter C. Spierenburg, *Judicial violence in the Dutch Republic. Corporal punishment, executions, and torture in Amsterdam, 1650–1750* (University of Amsterdam thesis, 1978).

[9] Douglas Greenberg, *Crime and law enforcement in the colony of New York* (Ithaca, N.Y., 1976), ch. 5.

in provincial Massachusetts than in New York. The high levels of criminality commonly associated with eighteenth-century England reflect conditions in London and its environs rather than high levels of serious crime in rural areas. Direct comparisons of the number of prosecutions at the Assizes in Massachusetts (1700–9) and in Essex (England) (ten available years from 1700 to 1714) reveal that the per capita crime rate was nevertheless 43 per cent higher in the Old World setting than in the new, primarily because of the much higher rate of prosecution for property offences in Essex. Massachusetts had a significantly higher rate of prosecution for crimes of violence, sexual offences, and miscellaneous crimes.[10]

The historian of crime must, of course, confront the perennial issue of unreported crime that plagues all criminal statistics.[11] In Massachusetts, cases tried at the Assizes were both known to the authorities and initially prosecuted before at least the grand jury. Obviously the occurrence of some serious crimes received no mention of any sort in contemporary accounts; other known crimes, including riots, adultery, and major thefts, did not lead to prosecutions. Contrary to the usual argument of criminologists and historians of crime, research for this study at least suggests that the level of serious unreported and unprosecuted crime in provincial Massachusetts was of modest proportions; social control worked well with respect to *serious* offences. An hypothesis suggesting the dominance of informal and extra-legal processing of persons suspected of criminal activities does not seem plausible for *serious* crimes as opposed to minor offences. The speeches, sermons, letters and diaries of contemporaries, as well as reports in the Boston newspapers, do not contain complaints about serious crime. Counterfeiting was the only offence that created much consternation; it was difficult to prosecute successfully because of evidentiary problems and was perceived as a significant threat to propertied interests and the state. No recurrent complaints surfaced in written sources about the incidence of murder, arson, assault, riots, burglary, and major thefts. When contemporaries complained about crime, it was fornication (bastardy), misbehaviour on the Sabbath, idleness, and selling liquor without a licence that concerned them. Much of the 'serious' crime from all parts of the province actually reported in the Boston newspapers later appeared on the docket of the Assizes, although in a number of instances the sketchy character of the initial description of a crime makes positive identification difficult. At least one-half of the forty-seven Massachusetts crimes reported in the available issues of the Boston *News Letter* during the 1720s were minor offences such as petty theft that would often be tried at General Sessions.[12] During the same decade

[10] See the discussion of urban versus rural crime rates in John Beattie, 'The pattern of crime in England, 1660–1800', *Past and Present*, no. 62 (1974), pp. 59–60, 74–85. The Essex data are derived from the Calendar of Essex Assize Records, Essex Record Office, Chelmsford.

[11] See the informative discussion of the problems associated with the 'dark figure' of unknown crime in J. M. Beattie, 'Towards a study of crime in eighteenth century England: a note on indictments', in David Williams and Paul Fritz, eds., *The triumph of culture: eighteenth-century perspectives* (Toronto, 1972), pp. 302–4.

[12] The figures used here for crime reported in the Massachusetts newspapers exclude servants who simply ran away, and episodes of piracy and smuggling.

reports on 186 crimes from other colonies and countries indicate that the newspaper regularly reported crime.

Even accepting the limitations of the evidence available to support the hypothesis that the incidence of serious criminal deviance in provincial Massachusetts was indeed of modest proportions, the historian must nevertheless seek to explain why the serious crime rate was apparently so low in the first half of the eighteenth century in Massachusetts. If a small amount of serious crime was indeed the norm in pre-industrial societies of this kind, how was this achieved? Although many aspects of the Massachusetts social structure may have contributed to the prevention and discouragement of crime, this essay will emphasize those factors usually identified as methods and institutions of social control that were in some measure unique to the New World, or at least New England, in the eighteenth century.

236

I

The factors that contributed to the modest amounts of deviant behaviour prosecuted at the Assizes in provincial Massachusetts are varied and closely interrelated. In the first place the population was small and relatively homogeneous, there was some out-migration, both temporary and permanent, of potentially disruptive young men, population density was low, and everyone lived within the physical confines and organizational framework of a township. The population that reached the 100,000 mark around the year 1725 was overwhelmingly native-born and Anglo-Saxon in derivation. The total population was approximately 56,000 in 1700 and 188,000 in 1750 with an average growth rate of 27·9 per cent per decade during this period.[13] Michael Zuckerman stresses ethnic and cultural homogeneity: 'Massachusetts was more nearly restricted to white Anglo-Saxon Protestants than any other province in English America, with the possible exception of its New England neighbours, Connecticut and New Hampshire.'[14] The degree of demographic homogeneity is especially striking in comparison with such heterogeneous colonies as New York and Pennsylvania. The work of Douglas Greenberg does suggest that lack of homogeneity in the New York populace was one of the factors contributing to the level of crime he found there.[15] Amost nothing is known about the amount of crime in eighteenth-century Pennsylvania. It would be much too simple-minded to argue that the absence of a homogeneous population ensured a high crime rate, although it does seem clear that in Massachusetts homogeneity helped to make control easier. Net migration into New England played only a minor role in eighteenth-century population growth.[16] Massachusetts itself attracted proportionately fewer immigrants than

---

[13] Basic population figures were derived from U.S. Bureau of the Census, *Historical statistics of the United States, colonial times to 1970* (Washington, D.C., 1975), part 2, p. Z, 1–23.

[14] Michael Zuckerman, 'The social context of democracy in Massachusetts', *William and Mary Quarterly*, xxv (1968), 538.

[15] Greenberg, *Crime and law enforcement in the colony of New York*, pp. 40–9, 139, 215–16.

[16] Daniel Scott Smith, 'The demographic history of colonial New England', *The Journal of Economic History*, xxxII (1972), 171.

the other major colonies and almost no transported British convicts.[17] Between
1713 and 1740 some immigration of Scots-Irish, English, and Huguenots
occurred, but on the whole both provincial and local leaders managed to
maintain homogeneity and stability in the population.

In addition to the absence of substantial immigration from other colonies
and abroad in the provincial era, there was a significant out-migration from
some towns to other parts of Massachusetts or to such neighbouring colonies
as New Hampshire, Connecticut, and New York.[18] In response to the
decreasing availability of resources in some older agricultural towns, a steady
flow of young men and women drifted away in search of improved economic
opportunities in new towns or those with a growing commercial character.[19]
The departure of some members of the younger generation from established
towns reduced the numbers in those youthful age groups that criminologists
and historians traditionally associate with deviant behaviour and problems of
social control.[20] Seafaring and military service functioned as additional and
recurrent safety-valves for provincial society. Young and unmarried men were
attracted to such service for a number of years. They were away from
Massachusetts on a regular basis and presumably had some money from
accumulated pay during intervals at home, and/or when they decided to settle
down. Persons in trouble with the law also sought (or were given) the escape
of maritime and military life on occasion, thus contributing to the maintenance
of control.[21]

Moreover, overall population density in Massachusetts remained low
throughout the colonial era, even if it was gradually increasing; a small number
of people lived in a large territorial expanse. Boston in Suffolk county was the
only urban centre of any consequence, with a population of about 15,000
persons from 1730 to 1770. Appendix table II indicates that it had more serious
crime than any other town. Everyone in the province lived within the

237

[17] See Clifford K. Shipton, 'Immigration to New England, 1680–1740', *Journal of Political Economy*, XLIV (1936), 225–38.

[18] This trend is well described in Philip J. Greven, Jr, *Four generations. Population, land, and family in colonial Andover, Massachusetts* (Ithaca, N.Y., 1970), pp. 161, 212–14, 250–1; Patricia U. Bonomi, *A factious people. Politics and society in colonial New York* (New York, 1971), pp. 200–24; and Richard L. Bushman, *From puritan to yankee. Character and the social order in Connecticut, 1690–1765* (Cambridge, Mass., 1967), pp. 83, 122.

[19] This theme of the interaction between population density and economic opportunity has been very well developed for New Hampshire towns in the last third of the eighteenth century. See Darrett B. Rutman, 'People in process. The New Hampshire town of the eighteenth century', *Journal of Urban History*, 1 (1975), 268–92.

[20] President's Commission on Law Enforcement and Administration of Justice, *The challenge of crime in a free society* (Washington, D.C., 1967), ch. 3; Natalie Zemon Davis, 'The reasons of misrule: youth groups and charivaris in sixteenth-century France', *Past and Present*, no. 50 (February, 1971), pp. 41–75; Olwen H. Hufton, 'Attitudes towards authority in eighteenth-century Languedoc', *Social History*, III (1978), 291–4; Keith Thomas, *Age and authority in early modern England* (London, 1976), pp. 16–18.

[21] These suggestions concerning seafaring and military service are based on an interpretation of the details of various criminal cases. However, the functions of these careers in colonial society deserve more direct investigation on these and many other points. For material that is at least partially supportive of my interpretation, see Jesse Lemisch, 'Jack Tar in the streets: merchant seamen in the politics of revolutionary America', *William and Mary Quarterly*, XXV (1968), 371–80.

geographic confines of an organized township. Such a manageable pattern of settlement contributed to the successful control of serious breaches of the peace. Although by the eighteenth century many 'outlivers' dwelt permanently on their outlying farmlands, each town retained a nuclear centre or at least several separate precincts, which tended to centralize political, legal, religious, and social activities, thereby easing the burden of control.

There were about eighty incorporated towns in Massachusetts in 1700, between 100 and 125 in the 1720s, and about 150 in 1750. The average population of a town grew from about 700 to 1,200 persons during the first half of the eighteenth century. In 1764 the median size of 200 established towns was 1,091.[22] Residents generally lived in small face-to-face communities, many of which included only several hundred persons. Members of families and extended kinship groups often remained in towns and counties over several generations, with the result that local people knew one another.[23] The Assize records indicate that most persons apprehended for crimes were not strangers or transients in a particular community. Persons living in small towns did not have much freedom to engage with impunity in serious criminal activity, except on those occasions when the interests of self and community coincided in outbreaks of popular protest.

Although county differences in crime rates do exist with respect to various categories of major offences, research findings to date indicate that serious crime occurred and was prosecuted at roughly comparable levels throughout the province. Boston is the main exception to this generalization. Even for the metropolis the number of criminal prosecutions at Suffolk General Sessions, which included eighteen towns in the county, declined from an annual average of 60·6 total cases from 1726–31 to 23·7 from 1744–53.[24] This decline may also reflect a tendency to try more theft cases at the Assizes during the 1740s. The lack of other urban centres makes further urban versus countryside distinctions of little value. No geographical area had a monopoly on crimes of violence, nor on the few serious sex crimes that appeared in the Assize records. With respect to property offences, Boston maintained its usual numerical and per capita superiority in terms of offences prosecuted; it also furnished the best economic opportunities for burglary and theft in the province. But these crimes and counterfeiting occurred all over the province, with the largest and wealthiest towns in each county generating the preponderance of serious criminal activity before the Assizes.

The success of community organization in controlling serious crime seems to be illustrated by the experience of Dedham, 'one of the largest and most influential country towns in Massachusetts'.[25] It enjoyed substantial population growth during the first half of the eighteenth century. The town, which was

[22] Flaherty, *Privacy in colonial New England*, p. 99.

[23] Ibid. pp. 97–103.

[24] The dates selected for comparison from Suffolk County General Sessions records are the only years from 1725 to 1755 for which such records exist.

[25] Kenneth A. Lockridge, *A New England town: The first hundred years: Dedham, Massachusetts, 1636–1736* (New York, 1970), pp. 93–4, 118, 148.

in Suffolk county only ten miles from Boston, had about 1,100 persons in the 1720s and 1,600 by 1750. Yet from 1688 to 1728 fewer than fifteen new persons a year moved into Dedham, so the town enjoyed a relatively stable and homogeneous character. Lockridge reports that in the seventeenth century 'the average inhabitant was a plaintiff or defendant in civil proceedings no more than once in his life-time and involvements in criminal proceedings were virtually nonexistent'.[26] Between 1693 and 1719 the available records indicate that only one resident of Dedham was tried at the Assizes. Joseph Hyde, an Indian, was convicted in 1695 for the murder of another Indian in Dedham.[27] During the 1720s inhabitants of Dedham appeared before the Assizes in three cases. Richard Bucket, a Dedham labourer, was the only person tried originally at the Assizes during this decade. On the night of 11 April 1728 he broke into the home of a Dedham husbandman and viciously assaulted the master of the house, probably because he was keeping Bucket's girlfriend from him. Six other Dedham residents brought two cases on appeal to the Assizes in 1727 and 1728 and received new trials.[28] On 19 December 1726 three men had assaulted a deputy who was trying to serve an attachment on one of them. Three others appealed against their conviction for disrupting a Dedham town meeting in March 1728 and assaulting the moderator. Each of the seven Dedhamites in the three cases before the Assizes during the 1720s was convicted.

239

Despite this evidence of some significant violence in eighteenth-century Dedham, the town's serious crime rate was only three cases from a population of just over 1,000 persons, not for one year, but for an entire decade. Even this rate for the 1720s was high.[29] During the 1730s Dedhamites produced only one case of bastardy on appeal. During the 1740s a solitary prosecution for riot against five men from Dedham and five from Roxbury was quashed by the Attorney General. In 1758 three of four Dedhamites who had broken into a dwelling house and terrified a woman were convicted and fined twenty shillings each. In 1763 a man and two women (with the same family name) were acquitted on a charge of assaulting a deputy sheriff.[30] In sum, Dedhamites were prosecuted in five original cases and three appeals at the Assizes from 1693 to 1769. Thus even in the eighteenth century the homogeneity and continuity within the population of Dedham, among other factors, helped to make involvement in serious crime both unlikely and virtually impossible on a

[26] Ibid. p. 65; Edward M. Cook, Jr, reaffirms the stable character of the Dedham population ('Social behavior and changing values in Dedham, Massachusetts, 1700-1775', *William and Mary Quarterly*, xxvii [1970], 572).
[27] Superior Court of Judicature, Records, 1692-5, pp. 149-50 [hereafter cited as SCJ, Recs.].
[28] SCJ, Recs., 1725-30, pp. 87, 182.
[29] For the six years 1726-31, an average of only one case a year from Dedham came before the General Sessions for Suffolk county. Two of these later appeared on appeal at the Assizes and are described briefly above. For the ten years 1744-53, Dedhamites averaged 1·3 cases per year at General Sessions. The total of 19 cases in 16 years broke down as follows: riot, 2; assault, 4; fornication (bastardy), 8; liquor offences, 3; and miscellaneous, 2. For 8 of the 16 years no case from Dedham came before the General Sessions.
[30] SCJ, Recs., 1736-8, pp. 43-4; 1739-40, p. 191; 1757-9, pp. 424-5; 1763-4, p. 132.

recurring basis. The evidence indicates that such conditions were repeated in town after town throughout the province.[31]

II

Within towns, counties, and the province as a whole, elite groups, who dominated the political and judicial life of their locality, made a significant contribution to law and order.[32] In remote Hampshire county a number of families maintained their dominance for long periods of time. Such individuals as John Pynchon, Samuel Partridge, John Stoddard, and Israel Williams ran this western county in successive leadership roles during the entire first half of the eighteenth century.[33] Partridge, for example, missed only one sitting of General Sessions for Hampshire from 1692 to 1737. These leading men and their families had close alliances with the leading clergymen of the region, including such ministers as Solomon Stoddard, John Williams and William Williams. This reinforced the commitment of local Congregational churches to the maintenance of good behaviour, which had its foremost manifestation in the exercise of supplementary discipline over full church members.[34] The associated ministers also served as a pressure group at the provincial level with respect to the discouragement of misbehaviour, although this concern was always at the level of such minor offences as breaches of the Sabbath.

Local community pressure made a related and important contribution to the maintenance of control over crime. Towns, for example, had formal and informal systems of surveillance.[35] Each had the power to refuse admittance to newcomers by means of residency laws. Unwanted individuals could simply be warned out of town by the constable. One of the purposes of residence requirements was to keep out 'vicious' persons, which would obviously include those with known criminal records or alleged criminal tendencies.[36] This power

[31] Andover in Essex county, another much studied town, produced no cases at the Assizes between 1694 and 1729, two during the 1730s, one in the 1740s, one in the 1750s (for an assault committed in Billerica), and an appeal in the 1760s. There were two prosecutions for counterfeiting and one for an attempted poisoning; the appeal of a conviction for killing a wild deer was reversed. Andover was somewhat larger than Dedham; both belonged among the leading 20 per cent of towns in the province in terms of population and wealth. In 1693 thirty-seven of the prosecutions for witchcraft at the Assizes involved accused persons from Andover. The Andover prosecutions resulted in four convictions against two persons. (SCJ, Recs., 1692–5, pp. 6–29, 56, 61.)

[32] Bushman has best described this commitment in *From puritan to yankee*, pp. 3–7, 10, 13. See also Edward M. Cook, Jr, *The fathers of the towns. Leadership and community structure in eighteenth-century New England* (Baltimore, 1976), ch. 2.

[33] Ronald Kingman Snell, 'The county magistracy in eighteenth-century Massachusetts: 1692–1750' (Ph.D diss., Princeton University, 1970), pp. 246–85.

[34] See Flaherty, *Privacy in colonial New England*, pp. 151–62; and Oberholzer, *Delinquent saints*.

[35] See Flaherty, *Privacy in colonial New England*, pp. 88–112, 170–5. For a modern illustration of the efficacy of local communities in controlling crime, see Marshall B. Clinard, *Cities with little crime. The case of Switzerland* (Cambridge, England, 1978), pp. 107, 113.

[36] See *Mass. Acts and Res.* II, 336–8; Flaherty, *Privacy in colonial New England*, pp. 170–5. Boston warned out 230 persons from 1701–15 and 330 from 1715–20, the latter increase in response to a sudden influx of Scotch-Irish (Carl Bridenbaugh, *Cities in the wilderness* [New York, 1938], p. 231).

was most frequently exercised to prevent poor people from settling in a town and acquiring the right of local welfare support.

Informal means of control in local communities were a potent factor in discouraging major forms of misbehaviour. In small New England towns people knew and observed one another; it was difficult to conceal illegal or even suspicious activity for very long. Edward Cook has estimated that only one-fifth of the population were adult males.[37] The uneventful character of life in small towns encouraged mutual surveillance and increased the risk of public censure for violations of laws and regulations. Suspicious persons could be easily kept under public observation. If they were truly transients, surveillance inspired by inquisitiveness was assured.[38] Scattered evidence hints that informal modes of control sometimes culminated in vigilante action, especially when elite groups made efforts to discipline individual members of commonly accepted 'deviant' groups in the society, such as Negroes.[39] Although the available evidence suggests that recourse to extra-legal remedies remained uncommon, an awareness on the part of individuals that such correction remained within the realm of possibility must have contributed to the discouragement of deviant behaviour.

The well-known centrality of the family in provincial society meant that its role in socialization and the internalization of behavioural norms was more important than in the modern industrial era. An admirable secondary literature develops the importance of the colonial family so effectively that this agrument about the family as an agency of social control does not require much elaboration in the context of discouraging serious crime. Nuclear families, extended families, and kinship groups furnished individuals and society with a sense of stability and orderliness.[40] The concept of patriarchal fatherhood had not yet died out. Parental supervision and control was a reality, sometimes long after an individual achieved majority. Young persons departing from their own families frequently acquired comparable dependent status and the accompanying supervision as servants in the homes of others.[41]

James Henretta has speculated recently that the patterns of childhood training characteristic of early New England contributed substantially to social stability.[42] In his opinion the inculcation of a system of social self-control emphasized an inner psychological commitment and the internalization of moral codes. A child learned conformity to culturally prescribed and inherently coercive behaviour patterns. Adults extended social approval to law-abiding

[37] Cook, *The fathers of the towns*, p. 24.
[38] See Flaherty, *Privacy in colonial New England*, pp. 97–112.
[39] For an exceptional episode, see the Boston *Evening Post*, 20 July 1741; Boston *News Letter*, 16–23 July 1741; Boston *Gazette*, 13–20 July 1741.
[40] See the discussion in Greven, *Four generations*, pp. 175–6, 215–21, 271–3.
[41] Valuable examples of the exercise of discipline, including physical beatings, over household servants are contained in *The diary of Samuel Pepys*, ed. R. Latham and W. Matthews (London, 1970–), I, 233, 307; II, 54–5, 206–7; III, 66, 105, 116; IV, 7, 12–13, 109. Colonial diaries are not as fruitful on this particular point, but see Flaherty, *Privacy in colonial New England*, pp. 59–64, 67–8.
[42] See the extended discussion in James A. Henretta, *The evolution of American society, 1700–1815. An interdisciplinary analysis* (Lexington, Mass., 1973), pp. 83, 94, 96, 100–1, 114–15, 175.

behaviour and responsible conduct. Together with other community agencies the family taught the child the precise distinctions between deviance and conformity and then subjected him to surveillance for good measure.

The practice of apprenticeship and indentured servitude obviously extended the role of the family in social control.[43] Families stood *in loco parentis* for all servants living with them. Masters had formal responsibility for the behaviour of their apprentices and servants, who agreed to obey their masters. Most adolescents served for an extended period in one form of servitude or another. Many new immigrants became indentured servants for a number of years, thus coming under the socializing influence of a native family. Since the majority of homes never housed hired servants or apprentices, the practice also reinforced the role of elite groups in the ordering of society by furnishing the 'better sort' of families with recurrent opportunities to inculcate appropriate standards of behaviour. The colonial authorities ordered poor, idle, dissolute, or orphaned children to be bound out as servants. On occasion they at least threatened to take children from parents who were failing to inculcate appropriate standards of behaviour. Servitude was also useful as a mode of controlling minority group members, such as Negroes and Indians, many of whom worked in this capacity. Any servant who ran away or committed a crime such as theft might have his or her term of service extended by a court as a part of punishment, if apprehension occurred.

The most repressive use of servitude as a form of control involved the practice of selling free persons into servitude for a limited term, if they could not pay fines, appropriate restitution in property offences, and occasionally even court and prison costs after an acquittal. Although such an occurrence was infrequent at the Assizes, it happened often enough each decade to keep the threat a credible one. During the 1730s, for example, at least nine persons in seven separate cases were sold into servitude for being unable to pay a fine in one instance and to pay restitution for theft in the others. Lawrence Towner found seventy-five cases of free white persons and twenty-three instances of Indians being sold into servitude by General Sessions in the first half of the eighteenth century.[44] Most involved the punishment of theft. More than fifty per cent of the white persons sold in this fashion were tried in Suffolk county. The crucial element in all of these instances is that society had continuing recourse to elite groups, the family and the community as a way of upholding law and order or at least seeking control over the level of deviant behaviour.

III

Law enforcement played the most central role in the control of serious crime. In the better established and more mature society of the eighteenth century, law enforcers may even have had fewer problems of control in this area than

---

[43] This paragraph is largely founded on the treatment of these matters in Lawrence W. Towner, 'A good master well served: a social history of servitude in Massachusetts, 1620–1750' (Ph.D. diss., Northwestern University, 1955), passim. See also the discussion in Flaherty, *Privacy in colonial New England*, pp. 59–66.   [44] Ibid. pp. 397–409, 413–14.

they had in the century of settlement. It was an initial advantage that the criminal code was thoroughly revised after the charter of 1691 and remained thereafter in a relatively coherent and intelligible form without frequent legislative tinkering; the criminal law was thus a viable tool in law enforcement. The local elite were kept aware of new and revised statues by the sheriffs of their respective counties, who were required to send copies to individual towns.[45] The Boston *News Letter* printed the titles of statutes enacted at each session of the legislature to alert the populace to alterations in the criminal law.[46] The legislature was also responsive to real or alleged problems in law enforcement, although these primarily related to the handling of relatively minor criminal offences. On a variety of occasions the General Court considered revisions of the criminal code on a number of subjects and finally decided not to enact new legislation.[47] For such episodes it is almost impossible to learn why the proposed revisions were not enacted.

243

Although Massachusetts did not have a police force in the nineteenth-century sense, the province did have a panoply of law enforcers, ranging from justices of the peace to sheriffs and deputies for counties, and constables in each town. This system worked much more effectively with respect to serious than to petty crime.[48] Because of preoccupation with their own affairs and the tendency to respond rather than to initiate activities, law enforcers in effect created a scale of the offensiveness of crimes in local society. Minor matters were easier to ignore and less likely to be reported than flagrant breaches of the peace. Justices of the peace living in particular towns were both judges and persons charged to investigate complaints and reports of criminal behaviour. As men of substance and power in their local communities, they had a substantial self-interest in the prevention of serious crime, even if some held the title for purposes of prestige only and did not perform any regular law enforcement functions. Sheriffs, deputy-sheriffs, county coroners, and constables also had an economic incentive to prosecute lawbreakers, since they were paid for every step of the criminal process once they apprehended an offender suspected of a significant offence. The more serious the alleged crime, the greater were the opportunities to earn profitable fees. This fee system helped to overcome the lassitude usually associated with such local law enforcers as constables. Nevertheless, constables probably remained the weakest link in the whole system of control, since they were annually elected, had limited access to consequential fees, and had to continue to earn a living at their regular occupation. The legislature had to pay considerable attention to the problem of persons who refused to serve as constables.[49]

A variety of law enforcement practices further contributed to the prevention

[45] *Journals of the House of Representatives of Massachusetts* (Boston, 1919–), 1, 165 (hereafter cited as *JHR*).

[46] See Boston *News Letter*, 12–19 Dec. 1720.

[47] See *JHR*, v, 18–292 passim; ibid. viii, 38–42.

[48] See Flaherty, 'Law and the enforcement of morals in early America', 225–44; and Flaherty, *Privacy in colonial New England*, pp. 189–218.

[49] See *JHR*, 1, 97; and Flaherty, *Privacy*, pp. 190–3.

of serious crime. Judges frequently imposed bonds for good behaviour on individuals to prevent deviant behaviour or its possible recurrence. Even acquitted persons could be bound to good behaviour. The threat of forfeiting a bond was a useful form of local control, especially since a breach of the peace could involve a significant financial loss not only for the accused but for those who had pledged their own resources in support of a friend or relative; it is a tribute to the law-abiding character of Massachusetts society that such forfeitures rarely occurred. Secondly, victims of property offences, especially theft, had strong financial incentives to prosecute and apprehend culprits, since the courts imposed a sentence of treble restitution on convicted thieves. A person who lost five pounds' worth of goods received fifteen pounds, for example, if the thief could be apprehended and convicted. Apprehension and conviction for theft could be a financial and personal disaster for the accused, and was thus a deterrent to property offences. Impecunious thieves were compelled to repay such amounts by means of forced servitude; the fact that this occurred only infrequently suggests the level of prosperity in the society. The authorities also promised rewards for the apprehension of persons guilty of particulary notable offences, such as counterfeiting. The lure of a substantial cash reward was of much consequence in a society where small cash incomes were the rule, even leading some counterfeiters to 'turn in' their brethren in order to collect the reward.[50]

The ready availability of legal redress through complaint, prosecution and punishment cannot be emphasized too strongly in explaining the success of Massachusetts law enforcement in controlling serious crime.[51] Justices of the peace received complaints and initiated prosecutions in every town of any size and bound over to the higher courts those suspected of more serious offences. County courts of General Sessions of the Peace met at least quarterly. The five judges on the bench of the Assizes visited every county at least once a year, travelling twice to the more populous ones, and sometimes adjourning for third and fourth sittings. A person who felt criminally aggrieved could find a judge readily at hand to initiate an apprehension and conduct a preliminary examination. The prosecution of an accused person and the punishment of those convicted was generally certain and swift at all levels of criminal justice, especially for crimes of violence and property offences. It is also evident that the punishments handed out lent a substantial degree of credibility to the system of social control. The Massachusetts experience amply illustrates Beccaria's contention in the 1760s that certainty of punishment is more necessary to prevent crimes than severity. A person who committed a serious crime knew that there was a credible threat of being apprehended, convicted, and punished. The high rates of conviction by juries in property cases suggest the degree of commitment of society as a whole to the maintenance of law and

---

[50] See *JHR*, vi, 18-19, 176; *Mass. Acts and Res.* x, 436.
[51] Kinvin Wroth stresses the role of the Massachusetts legal system as 'an independent and effective instrument of social control' ('Possible kingdoms: the New England town from the perspective of legal history', *American Journal of Legal History*, xv [1971], 319-24, also 327).

order. Moreover, the crucial role of representative grand and petty juries in the screening of prosecutions and determining guilt or innocence at the Assizes lent a substantial degree of credibility to the entire system of criminal justice.

IV

Although not as important a causal factor in explaining crime rates as the various methods of social control already discussed, the weakness of economic incentives to serious crime in provincial Massachusetts, especially the absence of substantial poverty and similar supposed economic determinants of criminal activity, did make a direct contribution to the modest serious crime rates in the province. The American colonists generally achieved a very high standard of living during the eighteenth century.[52] This is not to suggest that there were no poor people, nor that the amount of poverty remained stable during the decades studied. Some recent research suggests that the stratification of society increased as the eighteenth century progressed. Nor was poverty evenly distributed; some towns, like Boston, evidently suffered more poverty than others. Nevertheless the large middling classes dominated provincial society, since neither the very rich nor the very poor made up sizeable segments of the population. The limited number of well-to-do persons reduced the targets available for major property offences, while the limited range of poverty reduced the numbers attracted to major criminal activities. The vast majority of the population lived in an ordinary lifestyle, ranging from the edge of poverty to the edge of wealth. The social structure and the distribution of property were predominantly egalitarian.[53] The number of those condemned to a life of abject poverty was small; for many, individual towns bore the brunt of public welfare in periodic times of need. A New England town accepted responsibility for its poor; the concern existed and could be activated at seasonal or exceptional times of distress. Moreover, criminal activity was not a credible outlet for such distressed individuals as the sick, the disabled, the very young, and the very old.

Lockridge has argued that in Dedham a lower class appeared during the eighteenth century. These victims of scarcity moved from 'near-independence' to 'scrabbling inadequacy', leading to the emergence of a class of have-nots. The share of the town's wealth held by the poorest 20 per cent of the taxpayers dropped from 10 per cent in 1690 to 5 per cent in 1730, while the landless formed 5 per cent of the taxpayers in 1690 and 10 per cent in 1730.[54] None the less the modest significance of the extent of poverty in Dedham can be further seen in the data used by Edward Cook to illustrate the 'steady increase in the number of poor' in Dedham. From 1715 to 1735 there were 15 cases of poor relief, usually for short periods of time. From 1735 to 1750 there were

245

[52] Gary M. Walton and James F. Shepherd, *Economic rise of early America* (Cambridge, England, 1979), pp. 142–5.
[53] Cook, *Fathers of the towns*, p. 70.
[54] Lockridge, *A New England town*, p. 151.

16 cases. In both of these periods the number of 'poor' was less than 1 per cent of the town's population.[55] The impressive aspect of these figures is their paltry character, not in terms of the potential for human suffering, but in comparison with the situation in England or France, even as reported in colonial newspapers.[56] Residents of Massachusetts had only limited experience with poverty in comparison to their fellow countrymen in Great Britain. As much as one-third of the English population may not have been able to feed and clothe themselves adequately;[57] however much the number of poor may have increased in colonial America, the figures never approached the English totals.

Boston suffered more from poverty and crime than any other Massachusetts town. G. B. Warden has described the experience of Boston in the 1720s as follows: 'The number of vagabonds and poor people increased, as taxes rose and the price of wheat doubled. Violence, crime, and restlessness tended to appear with increasing frequency and vehemence. To make matters worse, a disastrous smallpox epidemic literally decimated the town after 1720, a calamity from which Boston never really recovered in the eighteenth century.[58] To the extent that this characterization of an unusually violent decade is accurate, it simply highlights the unique qualities of Boston during and after the 1720s. Workhouses were built. In the mid-1730s the town cried poverty to Governor Belcher on several occasions, arguing in 1734 that the amount spent by the town in support of the poor had doubled in the previous five years. In 1738 the town told the governor that Boston was 'the Receptacle of almost all the Poor that come into this Province, by reason that most Foreigners fix here'.[59] Yet on the eve of the Revolution when the percentage of poor had ostensibly increased in Boston, Allan Kulikoff has found that 'the percentage of poor can be roughly estimated at seven per cent of the population in 1771 and ten per cent in 1790'.[60]

Epidemics struck Boston more severely than other towns because of its concentrated population. Yet the extent of poverty brought on by the spread of smallpox in 1721, for example, was a temporary and unusual phenomenon according to a petition to the House of Representatives: 'Many persons are reduced to very great straits, and necessitious circumstances, who otherwise would have been in a capacity to have subsisted their Families in comfortable circumstances'.[61] The House voted £1,000 for distribution to the people of the

[55] Cook, 'Social behaviour and changing values in Dedham', *William and Mary Quarterly*, xxvii (1970), 568.

[56] Compare Olwen H. Hufton, *The poor of eighteenth-century France* (Oxford, 1974).

[57] See R. M. Hartwell, *The industrial revolution and economic growth* (London, 1971), p. 61; Peter Clark and Paul Slack, *English towns in transition, 1500–1700* (London, 1976), pp. 112–14, 121–5, and Alan Macfarlane, *The origins of English individualism* (Oxford, 1978), pp. 69–71, 77.

[58] G. B. Warden, *Boston, 1689–1776* (Boston, 1970), p. 81.

[59] *Records relating to the early history of Boston*, ed. William H. Whitmore et al. (Boston, 1876–1909), xii, 121–2 (1734), 207 (1738).

[60] Allan Kulikoff, 'The progress of inequality in revolutionary Boston', *William and Mary Quarterly*, xxviii (1971), 383.

[61] *JHR*, iii, 147.

town. But even Boston took such tragedies in stride; there seems to have been no dramatic rise in the crime rate in Boston because of smallpox or attendant economic necessity.

The economic difficulties of the 1720s make this decade particularly appropriate for analysing the role of hard times in initiating criminal activity during the first half of the eighteenth century. Inflation became a very serious problem in the late 1710s and early 1720s, as the paper bills of credit issued by the province as a medium of trade since the early years of the century continued to depreciate in value. The newly arrived Governor Shute urged the House in 1717 to do something about the 'intolerable' depreciation in the value of paper money. In 1720 he looked backward to the time of his arrival and concluded that 'the value of the Bills of Credit have been very much sunk since that time'.[62] In 1723 Chief Justice Sewall commiserated with a prominent friend about the impact of depreciation: 'I confess my Failure, in that having been some part of the Government, I did no more to have prevented the Bills from sinking in their Credit; which ought in Justice to have been done.'[63] In 1728 the Bristol Assizes convicted a cordwainer of seditious libel for asserting 'that there was a scarcity of Bills which occasioned the grinding of the faces of the poor and that the General Court would not make any more Bills'.[64] There were other signs of economic unrest. In 1720 the House failed in an attempt to regulate the price of silver by statute. In 1721 the General Court enacted an addition to the act against taking excessive usury. In 1726 it passed a statute for the relief of debtors.[65]

What was the impact of such hard times on the crime rate? As the Appendix tables indicate, the serious crime rate did not change dramatically in the 1720s; in fact, on a per capita basis the crime rate declined in comparison with the previous decades of the century. General Sessions records studied to date indicate that ordinary property offences did not increase in any significant way. Middlesex General Sessions tried 4 cases of theft in 1720 and 1721, 1 in 1772, 2 in 1723, and none in 1724. The number of prosecutions for theft at the Suffolk General Sessions declined from 14·5 cases per year in 1726–31 to 4·4 cases per year in 1744–53.[66] In fact, it is unusual to find direct evidence that actual economic need inspired a particular criminal act. Such information does exist for a conviction at the Suffolk Assizes in August 1729. One Benjamin Farr admitted that he had come ashore from an English naval vessel on a Tuesday: 'That on Wednesday he was walking about Town, looking for Work, meeting with no Work and being something in Drink', he saw a parcel of linen hanging in a garden and stole it. He was discovered in the process of peddling the clothes to local residents during the next several days.[67] Economic motives

247

[62] *JHR*, I, 169, 182 (1717); ibid. II, 252 (1720).
[63] 'Letter book of Samuel Sewall', Massachusetts Historical Society, *Collections*, 6th ser. I–II (Boston, 1886–8), II, 152.
[64] SCJ, Recs., 1725–9, p. 214.
[65] *JHR*, II, 324–73 (1720), 379–84 (1721); ibid. VII, 47–53 (1726).
[66] See note 24.
[67] Early files in the office of the Clerk of the Supreme Judicial Court, no. 23170:2, Suffolk County Court House, Boston.

were no doubt more common than the surviving records indicate. Yet it still appears that in a period of significant economic distress during the 1720s the populace did not turn to crime as a solution to their problems.

Some of the recent literature on Massachusetts history has suggested that life in the province might have been very different in the second half of the eighteenth century from what it had been in the first. Gary B. Nash claims that the third quarter of the century was a period of severe economic and social dislocation and that poverty struck harder at the town than that in earlier decades.[68] At the same time, Warden has persuasively concluded that 'the arguments for increasing socio-economic inequality in pre-revolutionary Boston are hardly convincing since they rely on evidence like probate inventories and tax records which reflect a mammoth display of spectacular clerical error'.[69] Douglas L. Jones has presented evidence for an increase in transiency and declining levels of residential continuity in the province as a whole as the eighteenth century progressed.[70] Mobility did increase, but the continuity of population still remained high. Jones's work further illustrates the persistent efforts to exercise social control over transients. The search for adequate evidence on these and other matters will necessitate extensive use of court records for the second half of the eighteenth century both for Boston and elsewhere. The kind of detail recorded in civil and criminal trials may furnish important clues. The Assize records to 1769 indicate that crime rates were lower after 1750 than in any earlier decades.

V

The residents of Massachusetts did not believe that serious crime was a significant problem in the first half of the eighteenth century. Crime existed and was a matter of concern to persons on specific occasions (especially if they were victimized). The populace discussed spectacular outbreaks and the pious lamented the prevalence of minor moral offences. But on the whole serious crime was so infrequent an event in daily life as to be of only minimal concern to individuals. Readers of the Boston newspapers were constantly reminded by news reports from other colonies and abroad that serious crime was more prevalent elsewhere, especially in England and on the continent. Perhaps the only ones really surprised at the limited extent of serious crime in eighteenth-century America are residents of twentieth-century North America, accustomed to spiralling crime rates.

Provincial Massachusetts was remarkably free of serious crime (and probably of all crime) because of the efficacy of the instruments of social control. Living

[68] G. B. Nash, 'Urban wealth and poverty in pre-revolutionary America', *Journal of Interdisciplinary History*, VI (1976), 559–630.

[69] G. B. Warden, 'Inequality and instability in eighteenth-century Boston: a reappraisal', ibid. VI (1976), 613.

[70] D. L. Jones, 'The strolling poor: transiency in eighteenth-century Massachusetts', *Journal of Social History*, VIII (1975), 28–54.

in a homogeneous society with a low population density reinforced the traits
of order and stability in community and family life. A variety of local measures
at the township level performed general and individualized functions in the
interests of social control. The machinery of local government, elite groups in
town and country, the individual, family, and extended kinship networks, and
the town church made vital contributions. An individual ultimately unresponsive to these general modes of social control confronted an efficient system
of law enforcement that further discouraged serious deviant behaviour.

The discussion in this essay of the various components of the control system
makes it easier to understand why there were so few cases of crime prosecuted
at the Assizes. But this is not to suggest that Massachusetts society was free
from crime, or that there was no unreported crime. The system of social control
was not always successful in preventing serious crime, since persons varied in
their susceptibility to the same influences, but it did successfully discourage it.
The Assize records reveal very little recidivism. Unfortunately, the nature of
the surviving evidence makes it almost impossible to explore why the system
did not always work for particular persons or for particular offences. Additional
research will permit the further exploration of such intriguing questions as
comparative crime rates, the amount of unreported crime, and the causes of
changes in serious crime rates over time.

It should be clearly understood that the characteristics of Massachusetts
society described in this essay were the dominant ones – it was for the most
part a homogeneous law-abiding society dominated by the rule of law and at
least the search for consensus and order. But the province did not achieve the
ranks of an earthly paradise, despite its efforts in this direction and the
toleration of repressive practices. Civil conflict was endemic in the courts and
sometimes led to outbreaks of physical violence. Instances of assault, fornication,
and minor thefts of property regularly appeared on the dockets of justices of the
peace and General Sessions. Riots did break out. Individuals resorted to violence
on a regular basis to assert their own definition of their rights. But overall the
system of social control did function effectively for the prevention and
prosecution of serious crime. At least a few of these components remain worthy
of consideration and perhaps application in modern industrial societies. Such
aims as a speedy trial and prompt and certain punishment remain worthy if
elusive goals.

APPENDIX
Sources for the tables

Superior Court of Judicature, Records and Minutes Books, Suffolk County Court House, Boston, Massachusetts.

The population figures are for the mid-year of each decade and assume a constant annual rate of growth from each decennial estimate to the next. Data include the total population of the province of Massachusetts Bay (including the counties of what became the state of Maine). They are derived from U.S. Bureau of the Census, *Historical statistics of the United States, colonial times to 1970* (Washington, D.C., 1975), part 2, p. Z, 1–23.

250   The figures for all the decades except 1700–9, 1720–9, and 1740–9 are based solely upon the information furnished in the formal record books of the court, not including a supplementary search of the file papers. When the nature of the offence is not specified in the record books, I have assigned the case to the miscellaneous category in the several tables; it is very unlikely that this has resulted in substantial distortions in the finished product.

Several guidelines followed in counting the criminal cases should also be noted. Even though a single indictment included allegations against several people, it is counted as one case in these tables. Each case thus represents one indictment. A series of indictments, presentments or informations against the same person are counted as separate prosecutions. If at least one person charged in an indictment is convicted, even of a lesser charge, the case is counted (for numerical purposes only) as a conviction; this results in some inflation of the rates of conviction in Table 1. Since the Assizes first began to sit in January 1693, there are only seven years of data for the 1690s; the overall figures for this period are also misleading, because of fifty-six prosecutions for witchcraft in 1693, which resulted in six convictions against three persons.

The basic records of the Superior Court appear to be complete from January 1693 to December 1769, except for a gap between May and August 1750. Further research may uncover the records for the six sittings in these months that are currently missing from the above tables.

Table 1. *Criminal prosecutions before the Massachusetts Assizes, 1693–1769*

Decade	Total	Original juris-diction	Convictions No.	%	Appellate juris-diction	Total population
1693–9	120	115	32	(27·8)	5 (4·2)	53,927
1700–9	110	89	50	(56·2)	21 (19·1)	58,436
1710–19	165	122	59	(48·4)	43 (26·1)	72,561
1720–9	181	125	47	(37·6)	56 (30·1)	99,629
1730–9	207	166	93	(56·0)	41 (19·8)	127,851
1740–9	202	155	90	(58·1)	47 (23·3)	165,236
1750–9	145	132	107	(81·0)	13 (9·0)	204,570
1760–9	331	288	197	(68·4)	43 (13·0)	243,593
Totals	1,461	1,192	675	(56·6)	269 (18·4)	

DAVID H. FLAHERTY

Table 2. *Categories of prosecutions: Massachusetts Assizes, 1693–1769*

Decade	Violence	Sex	Property	Miscel-laneous	Total
Total prosecutions: original and appellate					
1693–9	19	8	13	80	120
1700–9	22	14	39	35	110
1710–19	20	26	76	43	165
1720–9	63	17	53	48	181
1730–9	56	25	82	44	207
1740–9	67	7	86	42	202
1750–9	41	17	67	20	145
1760–9	70	20	145	96	331
Totals	358	134	561	408	1,461
Original prosecutions only					
1693–9	19	8	11	77	115
1700–9	17	12	36	24	89
1710–19	20	16	68	18	122
1720–9	47	9	43	26	125
1730–9	49	15	78	24	166
1740–9	51	3	81	20	155
1750–9	38	15	65	14	132
1760–9	58	17	138	75	288
Totals	299	95	520	278	1,192
Original prosecutions: Suffolk county only					
1693–9	7	3	7	18	35
1700–9	7	4	21	6	38
1710–19	7	8	41	10	66
1720–9	16	3	17	12	48
1730–9	12	7	27	8	54
1740–9	20	1	41	9	71
1750–9	13	3	30	7	53
1760–9	20	6	56	12	94
Totals	102	35	240	82	459
Percentage of all original prosecutions	34·1%	36·8%	46·2%	29·5%	38·5%

Table 3. *Massachusetts Court of Assize, 1693–1769: total prosecutions for crime per 1,000 persons per decade*

Decade	Total crime rate	Violent crime rate	Sex crime rate	Property crime rate	Miscel-laneous crime rate
1690s (7 years)	2·22	0·35	0·15	0·24	1·48
1700s	1·88	0·38	0·24	0·67	0·60
1710s	2·27	0·28	0·36	1·05	0·59
1720s	1·82	0·63	0·17	0·53	0·48
1730s	1·62	0·44	0·20	0·64	0·34
1740s	1·22	0·41	0·04	0·52	0·25
1750s	0·71	0·20	0·08	0·33	0·10
1760s	1·28	0·29	0·08	0·60	0·39
Mean	1·63	0·37	0·17	0·57	0·53
Median	1·72	0·37	0·16	0·57	0·44

Table 4. *Massachusetts Court of Assize, 1693–1769: original prosecutions for crime per 1,000 persons per decade*

Decade	Total crime rate	Violent crime rate	Sex crime rate	Property crime rate	Miscel-laneous crime rate
1690s (7 years)	2·13	0·35	0·15	0·20	1·43
1700s	1·52	0·29	0·21	0·62	0·41
1710s	1·68	0·28	0·22	0·94	0·25
1720s	1·25	0·47	0·09	0·43	0·26
1730s	1·30	0·38	0·12	0·61	0·19
1740s	0·94	0·31	0·02	0·49	0·12
1750s	0·65	0·19	0·07	0·32	0·07
1760s	1·18	0·24	0·07	0·57	0·31
Mean	1·33	0·32	0·12	0·52	0·38
Median	1·28	0·30	0·11	0·53	0·26

252

Table 5. *Massachusetts Court of Assize, 1693–1769: convictions in original prosecutions for crime per 1,000 persons per decade*

Decade	Total crime rate	Violent crime rate	Sex crime rate	Property crime rate	Miscellaneous crime rate
1690s (7 years)	0·59	0·22	0·06	0·09	0·22
1700s	0·86	0·17	0·07	0·36	0·26
1710s	0·81	0·10	0·04	0·55	0·12
1720s	0·47	0·15	0·04	0·22	0·06
1730s	0·73	0·19	0·05	0·41	0·08
1740s	0·54	0·21	0·01	0·28	0·04
1750s	0·52	0·13	0·07	0·26	0·07
1760s	0·81	0·14	0·04	0·48	0·16
Mean	0·67	0·17	0·05	0·33	0·13
Median	0·66	0·16	0·05	0·32	0·10

Family, Inheritance, and Migration in Colonial New England: The Evidence from Guilford, Connecticut

John J. Waters

THE "new social history" of the past fifteen years has produced a large, methodologically innovative, and technically intriguing literature about families and small communities in pre-industrial New England. We now have solid sociodemographic evidence to show that the life expectancy and family size of New England's inhabitants exceeded general European norms as well as those of both England and the southern colonies.[1] These findings lend substance to the remark of Philip Vincent in the 1630s that New England families were bringing "forth more children than any other nation of the world."[2]

What were these families like? How were they composed and organized? Treating these questions, some scholars have argued, as John Demos does for Plymouth, that "the family was nuclear in its basic composition." Demos shows us a people on the move, to whom the baggage of the multigenerational household was a burden; his interpreta-

Mr. Waters is a member of the Department of History at the University of Rochester. He wishes to thank F. Gamst, Alfred Harris, James A. Henretta, Marc Raeff, Darrett B. Rutman, Ralph Sell, Daniel Scott Smith, Lorena S. Walsh, and Maris A. Vinovskis for their interest and assistance in the shaping of this essay.

[1] See Daniel Scott Smith, "The Demographic History of Colonial New England," *Journal of Economic History*, XXXII (1972), 165-183; Robert V. Wells, "Quaker Marriage Patterns in a Colonial Perspective," *William and Mary Quarterly*, 3d Ser., XXIX (1972), 429, 438; and Daniel Blake Smith, "Mortality and Family in the Colonial Chesapeake," *Journal of Interdisciplinary History*, VIII (1977), 403-427, for summary views of the colonial period, and compare this material with J. Hajnal, "European Marriage Patterns in Perspective," in D. V. Glass and D.E.C. Eversley, eds., *Population in History: Essays in Historical Demography* (London, 1965), 101-103, 131-135; Pierre Goubert, "Historical Demography and the Reinterpretation of Early Modern French History: A Research Review," *JIH*, I (1970), 37-48; Hubert Charbonneau, *Vie et mort de nos ancêtres: Étude démographique* (Montreal, 1975), 195, for French Canada; and Lawrence Stone, *The Family, Sex and Marriage in England, 1500-1800* (New York, 1977), chap. 2.

[2] Vincent, "A True Relation of the Late Battell Fought in *New-England* . . ." (London, 1638), in Massachusetts Historical Society, *Collections*, 3d Ser., VI (1837), 42.

tion stresses mobility, fragmentation, modernity.[3] Other historians paint a strikingly different picture in which New England's colonial communities appear as prototypes of "Our Town," wedded to ideals of social and familial stability. These scholars find strong evidence of extended family structures, examine generational exchanges of property and responsibility, and emphasize the traditional agrarian *mentalité* of early New England.[4] Such differences of interpretation give an impression of intractable contradiction with seriously problematic consequences for our understanding of New England culture.

But are the families so differently viewed actually the same families? I think not. We find that in eighteenth-century Guilford, Connecticut, the persisting families were those with one or two male heirs or stem families with a chosen male heir. Such families composed the major part of the landed taxpayers in Guilford at all times. It was the minority, those families with more sons and daughters than land or cattle for marriage portions, that supplied the migrants. The strategies of farm families, as revealed in arranged marriages between cousins, marriages of siblings between families, and generational transfers of land, yield persuasive evidence that these New Englanders valued above all households of fathers, sons, and related females. Moreover, East Guilford, with even more richly detailed documents than the town's other parishes, yields evidence that a majority of its seventy-six householders on the 1732 tax rolls participated in a multifamily situation at some point in their lifetimes. The sum of these practices produced a community composed mainly of interrelated and interdependent families. These lineal families dominate the historical panorama. The overlooked background shows a bleak, marginal world of minorities composed of singles, lone females, the childless, and above all males without land.[5]

255

---

[3] Demos, *A Little Commonwealth: Family Life in Plymouth Colony* (New York, 1970), 180-181, and his reiteration of this theme in "Images of the American Family, Then and Now," in Virginia Tufte and Barbara Myerhoff, eds., *Changing Images of the Family* (New Haven, Conn., 1979), 47.

[4] John J. Waters, "The Traditional World of the New England Peasants: A View from Seventeenth-Century Barnstable," *New England Historical and Genealogical Register*, CXXX (1976), 3-21; Thomas R. Cole, "Family, Settlement, and Migration in Southeastern Massachusetts, 1650-1805: The Case for Regional Analysis," *ibid.*, CXXXII (1978), 171-185; James A. Henretta, "Families and Farms: *Mentalité* in Pre-Industrial America," *WMQ*, 3d Ser., XXXV (1978), 3-32.

[5] R. J. Johnston's study of West Yorkshire shows the persisting properties of "extensive kinship networks ... especially among farming families" and the tendency "to remain at the same place (or in the same local area) for very long periods" ("Resistance to Migration and the Mover/Stayer Dichotomy: Aspects of Kinship and Population Stability in an English Rural Area," *Geografiska Annaler*, LIII [1971], 25). J. A. Raftis finds analogous characteristics for his medieval "main line" families in "Social Structures in Five East Midland Villages: A Study of Possibilities in the Use of Court Roll Data," *Economic History Review*, 2d Ser., XVIII (1965), 83-99.

Like its predecessors, this study starts with "reconstituted" individual families. I have systematically collected the vital statistics for the 135 taxpayers found on East Guilford's 1732 and 1740 cadastral lists. The resulting demographic profile shows that the males on these lists lived on the average to 64.54 years, their spouses and other females to 64.64 years; that males first married at 26.23 years, females at 22.6 years; and that 93 percent of these people who married produced 6.1 children per family, or 4 adults after discounting for infant and adolescent mortality.[6] The data show that the select number of adults who survived to age twenty or beyond could expect to live long enough to know their grandchildren. Collectively, the reconstituted families had forty family names; one-third of the 135 taxpayers came from but five families. I have kept track of the number of male and female heirs per family by order of birth; after all, their culture valued the "primogenitive and due of birth, Prerogative of age."[7] Moreover, the world of kin played an important part in arranging nuptials: in 27 percent of families with children at least one child married his or her cousin, and another (and distinct) 12 percent engaged in the marital exchange of siblings. Thus almost 40 percent of these East Guilford families were re-related to each other.

These figures, the first on marriage patterns in New England, are significant new findings. They demonstrate the structural function of large families: many surviving children made possible the formation of extensive kinship networks. These patterns reveal norms favoring cousin marriages as a basic ideal of community life in eighteenth-century New England. It is precisely such a belief in the centrality of kin that the Rev. Joseph Emerson of Pepperell, Massachusetts, had in mind when he remarked that he "sometimes regretted that he did not marry a Shattuck, for he should then have been related to the whole town." Tina Jolas and Françoise Zonabend, looking at traditional agrarian life in Burgundy, France, observed that "one always married the same people" and that "it was always a matter of fields."[8] In such a world, where in the words of the early New England historian William Hubbard, "the greater part of the

---

[6] These updated vital statistics differ slightly from the figures presented in Waters, "Patrimony, Succession, and Social Stability: Guilford, Connecticut in the Eighteenth Century," *Perspectives in American History*, X (1976), 146. While I have decreased the number of observations based on estimated data, the principal change has been the reduction of taxpayers from 136 to 135 as close scrutiny proved that the Samuel Meigs listed as the 53rd taxpayer and the Samuel Meigs listed as the 81st on the 1732 list were in reality the same man. These Guilford data agree with the findings of Alan Swedlund *et al.*, "Population Studies in the Connecticut Valley: Prospectus," *Journal of Human Evolution*, V (1976), 85-89. Under "AGROS," they are from the "Early American Social Data Tape HST075," with access through the "Statistical Package for the Social Sciences," University of Rochester, Computing Center, Rochester, N.Y.

[7] *Troilus and Cressida*, I, iii, 106.

[8] Lemuel Shattuck, *Memorials of the Descendants of William Shattuck...* (Boston, 1855), 11. For the import of these kinds of marriage exchanges see Alain Collomp, "Alliance et filiation en haute Provence au XVIIIe siècle," *Annales*, XXXII

people" were "wholly devoted to the Plow," we find practices indicating that marriage was a family arrangement as much as a union of a couple. The Shropshire prayer, "God give him his blessing, and grant that by him the name and family . . . may be propagated in the Parish," perfectly mirrors values common to both old and New England.[9]

Families, lines, names—simple enough terms, but what did they mean in the context of colonial America? The replies of the new social historians to this central question project two different lines of interpretation. The first derives from the nineteenth-century French sociologist Pierre LePlay, whose *L'Organisation de la famille* furnished a nomenclature and a taxonomic system of analysis that established the meaning of such key terms as the extended or joint, the stem, and the nuclear family.[10] As an example, in speaking of an extended or joint family we think of the structure envisioned by Gov. Thomas Hinckley of Plymouth Colony when he made plans for his two sons and their families to live together in his large mansion. Similarly, in Guilford both the two Fowler and the two Munger brothers raised their families under the same roof and jointly worked their fields. We also see this idea expressed in the Georgian double-house built by the Stone brothers of Belmont, Massachusetts, for their joint occupancy—a purpose it served their heirs well into the nineteenth century. The large houses needed for these kinds of arrangements were few and as highly visible as their elite inhabitants. A more common form of joint living was the stem family (*la famille-souche*) in which one son brought his new wife to live with his parents, inherited the homestead, and raised the next generation. The Richard Handy family of Sandwich, Massachusetts, aptly illustrates this pattern and also shows how the other brothers and sisters either remained home as celibates or moved elsewhere to establish families. In this instance, the younger of two brothers stayed at home, thus forming a three-generational stem family. The older brother moved out; his family exemplifies the nuclear model for it consisted only of the conjugal couple and their children.[11]

257

(1977), 450-451. The quotation is from Jolas and Zonabend, "Tillers of the Fields and Woodspeople," trans. Elborg Forster, in *Rural Society in France: Selections from the Annales* (Baltimore, 1977), 134. Cf. Bernard Farber, *Guardians of Virtue: Salem Families in 1800* (New York, 1972), 127.

[9] Hubbard, *A General History of New England* . . . (Mass. Hist. Soc., Colls., 2d Ser., V [Boston, 1815]), 242; Richard Gough, *Antiquities and Memoirs of the Parish of Myddle, County of Salop* . . . *A.D. 1700* (Shrewsbury, Eng., 1875), 32.

[10] LePlay, *L'Organisation de la famille* (Paris, 1871), 9-11. For a modern evaluation of the stem tradition see William L. Parish, Jr., and Moshe Schwartz, "Household Complexity in Nineteenth Century France," *American Sociological Review*, XXXVII (1972), 154-156, 169.

[11] Waters, "American Colonial Stem Families: Persisting European Patterns in the New World" (unpubl. paper, Social Science History Association, 1978), 1-2; "Guilford List 1716," Guilford Keeping Society, Guilford Public Library, Guilford, Conn. For the Stone brothers see Richard B. Betts, *The Streets of Belmont and How They Were Named* . . . (Belmont, Mass., 1974), 137-139.

LePlay's historical sociology was far from neutral; he championed the joint and stem families as preservers of traditional French values, and he condemned the nuclear family as "unstable," rootless, modern. Peter Laslett and the Cambridge Group for the History of Population and Social Structure display a different preference. Their favor falls on the nuclear family as the modern form; Laslett has given his opinion that it was the predominance of the nuclear family that enabled England to lead the Industrial Revolution. More fundamental than these opposing opinions, however, is the fact that French and English students of the family in history have a common vocabulary and pursue the same line of analysis—essentially, a taxonomic approach. Therein lie problems, for the result is a virtually static picture of society that fails to capture the actual dynamics of family life in the past.[12]

Anthropologists Meyer Fortes and Jack Goody have offered the second line of interpretation; they argue for the holistic view obtained from following the flow of life experience through time.[13] After all, a person could start out as a grandchild in a stem family, establish a nuclear household as one-half of a young couple, form a stem family in middle age, and finally become an honored patriarch in a joint household with many extensions. This is far from a fanciful example. If a census or nominal list had been taken in 1655, John Meigs of Guilford would have been classified as head of a nuclear household, but this fact is not a fixed tag

[12] Laslett and John Harrison first presented their ideas on the dominance of the English nuclear family in "Clayworth and Cogenhoe," in H. E. Bell and R. L. Ollard, eds., *Historical Essays, 1600-1750: Presented to David Ogg* (London, 1963), 168. Restatements may be found in Laslett's *The World We Have Lost* (London, 1965), 90-93, 128-132, 236, and his "Mean Household Size in England since the Sixteenth Century," in Peter Laslett and Richard Wall, eds., *Household and Family in Past Time* (Cambridge, 1972), 125-158. For its connection with the Industrial Revolution see Laslett's lecture of Mar. 23, 1977, at the University of Rochester. Laslett counts types, not individual experiences, and he is not concerned with social aspirations or ideals. Thus his most recent study correctly states that "solitaries" were 13% of all households in "Stafford" but neglects to calculate that they were only 3.2% of that town's population (cf. "The English Evidence on Household Structure Compared with the Outcomes of Microsimulation," in Kenneth W. Wachter *et al.*, eds., *Statistical Studies of Historical Social Structure* [New York, 1978], 70-73, 80). Collomp asserts that this "nuclear" interpretation does violence to the deepest cultural aspirations of our ancestors ("Ménage et famille: Études comparatives sur la dimension et la structure du groupe domestique," *Annales*, XXIX [1974], 784-786). For the historiographical debate see Jean-Louis Flandrin, *Familles: parenté, maison, sexualité dans l'ancienne société* (Paris, 1976), 54-91.

[13] Fortes, "Time and Social Structure: An Ashanti Case Study," in Fortes, ed., *Social Structure: Studies Presented to A. R. Radcliffe-Brown* (Oxford, 1949), 64-67; Goody, "The Fission of Domestic Groups among the LoDagaba," in Goody, ed., *The Developmental Cycle in Domestic Groups* (Cambridge, 1958), 83-89. For a detailed critique of the taxonomic approach see Lutz K. Berkner, "The Use and Misuse of Census Data for the Historical Analysis of Family Structure," *JIH*, V (1975), 727.

FIGURE I: THE HOUSEHOLD OF JOHN MEIGS I (1670)

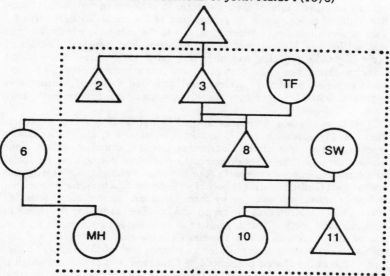

The dotted rectangle contains the John Meigs household members as of 1670. They were John I (#3), wife Tamezine Frye, bachelor uncle Vincent (#2), son John II (#8), and his wife Sarah Wilcox and their children Sarah (#10) and John III (#11). The household also included granddaughter Mary Hubbell, the child of John I's deceased daughter Elizabeth, who had been sent to this household (the Hubbells kept her brothers) and was promised £30 if she remained with her grandmother "to the day of her ... death." Her mother Elizabeth (#6) had been part of this household before her marriage in 1650, while her grandfather Vincent (#1) had died there in 1658. For the assigned family numbers see Henry B. Meigs, *Record of the Decendants of Vincent Meigs* ... (Baltimore, 1901).

forever labeling John Meigs. Had a count been taken in 1658, when Meigs's father moved in from New Haven, it would have revealed a classic three-generational stem family. Finally, if a census taker had recorded Meigs's household in December 1670, he would have found John, his wife, his bachelor brother, his son and grandson, his daughter-in-law, and his granddaughter Elizabeth, the female child of his deceased daughter (see Figure 1).[14] Life-cycle analysis reveals the specific intent of this family

[14] John Meigs, Sr., Will, Jan. 1672, Killingworth Deeds, II, 62, Killingworth Town Hall; distribution of the goods of Vincent Meigs II, Dec. 17, 1700, transcription in Henry B. Meigs, *Record of the Descendants of Vincent Meigs* ... (Baltimore, 1901), 169-171; Walter Hubbell, *History of the Hubbell Family* (New York, 1915 [orig. publ. 1881]), 5-6. We know that the founder of this line, Vincent Meigs, lived and died in his son's Guilford household because his "oral" will of Dec. 2, 1658, was presented from there.

to cluster together in a sustaining multigenerational relationship. As
parents had taken care of their children, so children in turn would "rock
the cradle of reposing age" in recognition of the mutuality of family life.
Two observations are in order: first, it was the temporal overlaps of the
married lives of Meigs's parents and children—the personal specifics of
New England's mortality and nuptiality rates, as it were—that enabled
three generations to know each other and live together; second, a person
could experience solitary, nuclear, and extended living arrangements in
sequence. Social life develops, unfolds, contracts; it is process with many
states and stages.[15]

How common was multigenerational living? This is a key structural
question. My approach to it is to take a nominal list, analyze its family
types (the technique of the Cambridge Group), and then follow these
families through "their developmental cycle" (the method of the social
structuralists). Eugene Hammel's four household classifications easily sort
out the East Guilford data: (1) bachelors—Aaron Blachley, for example—
and other individuals who live by themselves are counted as *solitaries;* (2)
couples with children such as Joseph and Lois Lee, as well as the childless
Nathaniel and Jemima Hand, register as *nuclears;* (3) households such as
that of the senior and junior Thomas Cruttendens, their wives, and the
younger Cruttendens' four children constitute *multiple lineals;* (4) finally,
forms such as the shared household of Capt. and Mrs. Thomas Hodgkin
and his nephew (and future heir) Joseph are included in the term *other
extensions.*[16]

We start our enumeration with the 1732 East Guilford listing of
seventy-six households containing in all 406 men, women, and children.
The distribution displayed in Table I shows that a substantial majority of
households were *nuclear* at that moment in time and that a substantial
majority of the town's people lived in those households; it also reveals that
the number of *multiple lineal* (or stem) households falls short of accurately
reflecting the number of people living in them. These findings are
important, yet subject to still more important qualifications, for a tabulation based only on household types does not reveal the lifetime coresiden-
tial experiences of these seventy-six heads of household. We find that
twenty-one of the fifty-two *nuclears* would later join the ranks of *multiple
lineals,* usually in their mid-fifties when a resident son and daughter-in-law
presented them with a grandchild. By adding these twenty-one household
heads to the twelve *multiple lineals* on the 1732 list, and by including the
seven *other extension* householders from that list, we obtain a total of forty

[15] Quotation from John W. Walzer, "A Period of Ambivalence: Eighteenth-
Century American Childhood," in Lloyd deMause, ed., *The History of Childhood*
(New York, 1974), 363. Darrett B. Rutman, "People in Process: The New
Hampshire Towns of the Eighteenth Century," *Journal of Urban History,* I (1975),
268-292, applies generational mortality and growth to settlement seen as developmental process.
[16] Wachter *et al., Statistical Studies,* 15-27, 39-42, 98.

TABLE I
EAST GUILFORD HOUSEHOLD CLASSIFICATIONS, 1732

Categories	Household Types		Household Population		Mean Household Size	Standard Deviation
	N	%	N	%		
Solitaries	5	6.58	5	1.23	1.00	0
Nuclears	52	68.42	285	70.20	5.48	2.2142
Multiple Lineals (Stems)	12	15.79	82	20.20	6.83	1.5578
Other Extensions	7	9.21	34	8.37	4.85	2.1663
Summary	76	100.00	406	100.00	5.34	

(out of seventy-six of our original households) who experienced multigenerational living arrangements at some time in their life cycles.[17] This is 53 percent of the whole. Context remains central in this analysis. To illustrate this let us focus on the interrelations of property holdings, marriages, residency patterns, and outmigration of four Guilford families.

The Cruttendens were a clan of classic averages. The first of its five Abrahams came from Kent as part of a "circle of young people" who followed their charismatic pastor, Henry Whitfield, to the New Jerusalem. Abraham Cruttenden was one of the twenty-five signers of Guilford's covenant of 1639 who intended to "walk worthy of the fellowship in Christ our hope." The Cruttendens were thus one of the founding families of Guilford.[18] For four generations thereafter, its collective profile was

[17] Central to the reliability of this analysis is the inclusiveness of the key document, "A List Book for East Guilford, Ano [sic] Domini 1732," New-York Historical Society, New York City. Jeffrey L. Beneke's paper, "The Artisans of Eighteenth Century Guilford, Connecticut" (seminar paper, University of Rochester, 1978), shows that the town did enumerate on this list artisans who moved in, and James J. Newman demonstrates that the public viewing of these tax lists, coupled with the sharing of tax evasion penalties with informers, insured near universal tax registration ("Tax Evasion in a Colonial Connecticut Town" [A.M. thesis, University of Rochester, 1979]). For a 19th-century commentary on the high level of multifamily living see David Dudley Field, "A History of the Town of Guilford . . . ," I, Guilford MS, 64-65, Connecticut Historical Society, Hartford, Conn.

[18] Richard Davenport to Hugh Peter, Guilford, July 1637, in Joel E. Helander, Oxpasture to Summer Colony: The Story of Sachem's Head in Guilford, Connecticut ([Guilford, Conn.], 1976), 2; Bernard Christian Steiner, A History of the Plantation of Menunkatuck and of the Original Town of Guilford, Connecticut . . . (Baltimore, 1897), 17.

virtually identical with East Guilford's statistical averages: fifty-four of this clan's sixty-two adults married (87 percent); they produced an average of 6.25 children; and they had male and female longevities of 64.74 and 64.51 years, respectively. They married, as Shakespeare said, of their "own clime, complexion, and degree."[19] Most of the Cruttendens in the eighteenth century consistently ranked in the third quintile of assessed wealth. Socially, the family was one of the ordinary middling sort. Only in the third generation did it produce a church deacon, a militia ensign, and a militia lieutenant (and first- and second-quintile wealth standing), but these three above-average Cruttendens did not pass on their distinction to the next generation. For the period 1728-1784, this clan speaks to us mainly through its seventy-five recorded land deeds. We see twenty-six transfers of land from fathers to sons, eighteen transfers involving in-laws, six family agreements, four brother-to-brother deeds, and one homelot gift from a father to his daughter.[20] Thus 72 percent of the Cruttenden land transfers involved family and family concerns. Their land dealings reflect the boundaries of a kin-centered universe.

The Lees exemplify the movement of upwardly mobile outsiders into Guilford's elite. Edward Lee came to the town through marriage to one of the three daughters of the wealthy Benjamin Wright, as did Joseph Hand and John Walstone. For these three men, biology shaped destiny. The customary marriage contract in these cases required the groom to agree that should he "bury" his bride and "take another wife," all the maternal land should pass to the children of his first wife. (In fact, Edward Lee did remarry after the death of his young wife, Elizabeth, and her portion of the Wright fields went to her only surviving son, Samuel.)[21] Thus what Lee

262

[19] See Sara Goldstein, "Three Generations: An Analysis of the Cruttenden Family of Guilford" (workshop paper, University of Rochester, 1976), 1-3, 10. *Othello*, III, iii, 230.

[20] Michael Szkolka, "The Cruttenden Family of Colonial Guilford, Connecticut: A Study of an Ordinary, Non-Political Family and the Land They Inhabited" (A.M. thesis, University of Massachusetts, Boston, 1980), 56-59, 86.

[21] See Sue Eddy, "The Lee Family of Guilford" (workshop paper, University of Rochester, 1976), 10-14, and Alexander Von Hoffman, "Advancements and Settlements in the World: The Lee Family in 18th Century, Guilford, Connecticut" (seminar paper, University of Massachusetts, 1977), 6-7, 16-22. For the Jordan marriage agreement see Bernard C. Steiner, "John and Thomas Jordan of Guilford, Conn., and Their Descendants," *NEHGR*, LXII (1908), 333. For the marriages of the Wright females see Ralph D. Smyth, "Descendants of Edward and John Lee of Guilford, Conn.," *ibid.*, LIII (1899), 53-54, "Joseph Hand of East Guilford (Now Madison), Conn., and His Descendants," *ibid.*, LV (1901), 31, and "John Walstone of Guilford, Conn., and His Descendants," *ibid.*, LIX (1905), 385. In 18th-century Guilford a David Naughty, holding "Large Estates in Lands" and having only a daughter, willed his land to her child David Naughty Benton "upon Condition of his procuring Liberty to change his Surname into that of Naughty" ("Petition," Oct. 13, 1772, Connecticut Archives, Miscellaneous, 1st Ser., III, Pt. ii, 215-216, Hartford, Conn.).

gained was the "use" of fields but not their ultimate disposition.[22] However, he was able to help make a place for his brother, the cooper John, and this close-linked family achieved a modicum of prosperity. The next generation of Lee brothers jointly owned fields and crowbars, innovatively grew tobacco as a cash crop, built houses, took an active part in the Congregational church, and married the daughters of deacons Morse and Meigs.

Here we have a generational success story based on marriage to an heiress but built by hard work, close brotherly cooperation for two generations, crop innovation, no male deaths in mid-life, and, finally, marriages into the parochial elite.[23] I suggest that it was the need to find husbands for heiresses that gave outsiders their principal entrée into town life. Moreover, the failure of male lines recurred each generation. Nineteen of the one hundred nine taxpayers with issue, as recorded on the East Guilford lists of 1732 and 1740, had only females as direct heirs. Thus 17.4 percent, or one out of six, of these landholding families faced the problem of finding husbands for their daughters and male tillers for their fields. In a patrilineal society these husbands, who in Guilford tended to be outsiders, rank as second-status males. Some of the resentment arising from this anomalous situation may still be heard in the ballad tale about Johnny Sands who

> Had married Betty Hague,
> And though she brought him gold and lands,
> She prov'd a terrible plague,
> For Oh! she was a scolding wife.[24]

This tale does not tell us so much about wives as it does about the right of property holders to speak loudly and to be heard in a landowning society, be they male or female.

Historians do not usually study failures, and genealogists rarely look at families marked by demographic attrition.[25] The Blachleys constitute such

[22] For this custom see Barbara M. Cross, ed., *The Autobiography of Lyman Beecher*, I (Cambridge, Mass., 1961), 32, and Jay Heffron, "The Female Presence: New Perspectives on Land Transfer and Succession in Pre-Industrial New England" (seminar paper, University of Rochester, 1978).

[23] Cf. Edward Lee to Samuel Lee, Guilford, May 15, 1718, Guilford Deeds, II, 138, Guilford Town Hall, Guilford, Conn.

[24] B. A. Botkin, ed., *A Treasury of New England Folklore: Stories, Ballads, and Traditions of Yankee Folk*, rev. ed. (New York, 1965), 575. P.D.A. Harvey points out that if a man "entered a tenement by marrying a widow, he normally assumed the surname of her first husband" (*A Medieval Oxfordshire Village: Cuxham, 1240 to 1400* [Oxford, 1965], 127). Cf. Emmanuel Le Roy Ladurie, *Montaillou: The Promised Land of Error*, trans. Barbara Bray (New York, 1978), 34.

[25] John W. Adams and Alice B. Kasakoff, "Migration at Marriage in Colonial New England: A Comparison of Rates Derived from Genealogies with Rates from Vital Records," in Bennett Dyke and Warren T. Morrill, eds., *Genealogical Demography* (New York, 1980), 115-138.

a family. The line started with Thomas Blachley, a merchant who worked the Hartford-Boston axis, was admitted a Guilford "inhabitant" in 1668, and gained election to the Connecticut General Court from the neighboring town of Branford for 1667, 1668, and 1669. Clearly, his mercantile connections supplied contacts not found in the original Guilford settlement pool. Yet, this family starting high, spent its next three generations moving downhill. Thomas's two sons lived on adjacent homelots, and we know that the elder gave to his first son in anticipation of marriage "my Dwelling House together with all that my Lot of Land . . . forever," but within five months this chosen heir was dead. This family thus lost an early opportunity to set up a multiple lineal household, and later generations had equally poor luck. These Blachley males registered a mean longevity of 46.62 years, while the family celibacy rate was 20 percent (N = 11/53).[26] Thus generation after generation, the family lost its males at early midlife when they should have started their major period of property accumulation. This quickening of death put a pall on the family's expectations and gave a special poignancy to the ritual expression, "he was gathered to his fathers."[27] The large percentage of Blachley children who did not marry—and note that their one-out-of-five figure matches that of the Guilford "poor relief" cases in 1791—suggests that their society insisted on a property base for family formation.[28] That the Blachley clan lacked such a base is indicated by their inability to form matrimonial alliances and create kin networks. Moreover, only one Blachley ever left a will—an only son received half the bequest and his six sisters shared the other half—while the family members rarely appear on church rolls or held any of the town's many public offices.[29]

Our fourth family, the Meigses, formed a continuing parochial elite and maintained first-quintile wealth status and concomitant social position throughout the colonial period. They were not one of the Kentish founding families as were the Cruttendens, nor did they marry into Guilford land like Edward Lee, nor did they engage in trade like Thomas Blachley. Rather, John Meigs, their progenitor in Guilford, was recruited because of his skill as a tanner. In 1661, after a period of friction with his predominantly Kentish neighbors, this Somersetshire man proved himself by his "speedy" warning of two of the Puritan regicides to flee from

[26] William J. Walczak, "Aaron and Moses Blachley and Their Progeny" (seminar paper, University of Massachusetts, 1977), 9; Smyth, "Thomas Blatchley, or Blachley, and His Descendants," *NEHGR*, LVIII (1904), 357-359; Aaron Blachley to Thomas Blachley, July 19, 1692, Guilford Deeds, II, 49.

[27] Field, "History of Guilford," I, Guilford MS, 69.

[28] Douglas L. Lowell, "The Guilford Poor: A Study of Public Poor Relief in Colonial America" (senior paper, University of Rochester, 1979), 10-14; David Levine, *Family Formation in an Age of Nascent Capitalism* (New York, 1977), 9.

[29] Walczak, "Aaron and Moses Blachley," 11.

Charles II's agents who followed close on their trail.[30] Meigs became Guilford's first local hero. He joined the church, mended his ways, and concluded his days as an established pater familias (see Figure 1). Each of the next three generations supplied deacons to the service of the Lord, and the town fondly remembered one of these, Timothy Meigs, A.B. Yale 1732, as "Our Israel's sweet singer." Three members of the family represented Guilford at the General Court; two of these three also served as militia officers; and three others held military posts, the most famous being Phineas Meigs who died in the little known Guilford battle of 1782 "Contending for the Freedom of his Country in the 74th Year of his Age." His tombstone proclaims his heroic stature; the family plot in which it stands holds the remains of this elite clan of landed farmer-artisans whose life was dominated by family and rooted in their fields.[31] Lovingly the Meigses spoke of this earth as the "Land called the Maj[o]rs," the "jed Pierson Lot," the "Lot called the Felix [Meigs] Lot," while in their deeds they wrote proudly that this soil had belonged to an "Honoured Father" or had come to them from "our Honoured Grandfather."[32]

265

In a double sense, the Meigses followed Isaiah's words, "I have named thee, thou art mine" (43:1), for they named both their sons and their fields. Naming first sons after their grandfathers, in accordance with the patrilineal tradition of their culture, they produced five Johns, three Jameses, and three Ebenezers. It is noteworthy that the persistence rate for the progeny of East Guilford families with such patterns was 50 percent greater than for families that did not follow this old European peasant naming custom. The Meigses in their testaments as well as in their marriage settlements favored first-born sons over other sons, and sons over daughters. In fact, their first-born males married at 23.19 years on average, while the mean age for other sons was 25.29. These males had a mean longevity of 64.24 years, and fourteen of the sixteen lines studied had surviving male issue (87.5 percent). Finally, the Meigses married off

---

[30] Steiner, *History of Guilford*, 88, 96, 110. The early friction resulted in part from oral sales and agreements such as the transfer from John Meigs to Edward Benton with "no Bill of Sale given" (Feb. 20, 1671/2, Guilford Deeds, C, fol. 30), or the "told" word of Mr. Leete to his manservant Thomas (Oct. 11, 1687, Conn. Hist. Soc., *Collections*, XXII [1924], 178).

[31] The testimonials to this extended family are Meigs, *Record of Descendants*, 15, 19-22, and William M. Meigs, *Life of Josiah Meigs* (Philadelphia, 1887), 2-4. The 16th-century translation of *"Familiam Tuam quaesumus, Domine . . . custodi"* from the Gregorian Sacramentary as "O Lord, we beseech Thee to keep Thy Church and household" shows that "family" as a concept then included both the household and the village congregation. See John Henry Blunt, ed., *The Annotated Book of Common Prayer* . . . (New York, 1889 [orig. publ. London, 1866]), 262-263.

[32] Inventory, Estate of Capt. Jehiel Meigs, Mar. 15, 1791, Guilford Probate, XIV, 91, Guilford Town Hall; Samuel Fish *et al.*, Falmouth, to Jehiel Meigs, Dec. 8, 1730, Ebenezer Meigs to Jehiel Meigs, Dec. 9, 1730, and Return Meigs to Jehiel Meigs, June 9, 1744, Guilford Deeds, IV, 210, VII, 13.

90 percent of their adult progeny (N = 72/80)—the highest rate of these four families—thus testifying to the desirability of their males and females as marriage partners and of course as the prospective possessors of inherited wealth. The Meigses followed the convention that assigned ownership of land and the principal bed to males, while cattle, blankets, chests, and kitchen utensils belonged to females; this distribution of possessions reified the world view of their owners.[33]

In contrast to the Cruttendens, for whom 72 percent of all land transfers involved family members, the figure for the Meigses comes to 41 percent (N = 70/171). However, this major land-trading family was far from indifferent to the acquisition and retention of land for family needs; their 171 deeds show that, on average, swaps or exchanges amounted to 5.17 acres; in-law transfers, 8.75; commercial transfers, 9.02; Meigs males selling to other Meigs males, 11.26; and gifts from fathers to their progeny, 42.34. These figures suggest that the family entered the land market to secure real estate for heirs. Furthermore, of the Meigs's twelve recorded homestead transfers from the 1650s to the 1760s, six were wedding settlements, four were sales within the family, one was a "purchase" from a future father-in-law, and one a purchase of a vacant homestead from out-of-town heirs. Sixty-three percent of these deeds involved lands that bordered properties held either by the buyer or by one of his brothers. Thus the twelve-and-one-half acres that Josiah Meigs bought from Nathaniel Stevens was "bounded westerly part by the Land of Reuben Meigs and part by the Land of Joseph Meigs, and part by the Land of Jehiel Meigs . . . and part of the Land of Lt. Janna Meigs."[34] For five generations this family traded small plots as did their medieval English

[33] Cf. "Listings" of a bride's portion in goods, Mar. 11, 1777, document #902206, Henry Whitfield Historical Museum, Guilford, Conn.; and observe the provisions of the will of John Meigs III, Feb. 18, 1717/8: "My two daughters" shall "have theire part out of my Moveables & if yt be not sufficient to make th[e]m Equal they shall have no more" (New Haven Probate District, #6886, New Haven, Conn.). Cicely Howell reminds us that the Norfolk custom had the husband promise his bride that "with all my worldely catel I thee endow" ("Peasant Inheritance Customs in the Midlands, 1280-1700," in Jack Goody *et al.*, eds., *Family and Inheritance: Rural Society in Western Europe, 1200-1800* [Cambridge, 1976], 144).

[34] Nathaniel Stevens to Josiah Meigs, Aug. 12, 1730, Guilford Deeds, IV, 199; Joseph Hand to Josiah Meigs, July 9, 1736, *ibid.*, V, 272. Such clustering of kin had been commented on as a way of organizing society by the Stuart divine George Lawson when he wrote that a family over time "may multiply into severall familys, and they into Vicinityes" (*Theo-Politica: Or, a Body of Divinity* . . . [London, 1659], 186-187). The settlement map of 1740 shows this to have been the practice of the Turner, Evarts, Crampton, and Bishop families (Conn. Archs., 1st Ser., Ecclesiastical, IX, 77). In fact, this remained a social principle well into the 19th century. See Jane Finch Bushnell, "An Old Neighborhood: Boston Street, Madison [Guilford] Conn.," *Connecticut Quarterly*, III (1897), 309.

forbears; brothers tended to cluster their lands together; and homesteads were never sold to anyone who was not a member of their clan.[35] The Guilford properties of the Meigses speak of their family concerns.

Guilford families assembled spreads and reserved homesteads for their sons. This was a deeply reciprocal arrangement, for a farmer's sons were the "main source of labor,"[36] and the ten years of work between a young man's sixteenth birthday and the mean statistical marriage age of twenty-six made an important contribution to his father's wherewithal. An early recognition of this mutuality of interest may be seen in the 1694 deed of sale of a field by John Meigs "by and w[it]h the consent" of his two sons although he alone held title to it.[37] The 1732 and 1740 Guilford cadastral lists show systematically that the families that had sons to work their fields also owned the ox teams and were the wealthiest households (the correlation coefficients being .51 and .67). These deeds and lists mark the furrows of families that plowed together. Like the countrymen of Ralph Waldo Emerson's *Hamatreya*, "Each . . . walked admist his farm, / Saying, ' 'Tis mine, my children's, and my name's.' "[38]

The marital patterns of sons and daughters in early New England show that the family farm was a way of life.[39] Marriage heralded the coming of a new generation and the waning of the old. In late medieval England the heir-groom took over by paying "for his father's land and for licence to

[35] For the analogous English practices see W. G. Hoskins, *The Midland Peasant: The Economic and Social History of a Leicestershire Village* (London, 1957), 31, 52, 116, 189, and George Caspar Homans, *English Villagers of the Thirteenth Century* (Cambridge, Mass., 1941), 110, 139, 164-165, 187, 206.

[36] Rose Ann Lockwood, "Birth, Illness and Death in 18th-Century New England," *Journal of Social History*, XII (1978), 120.

[37] John Meigs, Sr., John Meigs, Jr., and Janna Meigs to Thomas Cook, July 2, 1694, Guilford Deeds, I, 117. Note the exchange by "We John Megs Senior and Junior" with Nathan Bradley, Feb. 20, 1668/9, "Terrier," I, 14, Guilford Town Hall. These findings are in sharp contrast to the thesis of Alan Macfarlane, *The Origins of English Individualism: The Family, Property and Social Transition* (Oxford, 1978), 77-79.

[38] Ronald G. Gottesman *et al.*, eds., *The Norton Anthology of American Literature*, I (New York, 1979), 836. In Guilford references are still made to "Bartlet's Pond," "Caldwell Point," and "Meigs Island" (see Arthur H. Hughes and Morse S. Allen, *Connecticut Place Names* [Hartford, Conn., 1976], 215).

[39] This was the position of *American Husbandry*, ed. Harry J. Carman (New York, 1939 [orig. publ. London, 1775]), 50, and it has been reaffirmed by Henretta, "Families and Farms," *WMQ*, 3d Ser., XXXV (1978), 19-21, and Christopher Clark, "The Household Economy, Market Exchange and the Rise of Capitalism in the Connecticut Valley, 1800-1860," *Jour. Soc. Hist.*, XIII (1979), 169-189. My use of the concept of the family farm depends on the work of Alexei Vasilevich Chayanov, *The Theory of Peasant Economy*, ed. Daniel Thorner *et al.* (Homewood, Ill., 1966), 116-117, 128-132. Cf. Evgeniĭ Alekseevich Kosminskiĭ, *Studies in the Agrarian History of England in the Thirteenth Century*, ed. R. H. Hilton, trans. Ruth Kisch (New York, [1956]), xii, 332-334.

marry" from the lord.[40] New Englanders, while influenced by this custom, had neither an agreed-on time for the transfer of land nor any requirement that the devolution be written. The event could occur as early as a son's twenty-first birthday, as shown in the simple diary entry of the North Guilford school master Abraham Pierson—"my Dady gave me a Deed of 12 acres of land " or as late as his fortieth, the point at which Samuel Lee obtained "his whole portion." Such transfers could take the form of a marriage settlement, which, as Sam Scranton told his son, counted as part of "his portion of my estate intended for him." An even more explicit transfer was Comfort Starr's deed-will gift of his "Dwelling House Barn out Houses" and lands "where I now dwell" to his son as a "Clear & absolute Estate of Inheritance," only reserving residency rights for himself, his wife, and his daughters while single.[41]

These documents indicate how "inheritance and dowry, heritage and donation, are part of the more general process of devolution." Guilford marriages reveal family strategies aimed at balancing the resources of each generation against its numbers and governed by concern that human fertility not overreach the supply of land. In both England and New England a rule of parity operated in matchmaking, for partners were expected to bring equivalent wealth to a marriage: as the antiquarian Richard Gough put it, one "had an estate to balance such a portion."[42] The

---

[40] Rosamond Jane Faith, "Peasant Families and Inheritance Customs in Medieval England," *Agricultural History Review*, XIV (1966), 83, 87. Alan R. H. Baker shows the existence of partible practices for some Kent fields ("Open Fields and Partible Inheritance on a Kent Manor, *Econ. Hist. Rev.*, 2d Ser., XVII [1964], 1-23), while Barbara Dodwell notes the custom of an "extra" portion for the eldest son ("Holdings and Inheritance in Medieval East Anglia," *ibid.*, XX [1967], 53-65). Scholars no longer believe that primogeniture was the general rule in early modern England, for as the 17th-century antiquarian John Norden stated, *"Surely differences there are in sundry Mannors"* (*The Surveiors Dialogue* . . . [London, 1738 (orig. publ. 1610)], 152). For New England practices see George Lee Haskins, *Law and Authority in Early Massachusetts: A Study in Tradition and Design* (New York, 1960), 171, and Philip J. Greven, Jr., *Four Generations: Population, Land, and Family in Colonial Andover, Massachusetts* (Ithaca, N.Y., 1970), 133-135.

[41] "Abraham Pierson's Journal," Conn. Hist. Soc., *Bulletin*, XV (1950), 18-24; Edward Lee to Samuel Lee, May 15, 1718, Guilford Deeds, II, 138; Samuel Scranton to Samuel Scranton, Jr., Aug. 21, 1749, Scranton Deeds, 1730-1757, doc. #911036, Henry Whitfield Historical Museum; Comfort Starr to Jehoshaphat Starr, Jan. 12, 1734/5, Guilford Deeds, V, 133; cf. Will of William Leete, Esq., Apr. 2, 1683, in Charles William Manwaring, comp., *A Digest of the Early Connecticut Probate Records: Hartford District, 1635-1700* (Hartford, Conn., 1904), 330.

[42] Goody, "Inheritance, Property and Women: Some Comparative Considerations," in Goody *et al.*, eds., *Family and Inheritance*, 15, and Gough, *Antiquities*, 17. New England's values may be seen in its chosen sons "who live upon a part of a Paternal estate, expecting the Fee thereof," in adult celibacy rates that correlate with the availability of family resources, and in an increasing age of marriage and with it a decreasing number of children for the land-short fifth, sixth, and seventh

Guilford records show distinct life patterns for parents and children in families where there were one and two male heirs, other life strategies for families having three or more male heirs, a special set of priorities for families having only female heirs, and finally a distinct social role for single persons and the childless. From the 1730s through the 1770s, the single most consistent pattern of devolution favored a chosen heir as homestead successor. This finding brings into question Philip Greven's view, based on cohort analysis, of a decline in parental power and care. It seems highly probable that a recasting of Greven's data would uncover persistent patterns of either primogenitural or ultimogenitural choices by Andover's patriarchs.[43]

In Guilford the most privileged marriage partners came from the pools of sole heirs and heiresses. Thus John Meigs turned over "all my lands . . . Unto Myne only and Beloved Son John Megs Junior" on the latter's wedding date in 1666. We find that 24 of the 109 father-taxpayers on the East Guilford 1732 and 1740 cadastrals had only one male heir; these fathers constituted 22 percent of those with issue and 17.8 percent of all the taxpayers under survey (see Tables II and III). These sole heirs presented no problems to their fathers in the disposition of fields; for three of these families they offered in addition the attractive option of marriages to cousins.[44] A female example of this practice was the marriage of Abigail Meigs, the only child of Phineas, to her cousin Jehiel Meigs, Jr., in 1764. The fathers of the couple were friendly cousins, militia officers, and business associates. Phineas Meigs's tax rating of £97.85 placed him in

---

generations. See Oscar and Mary Handlin, eds., *The Popular Sources of Political Authority: Documents on the Massachusetts Constitution of 1780* (Cambridge, Mass., 1966), 437. H. Temkin-Greener and A. C. Swedlund cast light on the demographic governors in "Fertility Transition in the Connecticut Valley: 1740-1850," *Population Studies*, XXXII (1978), 34, 38-39. As Pierre Bourdieu comments, "Marriages took place between families on the same economic level" ("Marriage Strategies as Strategies of Social Reproduction," trans. Elborg Forster, in Robert Forster and Orest Ranum, eds., *Family and Society: Selections from the Annales . . .* [Baltimore, 1976], 122). This is also the finding of Daniel Scott Smith, "Parental Power and Marriage Patterns: An Analysis of Historical Trends in Hingham, Massachusetts," *Journal of Marriage and the Family*, XXXV (1973), 420-427.

[43] The Ballard, Barker, Lovejoy, and Farnum cases cited by Greven in *Four Generations*, 85, 88, 95, 149-150, are on examination all ultimogenitural household successions, and this holds true for the Browns in Robert A. Gross, *The Minutemen and Their World* (New York, 1976), 178.

[44] See John Meigs, Sr., to John Meigs, Jr., Mar. 7, 1665/6, "Terrier," I, 105. For verification that this was the wedding day see Reynold Webb Wilcox, *The Descendants of William Wilcoxson . . .* (New York, 1893), 5-6. The information on cousin marriages comes from Alvan Talcott's studies of Nathaniel Allis and Hannah Norton, Joshua Blachley and Abigail Dudley, and Jesse Crampton and Submit Crampton, "Guilford Genealogy," 3 vols., I, 3, 55, 127, Connecticut State Library Photostat, Hartford, Conn. Cf. Claude Lévi-Strauss, *The Elementary Structures of Kinship*, trans. James H. Bell *et al.* (Boston, 1969), 132-135, 480-481.

TABLE II
MALE HEIR PERSISTENCE

Male Heirs per Father	Fathers with Male Heirs		Fathers with Persistent Male Heirs Only		Male Heirs		
N	N	%	N	%	N	N Persisting	%
1	24	26	20	83	24	20	83
2	25	28	18	72	50	39	78
3	25	28	9	36	75	47	63
4+	16	18	1	6	74	45	61
Summary	90[a]	100	48	53	223	151	68

[a]Another 19 (17% of the total number of fathers) had no male heirs.

TABLE III
EAST GUILFORD TAXED WEALTH DISTRIBUTION

Categories	Taxpayers		Married with Issue		Percentage of Taxed Wealth
	N(135)	%	N(109)	%	
Taxpayers without Progeny	26	19			10
Taxpayers with Only Female Heirs	19	14	19	17	12
Taxpayers with Male Heirs	90	67	90	83	78

the top quintile of East Guilford's landlords; Abigail's desirability can be inferred from the fact that she became enshrined in family oral tradition as the "Heiress"; and young Jehiel brought to this perfect "patriline repair" marriage a settlement worth £70 in land. This cousin match followed the custom of "acre for acre" (although the settlement was to the disadvantage of Jehiel's two brothers), and circumstantial evidence indicates that the groom moved in with the bride's family.[45] Two patterns emerge for these

[45] For the marriage settlement see Jehiel Meigs I to Jehiel Meigs II, Oct. 31, 1765, Guilford Deeds, IX, 81. Jehiel II's list of £69 10s. 9d. and his father-in-law's list of £97 17s. may be found in the "East Guilford Book . . . 1765" [#116, #121], N.-Y. Hist. Soc. Cf. Wachter *et al.*, *Statistical Studies*, 98.

single-heir Guilford families: first, they could avoid the entire probate process by a de facto property transfer, as seen on the tax rolls; second, the tax rolls are the key documents testifying to the persistence of their unique heirs.[46] The evidence shows that twenty of the twenty-four sole surviving sons remained in Guilford.

Twenty-five fathers with two male heirs formed a second privileged group. Their optimal life strategy called for a dowered wife, some twenty years of fruitful work that would double one's landholdings, and then a division of this spread between sons. One quarter of Guilford wills explicitly divided the homelot between two sons,[47] an arrangement that strongly implies day-to-day, face-to-face relationships. Thus Judah Evarts willed his first son, Caleb, "one half of my homelot . . . with a Dwelling house [his own] & barn"; the "northerly half of my homelot with the [other] Dwelling house and barn" went to his other son, Amos.[48] Such divisions could be made by means other than a will: the patriarch Ebenezer Dowd simply took his two sons and two stakes into his fields and said to the elder, "the land on this side of the line joining these stakes is yours," and to the younger, the "land on that side is yours." This vignette of an oral transfer survives because Ebenezer's heirs proudly marked the spot as a family monument.[49] Another method of transfer is seen in the 1758 *inter vivos* deed by which Recompence Meigs gave his youngest son, Elias, the "eastermost half of my Dwelling House with half the Cellar and the benefit of useing the ovens and well and the improvement of half my Garden South of my House and also half of my Barn," in anticipation of his son's marriage. That winter Elias brought home his bride, Rachel Bishop, to share with him and his parents this newly formed multiple lineal household (see Figure 2).[50] Eighteen of these twenty-five fathers (72

271

[46] Neither Phineas Meigs nor his son-in-law Jehiel II had a will proven or other probate documentation, although we see the daughter-widow Abigail Meigs's assumption of their properties in "Guilford . . . 1777" [#134], and "East Guilford List . . . 1789," fol. 8 [#9], N.-Y. Hist. Soc. For a heavy dependence on probate files see Jackson Turner Main, "The Distribution of Property in Colonial Connecticut," in James Kirby Martin, ed., *The Human Dimensions of Nation Making: Essays on Colonial and Revolutionary America* (Madison, Wis., 1976), 81-99, and Jacob M. Price's words of caution in "Quantifying Colonial America: A Comment on Nash and Warden," *JIH*, VI (1976), 701-709.

[47] Waters, "Patrimony, Succession, and Social Stability," *Perspectives Am. Hist.*, X (1976), 150.

[48] Judah Evarts, Will, Nov. 28, 1744, Guilford Probate, IV, 487-488.

[49] Willis W. Dowd, comp., *The Descendants of Henry Doude, Who Came from England in 1639* (Hartford, Conn., 1885), 8. John Bishop (1692-1782) also divided his property among his children by his spoken word (William Whitney Cone, comp., *Record of the Descendants of John Bishop* . . . [Nyack, N.Y., 1951], 3).

[50] Recompence Meigs to Elias Meigs, May 3, 1758, Guilford Deeds, VIII, 95. Eight of twelve of this family's lines over a span of five generations established multiple lineal households. For the model see Berkner, "The Stem Family and the Developmental Cycle of the Peasant Household: An Eighteenth-Century Austrian Example," *American Historical Review*, LXXVII (1972), 398-418.

FIGURE 2: THE HOUSEHOLDS OF RECOMPENCE MEIGS (1760)
AND HIS SON ELIAS (1771)

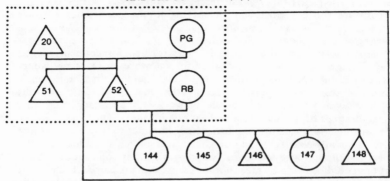

The dotted rectangle contains the Recompence Meigs household members as of 1760. They were Recompence (#20), wife Phebe Goodale, single son Nathan (#51), married son Elias (#52), and his wife Rachel Bishop. Recompence's death in April of 1760 precluded his knowing his first grandchild Rhoda (#144), although he had established a multiple lineal family. The solid rectangle contains the household of his son Elias as of the death of his mother in 1771. It included Elias (#52), his wife Rachel Bishop, five grandchildren (#144-148), and the widow-grandmother Phebe Goodale Meigs.

percent) successfully placed their two sons upon the parental land; all told, thirty-nine persisting sons, or 78 percent of the population at risk, composed this favored group. Both the one- and two-male-heir families illustrate the power of traditional patrilineal and patrilocal custom. When Timothy Dwight praised the Guilford folk for retaining the "ancient manners of the New England colonists," these were the farmers he saw.[51] For these heirs, life was predictable, stable, and essentially familial.

Twenty-five men with three male heirs form a third group, comprising 23 percent of the village fathers (N = 109) and 18.5 percent of the East Guilfordians in this study (N = 135). While only nine (36 percent) of these men had sufficient land to settle all three sons, in toto they were able to place two-thirds of their male progeny in Guilford (N = 47/75). That William Bartlet endowed his third son with a horse, a team of oxen, and eight cows indicates that livestock could be used to provide for a son who received no land. For the sixteen families with four or more sons the prospects were bleaker—only forty-five of the seventy-four sons in this category remained in the town. It was these large families that furnished the bulk of those who left Guilford. In summary, forty-eight fathers lost no sons to migration, twenty-five saw one depart, ten had two sons move

[51] Barbara Miller Solomon, ed., *Travels in New England and New York*, II (Cambridge, Mass., 1969), 360.

out, and seven supplied three or more migrants apiece. "Our Town" belonged to the forty-eight and their persisting heirs, while their lines lasted.[52]

The groups we have examined so far comprise ninety fathers with male heirs. They constitute two-thirds of all the taxpayers in this study and held 78 percent of the total enumerated wealth (see Table III). These families possessed several characteristics: they were most likely to live in multiple lineal (or stem) families; they were relatively well-to-do; they had a high rate of marriage and remarriage; and they persisted. Consequently, their records and oral traditions became the collective memory of the New England way.[53]

The remaining third of East Guilford's taxpayers still require an accounting. Nineteen were fathers who had one or more daughters but no sons. They constituted 14 percent of the taxpayers and held 12 percent of the listed wealth. On average they had one-third less wealth per capita than fathers whose heirs were male.[54] This was no great handicap for the ten fathers with but a single heiress, eight of whose daughters remained in Guilford, or for the five fathers with two female heirs, six of whom persisted. These patterns are remarkably similar to the analogous experience of sons. By contrast, nine of the fifteen daughters of the four fathers who had three or more female heirs left the town, a rate of outmigration that indicates insufficient material resources to provide for them there. As in the case of males, this evidence for females shows that persisters and migrants came from different subgroups of the population.[55]

273

[52] When the Cruttendens, Evarts, Lees, and Meigses did depart, they disposed of their land to their Guilford relatives in a manner suggestive of the *retrait lignager*. For examples of this see Return Meigs to Jehiel Meigs, Apr. 2, 1737, and John Meigs to Jehiel Meigs, July 4, 1737, Guilford Deeds, V, 268, VI, 5. If a female inherited land rights, the belief existed that she did so "in trust" for males as seen in the option claim of the "Eldest son of Mary Shilley who was the Daughter of Alexander Bow formerly of . . . Middletown," in Ebenezer Shelley to Seth Wetmore, Guilford, Dec. 31, 1754, Chauncey Whittelsey Papers, Box I, Newberry Library, Chicago, Ill.

[53] Roy Ekland, "Guilford Condescriptive Run," Computer Printout, June 1975, demonstrates that the richest quintile of Guilford's 403 taxpayers in the 1730s had a third more kin than the poorest. Observe also that the single variable in this Guilford analysis that correlates with the marriage of sons is the *inter vivos* transfer of property, with a Pearson Correlation of .46.

[54] The Guilford total taxed-wealth variable is a summary of individual listings for 1716, 1732, 1740, 1749, 1756, and 1777. For these documents see Waters, "Patrimony, Succession, and Social Stability," *Perspectives Am. Hist.*, X (1976), 143, 157-159, and cf. Alice Hanson Jones, *Wealth of a Nation to Be: The American Colonies on the Eve of the Revolution* (New York, 1980), 206-210, 382-388.

[55] Edward Britton, *The Community of the Vill: A Study in the History of the Family and Village Life in Fourteenth-Century England* (Toronto, 1977), 149, and Albert I. Hermalin and Etienne van de Walle, "The Civil Code and Nuptiality: Empirical Investigation of a Hypothesis," in Ronald Demos Lee, ed., *Population Patterns in the Past* (New York, 1977), 90, connect marriage with land and the lack of it with outmigration.

Clearly, fathers with many daughters faced special difficulties. The arrangements Deacon Josiah Meigs made for his wife and three daughters illustrate this point. Meigs had girls needing husbands and land needing workers. He found both in the Ward brothers, whose prospects in their father's large family and in Killingworth were close to nil. Levi and Ambrose Ward married Mary and Lois Meigs, although these brides were seven and four years older than the respective grooms. Evidence suggests that the deacon lived on his homestead with his wife, Mary, his single daughter, Betty, his two married daughters, Mary and Lois, their husbands, the brothers Levi and Ambrose, and grandchildren. Probate records outline the household's complexity. In the distribution of Josiah Meigs's estate, the widow received her dower share, and the single daughter "one Sixth Part of the dwelling House," while Mary Ward and Lois Ward each received "one Quarter of the Dwelling House" and half of the "Homestead" fields. Figure 3 shows this ménage of mother-in-law, two married daughters, their husbands, their children, and a spinster sister.[56] The lack of sons created openings for the Ward brothers; similar situations provided places for such other outsiders as the men of the Hand, Walstone, and Lee families. One of every six fathers in East Guilford faced the problem of making some such special arrangements for his female heirs.

In addition to fathers without sons, the records yield twenty-six men and women who had no issue at all. They composed 19 percent of East Guilford's taxpayers and held 10 percent of the wealth. Their properties, small though they might be, could provide for the welfare of a younger kinsman, as in the instance of the third Abraham Cruttenden, to whom his uncle, a bachelor farmer-tailor, left his lands.[57] Together, Guilfordians who produced no male heirs contributed significantly to the redistribution of wealth in the town. In each generation lack of sons led to the recirculation of slightly more than a fifth of all property in Guilford to kinfolk, friends, and newcomers such as the Ward brothers. In all, this usually silent third played an essential part in Guilford society.

The evidence now at hand argues that in the colonial American context New Englanders had a unique regional social system. Puritanism—which excluded "such whose dispositions do not suit us, whose society will be

---

[56] Fathers without adult sons and women without males would have to work with or hire relatives (the preferred option) or use strangers to plow their fields as seen in the 1744-1747 entries of "Nathaniel Bartlet His Book 1721," 35-43, Henry Whitfield Historical Museum, and "Mary Leetes book," 1780 spring entries, n.p., N.-Y. Hist. Soc. See the petition of Daniel Leete, 1775, Conn. Archs., 2d Ser., Finance and Currency, VIII, 190a, 190b, for the destruction of the Guilford Rate Books. The "Distribution of the Estate of Josiah Meigs, Esq.," 1775, may be found under Guilford Probate, XII, 421-423. For Levi and Ambrose Ward see George K. Warde, *Andrew Warde and His Descendants, 1597-1910* (New York, 1910), 85-86.

[57] Smyth, "Abraham Cruttenden of Guilford, Conn., and His Descendants," *NEHGR*, LII (1898), 466.

FIGURE 3: THE PROBABLE HOUSEHOLD OF JOSIAH MEIGS (1774)

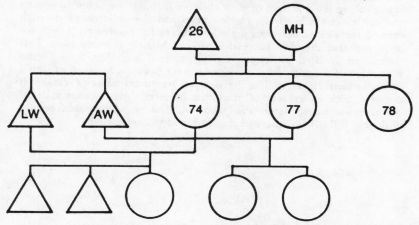

275

This household contained Josiah (#26), wife Mary Hand, single daughter Betty (#78), daughters Mary (#74)—who married Levi Ward—and Lois (#77)—who married Ambrose Ward—and assorted grandchildren.

hurtful to us," and included settlers who believed in patriarchal government and family worship—certainly helped shape the texture of that society.[58] Furthermore, New Englanders' creation of Thanksgiving Day as their special feast confirmed their sense of being a chosen people; on that day they ritually recalled the "mercies of God in his dealing with their family."[59] And when these folk spoke of family, they meant fathers, brothers, sisters, and cousins living next to each other and working their beloved fields. In Guilford these farmers made a kin-centered universe that formally favored males and related females. They talked about their ancestors, their lands carried their names, and they remembered them in the naming of their children.[60] For them, their historical past was a "sort of family history."[61]

This essay shows that New England families were shaped consciously,

[58] Sumner Chilton Powell, *Puritan Village: The Formation of a New England Town* (Middletown, Conn., 1963), xviii.

[59] Harriet Beecher Stowe, *Oldtown Folks* (Boston, 1869), 347.

[60] See Daniel Scott Smith, "Child-Naming Patterns and Family Structure Change: Hingham, Massachusetts, 1640-1880" (Newberry Papers in Family History, 76-5, Chicago, 1977), 19; for the medieval background, Clair Hayden Bell, *Peasant Life in Old German Epics: Meier Helmbrecht and Der Arme Heinrich . . .* (New York, 1931), lines 913-915; and, of course, Conrad M. Arensberg, *The Irish Countryman: An Anthropological Study* (New York, 1968 [orig. publ. 1937]), 82-83.

[61] Stowe, *Oldtown Folks*, 345-349, quotation on p. 347.

that they embodied values emphasizing the line, and that parents took an active role in the marriage of their children through their control of land and cattle. In Guilford the chosen heirs and the children of the rich formed families earlier than their less successful neighbors; it was not accidental that the least successful had the highest celibacy rates. This community insisted on either the promise of an inheritance or the possession of property for a marriage to take place. It believed in family order, in birth rights, and in the unequal treatment of heirs. Finally, it operated with an evident calculus that balanced heirs against material resources and largely determined who would marry, who would take care of the old folks, who inherited the land, and who migrated.

Ministers vs. Laymen: The Singing Controversy in Puritan New England, 1720–1740

LAURA L. BECKER

THE singing controversy in early eighteenth-century New England has long intrigued scholars. Most of the writing on this colorful debate over how psalms should be sung has been the work of musicologists who have sought to place it within the context of Anglo-American musical developments.[1] But historians have been interested as well. Ola Winslow portrayed the dispute as a typical manifestation of Puritan contentiousness, while Joyce Irwin has suggested that the introduction of the "New Way" of psalm singing reflected the intrusion of rationalism, pietism, and baroque ideas into the New England mind.[2]

Whereas all of this work has illuminated the nature and significance of the singing controversy, it has failed to give adequate weight to the fact that the reform was initiated and championed by the clergy against substantial lay opposition at a time when New England ministers were feeling generally besieged by their parishioners. The reformers did have some lay support on this issue, but the majority of citizens seem to

---

[1] See, e.g., George Hood, *History of Music in New England* (Boston: Wilkins, Carter and Company, 1846), pp. 65–152, 211–18; Henry Foote, *Three Centuries of American Hymnody* (Cambridge: Harvard University Press, 1940), pp. 91–111, 383–86; Allen Brinton, "Theoretical Introductions in American Tune Books to 1800" (Ph.D. diss., University of Michigan, 1949), pp. 75–108; Gilbert Chase, *America's Music*, 2d ed. (New York: McGraw Hill, 1966), chap. 2; Donald McKay and Richard Crawford, *William Billings of Boston* (Princeton: Princeton University Press, 1975), pp. 9–20.

[2] Ola Winslow, *Meetinghouse Hill* (New York: MacMillan Company, 1952), chap. 10; Joyce Irwin, "The Theology of Regular Singing," *New England Quarterly* 51 (1978): 176–92.

have opposed the movement, while only one preacher—Samuel Niles of Braintree—is known to have disagreed with his fellow clergymen.[3] Moreover, the timing of the reform is as significant as the clergy's unified stand. The tunebooks published, the sermons delivered, the singing societies founded, and the church councils devoted to this issue must be viewed within the context of broader ministerial anxieties and goals during the decades preceding the Great Awakening. The debate did involve musical taste and a specific set of intellectual assumptions, but it was the clergy's concern with irreligion, cultural decline, and their own status that fueled their passion for the New Way of singing.

Psalm singing was an integral part of worship in the Puritan churches. Its propriety had evidently been questioned in the early seventeenth century, but John Cotton's definitive treatise entitled *Singing of Psalms a Gospel Ordinance* (Boston, 1647) put an end to that debate. By 1720, the New Englanders' revered *Bay Psalm Book* had quietly gone through twenty editions when suddenly a stream of spirited pamphlets appeared, written by ministers intent upon "reforming the Depravations and Debasements our Psalmody labors under." The prevailing or "Old Way" of singing was an essentially oral tradition consisting of a limited number of tunes sung from memory in a slow tempo with considerable embellishment.[4] The New England clergy sought to replace this individualistic, improvised, and ever changing oral tradition with "Regular Singing," or "Singing by Note," which involved learning how to read, and maintaining strict fidelity to, the music as printed.

The first recorded sign of distress appeared in the 1698 edition of the *Bay Psalm Book*. Previously, this psalter had in-

---

[3] For his unusual story, see Foote, *Three Centuries of American Hymnody*, pp. 383–86.

[4] Modern scholars believe that this style evolved as a result of a shortage of music books, a low level of musical literacy, and the influence of secular folksong style. Congregational singing was also characterized by "lining out," wherein a deacon sang each line for the congregation to repeat after him. This practice did not come under heavy attack until the 1770s, however. See Chase, *America's Music*, pp. 30–39; McKay and Crawford, *William Billings*, pp. 14–19.

cluded only texts, but the new edition appended thirteen tunes accompanied by "some few directions for Ordering the Voice," designed to enable people to sing "without Squeaking above, or Grumbling below." The decision to print tunes and vocal directions was undoubtedly made by clergymen since they were largely responsible for other revisions, but their instructions apparently had minimal effect. As tune-setter for his church, Judge Samuel Sewall was embarrassed on a number of occasions by his own and his congregation's inability to hold a tune, and Cotton Mather declared: "The Psalmody is but poorly carried on in my Flock . . . I would see about it."[5]

279

The first tract connected with the singing reform movement seems to have been the Reverend Thomas Symmes's pamphlet *The Reasonableness of Regular Singing, or Singing by Note. In an Essay to Revive the True and Ancient Mode of Singing Psalm-Tunes . . . the Knowledge and Practice of Which is Greatly Decayed in Most Congregations* (Boston, 1720). It was followed by two of America's earliest musical instruction books: the Reverend John Tufts's *Introduction to the Singing of Psalm-Tunes* (Boston, 1721)[6] and the Reverend Thomas Walter's *The Grounds and Rules of Musick Explained* (Boston, 1721). Both of these works provided "rules for tuning the voice" (how to sing sweetly) and "rules for singing by note" (how to read music).

Symmes, Tufts, and Walter undoubtedly possessed unusual interest and skill in music, which made them the prime movers of the singing reform movement, but their ideas and goals met with immediate widespread approbation from their fellow pastors. Between 1722 and 1728, at least twelve more

---

[5] Thomas Halsey, ed., *The Diary of Samuel Sewall*, 2 vols. (New York: Farrar, Straus, Giroux, 1973), 1:436, 538; 2:720, 881, 885; Cotton Mather, *The Diary of Cotton Mather*, 2 vols. (New York: Frederick Ungar Publishing, 1957), 2:373, 560, 606, 624.

[6] The exact date Tufts's work first appeared is in doubt. Evans listed it as 1715, but Irving Lowens's date of 1721 is now more widely accepted. See Lowens's *Music and Musicians in Early America* (New York: W. W. Norton and Co., 1964), pp. 39–57. For a brief history of Tufts's life and work, see John H. Butler, "John Tufts: Aurora Unaware," *Music Educators Journal* 55 (January 1969): 44–46, 105–6.

addresses were delivered on the subject, nine of which were published. By 1731, Tufts's *Introduction* was in its eighth edition, and Walter's *Grounds and Rules* was in its second. "A Society for Promoting Regular Singing in The Worship of God" was established in Boston; it sponsored "singing lectures" consisting of discourses by clergymen and psalm singing in the New Way.[7] Although the reform movement seems to have gotten under way in the vicinity of Boston, it soon spread. Town and church records show that between 1722 and 1744, the issue of how to sing psalms was publicly debated in many communities, including Barnstable, Beverly, Braintree, Mattapoisett, Newbury, Westborough, Weston, and Worcester, Massachusetts; Eastbury, Fairfield, Farmington, Glastonbury, Kensington, New Milford, Wallingford, and Woodbury, Connecticut.[8]

Existing documents do not explain precisely how the reforming spirit spread, but clerical gatherings probably played a significant role. *Cases of Conscience About Singing Psalms*, by Peter Thacher, John Danforth, and Samuel Danforth (Boston, 1723), was "printed at the Desire of Honourable, Rever-

280

[7] References to such lectures can be found in Halsey, *The Diary of Samuel Sewall*, 2:285; *The New England Courant*, 26 February–6 March 1722; 12–19 March 1722; 7–14 May 1722; 28 May–4 June 1722; 23–30 September 1723.

[8] Alonzo Chapin, *Glastonbury for Two Hundred Years* (Hartford: Tiffany and Co., 1853), pp. 77–78; William Cothren, *History of Ancient Woodbury, Connecticut* (Waterbury: Bronson Brothers, 1854), p. 226; John Currier, *History of Newbury, Massachusetts* (Boston: Damrell and Upton, 1902), pp. 337, 356; Charles Davis, *History of Wallingford, Connecticut* (Meriden: By the Author, 1870), p. 403; Heman DeForest, *The History of Westborough, Massachusetts* (Westborough: By the Town, 1891), pp. 115–16; Hamilton Hurd, ed., *History of Fairfield County, Connecticut* (Philadelphia: J. Lewis and Co., 1881), p. 271; William Lincoln, *History of Worcester* (Worcester: Moses D. Phillips and Co., 1837), p. 178; *Mattapoisett and Old Rochester* (New York: By a Town Committee, 1907), p. 196; *New England Courant*, 2–9 April 1723, 12–19 August 1723, 9–16 September 1723; Heman Timlow, *Ecclesiastical and Other Sketches of Southington, Connecticut* (Hartford: Case, Lockwood and Brainard Co., 1875), p. 193; *Town of Weston, Church Records 1709–1825* (Boston: McIndol Brothers, 1901), p. 528; Donald Trayser, *Barnstable—Three Centuries of a Cape Cod Town* (Hyannis: P. B. and F. P. Goss, 1939), p. 47; J. Hammond Trumbell, ed., *The Memorial History of Hartford County, Connecticut* (Boston: Edward Osgood, 1886), p. 224; *Two Centuries of New Milford, Connecticut* (New York: Grafton Press, 1907), p. 13; *Two Hundredth Anniversary, Kensington Congregational Church* (Kensington: n.p., 1912), p. 38; Winslow, *Meetinghouse Hill*, p. 166.

end and Worthy Persons, to whom it was communicated, in a
Venerable Council of Churches, January 30, 1722–3." The
author of *A Brief Discourse Concerning Regular Singing* (Boston, 1725) dedicated his work to "the honorable Council of
Churches, Patrons of Regular Singing." Nathaniel Chauncey's
sermon *Regular Singing Defended* (Hartford, 1728) was "read
and approved by the General Association at Hartford, May
the 12th, 1727," and was printed "with their recommendation
of it to the Publick." This same body issued a formal endorsement of the New Way and sponsored a singing lecture in
June of that year.[9]

Other evidence further supports the idea that the promo-
tion of a reform in psalm singing was a collective effort on the
part of New England clergymen. The title page of Symmes's
sermon on *The Reasonableness of Regular Singing* indicates
that his work was "Perused by Several Ministers in the Town
& Country, and Published with the Approbation of All who
Read It." Walter's *The Grounds and Rules of Musick Explained* was accompanied by a "Recommendatory Preface"
signed by more than fifteen ministers who undoubtedly discussed the issue at some point, if not at a council, then in-
formally. The "several ministers" who urged Walter to publish his *Sweet Psalmist of Israel* (Boston, 1722) and the four
who endorsed Symmes's *Utile Dulci, Or, A Joco-Serious Dialogue Concerning Regular Singing* (Boston, 1723) must have
done likewise.

Between 1720 and 1730, no fewer than thirty-one clergymen
preached in favor of the New Way or signed their names in
support of someone else's sermon or tunebook (see appendix),
and a thorough examination of ministers' diaries would undoubtedly reveal the names of others who advocated the
reform. Furthermore, there are definite indications that ministers were aware of what was happening in other communities. Some made specific references to towns where the reform
had already been enacted, while others remarked on how wide-

281

9 George Walker, *History of the First Church in Hartford* (Hartford: Brown and Goss, 1884), p. 226.

spread the contention was.[10] Finally, the great similarity in the arguments presented in the various published essays strongly suggests that the clergy involved in this effort shared their ideas with one another.

The ministers' arguments focus on two broad issues: the intrinsic merits of Regular Singing and its benefits to society. They argued first that singing by note was in accord with God's will. It required more skill and care than the Old Way and thus made better use of the "tuneable voices" and "organs for hearing" the Lord had provided. "To act below the powers and faculties with which God has endowed us" was wrong, the clergy maintained. In fact, it was man's duty to improve himself in all things, including singing. By so doing man would distinguish himself from the random or rote behavior of "bruit creatures" by calling upon his rational faculties.[11] The New Way also suited God's love of order. "God is not the Author of Confusion," claimed one minister as he elaborated on a passage from Corinthians: "discord and confusion are contrary to God." Others argued that Regular Singing was aesthetically superior. Whereas the Old Way produced "uncouth noise" and "hideous howlings," the New Way was "most melodious."[12]

Although the clergy invoked God's Will, human reason, and music's "Doctrine of Concords" to support their position,[13] and they welcomed the pleasure which people could derive from an activity well done, they clearly saw the singing reform as a means to certain greater ends. Paramount among

10 See, e.g., Thacher et al., *Cases of Conscience*, p. 7; Timothy Woodbridge, *The Duty of God's Professing People, in Glorifying their Heavenly Father* (New London, 1727), p. 1; *A Pacificatory Letter About Psalmody* (Boston, 1724), p. 2.

11 *A Brief Discourse*, pp. 8–10, 14; Chauncey, *Regular Singing Defended*, pp. 15–16, 23; Thacher et al., *Cases of Conscience*, pp. 3–5, 17; Symmes, *The Reasonableness of Regular Singing*, pp. 10–12.

12 *A Pacificatory Letter*, p. 6; Symmes, *The Reasonableness of Regular Singing*, pp. 9, 11; Symmes, *Utile Dulci*, pp. 19–20; Walter, *The Sweet Psalmist of Israel*, pp. 9, 26; Thacher et al., *Cases of Conscience*, pp. 3, 7; Cotton Mather, *The Accomplished Singer* (Boston, 1721), pp. 22–23.

13 For an excellent analysis of the way in which these arguments reflect the impact of rationalism and baroque ideas on traditional Puritan thought, see Irwin, "The Theology of Regular Singing."

these was the restoration of religion to its earlier prominence in the lives of the people.

The idea that the late seventeenth and early eighteenth centuries were a time of religious declension has come under considerable attack recently. For the purposes of this study, however, the reality of the decline is less important than the clergymen's belief that it was real. Their public jeremiads and private soul searchings attest to their great concern over the increasing worldliness, wickedness, and religious indifference they saw around them. The problem was evident, but solutions were evasive. Pleas for reformation and warnings of dire consequences if New Englanders failed to mend their ways yielded to the encouragement of outward things; religious practice was viewed as a means to religious fervor. Early eighteenth-century ministers urged the people to observe the Sabbath, to attend church regularly, to read the Bible, and to pray often. They also promoted the singing of psalms.

Most of the clergymen involved in the singing controversy focused on the virtues of the New Way in particular, but those who began at the beginning and explained the need for psalm singing in general suggested that it had a wide range of benefits for the singer. It was a fulfillment of a religious duty, an act of devotion which pleased God; it provided an effective "chariot" on which prayers could be "sweetly and gloriously conveyed to heaven"; it soothed "unhappy emotions"; and it promoted a sense of brotherhood. Most important, psalm singing helped an individual resist Satan and turn instead to the Lord. "Music happily serves to fix the mind upon religious objects, abstracting the soul from every Diversion," claimed one minister. It "prepares our souls for the entrance of the Holy Ghost." Another writer advocated the founding of psalm singing schools, arguing that such institutions would "divert young people from learning Idle, Foolish, yea pernicious Songs and ballads, and banish all such Trash from their minds."[14]

14 Mather, *The Accomplished Singer*, pp. 8–10, 16; preface to Walter's *The Grounds and Rules of Musick Explained*, p. ii; Walter, *The Sweet Psalmist of Israel*, pp. 11–20; Symmes, *The Reasonableness of Regular Singing*, p. 20.

New England clergymen writing on music during this period were unanimous in their opinion that the New Way was more likely to effect these ends than the Old Way. First, they expected the reform to bring into the fold that "multitude of persons" who "open not their mouths to praise God . . . because they know not how to sing." Indeed, if people learned to read notes, they would be able to sing psalms outside as well as inside the church, since they would no longer be dependent on the deacons to set the tune and lead them in their singing. A revival of psalmody in the home was deemed particularly important because it would bolster family cohesiveness (a major ministerial concern) and allow people to experience psalm singing's spiritually uplifting power more frequently.[15]

The clergy also claimed that the New Way would produce a spiritually enriching variety of tunes. Under the uncertainties of oral tradition, the Puritans had forgotten most of the psalm tunes that their forefathers had brought over from England. As a result, Thomas Walter wrote in 1721, "at present we are confined to eight or ten Tunes, and in some congregations to little more than half that Number, which being sung over, are too apt, if not to create a Distaste, yet at least mightily to lessen the Relish of them." The New Way would enable people to master a stimulating assortment of new melodies.[16]

The ministers further held that Regular Singing was more conducive to solemn thoughts and proper devotion because, being orderly and dignified, it encouraged discipline. Nathaniel Chauncey argued vigorously that man needs rules, that without them there is no way to "rectify anything amiss . . . no possibility of passing any judgment on the work or duty done, whether it be well done or ill done." Knowing this, God pro-

---

15 Chauncey, *Regular Singing Defended*, p. 10; Symmes, *The Reasonableness of Regular Singing*, pp. 3, 15; Increase Mather's preface to Cotton Mather's *The Accomplished Singer;* preface to Walter's *The Grounds and Rules of Musick Explained*, p. ii. See also the statements of the North Association of Hartford, 6 June 1727, cited in Walker, *History of the First Church in Hartford*, p. 226.

16 Walter, *The Grounds of Music Explained*, p. 4. See also Symmes, *Utile Dulci*, p. 25.

vided rules for guidance in all things. Therefore, it was man's duty not only to sing psalms, but to sing them in the New Way, in accordance with God's rules of harmony and order. This would help to remind people that all aspects of their lives were to be similarly governed.[17]

The New England clergy believed that the replacement of "fancy" by "rule" would help to achieve another aim dear to their hearts: uniformity within and among their churches. Several writers commented that "disunity is unbecoming" and hinted that a congregation which could not or would not sing as one was unlikely to be unified in other endeavors. The New Way, they argued, would eliminate those individual "quaverings and turnings" that created "perpetual interferings" and made the singing of one congregation sound "like five hundred different tunes roared out at the same time." Through Regular Singing, "a whole congregation may be said to make but one Sound"; a peaceful blending of voices to encourage or, better yet, to mirror a peaceful blending of minds and spirits.[18]

That goal achieved, it could be expanded to include diverse congregations. "There are no two churches that sing alike," complained Thomas Walter. "I have myself heard, for instance, Oxford tune sung in three churches . . . with as much difference as there can possibly be between York and Oxford, or any two other different tunes." If the same tunes were sung in a Regular manner in all congregations, argued another, people attending services at a church other than their own could join in the psalm singing much more readily.[19]

The desire for uniformity in psalm singing, however, went beyond such practical considerations as concern for the plight

285

[17] Chauncey, *Regular Singing Defended*, pp. 32–39, 47; Symmes, *The Reasonableness of Regular Singing*, p. 6; *A Brief Discourse*, pp. 2–3; Walter, *Sweet Psalmist of Israel*, p. 26.

[18] Walter, *The Grounds and Rules of Musick Explained*, pp. 3–5; *A Brief Discourse Concerning Regular Singing*, p. 7; Chauncey, *Regular Singing Defended*, p. 28; *A Pacificatory Letter About Psalmody*, p. 7.

[19] Walter, *The Grounds and Rules of Musick Explained*, p. 3; Chauncey, *Regular Singing Defended*, p. 43; *A Pacificatory Letter about Psalmody*, p. 7; *A Brief Discourse Concerning Regular Singing*, p. 7.

of visitors. The variation which the clergy detected in this aspect of worship probably disturbed them in large part because it symbolized a lack of uniformity among the Puritan churches in a host of other, more important matters. During the early eighteenth century, many New England ministers seriously began to question the congregational system. They feared that autonomy had gotten out of hand, that standards needed to be reasserted and individual churches made to conform. This concern contributed to the growth of clerical councils and associations as well as to the intense debate between the Mather "conservatives" and their "liberal" opponents. Not surprisingly, those in favor of strict standards were among the most active advocates of the New Way.[20]

The revival of psalm singing was a relatively minor issue, but Puritan ministers clearly saw it as a means to achieve a variety of religious ends. These included more frequent, better ordered, more inspiring, and more uniform worship; in short, a revival of religion. While this was their primary concern, the clergy were also alarmed by what they perceived to be a general decline in learning in the late seventeenth and early eighteenth centuries. In the mid-1600s, laws had been enacted requiring each town with more than fifty families to hire a schoolmaster and each with more than one hundred families to provide a college-preparatory education for those interested and qualified. As early as the 1670s, however, there were definite indications that the system was not achieving its goals, and lamentations over the "low and languishing state" of learning emanated from the pulpit with increasing frequency. Connecticut officials apparently gave up and waived the requirement for all but the largest towns in 1700. Massachusetts officials persisted: in 1701 the General Court doubled the penalty for towns which failed to comply with the law.

[20] See Perry Miller, *The New England Mind: From Colony to Province* (Cambridge: Harvard University Press, 1953), chaps. 16–18; Richard Bushman, *From Puritan to Yankee* (New York: W. W. Norton and Co., 1970), chap. 10; J. William T. Youngs, *God's Messengers: Religious Leadership in Colonial New England, 1700–1750* (Baltimore: Johns Hopkins University Press, 1976), chap. 4. A few leading liberals joined the conservatives, undoubtedly because they shared other goals discussed below.

Nevertheless, many towns simply paid the fine and continued to show little concern for the formal education of their children.[21]

A number of the ministers who advocated Regular Singing expressed themselves vigorously on this issue. Joseph Belcher of Dedham worried aloud about "the coldness, indisposition, not to say opposition" to secondary schools on the part of "too many of our unlearned." Cotton Mather declared that "a lively discourse about the Benefit and Importance of *Education* should be given to the Country. The Country is perishing for want of it; they are sinking apace into Barbarism and all Wickedness." In their sermon on the New Way, Peter Thacher, John Danforth, and Samuel Danforth commented, "we cannot but think that some of our congregations have too much indulged themselves in Ignorance and Carelessness."[22]

Thacher and the Danforths were not alone in drawing a connection between education and psalm singing. Many of their fellow advocates argued that the Old Way was itself proof and product of a decline in learning. Several noted that music and its rules were well known to the founders of New England, but through a lack of instruction and books knowledge degenerated into an oral tradition. "And whatsoever is conveyed down to us" in this poor manner, wrote Symmes, "it is a thousand to one if it be not miserably corrupted in three or four score years time." Cotton Mather asserted that "to recover Regular Singing would be really a Reformation, a recovery out of an apostacy."[23]

Many advocates of the New Way went one step further and denegrated their opponents as intellectually inferior. The au-

287

[21] Robert Middlekauff, *Ancients and Axioms: Secondary Education in Eighteenth-Century New England* (New Haven: Yale University Press, 1963), pp. 32–40; James Axtell, *The School Upon A Hill: Education and Society in Colonial New England* (New York: W. W. Norton, 1976), pp. 176–83.

[22] Axtell, *The School Upon a Hill,* p. 180; Mather, *Diary,* 2:51; Thacher et al., *Cases of Conscience,* pp. 13–14.

[23] Symmes, *The Reasonableness of Regular Singing,* pp. 5–9; Mather, *The Accomplished Singer,* p. 22. See also Walter, *The Grounds and Rules of Musick Explained,* p. 4; Chauncey, *Regular Singing Defended,* p. 31; *A Pacificatory Letter About Psalmody,* p. 7; Woodbridge, *The Duty of God's Professing People.*

thor of *A Brief Discourse* claimed that his pamphlet was "designed for the Unlearned, who applaud 'the good Old Way.'" Nathaniel Chauncey asserted that Singing by Note was the method favored by "the learned," while Cotton Mather and Thomas Walter each made disparaging remarks about "rustik" or "country" people. Thomas Symmes suggested that "anti-Regular Singers" tended to be "shy" of books in general and asserted that all "rational," "unprejudiced," and "qualified" people preferred the New Way. At the end of one essay, he commented pointedly that "what I have writ was designed chiefly for the common Country People, and I have endeavored to accommodate it to their capacities. If it had been designed for Men of Letters, some arguments would have been fetched from some other Topicks, and proposed in another Method and Stile, but this is needless." Symmes's *Utile Dulci* is heavy with sarcasm from start to finish. It pits an urbane minister against a self-deprecating common man, who humbly confesses to the minister, "I don't know whether I've skill enough to range my objections to your mind."[24]

Comments of this nature support J. William T. Youngs's contention that the New England clergymen of this era had a strong sense of superiority. Individually and collectively, they sought to preserve their elite standing and to enhance their profession through clerical councils, revised ordination procedures, sermons on their unique and vital role, and attempts to restrict the power of the laity, as well as efforts to revive the religious fervor and respect for learning on which their preeminence rested.[25] The singing reform movement clearly fit in with this general program because, aside from its perceived benefits for spiritual and cultural life, it provided new opportunities for ministerial leadership.

The leadership theme appeared in many of the discourses

[24] *A Brief Discourse*, pp. 1, 7, 14; Chauncey, *Regular Singing Defended*, p. 42; Cotton Mather to Thomas Hollis, Jr., 5 November 1723, in *Selected Letters of Cotton Mather*, ed. Kenneth Silverman (Baton Rouge: Louisiana State University Press, 1971), pp. 376–77; Walter, *The Grounds and Rules of Musick Explained*, p. 4; Symmes, *The Reasonableness of Regular Singing*, pp. 5, 9, 21; Symmes, *Utile Dulci*, pp. 10, 23.

[25] Youngs, *God's Messengers*, chaps. 1, 2, 4, 5.

on Regular Singing. Cotton Mather recommended that pastors aid in the revitalization of psalmody by giving a special exposition on each text before it was sung. Another writer noted, "The Levites were leaders in this holy exercise [psalm singing] and these (many of them) excelled in skill and instructed others, which shows that the ministers of the Gospel ... should instruct and lead their people." Thomas Symmes added that the pastor, not the deacon, had the right to set the psalm.[26]

Symmes was, in fact, quite belligerent on the sensitive issue of clerical rights. In *Utile Dulci, Or a Joco-Serious Dialogue,* the minister insists that the discussion can take place only if he is accorded proper respect: "If those that should come to learn of me and be instructed by me, come rather to dictate to me, and instead of (as the Apostle directs) Entreating me as a Father ... arraign my Administrations ... I have just reason to be angry. ... I should sin against God, and betray the authority I'm vested with ... if I should tamely suffer myself to be insulted." Elsewhere in the dialogue, Symmes's minister complains of the "impertinences" of "anti-Regular Singers" and is indignant that they are not swayed even when they learn that the reform is favored by Cotton Mather, Increase Mather, and many other eminent ministers. "Is this to obey the voice of the Lord's Servants?" he thunders; "To believe his prophets? To learn the law at the mouth of Christ's messengers? I have told you often, and now tell you even weeping,—'tis a lamentation." Asserting that it was up to the pastor, not the congregation, to decide matters of doctrine and forms of worship, he adds, "I shan't be determined by those that understand neither what they say nor whereof they affirm. And if any will be so hardy as to arraign my administration on this score, I appeal to council."[27]

Thomas Symmes seems to have been unusually preoccupied with ministerial rights and authority: he published *A Discourse Concerning Prejudice in Matters of Religion* (Boston,

289

[26] Mather, *The Accomplished Singer*, p. 12; *A Brief Discourse*, pp. 5–6, 14–15; Symmes, *The Reasonableness of Regular Singing*, pp. 20–21.

[27] Symmes, *Utile Dulci*, pp. 9–10, 27, 46–56.

1722), in which he once again condemned those who refused to be guided by clerical wisdom, as well as *The People's Interest . . . Or a Sermon Showing that it is the Interest of the People of God, to do their Duty Toward the Subsistence of Such as Preach the Gospel to Them* (Boston, 1724). But Symmes's concerns were shared by other reformers. His *Discourse on Prejudice* was printed, he claimed, at the urging of "Sundry . . . Brethren in the Ministry," and one of his co-leaders in the singing movement, John Tufts, wrote an even more acrimonious essay on this same subject entitled *Anti-Ministerial Objections Considered, Or the Unreasonable Pleas Made By Some Against Their Duty To Their Ministers, With Respect To Their Maintenance Answered* (Boston, 1725). Between 1715 and 1730, at least ten other advocates of the New Way published discourses on the rights and responsibilities of the clergy.[28] These men undoubtedly welcomed the effort to reform psalmody as a chance to perform their rightful roles as leaders within the colony in general and their own communities in particular.

However, as numerous scholars have pointed out, Puritan clergymen were on the defensive during much of the early eighteenth century. James Schmotter has documented a steady rise in the number of serious quarrels between pastors and their congregations, especially over salary and doctrine. Youngs claims that the ministers were "losing their audience" due to lay ignorance and worldliness, and Clifford Shipton argues that even the more conservative clergy were too liberal for the masses. Clerical meddling in nonspiritual affairs, such as the controversies over smallpox and paper money, was harshly condemned in the 1720s, as were clerical attempts to assert power through exclusive councils.[29] Thus, it is not sur-

---

[28] These include Samuel Checkley, Benjamin Colman, Nathaniel Eells, Thomas Foxcroft, Cotton Mather, Increase Mather, Thomas Prince, Benjamin Wadsworth, Nehemiah Walter, and John Webb. Their sermons are available on the Readex Microprint of Charles Evans's *Early American Imprints*.

[29] James Schmotter, "Ministerial Careers in Eighteenth-Century New England: The Social Context, 1700–1760," *Journal of Social History* 9 (1975): 256–58; Youngs, *God's Messengers*, pp. 27–28, 37–38, 63–64, 92–108; Clifford Shipton, "The New England Clergy of the 'Glacial Age,'" Publications of the Colonial

prising that the ministers' efforts to introduce the New Way also generated strong lay opposition.

Town and church records from this period generally do not include votes on issues but simply indicate that a matter was discussed and/or a particular decision reached. There is ample evidence, however, that Regular Singing was not greeted with enthusiasm. Many communities did not even consider adopting the New Way until well into the 1730s, and even then a final decision was sometimes deferred, as in Wallingford and Hartford, Connecticut. In Kensington and New Milford, split votes were recorded, while Eastbury, Connecticut, and Westborough, Massachusetts, accepted the change, then reconsidered. Compromise was necessary in Barnstable, Massachusetts, and Glastonbury, Connecticut, where residents voted "to sing for half a year in the old way, and the other half in the Regular." In Braintree, Worcester, and Farmington, the issue seems to have been fought out during worship itself, with "regular singers" and "irregular singers" trying to drown out each other.[30] Virtually all of the essays written in support of the New Way (except those which started the movement) contain references to the widespread "Contention and Discord" the projected change engendered.

Although such dissension clearly indicates substantial lay opposition to Singing by Note, it also indicates that the ministers had lay allies. Judging from statements by various clergymen, most of those allies seem to have been either young people or Bostonians.[31] Widespread support of the New Way among young people probably stemmed from extrinsic factors

Society of Massachusetts, *Transactions* 32 (1933–37): 24–54; G. B. Warden, *Boston 1689–1776* (Boston: Little, Brown, 1970), pp. 80–90; Paul Lucas, *Valley of Discord: Church and Society Along the Connecticut River, 1636–1725* (Hanover: University Press of New England, 1976), pp. 189–204; H. B. Parkes, "New England in the Seventeen Thirties," *New England Quarterly* 3 (1930): 409–13.

30 See n. 8 for citations.

31 Cotton Mather to Thomas Hollis, 5 November 1723, in Silverman, *Selected Letters of Cotton Mather*, pp. 376–77; Symmes, *Utile Dulci*, p. 30; Dwight, *An Essay to Silence the Outcry*, p. 10; Woodbridge, *The Duty of God's Professing People*, p. 8; Thacher et al., *Cases of Conscience*, pp. 8, 16; Symmes, *The Reasonableness of Regular Singing*, p. 17; *A Pacificatory Letter*, p. 12.

such as openness to change, a desire to rebel against parents, and the social attraction of coed singing schools. Mather and Symmes used the support of Bostonians to bolster their assertion that anyone who was at all sophisticated accepted Regular Singing. However, letters to the editor in the 2–9 April and the 19–26 November 1722 issues of the *New England Courant* indicate that even here there was some opposition.

Most, though not all, of the information on the opposition appears in the form of objections answered by the clergy in their discourses on Regular Singing. Since these sources are clearly biased, any analysis of lay views must be tentative. Nevertheless the evidence suggests that aesthetic judgment—a frank preference for the sound of the Old Way—plus a general cultural conservatism—a desire to perpetuate tradition for its own sake—were of prime importance.[32] The reforming clergy claimed that these inclinations were the product of ignorance, but several musicologists have argued that the Old Way was an indigenous musical form, a manifestation of the Anglo-American folksong style, and not a degeneration. The New Way, they contend, was a "high art" form derived from elite traditions and imposed on the innately conservative "folk."[33]

In any case, resentment and mistrust of the clergy clearly reinforced matters of taste in arousing hostility to Regular Singing. Several reformers stated openly that much of the opposition was based on feelings "against the persons that are the promoters." Some opponents were concerned that the ministers were "endeavoring to bring . . . superstitious Ceremonies into the Church," a charge that underscores both the conservatism of the laity and their reluctance to yield readily to the will of the clergy. Others asserted that the reform was merely "a contrivance to get money." There were complaints

[32] Objections are noted in Chauncey, *Regular Singing Defended*, pp. 30, 49; Dwight, *An Essay to Silence the Outcry*, pp. 11–12; Symmes, *The Reasonableness of Regular Singing*, pp. 9, 17, 18; *A Brief Discourse*, p. 13; Woodbridge, *The Duty of God's Professing People*, p. 10; Thacher et al., *Cases of Conscience*, pp. 13, 17; Symmes, *Utile Dulci*, pp. 21, 38.

[33] See, e.g., Chase, *America's Music*, pp. 30–39; Britton, "Theoretical Introductions in American Tunebooks," p. 87.

that the people were not "advised with and consulted in the Case," that the ministers were "intruding" their views on their congregations. The fact that the clergy were united behind Regular Singing did not strengthen their cause: Thomas Symmes noted the people's "perverse" tendency to dismiss this unity as insignificant on the grounds that "ministers will hang together, right or wrong." Nathaniel Chauncey leveled an even stronger charge against opponents of the New Way when he remarked pointedly that "sometimes persons are moved to reject a thing urged, as a duty, from a spirit of Corahism, or a forward disposition to oppose ministers."[34]

293

The ministers eventually won the battle: by the mid-1740s, most congregations sang in the New Way. Disagreements over other aspects of church music, however—lining out, the use of musical instruments, the introduction of hymns—stirred passions in New England throughout the eighteenth century and on into the nineteenth.[35] More significantly, the underlying issues which made the singing reform so important to the clergy in the first place—religious indifference, a decline in learning, and a disconcerting lack of deference on the part of the masses—remained largely unresolved. Thus, while the triumph of the New Way was indeed a victory over the laymen, it was a far narrower victory than the Puritan clergy had sought.

[34] Dwight, *An Essay to Silence the Outcry*, p. 3; Woodbridge, *The Duty of God's Professing People*, p. 8; Symmes, *Utile Dulci*, pp. 12, 47, 50; Thacher et al., *Cases of Conscience*, p. 7; *A Pacificatory Letter*, p. 9; Chauncey, *Regular Singing Defended*, p. 6. The basis for the charge that the reform was "a contrivance to get money" is unclear. Perhaps it was a reference to the fact that ministers compiled the tunebooks and may have given lessons in singing by note.

[35] See Foote, *Three Centuries of American Hymnody*, chaps. 3, 5.

Laura L. Becker *is Assistant Professor of History at Clemson University.*

APPENDIX

The following list includes all clergymen known to have preached, written, or signed their names in support of the New Way. Those starred gave oral or written discourses on the subject; the others simply signified their approval.

294

*John Barnard	(Marblehead, Massachusetts)
Joseph Belcher	(Dedham, Massachusetts)
Thomas Blowers	(Beverly, Massachusetts)
*Richard Brown	(Reading, Massachusetts)
*Nathaniel Chauncey	(Durham, Connecticut)
Samuel Checkley	(Boston, Massachusetts)
Benjamin Colman	(Boston, Massachusetts)
William Cooper	(Boston, Massachusetts)
*John Danforth	(Dorchester, Massachusetts)
*Samuel Danforth	(Taunton, Massachusetts)
*Josiah Dwight	(Woodstock, Connecticut)
Nathaniel Eells	(Norwell, Massachusetts)
*Samuel Fiske	(Salem, Massachusetts)
Thomas Foxcroft	(Boston, Massachusetts)
Nathaniel Hunting	(East Hampton, Long Island)
*Cotton Mather	(Boston, Massachusetts)
Increase Mather	(Boston, Massachusetts)
Samuel Moody	(York, Massachusetts [Maine])
Thomas Prince	(Boston, Massachusetts)
John Rogers	(Boxford, Massachusetts)
Joseph Sewall	(Boston, Massachusetts)
*Thomas Symmes	(Bradford, Massachusetts)
*Peter Thacher	(Milton, Massachusetts)
*John Tufts	(West Newbury, Massachusetts)
Benjamin Wadsworth	(Boston, Massachusetts)
Nehemiah Walter	(Roxbury, Massachusetts)
*Thomas Walter	(Roxbury, Massachusetts)
*Valentine Wightman	(Groton, Connecticut)
John Webb	(Boston, Massachusetts)
Nathaniel Williams	(Boston, Massachusetts)
*Timothy Woodbridge	(Hartford, Connecticut)

Journal of Historical Geography, 8, 4 (1982) 333–346

Village and community in early colonial New England

Joseph S. Wood

The long-standing correlation between community function and nucleated settlement form in early colonial New England is mistaken. Puritan communities were established, but new communities—often called villages in colonial records—were developed and survived quite well regardless of settlement form. As in England at the time, village meant community and community was a social web. Village status in New England provided a community with land and thus enabled the community to undertake settlement. But the social web that comprised community did not require nucleated settlement, and the dispersed settlement form that many colonists had known in England dominated the village landscape of early colonial New England.

Early New England colonists, it is widely believed, established nucleated settlements, and these nucleated settlements enhanced community life.[1] This correlation between community function and settlement form was so important, it is further believed, that community was diminished in the eighteenth century as settlement form was loosened and many community members dispersed from nucleated villages to individual farms. But was community forbearance so dependent upon nucleated settlement? Or has the rhetoric about Puritan community been so linked with the particular settlement form of the New England town as "to effect an implicit definition of community as the ideal Puritan town", and so confuse the settlement form with community?[2] The argument that follows suggests that a simple correlation between community function and nucleated settlement form in early colonial New England is mistaken. Highly structured communities were established; but, as in England, whence the colonists came, new communities—often called villages—developed and survived quite well without the necessity of nucleated settlement.

Community is a "social web" or, more explicitly, "a network of social relations marked by mutuality and emotional bonds".[3] Community is dependent upon common purpose, shared understanding and values, a sense of obligation and reciprocity, and collective action. As traditional community interaction was interpersonal and frequent, common space is also implied in most definitions. Space and place denote common experience; and, in the traditional view, community as experience and community as place were one.[4] The organization of the common space—the settlement form—reflects in large measure the configuration or spatial structure of the social web.[5]

The prevalent settlement form attributed to the place associated with traditional, pre-industrial community is the village, or "collection of dwelling houses and other buildings, forming a centre of habitation in a country district".[6] Village and

0305-7488/82/040333 + 14 $03.00/0   333

community, like place and community, are often considered one and the same and the terms used interchangeably; but, in the primary definition of village, nucleation is strongly implied:[7] a kind of cosmological predeliction to have a nucleated settlement located at the centre of a community's area prevails and, in the geographical literature, is reinforced by a spatial view based on Von Thünen land-use rings, agglomeration economies, and central places. Quite simply, nucleated forms provided the functional requirements for successful community and economy.[8]

No settlement form would have better ensured community forbearance as seventeenth-century colonists ventured into the wilderness of New England. The conventional view that New England's colonial communities formed compact villages gathered around a central meetinghouse correlates nicely with an idealized social order attributed to hard-bitten, theocratic Puritans; with recorded plans for villages; with literary and circumstantial historical reference to villages; with nineteenth-century maps and sketches of villages; and with present-day landscape. Yet, for all that has been said about community and settlement form in New England, it is instructive to examine once more the New England village. First, a number of scholars have shown that villages need not be nucleated settlement forms at all. Villages in Europe, including England, have ranged in form from quite compact, to linear, to widely dispersed neighbourhoods.[9] Dispersed villages were common in south-east England, the major source area of New England colonists in the seventeenth century.[10] Second, recent studies of New England communities have dealt largely with the question of the essence of pre-industrial village life in New England, the extent to which this way of life reflected its particular English origins, and the particularly American experience of these communities.[11] As a result of these studies, it has become evident to some historians that nucleation was not the constant rule for settlement form in early colonial New England.[12]

Close inspection of seventeenth-century New England villages—places specifically called villages in records of towns and governing colonial assemblies—suggests that village was an official designation of a community, like town, and that villages were subordinate to towns. Also like towns, villages were not necessarily nucleated in form. Indeed, detailed accounts of settlement form indicate that the modal form of settlement was dispersed from the 1630s onward and even many nucleated settlements were short-lived.[13] Nevertheless, New England communities existed and functioned quite well. Even when social structure or settlement form was altered, the social web that constituted community persisted. Village status encouraged such community forbearance by providing a community with land resources and placing the community and its assigned land under the auspices, guidance, and taxing power of a parent town. This status enabled the community to establish its own ecclesiastical society, or parish, or, if unsettled, to undertake settlement beyond the pale of what in time might become a town in its own right.

"In the village manner"

New England colonists' yearning for land was great, and available land was a critical factor in the establishment of New England villages. Civil and religious liberty was important for settlers who came to New England, of course, but owning land and all that implied were the most impelling reasons for initial colonization and inland settlement alike.[14] The goal of Puritan settlement in New England was noble: there was to be a covenanted community of men established in a new England, a congregation of individuals bound by special compact. But abundant land had an unsettling effect. Settlement expansion took place by replication, by increasing the number of communities, not by enlarging any one. Not satisfied with crowding along the shoreline, in Salem or about Boston Bay, settlers spread inland when and wherever they could. Much of New England is hardscrabble; and once salt marshes, Indian old fields, and riverine meadows called intervales were taken, settlers were forced to settle land more marginal than what the first settlers had found. As New Englanders spread across the land, they established a settled landscape of places, many called villages, and all designed to foster community well-being.

The New England town system was designed to bring order to these communities. The town was a community of settlers incorporated as an administrative unit to encourage settlement and establish political and religious institutions within clearly defined geographic boundaries and, thus, perpetuate community. But a town was not a settlement. Only through land proprietors, in whom was vested local authority and who were responsible for distributing land, did towns come to be instruments of settlement. Colonial magistrates made extensive grants of land to town proprietors and to individuals in their favour, so, according to Governor Winthrop,

297

> that (when the towns should be increased by their children and servants growing up, etc.) they might have place to erect villages, where they might be planted, and so the land improved to the more common benefit.[15]

These "villages or plantations" were to be developed into new, freestanding communities with certain conditions required to assure success of the comunity.[16] The Town of Lynn, Massachusetts, one of the original towns about Massachusetts Bay, was especially in need of the grant for Lynn Village. The 50 families that came to Lynn in 1630 had laid out farms from 10 to 200 acres in size and had settled these farms in all parts of the original town grant.[17] But by 1639 more land was required, and the General Court was generous:

> The petition of the inhabitants of Linn for an inland plantation at the head of their bounds is granted them 4 miles square, as the place will affoard, upon condition that the petitioners shall within 2 years make some good proceeding in planting, so as it may bee a village fit to conteine a convenient number of inhabitants, which may in dewe time have a churche there, & so as such as shall remove to inhabit there shall not with all keepe their accomodations in Linn above 2 years after their removall to the said village, upon paine to forfeit their interest in one of them, at their owne election, except this Court shall see just cause to dispense further with them; & this village is to bee 4 mile square at least by just content.[18]

New England towns were thus settled, according to Timothy Dwight, widely travelled president of Yale College, in "*the village manner:* the inhabitants having originally planted themselves in small towns".[19] Dwight continued:

> A town in the language of New England, denotes a collection of houses in the first parish, if the township contains more than one, constituting the principal, and ordinarily the original, settlement in the Parish. . . . A Street is the way, on which such a collection of houses is built; but does not at all include the fact, that the way is paved. . . . *Nor is it intended that the houses are contiguous, or even very near to each other.*[20]

336   J. S. WOOD

While Dwight's statement is characteristic of the eighteenth-century landscape with which he was familiar, his description is appropriate for the seventeenth century as well. A century and a half before Dwight wrote, Captain Edward Johnson described Watertown, like Lynn one of the original towns about Massachusetts Bay, as:

> a fruitful plat, and of large extent, watered with many pleasant Springs, and small Rivulets, running like veines throughout her Body, which hath caused her *inhabitants to scatter in such manner*, that their Sabbath-Assemblies prove very thin if the season favour not.[21]

Similar descriptions, individual town records and maps, and even idiosyncratic town histories confirm that seventeenth-century settlements, like Lynn or Watertown, were more often than not settled in a dispersed fashion.

298

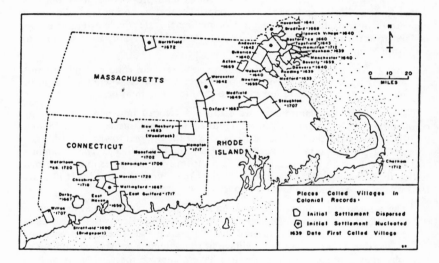

Figure 1. Places called villages in colonial records and their corresponding settlement forms.

Dispersal was especially characteristic of places explicitly called villages in colonial records (Fig. 1). Some of these places, like Billerica, first mentioned as a village in the colonial records of Massachusetts Bay in 1642, received new grants of land:

> All the land lying upon Saweshine River & between that & Concord Ryver, & between that & Merrimack Ryver, not formerly granted by this Court, are granted to Cambridge, so as they may erect a village there within 5 yeares, & so as it shall not extend to prejudice Charlstowne village [Woburn], or the village of Cochitawit [Andover], nor the farmes formerly granted to the now Governor of 1260 acres.[22]

By 1660 over 40 families had established farms in Billerica, forming a settlement that partially paralleled the Concord River but otherwise was dispersed (Fig. 2).[23]

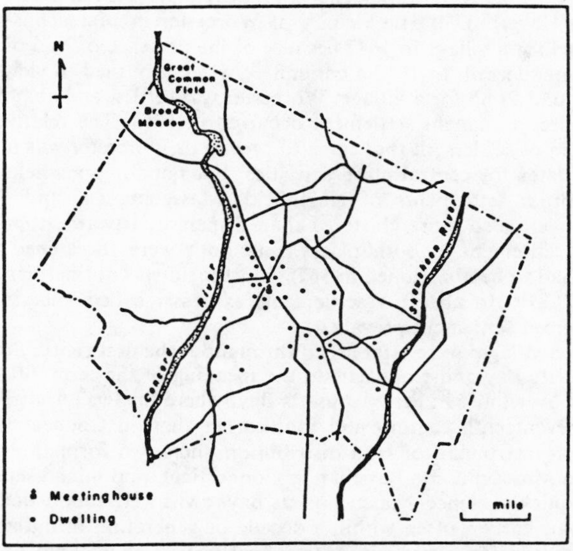

Figure 2. Billerica, Massachusetts, *c.* 1660. Settlers in early Billerica did not establish a nucleated settlement.

Other villages, like Manchester, Beverly, and Salem Village, now the Town of Danvers, were outlying neighbourhoods of the original Town of Salem. The dispersed inhabitants of Salem Village, called the "farmers of Salem", broke off from "Salem Town", where Salem's merchants resided. Salem Town was not becoming too crowded for farmers, but farmers had long before moved out into an interstitial area beyond the reach of comfortable weekly commuting to the meetinghouse.[24] As in many other towns in Massachusetts and Connecticut, Salem's settlers were simply too widely dispersed from homesteading on great lots, distant divisions of land, not to split into more manageable social, religious, and eventually political units—villages.

The meaning of village

A number of issues follow from the manner in which the term village was used in early colonial New England. First, not all settlements were called villages and not all villages were dispersed settlements. Villages seem generally to have been secondary settlements, for a time part of or subordinate to another town. None of the very first settled towns in either Massachusetts Bay or Connecticut, and few primary or first-order towns, granted independently of any other town, were called villages.[25] There were three exceptions. Andover and Haverhill were first-order towns reserved by the Massachusetts Court as villages and granted to companies of men from a number of the original towns about Massachusetts Bay. The nucleated settlements of both towns were short-lived. As at Sudbury and Dedham, nucleated forms proved useful in establishing initial settlements in the deep woods but not for general farming; and farmers dispersed within a generation, leaving no nucleated settlement in Andover and only a small commercial settlement in Haverhill.[26] The vicinity of Worcester in Massachusetts Bay was first mentioned for a village in 1642 because of the presence of lead mines, but the venture did not succeed. In 1667 a committee was established to view the vicinity of Quinsigamond Pond for a village. Worcester was settled and abandoned twice, however, before permanent settlement occurred in 1713. The relatively compact but linear form of settlement that came to prevail in Worcester was important for defence, and later for central-place activities, but not for open-field farming.[27] The second-order settlements of Northfield, Massachusetts, and Wallingford, Connecticut, were also more clustered than dispersed. Riverine topography favoured linear settlement in both places, and both were threatened by Indians. Wallingford had to be abandoned in 1675. Northfield was not permanently settled until after 1713.[28] In all other settlements expressly called villages in colonial records, dispersed settlement prevailed.

300

Though such villages were established throughout the first century of settlement in Massachusetts Bay and Connecticut, the meaning of the term village seems to have changed over time. In Massachusetts Bay, where the term was generally used only in the seventeenth century and thus earlier than in Connecticut, a village charter was an instrument of land distribution and town formation. Population was greater in Massachusetts Bay than in Connecticut, and inland settlement proceeded more quickly. Hence, Massachusetts Bay towns were subdivided or required new land grants earlier, often within a decade or generation of initial settlement. The area allocated for a town in Massachusetts Bay could hold only so many people before the community split into new communities or overflowed. In Connecticut, on the other hand, dispersed settlements were divided from older towns as well, but only long after the same process had generally occurred in Massachusetts Bay. In contrast to Massachusetts Bay, English agricultural practice, including common-field agriculture, persisted longer in Connecticut, larger reserves of land were held for future generations, and stricter control was placed on land division. Moreover, with a smaller initial population, population pressure took longer to build up. Hence, there were fewer requests for new communities, and until the end of the seventeenth century the Connecticut Court and Assembly were reluctant about liberally granting new villages.[29]

By then, village had come to mean something different in Connecticut than in Massachusetts. As early as 1659, some dispersed inhabitants of New Haven, Connecticut, were asking to be a separate village of East Haven. They agreed to meet conditions of their "Village grant" by laying out a five-acre meetinghouse lot, constructing a meetinghouse, and settling a minister.[30] Village status was finally granted in 1707, and records of the subsequent dialogue between inhabitants of East Haven and the Connecticut Assembly reveal the changing meaning of village:

> This Assembly considering the petition of the East Village of New Haven, do see cause to order that they shall be a village distinct from the township of Newhaven, and invested and privileged with all immunities and privileges that are proper and necessary for a village for the upholding of the publick worship of God, as also their own civil concerns; and in order thereunto, do grant them libertie of all such offices as are proper and necessary for a town, and to be chosen by themselves in order and form as allowed by law for each and any town. . . . As also the said village have libertie to have a school

amongst themselves with the privilege of the fortie schillings upon the thousand pound estate as every town hath by law; and also shall free their own village charge, and maintain their own poor, as all towns are obliged by law to do; and be fully freed from paying any taxes to the town of New-haven.[31]

East Haven residents read more into their charter than the Assembly had meant to concede them and, in 1710, the order had to be qualified to read that "there is nothing in the said act that concerns property of lands, or that excludes the village from being within the township of New Haven".[32] Even this failed to settle the matter. In 1716, East Haven was "to have no other powers than those that are common to other parishes".[33] In short, land distribution was no longer the purpose or prerogative of the village, but a village still formed a community for social and religious functions. Consequently, when the inhabitants of Wilton petitioned for separation from Norwalk in 1726, the Assembly was quite specific about what village had come to mean in Connecticut:

> Upon the petition . . . praying to be a village by themselves enjoying parish privileges, and that they may be called by the name of Wilton Parish: This Assembly do hereby grant the said inhabitants be one village.[34]

Occasional references not specifying any particular place suggest that village was used by some to mean any settlement, especially any recent or prospective settlement.[35] But in most cases, a village was self-consciously and legally ordained as a community. In the seventeenth century, a village had sufficient independent status and authority to establish and foster spiritual as well as economic, social, and political well-being for its inhabitants while still constituting a part of a parent town. By the eighteenth century, a village was at least an ecclesiastical parish.

The cultural context

The traditional view that colonial New England villages were necessarily nucleated settlements housing rural communities practising open-field agriculture is based on the premise that New Englanders were so predisposed. That is what Englishmen were supposed to do. Moreover, nucleated settlements met the requirements of both mutual protection in the wilderness and Puritan tenets about how communities should be organized spatially to maximize political and religious order.[36] But though English colonists shared a common heritage, England was hardly homogeneous in social structure. Englishmen came from a variety of social backgrounds and regional subcultures. Most had some familiarity with agriculture, but rural England in the seventeenth century was not composed exclusively, even largely, of corn-and-stock peasants farming open fields and living in nucleated settlements. Areas devoted more to livestock and less to grain tended towards dispersed settlement.[37] Thus, no singular folk tradition or set of rules and material forms existed. No single model of how an agricultural community was to operate or how a settlement was to be formed prevailed.[38] The English village that many colonists left behind was not necessarily a nucleated cluster of dwellings and outbuildings adjacent to a church and manor and encircled by common fields. How an English village functioned to provide a sense of community was more important than the form it took. The village was an interdependent, rural society carrying on family-oriented agriculture. The village functioned to provide economic

301

security for its inhabitants, and its inhabitants shared a common social purpose.[39]

Not only did England embody a heterogeneous landscape of settlement forms, but the society colonists were leaving behind in England was in the throes of significant institutional changes, including changes in land division and tenure. England was experiencing a crumbling of old customs of farming in the face of subtly increasing commercialization of agriculture and voluntary enclosure. The bulk of New England colonists, though not necessarily the dispossessed, came from portions of the east and south of England especially undergoing change. They brought with them to New England a strong notion that land ownership would provide both prestige and economic security.[40] Their desire for land was compounded by a spirit of individualism in politics, society, and ideas that had grown and developed in sixteenth and seventeenth century England. Hence, New England settlement must be viewed in the context of a tension between a longing for individual private control of land in a garden—and individual economic security—and a communal forbearance in a wilderness—social security. In all of their endeavours, large numbers of English colonists were driven to seek individual expression and convenanted communities alike.[41]

Driven as they were, and with no vested interests in a complex and finely woven cultural landscape as in England, the intricate weave of social structure that was itself undergoing change in England would not be rewoven in the same fashion. Englishmen in New England could mould a new cultural landscape. Thus, while colonists drew upon familiar forms and ways of doing things, they probably brought with them little excess cultural baggage, few vestiges of medieval institutions in community, church, governance, or agricultural practice. As a result, English local institutions were reshaped within each New England community to meet the particular needs and the particular English backgrounds of the inhabitants.[42] But because people of a common cultural heritage yet quite different social backgrounds and regional subcultures, each with their own customs and material forms, were intermingling, further reduction of vestigial ways and forms and a process of adaptation and innovation eventually took place. Such intermingling led towards more common ways of doing things and more common material culture.[43] By the end of the seventeenth century, much individual town distinctiveness inherited from England was gone.[44]

Both the common English notion of community and dispersed settlement survived the cultural transfer of English ways to the wilderness of New England. Such community not only could accommodate the centripetal requirements of venturing into the wilderness, but in its English variety of settlement forms, it could also accommodate the variety of individual needs and experiences of New England's colonists. Requirements of defence and economic and spiritual well-being easily gave way to direct transfer from England of well-established cultural predispositions for certain kinds of economic endeavour, land-division practices, and preferences for particular environmental conditions, that could not all be accommodated in a nucleated settlement form. As livestock raising was especially significant in early colonial New England, settlers were prompted to secure as much intervale or salt marsh as they could, while still remaining loyal to the evolving concept of the New England town.[45] One could choose either nucleated or dispersed settlement; but the modal form of community settlement that characteristically emerged in an early colonial New England, torn between individual expression and community covenant, was the dispersed village; and English custom encouraged it.

Village and community

What is important from the foregoing discussion of settlement form is not only that villages were often not nucleated settlements in early colonial New England, but that villages functioned as communities regardless of settlement form. No one doubts that community was achieved in early colonial New England villages. The process of community building was not necessarily easy; but, aided by the common English heritage of the colonists, by the fact that many communities were purposefully gathered from parent communities in England or were formed in New England of old neighbours or acquaintances, and by the provision for land distribution, community building was accomplished. As in England, village meant community. As in England, villages were well-knit rural societies carrying on family-oriented agriculture, constituting distinct social and religious groups, and providing collective security for inhabitants. Indeed, community cohesion may have grown stronger in New England, and New Englanders continued to nourish such localism as a value to be cherished.[46] Congregational control of the church and local political control, including collective regulation of land distribution, encouragement of local enterprise, and coordination of communal activities, provided for a distinctive sense of community identity. Shared ideology insured societal uniformity and cohesion. Even economic exchange was fundamentally local. Trading relationships were familiar and intimate. Moreover, available land had released colonists from an age-old cultural tradition of communal frugality in land utilization. Finally, available land meant political responsibility based on freeholding could actually be more widely held within the community.[47]

303

Dispersed settlement did not necessarily imply remoteness and isolation, a denial of community, even in a society driven to individual expression. Interaction caused by daily, weekly, seasonal, and annual congregational and political responsibilities took place within an established social structure, and the interaction itself was more important than the degree to which settlement·was nucleated. The real colonial New England village was a network of social and economic linkages, a social web, not a cluster of dwellings. Within the social web, a basic conflict between human striving for individual expression and a similar strong need for collective experience and a place to belong was played out. People were villagers, within an umbrella of social control and economic security, while living dispersed upon their own farms.

The New England community's network of interaction had a physical manifestation. Common cultural features of colonial maps of New England villages and towns are a node, paths, and edges—or the meetinghouse, roads, and town boundaries. Other buildings or dwellings and property boundaries are less often shown, especially on the earliest extant maps. The meetinghouse, the focus of community activity, was often exaggerated beyond proportion to indicate its location. Indeed, the meetinghouse, well situated often at an elevation, standing alone or accompanied by a parsonage, in time a tavern, perhaps a blacksmith, and by chance a farmhouse or two, was the dominant feature of the village landscape throughout the colonial period. No particular sacredness was attached to the meetinghouse itself, but the meetinghouse was the embodiment of the community, a tangible manifestation of the intangible political and religious life of the community—even if it stood alone as Captain Edward Johnson described the meetinghouse in Roxbury, Massachusetts, in the 1630s. "Their streets are large, and some fayre Houses, yet they have built the House for Church-assembly, destitute and unbeautified with other buildings."[48] One hundred and fifty years later, community centres looked little different, as Meriden, Connecticut, first called a village

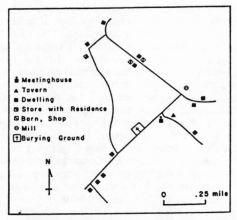

Figure 3. The central portion of Meriden, Connecticut, *c.* 1780. Meetinghouses were the symbolic and geographic centres of New England communities, but meetinghouses were not necessarily the centres of nucleated settlements.

in 1728, illustrated (Fig. 3).[49] The town road network, extended to interconnect dispersed farmsteads, enhanced the situation of the meetinghouse, providing access for all in the community. The physical circumscription of bounds added to the sense of place, and the annual perambulation and intertown contentiousness over bounds recorded by provincial assemblies attest to the significance of town boundaries.[50]

Bounds, of course, could not be too extensive, or intra-town contentiousness also recorded by town meetings and provincial assemblies might arise and a new community might need to be established. Equitable organization of space within reasonable bounds for dispersed settlements was the overriding consideration in the formation of new communities. As seventeenth-century settlement reached into extensions of land granted for villages and plantations, and more distant settlers were required to travel considerable distances to meeting and so often petitioned for establishment of a separate community, a village with its own meetinghouse could be sanctioned and social order maintained. As residents withdrew still further from the affairs of the original community, the town, they might petition for their own separate town incorporation. Because parent towns were reluctant often to release such communities within their bounds and thus reduce their tax base, as residents of East Haven, Connecticut, had learned, such division was slow. Nevertheless, division of dispersed communities into new villages and towns was an important process in the evolution of the New England settlement landscape.[51] As long as social and economic linkages remained unbroken, community prevailed. When linkages were stretched too far, the effect was hardly a rejection of the idea of community. As in 1630, when too many settlers had gathered on the shores of Massachusetts Bay to form a single community, division created new communities.[52] By the end of the colonial period, early settled towns had been subdivided and more recently settled towns granted in such a fashion that the landscape of New England came to resemble a great mosaic of equal-sized communities.

Also by the end of the colonial period, the notion of community as it had been known in early colonial New England was being challenged. Economic and social linkages that maintained community were strained. Yet the informal and intimate relationship of self-conscious, colonial communities bridged differences, including the new abstract theological differences of the Great Awakening that had given rise to dissenting congregations within communities and that had assumed great rhetorical importance in provincial politics. A multiplicity of operating cultures— a pragmatic, family-based community culture concerned with local economic and social affairs, superficially overlain by a more abstract culture concerned with religious and political issues, all interpenetrated by emerging external associations —helps explain the apparent persistence of "peaceable kingdoms" well into the eighteenth century. Community was not necessarily diminished; it simply accommodated change; and settlement form, long dispersed, had little to do with it.[53] Methods of land distribution within towns on the other hand, increasingly individualistic and competitive rather than community-based as the colonial period passed, may have had much to do with transforming what was recognized as community in the seventeenth century to a form of community more appropriate to the eighteenth century.[54] That, however, is another study.

305

Conclusion

David Lowenthal reminds us that the preservation of relict artifacts may overemphasize the role an artifact played in a past landscape.[55] The village encountered in New England today, white-painted, black-shuttered, classical-revival dwellings, churches, and stores abutting a tree-shaded green, reflects not continuity with New England's colonial past but a most dramatic change. The change took place in the Federal period, in the last generation of the eighteenth century and the first generation of the nineteenth century. Economic affairs became increasingly regional, and New Englanders broke out of traditional culture moulds to create a landscape of commercial places where meetinghouses had long stood alone.[56]

Only then, as the form of settlement changed to become nucleated, did the term village take on its present-day connotation. To early colonial New Englanders, who were not necessarily predisposed towards nucleated settlement, village only meant community. The New England town was the source of land for most individuals and thus initially the instrument for providing economic security and encouraging settlement. A well-bounded corporate space, inhabited by people who sensed they comprised a community distinct from any other, was sufficient to provide the order and cohesion long attributed to nucleated settlement. Indeed, closely interdependent, collaborative communities of colonial New England themselves allowed nucleated settlement, where it had been implanted, to wither. Social order did not require nucleation. In the colonial meaning, the village was a social web in which Puritan tenets worked well enough.[57]

University of Nebraska at Omaha

Notes

[1] On settlement form see Edna Scofield, The origin of settlement patterns in rural New
England *Geographical Review* **28** (1938) 652–63; Glenn T. Trewartha, Types of rural
settlement in colonial America *Geographical Review* **36** (1946) 568–96; F. Grave Morris,
Some aspects of the rural settlement of New England in colonial times in L. D. Stamp and
S. W. Wooldridge (Eds), *London essays in geography* (London 1951) 219–27; D. R. Mc-
Manis, *Colonial New England: a historical geography* (New York 1975). On New England
communities see S. C. Powell, *The Puritan village; the formation of a New England town*
(Middletown, Conn. 1963); R. L. Bushman, *From Puritan to yankee: character and social
order in Connecticut, 1690–1765* (Cambridge, Mass. 1967); K. Lockridge, *A New England
town: the first hundred years* (New York 1970); P. J. Greven, Jr., *Four generations: population, land, and family life in colonial Andover, Massachusetts* (Ithaca, N.Y. 1970); B. C.
Daniels, *The Connecticut town: growth and development, 1635–1790* (Middletown, Conn.
1979)

[2] Darrett B. Rutman, The social web: a prospectus for the study of the early American
community, in W. L. O'Neill (Ed.), *Insights and parallels: problems and issues of American
social history* (Minneapolis 1973) 58

[3] *Ibid.* 62–3; T. Bender, *Community and social change in America* (New Brunswick, N.J.
1978) 7 including note 4

[4] Yi-Fu Tuan, *Space and place: the perspective of experience* (Minneapolis 1977) 3; see also
Bender, *op. cit.* 61; Rutman, *op. cit.* 62–3; Harold R. Kaufman, Toward an interactional
conception of community *Social Forces* **38** (1959) 9–17

[5] Milton B. Newton, Jr., Settlement patterns as artifacts of social structure, in M. Richardson
(Ed.), *The human mirror: material and spatial images of man* (Baton Rouge, La. 1974) 339–61

[6] *Oxford English dictionary* XII (Oxford 1933) 204

[7] *Webster's third new international dictionary of the English language* (Springfield, Mass.
1971) 2552

[8] Albert Demangeon, La geographie de l'habitat rural *Annales de Geographie* **36** (1927) 1–23,
97–114; W. Christaller, *Central places of southern Germany* (Englewood Cliffs, N.J. 1966).
As an objective measure, Martyn J. Bowden, Clark University, personal communication,
December 1975, has suggested that a nucleated settlement be one in which more than four
neighbours dwell purposefully within hailing distance of one another, perhaps 100 m.
Four houses located by chance at a crossroads need not be considered nucleated settlement

[9] Robert E. Dickinson, Rural settlements in the German lands *Annals of the Association of
American Geographers* **39** (1949) 239–63; Gottfried Pfeifer, The quality of peasant living in
Central Europe, in W. L. Thomas (Ed.), *Man's role in changing the face of the earth* (Chicago
1956) 240–77

[10] Joan Thirsk, The farming regions of England, in J. Thirsk (Ed.), *The agrarian history of
England and Wales, 1500–1640* IV (Cambridge 1967) 1–112; see also George C. Homans,
The explanation of English regional differences *Past and Present* **42** (1969) 18–34

[11] See for instance Powell, *op. cit.*; Lockridge, *op. cit.*; Greven, *Four generations*

[12] Rutman, *op. cit.* 67 note 29; T. H. Breen, Persistent localism: English social change and the
shaping of New England institutions *William and Mary Quarterly* Series 3 **32** (1975) 20;
idem, Transfer of culture: chance and design in shaping Massachusetts Bay, 1630–1660
New England Historical and Genealogical Register **132** (1978) 9

[13] J. S. Wood, The origin of the New England village (unpubl. Ph.D. thesis, Pennsylvania
State University 1978) 58–202

[14] D. G. Allen, *In English ways: the movement of societies and the transferal of English local
custom to Massachusetts Bay in the seventeenth century* (Chapel Hill, N.C. 1981); T. H.
Breen and Stephen Foster, Moving to the new world *William and Mary Quarterly* Series 3
30 (1973) 189–222; James T. Lemon, Early Americans and their social environment *Journal
of Historical Geography* **6** (1980) 119–21

[15] J. Winthrop, *The history of New England from 1630–1649* II (New York 1825–26) 263. See
also *Records of the Governor and Company of the Massachusetts Bay in New England,
1628–1686* II (Boston 1853–54) 135

[16] W. Haller, Jr., *The Puritan frontier: town planting in New England colonial development,
1630–1660* (New York 1951); H. R. McCutcheon, Town formation in eastern Massachusetts 1630–1802: a case study in political area organization (unpubl. Ph.D. thesis,
Clark University 1970)

[17] A. Lewis and J. R. Newhall, *History of Lynn, Essex County, Massachusetts* (Boston 1865) 131; Richard B. Johnson, Swampscott, Massachusetts, in the seventeenth century *Essex Institute Historical Collections* 109 (1973) 251

[18] *Records of Massachusetts Bay, op. cit.* I 272; III 7

[19] T. Dwight, *Travels in New England and New York* I (New Haven, Conn. 1821–1822) 216

[20] *Ibid.* Italics mine

[21] Captain E. Johnson, *Wonder-working providence of Sions Savior in New England* (London 1654; reprint ed., Andover, Mass. 1867) 46. Italics mine

[22] *Records of Massachusetts Bay, op. cit.* II 17

[23] H. A. Hazen, *History of Billerica, Massachusetts* (Boston 1883) 24–6

[24] *Records of Massachusetts Bay, op. cit.* V 247–8; C. W. Upham, *Salem witchcraft* (Boston 1867); Sidney Perley, Part of Salem village in 1700 *Essex Institute Historical Collections* 52 (1916) 177–91; P. Boyer and S. Nissenbaum, *Salem possessed: the social origins of witchcraft* (Cambridge, Mass. 1974); R. P. Gildrie, *Salem, Massachusetts, 1628–1683: a covenanted community* (Charlottesville, Va. 1975). The use of the term town in this context suggests that, like village, town could be ambiguous in colonial New England. In New England as in England, town could refer to a major market centre, like Salem or Boston, as well as an incorporated area. For elaboration see Carville E. Earle, The first English towns in North America *Geographical Review* 67 (1977) 34–50

[25] On the classification of towns by order see McCutcheon, *op. cit.*

[26] *Records of Massachusetts Bay, op. cit.* I 306, 319; II 10–11, 17; A. Abbot, *History of Andover from its settlement to 1829* (Andover, Mass. 1829) 12, 47, 74–6; Philip J. Greven, Jr., Old patterns in the new world: the distribution of land in seventeenth-century Andover *Essex Institute Historical Collections* 101 (1965) 133–48; G. W. Chase, *The history of Haverhill, Massachusetts, from its first settlement, in 1640, to 1860* (Haverhill, Mass. 1861) 42, 61. See also Powell, *op. cit.*; and Lockridge, *op. cit*

[27] *Records of Massachusetts Bay, op. cit.* II 11; IV part 2, 408–9; W. Lincoln, *History of Worcester, Massachusetts* (Worcester, Mass. 1837) 6–7, 30–1, 43

[28] *Records of Massachusetts Bay, op. cit.* IV part 2, 528–9; J. H. Temple and G. Sheldon, *History of the Town of Northfield, Massachusetts* (Albany, N.Y. 1975) 165; *Public Records of the Colony of Connecticut, 1636–1776* (Hartford, Conn. 1850–90) II 255; III 1; C. H. S. Davis, *History of Wallingford, Connecticut, from its settlement in 1670 to the present time* (Meriden, Conn. 1870) 78–9

[29] Wood, *op. cit.* 102–7, 117–36; Daniels, *op. cit.* 97; and Bender, *op. cit.* 72 note 70

[30] S. E. Hughes, *History of East Haven* (New Haven, Conn. 1908) 67–75; D. Deming, *The settlement of Connecticut towns* (New Haven, Conn. 1933) 68

[31] *Records of Connecticut, op. cit.* IV 15–16

[32] *Ibid.* IV 123–4

[33] *Ibid.* V 63

[34] *Ibid.* V 521

[35] *Ibid.* III 190; *Records of Massachusetts Bay, op. cit.* V 213–4, 311–12

[36] Scofield, *op. cit.*; Trewartha, *op. cit*

[37] Thirsk, The farming regions of England; Homans, *op. cit.* See Allen, *op. cit.*, for detailed discussion of several source communities

[38] A significant statement of this point is Allen, *op. cit*

[39] P. Laslett, *The world we have lost* (New York 1965) 53–80 may overstate the case. See also R. Cole Harris, The simplification of Europe overseas *Annals of the Association of American Geographers* 67 (1977) 471, especially note 6; Joan Thirsk, Enclosing and engrossing, in Thirsk, *The agrarian history of England and Wales* 225

[40] C. Hill, *Change and continuity in seventeenth-century England* (London 1974); Thirsk, The farming regions of England 6–7; H. S. Russell, *A long deep furrow: three centuries of farming in New England* (Hanover, N.H. 1976) 26–7; J. R. Stilgoe, Pattern on the land: the making of a colonial landscape, 1633–1800 (Unpubl. Ph.D. thesis, Harvard University 1976)

[41] Michael Zuckerman, The fabrication of identity in early America *William and Mary Quarterly* Series 3 34 (1977) 183–214; see also P. N. Carroll, *Puritanism and the wilderness: the intellectual significance of the New England frontier, 1629–1700* (New York 1969) 133, 140–7, 182–7

[42] Allen, *op. cit.*; Breen, Transfer of culture 5 note 5; G. B. Warden, Law reform in England and New England *William and Mary Quarterly* Series 3, 35 (1978) 687–8

[43] Harris, *op. cit.*, elaborates on this process; see also Robert D. Mitchell, Comment on the

307

simplification of Europe overseas; Adrian Pollock, Commentary—Europe simplified; R. Cole Harris, Comment in reply *Annals of Association of American Geographers* **69** (1979) 474–80. Allen, *op. cit.* 222, argues that the trend away from open fields was faster in New England than was possible in England. On material culture see A. L. Cummings, *The framed houses of Massachusetts Bay, 1625–1725* (Cambridge, Mass. 1979)

[44] Allen, *op. cit.* 231–2
[45] McManis, *op. cit.* 93–102
[46] John Murrin, Review essay *Historical Theory* **11** (1972) 231
[47] Bender, *op. cit.* 63–8, provides a summary of community in New England. See also Rutman, *op. cit.*; James A. Henretta, Families and farms: *mentalité* in preindustrial America *William and Mary Quarterly* Series 3 **35** (1978) 3–32; Timothy H. Breen and Stephen Foster, The Puritans' greatest achievement: a study of social cohesion in seventeenth-century Massachusetts *Journal of American History* **60** (1973) 5–22; Breen, Transfer of culture
[48] Johnson, *op. cit.* 44
[49] *Records of Connecticut, op. cit.* VI 121; Davis, *op. cit.* 125; C. B. Gillespie (Comp.), *A century of Meriden* (Meriden, Conn. 1906)
[50] Tuan, *op. cit.* 166. James T. Lemon, The weakness of place and community in early Pennsylvania, in J. R. Gibson (Ed.), *European settlement and development in North America: essays in honour and memory of A. H. Clark* (Toronto 1978) 198–9, argues that a critical difference between community in Pennsylvania and community in New England was the fixing of parish or town bounds to provide a sense of place for community groups
[51] McCutcheon, *op. cit.*; Daniels, *op. cit.* are good sources on the division of towns. The process of towns dividing into smaller units or sending out new villages, parishes, or towns has long been called hiving off. The analogy is inappropriate because it suggests a nucleated settlement splitting to form another nucleated settlement, or hive
[52] Bender, *op. cit.* 72–3; Rutman, *op. cit.* 68
[53] M. Zuckerman, *Peaceable kingdoms: New England towns in the eighteenth century* (New York 1970). Bender, *op. cit.* 3–13, 75–8, argues that a historically grounded concept of community is one that allows a community to alter its social structure, and by implication its spatial structure, to meet new conditions without necessarily breaking down
[54] See Daniels, *op. cit.* 173; Lemon, Early Americans and their social environment 129–30
[55] David Lowenthal, Age and artifact: dilemmas of appreciation, in D. W. Meinig (Ed.), *The interpretation of ordinary landscapes* (New York 1979) 103–27
[56] Wood, *op. cit.* 203–85
[57] The University Research Committee, The University of Nebraska at Omaha, has funded portions of the research reported in this paper

The "Particular Courts" of Local Government: Town Councils in Eighteenth-Century Rhode Island

by Bruce C. Daniels*

* Mr. Daniels is a professor of history at the University of Winnipeg. He wishes to thank the Social Sciences and Humanities Research Council of Canada for its generous financial support.

Local history is by far the most prevalent form of historical writing in the United States but, paradoxically, we know less about local institutions than any others. Over the past two hundred years, tens of thousands of books have been written about specific parishes, towns, and counties, but we have only a handful of solid historical studies of *the* parish, *the* town, or *the* county. Local history writing has traditionally been an antiquarian pastime in which narratives extol the virtues of ancestors and charm descendents with anecdotes and tales of bravery and hardship. Indeed, these local histories are usually charming if one knows the place and the people being described; moreover, they frequently function as a ritual in community-building by renewing and personalizing the relationship people feel with the past. By labeling local history antiquarian or by saying it does not tell us much about local institutions, I do not mean to imply that the genre itself is insignificant. Professional analysis was seldom its goal. But, because of its primary concern with specific incidents and people, we have learned little about the general principles and institutions that have governed our communities. Analyses of local governments have usually been left to political scientists who tend to write about the present and not about the past.

Over the past two decades, however, academic historians have begun to see the local community as a subject worth investigating, and an early trickle of professional studies in the 1960s has become a flood of theses, dissertations, and articles in the 1970s. While vastly expanding our knowledge of early American communities, recent local history nevertheless suffers from two problems. First, almost all of it has been written with a case-study methodology, and although the authors hope to establish general principles, the typicality of each case is usually unproven. Second, the questions asked in the case studies reflect a present societal concern with inequalities and inequities, and have emphasized analyses of power relationships and social structures and have neglected institutions and structures—in short, social history has almost entirely eclipsed constitutional history at the local level. In-depth community studies, of course, penetrate deeply into the lives of a locale and tell us much that is suggestive, and social history has given us a crucial new perspective on economic and demographic forces that shaped our past; the value of both the methodology and the substance is immense. But, unless we wish to run the risks of "balkanizing" early American history and of pretending that social pressures do not manifest themselves in institutions, we also need to pay some attention to general principles and institutional arrangements operating at the local level.[1] The following analysis of Rhode Island's town councils in the eighteenth century attempts to do this. Using a sample of nearly half of colonial Rhode Island's towns, it describes and analyzes the practices and functions of the towns' key executive bodies.

Rhode Island's distinctive use of the term "town council" requires some explanation. No other colony used the term widely to designate a community's senior officers. In the rest of New England, the towns' executives were called selectmen or townsmen; in the middle colonies of New York and Pennsylvania, a variety of names were used for local executives; and in the southern colonies, vestrymen and county court justices administered local affairs. The term "town council" was not extensively used in England prior to the settlement of British North America, although a group of advisors to the mayors of some municipal corporations were called the council or "mayor's peers" or "mayor's brethren." But such bodies were not direct predecessors of the Rhode Island town councils: the councils in England were larger, subordinate advisors to the mayor, and had different functions.[2] Thus, while the name has some connection to the English past, and while English common law and practices of borough administration guided much of their actions, the Rhode Island town councils were essentially a New World creation, part of the process of selective borrowing by which every colony derived a system of local government distinct from its fellow colonies but fashioned eclectically from a heterogeneous English institutional background.

In Rhode Island's founding decade, different names were used for executives elected by the towns. The General Court for Newport and Portsmouth specified in 1640 that magistrates in each of the towns were to meet monthly in a "particular court" to administer the affairs of the towns. In the same year the constitution adopted by Providence created a five-member board of "disposers" whose main function was to supervise the allotment of lands but who also acted as an executive board for local matters. Warwick did not constitute a formal government in its first few years and governed itself, it would seem, without an executive body. In May 1647, the four towns meeting together in a General Court set up rules to implement the Charter of 1644 which made them a colony and ordered each town to choose a six-man town council at its town meeting. Each town did so in the following year, and it is from this act that the town councils derived.[3]

The power and authority of the new town councils were not precisely delineated in the legislation but it was clear that the town meetings were to be supreme in local matters and that the town councils

1. There have been some exceptions to this tendency to overlook institutions and general patterns in local life. The essayists in Bruce C. Daniels, ed., *Town and County: Essays on The Structure of Local Government in the American Colonies* (Middletown, Conn., 1978), have written in this volume and elsewhere on local government. Edward M. Cook, Jr., in *The Fathers of the Towns: Leadership and Community Structure in Eighteenth-Century New England* (Baltimore, 1976), comments perceptively on general patterns of officeholding in New England and analyzes how these patterns intersected with institutional arrangements. Other examples could be cited but in the main they only scratch the surface and dozens of additional specialized studies are needed to provide a secure picture of local government.

2. Sydney and Beatrice Webb, *English Local Government From the Revolution to the Municipal Corporation Act: The Manor and the Borough*, Part I (London and New York, 1908), 336–377.

3. John Russell Bartlett, ed., *Records of the Colony of Rhode Island and Providence Plantations*, 10 vols. (Providence, R.I., 1856–1862), I, (Aug. 1640), 106, (May 1647), 151, hereafter cited as *R.I.C.R.* The Providence constitution can be found in Samuel Greene Arnold, *History of the State of Rhode Island and Providence Plantations*, 2 vols. (New York, 1859–1860), 108.

4. *Digest of 1744* (Newport, R.I.,
1744), 177–178.
5. For the acts passed by the General
Assembly dealing with town councils see
R.I.C.R., II (May 1667), 189; II (July 1667),
212; III (May 1678), 15; III (May 1680), 89;
IV (Mar. 1709), 64–65; IV (June 1719),
253–254; IV (Oct. 1719), 263; the acts of
Nov. 1742 and Feb. 1743 in *Digest of
1744*, 250–251 and 275–278; and acts of
1663, 1711, 1717, 1724, 1728, and 1737 in
The Digest of 1767 (Newport, R.I., 1767),
214–219.

were to have limited authority to act only on specific matters and were
not to make broad policy. The council thus was to function as a "particular court" and handle the details of individual cases under the general guidance of the town meeting. In addition to the six members of
the town council elected by the town meeting, any magistrates of the
colony living in the town (and each town had at least two) were automatically members of the local council. When the magistracy was increased by the creation of justices of the peace, these colony-appointed
officials were also made members of the town councils. Not until 1733
did the colony government, mindful that towns were "defeated of the
privilege of having their prudential affairs carried on by persons of their
own choosing," exclude magistrates from the town council and make it
a body elected entirely by the local town meeting.[4]

Even though the General Assembly passed many laws throughout
the colonial period strengthening the powers of the town council to act
on delegated matters, the council was never elevated to a policy-making position and was never able to transcend the limits of being a particular court. The belief in participatory government proved too strong
to allow inroads to be made on the authority of the town meeting to set
all policy.[5] Moreover, many of the General Assembly statutes set policies within which the town councils were forced to operate which also
limited their discretionary powers. Even in its function as a particular
court, the town council had limits on its power. In matters which involved punishment of a person by fining, or whipping, or warning out
of town, the council had to apply to a justice of the peace for a warrant
to put the punishment into effect.

Despite the restricted nature of their authority, however, the town
councils were institutions of enormous importance in local governance. If, for example, the town meeting passed a bylaw stipulating
that a new highway was to be laid out, it was the town council who
decided how much money would be given to compensate land-owners
for their losses. If the General Assembly passed laws outlining procedures for probating wills and inventorying estates, it was the town
council who decided if the executors of a decedent carried out these
procedures with fairness and justice. If a justice of the peace ordered a
transient warned out of town or whipped for vagrancy, he usually did so
on the recommendation of the town council. The details of administering justice within broad guidelines were immensely important: almost
every man in colonial Rhode Island was directly affected at some point
by a town council decision.

To handle all of these details, the town councils met frequently. The
ideal model seemed to be monthly meetings, although some years they
met more than twelve times and some years less, depending upon
need. From 1710, the approximate year from which extant council records date, to 1790, the end of the Revolutionary period, the towns averaged just about twelve meetings per year. However, this average of one
meeting per month disguises some fluctuations. Out of a sample of ten

311

towns,* seven of them had years in which the council met only six times and the remaining three towns had lows of seven, eight, and nine meetings respectively in at least one year. At the other extreme, the Providence council met fifty-two times in one year and the East Greenwich council met forty-one times. No clear trend of meeting frequency emerged over the eighteenth century, but in the 1770s and 1780s the councils met much more often primarily to deal with the details of implementing the Revolutionary war effort at the local level: increased poor-relief needs caused by the war, obtaining military supplies, additional probate work, and other war-related matters, all necessitated more meetings than usual. The decade with the highest number of meetings prior to the Revolution was the 1750s, also a decade of war. During the 1760s and the early 1770s, when town meetings were held more frequently to discuss and debate the imperial problem, town councils did not do so because the imperial debate involved matters of policy-making and not of administrative detail. While none of the ten towns in the sample deviated tremendously from the average throughout the colony, Providence, the most populous town in the sample, had the most council meetings. Despite these variations, extremes were unusual and all the quantitative evidence shows that townspeople could usually expect a town council meeting on an average of once a month. Occasionally, town councils met even when there was no evident business to consider, which nonetheless gave people the opportunity to bring matters to their attention. And if no business was forthcoming the councils simply adjourned. About once a year, for instance, the Cranston town council would record that "there appears no business of consequence to be done," and would then adjourn.

An average of twelve meetings a year and an occasionally much higher number must have placed a substantial strain on the energies of the town councilmen. Given this, attendance was surprisingly high at town council meetings and only one town, Providence, had a problem more than once or twice in ninety years in mustering the required

312

6. A sample of ten may seem small, but at the end of the colonial period Rhode Island had only thirty incorporated towns and ten of them were new towns founded after 1735. Only Cranston of the above ten in the sample was one of these new towns. Several of the towns do not have usable town council records, so the sample includes over three-fourths of the towns in the colony with lengthy town council minutes. Regrettably, the council records of Newport, the most important town in the colony, are not readable.

TABLE I
THE AVERAGE ANNUAL NUMBER OF MEETINGS OF TOWN COUNCILS BY DECADE 1710–1790

	1710s	1720s	1730s	1740s	1750s	1760s	1770s	1780s	least	most
Bristol						12	11	13	9	16
Cranston					10	10	17	14	6	33
East Greenwich	7	9			14	10	18	15	6	41
Portsmouth	9	9	11	13	14	12	11	13	6	17
Providence	13	11	11	13	18	12	26	34	8	52
South Kingstown		12	13	12	16	14	13	14	7	21
Scituate				10	10	9	13	9	6	22
Tiverton				11	9	10	10	9	6	15
Warwick				7	8	8	16	12	6	26
Westerly			10	12	12	12	12	14	6	26
All	9.7	10.3	11.3	11.1	12.3	10.8	14.7	14.7		

TABLE II
ATTENDANCE OF COUNCILMEN AT TOWN COUNCIL MEETINGS 1710–1790

Town	Average # attending each meeting
Bristol	5.20
Cranston	5.13
East Greenwich	5.11
Providence	4.79
Portsmouth	5.17
South Kingstown	4.98
Scituate	5.15
Tiverton	5.18
Warwick	5.31
Westerly	5.51

313

7. Scituate Town Council Minutes, Scituate Town Hall (Nov. 1790); Portsmouth Town Council Minutes, Portsmouth Town Hall, 1750s–1790s.

quorum of four for a council meeting. Even Providence's problems of attendance were slight: only about once every three or four years did less than four councilmen show up and in 1756 the Providence town council members showed their dissatisfaction with their absent fellows by instituting a fine of ten shillings for missing a meeting. Eight of the ten towns whose attendance records were analyzed averaged over five members present per meeting, including Westerly which averaged 5.51. Providence, with an average attendance of 4.79 per meeting (out of a possible 6) was the lowest; undoubtedly this was no accident since Providence, of course, had the highest number of meetings of any town. Still, when one considers that Providence averaged twenty-six and thirty-four meetings per year in the 1770s and 1780s respectively, the attendance of its council members might also be considered high. When one also considers that some members had to travel distances of up to five or six miles and the inevitable sickness that must have befallen some councilmen, the record of attendance shows an extraordinary commitment to duty.

Town councils met in a variety of places and sometimes rotated the location of their meetings in order to be fair to all the members or sometimes met in one fixed location for a number of years. South Kingstown always rotated the meetings among councilmen's houses. The Scituate council met for years at the house of Richard Smith, who was not a councilman, but apparently had convenient and commodious quarters. Smith, although not normally a tavern keeper, had a special license to sell "victuals and drink" on council-meeting days. The Portsmouth council met for over two decades at Christopher Turner's tavern and then switched to a tavern run by David Gifford.' Warwick had no fixed place or rotation schedule but decided at each meeting where the next one would be. Similarly, the time of the council meetings varied within and among the towns but more often than not they began in the early afternoon and adjourned before dark. This arrangement gave councilmen time to arrive with convenience and to reach

TABLE III
BUSINESS OF TOWN COUNCILS 1725–1790

Item	Percentage of Total Activity			
	1725*	1750**	1775***	1790***
Probate	45	26	27	21
Authorizing				
Payments	15	18	34	42
Liquor Licenses	14	13	12	14
Warning Out	8	10	10	10
Guardianships and				
Apprenticeships	8	7	6	3
Highway Matters	4	5	2	5
Granting Certificates	1	9	2	3
Miscellaneous	5	3	3	2

*Six towns in sample.
**Nine towns in sample.
***Ten towns in sample.

314

home before the late evening. Portsmouth and Providence, however, would occasionally meet as early as 9:00 A.M.; the afternoon meeting was the ideal but if the press of business was heavy, councilmen would have to get up earlier to accommodate the need. Accessibility in terms of location and time was not solely designed for the convenience of the councilmen. The town clerk and town sergeant had to attend all council meetings, and a large number of people applying for licenses, registering probate materials, asking for payment for services, all streamed through many of the meetings. It was not rare for a meeting to deal with ten or fifteen separate items, each one requiring one or several people to appear before it.

This large volume of work would have taxed the energies of any six men, and even if most of the decisions were routine, they still required at least a cursory appraisal. Over the course of the eighteenth century the average annual number of items dealt with by each council increased from twenty-nine items per year in 1725 to seventy-seven in 1790. Not surprisingly, the amount of business varied proportionately with the size of the town. Small towns such as Cranston and Scituate dealt with about twenty-five items of business in 1790, while Providence, the largest town with extant council records, dealt with slightly over 200 items in the same year. Administering the probate processes and authorizing payments of town monies were the two largest items of business, comprising over 60 percent of the councils' activities. The remaining time was spent licensing taverns and public houses, warning people out of town (to avoid assuming the responsibility of poor relief for them), dealing with highway matters, arranging and authorizing guardianships and apprenticeships, granting certificates to people moving out of town (to indicate that the hometown would accept responsibility for their support if they became indigent), and a variety of miscellaneous items. Of course, these categories could be rearranged under other headings which would yield different percentiles.[8]

8. Much of the authorization of payments, warning out of undesirables, binding out of children, and granting of certificates, for example, could be grouped under a single category of poor relief, but this would not serve the purposes of analysis as well.

TABLE IV
AVERAGE NUMBER OF ITEMS DEALT WITH PER TOWN PER YEAR

1725*	1750**	1775***	1790***
29	43	48	77

*Six towns in sample.
**Nine towns in sample.
***Ten towns in sample.

In terms of sheer quantity, the town council's greatest amount of business was spent on authorizing payment of town monies to various individuals. This function as the auditor of all accounts steadily increased relative to other functions as the eighteenth century progressed. It is doubtful, however, if approving payments took the largest part of the council's time; most of the payments were routine and required little in the way of difficult decision-making. Over three-fourths of the payments authorized were to people for taking care of the towns' poor, and most of the rest were for services rendered the town by one of the local officers. Usually, each payment item required a one-line statement in the town council records. Such statements were generally brief: "account of Thomas Shepherd for £3 for the keeping of widow Smith for two months approved." The evidence suggests that accounts were seldom disputed, yet, every person had to be able to justify his expenses to the town council. Petitioners knew that if they appeared suspicious or even unreasonable they could be closely questioned, and this in turn imparted a high degree of accountability to the financial structure of the town. No monies, no matter how small, would be paid out of the town treasury without the council's approbation.

Probate matters, quantitatively the second most numerous item that the councils had to deal with, consumed much more space in council records than all other items taken together. This does not mean, however, that the probating process was controversial; contention seldom surfaced, but the various stages involved in settling an estate each entailed documentation. First, a letter of administration would be issued by the council to someone (usually a close relative of the decedent) who would authorize the supervision of the out-of-council process. Second, if a will was extant it would be presented to the council, usually approved and then entered into the council records. Third, a detailed inventory of all goods and their value would be presented by the executor and two others to the council for entry into the records. Fourth, any debts due or owed by the estate would be collected or paid under the supervision of the council. Finally, the council would approve the distribution of the estate to the heirs under the terms of the will or under the terms of colony law (in cases where no will was extant). In most instances, the process of settling an estate dragged out over several council meetings. Seldom was anything out of the routine involved; the biggest problem councils usually encountered developed if people refused to accept the letter of administration.

315

Much other business was also routine to the point of being *pro forma*. Licenses for keeping taverns or public houses, once issued, were regularly reissued year after year although the matter of fees for them might provoke some discussion. The issuance of certificates to people moving to another town was nearly automatic. Highway business, although it could involve a decision of great importance to an individual, was seldom contentious at the town council level. Highway planning often prompted heated debates among townspeople, but the town meeting handled this problem, not the town council. The council was called upon merely to adjust little details of highway programs the town meeting had already approved. Similarly, warning people out of town did not usually involve the council in any agonizing over the nature of justice. The town council simply recommended to a justice of the peace that any individuals that the town did not have a clear responsibility to support and who could not support themselves should be ordered out of town and sent back to the town of their last legal settlement, usually their birthplace. If a newcomer to town could not produce a certificate from his hometown guaranteeing the hometown's support in case of financial need, or if a person admitted with a certificate from another town needed relief, the council invariably asked for a warning-out warrant to be issued. Compassion played little role in this process, and if a town could legally avoid the cost of poor relief for a person it did so by warning him out. Only when travel would hazard a person's life did the council deliberate whether or not he should be warned out. Still, even if the decisions on warning out were nearly automatic, they did sometimes involve a hearing to determine which town was responsible for an individual's welfare. Not infrequently towns disputed the assignment of responsibility, and the town councils were required to negotiate an agreement with other town councils or go to court over the matter.

Matters of guardianship and binding out of children as apprentices were also usually routine but could involve some difficult decision-making. Orphaned children fourteen years of age or older were allowed to choose their own guardians and generally the council merely ratified the choice of an uncle, grandparent, or neighbor. At times, however, people refused to accept the guardianship and finding a suitable person to care for an adolescent and manage his property could be a problem. If an orphaned child was under fourteen or if a child under that age could not be adequately cared for by his parents, the child would be "bound out" to some willing town resident. These decisions required careful thought and choice on the part of the town council because it wanted to make certain that the child would be placed in a proper environment. The situation could, of course, invite abuse of the child if he or she was overworked and undercared for.

The most nettlesome problem with guardianships, however, involved the management of the estates of people termed *non compos mentis* by the council. In a society without institutions to provide care

9. South Kingstown Town Council Minutes, South Kingstown Town Hall, Feb. 1752.
10. Portsmouth Town Council Minutes, Mar. 1725, Jan. 1741.
11. Providence Town Council Minutes, Providence City Hall, July 1726.
12. South Kingstown Town Council Minutes, May 1727, June 1727.

for the feebleminded and elderly, many people with enough to sustain themselves proved unable to manage their property. The council could either initiate action on its own to assign guardians for these people or, as it more frequently did, act on a petition by some concerned person to have a guardian appointed for one of these unfortunates. This occasionally involved some controversy. The delicate nature of determining someone to be unresponsible for himself and the potential for abuse of the individual's finances ensured that the council took these decisions under very serious consideration.

Some unusual decisions were occasionally required of the council and broke the normal humdrum of routine. The most dramatic of these occurred periodically in every town when smallpox epidemics struck and the town councils responded with frenzied activity in an attempt to contain the contagion. In these emergencies, the councils assumed extraordinary power and acted in ways to limit freedom of movement and action that would have been unthinkable in normal times. They ordered people confined to homes or removed to buildings set up as "pest houses" and posted guards around affected areas. The councils often prohibited all unauthorized travel in the vicinity, appointed special persons to treat the infected, closed harbors and roads, directed the process of burials, and in general would try anything that might prevent the disease from being spread throughout the community. The dread of smallpox ran so deeply that no matter how highhanded the councils' orders may have seemed if issued in other matters, they were accepted with alacrity during epidemics. Each town experienced about five or six such emergencies in the eighteenth century.

Small and unusual matters would sometimes come under the town council's purview. Although questions of morality were usually brought to a justice of the peace, they could be brought to the council if they involved conduct in taverns (since the council licensed them), or if they involved people who might be warned out of town. South Kingstown's town council, for example, summoned Jacob Mott to answer charges that he was keeping "a disorderly house, frolicking, [and] entertaining servants." Mott appeared before the council and was not punished because he promised that these practices would end.[9] John Butts of Portsmouth was not so fortunate: when the town council found him guilty of "suffering card playing," it revoked his license and ordered him "to take down his sign." Portsmouth also ordered Elizabeth Stone, "a woman of ill fame and of lewd conversation [who] is frequently entertained" to be shipped and warned out of town because of her moral character.[10] The Providence council similarly ordered "the girl that lives at Captain David Abbott's . . . to depart" because it thought her conduct somewhat less than wholesome.[11] The council was not beyond interfering in internal family matters if it felt decency required official action. The South Kingstown council ordered one of its members to investigate Letiah Cottrell's complaint that she was "much abused by her son Stephen and his wife."[12]

317

Few matters were too trivial to be brought to the council for action: the Bristol council loaned Joseph Maxfield the money to buy a cord of wood which was to be repaid "when he gets his money from Mr. Bosworth."[13] When Henry Jones told the Providence town council that he "lay in a very poor condition and especially for want of lodging . . . and that there being a bed in the hands of [the town sergeant] . . . which was part of the estate of John Jones," the council "thought it proper that the sergeant let the bed go to the use of the said Henry Jones for his present relief."[14] In an even more unusual case, Caleb Arnold, a tavernkeeper, asked for and received the Warwick council's help in getting a supply of rum from East Greenwich for his tavern.[15]

For all of their diligence in assisting needy townspeople, probating estates, and auditing the town's expenses, the town councilmen usually received something in the way of a financial reward but it was invariably only honorific and not equal to the effort expended. Portsmouth first paid its councilmen in 1682 when the town meeting "taking into consideration the many services the town council has these several years done for which they have had nothing allowed in compensation," ordered that the money the council collected for liquor licenses be divided among them for pay. This amounted to less than one pound per councilman, not a very substantial sum, and two years later the town meeting reduced this to half of the license money.[16] Other towns also usually paid their councilmen a token fee but not all did. As late as 1765 two Newport councilmen complained to the town meeting that they had served for many years without any pay and would no longer stand for reelection unless some "proper allowance" was forthcoming. The town meeting responded, in a way undoubtedly regarded as inadequate by the complainants, by authorizing payments only for times of unusual activity such as smallpox epidemics.[17]

Almost invariably, however, councilmen were provided free dinners and liquor on the days of their meetings—the South Kingstown council's last act at each meeting was always to authorize funds for their own "victuals and drink"—but occasionally even these perquisites could fall victim to the towns' penuriousness. When Warwick experienced severe financial problems during the 1760s, one of the casualties was payment for the dinners of the councilmen which had been paid for by the town for the first sixty-five years of the eighteenth century. Not until 1777 were free dinners for councilmen restored to them.[18] Similarly, East Greenwich's town meeting voted "no dinner [for the council] at the town's cost," but it took only seven years of complaining for the town councilmen to get them back.[19] These extreme examples of tightfistedness toward the town councils are unusual but even in the most generous towns the councilmen could expect only meals and a few glasses of rum, or a token payment, for the long hours they served. Prestige, status, and a sense of satisfaction from doing one's duty were the real rewards councilmen enjoyed.

Apparently, the prestige, status, and sense of satisfaction were usu-

13. Bristol Town Council Minutes, Bristol Town Hall, Feb. 1763.

14. Providence Town Council Minutes, Dec. 1734.

15. Warwick Town Council Minutes, Warwick City Hall, June 1777.

16. Portsmouth Town Meeting Minutes, Portsmouth Town Hall, Aug. 1683, June 1685.

17. Newport Town Meeting Minutes, Newport Historical Society, Jan. 1765.

18. Warwick Town Meeting Minutes, Warwick City Hall, June 1765, June 1777.

19. East Greenwich Town Meeting Minutes, East Greenwich Town Hall, Oct. 1724, May 1741.

318

20. For contention on the colony level see David Lovejoy, *Rhode Island Politics and the American Revolution. 1760–1770* (Providence, R.I., 1958), and Sydney V. James, *Colonial Rhode Island: A History* (New York, 1975). For problems at the town meeting level see Bruce C. Daniels, "Poor Relief, Local Finance, and Town Government in Eighteenth-Century Rhode Island," *Rhode Island History*, XL (1981), 75–87.

ally adequate: despite a significant number of men who refused to serve on the council, between 1700 and 1760 town councils averaged a turnover rate of 27.3 percent, which meant that on a yearly average between four and five of the councilmen were reelected. The average town councilman served 5.3 terms, and some, such as Thomas Nickols of East Greenwich and Joseph Crandall of Westerly, served over thirty terms. Of the seven towns whose town council records span all sixty of these years, all had at least one councilman who served twenty terms or more.

It is a moot question whether or not this low turnover rate and the long tenures in office reflect an absence of democracy in the power structures of the towns. Undoubtedly, family connections and wealth as well as leadership ability affected the choice of councilmen. The important fact to note, however, is that the councils exhibited a remarkably high degree of stability—many men were willing to serve and the voters were usually pleased with those who did and reelected them. Nor did this change over the course of the eighteenth century as town council meetings grew lengthier and dealt with more items at each meeting. The pattern of officeholding was just as stable on the eve of the Revolutionary struggles as it was in 1700.

In the final analysis when one combines all the details of Rhode Island's town councils into a coherent whole, a rather clear picture emerges. The council always functioned as a "particular court," as its institutional predecessors in Newport and Portsmouth were called. It never made policy *per se* but instead unified the administrative functions of government on the local level. Any "particular" that required town action came before the town council and it decided the particular to the best of its ability according to colony statutes and town bylaws. Items such as probate, the authorizing of town expenditures, and the warning out of undesirables, were regular and routine items of business; but almost no detail of local life was too trivial for a council to entertain. And, despite the minutiae that characterized the meetings, the lack of a policy-making function, the increasing amount of business, and the lack of adequate compensation, the councilmen were diligent in their duty as shown by their high attendance and their willing-

TABLE V
OFFICEHOLDING AMONG TOWN COUNCILMEN 1700–1785

	Overall*	1701–1720	1721–1740	1741–1760
Turnover Rate	27.3%	27.7%	29.0%	24.3%
Average # of terms per Councilman	5.3	4.8	4.4	4.5

*Twelve towns in sample. The overall average number of terms served is higher than that of any period because periodization artificially lowers the average since most men served terms in more than one period.

ness to serve many terms. The conduct of the town councils in the Revolution adds more support to this interpretation. They did not enter the debates over the Imperial connection, declaring independence, writing a new state constitution, or ratifying the Federal Constitution. Instead, guided by the decisions of the town meetings and the policies of the colony, they expanded their meetings to carry on the particulars of organizing men and munitions and dealing with the many quotidian problems caused by war. If, as all analyses indicate, the General Assembly of colonial Rhode Island was wracked with chronic and vituperative political wrangling and instability, and the town meetings frequently acted with financial irresponsibility,[30] the town councils provided a sense of stability, balance, and order in the day-to-day particulars of life that was lacking elsewhere in the colony.

320

Public Poor Relief and the Massachusetts Community, 1620–1715

CHARLES R. LEE

IN 1624 secretary for the Merchant Adventurers, James Sherley, sent the inhabitants of Plymouth Colony one red heifer "to begin a stock for the poor." Five years later, preparing for the Winthrop fleet to sail, the Massachusetts Bay Company instructed John Endecott, its resident governor of the settlement at Salem, to raise a general stock for community purposes, including the relief of the poor.[1] These actions were the first formal steps taken to provide public poor relief in Massachusetts. Thereafter, settlement and provision for public poor relief advanced hand in hand. With one possible exception, every community in the Plymouth and Massachusetts Bay colonies provided for relief in the initial stages of settlement and subsequently administered relief as a regular town function.[2] Public poor relief, it appears, was basic to the Massachusetts community experience.

So basic was the association, in fact, that public poor relief

The author wishes to acknowledge the contributions of Robert MacCameron and Scott Eberle, colleagues who carefully read and critiqued this essay.

[1] James Sherley et al. to Bradford, in William Bradford, *Of Plymouth Plantation, 1620–1647*, ed. Samuel Eliot Morison (New York: A. A. Knopf, 1966), p. 174. Darrett B. Rutman, *Husbandmen of Plymouth: Farms and Villages in the Old Colony, 1620–1692* (Boston: Beacon Press, 1968), p. 6; "Records of the Governor and Company," in Alexander Young, ed., *Chronicles of the First Planters of the Colony of Massachusetts Bay, From 1623 to 1636* (Boston: C. C. Little and J. Brown, 1846), pp. 120–21; Richard P. Gildrie, *Salem, Massachusetts, 1626–1683: A Covenant Community* (Charlottesville: University Press of Virginia, 1975), p. 12.

[2] Nathaniel B. Shurtleff and David Pulsifer, eds., *Records of the Colony of New Plymouth in New England*, 12 vols. (Boston: W. White, 1855–61), 3:37, 132, 134. The exception is the town of Taunton, in Plymouth Colony, which was cited for not providing poor relief during the 1650s.

in seventeenth-century Massachusetts had significance beyond its practical application. Imbued with religious and civic importance, public poor relief symbolized for many colonials the well-ordered community and commonwealth and, in this respect, helped define the Massachusetts community. As Massachusetts society changed during the first hundred years of European settlement, the methods used for and, in some locales, the function of relief altered. Nevertheless, the importance of public relief in colonial life remained relatively unaltered. The task of "mapping the social network" of Massachusetts communities, to borrow Thomas Bender's phrase, can be advanced by focusing on this key element of seventeenth-century social organization, by analyzing Massachusetts communities and their records regarding poor relief in three periods—the early period, 1620–45; mid-century, 1660–75; and the beginning of the provincial era, 1690–1715.[3]

Like Cotton Mather counting the widows seated before him in his Second Church congregation, historians in recent years have sought to detail the problem of poverty in early America.[4] Scholars have documented the daily effects of poverty by means

322

[3] The fullest expression of the periodization employed in this essay is in David Thomas Konig's *Law and Society in Puritan Massachusetts, 1629–1692* (Chapel Hill: University of North Carolina Press, 1979). The theory of social change used here has been expressed by: Richard R. Beeman, "The New Social History and the Search for 'Community' in Colonial America," *American Quarterly* 29 (Fall 1977): 422–44; Thomas Bender, *Community and Social Change in America* (New Brunswick, N.J.: Rutgers University Press, 1978); John Higham, "Hanging Together: Divergent Unities in American History," *Journal of American History* 61 (June 1974): 5–29; Darrett B. Rutman, "The Social Web: A Prospectus for the Study of the Early American Community," in *Insights and Parallels: Problems and Issues of American Social History*, ed. William L. O'Neill (Minneapolis: Burgess Publishing Co., 1973), pp. 57–89; Roland L. Warren, *The Community in America* (Chicago: Rand McNally, 1963). Massachusetts churches also played a role in local poor relief. Their efforts were not included here due to lack of space.

[4] A sample of the best recent work would include: Gary B. Nash, *The Urban Crucible: Social Change, Political Consciousness, and the Origins of the American Revolution* (Cambridge: Harvard University Press, 1979); Douglas Lamar Jones, "Poverty and Vagabondage: The Process of Survival in Eighteenth-Century Massachusetts," *New England Historical and Genealogical Register* 133 (October 1979): 243–55; John A. Garraty, *Unemployment in History: Economic Thought and Public Policy* (New York: Harper & Row, 1978), chap. 1; David S. Rothman, *The Discovery of the Asylum: Social Order and Disorder in the New Republic* (Boston: Little, Brown, 1971), chap. 1.

of annual town rates levied to pay for maintenance, service agreements to provide for the care of indigent children, accounts of clothing and shelter found for old persons without families, prospects of itinerants, and burial arrangements made for paupers. Whereas historians have recognized that public relief was a central concern of Massachusetts communities, the marked variability among the communities' responses has not been acknowledged. Furthermore, most recent accounts have focused on the social transformation of the late eighteenth and early nineteenth centuries and relied upon old, unexamined assumptions about the colonial past.[5] The evidence presented here is intended to serve as a partial corrective.

323

The story begins with James Sherley's heifer. The gift was a particularly fitting one since it could answer many needs. From initial settlement until the mid-1640s a relatively unstructured, decentralized approach to the problem of poverty was characteristic of both the Plymouth and Massachusetts Bay colonies. Magistrates of both colonies entertained individual petitions for relief. Moreover, the towns of Plymouth, Boston, Salem, Charlestown, Dedham, Dorchester, Cambridge, Ipswich, and Watertown exercised community initiative. The well-known "Town Act" of 1635, which gave towns in the Bay Colony responsibility for local affairs, neither instituted nor interrupted ongoing local relief actions. Despite local variations, there appears to have been a consensus among the founders regarding the relief of the poor—a consensus built upon the foundation of English law and local custom and buttressed by the circumstances of settling the wilderness.

The community, according to English law, was responsible for the local poor. The Elizabethan Poor Law of 1601 con-

[5] The most prominent of these assumptions are: poverty was not a "problem" in colonial Massachusetts since there were relatively few indigent persons; those who were poor were cared for in the family home; no specialized institutions were required until the eighteenth century; and, thus, the seventeenth century represents a "simple past." For an example of these assumptions at work, see Rothman, *Discovery of the Asylum*, chap. 1.

firmed the principle but did not stipulate the manner in which it should be practiced. According to David Grayson Allen, poor relief was the single most important public function in those towns where manorial relationships were weak, for instance, in portions of East Anglia; in other areas manorial or ecclesiastical institutions assumed the major burden.[6] In any case, the custom of local responsibility, as Plymouth first demonstrated, survived transplantation. Regard for the local poor was a civic virtue carried to New England by the founders.

During their short experiment with communal organization, leaders of the Plymouth plantation time and again stressed the community's responsibility for maintaining the general welfare, specifically the welfare of those in need. In part, the founders emphasized charity to moderate individualism. In 1621 Robert Cushman, a member of the Leyden congregation and an agent for the Merchant Adventurers, visited the settlement to help quiet a disturbance that had arisen over land allotments. He used the visit to remind the settlers that the community should serve the needs of all its members. They should not, he told them, look "gapingly one upon other, pleading your goodness, your birth, your life you lived, your means you had and might have had." Those who were poor, sick, weak, or of indifferent abilities should be accommodated. Later, Cushman posed the matter of community ties this way: "Eats he coarse fare, bread and water, and I have better? Why, surely we will part stakes." The community and the "General Conveniency," as Pastor John Robinson put it, were one. Cushman, Robinson, William Bradford, Edward Winslow, and other leading lights of the settlement shared this notion of what was to be done in Plymouth. The *Mayflower Compact* had expressed the same ideal.[7] Although its context was prac-

324

----

[6] David Grayson Allen, *In English Ways: The Movement of Societies and the Transferral of English Local Law and Custom to Massachusetts Bay in the Seventeenth Century* (Chapel Hill: University of North Carolina Press, 1981), p. 117. See also, Wilbur K. Jordan, *Philanthropy in England, 1480–1660* (New York: Russell Sage Foundation, 1959).

[7] Robert Cushman, "Of the State of the Colony, and the Need of Public Spirit in the Colonists," in Alexander Young, ed., *Chronicles of the Pilgrim Fathers of the Colony of Plymouth, 1602–1625* (New York: Da Capo Press, 1971), pp. 264.

tical, political, and financial, the founders clearly meant to equate community with welfare responsibilities. Soon the ideal was translated into system. After 1623, when Plymouth abandoned its communal organization, the simple Christian charity that Cushman preached was replaced by a system of poor relief administered by colony and town officials. Cushman decried the new order, referring to it as "skins and gymocks," but apparently few agreed with him. In 1624 Sherley's gift for a "poor stock" arrived. Some of the first settlers were still living in crude shelters or tents, in part due to the dissension caused by the colony's original "common course" of settlement and agriculture. Whereas the colonists were no longer subsisting on groundnuts and mussels, as they had the first year, the yield realized from English grains was meager,[8] and the community's livestock numbered only three heifers and one bull. One red heifer for the poor was a significant addition, and its significance grew as the townspeople of Plymouth carefully administered it and its "increase" for the next thirty years.

The stock came to answer multiple needs in the agrarian community. The cattle were used as payment for the relief of the aged, infirm, and insane. Most early relief cases involved individuals who were separated from a means of support because of one of these conditions and also from a household. The stock could be used to benefit or pay the family—not usually the indigent person's own—that agreed to care for him or her. Arrangements and accounting procedures often became quite complicated, for instance, when half or quarter shares or future calves were promised to individuals for a set period of time in return for their part in providing necessary items for the relief of a particular person. Most of the Plym-

325

267–68. "Letter of John Robinson to the Pilgrims," in *Plymouth Church Records: 1620–1859*, Publications of the Colonial Society of Massachusetts, vol. 22 (Boston: Colonial Society, 1920), p. 47. George F. Willison, *Saints and Strangers* (New York: Reynal & Hitchcock, 1945), p. 193.

[8] See Rutman, *Husbandmen of Plymouth,* for the best portrait of life in Plymouth at this time. The groundnut is a tuber from the plant *Apios americana,* common to the area from the Gulf of Mexico to the Gulf of St. Lawrence and to the Wampanoag diet.

outh poor were cared for in this fashion (one or two were shipped back to their families in England), and all orphans and servants were "ranged" under some family.

Initially the Plymouth town meeting shared responsibility for relief with colony officials, but during the 1630s the town became more active, and in 1649 town inhabitants delegated the task to their selectmen. Although the administration of relief was a complex affair, the burden it imposed upon the community was not great in other respects. The livestock cost the town nothing to keep since they were sheltered and fed by persons granted their "increase"—milk and calves. There were fifty-seven different relief cases recorded by colony and Plymouth town officials between 1630 and 1645. Some individuals were carried by relief from year to year; some names appeared only once. Even with a relatively small population, estimated to be between 400 and 500 persons in 1630 and close to 700 in 1643, Plymouth Colony managed poor relief easily.[9]

The record of the Massachusetts Bay Colony regarding poor relief during the early period parallels Plymouth's, although the chronology is somewhat compressed. Bay Colony leaders like John White and John Winthrop were given to the same kind of charitable ethic that had inspired Cushman and his colleagues. This facet of the Puritan mission was first expressed by Winthrop in his *Modell of Christian Charity*, when he counseled that the supplies, joys, and labors of any one member must be shared by all, as all share in "our Commission and Community." In 1631 when the *Dartmouth* landed at Boston laden with provisions from Ireland, Winthrop and the other Assistants bought the entire cargo for the general stock and then distributed it to families "as every man had need." The needy, the "poorer sort of people" as Winthrop

9 *Records of the Town of Plymouth, 1638–1783*, 3 vols. (Plymouth: Avery & Doten, 1889–1903), 1:30. For the problem of population, I consulted Evarts B. Greene and Virginia D. Harrington, *American Population before the Federal Census of 1790* (New York: Columbia University Press, 1932), and Kenneth Lockridge, "Population of Dedham, Massachusetts, 1636–1736," *Economic History Review*, 2d ser. 19 (1966): 318–44. The number of relief cases and thus the burden of poverty is likely understated by the figures given in this essay. The records are not consistently specific about the number of individuals on relief.

called them, had spent the first winter living in tents, where many fell victim to scurvy.[10] These provisions may have been the first purchase for the general stock Endecott was instructed to raise in 1629. Soon thereafter, however, the colony and its towns developed methods of granting relief that would be characteristic of the remainder of the early period.

Although the Bay Colony administered poor relief during the fifteen-year period, until 1645, the towns gradually assumed the greater burden. The General Court primarily limited its relief efforts to a certain type of poor person. On 5 August 1634, for example, the Court ordered the treasurer to lay out monies for the maintenance of widow Bosworth and her family. That same year, Thomas Land, brought to New England in the service of John Burslyn, completed his term of indenture and subsequently traveled from Wessacucon (later renamed Newbury) to Dorchester, where he fell "lame and impotent" and required relief. The Court supplied him. John Stanley died intestate en route to New England in 1635 and left two children who had to be maintained. Little can be learned about the lives of these individuals, other than that they were persons caught by misfortune in transit from one place to another, residents of no town. They petitioned the Court for relief or had others submit petitions in their names, and they were supplied for indefinite periods of time in indefinite ways. Providing medicine, transportation, land to plant, or corn, the magistrates continued to entertain similar petitions even after 1635, when all relief matters were officially delegated to the towns. In fact, whereas the Court responded to eighteen individual petitions between 1630 and 1639, the number doubled between 1640 and 1645.[11]

327

10 John Winthrop, "A Model of Christian Charity," in *Puritan Political Ideas, 1558–1794*, ed. Edmund S. Morgan (Indianapolis: Bobbs-Merrill, 1965), p. 92. "Early Records of Charlestown," and "The Memoirs of Roger Clap," in *Chronicles of the First Planters*, pp. 353, 385. James Kendall Hosmer, ed., *Winthrop's Journal: "History of New England," 1630–1649*, 3 vols. (New York: Charles Scribner's Sons, 1908), 1:58.

11 Nathaniel B. Shurtleff, ed., *Records of the Governor and Company of the Massachusetts Bay in New England*, 5 vols. (Boston: W. White, 1853–54), 1:121, 123, 134, 143–44, 151, 183, 230; 2:45–56, 48, 51, 52, 54, 97.

Bay Colony towns had not waited for the delegation of powers. Most towns had covenants, written by the town founders, to which all persons had to swear in order to be admitted to residence. The typical civic covenant expressed the goal of a godly and harmonious community life and commitment to community welfare. A renewal of shared ideals, the documents gave shape to town life.[12] Beyond this common ethic, town actions were determined partly by the character and composition of the town poor and partly by local resources. Charlestown had few cases—only four were recorded for the period 1630 to 1645—but one required extensive relief. In October 1635 the town meeting voted that "widow Morley be monthly kept from House to House throughout the town, at 3s. in winter, and 2s. in summer, per week." In 1637 the town provided a room for her in the watch house, where she remained for a number of years. Cambridge set aside fifty acres of land close to the town center in 1638 for the "Impotent" poor. Watertown began setting regular rates to cover "charges to ye Poore" early in the 1640s. The town recorded six relief cases between 1630 and 1645; by 1650 its yearly expenditure for relief was over £10.

In the 1640s Boston also increased its rate to pay for its half dozen cases. The town began to pay individuals to take some of the poor into their homes; a few who were indigent and ill were housed in the Boston jail. In addition, many of the "country poor," relieved by the General Court, resided in the port town. Dedham, with five recorded cases, allowed a few people who were "destitute of Corne," either because of fire or other causes, to cut trees for planks which they then could sell. Having also recorded five relief cases, the Salem townsmen, after receiving a cow in 1645 from a man in London, sought out the poorest man in town and gave the cow to him, and in 1647 the town fathers placed Ruben Guppey's two eldest children in service to free him of their expense.[13]

12 Gildrie, *Salem*, pp. ix–x, 38, 39.

13 *Boston Records, 1634–1728*, 3 vols., vols. 2, 7, and 10 of Reports of the Record Commissioners of the City of Boston (Boston, 1881, 1883, 1886), 2:80, 81,

THE NEW ENGLAND QUARTERLY

In the towns, the means of relief were often tailored to fit the case. Boarding is the easiest method to define. Poor persons, like widow Morley, who had no families of their own were placed with families that would provide food, clothing, shelter, and perhaps something to do. Many who were boarded were old, ill, or incapacitated, and thus their condition determined their care, at least in part. Town fathers also had to find a family willing to take in the indigent person. A great many other cases can be placed in the category of outdoor relief. If family members were present who could provide some but not all necessities, if individuals were capable of helping themselves, or if other circumstances seemed to rule out boarding a person with a family, then individuals were given relief but their household status was not changed. The Cambridge and Dedham actions are examples of this type of relief. As far as can be determined, no generalization governed the type of relief a town provided. All towns used both boarding and outdoor relief during this period, and neither type was clearly predominant.

The record Massachusetts colony and town officials established from 1620 to 1645 bears the unmistakable mark of English legal and customary precedent and the special imprint of the migration. The first generation assumed public responsibility for the worthy poor: those whose condition was entirely fortuitous. Distinguishing between the worthy and unworthy poor had been customary in Europe since the fourteenth century. The worthy poor were indigent through no fault of their own and deserved aid. The unworthy poor had contributed to their own decline and thus were not, properly speaking, poor at all but criminal and deserved nothing more than correction.

83. *The Records of the Town of Cambridge, 1630–1703* (Cambridge, 1901), p. 32. Don Gleason Hill, ed., *The Early Records of the Town of Dedham, Massachusetts, 1636–1706*, 5 vols. (Dedham: Dedham Transcript Press, 1886–99), 3:83. *Town Records of Salem, Massachusetts, 1630–1691*, 3 vols. (Salem: The Essex Institute, 1868–1934), 1:64, 118, 138, 151. *Watertown Records, 1634–1745*, 4 vols. (Watertown, 1894–1928), 2:9, 12, 16, 20. Most of these towns had populations of roughly 350 to 450 persons, with Salem somewhat over 1,000 individuals in 1645 and Boston close to 2,000.

The justice of this historical formula and the justice envisioned by both Pilgrims and Puritans in their "New World" societies were nearly the same.[14]

The settlements did not mirror their ideal, but they did not fail for want of effort. Public poor relief was an article of civic and Christian faith, part of an organic world view. Perry Miller and Edmund Morgan, among others, have identified that the Puritans viewed the family as the keystone of community and commonwealth.[15] On this point, at least, the Pilgrim mind was similarly cast. Communities were aggregates of families or households whose strengths or weaknesses determined the health of the larger social unit. The commonwealth, in this case the Holy Commonwealth of Massachusetts or that of Plymouth Colony, was in turn a chain composed of community links. Thus, poverty to Pilgrim and Puritan involved more than economic need. Poverty was the failure—a complex social, economic, and psychological event—of the family or of the household. Public responsibility for the poor began here, where the family or even a distant member of it could not fulfill its responsibility for justifiable reasons. Since the migration to Massachusetts was dominated by families that were relatively young, healthy, and intact, the poor during this early period were orphans, widows, servants, and transients who suffered calamity.

It was in this light that the founders viewed poverty as a significant problem. Those fresh over from England, like Thomas Lechford in 1642, saw plenty and prosperity everywhere they turned. The land was sufficiently bountiful and

14 Brian Tierney, *Medieval Poor Law: A Sketch of Canonical Theory and Its Application in England* (Berkeley: University of California Press, 1959); Michael Walzer, *The Revolution of the Saints: A Study in the Origins of Radical Politics* (New York: Atheneum, 1974), pp. 216–17; Garraty, *Unemployment in History*, chap. 1.

15 Perry Miller, *The New England Mind: The Seventeenth Century* (1939; Cambridge: Harvard University Press, 1967), p. 420; Edmund S. Morgan, *The Puritan Family: Religion and Domestic Relations in Seventeenth-Century New England* (New York: Harper & Row, 1966), p. 143; Oscar Handlin, "Poverty from the Civil War to World War II," in *Poverty Amid Affluence*, ed. Leo Fishman (New Haven: Yale University Press, 1966), pp. 3–18.

there were few poor; conditions were much worse in England. The number of relief cases recorded by Massachusetts towns seems to confirm Lechford's judgment. Including all of the jurisdictions (towns, counties, and colonies) surveyed for this study, the total number of relief cases in any one decade exceeded one hundred only three times between 1620 and 1715: during the 1670s there were 164 cases; the 1680s include 130 recorded cases; and the years 1700 to 1709 account for 157 recorded cases. The 1630s and the 1690s have 66 and 63 recorded cases respectively; all other decades have totals between 90 and 100. Considering the great population growth of the seventeenth century, the number of relief cases recorded during the same period rose slowly and remained small.

331

For contemporaries, though, numbers told only part of the story. The spectre of poverty crept into the speech and writings of those who lived in the fledgling towns and remained a part of the colonial lexicon. During the 1640s, the official communications of Bay Colony magistrates began to include references to the "straites" of New England society and the "povrty" of the country. Several years later Nathaniel Morton of Plymouth, working from Bradford's notes and records, described the effect upon the Plymouth church of the dispersal of several families to outlying farms. It was, he said, like an "Ancient Mother Growne old and forsaken of her children, . . . left onely to trust in God thuse shee that had made many Rich, became her selfe poor."[16]

❖❖❖   ❖❖❖   ❖❖❖

The second generation—the children of Morton's figurative "children"—came of age during the period 1660 to 1675, when both the substance and structure of social welfare in Massachusetts were changing. In some locales, interaction among juris-

[16] *Massachusetts Bay Records*, 2:16, 34, 185. *Plymouth Church Records*, 1:85. The total number of relief cases equals 960. The jurisdictions surveyed include: Massachusetts and Plymouth colonies; Essex, Suffolk, and Middlesex counties; and the towns of Boston, Charlestown, Cambridge, Watertown, Worcester, Plymouth, Taunton, Salem, Boxford, Dedham, Ipswich, Springfield, Dorchester, Lancaster, Milton, and Topsfield.

dictions produced structures that were more formal and patterned than in the earlier period. The characteristic diversity of relief methods remained and, in fact, intensified as conditions, and the range of experience associated with them, came to vary from one town to another.

Boston, the recognized center of New England affairs, was by mid-century rapidly becoming a town unlike any other. Its size, relative pluralism, public function, and ties with the Atlantic trading world set it apart and influenced life within the town. Public poor relief as a result was conducted differently than in other places. During the 1650s Boston had relied solely upon monetary or commodity exchanges for relief purposes; using boarding and outdoor methods, the town spent an average of £50 per year on relief. In 1660 the town received a £100 bequest from Henry Webb, and the selectmen decided to use it to establish an almshouse. Adding Robert Keayne's £120 legacy for the poor and other subscriptions to Webb's gift, the selectmen opened an almshouse in 1662. Only a few poor persons were admitted to it, however, before it burned down a year or so later. The town received another legacy of £80 in 1676 from Peter Lidget. This time, however, the selectmen gave a list of the town's poor to his widow so that she could distribute the bequest among them. This action was more characteristic of Boston's relief efforts during the period; simple maintenance was the characteristic form of relief given the poor. In most cases—there were twenty-nine recorded cases during the period—the method was outdoor relief.

The town no longer boarded many of those who in earlier years would have been placed with a family. The almshouse, thought to be a public alternative to the private household, was intended to replace boarding, which was increasingly less acceptable in a time of social flux. Residents were to create a family-like atmosphere and structure within the institution.[17]

17 *Boston Records,* 7:7, 24, 104, 105, 125, 158, and Josiah Quincy, *A Municipal History of the Town and City of Boston* (Boston: C. C. Little & J. Brown, 1852), pp. 8–9.

Its almshouse destroyed, however, Boston demonstrated the paradox that as it expanded as a town, its relief options appeared to be shrinking.

A wider array of options were used in a great many other towns in the Bay Colony and Plymouth. These towns--Cambridge, Watertown, Dorchester, Dedham, Springfield, Salem, and Plymouth—were smaller than Boston, less wealthy, and used a variety of methods to cope with poverty. Officials as a rule surveyed their towns to locate the poor, commanded more public funds for relief, used emerging local economic opportunities for relief purposes, and yet still maintained the familiar methods established by the first generation. Even while using new or expanding service enterprises (like inns and ferries) to employ the poor and negotiating apprenticeship agreements with local tradesmen, towns continued to board the poor and give some others outdoor relief. The towns of Ipswich, Cambridge, Sudbury, Lancaster, and Springfield combined apprenticeship agreements for some poor youth with relief in kind—materials like building supplies, land, and crops—for poor families.[18]

In Salem, a promising mercantile center of over one thousand persons, simple maintenance and public employment were the two most prevalent forms of relief. Costs for boarding and outdoor maintenance, accorded widows, unwed mothers, and other individuals of whom the records give no information, rose from approximately £5 per year in 1662 to approximately £12–13 per year in the 1670s. Salem had several long-term responsibilities. Sarah Lambert received continuous relief during the entire period, 1660–75, despite efforts by the selectmen either to "dispose" of her into a family or send her out of the colony to Virginia. In 1673 she gave birth to a child whom the selectmen successfully placed with a family, but

333

[18] *Salem Records*, 2:187; *Dedham Records*, 5:117; Henry M. Burt, ed., *The First Century of the History of Springfield: The Official Records from 1636 to 1736*, 2 vols. (Springfield: H. M. Burt, 1898), 1:85–86, 2:359; Thomas Franklin Waters, *Ipswich in the Massachusetts Bay Colony*, 2 vols. (Ipswich: Ipswich Historical Society, 1905–17), 2:388, 390.

Sarah herself remained outside the family orbit. Most poor persons were maintained for a year or two, typically, but a few were on the public rolls for up to five years. The annual cost of relief in Salem is a poor measure of the incidence of poverty because the town was more successful than most in keeping individuals off the relief rolls. Town officials used servitude, apprenticeship, and public enterprises to rebuild household sufficiency. Local craftsmen, public inns, and the ferry provided valuable opportunities for employing the poor.[19]

334

Watertown recorded forty-eight poverty cases between 1660 and 1675. In January 1661 the town meeting instructed the selectmen to survey the town's inhabitants and report the needs of poor families. Their survey identified four families, including a total of eighteen children, in need of immediate relief. The records identify twenty-one other individuals (but do not specify the existence or extent of their families) who also received maintenance relief during this period. The widow Bradbook and Thomas Philpot, once cited as mentally ill, received relief for the entire period. Most others were on the rolls for short periods of time. As usual, older persons— widows and widowers—received most of the outdoor mainte- nance relief. Some of the indigent were boarded with families. The town did not use servitude, apprenticeship, or employ- ment extensively for relief. Partly for this reason, the cost of relief for the town was consistently between £10 and £20 during the period, roughly 20 to 30 percent of all town expenses.

The selectmen provided specific, practical items for poor relief when the circumstances allowed. They gave Hugh Pas- son two cords of wood and two bushels of corn. Richard Beech was given wood for "fireing" and some clothing. Goodman Thorp got two shirts.[20] The records do not reveal the specifics

19 *Salem Records*, 2:27, 29, 32, 35, 39, 41, 48, 53, 59, 68, 71–74, 100, 123, 128, 138, 154, 171, 190, 193–94, 218, 221, 289, 298–99, 310, 317, 323–26.

20 *Watertown Records*, 1:59, 70, 71, 78, 80, 87, 89, 93, 94, 97, 98, 102, 103, 107, 110, 111, 115, 122, 125, 129, 132, 134, 143. David Pulsifer, transcr., *Middlesex County Court Records, 1649–1686*, 1:272, 279–80 (the four volumes, transcribed in 1851 but not published, are stored in the county clerk's office).

of the majority of cases, however; brief ledger entries provide
a name and a sum, nothing more. Even without detailed information, however, the record dramatizes the social transformation in progress in Watertown. The town was in the
midst of a period of prolonged, slow population growth; it
was larger than Dedham but still smaller than Salem. Wealth
in Watertown was in the form of land, not commerce, and was
more evenly distributed than in the commercial centers. Public relief was marked by familiarity, boarding and outdoor
methods, and yet was also subject to a formal annual survey.
Innovation combined with established patterns of action to
adapt the relief system to changing social conditions.

According to an account recorded by William Bradford,
Plymouth was still using its poor stock of cows for relief in
1655, but the stock was dwindling. Two cows "boged and
dyed" without increase in 1655, and two calves were lost, one
to a wolf. Plymouth, however, did not depend totally on its
livestock, for in 1649 the town meeting had authorized the
first annual rate, not then to exceed £3.[21] The amount spent
on relief did not increase greatly, since Plymouth recorded
only eleven relief cases from 1660–75. Dependent upon Boston
commercially, poor by comparison with Massachusetts towns,
and with its population dispersed and stable, Plymouth nevertheless adopted methods and administration similar to those
of Bay Colony towns.

Yet a third group of New England towns—Lancaster and
Sudbury are examples—were still relieving the poor as the
founders had. With fewer relief cases and smaller populations
than the towns mentioned above, no almshouses were built
here, no surveys were conducted to identify the needy, and no
regular annual rates for poor relief were necessary. Town officials used either land, boarding, outdoor relief, or servitude
to relieve poverty. Each case commanded the undivided attention of the town meeting.[22]

335

21 *Plymouth Town Records*, 1:29–30.

22 Waters, *Ipswich*, pp. 388–91; A. S. Hudson, *The History of Sudbury, Massachusetts* (Boston: A. H. Blodgett, 1889), p. 137; Henry S. Nourse, ed., *The
Early Records of Lancaster, Massachusetts, 1643–1725* (Lancaster: W. J. Coulter,
1884), p. 29.

Direct community involvement was still evident in the methods all Massachusetts towns used for poor relief at mid-century. In towns like Lancaster and Sudbury, especially, townspeople deciding on cases were familiar with those in need. Elsewhere, however, social change was leading to anonymity. The growing diversity of public response suggests a greater variety of individual needs as well as a greater variety of town circumstances. The almshouse in Boston and the selectmen's surveys in Watertown were early efforts toward specialization. Factors similar to those justifying these special responses also prompted increased interaction between towns and between the towns and colony officials.

The towns of Boston, Cambridge, Dorchester, and Ipswich pioneered the practice of issuing certificates verifying legal residence to poor persons who wanted to move elsewhere and test their prospects. These certificates were accepted as bonds and granted the person entry into neighboring towns. The towns interacted even more with the Quarterly Courts, created in 1636 and staffed by Bay Colony magistrates to supervise town affairs. By 1660 Quarterly Courts were beginning to play a significant role in poor relief, especially cases involving individuals who found themselves without family support and town residency. The courts "settled" such an individual in a town or with the persons who bore the closest discoverable relationship to him. For example, Charlestown selectmen were ordered by the Middlesex County Court to provide for the care of the children of Sarah Stretcher, who had died in their town without being admitted as an inhabitant.[23] Such cases, as well as a number of others involving mental illness, formed

23 *Cambridge Records*, pp. 145–46. *Boston Records*, 7:142, 146, 149. *Watertown Records*, 1:109. *Dorchester Town Records, 1632–1686*, vol. 4 of Reports of the Record Commissioners of the City of Boston (Boston, 1898), 4:130–31. *Middlesex County Court Records*, 3:218, 245, 300. Samuel E. Morison, ed., *Records of the Suffolk County Court, 1671–1680*, vols. 29 and 30 of Collections of the Colonial Society of Massachusetts (Boston: Colonial Society, 1933), 1:264, 345; 2:925. George F. Dow, ed., *Records and Files of the Quarterly Courts of Essex County, Massachusetts, 1638–1683*, 8 vols. (Salem: Essex Institute, 1911–21), 3:218; 5:312. Lucius R. Paige, *History of Cambridge, Massachusetts, 1630–1877* (Boston: H. O. Houghton & Co.; New York: Hurd & Houghton, 1877), p. 218.

the bulk of the courts' relief efforts. Significant magisterial participation in local poor relief and an increasingly complex social environment developed in parallel.

❖❖❖   ❖❖❖   ❖❖❖

The final period under consideration, 1690 to 1715, was one of sweeping change. Increase Mather brought home the new charter, which established the preeminence of the new commercial elite, in 1692, and 1689 marked the beginning of a long series of colonial wars that profoundly affected the colonial economy and life-style.[24] Still, these forces were not strong enough to sever the ties binding Massachusetts communities to earlier ways. The community consensus regarding relief and the definition of poverty, the variety of types of relief, and sharply contrasting local conditions remained relatively unaltered by 1715. Extralocal administrative connections and initiatives became more important in Massachusetts, and public buildings to house the poor were erected outside the limits of Boston. Nevertheless, changes were fully within the limits of past practice.

Boston is a good example of how changes in poor relief were a matter of degree rather than of kind. In 1682 the town had voted to rebuild the old, burned-out almshouse and reopen it as a workhouse (although theoretically different, the terms workhouse and almshouse were often used interchangeably) for those either unable to work or unable to find work. Those who could work would help defray the costs of the institution. One thousand pounds, local currency, was the figure the town decided to spend building and stocking the institution. The town was quite specific about its motives: the workhouse was to provide *economical* relief, and costs were to be kept down through the sale of some finished product. Completing the structure, however, depended upon some private contributions, and when these fell short, the project had to be abandoned.

---

[24] See G. B. Warden, *Boston, 1689–1776* (Boston: Little, Brown, 1970), and Howard H. Peckham, *The Colonial Wars, 1689–1762* (Chicago: University of Chicago Press, 1964).

Boston was becoming, according to many accounts, a haven for the provincial poor. Refugees from the wars, the town claimed, "by shifting from place to place," added to the town's own "other poor and idle persons ... [and] ... Presage great Poverty to be hastening upon this Town." A petition from the town to Dominion officials in 1686 referred to the "considerable visible decayes in the Estates" of Boston and claimed that the "number of the poor is much increased." In 1692, in its first meeting after the new charter was in effect, Boston elected four Overseers of the Poor and charged them with acting as liaisons between the town and the General and County courts and to administer poor relief.[25]

Due to the variations in record keeping instituted by the overseers, a reliable count of relief cases in Boston for the period 1690 to 1715 is not possible. The cost of relief was almost twice what it had been at mid-century, but the badly inflated currency and population growth must be taken into account. During the 1690s, Boston never spent over £100 per year for relief. In 1700 the town raised £100 for the poor, only 25 percent of its expenses that year. Figures for later years are less precise, but in 1715 the town raised a total rate of £2,000, a portion of which was for the poor. Assuming that the proportion of the total allocated for relief remained relatively constant, relief costs in 1715 would have been in the vicinity of £500. In 1692 there were 7,000 regular residents of Boston; in 1720 the number reached 12,000.[26] All public expenses increased in the burgeoning port town, and in relative terms the cost of relief does not appear to have risen disproportionately. Even with special administrators, the workhouse project, and wartime transients, poor relief in Boston remained to a great degree a community expression of social familiarity. The

25 *Boston Records*, 7:157-58, 174, 206, 241. M. Halsey Thomas, ed., *The Diary of Samuel Sewall, 1674-1729*, 2 vols. (New York: Farrar, Straus, & Giroux, 1973), 1:219, 276, 289.

26 Warden, *Boston*, pp. 25, 37, 64-71; Wesley Frank Craven, *The Colonies in Transition, 1660-1713* (New York: Harper & Row, 1968), pp. 305-10; Carl Bridenbaugh, *Cities in the Wilderness: The First Century of Urban Life in America, 1625-1742* (New York: A. A. Knopf, 1968), pp. 233-34. Nash, *Urban Crucible*, pp. 21-22.

338

Overseers of the Poor dispensed relief money for outdoor and boarding relief, though boarding was used rarely by this date. When paupers died, the Overseers had them properly buried. Orphans, the aged, and the infirm were still the chief beneficiaries of the system. Cotton Mather, dispensing counsel, prayer, and charity, chronicled his visits to the "ancient widows" of his neighborhood.

External affairs also intruded upon community relief responsibilities in the hinterland. When war broke out or Indian raids disrupted small farming villages like Boxford (with a population of approximately 184), Topsfield (with a population of approximately 279), Lexington, and Lancaster, poor relief took on a new meaning. Many small towns, claiming that they were too pressed to support taxes, periodically applied to the General Court for abatement of all country rates.[27] Infant communities with fully mature concerns, these towns shared both the experience of the founders and that of turn-of-the-century Boston.

During the 1690s Watertown, Dorchester, Dedham, Plymouth, Salem, Cambridge, Charlestown, Plymouth, and Ipswich continued to rely upon outdoor and boarding relief, but by 1715 most had entertained building or been encouraged or ordered to establish an almshouse. The burden for poor relief supported by towns from 1690 to 1715 is not easily measured, partly due to eccentricities of town record keeping. The Watertown records provide the most detailed picture. After a twenty-year boom, the population of Watertown was approximately 1,000 persons in 1708. The number of individuals receiving relief also rose; one hundred cases were recorded between 1690 and 1715. Thirty cases were recorded in the 1690s; thirty-two were recorded between 1700 and 1709; and thirty-eight were recorded between 1710 and 1715. The cost of relief

339

---

[27] *Lancaster Town Records*, pp. 181, 209; Franklin P. Rice, ed., *Records of the Proprietors of Worcester, Massachusetts* (Worcester: Worcester Society of Antiquity, 1881), p. 60; Charles Hudson, *History of the Town of Lexington, Middlesex County, Massachusetts* (Boston and New York: Houghton Mifflin Co., 1913), pp. 63–64, 209; Sidney Perley, *The History of Boxford, Essex County, Massachusetts* (Boxford: S. Perley, 1880), pp. 154, 165.

fluctuated from year to year but never exceeded £34. In many of these years the cost of relief accounted for one third of all town expenses.

Salem faced a similar burden. A much larger town than Watertown, with a population reaching 2,500 by 1700, Salem recorded twenty-nine relief cases in the 1690s and spent from £50 to £70 annually on relief. Dedham, with a population of 750 in 1700, recorded thirteen relief cases during the period under discussion. Ipswich, a community in which agriculture and commerce produced a highly stratified social structure, spent only £6 on relief in 1716 out of a total town rate of £100. Plymouth in 1710 spent £5 on relief, with total town expenses of £65. In 1715 the amount spent on relief in Plymouth rose to £10. The burden of relief in these last three towns does not appear to have been significantly greater than it had been at mid-century. Relief responsibilities grew in Watertown and Salem but not out of proportion to other measures of growth.

Variations in the methods of providing poor relief were still evident. In Watertown the town jail was used to house at least one poor person. Shuball Childs had been ruled a "distracted" person by the County Court and confined to the jail, where it was thought he could be most easily maintained. While there, his feet froze due to the unimproved condition of the facility.[28] Colony magistrates, sensitive to the inconveniences of housing the poor in community households or makeshift facilities, began to press towns to build almshouses or workhouses. The towns, arguing that institutions cost too much to build and maintain, resisted. Salem talked about building an almshouse during the 1690s, but the talk did not lead to action. For several years the town had been placing "inmates" with Goody Thorne, who housed them and was reimbursed by the town for their care. In effect, her house was the Salem almshouse. Watertown discussed building an almshouse in 1711, but the town voted against the project. In 1713 county magistrates ordered Worcester to build an almshouse and, a year later,

28 *Watertown Records*, 3:62, 64, 76, 77, 83, 86–87.

likewise ordered Ipswich, Charlestown, and Plymouth.[29] Records do not indicate whether Worcester complied, but the other three towns did. In Boston, meanwhile, the townspeople were discussing elaborate plans to coordinate its still unfinished workhouse with a house of correction and spinning school.

Specialized institutions like the almshouse/workhouse represented both change and continuity. The impact of population growth and mobility made former methods less acceptable. Towns were less able or less willing to impose poor people upon established households than in earlier years. Boarding neighbors and life-long town inhabitants was one thing; trying to board court-imposed poor persons or those not fully accepted as part of the community was quite another.

Although the almshouse/workhouse was an institutionalized and, therefore, anonymous method of providing for the poor and although almshouses at times appeared to be discussed more in terms of boosting a commercialized civic pride than in providing a practical social service, many of the founders' values were still evident.[30] While providing day-to-day maintenance relief, the almshouse/workhouse ideally would instruct the poor in productive habits and skills. At the very least the institution would approximate the family environment. Family sufficiency, not simply maintenance for the individual, was the goal.

The community context had changed, to some extent the function of relief had changed, but the ideal remained the same. While answering immediate needs, poor relief in Massachusetts, by focusing on the family, was designed to strike at the source of poverty. The ideal, of course, was not always

341

29 *Salem Records*, 3:174, 246; *Watertown Records*, 3:200. *Plymouth Town Records*, 2:254, 260, 274, 318; Franklin P. Rice, ed., *Records of the Court of General Sessions of the Peace for the County of Worcester, Massachusetts, From 1731-1737*, 2 vols. (Worcester: Worcester Society of Antiquity, 1882), 1:26-27; Richard Frothingham, *The History of Charlestown, Massachusetts* (Charlestown: C. P. Emmons; Boston: C. C. Little & J. Brown, 1845-49), pp. 252, 258, 259. Waters, *Ipswich*, pp. 396-98.
30 Elvin Hatch, *Biography of a Small Town* (New York: Columbia University Press, 1979), pp. 260-61.

realized, but it was an abiding measure of success or failure. The continuity of this commitment and outlook throughout one hundred years is remarkable. The almshouse, then, was not so radically different from James Sherley's red heifer, for both represented a crucial aspect of community life in Massachusetts, the importance of civic virtue expressed through Christian charity.

342

Charles R. Lee *is Lecturer of History at the University of Wisconsin, La Crosse.*

James Davenport and the Great Awakening in New London

Harry S. Stout and Peter Onuf

By 1743, readers of colonial newspapers had grown accustomed to reports of the religious revivals inaugurated by the English itinerant George Whitefield. But few were prepared for accounts of the bizarre and sensational events that took place in the port city of New London, Connecticut, in March of that year. According to the *Boston Evening Post*, the central character in the affair was the ailing and fanatical native-born itinerant James Davenport, whose "theatrical" preaching style and wild accusations against his fellow ministers had led to his arrest earlier in both Hartford and Boston. His chief accomplices were a devoted group of radical "New Lights" who, with Davenport's encouragement, had separated themselves from the Congregational church fifteen months earlier and formed their own church and an evangelical seminary known as the "Shepherd's Tent." Under the impression of messages "received from the Spirit in Dreams," Davenport carried his band of Separates into an orgy of religious enthusiasm that exceeded all bounds of decency and good order. By Sabbath afternoon, March 6, he had worked the people into such a frenzy that townsmen "ran to see if Murder or some other Mischief was not about to be done." Instead they witnessed the most remarkable event of the Great Awakening in New England. There, at Christophers's town wharf, Davenport and his followers gathered around a bonfire and cast into it a veritable library of Puritan classics. The catalogue of burned books was said to include works by such celebrated divines as Matthew Henry, Richard Sibbes, Increase Mather, and Benjamin Colman. The *Post*'s writer heard the book-burners "sing *Hallehuahs* and *Gloria Patri* over the Pile, and I heard them with a loud voice declare, *That the smoak of the Torments of such of the Authors of the above said Books as died in the same Belief as when they set them out, was now ascending in Hell in like manner as they saw the smoak of them books rise.*"[1]

Harry S. Stout is associate professor of history, University of Connecticut. Peter Onuf is assistant professor of history, Worcester Polytechnic Institute, Worcester, Mass.

[1] *Boston Evening Post*, April 11, 1743.

Once begun, there was no stopping the wanton assault on material posses-sions. The next day Davenport's group built another bonfire, this time made out of "wigs, cloaks and breeches, Hoods, Gowns, Rings, Jewels and Neck-laces," and anything else that represented the "world." Shocked by these abuses, civil authorities acted quickly to stop the fever and bring the ringleaders to trial. At the same time a ministerial assembly dominated by moderate prorevivalists denounced the enthusiasts. Davenport immediately left town and shortly thereafter disavowed his own excesses. The participants themselves were shaken beyond recovery. With their leader gone and their actions the talk of New England, the church and college dissolved, never to be heard from again.[2]

It is difficult to understand the extent to which the book burning shocked the sensibilities of eighteenth-century New England society. Word of the radical "excesses" spread rapidly, lifting the episode out of its local context and making it the cause célèbre of the Great Awakening. Commentators used strong adjectives to describe the New London events: they were "wild," "extravagant," and "indecent." The "thronging multitudes" who partici-pated in the carnage were "mad men" consumed by their "flaming zeal" and "enthusiastic fury"; they were clearly suffering the mental disorders of the pathologically pious. While New Lights and Old Lights strenuously disagreed over whether true revivals were taking place in the Great Awakening, they joined in condemning Davenport's particular brand of revivalism. Old Lights detected throughout the ranks of their opponents symptoms of "enthusiasm," which Davenport exhibited in acute form. Crowd behavior in New London showed them how people caught up in the revivals inevitably turned against established order and authority. New Lights thought Davenport was peculiarly afflicted and were deeply embarrassed ("at a loss how to conduct themselves") by the whole affair.[3] The revivals, they insisted, did not have to lead to anarchy. But all—even his friends and relatives and, in the afterglow of the bonfire, Davenport himself—believed that Davenport had been at least tem-porarily insane.[4] The whole episode was too outrageous to be explained in any other way.

Surprisingly, historians have done little to advance beyond the original explanation offered by contemporaries. Instead they have simply retold the sensational story, accepting at face value the judgment of eighteenth-century interpreters.[5] While recent empirical studies of the Awakening in particular

344

---

[2] Ibid.; Joseph Tracy, The Great Awakening: A History of the Revival of Religion in the Time of Edwards and Whitefield (Boston, 1845), 230–55.

[3] Boston Evening Post, April 11, 1743. For Old Light criticisms of James Davenport, see John Hancock, The Danger of an Unqualified Ministry: Represented in a Sermon Preached at Ashford, in the Colony of Connecticut, Sept. 7th, 1743 (Boston, 1743), 28–29; The Testimony and Advice of a Number of Laymen Respecting Religion, and the Teaching of It. Address'd to the Pastors of New-England (Boston, 1743), 5–6; and The Testimony and Advice of an Assembly of Pastors of Churches in New-England at a Meeting in Boston, July 7, 1743, Occasion'd by the Late Happy Revival of Religion in Many Parts of the Land (Boston, 1743), 11–12.

[4] James Davenport, Confession and Retractions, in The Great Awakening: Documents on the Revival of Religion, 1740–1745, ed. Richard L. Bushman (New York, 1969), 53–55.

[5] For pathological explanations of Davenport's behavior and the New London revivals, see, for example, Frances Manwaring Caulkins, History of New London, Connecticut, from the First

towns have improved our understanding of the social dynamics of the revivals in significant regards, the participants in this most notorious of episodes have gone virtually unexamined. Their identities and goals remain as mysterious today as they were then, despite the surprising amount of information on their activities that survives in town and parish records.[6] In like manner little effort has been extended to understand the peculiar appeal of Davenport's preaching style, even though he was, by all accounts, the most successful revivalist in Connecticut. What accounts for the peculiar potency of his address, and why did it strike such resonant chords with so many colonists? At the same time, why did others fear it so deeply? By failing to explore these questions, historians have deprived themselves of an invaluable index to the extent and limitations of religious radicalism in prerevolutionary New England.

345

This article offers an account of the brief history of the New London Separates and their leader Davenport and of the circumstances that brought them to their ill-fated climax at Christophers's wharf. The book burning was not a spontaneous combustion ignited on March 6, 1743, and extinguished the next day but the product of a complicated sequence of events that brought Davenport and his audience together in a new and explosive configuration. When the bonfire is placed in the context of mid-eighteenth-century New England society, a complex story appears in which a crisis in the ministerial profession, rapid social change, popular rebellion against established authority, lay congregationalism, and economic and social factors all played a part. If the New London bonfire was unique, the circumstances that gave rise to it were not, and this fact is what made the event so terrifying to the established authorities. They glimpsed a frighteningly new cultural landscape in Davenport's career. This new order of things was not simply a precocious aberration, brought on by one man's deranged mental state. It was implicit in the revivals themselves, particularly in the response to New Light rhetoric.

Religious revivals were a familiar occurrence in the interior life of New England churches. Each generation could point to at least one spiritual "harvest" when, in the space of several months or a year, significant numbers of new converts were added to the churches. Thus when Whitefield began his preaching tour of New England in 1740, most ministers welcomed him to their pulpits, expecting that his revivals would secure the religious foundations of communal life—and their own preeminence. Often they were correct. By adopting the Grand Itinerant's popular pulpit style and issuing their own impassioned calls for a "New Birth," many local ministers greatly enlarged church memberships and, in the process, restored some measure of order and

Survey of the Coast in 1612 (New London, 1895), 454–55; David S. Lovejoy, *Religious Enthusiasm and the Great Awakening* (Englewood Cliffs, 1969), 67; C. C. Goen, *Revivalism and Separatism in New England, 1740–1800: Strict Congregationalists and Separate Baptists in the Great Awakening* (New Haven, 1962), 26–27; Edwin Gaustad, *The Great Awakening in New England* (New York, 1957), 38–39; and Tracy, *Great Awakening*, 252–53. A recent exception, which examines the social context of Davenport's revivals in Boston, is Gary B. Nash, *The Urban Crucible: Social Change, Political Consciousness, and the Origins of the American Revolution* (Cambridge, Mass., 1979), 204–21.

[6] For a description and analysis of these records, see Peter Onuf, "New Lights in New London: A Group Portrait of the Separatists," *William and Mary Quarterly*, 37 (Oct. 1980), 627–43.

harmony to communal life.[7] Other ministers, however, had a very different experience. Rather than restoring harmony, the revivals merely exacerbated preexisting tensions and drove an even deeper wedge of contention into the heart of their communities. These ministers discovered that the Awakening, in frightening contrast to earlier revivals, could not be contained within the church. Instead it became a revival *against* the established church.

There were many reasons why particular communities exposed to the Great Awakening failed to follow the traditional pattern of renewed harmony. Sometimes divisions ensued when a minister refused to support the revival and adopt the message of the New Birth. Such clerical opposition often set in motion a popular backlash calling for the "unconverted" minister's dismissal or, failing that, for a branching off into independent "Separate" churches.[8] Elsewhere, ministers supported the revivals, but found that their communities were simply too diverse—with divisions too deep and institutionalized—ever to achieve communal harmony. New London was such a place.

Like other large towns and cities in New England, New London needed reviving. But the obstacles were forbidding: the town bore little resemblance to the small agricultural villages where the New England Way had first flourished and which country towns might still emulate. It was "the seat of his Majesty's custom-house and so the port of greatest note in the colony," according to a contemporary description. The distribution of wealth reflected the commercial character of the port and its agricultural hinterland. By contemporary standards the leading merchants and farmers were fabulously wealthy.[9]

The relatively complex and differentiated economic and social structure was reflected in New London's religious life. The number of churches multiplied during the pastorate (1709–1753) of Eliphalet Adams at the Congregational

---

[7] Gerald Moran traces revivals occurring in Connecticut church membership every twenty-five to thirty-five years in Gerald Moran, "The Puritan Saint: Religious Experience, Church Membership, and Piety in Connecticut, 1656–1776" (Ph.D. diss., Rutgers University, 1974). Such revivals were especially noted in small country towns where membership was already large—following earlier revivals—and where the established church still enjoyed a religious monopoly. At the outset of the Great Awakening, Baptists and Anglicans had not yet penetrated the interior. See Kennth Walter Cameron, ed., *Historical Resources of the Episcopal Diocese of Connecticut* (Hartford, 1966), 277, map facing 285; William G. McLoughlin, *New England Dissent, 1630–1833: The Baptists and the Separation of Church and State* (2 vols., Cambridge, Mass., 1971), I, 421–88; M. Louise Greene, *The Development of Religious Liberty in Connecticut* (Boston, 1905), 146–269.

[8] For a description of Separate movements, see Goen, *Revivalism and Separatism*; and McLoughlin, *New England Dissent*, I, 329–419.

[9] Robert A. Hallam, *Annals of St. James Church, New London, Connecticut for One Hundred and Fifty Years* (Hartford, 1873), 35. See also Bruce C. Daniels, *The Connecticut Town: Growth and Development, 1635–1790* (Middletown, Conn., 1979), 146. On life in New London, consult the invaluable *Diary of Joshua Hempstead of New London, Connecticut, Covering a Period of Forty-Seven Years, from September, 1711, to November, 1758* (New London, 1901); and Caulkins, *History of New London*. Among wealthy New Londoners, the Congregationalist John Savel left an estate worth more than £17,000, and the Rogerene John Rogers left one worth more than £20,000. Matthew Stewart, an Anglican, was assessed £553, by far the highest on the 1749 tax list for New London. See inventory of John Savel, 1754, file 4694, New London County Probate Records (Connecticut State Library, Hartford); inventory of John Rogers, 1753, file 4543, *ibid.*; New London tax list, 1749, New London Tax Lists, *ibid.*

church. The northern part of town was set off as a distinct parish in 1721. Dissenting (non-Congregational) churches gained an early foothold and were exempted from supporting the established churches. The richest New Londoners, including many "Europeans not long settled here, or persons brought up in other colonies," generally favored the Anglican St. James Church, founded in 1725. Baptists represented the popular alternative to Congregationalism throughout southeastern Connecticut: the Fort Hill Church in New London dated from 1704 and grew rapidly after 1720. The ranks of the Rogerenes—who broke away from Seventh-Day Baptism in the late 1670s— were swollen by the heroic generative efforts of the first John Rogers and his three wives. Thus, on the eve of the Great Awakening the established church no longer enjoyed a religious monopoly: it was a minority church, eschewed by many of the town's leading men and common inhabitants. In 1740 only about 16 percent of all parish residents were Congregational church members, despite notoriously lax admission standards. About one-third of the female adults in the parish and only one-sixth of the men took communion with the Congregationalists.[10]

While in many country towns in the decades before the Awakening the established church grew proportionately to population, Adams's New London church lost members to other churches. The potential for a revival *within* the church consequently diminished. Children of regular church members were the prize candidates for conversion in most places, but this pool of potential converts was small in New London. If there were to be a large influx of new members, many would necessarily be drawn from other communions or from the hitherto unchurched. The difficulty of assimilating these new elements jeopardized the promise of communal harmony.[11]

The Great Awakening came to New London in March 1741 when the Pennsylvania itinerant Gilbert Tennent delivered seven sermons in two days,

[10] For descriptions of New London's ecclesiastical mosaic, see *Sibley's Harvard Graduates* (17 vols., Boston and Cambridge, Mass., 1873–), IV, 189–98; S. Leroy Blake, *The Later History of the First Church of Christ, New London, Conn.* (New London, 1900), 17–136; Caulkins, *History of New London*, 436–39; Hallam, *Annals of St. James Church*, 7–39; James Swift Rogers, *James Rogers of New London, Connecticut and His Descendants* (Boston, 1902), 16–23; and Anna B. Williams, *The Rogerenes: Some Hitherto Unpublished Annals Belonging to the Colonial History of Connecticut* (Boston, 1904). Membership data are taken from New London First Church of Christ Records, 1670–1888, vol. 3, pp. 5–30 (Connecticut State Library). The parish population is estimated at 1,100 by extrapolation from the 1708–1709 list of tithables and the 1756 census, both reprinted in Evarts B. Greene and Virginia D. Harrington, *American Population before the Federal Census of 1790* (New York, 1932), 58–60.

[11] Moran, "Puritan Saint," 247. On the importance of family connections for revival converts, see Gerald F. Moran, "Conditions of Religious Conversion in the First Society of Norwich, Connecticut, 1718–1744," *Journal of Social History*, 5 (Spring 1972), 331–41; William Willingham, "Religious Conversion in the Second Society of Windham, Connecticut 1723–1743; A Case Study," *Societas*, 6 (Spring 1976), 109–19; and James Walsh, "The Great Awakening in the First Congregational Church of Woodbury, Connecticut," *William and Mary Quarterly*, 28 (Oct. 1971), 543–62. Jonathan Parsons's revival at Lyme, Connecticut, provides a good example of the difficulty of assimilating large numbers of new members. According to Parsons, new members flaunted their "experimental acquaintance with the regenerating influences of the holy Spirit" and challenged the spiritual credentials of old members. Jonathan Parsons, *A Needful Caution in a Critical Day, Or, the Christians Urged to Strict Watchfulness, That the Contrary Part may have no Evil Thing to Say of Him. A Discourse Preached at Lyme, Feb. 4, 1741. 2* (New London, 1742), 41.

347

including three at night. The first great outburst of popular enthusiasm, however, did not occur until late May and early June, in response to the preaching of Jedidiah Mills of Ripton parish in Stratford and Nathaniel Eels of Stonington. According to diarist Joshua Hempstead, "there hath been the wonderfull work of God made Evident in the powerfull Convictions Conversion of Divers persons in an Extreordinary manner . . . this week hath been kept as a Sabbath most of it, & with the greatest Success Imaginable & beyond what is Rational to Conceive. . . . Never any Such time here & Scarce any where Else."[12]

New converts flocked into the church: 81 admissions from May to November swelled the prerevival membership by 48 percent. Women and children responded enthusiastically to the new preaching, but a remarkable number of "Strong men" were also counted among the "Wounded." An outburst of adult baptism reflected an overwhelming reaction throughout the town, even among families who had shunned the church for generations. On two dates in June, for instance, first 9 then "20 grown people were Baptized." That so many New Londoners were eligible for this sacrament showed how tenuous the church's position had become in the community. But the "mighty works" now being accomplished by the revivalists with Adams's encouragement promised to recover many lost souls.[13]

Such sanguine expectations were soon abandoned, however. Enthusiastic converts had barely joined the church before they began sniping at Adams (a "Pillar of our Churches," according to his colleagues) and other supposedly unregenerate church members. Local preachers—most of whom favored the revivals and participated in them—found themselves on the defensive against radical attacks. Jonathan Parsons reported that "mutual jealousies" in New London had resulted in an "open separation." On June 16, 1741, Parsons preached twice at the meetinghouse and later to the dissidents gathered at John Curtis's home. But notwithstanding "a very great display of Grace on both sides," Parsons could not effect a reconciliation.[14]

Although technically members of the Congregational church, the new converts were never assimilated into the larger body, and they continued to meet separately at Curtis's home. Old Light critics refused to accept such religious dissent at face value and assumed that it was grounded in deeper, class-based antagonisms. According to newspaper accounts, most separatists were "idle or ignorant persons, and those of the lowest Rank." Boston's Charles Chauncy believed they were chiefly "young and illiterate" and predominantly female.[15] In all such descriptions the dissidents' rebellious behavior was, perhaps intentionally, confused with their supposedly obscure social background.

[12] Diary of Joshua Hempstead, 375, 377.

[13] Ibid., 378, 380.

[14] Solomon Williams to Eleazar Wheelock, July 17, 1741, item 741417, Eleazar Wheelock Papers (Dartmouth College Library, Hanover, N.H.); Boston Weekly Post-Boy, Sept. 28, 1741; Jonathan Parsons, "Account of the Revival at Lyme," in The Christian History for the Year 1743, ed. Thomas Prince (Boston, 1744), 143; Diary of Joshua Hempstead, 378.

[15] Boston Evening Post, Aug. 2, 1742; Boston Weekly Post-Boy, Sept. 28, 1741; Charles Chauncy, Enthusiasm Described and Cautioned Against: A Sermon Preached at the Old Brick Meeting-House in Boston, the Lord's Day after the Commencement 1742 (Boston, 1742), 5-9.

There was some justification for these descriptions, but they also involved significant distortions, as for instance in their suggesting that religious dissent was rooted in prior occupational and geographic associations. When information about the 115 individuals who would eventually form the New London Separate church is compiled, no clear geographic or occupational pattern appears. The geographic range of the group was remarkable. While at least eight dissident families lived in the densely populated town center, six came from Niantic, and three others from the north parish. At least one dissident, and probably more, commuted across the Thames River from Groton. Several were recent arrivals in town, including Curtis from Wethersfield, Michael Hill from Guilford, and Daniel Whitemore from Boston. The occupational range was similarly diverse. The group contained farmers, merchants, small tradesmen, craftsmen, and at least one day laborer. While none of the town's wealthiest men joined in the dissent, the "idle poor" appeared equally immune.[16]

Far more important than common occupation or residence in distinguishing the dissenters were demographic and kinship connections. Like revival converts in other New England towns, many were young, and a substantial proportion (46 percent) were male. The age differential between separatists and the Congregationalists is striking: at 25.3 years old, the average male separatist was nearly 20 years younger than the average Congregationalist; the average age for female separatists (including many mothers) was 29.8, 12 years below the average among Congregationalist women. Family connections provided the strongest pull toward separatism—a finding confirming recent studies that point to the family as the primary carrier of religious piety in New England. An extraordinary number of separatists were related to each other; comparatively few were connected with Congregationalists. Of sixty-seven married dissidents, forty-two were married to other separatists and only three to regular church members. Maternal connections were particularly important. Most separatist teenagers—including an equal number of boys and girls—joined along with their parents, particularly their mothers.[17]

349

[16] The reconstruction of the separatist church membership is based on county court documents. See memorial of Christopher Christophers et al., [late 1742], "Meeting House" file, miscellaneous papers 1700–1855 box, New London County Court Records (Connecticut State Library); petition from Separates signifying choice of Timothy Allen and John Curtis as teachers, Nov. 1742, ibid.; and Separates' subscriptions before the county court, Nov. 27, 1742, Feb. 1743, ibid. To determine residences, we used the published sources cited in notes 9 and 10 and genealogies, New London County probate records, and records of the New London First Church of Christ and the Montville Congregational Church located at the Connecticut State Library. For a summary of Separates' tax assessments for 1733 and 1749, see Onuf, "New Lights in New London," 638.
[17] Family connections for separatists and regular church members were reconstructed with the aid of the superb genealogical collections at the Connecticut State Library. Particularly useful was Charles Dyer Parkhurst, "Early Families of New London and Vicinity," photocopy (Connecticut State Library). Three extended families—Shapleys, Caulkinses, and Rogerses (cousins of the Rogerene line)—and three other related nuclear families—headed by Ebenezer Howard, George Richards, and Nathan Howard—included over half of the native New Londoners in the separatist church. On the importance of family to religion, see Philip Greven, The Protestant Temperament: Patterns of Child-Rearing, Religious Experience, and the Self in Early America (New York, 1977); and Gerald F. Moran and Maris A. Vinovskis, "The Puritan Family and Religion: A Critical Reappraisal," William and Mary Quarterly, 39 (Jan. 1982), 29–63. The data on the separatists are summarized in Onuf, "New Lights in New London," 636.

Although many of the dissident families had lived in New London as long as Congregational families had, they were not well entrenched in the religious or civil hierarchies of town life. Unlike converts in other Connecticut towns, most were not church members before 1741, nor did they come from families who traced a long ancestry in the Congregational church. If not of the "lowest Rank," they were poorer than established church members and held no important offices in town government. Curtis, their lay leader, had a long history of quarrels with established authority before his arrival in New London. He prepared for the ministry at Yale and in 1727 received a unanimous invitation to settle at Glastonbury. The call was, in effect, withdrawn, however, when the local ministerial association refused to ordain him. Curtis's subsequent success as a merchant led him to New London where he was treasurer of the New London Society of Trade and Commerce. But once again, the intervention of authority—this time the General Assembly, which outlawed the society's bills—led to a serious setback in Curtis's career.[18]

Although shared religious concerns drew Curtis and his fellow dissidents together, their youth, lack of connections with the church, and location on the periphery of New London society prepared them to express their new-found piety outside the established church. The tendency toward separation grew when their enthusiasm began to alienate older, more respectable members. Still, before Davenport's visit in July 1741 they probably did not contemplate a complete break with the church. Their radicalism was limited, and they needed support ·from within the ministerial establishment to justify a separation from the church. Until Davenport's arrival visiting revivalists had treated Adams as an "eminent servant of God," thus connecting the revivals with the regular church as a cooperative ministerial effort. Davenport exploded that connection in New London (as he had exploded similar connections elsewhere) when he labeled Adams a "carnal Pharisee" not fit to minister to the true converts in his flock. This was exactly what his audience was ready to hear. At the same time the accusation rendered Davenport a traitor to his own class. When the ministry destroyed its own authority, as Old Lights claimed that Davenport and his New Light friends were doing, chaos and disorder would surely follow. *"If the Shepherds are divided, the sheep will be scattered."*[19]

<code>350</code>

---

[18] Major town offices are recorded in Frances M. Caulkins, comp., "Town Officers of New London," typescript (New London County Historical Society, New London). Between 1700 and 1750 no separatist served in a high town office (selectman, deputy, justice of the peace, clerk, assessor, treasurer, moderator); Congregationalists served a total of eighty-four terms. Separatists such as Daniel Shapley, Daniel Starr, Peter Harris, and Christopher Christophers served the town as fence menders, highway surveyors, and hog reeves. Christophers, Yale graduate and scion of a distinguished New London family, later achieved local prominence as a sheriff. John Curtis had the most distinguished public career of any separatist: he sat in the General Assembly before and after his sojourn in New London (for Wethersfield, 1725-1731, and Canterbury, 1760-1764). No separatist could be counted a town or church leader before or during the Awakening. See Franklin B. Dexter, ed., *Biographical Sketches of the Graduates of Yale College* (6 vols., New York, 1885-1912), I, 203-06, 573; and Caulkins, *History of New London*, 243-44.

[19] Williams to Wheelock, July 17, 1741, item 741417, Wheelock Papers; *Boston Weekly Post-Boy*, Sept. 28, 1741; Nathaniel Eels, *Religion is the Life of GOD's People: A Sermon Preach'd at Boston* (Boston, 1743), 29. Curtis and other leading dissidents continued to take communion with the Congregationalists until Davenport's visit. See Goen, *Revivalism and Separatism*, 20-21; and *Diary of Joshua Hempstead*, 385.

Davenport's attitude toward his vocation was more complex than his critics imagined. Because of his illustrious family background, he was ranked at the top of the class of 1732 at Yale College. The character of the Yale student body had begun to change during Davenport's student days: the proportion of graduates headed for the ministry was declining, and, unlike Davenport, many scholars with distinguished backgrounds and high class rankings chose careers in law, politics, or business. Davenport's college experience was shaped by this diversification of career orientations and by the declining status and prospects of future ministers. Plenty of pulpits were available in Connecticut, but these were located predominantly in new parishes in poor, underpopulated frontier areas.[20] To accept a low-paying pulpit in an obscure country town must have seemed tantamount to forfeiting the prestige and status associated with a college education.

Davenport and his friends were nonetheless determined to become preachers. To support each other in their commitment, these pious students formed religious clubs. The clubs attested to the changing character of the student body; they also betrayed a growing suspicion of the purposes and piety of school authorities. Pious students with a ministerial vocation increasingly found themselves in an adversary relationship with the college. David Brainerd reportedly stated that tutor Chauncey Whittlesey had no more grace than a chair. They taught themselves to distinguish between spiritual truths and the Yale curriculum. According to Timothy Allen, who would soon migrate to New London, "I WANTED NOT HUMAN LEARNING, in order *to declare the will of GOD to the World.*"[21] Davenport, Timothy Allen, and other future

351

[20] Dexter, ed., *Biographical Sketches*, I, 447-50. Class rankings were based on social credentials, not academic merit. See Clifford K. Shipton, "Ye Mystery of Ye Ages Solved, or How Placing Worked at Colonial Harvard and Yale," *Harvard Alumni Bulletin*, 57 (1954-55), 258-59, 262-63. Of the forty-five graduates of the Yale classes of 1728-1737 who became ministers in Connecticut, only eleven, less than a quarter, were ranked in the top half of their classes. Of the forty-three pre-1728 graduates still preaching in the late 1740s, twenty-two (51 percent) had placed in the top half of their classes. Dexter, *Biographical Sketches*, I. For general treatments of declining ministerial status, see John William T. Youngs, Jr., *God's Messengers: Religious Leadership in Colonial New England, 1700-1750* (Baltimore, 1976); James W. Schmotter, "Provincial Professionalism: The New England Ministry, 1692-1742" (Ph.D. diss., Northwestern University, 1973); Christopher M. Jedrey, *The World of John Cleaveland: Family and Community in Eighteenth-Century New England* (New York, 1979), 17-41; and Joseph A. Conforti, *Samuel Hopkins and the New Divinity Movement: Calvinism, the Congregational Ministry, and Reform in New England between the Great Awakenings* (Grand Rapids, 1981), 9-22. On Connecticut parishes, see Connecticut Historical Society, *A List of Congregational Ecclesiastical Societies* (n.p., n.d.); and *Contributions to the Ecclesiastical History of Connecticut* (2 vols., New Haven, 1861), I.

[21] Leonard Bacon, *Thirteen Historical Discourses on the Completion of Two Hundred Years, from the Beginning of the First Church in New Haven* (New Haven, 1839), 246; Charles Chauncy, *Seasonable Thoughts on the State of Religion in New England* (Boston, 1743), 213-15. Davenport was attached to a group of "gloomy young persons" who were admirers of David Ferris, a student from New Milford who had been a leader of the revival in that town in 1727. Ferris was older and more experienced than his acolytes. (He was nine years older than Davenport who, at age sixteen, was the youngest graduate in the history of Yale College.) The group also included Eleazar Wheelock—Davenport's future brother-in-law—and Benjamin Pomeroy—Wheelock's future brother-in-law (both class of 1733). Ferris never graduated, demonstrating an inspired and inspiring contempt for formal education. See *ibid.*; and Dexter, ed., *Biographical Sketches*, I, 378,

revivalists thus learned to distrust established institutions at the very time that they embraced their ministerial vocations. The adversary mode adopted at Yale would become an evangelical tool of unprecedented and unpredictable power.

But these pious dissidents were not necessarily enemies of established order. Dissidence was a necessary component of their vocation, and their vocation was to fill pulpits—and, from them, pews—to secure the hegemony of the church and traditional religious values in a period of rapid growth and expansion throughout the colony. They meant to be revivalists, and revivalism had long been the clergy's favorite panacea for immorality, pride, and (worst of all) indifference.[22]

352

At the outset of the Awakening, most clergymen would have agreed that what most needed reviving was their own professional morale and evangelical vocation. "Reformation must begin at the house of God," Gov. Jonathan Belcher of Massachusetts told Whitefield, at the beginning of the young English itinerant's wildly successful preaching tour through New England in 1740. "A dead ministry will always make a dead people," thought Whitefield. And yet, he exulted, many preachers appeared to be coming to life under his ministrations. When Whitefield left Connecticut in 1740, William Gaylord of Wilton wrote that he had been "received by the generality of the ministers in these parts with sincere respect love and joy." The great itinerant had been "an instrument of much good among us, especially by stirring up ministers." Indeed, the first and most enduring phase of the Awakening coupled a new popular interest in religion with a revival in the ministry itself. Whitefield imparted the secret of his own astonishing evangelical successes to admiring colleagues: they must experience a New Birth themselves before they could call forth that experience in their flocks.[23] Davenport was among the many preachers who took this message to heart.

Davenport had accepted a call to the Congregational church at Southold, Long Island, in 1738. Southold was one of the most important parishes in the eastern part of the island where the cultural influence of Connecticut, across Long Island Sound, had long predominated. The Long Island towns were closely linked by trade and family with New London, the leading Connecticut port. Thus it was no accident that Davenport's spiritual travels and travails in New England should begin—and end—at New London. It was at Southold in 1740 that Davenport, stirred by an inspirational meeting with Whitefield in New York City, conducted his first revival meetings and experimented with

439, 447, 485-88, 493-99, 551. Student pietists felt compelled to meet in secret. Their sense of suspicious isolation is apparent in the complaint by Timothy Allen (another key figure in the New London events) that "there are those who continually watch for my halting." Appropriately, the letter was intercepted by college authorities. See Chauncy, *Seasonable Thoughts*, 215.

[22] James Walsh, "The Pure Church in Eighteenth Century Connecticut" (Ph.D. diss., Columbia University, 1967), 53-55.

[23] *George Whitefield's Journals* (London, 1960), 475; *Boston Gazette*, March 16, 1742; William Gaylord to Wheelock, Nov. 24, 1740, item 740624, Wheelock Papers. On George Whitefield's career in America, see William Howland Kenney III, "George Whitefield, Dissenter Priest of the Great Awakening," *William and Mary Quarterly*, 26 (Jan. 1969), 75-93.

new evangelical rhetorical techniques that he would take to unprecedented extremes.[24]

Davenport's chief contributions to the new evangelicalism flowed from his adversarial attitude toward the establishment—born at Yale and nurtured by Whitefield. "The more I am opposed the more joy I feel," Whitefield wrote in 1740. "O this is pleasant," echoed Davenport in 1741, "to suffer Reproach for the Blessed Jesus." But while Whitefield, following Tennent, attacked unconverted ministers *as a class* in order to bring about the ministerial revival that was a necssary precondition to a general reformation, Davenport discovered that attacks on the spiritual condition of *particular* ministers produced conversions among the people. Davenport's first task was to silence the voice of established authority. In every parish along his route he demanded an audience with the settled pastor. Invariably dissatisfied with the pastor's account of his spiritual condition, Davenport then led public prayers for his conversion. The logic of his evangelicalism led to an extraordinary inversion. Traditional exhortations to the ministry to revive itself had been premised on the spiritual preeminence and leadership of the clergy—even Whitefield hoped to work through the clergy—but Davenport's success depended on the unregenerate status of his colleagues. Indeed, in the new order the spiritual pretensions of born-again laymen were inherently more credible than the claims of "hireling" (tax-supported) preachers. "There is every place some dear X⁼ [Christians]," according to Davenport's lay speaking companion Hill, "but they are all most starved with dead preachers."[25]

Davenport's preaching was an extension of the techniques he had learned from Whitefield. But these techniques were radically transformed when he lifted them out of their original context. As the evangelical campaign moved out-of-doors, Davenport betrayed his clerical associates by making "his *private* judgment the ground of *Public* Actions." (Italics added.) He exploited anticlericalism for evangelical purposes, thereby tapping popular religious impulses that had never been adequately expressed. In their struggle against the supposed enemies of the Awakening, Davenport and his angry allies were freed from powerful cultural restraints against insubordination and contentiousness. Parsons—a prorevival preacher who, like Adams, would soon run afoul of Davenport—preferred "strife" to "quietness in the churches with a corrupt ministry." As the New Haven separatists reputedly claimed, "*where any Congregation is in Peace, the Devil is their Ruler.*" For most in the minis-

353

[24] James Davenport to Wheelock, Oct. 5, 1740, item 740555, Wheelock Papers; Chauncy, *Seasonable Thoughts*, 189–91; *George Whitefield's Journals*, 416–17; Daniels, *Connecticut Town*, 146–49. For a description of evangelical techniques, see Harry S. Stout, "Religion, Communications, and the Ideological Origins of the American Revolution," *William and Mary Quarterly*, 34 (Oct. 1977), 519–41.

[25] *New England Weekly Journal* (Boston), May 20, 1740; Chauncy, *Seasonable Thoughts*, 153–54; Gilbert Tennent, *The Danger of an Unconverted Ministry* (Philadelphia, 1741); Williams to Wheelock, July 17, 1741, item 741417, Wheelock Papers; Michael Hill to Philemon Robbins, Aug. 30, 1742, Robbins Papers (Connecticut Historical Society, Hartford). For accounts of Davenport in Connecticut, see *Boston Weekly Post-Boy*, Aug. 10, Sept. 28, Oct. 5, 1741. Davenport's attacks are a central theme in Chauncy, *Seasonable Thoughts*.

terial profession, the risks attached to these strategies were unacceptable: itinerant revivalists threatened to "make the *Relation*, between *Passors and People*, a *meer Nothing*, a *Sound without Meaning*."[26]

Because he was denied access to most pulpits—and because his audiences were too large to squeeze into most churches anyway—Davenport, like other popular revivalists, preached in physical settings as subversive to established order as was the message itself. He preached the danger of unconverted ministers in everyday places such as fields, orchards, and barns—places lacking any sacred pretense save that invested in them by the participants. The church buildings stood as symbols of spiritual deadness and hostility. In like manner, sacred time as traditionally defined ceased to exist under Davenport's dispensation. He held meetings every day of the week, and at any time, although he apparently considered nighttime particularly propitious for true worship. Ordinary pursuits came to a sudden halt. Joshua Hempstead found that his hay had not been cut at Stonington: "all hands have been hearing Mr. Davenport th[i]s week." Revival meetings, Charles Chauncy complained, were held at the expense of "the Religion of the Family at home." Enthusiasts "continue abroad 'till late in the Night, and so as to unfit themselves for the Services of the following day."[27]

More than had any of his itinerant predecessors, Davenport exploited music as an important outlet for communal speech. New Englanders had traditionally sung psalms, but extrabiblical singing had never occupied the central place in worship that it did for Davenport and his followers. Davenport's "New songs" diverged widely from the colonial psalter. They were ecstatically christocentric and otherworldly, as this stanza from *A Song of Praise* shows.

> I see thy Face, I hear thy Voice,
> I taste thy sweetest Love;
> My Soul doth leap: But O for Wings
> the Wings of *Noah*'s Dove!
> Then should I flee far hence away,
> Leaving this World of Sin:
> Then should my Lord put forth his Hand,
> And kindly take me in.

The music also conveyed anger and confrontation. Of all the disorderly practices of Davenport's followers, singing in the streets, at the top of their lungs—often at night—was most disturbing to public order. Enthusiasts broke into song on any and every occasion. According to one report, Davenport's "manner, with those that follow him is to Sing as he goes to the Places of Worship, and returns from it. . . . When the Sermon is ended he calls aloud to the People to come unto the Lord Jesus Christ . . . he acknowledges them true Disciples, welcomes them into the Kingdom of Christ, and sings a Hymn over them: *A custom that we have not known, nor the Churches of God*." Through music Davenport's audience emerged from isolation and anonymity to occupy

---

[26] Davenport, *Confession and Retractions*, 54; Youngs, *God's Messengers*, 126; *Boston Weekly Post-Boy*, March 1, 1742; Chauncy, *Seasonable Thoughts*, 51.

[27] *Diary of Joshua Hempstead*, 380; Chauncy, *Seasonable Thoughts*, 301.

center stage in town life. Their songs expressed the solidarity they had discovered in the revival.[28]

Davenport preached his extraordinary message at extraordinary times and places. Still, all might have been forgiven—in the heat of a revival—had his solicitude for souls abeen combined with a due respect for the interests of religion in general, notably the prerogatives and preeminence of the ministry. But Davenport's overtly anticlerical evangelicalism implied a fundamental reorganization of the churches in favor of greater lay participation in worship. His subversive intentions were equally apparent in his contempt for traditional rhetorical conventions.

Before the Great Awakening most college-trained ministers agreed that public speaking must be "studied" and was necessarily distinct from spontaneous—*ex tempore*—speech. Carefully prepared notes assured an orderly progression from "doctrine" to "uses" or "applications." Although plain in vocabulary and syntax, pulpit speech was clearly distinguished from vulgar, everyday language. Ministers were enjoined to keep "to the substance of their Sermons and keep to their Notes"; parishioners were enjoined to sit still and listen.[29] But Davenport dispensed with notes, logical sequence, and the traditional captive audience in order to create a new form of speech in which the people were encouraged—indeed, required—to speak out in their own idiom. In like manner he disregarded the rules of pulpit decorum.

Colonial rhetoricians paid as much attention to gesture or delivery as to speech itself. Whether the standard was Ramist or Ciceronian, educated clergymen were taught that sublime subject matter required grave and restrained delivery. According to a preacher's manual written by Cotton Mather that was a gift to all Harvard graduates, "A *Well prepared* Sermon should be a *Well pronounced* One. Wherefore, Avoid forever, all *Inanes fine Mente Sonos*; and all *Indecencies*, everything that is *Ridiculous*. Be sure to speak *Deliberately*. Strike the *Accent* always upon that *Word* in the sentence which it properly belongs unto."[30]

Davenport's vulgar delivery, his critics thought, was more appropriate to the stage than to the pulpit. One commentator observed that "His *Gestures* in preaching are *theatrical*, his *Voice tumultous*, his whole Speech and Behavior

355

[28] James Davenport, "A Song of Praise," in *The Great Awakening: Documents Illustrating the Crisis and Its Consequences*, ed. Alan Heimert and Perry Miller (Indianapolis, 1967), 202–03; *Boston Weekly Post-Boy*, Aug. 10, 1741; Cyclone Covey, "Puritanism and Music in Colonial America," *William and Mary Quarterly*, 8 (July 1951), 378–88.

[29] Stout, "Religion, Communications, and the Ideological Origins of the American Revolution," 528–30; Jacob Eliot to Wheelock, Oct. 5, 1741, item 741475, Wheelock Papers. Eliphalet Adams cautioned in his ordination sermon, "Noise and Loudness and a great deal of Bustle and Adoe in the delivering of Things, tho' it may take Strangely with some injudicious People, yet it will be of little real service, if care not be taken at the Same time to Digest and Dispose what is Delivered into a proper Method." Eliphalet Adams, *The Work of Ministers Rightly to Divide the Word of Truth* (New London, 1725), 12.

[30] Cotton Mather, *Manuducia ad Ministerium: Directions for a Candidate of the Ministry* (Boston, 1726), 105; Eugene E. White, *Puritan Rhetoric: The Issue of Emotion in Religion* (Carbondale, Ill., 1972), 206.

discovering the *Freaks of Madness*, and *wilds of Enthusiasm*." The same criticisms applied to Davenport's method of prayer. According to another observer, Davenport worked himself up "into the most extravagant Gesture and Behaviour both in Prayer and Preaching—His expressions in Prayer are often indecently familiar." Indeed, Davenport had rejected everything he was taught about ministerial speech and deportment. He made himself speak in an idiom that he could share with his audiences. It was Davenport's theatrical concept of his vocation that was so incomprehensible to his contemporaries. "Were you to see him in his most violent Agitations, you would be apt to think, that he was a Madman just broke from his chains," according to one newspaper account. Davenport drew his admirers into his drama: he walked the streets "with a large mob at his heels, singing all the way." Indeed, it was his performance in a crowd and the crowd's response that attracted most comment. "They look'd more like a company of *Bacchanalians* after a mad Frolick, than sober Christians who had been worshipping God."[31] Sacred usage could not be distinguished from secular usage. Everything Davenport said was vulgar and offensive to his critics; yet there was a chilling method to this madness. If everyday language could be sacralized, everyman could speak it. One man's insanity could not topple the New England Way: an alternative order—most notably apparent in the joint careers of Davenport and the New London separatists—was what the establishment feared.

When Davenport arrived in New London in July 1741, he discovered an audience prepared for his new style. Joshua Hempstead's diary captured the confusion at the meeting house when Davenport first led New Londoners in worship.

Diverse women were terrified and cried out exceedingly. When Mr. Davenport had dismissed the congregation some went out and others stayed; he then went out into the broad alley, which was much crowded, and there he screamed out, "Come to Christ! come to Christ! come away! come away!" Then he went into the third pew on the women's side, and kept there, sometimes singing, sometimes praying; he and his companions all taking their turns, and the women fainting and in hysterics. This confusion continued till ten o'clock at night, and then he went off singing through the streets.

Gone were the traditional distinctions between preacher and parishioner, pulpit and pew. One heard a cacophony of voices speaking, singing, and testifying in no discernible order. The *Boston Weekly Post-Boy* noted how

a great Part of their carryings on was not by Praying, Singing and preaching upon a Text as usual; but one would make a short prayer, then another would give a Word of Exhortation, and so on without any certain Order or Method, so that in one Meeting of 2 or 3 Hours, there would be it may be, 20 or 30 distinct exercises carried on by 5 or 10 distinct Persons; some standing in the Pulpit, some in the Body of Seats, some in the Pews and some up Gallery; and oftentimes several of them would speak together; So that, some praying, some exhorting and terrifying. Some singing, some screaming, some crying, some laughing and some scolding, made the most amazing Confusion that was ever heard.

[31] *Boston Evening Post*, Aug. 2, July 5, 1742.

The loudest note was struck by the cries of terrified women; lay companions played a conspicuous role. The injunction to "come away"—from the unregenerate church—"to Christ" was a recurring motif.[32]

The assertive role played by the audience at New London is revealed time and again by references to the noise produced. The Anglican Ebenezer Punderson noted with amazement how many listeners "were *struck* as the phrase is, and made the most terrible and affecting noise, that was heard a mile from the place."[33] The use of speaking companions drew much adverse comment. By giving people with no particular claim to authority free rein at public address, Davenport reversed the conventional flow of speech in public assemblies. The right to speak was a gift of the Holy Spirit, dispensed without regard to social position, sex, or age. Anyone was a potential public speaker.

Davenport and his friends discovered new identities for themselves in the New Birth. "The Spirit of God, they say, witnesses with their spirits that they are converted and born again," Samuel Seabury reported.[34] These New Lights created a new kind of community in their shared experience and in their contempt for the pretensions of temporal authority. This community rested on its own rhetorical foundation, a revolutionary new language of worship.

In Southold, Davenport had segregated born-again "brothers" from their unconverted "neighbors." A similar purification in New London required withdrawal from the Congregational church. On November 29, 1741, four months after Davenport's first visit, five prominent dissidents—Curtis, John Hempstead (Joshua Hempstead's son), Peter Harris, Christopher Christophers, and John Christophers—absented themselves from communion at the Congregational church.[35] This was the break Davenport had helped to prepare them for: they denied not only the efficacy of Adams's preaching but also the sacramental monopoly of the regular church. New Lights no longer needed to detour through the established church; they were ready to establish a church of their own that would serve as a prototype for other "true converts" throughout the land.

In the summer of 1742 with the Separate church meeting openly (if not yet legally), Timothy Allen arrived with his wife Mary Allen from West Haven to set up the Shepherd's Tent. Like Curtis and Davenport, Timothy Allen had also run into trouble with the ministerial establishment. A 1736 Yale graduate, Timothy Allen had been an intimate of Davenport and his pious friends (who probably included fellow New London Separate Christopher Christophers from the class of 1737) while preparing for the ministry. He accepted a call to West Haven in 1738 but was dismissed by the church and censured by the Old Light county ministerial association in 1742 because of

---

[32] Caulkins, *History of New London*, 450; *Boston Weekly Post-Boy*, Sept. 28, 1741. The entry for July 18, 1741, is mangled in *Diary of Joshua Hempstead*, 379. The best account of Davenport's activities in New London is still Tracy, *Great Awakening*, 230-55.

[33] Oscar Zeichner, *Connecticut's Years of Controversy, 1750-1776* (Chapel Hill, 1949), 22.

[34] Hallam, *Annals of St. James Church*, 36.

[35] Goen, *Revivalism and Separatism*, 20-21; *Diary of Joshua Hempstead*, 385. The date is incorrectly given as 1742 by Caulkins, *History of New London*, 452. She also substitutes John Harris for John Hempstead, son of the diarist.

his enthusiastic prorevivalism. Timothy Allen and Curtis had been trained as ministers but had been rejected by the establishment. With Christopher Christophers they constituted the educated but alienated leadership of the new church. They shared the popular enthusiasm for Davenport's preaching; they also had shared Davenport's experience with the established church. A division of labor naturally followed: Davenport continued his itinerations, while they remained in New London as teachers.[36]

During its brief existence, the Shepherd's Tent provided a vital nucleus for the Separate church. Students preparing for itinerant careers—reportedly including young women as well as men—took a leading role in Separate worship. Admission was dependent on spiritual, rather than academic or sexual credentials. But these standards were rigorously selected, as one young would-be student discovered. According to Joshua Hempstead's diary:

> Natt Williams of Stonington Lodged here [at Hempstead's]. He went over in the Evening to Mr. [Michael] Hills alia [Timothy] allins at the House that was Samuel Harris's (now ye Shephards Tent) and thare Related his Christian Experiences in order to have their approbation but behold the Quite Contrary, for they upon Examination find him yet in an unconverted Estate & Judged him So & he Confesses the Justice of their Judgement & says that he hath Judged others Divers times and altho he is unwilling to believe it yet like others he is forced to bear it.[37]

Those who passed the spiritual screening were, like members of the Separate church, drawn from a wide geographic range. Young enthusiasts were attracted from as far away as West Haven, Windham, and Middletown, Connecticut, and West Springfield, Massachusetts. Common religious goals, not common occupations or prior familiarity, brought the community together.[38]

In addition to serving the Separate church, the Shepherd's Tent was intended to serve as a link between the New London revival and the rest of the awakened world. As long as the revivals continued to flourish, the outer-directed function of the school as the vanguard of lay evangelicalism was as important as its internal mission to the New London converts.

Davenport solicited contributions for the seminary during his travels, much as Whitefield had collected for his Georgia orphanage. Established ministers recognized the importance of the Shepherd's Tent and other New Light seminaries to the radicals' revival. They charged that Whitefield and his allies meant to "introduce a Sett of Ministers into our Churches, by other Ways and Means of Education." These usurpers would be trained at foreign universities —"the Orphan-House in Georgia, or the Shepherd's Tent." Unlike Harvard or Yale, however, these New Light schools were mere "Castles or Colleges in the

[36] Dexter, ed., *Biographical Sketches*, I, 203-06, 551-55; Benjamin Trumbull, *A Complete History of Connecticut, Civil and Ecclesiastical from the Emigration of Its First Planters from England in the Year 1630, to the Year 1764; and to the Close of the Indian Wars* (2 vols., New Haven, 1818), II, 195-96; Caulkins, *History of New London*, 243-44; West Haven First Congregational Church Records, vol. 1, Jan. 12, 1742 (Connecticut State Library).

[37] *Diary of Joshua Hempstead*, 405. See also the discussion in Richard Warch, "The Shepherd's Tent: Education and Enthusiasm in the Great Awakening," *American Quarterly*, 30 (Summer 1978), 188-89.

[38] See note 16.

Air." The Shepherd's Tent, for instance, had no grounding in classi   n-
ing, apparently no library (at least after March 1743), and no printed curriculum. It rejected the traditional organization of the New England colleges and
disdained their historic function, to outfit gentlemen for professional careers
in church and state. Instead its model, growing from the Separate church, was
the extended family, with Timothy Allen *in loco parentis* and the teen-age
students as the children.[39]

The New London Separates were recognized as legal dissenters (from
Congregationalism) by the New London County Court in November 1742,
almost a full year after the separation. Yet, at the very time when the
machinery for universal revival seemed fully engaged and ready to conquer,
ominous signs appeared from the outside. In May 1742 the Connecticut assembly had outlawed itinerancy, thus dividing the clergy into New Light and Old
Light factions. While this could not directly threaten the Separate church once
it was legally recognized, it did endanger lay exhorters and therefore the
evangelical mission of the Shepherd's Tent. Local authorities invoked the law
to harass the New London separatists: in June, Peter Thatcher, "a Stranger &
an Exhorter," was driven across the river to Groton (though the constable
there allowed him to return to New London, where he carried on more dis-
creetly), and in August, Timothy Allen was "Committed to Prison on his not
Procureing Sufficient Security for His Good Behavior," according to the
provision's of the law. The law thus had a sudden "chilling" effect on the
revival circuit and tended to isolate the radical New Lights in New London.[40]

Davenport also encountered increased hostility from civil and ecclesiastical
authorities. In 1741 when the Awakening was still in high gear, Davenport's
extreme tactics had met with great success. No one could deny that he had
brought many new members into the churches. His "Glorious Success
surpasses even any Mr. Tennent or Whitefield have recorded," reported
Andrew Croswell, in what Connecticut church records show to be an understatement. By 1742 the situation had changed dramatically. Itinerant New
Lights discovered they could not sustain the high level of religious fervor
indefinitely, and with the return to normality, most of them (save Davenport)
returned to their neglected flocks. In Connecticut, moreover, the anti-
itinerancy legislation effectively disestablished unauthorized itinerants by
threatening to deprive them of their home parish rates. Twice in 1742 Davenport was arrested and tried for disturbing the peace and inciting rebellion: his
crime was in his speech. Both times, in recognition of his distinguished
pedigree as well as of his powerful popular support, Davenport was treated
leniently. Authorities in Hartford and in Boston determined that he was

[39] *Boston Evening Post*, Aug. 2, 1742; *The Declaration of the Rector and Tutors of Yale-College
in New Haven Against the Reverend Mr. George Whitefield. His Principles and Designs. in a
Letter to Him* (Boston, 1745), 10; Samuel Niles, *Tristitiae Ecclesiarum. or. a Brief and Sorrowful
Account of the Present State of the Churches in New England* (Boston, 1745), 6.

[40] Entries no. 334, 338 for Nov. 23, 1742, term, Trial Dockets, 1729–1815, vol. 20, New London
County Court Records; *Boston News-Letter*, Dec. 16, 1742; *Diary of Joshua Hempstead*, 395, 405;
Warch, "Shepherd's Tent," 188–89; entry of June 26, 1742, New London County Justice of the
Peace Court Records, 1739–1779 (Connecticut State Library).

"non compos mentis"—out of his mind—and deported him. How else could they explain Davenport's betrayal of his own class?[41]

Davenport's effectiveness as an itinerant evangelist was further curtailed by the universal censure of his fellow ministers, including most New Lights. At a time when popular deference to an educated clergy still ran high, Davenport's success depended in part on his ambiguous status as a minister: he *was* admitted to ministerial studies to conduct his spiritual probings, and he *was* allowed to preach from most pulpits. Davenport's attacks on clergymen were powerful and persuasive because he spoke with the authority of an insider, positioned to see through the pretenses of unregenerate pastors. The regular clergy knew it had less to fear from Davenport as an outsider than from Davenport as a subversive working from within. In July 1742, Boston-area preachers —despite New Light sympathies—barred Davenport from their pulpits.[42] Other churches followed suit.

This professional ostracism released Davenport from any lingering scruples about attacking fellow preachers (now sight unseen), but it also denied him his position within the clerical fraternity. According to a report in the *Boston Evening Post*:

Mr. D–t I heard declare on the Hill near *Charlestown* Ferry, that *the greatest Part of the Ministers in this Country were unconverted, and that they were murdering of Souls by Thousands and by Millions.* In the Common I heard him say, *The greatest part* of the Ministers in Boston were *carnal unconverted men,* and exhort the people *to pray for the conversion of those miserable and wretched men.* At another Time, in the Common, I heard him say, The ministers of Boston *were going to Hell themselves, and drawing Multitudes after them.*

Though the wholesale condemnation of an altogether unconverted clergy was undoubtedly sensational to the thousands thronged in Boston Common, its impact was also bound to be ephemeral. If there were no longer any churches fit to join, or any converted ministers fit to hear, then what meaning could "revival" possibly have? What was left to revive? Thus, as Davenport repudiated the established churches, he necessarily ceased to be an effective evangelist, and the number of converts joining churches dwindled.[43]

Even as Congregational New Lights lined up against the "Persecuting laws" of 1742, their attitude toward revivalism became increasingly cautious and defensive. Davenport was their leading liability. Thus, just as the New London Separatists cut their remaining ties with the regular church and were perse-

[41] Charles J. Hoadly, ed., *The Public Records of the Colony of Connecticut* (15 vols., Hartford, 1850-1890), VIII, 454-57; *Boston Weekly Post-Boy,* Oct. 5, 1741; *Boston News-Letter,* Aug. 26, 1743; Ecclesiastical section, vol. 7, pp. 252-57, Connecticut Archives (Connecticut State Library). An analysis of extant church records in the Connecticut State Library shows that admissions to churches in parishes visited by Davenport in the month after his visit were 5.6 times the monthly average for the rest of the year. Wheelock, the next most successful itinerant, produced a 50 percent increase in admissions. See Peter Onuf, "Preachers and Politics: The Great Awakening in Connecticut," 1980 (in possession of Peter Onuf), 186.

[42] *The Declaration of a Number of the Associated Pastors of Boston and Charles-town relating to the Rev. Mr. James Davenport and His Conduct* (Boston, 1742), 3-4.

[43] *Boston Evening Post,* Aug. 2, 1742; Moran, "Puritan Saint," 248.

cuted by civil authorities, Davenport became more and more isolated from his
ministerial colleagues, including former friends. This parallel withdrawal—
partly voluntary, partly involuntary in both cases—drew Davenport and the
New London Separates closer together. We are "a little flock of Lambs, greatly
opposed especially since our Dear Brother Davenport was here," Curtis wrote
Eleazar Wheelock.[44] The evangelical hopes of 1741 began to give way to
feelings of isolation, fear, and anger in an increasingly hostile world.

As most New England communities returned to their normal course of
business in late 1742 and 1743, the Separates were faced with a crisis of identity they could not survive: was their pure church supposed to be an institution *in* the world, or was it to be the final, radical denial of this world? They
were not the first to confront this contradiction; it was the quintessential
"Puritan dilemma."[45] As long as the world listened and the revival flourished,
priority was given to the evangelical goal of spearheading a general reformation. When the world stopped listening, as it apparently had by late 1742, the
character of religious radicalism in New London also changed. If this world
was beyond help, the Separates' piety required that they reject it and turn their
eyes to the world to come.

361

The new apocalyptic note was sounded by Davenport during his 1742 tour.
With no established churches left to revive, and with, in the words of Davenport's companion Hill, all the ministers "bound in one bundle" to persecute
"all True Lovers of Jesus," Davenport turned to the millennium for perspective. Millennial speculations and concern with the next world were not unique
to Davenport. According to Samuel Cooke of Stratfield, the reborn "Believer
treads the Moon under his Feet, looks with Contempt on all the Sublunary
World, with its Pleasures, Profits and Honours." But again, it was a question
of degree. Whereas Jonathan Edwards and other New Lights optimistically
pointed to ministerial revivals as a sign of impending glory, Davenport pointed
to the ministry's failure as a sign of coming destruction and conflagration.
While preaching in Stratford, Davenport terrified his listeners "by pretending
some *extraordinary discovery & assurance* of the very near approach of the *end
of the world*; and that tho' he didn't assign the *very day*, yet that he then had it
clearly open'd to him, and strongly impressed upon his mind, that in a very
short time all these things will be involv'd in devouring flames."[46]

Meanwhile, by early 1743 an apocalyptic mood had also descended on the
Separates. "Truly in God's Light we see Light!" Timothy Allen exclaimed,
"this has let me into the most wonderfull, wonderfull views of Richest, Richest, freest Grace of God; Oh the Grace! Oh the Grace! My soul sees Oceans,

[44] John Curtis to Wheelock, Oct. 15, 1741, item 741565, Wheelock Papers; Richard L. Bushman,
From Puritan to Yankee: Character and the Social Order in Connecticut. 1690-1765 (Cambridge,
Mass., 1967), 235-66.

[45] Edmund S. Morgan, *The Puritan Dilemma: The Story of John Winthrop* (Boston, 1958).

[46] Samuel Cooke, *Divine Sovereignty in the Salvation of Sinners consider'd and improv'd in a
SERMON Preach'd before the Eastern Association of Fairfield County, on a Publick Lecture in
Danbury. July 29th, 1741* (Boston, 1741), 37; Hill to Robbins, Aug. 30, 1742, Robbins Papers;
Boston Weekly News-Letter, July 1, 1742. For Jonathan Edwards's millennialism, see Stephen J.
Stein, ed., *Apocalyptic Writings* (New Haven, 1977).

boundless Oceans of Grace." Anger also suffused this mood. His friends had a growing sense of the "unspeakable vileness of their Natures" and were prepared to spurn worldly possessions as a "heap of Stuff." "The blessed Lord seems to be coming to get to himself a Kingdom again," he predicted.[47] Davenport and the New London Separates together would soon participate in the final crisis of Davenport's career as an itinerant evangelist.

During one of his rare visits to his own church at Southold, Davenport prepared to rise to the climactic occasion, to help the New Londoners purify themselves and their church. Joshua Hempstead happened to be in Southold on Sunday, February 27, 1743, and "went to Town to Meeting to hear Mr. Davenport." It was a typical performance: "the praying was without form or Comelyness. it was difficult to distinguish between his praying & preaching for it was all Meer Confused medley." During the meeting Davenport reported direct communications from God—"Concerning the Shepherds Tent & other Such things"—that required him to hurry back across Long Island Sound to New London. His return would be the ultimate test of the Separates' piety and commitment. With the Separates faced with so many unsympathetic souls and poised at the edge of Armageddon, a public repudiation of the world seemed not only desirable but, in its own way, even logical if they were to escape the "devouring flames" of eternity.[48]

Davenport arrived in New London on March 2. The book burning occurred on March 6, and personal possessions were apparently burned the following day. To the Separates the raging acts against social order made perfect sense. The book burning symbolized their separation from "heresy"—the false faith on which their society rested. The apparel signified "idolatry," and its destruction proclaimed their rejection of pride and worldly attachments.[49] With enemies all around, and with the fires of judgment imminent, what better way to manifest saving faith than to burn the symbols of society and, in so doing, escape eternal hellfire?

At the same time that the fires were symbolic of the Separates' disengagement from their society they were a catharsis that, once completed, purged their resentment and rage. No sooner were the acts completed than outside voices prevailed and persuaded many that they had gone too far. When Davenport pulled off his "Breeches" to cast them into the flames, a "young Sister" pulled them out and "sent them at him, with as much Indignation, as tho' they had been the Hire of a W[hore] or the Price of a Dog. . . ." A separatist "brother" from a "neighbouring Town" further cooled passions by suggesting that the bonfire itself was a golden calf the Separates were using to idolize their external purity and superiority. Davenport himself was apparently stricken by the accusations. Charged with having the "D[evi]l in him," he replied contritely that "He tho't so too," and added "that he was under the Influence of an evil Spirit, and that God had left him." Later, in a "public Recantation" he recalled how at the time of the burnings he was temporarily delirious—a

[47] Timothy Allen to Wheelock, Feb. 27, 1743, item 743177, Wheelock Papers.
[48] Diary of Joshua Hempstead, 406.
[49] Blake, Later History of the First Church, 130-32; Boston Weekly Post-Boy, March 28, 1743.

condition brought about by a "long Fever . . . and the cankry Humour [in his leg] raging at once."[50]

Within days of the burning, Davenport was left doubly alone. His friends in the ministry had forsaken him, and now he had forsaken his friends in New London. A friend reported that "he rides from town to town without any attendance [attendants]."[51] Timothy Allen also left town, and with his departure the Shepherd's Tent folded. Left without a leader—presumably Curtis was no longer able or willing to be one—the Separates lost their sense of communal identity and mission. Their community had been based on shared language and a common alienation from and rage against the social order. When their brief moment had passed, they could no longer speak to the larger culture, as they had, or even to each other. The church dissolved into diverse fragments: a few separatists returned to the established church; others became Baptists or joined the North New London separatist church; some left town.[52]

Opponents of the radicals orchestrated their responses on several fronts. On Wednesday, March 30, 1743, a ministerial council convened at Adams's home to consider what measures to take concerning "the disorders . . . subsisting among those Called New Lights." In addition to Edwards, the conclave included Solomon Williams, Benjamin Lord, Benjamin Pomeroy, Joseph Bellamy, Asher Rosseter, and Samuel Buell. Most, perhaps all, of these prominent prorevivalists had been popular itinerants at one time. But they needed to distance themselves from the New London "excesses" as much as Adams and the established church needed their immediate protection. On Thursday morning Edwards—playing Davenport's role for the other side—delivered a sermon bearing "Wittness against ye prevailing disorders and destractions yt [that] are subsisting in the Country by Means of Enthusiasm." The great concourse attending Edwards then "adjourned to ye Courthouse," where the great Puritan texts would be redeemed from the flames in a ritual demonstration of power and moral authority to counter the iconoclastic celebrations of March 6 and 7.[53]

On March 29 the county court had issued writs against the most conspicuous book burners who were still in town. The case against the book burners was continued to April 5, "present J. Hempstead justice of the Peace." The pathos of the separatists' position is apparent in their plea. Those under arrest consisted of conscientious dissenters who had "qualified at the County Court" and a few others "by them then called to assist as teachers and persons to join in worship with said Society; that on the day mentioned in the writ, they all with many others were assembled for worship accordingly and that they in their consciences were then persuaded that heretical books in their custody ought publicly to be burned, that they accordingly burned those they thought to be such, that the same was solemnized with prayer, and singing praises to God, and that nothing in itself immoral was committed by them

363

[50] Davenport, *Confession and Retractions*, 55; *Boston Weekly Post-Boy*, March 28, 1743.
[51] Sarah Pierpont to Wheelock, May 30, 1743, item 743330, Wheelock Papers.
[52] Onuf, "New Lights in New London," 642.
[53] *Diary of Joshua Hempstead*, 407; Warch, "Shepherd's Tent," 192–94.

therein—that in that burning, praying and singing in such their separate society, was what they then judged in their consciences *Duty* and agreeable to the word of God." The separatists simply wanted to worship God according to their own reading of Scripture; they disclaimed any "other view or motive." Yet they did not keep to themselves. In practical terms, the burnings meant that they were not prepared to accept their status as dissenters, though they claimed it in their own defense at the trial. They did not want their church to become just another of the many different churches that grew so luxuriantly in New London. Their piety, their quarrel with this world, ran too deep to accept such a compromise. It demanded a conspicuous public denunciation of the world. "Many others" were implicated in their acts—acts with powerful repercussions in New England society and culture.[54]

The campaign against the New London New Lights did not require severe penalties against the wrongdoers. The small fines against the book burners, "severally guilty of the profanation of the Sabbath," could hardly have contributed significantly to the collapse of the separatist movement, already well on its way.[55] Instead, the fines were only a small part of a coordinated response to "enthusiasm"; they were symbolic acts to match the symbolism of the book burning itself.

The drama of Davenport and the Separates had played itself out. No estates were confiscated; no lives were lost; no dangerous radicals were incarcerated in prisons. Those Separates who, before the revivals, were unchurched found their faith and melded into other religious societies. Their ideal was nothing more than the old religious order radically revived and purified, with themselves at center stage. Gov. Jonathan Law could complain that revivalists were thinly disguised social incendiaries, intoxicated by the "Doctrine of the Community of Goods" and bent on turning their world upside down, but these were inflated fears of distant possibilities, not actualities. In their defense the Separates invoked their religious "conscience." And that conscience was seared by the God of New England, who eventually gave them peace. Davenport also recovered from his ills and lived to preach (quietly) for fourteen more years until his death in 1757 at age forty-one.[56]

Yet, if religious radicalism at New London proved ephemeral, and seemed tame in comparison to the widespread popular tumults (and ritual burnings) a generation later, we can also see why fears ran so high in 1743. Contemporaries would recall with horror and amazement the peak of New London's hysteria and popular rage, not the ease with which it was suppressed. Events in New London showed how revivalism, the ministry's favorite panacea, could no longer be counted on to preserve order and harmony. Defenders of the traditional order recognized that the Separates were, if not typical, prototypical. More and more colonists, for a variety of social, religious, and economic reasons, were moving beyond the familiar, comfortable confines of

[54] Caulkins, *History of New London*, 456–57.
[55] *Ibid.*
[56] Onuf, "New Lights in New London," 642; Bernard Lord Manning, *The Protestant Dissenting Deputies*, ed. Omerod Greenwood (Cambridge, Eng., 1952), 412.

community life. By successfully calling into question the integrity of the religious establishment and enjoining these people to act for themselves, Davenport demonstrated how tenuous were the bonds of social order and how fragile traditional controls could be in a rapidly changing society. His words and actions opened a Pandora's box that could never be shut tight. Thus the character of the Awakening that Davenport and his followers created at New London cannot be understood simply as an attempt to recreate a golden age of piety.[57] Instead, this Awakening—which released so much anger and discord—offered a glimpse into things as they were and were becoming in a world at war with itself.

[57] Jon Butler has called into question broad interpretations of the Great Awakening that emphasize religious radicalism and its social implications. The present study does not question the traditionalist sources of revival piety: religious—and political—radicalism in eighteenth-century America were grounded in efforts to preserve and revitalize traditional values. Nonetheless, the Awakening did constitute a major break in the history of revivalism. While the New London case is hardly typical, it does enable us to see why the religious establishment found "enthusiasm" so disturbing and why contemporaries perceived this revival to be so radically different from its predecessors. The redefinition of revivalism by New Light radicals and their Old Light critics reflected epochal changes in late provincial religious and social history. Historians should neither ignore nor attempt to explain away a development that the colonists themselves knew had to be taken seriously. See Jon Butler, "Enthusiasm Described and Decried: The Great Awakening as Interpretative Fiction," *Journal of American History*, 69 (Sept. 1982), 305-25.

365

The publisher and editor gratefully acknowledge the permission of the authors and the following journals and organizations to reprint the copyright material in this volume; any further reproduction is prohibited without permission:

The American Journal of Legal History; the *American Quarterly*; the *Journal of Social History* and Carnegie Mellon University Press for material in the *Journal*; *The William and Mary Quarterly*; the Rhode Island Historical Society for material in *Rhode Island History*; Cambridge University Press for material in *The Historical Journal*; *The New England Quarterly*; Academic Press, Inc. for material in the *Journal of Historical Geography*; *The Journal of American History* & Organization of American Historians for material in the *Journal*.

CONTENTS OF THE SET

9.
AFRICANS BECOME AFRO-AMERICANS
Selected Articles on Slavery in the American Colonies

10.
COMMERCE AND COMMUNITY
Selected Articles on the Middle Atlantic Colonies

11.
COLONIAL WOMEN AND DOMESTICITY
Selected Articles on Gender in Early America

12.
AMERICAN PATTERNS OF LIFE
Selected Articles on the Provincial Period of American History

13.
THE MARROW OF AMERICAN DIVINITY
Selected Articles on Colonial Religion

14.
AN AMERICAN ENLIGHTENMENT
Selected Articles on Colonial Intellectual History

15.
THE STRESSES OF EMPIRE
Selected Articles on the British Empire in the Eighteenth Century

16.
THE PACE OF CHANGE
Selected Articles on Politics and Society in Pre-Revolutionary
America

17.
A NATION IN THE WOMB OF TIME
Selected Articles on the Long-term Causes of the
American Revolution

18.
A RAGE FOR LIBERTY
Selected Articles on the Immediate Causes of the
American Revolution